CHIRICO?

D0574483

THEOLOGICAL ISSUES OF VATICAN II

Barnabas Ahern
Walter J. Burghardt
Christopher Butler
Carlo Colombo
Yves M. J. Congar
Henri de Lubac
Godfrey L. Diekmann
Joseph Gremillion
Bernard Häring
George G. Higgins
François Houtart
George A. Lindbeck
Mark G. McGrath

Jorge Medina Estevez
John Meyendorff
Paul S. Minear
Charles Moeller
John Courtney Murray
James J. Norris
Albert Outler
Gerard Philips
Karl Rahner
Joseph Sittler
Thomas F. Stransky
Marc H. Tanenbaum
Robert Tucci

ASSOCIATION PRESS : NEW YORK

VATICAN II

AN INTERFAITH

APPRAISAL

INTERNATIONAL THEOLOGICAL CONFERENCE
UNIVERSITY OF NOTRE DAME : MARCH 20-26, 1966

EDITED BY

JOHN H. MILLER, C.S.C.

UNIVERSITY OF NOTRE DAME PRESS : NOTRE DAME & LONDON

THE RENEWING FIRE

". . . primary aspect of the spirit of the Council is fervor. This is the real goal toward which the Council was directing its effort, the spirit that it was striving to infuse into the people of God, the spirit of awakening, of alertness, of goodwill, of spiritual devotion, of zeal, of force and fire; new prospects, new hopes, new activities."   POPE PAUL VI, Address January 5, 1966

Copyright © 1966 by
University of Notre Dame Press
Notre Dame, Indiana
and
Association Press
New York, New York
Library of Congress Catalog Card Number: 66-24920
Manufactured in the United States

The Catholic contributors to this book have received ecclesiastical approval.

Imprimatur:

LEO A. PURSLEY, D.D.
Bishop of Fort Wayne-South Bend
May 11, 1966

Designed by John B. Goetz

EDITOR'S NOTE

All quotations from documents promulgated by Vatican Council II are cited according to the translation appearing in Walter M. Abbott, S.J., *The Documents of Vatican II* (New York: America Press, 1966). The abbreviation of all biblical references follow the style of the *Catholic Biblical Quarterly*.

We are grateful to Piero L. Frattin for the compilation of the index to this book.

T HE FOUR YEARS OF VATICAN COUNCIL II were years of growing and expanding theological perspectives, as the Church developed a clearer vision of her true nature and her mission in the world of today. The unity of Christianity, as an idea and a hope, also grew during these years of enlarged understanding.

As the Council drew to a close, there were born a whole new series of problems, never before existing. How was a church of half a billion persons, spread all across a world, to come to an understanding of what had really happened theologically in Rome between the years of 1961 and 1965.

There were, of course, documents to be read and studied, theologians to be heard, articles and books to be read. But in a very real sense, the key task was to understand where we are now in relation to where we were prior to Vatican Council II.

There is the further problem of where we are going, what new directives and perspectives have been opened up for Catholic life, thought, and vision by Vatican Council II. The close of the Council was not a terminus, but a point of departure. The challenge has been sounded. What does it mean and what do we now do?

Because of all these questions raised for all Catholics by Vatican Council II, it seemed to us at the University of Notre Dame that here was a unique opportunity to demonstrate what a Catholic university really is: a beacon and a bridge, a point of mediation between darkness and light, ignorance and knowledge.

So we approached those who had worked over, prayed over, worried over, and written the documents of Vatican Council II. The litany of names is very distinguished: Diekmann, Butler, Ahern, Medina, Philips, Moeller, de Lubac, Stransky, Congar, Colombo, Häring, Tucci, Murray, Ligutti, Norris, Rahner, Houtart, Gremillion, and Higgins. Happily, all of them agreed to come to Notre Dame and to tell all of us, Catholics, Orthodox, Protestants, Anglicans, and Jews, what had really happened, what was said and why, what it meant, where it led for the future.

Those of other faiths also had their say about what had been written and what it meant to them and their churches.

All in all, it was an exciting, exhilarating, and spectacular week. It was a new experience for America to have over fifty press representatives present at a theological conference. Television carried the conference all over the campus at Notre Dame and abroad in ten major cities. All of us learned, all of us grew, all of us were thrilled by the perspectives of a brighter, more meaningful Christian life and greater Christian unity ahead. The windows that Pope John XXIII opened let in new light; the world-wide perspectives of the Church of Paul VI took on new meaning as we glimpsed the new vision.

We at Notre Dame are grateful to Bishop Mark McGrath, C.S.C., one of our graduates, who had the original idea for this Conference, and to Father Albert Schlitzer, C.S.C., head of our department of theology, who organized the Conference, and, of course, we are especially grateful to all the distinguished Catholic, Orthodox, Protestant, Anglican, and Jewish theologians who joined us to make this Conference a living, pulsating reality that will long be remembered and hopefully repeated.

REV. THEODORE M. HESBURGH, C.S.C.
President
University of Notre Dame

March 27, 1966

CONTENTS

BUTLER

SESSION I

Abbot Christopher Butler, o.s.b.
The Aggiornamento of Vatican II

Abbot Christopher Butler, o.s.b.

THE AGGIORNAMENTO OF VATICAN II

Toward the end of its second session, Vatican Council II, bereft of the great Pope who had convened it, and seeming for the moment to have lost its bearings, took some of its precious and expensive time to celebrate the fourth centenary of the closing of the Council of Trent. The Council that ended in 1563, after a total life of about eighteen years, has gone down to history as the Council of the Counter-Reformation. It seems likely that Vatican II will be known in the future as the *Aggiornamento* Council. *Aggiornamento* was in fact the task proposed to it by John XXIII.

What is *aggiornamento*? I am no Italian expert, but I believe the word means, etymologically, "a bringing up to date." The Church was to be brought up to date. But what should *this* mean?

Of course, any institution that lives and means to play an active, not to say aggressive, part in the mainstream of human history must from time to time, and even continuously, be making minor adaptations to its ever changing environment. Such change was already in progress long before the Council opened. We need only remind ourselves of the striking modifications in the law of the eucharistic fast, introduced by Pius XII after World War II; or of changes in the liturgy, of which perhaps the most striking had been the restoration of the night-vigil of Easter.

Change had been going on, and there was a machinery that made possible not only the proposal of more changes, but the deliberate study and coordination of these proposals, and the enactment of them as and when their introduction might seem prudent. The Curia existed. And there was the pope, with an authority more practically absolute, and less liable than ever to questioning and resistance, since Vatican I had formally promulgated his universal, supreme, ordinary jurisdiction and—under certain conditions, it is true—the infallibility of his doctrinal pronouncements. Has any institution in human history been better equipped for strong and pliant government than the Catholic Church of the first half of the twentieth century? And since Rome had such dogmatic and practical competence, it could be asked: Why incur the trouble and expense of an ecumenical council?

Before the Council opened, on October 11, 1962, it was not even publicly known with any certainty how John XXIII himself viewed this task of *aggiornamento*. He had associated the Council with two other proposals: a reform of the code of canon law (which might of course mean either much or little) and a synod of the local church of Rome, of which the successor of St. Peter is the diocesan bishop. The synod had been held, and its outcome had been a host of new regulations that would have made life in Rome even more difficult for Catholics if they had been observed; it was not a very hopeful augury for the ecumenical Council for which it might be considered to play the role of a pilot scheme. It is true the Pope had hinted that Catholics might look forward to the Council as to a second Pentecost. The hint was calculated to alarm rather than to encourage those who feared that the major result of Vatican II would be a firmer control of the new movements in the Church and consequent disillusionment.

Some light on the Pope's mind could be gained from the discourse with which he closed the inaugural ceremonies October 11, although his hearers were so wearied after a long and tedious service that they were perhaps less responsive than they should have been. He spoke, said Cardinal Montini (who was to succeed to his office and to the guidance of his council), like "a teacher who loved the world." So far from urging the manning of the threatened bastions, he suggested that the Council's task would not be to repeat the old dogmatic formulas but to render the eternal truth present to the men of the present day, with due regard for modern mentalities and for the progress of research. The Church must be made present to the world, whose progress does not escape God's overarching providence, but which has no need of a Council that should find no fresh way of expressing the abiding truth. Not only did the Pope thus evoke the shades of Modernism. He dared to suggest that there was room for hope even in the seventh decade of the twentieth century, and expressed his dissent from the "prophets of woe who tell us that our age is worse than former ones and behave as though they had learned nothing from history; yet history is the teacher of life."

The crisis of the Council came in the first session when, after a long debate, but no significant vote, on the draft of the *Constitution on the Liturgy*, a secret ballot determined the demise of the draft on the sources of revelation. This vote, which showed that the Council was prepared to listen to the so-called new theology and to the biblical scholars, was followed by a debate in which the draft *Constitution on the Church* (of which the first chapter was entitled "The Nature of the Church Militant") came under heavy fire. It was then that Bishop De Smedt made his celebrated attack on "triumphalism, clericalism, and juridicism." By the end of the session it was obvious that we were determined to consider *aggiornamento* in depth.

May I try to explain what I mean by *aggiornamento* in depth? The Curia was able and willing to carry out surface adaptations in the life and administration of the Church, and had in fact, as already indicated, been doing so. But the Council, it seemed, was ready to study the desirability of something more than this. Perhaps an illustration from biology will not be too misleading.

Plant and animal species are found to include a number of varieties within themselves; they have modified a basic structure, common to all the varieties of a single species, to meet slightly differing concrete situations. But a time may come when the survival and welfare of the species' biological inheritance requires some more radical change. A species is conceived by Bernard Lonergan as "an intelligible solution to a problem of living in a given environment."[1] When the environment changes beyond a certain limit, the species ceases to be a solution to it, and the alternatives now are extinction or evolution. If evolution occurs, the resultant species is a new solution to the new problem of living. It "rises upon and takes into account, as it were," the earlier solution, and is "the sort of thing that insight hits upon and not the sort that results from accumulated, observable differences."[2]

The Catholic Church is of course not a species with varieties and specimens. It is a communion of human beings, and man, being not only intelligible but intelligent, is "not just a higher system but a source of higher systems."[3] The closest analogy in human history to the emergence of a new species was the incarnation, when God the Son assumed a particular human nature into hypostatic union with the divine nature. This was certainly an entirely novel solution of the human problem of living, but it did not make man less but more himself. It was novel; it was also unique and final, within the limits of history. Yet, although the Church cannot evolve into something other and higher than herself, the fact that she is a communion of human beings means that, grace aiding, she can achieve ever new solutions of the sort that "insight hits upon, and not the sort that results from accumulated,

[1] *Insight*, 265.
[2] *Ibid.*
[3] *Ibid.*, 267.

observable differences." Such new solutions will have a radical quality and will entail a searching discrimination between what is, after all, of the immutable essence of the Church, and all in her contingent existence that, however venerable, is yet—at least in principle—expendable. The Curia would have operated by gradual accumulation of observable differences. The Council contemplated the possibility of a complex of radical solutions. John XXIII had, as we have seen, hinted at a new Pentecost.

If it be asked whether *aggiornamento* in depth was really necessary, our answer may be to refer to the changed environment in which the Church has to live and function. Of this, the *Constitution on the Church in the Modern World* goes so far as to say: "Today, the human race is passing through a new age of its history. Profound and rapid changes are spreading by degrees around the whole world. Triggered by the intelligence and creative energies of man, these changes recoil upon him, upon his decisions and desires both individual and collective, and upon his manner of thinking and acting with respect to things and to people. Hence we can already speak of a true social and cultural transformation, one which has repercussions on man's religious life as well"—it is a crisis of development (art. 4).[4]

What, now, of the pre-Conciliar Church? Like a stratified rock to the geologist, she was a fascinating object for the historian, not to say the antiquarian. She trailed strange clouds of glory from a past growing ever more remote and irrelevant—like the three crowns of the papal tiara. Her law was articulated on principles, not to say in a spirit, which were ultimately those of the Roman civil law. Her central administration was redolent of the *familia* of the Roman Emperors, as her ceremonial reflected that of a Byzantine court. It needed a critical eye to discern, in the action and theory of the papal primacy, what came from the gospel and what from Caesar. She had never recovered from the estrangement between Eastern and Western Catholicism, which was symbolized in the mutual excommunications of Rome and Constantinople. Lacking the counterpoise of the Eastern churches, the West had come practically to identify its local tradition with the universal tradition, so much so that the miniature Eastern churches actually in communion with the Holy See were treated as quaint appendages and exceptions to a general rule. The *koinonia* of ante-Nicene times had become the Latin

---

[4] Cf. F. Houtart, *L'Église et le Monde*, 18: "The rhythm of the development of a man's potentialities is extraordinary. His mastery over nature is growing day by day and an almost unimaginable future is opening up before him. Man is becoming the basic value for contemporary philosophies and social systems, however halting their efforts may be. Men are becoming aware of great collective tasks ahead of them, involving increased interdependence, socialization and cooperation. Never has there been a more powerful consciousness of humanity's engagement in a common adventure, driving it as with irresistible force to the achieving of a goal which will mean, perhaps, man's willingness to transcend himself." Houtart was one of the "experts" of the Joint Conciliar Commission responsible for the *Constitution on the Church in the Modern World*. His influence is manifest in the passage of the Constitution cited above.

societas, and that society, having been first imperialized, had been feudalized in the Middle Ages. Still, in the middle of the twentieth century, she seemed to be trembling from the shock of the Protestant Reformation, and following her reaction against the new theology of the sixteenth century she had reacted also against the whole general stream of progress in that area of the world's surface where she was, geographically but no longer spiritually, at home. The tremendous dynamic movement that had flung her upon the Graeco-Roman world of the early Christian centuries seemed to have taken shape in a parabolic curve, carrying her now ever further from the living, moving, center of human affairs.

A species, when no longer adapted to its actual environment, can evolve, or it can perish. The Church cannot perish. But there is a third possibility. Sometimes a species succeeds in taking refuge in a backwater of existence, where—in diminished numbers and with no further relevance except to historians of past evolution—it prolongs an insignificant story. As we look back on the Church before 1962, do we not sometimes seem to be catching a glimpse of what might have become a monumental irrelevance?

It may indeed be asked: Should the Church, *ought* the Church, to adapt herself to the changing fashion of the world? Did not Pius IX condemn the proposition that "the Roman Pontiff can and ought to come to terms with Progress, Liberalism, and the New Civilization"? Well, according to Newman, the value of the Syllabus of Errors, from which this proposition is taken, lies in its references, and Newman finds no formal condemnation of this pronouncement in the Allocution from which it is excerpted; what the Pope did say was, in effect, that the mid-nineteenth-century champions of Progress, Liberalism and the New Civilization made use of their cause "so seriously to the injury of the Faith and the Church, that it was both out of the power, and contrary to the duty, of the Pope to come to terms with them."[5] But the deeper answer to our question is simply that the Church has a mission and a message, and divine help, for all mankind; to fulfill her function she must be not only chronologically but spiritually the contemporary of those to whom she addresses herself. *Aggiornamento* in depth is thus seen to be a pastoral necessity.

The word "pastoral" has taken us to the heart of the Council. It is an old-fashioned word, but to the Council it signified something that must urgently be modern. The commission to the apostles is: to make disciples of all nations, teaching them to observe all that Christ had commanded them. We used to be warned in the first session of the Council that the Church's prime

---

[5] "Open Letter to the Duke of Norfolk," in *Difficulties of Anglicans* II, 283, 286. Contrast with this rejection of a policy, not necessarily involving rejection of the values inspiring it, John XXIII's rejection of the basic Marxist-Leninist philosophy yet readiness for some limited practical cooperation with its adherents.

duty was to protect the faith of her actual children. But it should be observed that in the text of St. Matthew's Gospel (28:19f.) to which I have just referred, the making of disciples is mentioned before the teaching of the commandments. Proclamation (kerygma) precedes instruction (didache). Unless the work of evangelization comes first, there is no one to instruct, none with a faith to be protected.

The Church is, therefore, necessarily outward-looking, not primarily introspective and conservative, but primarily an indomitable adventurer into new fields. What else could she be, since she is, as St. Augustine taught us, the incorporation of Christian love or charity? Charity is the least introspective of virtues, calling us always to transcend the self and its immediate horizon, not feeding on itself but projecting itself thither where previously there has been a lack of love. Charity has the audacity of the great military geniuses, who know by instinct that a strategy of defense can never in the end win a campaign.

Perhaps it is not altogether fantastic to seek for this motive of pastoral charity behind a number of interests which gave the Council its characteristic color. The widening of horizons, an inevitable consequence of the meeting of over two thousand prelates from almost every part of the world, was still further extended by the presence throughout the Council of the observers from the churches and ecclesial communities of our separated brethren. It was as though the Council became conscious, as it looked beyond the walls of the city set on a hill, of friends, brothers, fellow disciples of the world's Savior, just outside those walls. The Church, in these separated brethren, seemed visibly to transcend its own limits. From this transcendence there springs a set of theological problems, which have left their mark not only on the *Decree on Ecumenism* but on *Lumen Gentium* itself. The Council had to turn back behind Bellarmine with his Counter-Reformation ecclesiology, behind St. Thomas himself and the Fathers, to the biblical theology which governs the first two chapters of the *Constitution on the Church.*

Then, beyond the baptized and unbaptized disciples of our Lord, there was the people of the Jews, who before us had obtained the divine adoption, the visible presence and the covenant, the Torah and the Prophets; who could claim the patriarchs for their own, and of whom came the Messiah in his human nature (cf. Rom 9:4f.). Here we owe a great debt to the German Cardinal Bea and the German hierarchy, whose successful determination to obtain a pronouncement against anti-Semitism by and for the whole Church was a blessed outcome of unhappy events in their own country in this century.

And beyond the Jews there were Islam and the great Eastern religions. It was a triumph of charity that, surely for the first time in history, an ecumenical council came to pronounce on these great faiths with practically exclusive reference to their positive values, and with unqualified respect.

And so on to secularist humanism and to atheism. Once the question was posed, it was indeed difficult for the Council not to "reprobate" atheism, since in itself it is the professed denial of the ultimate basis of religion. But even here, in the words of Archbishop Garrone, the desire behind the Conciliar treatment of this subject (in the *Constitution on the Church in the Modern World*) was "to give a description of atheism of which an atheist would say: This is no caricature—here I recognize myself."

Charity is both cause and effect of intercommunication, or, to use our modern word, of dialogue. Throughout the Council's treatment of the themes just mentioned there is the underlying motif of dialogue; implying a respect for the interlocutor, too sincere to allow us to make compromises of truth, yet tireless in seeking points of contact, agreement, of common concern.

Christian love is a love of respect, because it is an affair of interpersonal communication and communion. It therefore carries us on to another basic characteristic of the spirit and work of Vatican II. The Archbishop of Turin, in one of his notable contributions to the debates of the fourth session, said, as it were in passing, that he thought there was something valuabe in modern subjectivism, properly conceived. The remark was sufficiently unusual, particularly as coming from an Italian prelate, to challenge attention. It might be said that the very hallmark of modern Catholicism has been its insistence on the order of objective truths, values and laws. In fact, this preoccupation with the objective is one reason why our manuals of moral theology have conveyed to some minds the impression of a positively algebraic irrelevance to the real drama of man's moral life. Yet it is at least arguable that precisely the ferment of the gospel has been the creative source of our contemporary concern with personal freedom and responsibility, if not of the agonies of modern existentialism. Charity, after all, being supernatural love, is always orientated toward the living person of our fellowman, and therefore to his needs and problems as they come alive in his personal subjectivity. And charity respects this person and this person's viewpoint. It respects him, and it warns us of our limited understanding of him. It is charity that says: Judge not, and you shall not be judged: who art thou, to pass judgment on another's servant? (Rom 14:4). If it is a principle of law to presume that those who infringe its prescriptions are morally to blame, it is a principle of charity to presume that those who differ from us—including those who differ from the defined dogmas of the faith—are nevertheless "men of good will."

Such was the presumption governing what *Lumen Gentium* and the *Decree on Ecumenism*, as also the *Declaration on the Relationship of the Church to Non-Christian Religions*, had to say about non-Catholics. Such too is the presumption of the *Constitution on the Church in the Modern*

World, when it addresses itself to all men of good will irrespective of their creeds, their ideologies or their professed agnosticism. The same presumption really lies behind the *Declaration on Religious Freedom*, though the grounds there stated for this feedom go deeper than presumed good will to the inherent rights of the human person even in error, and even in guilt. And this presumption triumphed once again, though with some difficulty, in the modest suggestion in the chapter on peace and war that civil law might make provision for conscientious objectors.

The pastoral aim, the instinct of a charity that goes beyond all boundaries, the sense of mission not so much to human nature or the abstract human species, but to human persons and the actually existing human family, demanded that our *aggiornamento* should be conceived in depth. The consequent need to discriminate between what the Church must always be, what the gospel forever is, and the contingent elements in which, at any given moment, the Church presents herself in history, was driving the Council to some criterion. And this drive took her gaze ever backwards, behind the counterrevolutionary Church, behind the Counter-Reformation, behind the medieval synthesis, back to the Church before the estrangement of East and West, to the Church before the confrontation with Greek culture and philosophy, to the primal source: to Christ in Palestine. As Cardinal Montini said, in his speech near the end of the first session, the Church by herself is nothing. She is not so much a society founded by Christ as Christ himself, using us as his instruments to bring salvation to mankind.[6] Christ himself is the fullness of the divine revelation, and the content of the sacred tradition is just revelation, the word of God made flesh. The Church's teaching authority, embodied in the ecumenical Council, is not above the word of God but the servant of that word, teaching only that which has been transmitted (*Constitution on Divine Revelation* 10).

Thus the very need of accommodating the Church to the world of today and tomorrow, if it was not to lead to compromise with the world, must throw us back to our source. The *Decree on the Appropriate Renewal of the Religious Life* has its own rendering of the word *aggiornamento*: it speaks of "an accommodated renewal." The word "accommodated" here refers to contemporary adaptation. The word "renewal," however, as the text of the decree shows, does not mean "innovation" but "recovery of the initial inspiration." The more immediate source of a religious order is the "spirit and special projects" of its founder, together with "healthy traditions." But the source of the Church is the Spirit and gospel of Jesus of Nazareth, ever living in the Church he founded, but needing always to be recovered and relived.

Modern man has a profound sense of his involvement in the time process.

---

[6] X. Rynne, *Letters from Vatican City*, 227.

For good or ill, he seems less interested in the fact that the definition of his species is *animal rationale* than that he is an existing person, caught in the trammels and the challenge of duration and therefore of change. In the realm of natural science, he is fascinated by the concept and the story of evolution. And within the general scheme of evolution he frames the history of the human race, which he studies also scientifically. If philosophy was the basic discipline of the medieval schools, history is today a basic discipline among all those that deal with man. For modern man, the return to Jesus of Nazareth must mean, at least among other things, the scientific, historical quest of Jesus. And this brings us to the Conciliar dialectic of scholasticism and biblical scholarship. Speaking as one who has taken an amateur interest in biblical studies for the greater part of my life, I rejoice that the Council's *Constitution on Divine Revelation* can be viewed as containing at least the first sketch of a charter of open biblical research. That there was much nervousness about biblical criticism in the Council cannot be denied. And perhaps we lacked the voice of some great Council orator to remind us of the already great achievements of New Testament scholarship in allowing us to penetrate, tentatively and inchoatively, behind even the primitive postresurrection formulations of the gospel to the words and person and spirit of him who spoke with authority and not as the scribes. The spirit of Jesus was not the spirit of unqualified conservatism. He took his stand within the Great Tradition of the holy community of Israel, centered in the Torah and the temple priesthood. But, in strong contrast to the Dead Sea sectarians, he subordinated law to charity and gave the impulse that was to change a predominantly national religion into one that was universal, catholic. It is that spirit which provokes audacious change in order to preserve, at a higher level and from a superior viewpoint, inherited values, which is the Spirit that animates the mystical body of Christ. In "the name of" that Spirit Vatican II was called together and congregated. I am less doubtful than I once was that it was gathered for a second Pentecost.

The purpose of our conference is not retrospective. Or rather, if it looks back upon the Council, it is not in order to contemplate it as an end achieved, but to understand it as a step toward the future. The great Council of Trent dominated the centuries that followed it, not merely by what it did but by the application made of its work by St. Charles Borromeo and those who, like him, were determined that it should not remain a dead letter. Vatican II is at once a first step and, I venture to suggest, a new orientation. Fascinated, it may be by theological rationalizations of Church history, or under the spell of Newman's theory of development, we have been too much inclined to suppose that as the Church has moved in but one direction over the past thousand years, therefore she could only so have moved, and must continue on the same line. But in fact the Church is a fountainhead of unpredictable freedom. The static element in her complex totality, the sacraments and especially the sacramental ministry, is subordinate to the dynamic moment whose immediate source is the charisms, the grace-gifts, of the Spirit of Christ, given—as *Lumen Gentium* reminds us—as and to whom God chooses, whether pope or humble lay man or woman—or, we may add, African bushman to whom the gospel has never been proclaimed by human lips. The Spirit bloweth where it listeth, and it is impossible to foretell, from the present state and condition of the Church, what her history in the coming generations will be. But at least for the moment, without rejecting or denying her past, without any surrender of her patrimony, she appears to have changed her course.

To attempt to define this change would be hazardous, but I nevertheless would point to two moments in the Council's life and work which, between them, seem to me to be suggestive.

The first is the reaffirmation, in *Lumen Gentium*, of a genuine sacramental episcopal collegiality, which had been thrown somewhat into the background by the work of the prematurely ended Vatican I. This seems to afford the basis for a recovery of the principle that the papacy—and now we must add the episcopate—is not the source of the actual life of the Church, but the coordinator of that life's various and peripheral spontaneities. This principle of subsidiarity is carried through to the point at which the lay Catholic is seen as a genuine creative force in the life of the People of God; and to the further point where it is realized that the whole human family, so far as good will prevails, is a theater of the operations of the grace-gifts of the Holy Spirit, is cooperating, if often incognito, in the building up of Christ's kingdom.

The second suggestive moment is the direction of the *Constitution on the Church in the Modern World* not only to Catholics, or only to Christians, but to all men of good will. Human good will is the liaison between the total human family and the visible Church. Father Fernandez, Prior General of the Order of Preachers, reminded the Council Fathers in a notable speech that by their common humanity the members of the human race were all bound by ties of duty to the whole of mankind, and that this link was prior to the bonds that bind us to more local groupings. In this fact there is found a moral constituent of human unity that supervenes upon and perfects our biological unity. Mankind *ought* to be morally united, to form a single spiritual communion. The signs of our aspiration to such unity are plain to see in past and present history. That the obligation and the aspiration are real, gives meaning to the Council's address to all men of good will. But past and present history show us also how halting and imperfect are the steps that man can take in his own strength to achieve that unity without which his own future is now more than ever clouded over with menace. Our faith, as

Christians, is that Christ came for a purpose of reconciliation; reconciling man with God, but thereby also reconciling man with man. The Church, the People of God, in which all hierarchy exists for the sake of service or ministry, is the Spirit-animated mystical body of Christ and makes ever contemporary the reality of his presence and the saving truth of his gospel; she is the sign and the instrument of the unity of the whole human race.

We, then, who believe these things, must study the Council's acts. But we must do more; we must catch and embody the Council's spirit. We must be members and representations of Christ in and to the world. And we have to show that we remember that the heart of Christ and the heart of his gospel were directed ultimately by adoration beyond humanity to God.

DIEKMANN

SESSION II

REV. GODFREY L. DIEKMANN, O.S.B.
The Constitution on the Sacred Liturgy

Rev. Godfrey L. Diekmann, O.S.B.

THE CONSTITUTION ON THE SACRED LITURGY

W HEN AT THE VERY FIRST general assembly of the Council, October 13, 1962, Cardinals Lienart of France and Frings of Germany requested that the Council Fathers themselves be given the opportunity of nominating the members of the ten Conciliar commissions instead of merely approving the slate of names proposed to them, something like an electric shock passed through the Catholic world. Thereby the bishops at the very outset had punctured the prevalent pessimistic assumption that the Council would be no more than an endorsement of a prepared agenda. They had equivalently declared their determination to have free and full discussion of all matters pertaining to that inner renewal of the Church which Pope John had set as the goal of the Council.

A second step, perhaps equally decisive for the subsequent evolution of the Council, though not at the time generally recognized as such, was taken at the second general assembly, October 16, when the liturgy schema was selected as the first subject of debate. Very probably its choice was due primarily to widespread discontent with the four other schemata originally scheduled to precede it. Unlike these, which smelled too much of the stale polemics of theology classroom disputes, the liturgy document seemed to embody the pastoral thrust that promised fresh air from open windows.

True, the full dimensions of its pastoral intent were not apparent to all, more especially during the first session. For the important "declarations" appended to the various articles by the liturgical preparatory commission, con-

17

taining theological and historical reasons for positions taken and reforms proposed, were not made available to the Council Fathers. These would indubitably have forestalled much of the early, often tedious debate, and the resultant feeling of frustration, which led one bishop to exclaim: "Rome is burning, and we are fiddling away merrily about whether this or that ceremony should be changed."

But these were initial delays and disappointments, complicated by the need of discovering satisfactory procedural rules for the daily conduct of the Conciliar business. Before long, it became apparent to most, however, that the choice of the liturgy schema had been a happy one, since it offered a sound foundation for the hoped-for revitalization of the Church's life.

The document was basically sound above all because its principles had been tested in the pastoral experiences of a liturgical movement of more than half a century's duration, dating back to the famous talk of Dom Lambert Beauduin at Malines in 1909. Moreover, the preparatory liturgical commission was a genuinely representative body. It was composed of recognized liturgical scholars and pastoral leaders drawn from all four continents, and nineteen countries, persons who had arrived at a substantial consensus through the personal confrontation made possible by seven international liturgical study weeks, of which those of Lugano in 1953 and Assisi in 1956 are the best-known instances. They had enjoyed unhindered freedom of discussion in their deliberations, and the final formulation of their document genuinely reflected the majority mind.

However, this was not the same document that reached the Council floor. In passing through the hands of the Central Commission, it had been altered by one of the latter's subcommissions in several crucially important points, notably in the articles on concelebration and communion under both species, in the question of the use of the vernacular in the praying of the Divine Office, and in that of the power to be granted to territorial groups of bishops to decide certain liturgical matters. But episcopal members of the preparatory commission alerted the Council Fathers to what had happened, and it is revelatory of the temper of the Council that in every such instance the Council Fathers did not content themselves with merely reverting to the original text, but decreed even more generous provisions. As a matter of surprising fact, except in one or two matters of quite minor import, every change which the Council voted in the text proposed was liberalizing rather than restrictive, in some instances—for example, that of the use of the vernacular—drastically so. The preparatory commission had been as bold in its proposals as it had dared be. For despite fifty years of liturgical movement, what evidence was there that even a sizable minority of the bishops of the world were seriously interested in thorough-going liturgical reform? The liberalizing revisions and the successive overwhelmingly positive votes on the liturgy schema were the first great convincing proof to a skeptical world, non-Catholic as well as Catholic, that Vatican Council II was courageously facing the issue of *Ecclesia semper reformanda*.

The liturgy schema had profoundly profited from the grass-roots experiences of two generations of liturgical movement. But since, as the Council was to declare, the most important self-manifestation of the Church is in the assembly of eucharistic worship (art. 2, 41), the liturgical movement had proved to be above all else "a providential . . . movement of the Holy Spirit in His Church" (art. 43)[1] whereby she attained a new awareness of herself: of her true nature and purpose. Romano Guardini, forty-four years ago, could already attest that through the liturgical movement the Church is coming to life in the hearts of men. But it came to life also in the minds as well as the hearts of her more perceptive theologians. By communal prayer and song, by common sharing at the tables of the word and of the bread, Catholics had newly discovered each other as brothers, whom Christ in their midst was forming into a community of love. In a word, the liturgical movement of its very nature involved a profound reorientation of ecclesiology, which, furthered by authoritative sanctions such as Pius XII's encyclical *Mystici Corporis* and *Mediator Dei*, found its hitherto clearest and most developed expression in the *Constitution on the Sacred Liturgy*. It was an ecclesiology that was not the product primarily of academic theological speculation; its insights had been gained through the existential Church attempting to live most fully her life of sanctifying and worshiping. The ecclesiology of the liturgy Constitution was, therefore, more inductive than deductive: a self-reflection of the Church based on her own most vital activities. This is borne out by the significant fact that the first chapter of the document, the exposition of principles, was composed by the preparatory commission only subsequent to its discussions and formulations concerning the liturgical actions themselves.

Here we find, too, the most important reason why the choice of the liturgy schema as first on the agenda proved so felicitous. It was not the theological construct of the post-Constantine or post-Tridentine eras, but the living Church describing her self-discovery in liturgical action that to a very large extent determined the ecclesiology basic to all the subsequent documents, including the great *Constitution on the Church*. A decisive turning point of the entire Council was its rejection of the proposed schema on the Church, because, as Archbishop Martin of Rouen, among others, pointed out, it did not correspond to the spirit and content of the ecclesiology already approved in the liturgy Constitution. Several elements of this self-understanding of the Church, proclaimed in the liturgy Constitution and gained largely through

[1] A quotation from Pius XII's address to the Assisi Pastoral-Liturgical Congress, September 22, 1956.

the experiences of the pastoral liturgical movement, may be adduced as of significance in the Council's formulation of ecclesiology.

The first, and perhaps most important, is the priority given to the entire people of God as actively and responsively constituting the Church, before consideration of the diverse ministries, inclusive of the *diakonia* based on holy orders. Already Pius XII in *Mediator Dei* had laid the foundations for this understanding of the Church when he defined liturgy as "the public worship which our Redeemer as head of the Church renders to the Father, as well as the worship which the *community of the faithful* renders to its Founder, and through him to the Heavenly Father. It is the worship rendered by the mystical body of Christ in the *entirety* of its head and members" (Par. 20, NCWC edition). There seems no point in adducing quotations from the liturgy Constitution illustrative of the same understanding of the Church, as the actively engaged People of God. The entire document collapses without it. Active, conscious participation of *all*, through and *together with* their lawfully ordained ministers, is its burden—as it had been the overriding concern of the liturgical movement, which it largely mirrors and now authoritatively sanctions.

Secondly, and correlative to this basic concept of the Church, is the Constitution's underscoring of the dignity and role of the laity, based on their sacramental deputation to cult through baptism (and confirmation). I am one of those who believe that Vatican Council II, despite all the publicity attached to the indubitably important matter of collegiality of bishops and their role and authority vis-à-vis the Holy See, will most radically affect the future polity and life of the Church by its honest effort to restore full responsible citizenship to the layman. The Church, St. Paul reminds us, is founded "on the apostles *and prophets*, with Christ himself the chief cornerstone" (Eph 2:20). The liturgy, as the Constitution states, is both summit and source of the Church's activity and power (art. 10). "Full, conscious and active participation in it by the Christian people . . . is their right and duty by reason of their baptism" (art. 14). It is the root that demands and makes possible flowering in apostolic work. Not the sacrament of holy orders, as the recent 1958 Instruction of the Congregation of Rites still presupposed when it spoke of commentators, readers and choir members having a "delegated" ministry, but the sacraments of baptism and confirmation confer full worshiping and teaching and ruling rights according to rank in "the chosen race, the royal priesthood" (1 Pt 2:9). It is significant that this passage from 1 Peter is one of the most frequently quoted Scripture texts in the Conciliar documents—and all of them, in treating of the laity's role, invariably call attention to its baptismal, liturgical foundation. The clericalization of the Church, the most injurious imbalance reaching back certainly to the sixth century, by which an ecclesiology had become a hierarchology, had found its first and most ramifying expression in liturgical worship. It was therefore appropriate that in liturgical action and theory it be first and most radically abolished.

It can only be regretted, however, that this active role of the laity, so urgently proclaimed by the liturgy Constitution in theory, was completely overlooked in practice in the composition of the document which was chiefly for their benefit. No lay person, so far as I know, was directly asked to give advice. Certainly none was part of the preparatory liturgical commission or the commission that functioned during the Council. This, I believe, is the most flagrant flaw of the Constitution: a house was built without consulting the persons who are to live in it. As to that, I further believe that the commissions would have been significantly aided in their work had they enlisted the collaboration of competent spokesmen of the worship traditions of other Christian communities, not only of the so-called liturgical Churches, those of Anglicans and Lutherans, but also of the evangelical and free Churches. The Quakers, for instance, would have valuable advice for us about the community-formative power of silence.

A third component part of the Church's process of self-awareness, expressed first in the liturgy Constitution, and then re-echoed in the ecclesiology of subsequent documents, is the rediscovery that the local worshiping community, of diocese and parish (or its equivalent), constitutes not only a geographic or administrative division of the universal Church, but is her pre-eminent manifestation or self-realization, her most spiritually significant epiphany. Articles 41 and 42, which treat of this, and which ecclesiologically rank among the weightiest statements of the liturgy Constitution, embody a theology of the assembly, of the *ecclesia*, as the *qahal Yahweh*, which contemporary biblical and patristic scholarship as well as the pastoral experience of the liturgical movement had served to bring once again to the fore of consciousness. The liturgical movement had been forced to come of age during the war years, not least of all in the horror of the concentration camps. All customary props of ecclesiastical society had been swept away. Restricted to the minimum essentials of worship, the men and women who gathered about the sacrificial altar and ate of its meal experienced as never before the unsuspected depth and consolation of St. Paul's assurance: "We, though many, are one body, because we partake of the one bread" (1 Cor 10:17). One of the most moving moments in the work of the preparatory liturgical commission was when a bishop from behind the Iron Curtain described how in his country it is exclusively from the Sunday worship that his people can find the strength of Christian community, which enables them to live through the rest of the week without despair. "In strict truth," he said, "we now know that *eucharistia facit ecclesiam*" (the eucharist makes, creates the Church). And he pleaded passionately for liturgical reforms of language especially, but also of rite, in order that the Sunday Mass might even more effectively transform his scattered flock into strong local *ecclesiae*. It should be added that it is this same article 41 of the liturgy Constitution, which speaks of the bishop as the high priest of his flock and, reflecting the ecclesiology of Ignatius of Antioch, identifies him above all as the celebrant of the eucharist, that other Conciliar documents echo in portraying the episcopal office. The bishop, even the Bishop of Rome, is he who ministers the euchaarist, who re-enacts the covenant by making present again for his people the saving death and resurrection of Christ. And, as the examples of Popes John and Paul have so splendidly brought to life article 41 of the Constitution, if his people do not come to him, he seeks them out where they are.

These very actions of the Popes, however, make us more aware of another weakness of the Constitution. Articles 41 and 42 do restore a sound biblical and early traditional theology of the local Church, of the diocese and parish. But, given our modern phenomenon that the vast majority of Catholics belong to huge city parishes, in which even the eucharist cannot transform the multitudes into true communities, something more was called for than the stated theological principles. True, an opening to a solution underlies the phrase "lesser groupings of the faithful. . . . Among these the parishes . . . are the most important" (art. 42). The presence of some expert religious sociologists on the commissions responsible for the text might have produced a more forthright grappling with the problem that many believe to be the most serious confronting the revitalization of the Church through the liturgy today. One might say, that in this respect, the document is strong in theology, faltering in what might be called its "anthropology."

A fourth area in which the liturgy Constitution led the way in reorienting the ecclesiology of the Council are its revolutionary principles of the need of adaptation to the culture and traditions of peoples (art. 37–40). How revolutionary these common-sense principles are is evident from the history of the liturgy. Popes ever since Benedict XV had, it is true, spoken eloquently of the need of cultural adaptation in the missionary activities of the Church, and some indults had been granted for liturgical adaptations in mission lands. But the rigid fixation of rites for the Church at large, achieved in the publication of the "typical editions" of liturgical books resulting from Trent, had seemed indeed "ad perpetuam rei memoriam." In its early development, the Roman liturgy had as a matter of course embodied multiple cultural elements: Jewish, Hellenistic, and Roman. The legitimacy of such adaptations, within due bounds, was too obviously grounded in the fact of the incarnation to be questioned. The next major ritual adjustment occurred after the barbarian invasion, when Frankish and Germanic liturgies developed, and then in turn modified their common Roman source. But that adaptation did not go so far as to include the adoption of the vernaculars. When in the sixteenth century the great missionary activity of the Church brought the faith to the newly discovered lands, the by-then established principle of centralization of liturgical legislation and of rigid ritual uniformity prevented a normal incarnational growth. It is fascinating to speculate how different contemporary political history might be, had the Chinese rites controversy been resolved less disastrously.

The experiences of the liturgical movement had left no doubt that St. Pius X's ideal of active and intelligent participation could not be achieved without changes in text and rites, *and further*, a generous measure of flexibility in adapting them to given cultures and local requirements. "The liturgy is for men, and not men for the liturgy," Cardinal Montini stated at the fourth general assembly, October 22, 1962.

One of the great achievements of the Council is its demolition of the image of the monolithic Church, of the *de facto* canonization of uniformity in the name of unity. The measure of confusion in the minds of our people today is, not in last instance, witness to the effectiveness with which we had, often for polemical reasons, previously oversold the idea of the unchanging Church, not distinguishing adequately between what is essential and what is of human accretion. And because this canonization of uniformity had obtained so triumphantly in the liturgy, and for so long, its firm rejection in the liturgy Constitution set a liberating precedent for the following documents.

The Constitution carefully provides for the needed permanence or stability amid legitimate diversity (cf. art. 21, 23). A certain degree of decentralization of liturgical legislation was clearly imperative, however, in order to achieve suitable adaptation. For this reason the liturgy Constitution took for granted one of the momentous structural changes in Church administration effected by the Council even before the latter had thoroughly discussed or sanctioned it: the legislative competence of territorial bodies of bishops. To objections voiced by some Fathers, the liturgy commission replied: "The matter is of ·the highest consequence. The entire scope of the liturgical Constitution presupposes that the renewal of liturgy be achieved for the most part by the bishops according to the respective conditions and needs of their people." The Constitution, in like manner, basing itself on the same principle of adaptation to diverse needs, simply assumed the existence of a functional diaconate even before the Council had had an opportunity to decree its restoration (art. 35, 68).

Noteworthy especially in the light of past rigidity is the scope of possible adaptation. No liturgical rite, not even the Canon of the Mass, is *a priori* excluded; and, "providing that the substantial unity of the Roman rite is maintained" (art. 38), no restriction, whether geographical, cultural, or sociological, limits the situations that may prompt adaptation: variety is in principle approved not only according to the needs of peoples and regions, but also of "different groups," a term that allows of astonishingly wide application. The pertinent article 37 amounts to a frank recognition that the inherited sign language of the Roman liturgy is as much in danger of becoming irrelevant to technological man as it had in many respects proved meaningless in mission lands.

More specifically, the liturgy commission reported to the Council that even a vernacular Canon would be among the possible "more radical adaptations" for which territorial bodies of bishops may petition the Holy See (cf. art. 40). And while only one Council Father, Bishop Duschak of the Philippines, had asked for a drastic recasting of the Canon, or at least for an alternate Canon, simpler, shorter, and more biblical, the idea has gained considerable support in the few years since the promulgation of the Constitution. It would not seem beyond the realm of the possible, therefore, that the Consilium (the post-Conciliar liturgical commission) may produce such an alternate anaphora, perhaps similar to the eucharistic prayer of Hippolytus' *Apostolic Tradition* —one in all events which will constitute a more explicit "*sacrificium laudis*" (*berakah*), a proclaiming of the *magnalia Dei*, God's deeds in salvation history, such as several Protestant communions have already admirably achieved in recent liturgical reforms.

The principle of diversity in unity was well implemented by the Consilium itself in its Instruction of September 26, 1964. A quite unexpected variety of rubrical choice and flexibility of ritual action were therein permitted, which one can only hope will not be nullified by national or diocesan directives in the name of uniformity that edifies. Liturgical law had at long last sanctioned a balancing degree of liturgical liberty. Only experimentation within established limits, such as the Constitution calls for and the Instruction now permits, can establish what is or is not genuinely edifying.

Premise of adaptation and of the exercise of hitherto forbidden liturgical liberty is another and, to my thinking, the most consequential note of the Constitution: its profound respect for the mysterious, inviolable dignity of the human person. "Liturgy is for man, not man for the liturgy." This personalist approach determines the argument of the entire document like a leitmotif. The liturgical movement, with its stress on personal participation in community, its invoking among others the ancient principle of distribution of roles, had in the preceding decades been a religious counterpart of, and was no doubt reciprocally deeply affected by, the foremost concern of contemporary civilization: the rights and responsibilities of free man, and the interpersonal nature of societal relationships. Now woven into the texture of the first Conciliar pronouncement, its various dimensions more clearly appreciated after protracted debate on the Council floor, affirmation of the innate worth of the human person could not but become a dominant and integrating component also of the succeeding discussions and documents. It seems not improbable, indeed, that its highlighting of responsible personhood will historically be deemed the Council's most far-reaching over-all achievement.

So far as the liturgy Constitution is concerned, the very tone of its legislation strikes a new note. Direct commands are kept to a minimum. Instead, intent on encouraging free human initiative and/or obedience, it prefers to state a goal, and then contents itself with recommending it with lesser or greater urgency as the case may seem to require. The Latin language is rich in ways of expressing such optatives—not easily conveyed, by the way, with due nuance in translations. In any event, this unaccustomed approach has already resulted in misunderstandings, for example, in the matter of the use of the vernacular. Minds conditioned by the legalism of the past are all too apt to conclude that what is not expressly ordered may be ignored, or is at most permissive. The letter of the law is observed at the expense of the clear intent of the total context.

The willing engagement of free persons is the obvious aim, too, of the Constitution's repetitive insistence on continuing instruction of priests and people in the principles and practices of liturgical action. It is consideration for Christian persons, of their rights and needs, that ultimately prompted the new departures in adaptation, in enlisting the liturgical legislative power of territorial groups of bishops, in restoring the ecclesial dignity of the local eucharistic community, and in recognizing that the layman has an essential role in official worship that is peculiarly his by virtue of his baptism. The integrity of the human person is being violated when he is forced to worship through rites that have become misleading if not actually meaningless, through texts so notoriously indifferent to historical veracity as to occasion the saying "He lies like a second Nocturn." And if the use of one's native tongue is generally recognized as among man's inalienable rights, by what title does man forfeit this right when he worships as a Roman Catholic?

Regard for persons and for their free and responsible involvement underlies .also the Constitution's new understanding of the very meaning of liturgy. While it refrains from giving a definition of its own, there can be no doubt that it attempts to redress the imbalance of the excessively cultic definitions of more recent centuries. It makes clear that the sanctification of man is not merely an objective of the liturgy, but is constitutive of it. Liturgy is an exercise of the priestly office of Christ whereby he sanctifies man through signs (art. 7). The glorification of God is, of course, the ultimate aim of the liturgy; it is primary in order of intention, but God is glorified in sacramental action precisely by the transformation of man, and by man's conscious turning to God in faith and love, which the sacramental action accomplishes. Liturgy is the highest exemplification of the principle that we have not loved God first, but he has first loved us, and his love is a creative, transfiguring love. Liturgy is latreutic to the degree that it is soteriological; it is dialogic, a sac-

rum commercium, rather than solely cultic. Even the sacrifice of the Mass is no exception: in the service of the word God first enlivens man's faith and stirs up the response of love whereby man is enabled to enter worthily upon the eucharistic action of worship. Formed by the word of God, we dare to say *Gratias agamus*. Indicative of how consistently and how firmly the liturgy schema stressed the priority of sanctification of man as constituent of the *esse* of liturgical action, and as first in the order of achievement, is the fact that the Council, in order to forestall possible misconceptions, thought it prudent to insert in several additional instances explicit mention of worship.

Pius XII in *Mediator Dei* had, it is true, presented well the fuller context of Christ's saving priestly action in the liturgy. But the cultic emphasis was so thoroughly entrenched, so favored by the code of Canon Law, that his definition of liturgy as "the worship rendered by the mystical body of Christ in the entirety of its head and members," that is, a purely cultic definition, was remembered apart from its context. Indeed, what other understanding of the liturgy is possible, if liturgy is categorized as the external exercise of the virtue of religion, itself a subdivision of the cardinal virtue of justice—as it had *de facto* been classified quite unanimously ever since the days of St. Thomas. (Whether this simplistic view does justice to Thomas is another matter.) Liturgy is then an obligatory ritual action for the glorification of God. Man is for the liturgy, not vice versa. Sacramental absolutism is the inevitable result: the more ritual, the greater the honor to God. Witness the rationalization— until very recently accepted without question—of the graded stipend system: a solemn Mass, by the very fact of having sacred ministers, is the cultic equivalent of some twenty-five low Masses. Even *Mediator Dei*, in an unfortunate passage, contributes to this caricature: "A 'dialogue Mass' [with active participation of the people] cannot replace the High Mass, which, as a matter of fact, though it should be offered *with only the sacred ministers* possesses its own special dignity due to the impressive character of its ritual and the magnificence of its ceremonies" (No. 106, NCWC edition). The *Ecclesia quae offert* to all intents and purposes has been reduced to an abstraction.

The conclusion, however unintended and distorted, lies at hand: God is glorified by an action, rather than by the persons who perform the action; by an *opus operatum*, interpreted in a mechanistic fashion that perhaps more than anything else sparked the Reformers' protest, instead of in the true traditional and Thomistic and personalist sense of *actio Christi*.

Perhaps no other single item so clearly pinpoints the personalist concern of the Constitution as its deliberate avoidance of the theological phrase *ex opere operato* in describing sacramental efficacy, though some of the Council Fathers urged its use. Nor was this due solely to a determination to prefer wherever possible biblical and patristic over scholastic terminology. The majority of the men who composed the document had in their firsthand experience of the liturgical movement arrived at the conviction that *opus operatum*, however valuable for theological clarification, in pedagogical fact can only with the greatest difficulty be detached from an automatic, depersonalizing interpretation.

While amply maintaining the doctrinal content intended by the phrase, the Constitution concentrates rather on the interpersonal, dialogic character of the sacraments inherent in their nature as Christ's saving actions, sacred signs, signs of faith. "They not only presuppose faith, but by words and objects they also nourish, strengthen and express it; that is why they are called 'sacraments of faith'" (art. 59). The measure of fruitful reception of sacramental grace is according to the measure of the *fides et devotio*, which the sacramental celebration itself is meant most effectively to arouse. Though it be an exercise of the virtue of religion, commanded by justice, the Christian eucharistic "sacrifice of praise" is also and more importantly the personal and communal act of faith, hope, and charity of the People of God who constitute the given *ecclesia*. "The renewal in the Eucharist of the convenant between the Lord and man draws the faithful into the compelling love of Christ and sets them on fire" (art. 10). In other words, the pastoral dimension of liturgy is of its essence; the tautology inherent in the term "pastoral liturgical movement" can only be accounted for by the customary understanding of liturgy in one-sidedly cultic fashion.

It is, however, the Constitution's underscoring of the role of personal faith in the salvific action of the liturgy that deserves special attention. We are here worlds removed from the polemical preoccupations of Trent, which in its debate on original sin, for instance, eliminated the word "faith" from a proposed text, "The merit of Jesus Christ is applied both to adults and to infants by faith and the sacrament of baptism," because this sounded too much like article 2 of the Augsburg Confession, and substituted "Baptism rightly administered in the form of the Church" (Degree on Original Sin, 3). It would almost seem that the Constitution is trying to make amends; however belatedly, it associates itself frankly with the Catholic concern of the sixteenth century Reformers for the saving power of personal faith, making clear at the same time that this faith is operative most effectively through the signs of faith, the sacraments, the liturgy. Particularly apt, therefore, was the first liturgical reform since the promulgation of the Constitution: the personal faith-response of "Amen" by the recipient of holy communion.

Because faith comes through hearing, the Constitution restores due ritual prominence to the service of the word, and decrees that "the treasures of the Bible be opened up more lavishly, so that richer fare may be provided for the faithful at the table of God's Word" (art. 51). We may confidently look forward not only to a several years' cycle of more carefully chosen pericopes in Mass, but also to scriptural readings as an integral part of the rites of other sacraments. In the interest of deepening as well as evoking a responsive faith, too, are the Council's decrees about the homily, which it declares to be "part of the liturgical service" (art. 35), and its restoration of the ancient practice of the prayer of the faithful.

Article 33, finally, contradicts the facile distinction often invoked in discussions about liturgical language, that some parts of the liturgy are for the instruction and edification of the people, whereas others, particularly the Mass Canon, are purely theocentric, and hence need not and indeed should not be in the vernacular. "Not only when things are read 'which have been written for our instruction' [that is, in Scripture lessons], but also when the Church prays or sings or acts [that is, when the priest addresses prayers to God . . . which he always does 'in the name . . . of all present'], the faith of those taking part is nourished and their minds raised to God." What indeed can compare with the Canon of the Mass in power both to express and nourish the faith of the people most fully: for it is by this "memorial" above all that the Church proclaims the death of the Lord until he comes (1 Cor 11:26).

The importance attached by the Constitution to the willing and responsible action of each person of the assembly mirrored the self-discovery which the Church has been experiencing in recent years, perhaps most consciously in the liturgical movement. This had been achieved, above all, by a deliberate return to the sources. Working in close collaboration with the rapidly developing biblical and patristic movements, the liturgical revival had discovered anew some of the pastoral implications of the charismatic Church, the variety of the Holy Spirit's gifts to persons in the Church described by St. Paul immediately after his account of the eucharistic celebration (1 Cor 12).

This process of growing self-awareness by the Church was, however, unthinkable without a simultaneous and an even more profound fresh awareness of Christ. As a consequence of the Arian struggles, Christ-God at the right hand of the Father had occupied the thought of Christians. The Middle Ages had centered their devotion on the humanity of Jesus who had suffered and died for us. The *Constitution on the Liturgy*, returning to the sources, rejoices in the presence of the Emmanuel, the high priest of yesterday, of whose reign forever we already have a foretaste because of his saving presence in our midst today.

Articles 5–10 treat of this presence, and are without doubt the heart of the entire document, its most important theological as well as spiritual and devotional contribution to the renewing self-discovery of the Church. With unmistakable emphasis, article 7 states: *praesens adest* in the sacrifice of the Mass, in the person of his minister and in the eucharistic species. *Praesens adest* in the action of the sacraments. *Praesens adest* in his proclaimed word.

Praesens adest in the worshiping assembly.

This present activity of Christ in his Church, especially in all her liturgical celebrations, had already been declared by Pius XII in *Mediator Dei* (No. 20), but not with comparable emphasis: it seemed more incidental to his argument. Nor had Pius XII spoken of Christ's presence in the proclaimed Scripture. His citation, moreover, of Matthew 18:20, "Where two or three are gathered in my name, there I am in the midst of them," was more for the purpose of identifying the Divine Office as the prayer of Christ, than of asserting his presence in the assembly.

Too, the effective entry of Pius XII's statements into general Christian consciousness was obstructed by our centuries-old restriction of the term "real presence" exclusively to Christ's presence in the eucharistic species. Any other mode of presence must then logically be judged as somehow unreal, figurative. Some of the Council Fathers were, as a matter of fact, disturbed by article 7, especially by its assertion of Christ's presence in the proclaimed word, and asked that the document be submitted to the Theological Commission for a check on its orthodoxy. An emphatic and clear declaration was needed, and the Constitution has given it to us.

Equally emphatic is the Constitution's authoritative approbation of the contemporary biblical, liturgical and theological return to the sources in viewing Christ's death and resurrection as together constituting the saving "paschal mystery." In the "wondrous sacrament of the whole Church" (art. 5), the death and resurrection are not merely proclaimed but "accomplished," most especially in the celebration of the eucharist, whereby "the victory *and triumph* of his death are again made present" (art. 6). The Church is newly discovering herself today, is declaring the personal dignity of each member of her worshiping people, because the Church and each person are more clearly seen to be sacraments of the person Christ who is present in our midst, sharing with us his redeeming dying and rising.

In conclusion, I may be permitted a brief over-all judgment of the Constitution. My optimistic evaluation needs to be qualified by mention of its defects. Some have already been pointed out. Closer consultation with representatives of the Eastern Churches might have resulted in approximating those communities in their explicit extolling of the Holy Spirit and of his activity in the Church and her liturgy. The presence of Christ, which the Constitution so well highlights, is intrinsically bound up with his sending of the Spirit. The defect was adverted to by the Council Fathers, and three mentions of the Spirit were as a consequence added to the document. But the role of the Spirit is still not sufficiently stressed, nor integrated into the total theological presentation.

Another weakness is apparent in the Constitution's effort to correlate liturgical action to other areas of Christian life, whether devotional or apostolic.

Principles are stated but, given the divorce that has too long obtained, a more extended treatment was needed to carry conviction.

But even the positive achievements of the document may be looked at with a skeptical eye. What in it is really new? Leo the Great, who stated "Whatever was visible in the life of Christ has passed over into the sacraments" would probably find nothing particularly stimulating in it. Granted. But this very fact illustrates at least one of the Constitution's merits. It represents a willed return to the sources, of Scripture first of all. As one of the Protestant Observers remarked: "It may not quote the Bible as often as some of the other documents, but this thing surely has some convincing biblical theology."

The progress the document effects is the unexpectedly broad advance over positions occupied for centuries, and occasioned largely by polemics, both intra- and extramural. True to its own principles of change and adaptation, it retains what is valuable from those centuries, attempts to meet the changing conditions of today, and deliberately remains open to future changes. We have no reason to fear another liturgical ice age.

Pope John XXIII before the Council's opening stated that this program from Ephesians should be written over the portals of Vatican II: "Speaking the truth in love, we are to grow up in every way into him who is the head, into Christ, from whom the body, joined and knit together by every joint with which it is supplied, when each part is working properly, makes bodily growth and upbuilds itself in love" (Eph 4:15–16). I believe that, with the assistance of the Holy Spirit, the Council Fathers made a hearteningly good beginning of realizing that program through the *Constitution on the Sacred Liturgy*.

*Question: One of the most important details of the Consti-
tution on the Liturgy is its insistence on the word of God and
its basic importance for the liturgy. Now could you say something on this aspect and the way in which the Post-Conciliar
Commission intends to widen the scope and variety of the
readings from Scripture to be used, especially in the Mass, but
also in the Divine Office and maybe in the liturgy of the
sacraments?*

DIEKMANN: I spoke of Scripture only in passing, in relation to faith.
Obviously one of the great contributions of the *Constitution on the Liturgy*
is its restoration of Scripture in principle to that role which is its right as the
word of God, as an essential part of our dialogue with God. Not only does
the Constitution ask that there be a larger number and better selection of
Scripture readings, perhaps over a cycle of years, in the Mass. It also emphasizes the role of Scripture in personal devotional life, in Bible services, and
so on. It seems quite certain that, according to the principles of the Constitution and according to the mind of the people who have been working in
the Commission, there will be at least a three-year cycle of Scripture readings

31

for the Mass—i.e., a three-year cycle for Sundays and feast days, and perhaps on Sundays and feast days an optional third reading from the Old Testament. The problem is somewhat complicated by the obvious desirability of collaboration in this matter with other churches. Many of them have been experimenting with cycles of Scripture readings, and, therefore, there is a desire—I think on the part of all—that such collaboration be achieved and that together we work out a lectionary, again perhaps a three-year cycle of Scripture readings.

> Question: If the eucharist makes the Church, what about concelebration between Roman Catholics and other Christians as a means toward the unity of the Church? What does Father Diekmann think about this for the future? What are the difficult problems?

DIEKMANN: I am one of those who is convinced that the eucharist, since it is the most public declaration of our faith, of our unity in faith, of our belonging to the one Church, is and has been historically the sign of unity achieved in faith. Surely for those who participate in the eucharist it is the sign that accomplishes further unity. But I believe that historically the tradition has been—and it is sound theologically—that it presupposes the unity of faith *achieved*. This is not a problem that concerns merely us. I happen to have been at the Faith and Order Meeting at Montreal some years ago, and this was one of the most hotly discussed issues there. What the ultimate answer is, I do not know. We discussed this also at the Lutheran-Catholic dialogue in Chicago a few weeks ago, and it was one of the main points of discussion at the Episcopalian-Catholic meeting. Sacraments are for men. Surely there are exceptions: the famous incident of Lutherans in a concentration camp without a minister who believe in the real presence; certainly in such a case the eucharist should, I believe, be given to them. But this is an exception, a case of necessity. Whether this exception—an accepted case of exception—can be extended to other exceptions more broadly than at present, I do not know. Personally, I strongly incline to maintain the eucharist as the sign of the public—*the* public—sign of faith.

> Question: Might the Constitution on the Liturgy have been written differently had it been composed after schema 13, after the Church in the Modern World?

DIEKMANN: I am sure it would have been, just as I am sure that the Holy Spirit would have received his proper position in the entire theological exposition. Someone asked just before the meeting tonight, "What next?"

Well, sometimes I think that the liturgical movement at the present time can be compared to a boa constrictor in the process of swallowing a chicken.

It is so much occupied with the immediate present problems that it hasn't got time to think of the next step. Perhaps, as in the case of the ecumenical movement, we have to take the first step that now lies open and must be taken, and then hope that the next step will become clear.

However, it does seem to me that it is precisely the sociological dimension that calls for our attention now. It seems to me that we have an implicit theology of the Church in the *Constitution on the Liturgy*, made more explicit of course in subsequent documents; but the Church consists of men, and men live in the present, in given conditions, in given sociological structures, and I am sure that the Constitution does not wrestle with this problem as it might have, or give, let us say, indications of how this might be resolved. I do not think, to be very frank, that the members who composed the Constitution would be able to give those answers. And that is why I pleaded that religious sociologists be asked for their help in this essential matter of the liturgy coming to life in groups of people according to their needs. Msgr. Gremillion, would you have something to add there? What did you have in mind?

GREMILLION: I put the question to you as a pastor for some fifteen years and a person who now is full time in social action. The one hour of worship on Sunday is still relatively irrelevant to what Tom, Dick, Harry, Jane and Joan do on Tuesday night and Wednesday morning, and the other 167 hours of human life—I mean to the joys and sorrows and hopes of man, as schema 13 puts it. Frankly I don't know whether we should expect the liturgy to be that relevant; I sort of feel it should be. That is why I put the question. And you may have some further comeback on that. What I mean is that these people are worried about babies, bottles, colic, Telstar, astronauts, and building this building, etc. And how does all this experience of human creativity and striving for human unity join together with worshiping God as a group on Sunday in the liturgical setting?

DIEKMANN: I wonder whether Father Houtart would like to address himself to that problem?

HOUTART: Well, I think the problem is extremely vast, of course. There is not only a sociological problem, but I really think that in worship we have to have some kind of reference to the concrete life of people. Maybe the role of the homily has something to do with that, and also the prayers of the faithful before the Offertory. Concrete reference to some of their real problems should be made, it seems to me, in every liturgical celebration—the implications of faith in their daily life. I think a first step is already being made now.

HAY: This will be just a short one, Mr. Chairman, because possibly the question that I should like to talk about, the place of preaching in the liturgy, may come up later. Being a Presbyterian summoned to this assembly,

I must wave the flag in that direction—on behalf of my Lutheran friends too, perhaps. We need to have a more fully developed theology of preaching than I find in the *Constitution on the Liturgy*. Part of the answer to the question that has just been raised by Msgr. Gremillion is that liturgy becomes relevant when preaching is a real, living part of the liturgy.

BURGHARDT: I think my question has something to do with the socio-logical issue raised by Msgr. Gremillion; I also consider it to be a theological issue, and it is at the basis of a question that was previously asked. In what sense can it be said that the eucharist creates the Church? This has to do, I think, in a practical way, with Msgr. Gremillion's observations that in the concrete order the eucharist does not seem in any genuine sense to create the Church. If at all possible, I would like to get some sort of a theological understanding of this phrase. Is this saying any more than what you find, say, in the Fathers of the Church? For the Fathers of the Church, as I read them, the eucharist is the consummation, the perfection of the Church. Why? Because in the eucharist is realized, in an altogether unique fashion, the oneness of all men with God and with one another in God which had its radical beginning in the incarnation of God's Son in the womb of the Virgin. Are you saying anything more than that when you say the eucharist creates the Church?

DIEKMANN: I believe that the expression means more than this, Father. Not only the Church Fathers, but St. Thomas too insists that the "res huius sacramenti est unitas mystici corporis." The *res*, the purpose, the effect, of the sacrament is the unity of the mystical body. And Thomas frequently speaks of the eucharist as the sacrament of ecclesiastical unity, and by that he means the unity of the Church. It seems to me, then, that it means not merely the general union of ourselves with Christ in the Church, but it takes into account the Church as it becomes concrete locally. It seems to me that this is also the burden of—I bow to Scripture scholars here—the scriptural evidence for the theology of the assembly: that it was the community that came together; and that in coming together, its members had an experience of interpersonal relationship, of knowing each other, of loving each other—this thing became concrete. Love is not something abstract. And man needs this face-to-face confrontation. And that is why the eucharist is *the* opportunity of expressing this. That is, first of all, achieved by the eucharist itself; this is the grace of the eucharist. And furthermore, in the expression or cele-bration of the eucharist, this takes visible form, in singing together, in acting together, in meeting before and after, and so on. And so, in this matter we cannot abstract from the importance of the local community, particularly in view of the document, of theology's insistence on the meaning of *eccle-sia*, meaning not merely the universal Church but the local worshiping community.

DUNNE: I would like to pose a question about the matter that Father Diekmann mentioned earlier, that the liturgy is an expression of unity in faith, and the problem of concelebration and communion with other churches. I wonder if, at this point, we could make a distinction between faith and belief? By belief I would mean the notions that one holds, the religious notions that one holds; and by faith I would mean a sort of basic orientation of one's living and thinking. It seems, if you look at the general idea of the development of doctrine in the Church throughout the centuries that there is a development in belief. You could almost say something similar of the individual life; the individual person, no matter what church he belongs to, goes through a development of doctrine, a development of beliefs, so that his beliefs at one stage of his life are somewhat different than they are at another even though he recites the same creed. What it means at one point in his life is different from what it means at another. So I wonder if it would be possible to say that the liturgy is an expression of the unity of faith as distinct from belief. I myself feel that even within the Roman Catholic Church it would be difficult to say that there is a unity of belief, in the sense that everyone has exactly the same beliefs; yet I believe one can speak, with some assurance, of a unity of faith, in the sense of a basic orientation. I wonder if this wouldn't cast a different light on the problem of communion and concelebration with other churches.

DIEKMANN: Have we arrived perhaps at the ultimate possible expression of the visibility of the Church? Surely those who participate in the eucharistic service may have different understandings of the faith, maybe an error concerning that faith, yet all of them wish to accept the faith that is represented by this eucharistic service. It is the public, visible expression of adherence to *this* community which holds *this* faith, even though there may be a personal misunderstanding of what this implies. I believe this is what is at issue in this whole matter. I do not think it is a question merely of beliefs and faith, but a question of visibility that is involved.

DR. BROWN: Father Godfrey, could you expand just a little more on what this would mean about other liturgical actions in which we could participate? It would seem clear, from what you say, that you feel the line should be drawn in terms of concelebration, intercommunion. What is the principle in terms of which it would not violate your principles to have the sharing of hymns, of prayers, and so forth? What are the lines that you think should be drawn so that our liturgical actions together do not become a false sign?

DIEKMANN: I think it is precisely the eucharist that is the distinguishing rite; it is recognized historically and theologically as such. Other prayer services are not interpreted in that fashion, have not been interpreted in that fashion, and therefore are certainly possible. Therefore, union in prayer, common prayer, common Scripture service—all these things are quite another matter.

AHERN: Father Godfrey, how would you explain in this regard that period of about 150 years where we did have this practice with the Eastern Church?

DIEKMANN: I know. From what I have been able to understand of the Church's legislation as well as her present position, it does seem to me that there is an inconsistency here. If the interpretation I have presented does correspond to the theological principle underlying our rules so far, then I personally see an inconsistency here.

WOLF: I was the one who asked the question about concelebration. I would just like to make a further comment and see what your response to it would be, Father Diekmann. I agree with your interpretation of the historical situation. But it does seem to me that what you have just referred to as "inconsistency" may be traced further back. It seems to me that there is a sound biblical base for seeing the unity of the Church as being created through eucharistic action. I think particularly of some of the New Testament evidence that Father Cooke has recently published. And I just wonder if in the New Testament itself there is not some ground for thinking that the unity of the Church may be helped through eucharistic celebration, and not solely be the sign of unity achieved.

DIEKMANN: I am not acquainted sufficiently with the scriptural evidence. Father Cooke, would you like to tell us what your argument was?

COOKE: It wasn't exactly an argument; I was just trying to assemble the texts on both sides. I think you can gather a series of texts that point to the fact that one must presuppose some form of unity and community in faith which is then expressed in the eucharistic action. But there is also a series of texts which, when gathered, point to the fact that this eucharistic action itself is what is formative of the community. Actually I think it is a little bit of both. As far as I can see, the difficult question is going to be to determine what extent of unity of faith is required so as to make the liturgical celebration of the eucharist authentic, so that it will really say that you have a community of faith. It seemed to me, in puzzling over those texts in our meetings, that it was a difficulty of distinguishing between the operative faith-agreement in the people who celebrate the eucharist—that is to say their understanding of that action—and the organizational expression of that in a unified, organized community. I think, to some extent, it is going to have to be a matter of what you might call a disciplinary decision as you go along, safeguarding the genuine stability of the faith of the communities involved, so that it does not become an undisciplined approach to the thing; this, of course, would be disastrous both from the doctrinal and the community point of view.

DIEKMANN: Is there any opening, Father, for the possibility of such an interpretation in the adjective "indiscriminate" that has been added in the *Decree on Ecumenism?*

COOKE: Yes, that is one thing that was discussed. There were two things: first, it seemed that there was an exception made—or at least the difference of situation pointed out—with regard to the Anglican-Roman situation; and second, the remark that was made in there that we were not to proceed indiscriminately in the matter of intercommunion.

DIEKMANN: We have limited the discussion, so far this evening, to the question of faith. I wonder, Father, whether we can divorce the question of faith from that of submission to proper authority. The eucharist itself is not merely an expression of faith. Certainly if the ecclesiology of Ignatius of Antioch is to be more or less representative of the thought of early Christianity, then submission to authority was even more significant.

COOKE: Yes, actually that was introduced into the presentation. And I think that an even deeper question that we raised, and hope later on to discuss, is that if you were to have something like concelebration, the external manifestation of the ceremony points to a certain collegiality of ministry. And the question is: Does such a collegiality exist? And this question led us, not to specific questions of Anglican Orders or anything along that line, but to the deeper question of ministry, its nature and how it is involved.

> Question: A Protestant writer on the Council has said that the Council's Constitution on the Liturgy is the answer of the liturgical movement to Mediator Dei. He stresses that Mediator Dei emphasized the Church's action. The Constitution stresses Christ's action. Do you agree?

DIEKMANN: No. For many years I have been saying, and I am convinced this is correct, that *Mediator Dei's* greatest contribution was precisely this emphasis on the active presence of Christ. This was its great contribution but was not recognized at the time. It did not make the impact, for it was so new. What *Mediator Dei* gave us in this matter is now made much more explicit and more emphatic. But certainly *Mediator Dei* speaks again and again of Christ and his priestly ministry: "Christ acts each day to save us," and so on.

> Question: Does not the adaptation of liturgy to indigenous cultures present a real problem? Years of nonadaptation have left the African church, for example, without its own distinctive religious art forms. Today, therefore, adaptation requires creation of such forms, but today even Africa is feeling the pressure of Western civilization and will feel it even more so

*in the future. Is there reason to fear then that emphasis on
adaptation may be an anachronism?*

DIEKMANN: Father Ahern, you have been active in Africa for the last
several years. What would be your own answer to this?

AHERN: My own answer, Father Godfrey, is that it would be infinitely
desirable, but yet I wonder how practical. A very real example would be
this. The African has simply imported the European Christ. The European
changed the Semitic Christ to his own French or Italian form. The African
has merely accepted the European Christ. They have become so utterly
familiar with it that now I wonder whether an African Christ would really
and truly gain their love. They are starting it, but it's nearly null. Now as
far as religious music forms go they are certainly beginning that. But the
people are thoroughly familiar with the other forms.

DIEKMANN: But, Father, wouldn't the principle still hold good? Adaptation means that adjustment to conditions which are called for in a given
situation. If, therefore, in this particular situation adaptation is not applicable
in the same sense that it would be in other areas where there is an indigenous
culture, then this adaptation is not made. It is still the principle that souls
must be saved in the best possible way, given their situation. This, in itself,
it seems to me, is the principle of adaptation: that form should be used
which here and now speaks.

AHERN: Well, since I am speaking to the "hootenanny priest," you will
understand what I mean, and I agree with you, Father. In places like Tokyo,
where they are dancing the "frug," eventually their art forms may come to
be very much like ours. And in Africa where they love the Beatles, I think
their art forms may actually take those expressions. In other words, with this
progressive spread of Westernization, I wonder if the adaptation isn't going to
become much more uniform than the Constitution seems to speak of it here
and now.

HOUTART: I think it is here that we see the usefulness of anthropology,
ethnology and sociology. The discussion shows that there are different levels
of adaptation, and of adaptation of modern, of Western patterns of culture
and society. So we have to be very prudent. It is too easy to say that, on the
one hand, we have to adapt and, on the other, those people are now adapting
to our own culture. Things are much more complicated than that. The distinction between the different levels is a very important one.

> *Question: Could you explain more fully the presence of
> Christ in the Blessed Sacrament and his presence in each
> Christian, in the Church, in the proclaimed word, etc.?*

DIEKMANN: Well, not in ten minutes. I read this question because it gives me an opportunity to point out that the presentation in article 7 of the Constitution is somewhat unfortunate. It starts with the presence of Christ in the eucharist, instead of starting, as the encyclical *Mysterium Fidei* does, with the presence of Christ in the assembly, then in the word, then in the action of the sacrament and the eucharistic species. The presence of Christ in the Blessed Sacrament, or the eucharistic species, certainly is not an entity isolated from the other modes of presence, and its purpose is to deepen the presence of Christ in the assembly and in each member of the assembly.

CONGAR: It has always seemed to me that the *Constitution on the Liturgy* lacked a certain theology of the Christian cult. It seems that there is a question that has never been raised: What indeed is the nature of Christian cult? In the *Constitution on the Liturgy*, it has been clearly shown, there is somewhat of an answer to this question. The primary value in Christian cult seems to be the reception of God's sanctifying gift. But I for one would have liked the Constitution to go more deeply into the theological nature of cult. It seems to me that it presents the word of God as a preliminary condition rather than as an essential element of the cult which itself is essentially a cult of faith. If the Council had shown better that it is a cult of faith it would have been better able to integrate the human aspects mentioned by Abbe Houtart, the insertion in worship of the daily life of men. And I should like, therefore, to ask our speaker what he has to say in this connection?

DIEKMANN: I am not sure whether I got the total thrust of your question, Father. As far as Scripture is concerned, it is possible that it is not given that full significance which belongs to it as cult: the creative word of which in some sense the entire eucharistic action also is an expression. We can speak of the Mass itself as a *sacrificium laudis*, a sacrifice of praise, as Justin, for instance, speaks of it. So that in some ways the entire eucharistic action is nothing else than the creative word of God finding a twofold expression in the Scripture proclaimed and in the proclamation of the praise, in the *berakah*. I can only say, Father, that the intention of the Constitution, on the part of those who worked at its elaboration, was to restore precisely that emphasis on the word of God. Whether it succeeded is another matter. And also in this case, there were several changes made. For instance, the schema originally spoke of the table of the word and the table of the bread. This seemed too bold to some bishops and was therefore dropped, even though it was pointed out to them that this phrase is found in Book 4 of *Imitation* —and that author can hardly be called a very extreme person. Afterwards, however, the phrase "table of the word" was inserted.

CONGAR: I should like to press this point for a few moments, if you allow me. This admirable comparison of the two tables is found in the *Constitution on Divine Revelation* and the *Decree on the Ministry and Life of Priests*.

It is therefore commonplace in the Council, so to speak. But I would like to ask you, Father, how you view the development of the notion of priesthood itself corresponding to this rediscovery of the word as an essential element of cult? I believe that this figures explicitly in the Decree on priests, but I would be happy if you would explain this point now. Because, as I say, it seems that the word of God is a condition previous to rather than actually a part of the nature of cult itself?

DIEKMANN: If this is the impression given by the Constitution, then certainly it is a wrong impression. As far as I know, it is not the mind of the Constitution, certainly not the mind of those who spoke, of the use of Scripture. It is not preliminary to, but an essential expression of, the whole nature of cult and of worship. I think it was Irenaeus who said "Glorificatio Dei est homo," or something to that effect. That God is glorified by man, in man, in transfigured man, that the objective glorification of God is achieved through the word of God transforming men, the life-giving word. It is much more than a preamble, surely, Father.

BUTLER

MINEAR

AHERN

SESSION III

ABBOT CHRISTOPHER BUTLER, O.S.B.
The Constitution on Divine Revelation

REV. BARNABAS AHERN, C.P.
Scriptural Aspects

DR. PAUL S. MINEAR
A Protestant Point of View

Abbot Christopher Butler, O.S.B.

THE CONSTITUTION ON DIVINE REVELATION

O F THE SIXTEEN DOCUMENTS debated and enacted by Vatican Council II, only two—that on the Church and that on divine revelation—are accorded the title of Dogmatic Constitution. It will be in place to consider this title briefly here.

An ecumenical council is believed to have the God-given power of rendering infallible definition to some aspect of our inherited faith that has not hitherto been thus infallibly defined. Such defined doctrines are technically called "dogmas"—the noun corresponding to the verb used in Acts to introduce the decisions of the scriptural Council of Jerusalem: "It seemed good to us and to the Holy Spirit" (Acts 15:28).

As is well known, however, Vatican II issued no new dogmas—though it reaffirmed some old ones. This is sufficiently striking. Perhaps the simplest explanation to offer for it is that Vatican II was not that kind of council. As John XXIII said in his inaugural address October 11, 1962, "The salient point of this Council is not a discussion of one article or another of the fundamental doctrine of the Church which has been repeatedly taught by the Fathers and by ancient and modern theologians. . . . The Christian, Catholic and apostolic spirit of the whole world expects a step forward towards a doctrinal penetration . . . and perfect conformity to the authentic doctrine which, however, should be studied and expounded through the methods of research and through the literary forms of modern thought."[1]

[1] W. Abbott, S.J., *The Documents of Vatican II* (New York: America Press, 1966) 715.

Thus the word "dogmatic" in the title of our Constitution must be taken in a broad sense, corresponding to that of "doctrinal." This means that, except where it is repeating former definitions, nothing the Constitution says has the precise guarantee of infallibility, which a new dogma would have had. Short of that, its teaching has very high authority indeed, and it certainly could be rash to contravene it on any matter of substance on which the text itself shows that the Council meant to give a deliberate view. On the other hand, we should bear in mind that it is a fairly lengthy document, and that the Council Fathers as a whole had not given to many of its sentences that meticulous scrutiny which a dogmatic definition would have required. A clear example of this is the passage where the Constitution tells us that the Church "unhesitatingly asserts the historicity of the four Gospels" (art. 19). The word "historicity" would, I suggest, have been too elastic for a dogmatic definition.[2]

What we actually have, in this Constitution, is a presentation of the Church's doctrine on revelation which takes account of the "methods" and results "of research" in modern times, and (in some measure) conforms to the "literary forms of modern thought." As a surplus, we have a treatment of the notion of tradition which, while remaining imperfect and—to some extent—clumsily expressed, represents a very notable advance on anything hitherto found in the Church's official documents on this subject.

It remains to observe that this paper confines itself, in the main, to the first two chapters of the Constitution, and leaves the subject of Holy Scripture almost intact for treatment by one far more expert in that field than I can claim to be.

Chapter 1

Already at this point it is well to observe that the Constitution is not offering a theological explication and application of revelation considered formally as a communication of divine truth to the human intellect. Our concern is rather with a merciful intervention of God in human history: with what article 2 of the Constitution calls the "plan" or historical disposition of God's self-disclosure and self-giving.

This sentence is of vital importance and must be quoted in full: "This plan of revelation is realized by deeds and words having an inner unity: deeds wrought by God in the history of salvation manifest and confirm the teaching and the realities signified by the words, while the words proclaim the deeds and clarify the mystery contained in them."

We remark that revelation is not just a matter of "words" of God addressed

[2] Cf. the Constitution's own reference to parts of Scripture that are "history of one kind or another" (art. 12).

to our understanding. It is also a matter of divine *deeds*; and the deeds and words are not just a series of parallel phenomena, but are intrinsically inter-related, the deeds not merely confirming or miraculously attesting the truth of the words but giving visible body to the words, and the words giving expression to the implications of the deeds.

Christianity was born in a Jewish, indeed Palestinian *milieu* but rapidly, as though by a native instinct, turned away to confront the great Graeco-Roman civilization and culture, where its realistic claims were met by the alternative claims of Greek philosophy. When Emperor Justinian I closed the schools of Athens, it might seem that the Church had won her long war with Greek natural speculation. But in the process of that great conflict Christianity had itself become in great measure a Greek thing. The Fathers of the Church were often at home in the world of Plato; they were often, as their exegesis shows, out of their depth when it was a question of understanding the Bible. It was only too easy, and it occurred almost unconsciously, to present Christianity itself as a philosophy, superior to Plato mainly because it happened to have been revealed by God; as that divine "logos" or "word" dreamed of in the *Phaedo* of Plato, which Plato himself would have accepted as preferable to the best efforts and conclusions of merely human reason.

But Christianity is something more than a revealed philosophy. At its heart there is not simply an oracular enlightenment of the human intellect; there is a divine action in history, an action which becomes a part of the history in which it intervenes. The word "revelation" itself is from a Latin rendering of the Greek word *apocalypsis*, which reminds us more immediately of the latest strata of the Old Testament and of late noncanonical Jewish writings than of the great central foundation insights of religion of ancient Israel. These insights tended to revolve around, and to flow from, the Exodus from Egypt, interpreted as a marvelous act of divine redemption. And although the prophetic writings are full of the notion of divine "words," these are not merely pieces of information. They are, at the least, divine commands, and they tend to be regarded as pregnant with efficacious divine power. Hence, although it was natural that the Council should start its consideration of the Christian reality from the traditional approach of "revelation," it might have been truer to the genius of Christianity and to its own deepest insight if it had chosen to call our document "Concerning Divine Action." If the Jewish-Christian stream of faith believes in a "living God," its certainty is derived most properly from the manifestation of God's vitality provided in his historical interventions, of which the climax for the Church is his raising of Jesus Christ from the dead. God "speaks" to men by acting and his "words" (in the narrower sense of the term) are above all interpretations of this activity.

That this is the mind of the Constitution seems to emerge from its next sentence in article 2: "By this revelation, then, the deepest truth about God and man's salvation is made clear to us in Christ, who is the mediator and at the same time the fullness of all revelation." Christ, then, is not merely by his words the mediator of a message from God; he is, in the completeness of his historical factualness (words, works, sufferings, miraculous resurrection), God self-disclosed, but above all God self-given. When the Prologue of the Fourth Gospel reaches its summit in the affirmation that "the word became flesh and dwelt among us" (1:14), it is no doubt offering us a development of doctrine—at least a development of theological language—from the earlier Christian use of the term "word" of God. But this is a development that in fact rejoins and renders articulate the deepest Christian intuition. Christ is our Savior, is himself Good News from God, precisely by what he *is* in the fullness of his incarnate history. And Christianity is not just an enrichment of our intellect; it is a divine gift received in our heart and in our whole historical body-and-soul selves, a gift to which we respond by our total self-gift to God. Since we remain the heirs of Greek thought, we need to remind ourselves that, while the core of the Christian religion is the "knowledge" of God, the word "knowledge" has its own resonance in Scripture, where, if God knows his chosen ones and they know him, the knowledge in question is better compared to the mutual "knowledge" of matrimony than to the science and speculation of the Greeks. And for the interpretation of the *Constitution on Divine Revelation* we should bear in mind also that the word "truth" in the Old Testament similarly has a less cerebral flavor about it than it had in the writings of the Greek philosophers—and has in modern scientific writing. "Truth," in the Old Testament and in the New also, so far as the latter reflects Old Testament modes of thought, is both the divine trustworthiness and a concrete reality transcending the conceptual sphere. Such, it may be said in passing, is that "truth which God wanted put into the sacred writings for the sake of our salvation," in consequence of which "the books of Scripture . . . teach faithfully and without error" (art. 11).

The Constitution next gives a bird's-eye view of the history of salvation, from our first parents down to Christ, who, especially by his death and glorious resurrection, with the eventual mission of the Spirit of truth, completes, perfects and confirms the revelation that God is with us to free us from sin and death and to raise us up to eternal life. This Christian dispensation is the definitive covenant of God with man, and no new public revelation is henceforth to be expected till the "glorious manifestation of our Lord Jesus Christ" (art. 4).

The Constitution's first chapter concludes with two sections in the nature of appendices to the main theme.

The divine revelation is a gift that calls for acceptance. How does man accept it? The Council replies that we have to pay "the obedience of faith" to God in his act of revelation. This obedience amounts to a free and entire self-surrender to God, which takes shape in "a full submission of intellect and will to god who reveals" and a willed assent to the content of the revelation. Such faith itself presupposes the prior and concomitant help of God's grace and the interior assistance of the Holy Spirit to move our heart and turn it to God, to open our mind's eyes, and to give us "joy and ease . . . in assenting to the truth and believing it" (art. 5). There is thus, in the initial act of faith, a beginning of understanding of the revelation. This understanding can grow progressively with the continuing help of the Holy Spirit. The doctrine of this section, closely based on St. Paul, is also dependent on Vatican Council I.

The final section of the chapter deals with a subsidiary point. The divine plan for man's salvation, which is the central theme of revelation, is in itself something that transcends the natural order and can only be known *by* revelation. However, the Council reaffirms the teaching of Vatican Council I, that man's natural reason is not entirely hopeless in the sphere of divine truth: in theory, it can attain to a "certain knowledge of God" arising out of the created order. But the actual condition of mankind is not what, theoretically, it might have been. Sin has worked havoc not only on man's will but, consequently, on his power of attaining truth by his own efforts. A consequential benefit of revelation is to bestow on us stable certitude and freedom from error not only in the sphere of direct "salvation knowledge" but also in that of what would today be called "the philosophy of religion"—not that revelation provides us with philosophical arguments, but that it strengthens and clarifies our natural insight.

CHAPTER 2

The Christian message and religion hinge on the affirmation that "God has visited and redeemed his people"; that there is a particular nodal point in history where human act and divine act are identical in the identity of one self-same agent. It is at this point that the old tension between man's commitment to the relative, the contingent, the historical, and his aspiration for the Absolute is overcome.

By the nature of the case, however, this nodal point of history is both spatially and temporally conditioned. God's "only Son, our Lord . . . suffered under Pontius Pilate." What then of those who have never seen and heard and handled the Word of Life?

This is the problem of the transmission of divine revelation, announced in the preface of the Constitution and taken up in chapter 2. Let us remind ourselves that, while the Constitution speaks of the transmission of the revelation, it has already spoken of the "plan of revelation," of the "history of salvation"—meaning not history that is written but history that happens—and finally of Christ himself as not only the mediator of revelation but its fullness. The problem, then, is the transmission of Christ.

Christ was the fullness of revelation in his "whole work of making Himself present and manifesting Himself" (art. 4), as a historical reality. The Christian revelation is not merely historical as having been given at a moment of the human story; it is historical in its intrinsic nature. It saves inasmuch as it is a historical encounter. Therefore, it must retain its historical character in its mode of transmission, which must itself be historical. There is no intention here of denying that the act of faith, by which we respond to God's self-disclosure, places us in communion with the transhistorical Absolute. But it does so inasmuch as it is a time-conditioned response to a time-conditioned mediation of the Absolute.

God, the Constitution tells us (art. 7), so arranged that what he had revealed for the salvation of all peoples should be transmitted to every generation. Hence Christ commissioned the apostles that they should proclaim the gospel to all men, communicating to them the gifts of God. The last phrase is, I think, important. The apostles were not only to pass on a message; they were to communicate divine gifts—the very substance of the "plan of revelation," the saving reality of Christ himself.

This commission, we are told, was fulfilled in two ways. (1) The apostles "handed on, by their oral preaching, by example, and by ordinances, what they had received from the lips of Christ, from living with Him, and from what He did, or what they learned through the prompting of the Holy Spirit." (2) The commission was fulfilled "by those apostles and apostolic men who under the inspiration of the same Spirit committed the message of salvation to writing." (I would have preferred to write: "by those, whether apostles or apostolic men," since modern scholarship is not too sure that more than one apostle has, by immediate authorship, contributed to the New Testament. There is a further, I think unintentional, incoherence in the document at this point. The word "gospel" is used by those who composed the Constitution to mean the whole revelation, including the revealed ingredients of the Old Testament; and when the Constitution turns to the subject of the relations between "tradition" [as distinct from Scripture] and Holy Writ, it means by Holy Writ the whole Bible. Yet in article 7 only the New Testament is considered).

The first stage in the transmission of the revelation was thus fulfilled in the authorized teaching and work of the apostles (including the establishment of "ordinances," which presumably include the sacraments) and in the inspired authorship of those who composed the New Testament books. It was but a first stage, and obviously, if the revelation is for all men in every generation, something more was required. So the Constitution tells us that the apostles have left as their successors the bishops, to whom they passed on their own teaching authority. (I have translated the Latin *reliquerunt* as a true perfect, not an aorist. The *Constitution on the Church, Lumen gentium,* is careful not to assert that the nonepiscopal structure of the Church was established *as such* by the apostles.) Meanwhile, the Scriptures also survived the apostles, and we have the contemporary situation described, rather unfortunately, in the rejected predecessor of our Constitution as "the sources of revelation." Alike in Scripture and in the "sacred tradition," flowing like a stream from the work and teaching of the first commissioned envoys of Christ, we come face to face with Christ himself. And these two, sacred tradition and the Holy Writ of the Old and New Testament, are "like a mirror in which the pilgrim Church on earth looks at God . . . until she is brought to see Him as He is, face to face." We may observe that the Constitution speaks not of two mirrors, but of one. Sacred tradition and Holy Writ are, in fact, closely interconnected and interactive (*connectuntur et communicant inter se:* art. 9). They flow from the same divine source, combine so to say to form a single entity, and tend to the same end. Holy Writ is the utterance of God, and sacred tradition transmits the word of God, being enlightened at each moment of its continuing existence by the Spirit of truth, whose help is ever present to lead believers into all truth and to cause the word of Christ to indwell them abundantly. Hence the Church derives her certainty concerning all that has been revealed "not from sacred Scripture alone" (art. 9).

The last quoted clause deserves a comment. The Doctrinal Commission, which was mainly concerned with the final redaction of our Constitution, was under persistent pressure to commit itself to an explicit affirmation that Scripture does not contain the totality of the content of revelation. Our clause is a direct result of such pressure. It is therefore important to observe that it does not assert the "material insufficiency" of Scripture. Taken by itself, it would leave us free to hold that, explicitly or otherwise, the whole deposit of faith is contained in the Bible. It merely observes that the Church's *certainty* rests on two bases, Scripture and sacred tradition. These are converging, but not necessarily mutually complementing, grounds of certainty.

Elsewhere, it is true, the Constitution may seem to go further. Tradition, it is stated in article 8, is a means whereby the complete canon of Scripture is known by the Church; a statement which it is not easy to contradict. Moreover, it is of importance for the whole concept of the transmission of revelation to bear in mind that what is transmitted is not only a set of doctrines, or the content of the speculative act of faith, but the very reality of Christ as conveyed, for example, by the sacraments. Truth about the sacraments may well be found in Scripture, but not the sacraments themselves as factual institutions. The Church transmits to all generations not only "all that she believes" but "all that she *is*" (art. 8); and to say that the Church *is* in the Bible would be at least ambiguous.

Those who "swear to the words of Newman" will be glad to read the Council's affirmation that the apostolic tradition (a word which includes Holy Writ in its compass) "progresses" (*proficit*) in the Church under the assistance of the Holy Spirit (art. 8). There is a growth in our understanding of the tradition, resulting from study and contemplation of it, from an interior insight into the spiritual realities that believers experience, and from the preaching (praeconium, kerygma, official proclamation) of the bishops. Thus, as the ages roll on, the Church ever tends towards the fullness of divine truth, till the words of God are consummated in her.

There is, of course, no suggestion in this passage that the Church ever would or could make quantitative additions to the "deposit of faith"; as we have already been warned, the revelation in the historical Jesus puts a term to all "public revelations" (art. 4). What is affirmed is a growth in the Church's reflective grasp of the treasure entrusted to her. We might say that, from the beginning, she has possessed the fullness of the revelation in *re*; but her reflection upon revelation is a source of continuing further enlightenment by which the deposit becomes less opaque. The wisdom of babes is ever tending to become the wisdom of the perfect; and this is a process that will not be completed until Christ "comes again in the glory of his Father." It may be added that the prelate (Cardinal Florit) who officially, on behalf of the Doctrinal Commission, presented this chapter to the Council Fathers, while denying any material accretion to the deposit of faith, held that our paragraph does teach that the deposit itself is subject to the sort of intrinsic development which is found in living organisms, a development whereby the organism changes in order to maintain and deepen its own identity. The fact is that the deposit is itself a divine enrichment of our *intellect*, and as our intellectual grasp of it becomes more complete, it itself becomes more fully what it always had in it to become. Revelation implies a two-way traffic between God and man; it is not given till it is received, and it is given in so far as it is received.

Sacred tradition and Holy Writ, then, constitute a single sacred deposit of the word of God. This deposit is entrusted to the Church—by which the Council habitually means not simply those who wield hierarchical authority, but the whole People of God. There is, in fact, a singular agreement (*conspiratio*) of prelates and faithful in holding, putting into practice, and professing the transmitted faith (art. 10).

It is true that the college of bishops, inheriting the commission given by Christ to his apostles, has its own special function in regard to the transmitted word. This is a function of "authentic interpretation." As such, it places ecclesiastical authority not above God's word, but in the position of a servant of the word, to which it gives devout attention, and which it guards and faithfully expounds. The resulting interpretation of the deposit of faith can be trusted to be correct, because of the assistance of the Holy Spirit which is guaranteed to the college of Christ's envoys. We are reminded that ecclesiastical authority draws only from the single deposit of the word of God whatever it sets before men as divinely revealed.

I have referred to Newman. Students of his *Essay on the Development of Christian Doctrine* may remember how that great Christian and profound thinker was reluctant to admit that we could ever make an inventory of the contents of Holy Writ. Of no alleged truth, he held, could it be positively affirmed that it is *not* in Scripture—unless indeed it contradicts something already known to be true. He was equally convinced that our grasp of the contents of Scripture, nay, our grasp of the whole "idea" of Christianity, was capable of indefinite development. Such development, for him, was part and parcel of what is meant by sacred tradition. But he also argued that, if the process of development was not to lead the Church astray, it must be guaranteed by divine assistance; hence the place of ecclesiastical authority in the sphere of Christian belief. These three elements, Scripture, sacred tradition, and what is called the magisterium of the Church are the triple subject of our chapter. They are, it concludes, so intimately connected and allied together, that no one of them stands without the others, while all of them together, and each singly in its own fashion under the action of the one Holy Spirit, contribute effectively to the salvation of souls.

APPRAISAL

The time has perhaps not yet come for a definitive appraisal of the teaching contained in the first two chapters of *Dei verbum*. Already, however, we can usefully remind ourselves that they do not constitute a theological treatise on the subject of divine revelation and its transmission. A theologian, operating within limits laid down by the dogmas of the Church, would reflect upon his personal insights and would seek to convey a unified system of such insights. Those responsible for drafting the Council's dogmatic constitutions had a different task. They had to try to do justice to a sufficiently wide variety of opinions expressed in the Conciliar debates to produce a document that could command if possible a moral unanimity of assent, and yet constitute a real enrichment of the Christian mind. There is thus an ingredient of compromise in our document. This may be illustrated from a single sentence in its first chapter: " 'The obedience of faith' must be given to God who reveals, an obedience by which man entrusts his whole self freely to God, offering 'the full submission of intellect and will to God who reveals,' and freely assenting to the truth revealed by Him" (art. 5). The phrase "entrusts his whole self freely to God" is an attempt to render the richness of the biblical, and especially Pauline, notion of faith and, at the same time, to do justice to the profoundest existential insights of our own age. But since there were those to whom this seemed too vague and inarticulate a presentation of the act of faith, this phrase is coupled with another, quoted from Vatican I. There is, of course, in my judgment, no discrepancy between these two notions of faith; but they are placed side by side in our document, and it is left to theological reflection to show how they cohere or are indeed identical. Compromise may be more broadly illustrated by the fact that our document deliberately leaves substantially unsettled the current theological debate on what is called the material "sufficiency of Scripture."

Our Constitution is therefore a milestone on an uncompleted journey. But it is an important milestone. The very concrete, biblical, historical approach it takes to its primary subject is tremendously refreshing, and is capable of much further development, besides being highly serviceable to the cause of ecumenism. It should help to bridge the gap, from which Catholic reflection has suffered too long in recent years, between the manuals of dogmatic theology and the best work of our biblical theologians and scholars.

Hardly less important is the treatment of tradition in our second chapter. The quickest way to measure the progress effected here is to remind ourselves that the Council of Trent spoke not of tradition but of "unwritten traditions" in the plural. Our own document, on the other hand, considers the question of the transmission of divine revelation in all its amplitude. It recognizes that what is to be accounted for is not merely the preservation of a certain corpus of information received from the mouth of Christ or "the dictation of the Holy Spirit"[3] but the real presence of the Incarnate Word of God to the fullness of the humanity of the believer and in the fullness of the life of the People of God. Basically, as the almost inevitable term "real presence" suggests, this is a root problem of sacramental theology, transcending the problematic of the Greek schools and carrying us close to the heart of the Christian mystery. From this point of view, Scripture and tradition are not two separate issues; rather, Scripture enters as an ingredient into the total substance of tradition and lives ever contemporarily in that total substance. Here too, we may hope that the Constitution will prove to have paved the way to more fruitful dialogue both with our Eastern brethren, whose notion of tradition has habitually been less conceptual than our own, and who, I hope, will appreciate the Constitution's reminders that tradition itself lives with the infused life of the Holy Spirit; and with those Protestants who, starting it may seem from the opposite point of the theological compass, are coming to realize more reflectively the significance of tradition for a

---

[3] Council of Trent, Sessio IV, 8, Denzinger-Schönmetzer, 1501.

deeper understanding of the written word of God. For us Catholics, not the least pregnant sentence in the whole Constitution is that which tells us that, in virtue of sacred tradition (in its most inclusive sense), "the Church in her teaching, life, and worship perpetuates and hands on to all generations all that she herself is, and all that she believes" (art. 8).

The acts of Vatican Council II will be a tremendous stimulus to the work of the professional theologians. And among the lessons the Council as actually experienced could teach a man was that of the unique service theology has to perform for the Church. I should have liked to say that the three catalysts in the Council were the Eastern-rite churches of the Catholic communion, the new churches of Asia and Africa, and the theologians; but my dictionary asserts that catalysis is an effect produced by a substance that, without undergoing change itself, aids a chemical change in other bodies. And while change was certainly introduced into our inherited West-European Catholicism by the three named factors, I would be the last to suggest that they did not experience a beneficial change themselves. Certainly, the theology of the next fifty years will be deeply indebted to Vatican II.

But the Council is not to be conceived as just a private windfall for theologians, or as a new scheme of canon law for prelates and ecclesiastical administrators. More perhaps than any previous council, it is a challenge, and the promise of an inspiration, for the whole People of God. The layman must claim his share, the lion's share, in it. It is he who explores those frontiers between professed belief and professed unbelief that are ever summoning the Church to new adventures and new techniques of apostolate—those frontiers that moved John XXIII to convoke his pastoral council. It is for all of us, in a collaboration of renewed hope and charity, to carry the message of the Council to the whole human family; that message which is Christ, the Light of the nations, the Redeemer of mankind.

Rev. Barnabas Ahern, C.P.

SCRIPTURAL ASPECTS

A FIRST GLANCE AT THE *Constitution on Divine Revelation* indicates that the formal discussion of Scripture opens with chapter 3. Some might think, therefore, that a paper on the scriptural aspects of the Constitution should begin at that point. To do so, however, would result in writing sentences without directive context, like molding a body without a soul to give spirit and life. Scripture can be rightly understood only if it is seen as "the word of God inasmuch as it is consigned to writing under the inspiration of the divine Spirit" (art. 9). No one, therefore, can fully appreciate what the Constitution says of sacred Scripture, in chapters 3 to 6, unless he has first filled his mind with what the Constitution says of the word of God in chapters 1 and 2.

The divine word is a living communication of God himself to man. The grandeur and beauty of his being, the love and dynamism of his saving power —all this resounds in the words he speaks, even as his glory radiates through the earth "like shining from shook foil." The voice that speaks in revelation is the voice of God who lives and who gives himself lovingly to all who listen. His utterances, therefore, are alive with perennial invitation to union with himself.

This directive theme of the first chapter of the Constitution is crystallized in a single sentence: "Through this revelation the invisible God out of the abundance of His love, speaks to men as friends and lives among them, so

54

that He may invite and take them into fellowship with Himself" (art. 2).

This purpose, prompted by love, binds all of God's revelation into unity. But there is still a deeper reason for this oneness. As the Constitution repeatedly affirms,[1] all divine revelation centers in Christ. The Father of the Christian Trinity speaks only one Word; and that Word is his Son. Every utterance of God is but an echo of this single Word who sums up in himself everything the Father can say. All other particular truths and realities are seen truly and fully only in the Son; they are like colors of the spectrum refracted from the pure white light that is Christ. He gives meaning to all and sums up all. As the Constitution expresses it, "By this revelation the deepest truth about God and the salvation of man is made clear to us in Christ, who is the Mediator and at the same time the fullness of all revelation" (art. 2).

To this loving word of God in Christ man must respond. He must offer his whole being to the I-and-Thou dialogue of living faith. This means more than merely intellectual assent to doctrinal truth. For too long a time Trent's reaction against error has unwittingly affected common Catholic thinking on the nature of faith. So great has been the emphasis on mental acceptance of the truths of revelation that many have narrowed the perspective of faith to a level predominantly intellectual. In consequence, they have overlooked the full involvements of Pauline "faith," which envisions the whole man responding to God and receiving in return the whole of God through "Christ dwelling in the heart" (cf. Eph 3:17).

The Constitution happily restores the right perspective. It speaks of faith as an "obedience by which man entrusts his whole self freely to God" (art. 5). More than that, it sees the man of faith always growing in this spirit of self-surrender through the ceaseless activity of the Holy Spirit. An ever deeper knowledge of God, an ever stronger committal to God—this is the work of the Spirit in the man of faith. "To bring about an ever deeper understanding of revelation, the same Holy Spirit constantly brings faith to completion by His gifts" (art. 5).

What has just been said of the individual believer is eminently true of the Church herself. This spouse of Christ is ceaselessly involved in an I-and-Thou dialogue with God. Cherishing his word with love and responding faithfully to his voice, the Church grows constantly in that understanding of God which comes from persevering communion with him. Moreover, through the centuries "the Church, in her teaching, life and worship, perpetuates and hands on to all generations all that she herself is, all that she believes" (art. 8). The Constitution, therefore, bids us recognize "the living presence of this tradition, whose wealth is poured into the practice and life of the believing and praying Church" (art. 8).

Every member of the Church is empowered to strengthen and develop this tradition. Though the authoritative interpretation of revelation belongs solely to the magisterium of pope and bishops, nonetheless everyone who listens to the voice of God and seeks the assistance of the Holy Spirit has power to enrich the living tradition of the Church by ever new insights and by ever deeper understanding of the mystery of God in Christ Jesus. In one of its most beautiful paragraphs the Constitution emphasizes the dynamic process of growth which is always going on:

> This tradition which comes from the apostles develops in the Church with the help of the Holy Spirit. For there is a growth in the understanding of the realities and the words which have been handed down. This happens through the contemplation and study made by believers who treasure these things in their hearts (cf. Lk 2:19, 51), through the intimate understanding of spiritual things they experience, and through the preaching of those who have received through episcopal succession the sure gift of truth. For, as the centuries succeed one another, the Church constantly moves forward towards the fullness of divine truth until the words of God reach their complete fulfillment in her (art. 8).

All Christians, therefore—devout believers and theologians, saints and mystics, bishop-pastors of the flock—have power to make the voice of God more fully resonant in the Church and in the world. The magisterium itself cannot function outside this dynamic process. Its very competence as authentic interpreter of revelation, far from making it superior to the word of God, casts it in the role of the word's humble servant.[2] Its formulations can do nothing more or less than echo with infallible authority the voice of God as it resounds in the living tradition of the Church (art. 10).

It is only in the light of this doctrine on revelation that one can appreciate why the Constitution devotes so much space to the discussion of Scripture (chs. 3–6) and why it brings into prominence the explanations and directives which these chapters present. The simple truth is that two basic factors place Scripture within the perspectives of revelation itself. (1) Sacred Scripture, because it is an inspired book containing revelation, brings the word of God to the Church in a very special way. (2) Sacred Scripture, because it brings the word of God to the Church, is constantly open to an ever deeper understanding through the insights of a developing tradition.

Even when treating of revelation and its transmission, the Constitution weaves these basic facts together and gives them prominence in order that later, in the section on Scripture, it may apply to the sacred text everything it has already said of revelation:

> Through the same tradition . . . the sacred writings themselves are more profoundly understood and unceasingly made active in her [the Church]; and thus God, who spoke of old, uninterruptedly converses with the bride of His beloved

Son; and the Holy Spirit, through whom the living voice of the Gospel resounds in the Church, and through her, in the world, leads unto all truth those who believe and makes the word of Christ dwell abundantly in them (cf. Col 3:16) (art. 8).

These two themes of God's speaking in Scripture and the Church's responding with understanding and complete committal are dominant motifs in the Constitution's treatment of Scripture. Now one theme is to the fore and, again, the other. Many times both themes are gracefully fused.

Chapter 3

This chapter, which opens the formal discussion of Scripture, presents both themes with perfect balance. The very title of the chapter, "The Divine Inspiration and the Interpretation of Sacred Scripture," indicates the co-equal concern of the chapter for the realities of God's speaking and the Church's responding.[3]

The first paragraph is wholly concerned with the truth that God is author of sacred Scripture. As a dogma already in possession,[4] this truth of apostolic origin is affirmed simply, clearly and apodictically. Full recognition is taken of the fact that men also had part in the writing of the sacred books. The emphasis, however, rests on the action of God. Through the inspiration of his Holy Spirit he chose men, used their powers and faculties, and acted in and through them. Hence, whatever the Scriptures affirm God affirms. He is truly author of the inspired text. This doctrinal assertion is the only concern of the Constitution at this point; it seeks to emphasize the cardinal theme that God speaks to men through the Bible. There is no discussion here of the nature of inspiration; the Conciliar document does not raise, much less attempt to answer, the question as to how God used men in the writing of his book. The theological uncertainties of this question are still too many for a definitive pronouncement by the Church.[5] The Council, therefore, was content merely to affirm the life-giving truth of faith: "Those divinely revealed realities contained and presented in sacred Scripture have been committed to writing under the inspiration of the Holy Spirit" (art. 11).

It is not sufficient, however, to say simply that God is the author of Scripture. Chapters 1 and 2 of the Constitution have made clear that God always speaks for a purpose. Because he is a loving and saving God, his words always form a "message of salvation" (art. 7), "that He may invite and take them [men] into fellowship with Himself" (art. 2). The Constitution, therefore, sees an immediate and positive conclusion necessarily flowing from the very truth of inspiration. Since everything in Scripture is an assertion of the Holy Spirit it follows that "the books of Scripture must be acknowledged as teaching . . . without error the truth which God wanted put in the sacred writings for the sake of our salvation" (art. 11).[6]

This clear and precise statement restores to the teaching of the Church the exact meaning of biblical inerrancy as already expressed in 2 Timothy 3:16–17.[7] For too long a time popular teaching has presented inerrancy in a merely negative way or, worse still, it has applied inerrancy to elements that have no connection with the purpose of inspiration. Because of the enduring belief that the Bible, as God's book, had to be free of error, some tried to find in it a perfectly exact history book or manual of science. This distorted and naturalist view of inerrancy was bitterly cirticized by the Council Fathers.[8] Under their concerted action Vatican II has brought into the formal teaching of the Church a clear precision of what "biblical inerrancy" really means. God's authorship of the sacred text guarantees that the saving truths taught in this book and the saving realities described provide the sure way of salvation without error. This is the teaching of revelation itself (2 Tm 3:16–17); and so the Council has introduced this luminous and positive statement to crown its own treatment of this theme: "All Scripture is inspired by God and useful for teaching, for reproving, for correcting, and for instruction in justice, that the man of God may be perfect, equipped for every good work" (art. 11).

But if God speaks he must be listened to; the Church lives by his word. This necessity brings the chapter to develop its second part, on the interpretation of Scripture. For how can the voice of God be hearkened to if it is not understood? The living tradition of the Church, through the contemplation of her saints, the tireless labors of her scholars, and the Spirit-guided preaching of her bishops, must grow in an ever deeper understanding of the word of God. The way is twofold, through work in the present and through remembrance of the past. Both elements must be utilized and eventually fused.

The first article of this chapter (art. 11) has already affirmed that God made use of men in the composition of his book. Just as he manifested his goodness and loving kindness through the weaknesses and limitations of his son's humanness, so too he has shown the same "condescension" in communicating himself to men through the sacred Scriptures (art. 13). According to the memorable words of St. Augustine, quoted in this chapter of the Constitution, "God speaks in sacred Scripture through men in human fashion" (art. 12).

Obviously, therefore, to understand rightly and fully the message of God, one has to study what the inspired writers, as truly human authors, intended to say. This is not always an easy task; it will be, par excellence, the labor of the Church's scholars. Such investigation involves knowledge of the author's background, the ways of thinking and writing peculiar to his time, the problems, culture and attitudes of his age. All that Pope Pius XII has written in his encyclical *Divino Afflante Spiritu* on the exigencies of literary interpretation are summarily incorporated into this article of the Constitution. The methods that Scripture scholars, Catholic and non-Catholic alike, have consistently followed are here approved with all the force of a Conciliar constitution. Never again will there be any reason for benighted fundamentalism in the Church; no more will there be excuse for those unjust criticisms, which have so often blighted the lives and labors of the Church's devoted scholars.

On the contrary, this article of the Constitution implicitly affirms that the Scripture exegete is in the very forefront of the Church's living tradition. His scientific study of the sacred text often marks a degree of progress in the Church's resonant response to the word of God. The Constitution takes cognizance of such advances and praises their merit. It speaks of "the task of exegetes to work . . . towards a better understanding and explanation of the meaning of sacred Scripture, so that through this preparatory study the judgment of the Church may mature" (art. 12).

The Scripture scholar, like every true student, must often work alone. This solitariness is distinctive of his labor; it is the price he must pay to gain a deeper understanding of the sacred text. At the same time, however, he must also keep in touch with those who have already discovered the meaning of God's word and have faithfully responded to it. He can never stand apart from them, and his voice must synchronize with theirs. Careful attention to the living tradition of the Church and perfect agreement with what the Church herself, under the light of the Holy Spirit, has already come to find in the word of God form the second necessary norm which the Constitution provides for an ever fuller understanding of the sacred text. The Scripture exegete must be guided in his métier not only by the rules that govern all literary analysis, but also by that special rule frequently called the "analogy of faith."

This rule is based on the unique fact that Scripture is the book of God and that he has given it to the Church to be read under the guidance of his Holy Spirit. Fully to understand Scripture, therefore, Christian scholars must be ever mindful of the findings which the Spirit-guided Church has already achieved, above all, those which the magisterium has guaranteed. This perfect accord with the insights of the Church's living tradition is the best guide that anyone can have in studying God's word. Constant attention to the "analogy of faith" strengthens the student of Scripture with calm certainty and thus provides the basis for that true liberty which frees the spirit for ever new discoveries.[9]

Chapter 3 of the Constitution, therefore, shows clearly that sacred Scripture must be seen within the perspectives of revelation itself. It affirms that the Bible is God's book written by men and, at the same time, makes provision for the Church's response by presenting the basic principles of interpretation.

Thus this chapter lays a solid foundation for all that is to be said of the Old Testament in chapter 4, of the New Testament in chapter 5, and of the Church's use of Scripture in chapter 6.

Chapter 4

The treatment of the Old Testament (ch. 4) is the briefest unit on the Constitution; yet, when one finishes reading this section, one feels there is nothing more to be said, or better said. This chapter leaves one with the best of all convictions about the Old Testament: the Scriptures of Israel are alive with dynamic and perennial value; God still speaks to men from these pages.

All the insights of modern scholarship have been utilized here to make crystal clear the true meaning of biblical history. Faulty attitudes of the past that confounded the Old Testament with works of modern history writing failed to grasp the full momentum and pointed purpose of the biblical narrative. The first thirty years of the present century were marred by ill-advised efforts to match biblical history with the style and contents of modern historiography. As a result men missed the sublime unity of Israel's story. In the present chapter these mistaken attitudes and efforts are not even alluded to. Here the whole concern is to show that the Old Testament recountal presents salvation history (*Heilsgeschichte*) as a truly historical yet theologized record of God's saving action, which has power to save all those, past and present, who respond to his revelation through faith.[10]

History in the Old Testament, therefore, is seen as the working out of God's plan of salvation. Through the gradual unfolding of his plan God reveals himself—not merely by a conceptual communication of words and ideas, as some have thought, but also by dynamic self-manifestation in deeds. All that the Constitution says in chapter 4 on God's revelation in the Old Testament flows naturally from the principle already enunciated in the first chapter of the Constitution: "This plan of revelation is realized by deeds and words having an inner unity: the deeds wrought by God in the history of salvation manifest and confirm the teaching and realities signified by the words, while the words proclaim the deeds and clarify the mystery contained in them" (art. 2).

In accord with this perspective the opening paragraph of chapter 4 describes in lapidary phrases the whole development of God's dealings with the Chosen People. Dominant motifs of Old Testament theology are singled out with words and clauses that linger in the memory as guiding insights into the mystery of God and of his plans for men. The first sentence of the chapter begins the story of Israel with the sweeping vision of the most loving God solicitously planning and preparing the salvation of the whole human race. All his dealings with Israel, both the words he spoke and the deeds he wrought, are seen as a living communication. His one concern was to give himself to men through word and deed that they might know him and enter into fellowship with him. His saving action grew always more and more intense. Though centered in Israel it was intended for all the nations. Even more it was intended for all time, since the living God who revealed his person and his ways to Israel never changes. With good reason this article concludes with the words of St. Paul who knew so well the perennial value of the Old Testament: "For whatever things have been written have been written for our instruction, that through the patience and the consolation afforded by Scriptures we may have hope" (Rom 15:4).

But there is no history of salvation or manifestation of God which does not center in Christ. He is the fullness of revelation and the perfect Word of the Father. The second article of this chapter (art. 15), therefore, makes clear that all divine activity in the period of the Old Testament was intended to prepare for the full manifestation of God and the full execution of his saving plan in Christ.

In the earlier drafts of the Constitution this Christocentric tenor of the Old Testament was validated only by allusions to the prophecies and types found in its pages. In the Constitution as finally promulgated, the work of preparation is seen to be as vast as the Old Testament itself. All the wondrous elements of Israel's life—its living sense of God, its clear knowledge of the ways of God with men, its inspired treasury of prayers—all the perennial values that nourish the piety of Judaism even in our day are now seen to have their full meaning as a positive preparation of God's People to hear and answer the perfect Word of God, Christ Jesus (cf. art. 15). The conclusion, though not expressed, is unmistakable: Christians are truly children of Abraham; the faith and prayer and holiness of the perfect among God's People must be ours.[11]

"The New Testament," therefore, lies "hidden in the Old and the Old" becomes "manifest in the New" (art. 16). Though these words of St. Augustine[12] have been repeated to the point of becoming a cliché, they seem to sparkle anew with full meaning in the article concluding this chapter on the Old Testament. Everything in the previous treatment has shown how God's plan of salvation prepared for Christ and how the fullness of revelation in him marked the culmination of the revealing word of God. The books of the Old Testament, therefore, still echo the voice of God inviting the people of the New Covenant to prepare themselves for an ever fuller acceptance of Christ. As the Constitution states, "The books of the Old Testament with all their parts, caught up in the proclamation of the gospel, acquire and show forth their full meaning in the New Testament and in turn shed light on it and explain it" (art. 16).

CHAPTER 5

The motif of fulfillment pervades and integrates the Constitution's treatment of the New Testament in chapter 5. The first sentence of the opening article sums up all that can be said: "The word of God, which is the power of God for the salvation of all who believe, is set forth and shows its power in a most excellent way in the writings of the New Testament" (art. 17). This sentence is followed by a summary of the work of Christ with pointed reference to the significance of his redemptive life. Through the words and deeds of his Son, God consummates and gives full meaning to the words and deeds of Israel's salvation history. In and through Christ he manifests himself perfectly and gives himself to men completely. The writings of the New Testament, therefore, orchestrate the consummate revelation of God. Standing forever "as a perpetual and divine witness" to the realities of Christ (art. 17), they echo constantly in the hearts of men the voice of the Father speaking the one perfect Word which is his Son.

This thought naturally turns the development of the chapter to the gospels, which "among all the Scriptures, even those of the New Testament, have a special pre-eminence, and rightly so, for they are the principal witness of the life and teaching of the Incarnate Word" (art. 18).

The first article to treat of the gospels emphasizes their apostolic origin. Their materials were first preached by the apostles; their actual writing was the later work of the apostles themselves and of apostolic co-workers trained by them. Detailed problems of authorship are carefully avoided, for in this matter scholarship has not yet reached final conclusions.[13] To establish the fact that the fourfold gospel is the foundation of the faith, the Conciliar Fathers considered it sufficient to affirm that, humanly, they are of apostolic origin and, divinely, they are of God's inspiration.

The gospels, however, provide the foundation of faith precisely because they relate the saving realities of Christ's life, death and resurrection. It is imperative, then, that men be assured of their truly historical value. To do so is the purpose of the second article treating of the gospels. Here the Constitution clearly affirms that the gospels "faithfully hand on what Jesus Christ, while living among men, really did and taught for their eternal salvation until the day He was taken up into heaven" (art. 19). This affirmation is very simply stated. It needs no proof. It is at once the necessary presupposition of faith and the positive emergent of sound scholarship.[14]

At the same time, however, the Constitution takes care to add an important qualification. The history of Jesus, like salvation history in the Old Testament, differs from history in the modern sense of the word. It was not written to meet the requirements of historiographers of our century who follow constantly the principles in vogue since the Mommsen-Von Ranke school of the nineteenth century. The gospels, instead, follow the style of the ancient world where "history" was often enough an amalgam of earlier oral traditions, and where an interpretative philosophy of history was quite as important as the facts themselves. Utilizing with competence the emergents of gospel study in our present century, this article of the Constitution recognizes the validity of the sound and proven elements in the methods of Form-Criticism and Redaction-Criticism.[15]

An authoritative precedent for this approach to the gospels was already provided by the masterful instruction of the Pontifical Biblical Commission, *Sancta Mater Ecclesia*, published in April 1964.[16] This letter, while safeguarding the reliable historicity of the gospels, pointed out the significant fact that both the early apostolic community and the evangelists themselves have shaped the story of Jesus according to their own Spirit-guided understanding of its profound significance and have also given to the materials of this history the literary forms required to adapt the words and deeds of Jesus to the preaching of the early Church, to her liturgy, doctrinal instruction, controversy and other activities. Summarizing these formative influences, the Constitution has drawn its words almost verbatim from the earlier Instruction of the Biblical Commission:

> After the ascension of the Lord the apostles handed on to their hearers what He had said and done. They did this with that clearer understanding which they enjoyed after they had been instructed by the events of Christ's risen life and taught by the light of the Spirit of truth. The sacred authors wrote the four Gospels, selecting some things from the many which had been handed on by word of mouth or in writing, reducing some of them to a synthesis, explicating some things in view of the situation in their churches, and preserving the form of proclamation, but always in such fashion that they told us the honest truth about Jesus (art. 19).

It is clear, therefore, that the Constitution recognizes the full liberty which the gospel writers enjoyed as human authors to present their message in the way they wished and in the mode already determined by earlier apostolic use of the historical materials. At the same time, the Constitution guarantees that, in exercising this liberty, the evangelists present "the honest truth about Jesus"—the truth guaranteed by the faith of the apostles themselves and by the inspiration of the Spirit of truth.

The last article of this chapter may seem to treat rather summarily the rest of the New Testament writings.[17] Nevertheless this treatment, though brief, succinctly presents the precise nature of their rich contribution. Through the mystery of Christ fully set forth in the gospel, God speaks his perfect word and gives himself totally to men: "He who did not spare his own Son but gave him up for us all, will he not also give us *all things* with him?"

63

(Rom 8:32). Whatever else is written in the New Testament is but the unfolding of this perfect revelation of God. When, therefore, this chapter on the New Testament speaks (art. 20) of the Acts of the Apostles and the epistles, it views all these writings as a clarification and unfolding of the mystery of Christ:

> Besides the four Gospels, the canon of the New Testament also contains the epistles of St. Paul and other apostolic writings, composed under the inspiration of the Holy Spirit. In these writings, according to the wise plan of God, those matters which concern Christ the Lord are confirmed, his true teaching is more and more fully stated, the saving power of the divine work of Christ is preached, the story is told of the beginnings of the Church and of her marvelous growth, and her glorious fulfillment is foretold. For the Lord Jesus was with His apostles as He had promised and sent them as Paraclete the Spirit to lead them into the fullness of truth (art. 20).

Chapter 6

This last chapter is best described as the practical and pastoral conclusion of the light-giving truths the Constitution has developed. Because sacred Scripture is everywhere resonant with the living voice of God and because the People of God must respond to his voice with the self-committal of living faith, the Council Fathers were most concerned that the word of God, rightly understood, should be fruitfully listened to by the whole Church.

They have therefore concluded the Constitution with a beautiful and inspiring chapter that accords perfectly with the pastoral preoccupation of Vatican II. Here they voice their concordant appeal that the Scriptures should become once more for all men "the bread of life" (art. 21). God's word is both living and life-giving. No matter how or under what pretext many have neglected it in the past, it must now assume a primary role in the Church's spiritual life; for if religion means anything it is a loving communication between God and man, a continuing I-and-Thou dialogue between a devoted Father who speaks and an attentive child who faithfully responds.

This chapter, therefore, embraces every category in the Church when it urges constant and fruitful use of sacred Scripture. Priests are told that "all the preaching of the Church just as the Christian religion itself must be nourished and ruled by sacred Scripture" (art. 21). Theologians are reminded that the Bible is "the soul of sacred theology" (art. 24) and that a theologian's work "rests on the written word of God, together with sacred tradition, as its primary and perpetual foundation" (art. 24). Bishops are instructed to provide suitable training in the right use of the divine books (art. 25). All the faithful, and especially religious, are earnestly encouraged "to learn by frequent reading of the divine Scriptures 'the excelling knowledge of Jesus Christ'" (art. 25).

Naturally, this chapter contains a very special word for the Catholic exegete, the professional student of sacred Scripture, whose labors help the Church in a special way to come to a deeper understanding of God's word. These devoted scholars are encouraged to use the full apparatus of scientific scholarship; yet they are also reminded that, in their labors on God's book, they must be always animated by pastoral concern. It would be well if every student of Scripture were to keep ever before his eyes the inspiring directive the Fathers of Vatican II have prepared for him:

> Catholic exegetes, then, and other students of sacred theology, working diligently together and using appropriate means, should devote their energies, under the watchful care of the sacred teaching office of the Church, to an exploration and exposition of the divine writings. This task should be done in such a way that as many ministers of the divine word as possible will be able effectively to provide the nourishment of the Scriptures for the People of God, thereby enlightening their minds, strengthening their wills, and setting men's hearts on fire with the love of God. The sacred Synod encourages the sons of the Church who are biblical scholars to continue energetically with the work they have so well begun, with a constant renewal of vigor, and with loyalty to the mind of the Church (art. 23).

If only the recommendations of this final chapter of the Constitution are followed, a renewal of love for the Scriptures and practical, daily use of the Bible, especially the gospels, will bring fresh and dynamic power into the lives of all the People of God. His word is "spirit and life" (Jn 6:63). At the same time this renewal will forge a new bond with those sincere Christians who, though not members of the Church, have always cherished the sacred Scriptures and have often expressed wonderment that Catholics in general have so little familiarity with its pages.

The Constitution shows an awareness of the ecumenical value in a return to the Bible by our Catholic people. To strengthen this ecumenical rapport it endorses collaboration between Catholics and non-Catholics in translating the Scriptures.[18] This measure removes forever the wall of separation that has kept Catholics and Protestants apart even in their reading of that divine word which belongs to every true child of God.

Every chapter of this wondrous Constitution, therefore, serves to emphasize the life-giving truth that God is always speaking to the Church. It is for the Church, then, to listen attentively to his voice and to respond with living faith. Only the years to come will show what this means for the deepening and enriching of Christian life. The Council Fathers have done everything they could to make this enrichment possible. In the present Constitution they have centered attention on the Church's response to the voice of God speaking in the Scriptures. The fulfillment of their earnest recommendations rests with the Church itself. If only every Christian takes to heart the message of the Constitution, the promise of St. Paul, which is the very spirit of this document, will be certainly realized: "The gospel is the power of God for salvation to everyone who has faith" (Rom 1:16).

NOTES

1. Cf. articles 1, 2, 4, 7, 15, 17, 25.

2. Pope Pius XII, *Munificentissimus Deus*, has given classic expression to the relation between the magisterium and the living tradition of the Church. Cf. AAS 42 (1950) 756-7, 769.

3. In the original schema on revelation, rejected by the Council Fathers, the word "inerrancy" formed part of the title of this chapter. This emphasis on inerrancy, described in the chapter as outlawing the suggestion of any kind of error in the Bible, was typical of the first schema which merely reproduced what was customary in common teaching.

4. The reality of inspiration was solemnly attested by Vatican I in its dogmatic constiution on Catholic faith,·c. 2; cf. Denzinger-Schönmetzer, 3006.

5. The nature of inspiration, unlike the fact itself, has never been defined by the Church. Hence, apart from the reservations spelled out by Vatican I (cf. Denzinger-Schönmetzer, 3006), theologians are free to pursue their study of this delicate subject. Cf. Pierre Benoit, "Inspiration and Revelation," *Concilium* 10, 1 (1965) 6–10.

6. The Italian translation of the Constitution appearing in *L'Osservatore Romano*, Nov. 22–23, 1965, mistranslated the important phrase "quam Deus nostrae salutis causa." Whereas the members of the Theological Commission and the Conciliar Fathers used "causa" as an ablative ("for the sake of our salvation"), the *L'Osservatore* translation, unlike other vernacular translations, understood "causa" as a nominative ("che Dio causa della nostra salvezza"). This mistranslation completely distorts the meaning of this essential phrase and thus nullifies the Conciliar clarification of inerrancy.

7. Like many doctrines attested by ordinary magisterium yet not solemnly defined, the precise point of faith in the general statement "The Bible is free of error" was not always clearly seen. For this reason many thought that inerrancy precluded every kind of error. Vatican II, in its present statement, has now officially enunciated the exact meaning of inerrancy.

8. Cardinal Meyer of Chicago was the first to point out the inadequacy of the treatment of inerrancy that marred the rewritten schema on revelation presented to the Council in its second session. His criticism was complemented by the detailed attack on the schema formulation by Cardinal König of Vienna. Bishop Francis Simons of Indore (India) delivered the *coup de grâce* when he demanded a thorough reinvestigation of common teaching on inerrancy in order to correct exaggerated and false views.

9. The principle that truth makes one free is always valid. However, a long period of excessive caution in the Church (1900–1943) has labeled so many unwarranted positions as "true and unquestionable" that Catholic scholarship labored under repressive servitude. With the *Divino Afflante Spiritu* of Pope Pius XII (1943) the claims of sober discretion once more came to the fore. This encyclical provided a guide-line which, faithfully followed during the past twenty years, resulted in establishing an exact measure for truth and a corresponding liberty for the Church's scholars. In its doctrinal enactments Vatican II has guaranteed the permanence of this spirit in the Church.

10. The very theology that shapes the history of Israel into a salvation history is based upon and flows from the formative facts of that history. Hence, the theological aspect of this history, far from lessening its factual validity, offers proof positive that God's saving action was really present to change Israel from a disunited alien race in Egypt into a nation rich with a unique doctrinal faith and an unparalleled ethical code. The theologized history of Israel never could have been written unless the formative facts related in the account really took place.

11. Cf. Pius XI, *Mit brennender Sorge*, AAS 29 (1937) 151.

12. *Quaest-in Hept.* 2, 73; PL 34, 263.

13. The authorship of the Gospels of Matthew and John is still a matter of continuing discus-

sion. Many scholars see these two Gospels as the product of literary schools working with the materials and in the spirit of apostolic origins—and even, in the case of the Fourth Gospel, under the guidance of an apostle.

14. In our own time the historical validity of the Gospels has been seriously questioned by the school of Form Criticism. The postulates of this school, however, met with such thorough and reasoned critcism (first of all, from British scholars like C. H. Dodd, V. Taylor, T. W. Manson) that Form Criticism, except in its emphasis on the presence of oral forms in the written gospels, may now be considered passé. The most striking sign of this change is the fact that scholars of the Uppsala school, who were previously strongly influenced by German Form Criticism, are now writing in defense of the historical reliability of the gospels.

15. Apart from the unwarranted postulates, philosophical and theological, of these two schools, the emphasis which they have placed on the formative influence of the community (Form Criticism) and on the formative role of the evangelists themselves (Redaction Criticism) are solidly founded. Hence, the methods these two schools have used in studying the gospels (e.g., analysis of literary forms, careful attention to the unique qualities of each evangelist) can and must be used by all exegetes.

16. *AAS* 56 (1964) 715.

17. Archbishop Joseph Cordeiro of Karachi, in his intervention during the third session of the Council, pointed out the absence of St. Paul's name from the schema. His words secured the explicit mention of St. Paul in the final draft of the Constitution.

18. Collaboration between Catholics and non-Catholics in translating the Scriptures was already an actual fact in many parts of the world (e.g., Holland, France, parts of Africa, and elsewhere).

Dr. Paul S. Minear

A PROTESTANT POINT OF VIEW

W E ARE ALL AWARE OF THE IMPORTANCE of this subject and agree with Karl Rahner when he writes "If one single theological problem can stir up the whole of theology, we may be sure that it has been correctly asked."[1] We are also aware of the complexities of the problem. These complexities stem in part from the polemics of the past four centuries, in part from the impact of recent historical and theological research on inherited stereotypes, in part from the turbulent cross-currents of recent ecumenical dialogue, and in part from the semantic and linguistic difficulties inherent in using any of the major categories. There is as yet too much ferment of discussion and too many variables in the definition of each category to permit "dramatic magisterial solutions to an intricate complex of problems whose very formulation is frankly groping, whose positive data are in the process of accumulation, and whose points of insertion into the vast structure of systematic dogma are so numerous, so delicate, and so crucial."[2] All these difficulties notwithstanding, the treatment of this subject by the Council, though by no means achieving what could be called a solution, has carried the discussion a long step forward and has added opportunities and impetus to future explorations. In what follows I am primarily concerned with locating those opportunities.

I shall divide my analysis of the Constitution into sections according to the four key categories: revelation, Scripture, tradition, magisterium (these

I shall call for purposes of summary "the quadrilateral"). I am quite aware that these categories should not be isolated from one another, either historically or theologically. One of the fundamental values of the Constitution consists, in fact, in the affirmation that none of these four can stand alone (art. 10). Nevertheless, for the sake of analysis, a separation of the categories may be justified, if the motive for such separation is "for the sake of unifying."[3] So we begin with the doctrine of revelation which the Council explicitly wished to set forth.

A. The Description of Revelation

Basic to the thought of the Fathers are certain convictions about the reality of revelation which I am confident are shared with all Christian confessions, even though we would prefer to formulate descriptions of that reality in different ways. Quite apart from the diversity of doctrinal formulations, however, I believe that we may discern in the first six articles at least four basic convictions shared by us all.

1. Revelation should be primarily construed not in a substantive manner referring to an object[4] but verbally, since it connotes purposeful action, an action by which God discloses his goodness, wisdom and intention, and thus transforms the human situation, speaking to men, living with them, graciously drawing them into fellowship with himself and giving them eternal life (art. 1, 2).

2. When the Church speaks of revelation, her central intention is to point to disclosure of his will in a living person, Jesus Christ, "who is the mediator and at the same time the fullness of all revelation" (art. 2). In this disclosure, deeds and words possess an "inner unity," an interdependence by which the words proclaim the deeds and the deeds manifest the words. The reality requires both deeds and words, and yet transcends them both, a truth which is especially made clear by the gospel story of Jesus Christ (art. 4).[5]

3. When God thus discloses his purpose and goodness, man's response of obedience, that act of faith by which he submits himself totally to God, is gathered up within the event of revelation and becomes an intrinsic part of it. In such submission, the freedom of man itself comes to him as a gift of the grace of God through the help of the Holy Spirit in "moving the heart" and "opening the eyes of the mind." Man moves through this continuing help toward an ever deeper understanding of the action of God toward the world. (art. 5).

4. This action of revelation, seen in its wholeness, is a movement from hiddenness toward manifestation. The invisible becomes visible, at least to eyes of faith; the inaudible becomes audible, at least to ears that hear. Words and deeds emerge from the eternal mystery of God's will, and serve to clarify

that mystery. The mystery is, of course, not dispelled, since the treasures of divine life "totally transcend the understanding"(art. 6).

Although these four matters are debatable, I want to start with them as a common point of reference for further analysis. In this conception of the reality of God's self-disclosure, I call attention to the fact that the three other categories (Scripture, tradition, magisterium) are already present and play an essential role. *How* each is present, *how* each is integral to the revelation-reality as a whole—these are issues on which divergent attitudes are inescapable. As soon as we try to define any of these categories, the divergence becomes apparent. The problems of perception and definition are thus the key to our penetration into the issues. It is quite deceptive to affirm that there is agreement on the integral relation to the revelation-reality as conveyed by Scripture, tradition and teaching authority, unless at the same time we recognize the necessity of moving toward clear definitions of what is embraced by each of these categories, and how we accordingly conceive their interdependence. Even so, the basic convictions regarding revelation remain a viable starting point for this exploration. Let me then raise several questions which express the concern that the Constitution does not hold closely enough to these convictions.

1. When we have centered upon revelation as the reality of God's action in initiating communication with men with a view to transmitting to them participation in his eternal life (art. 1), i.e., when we locate revelation by this life-giving action of God, do we not go astray almost immediately by accepting as virtual equivalents for the term revelation, such terms as "the message of salvation," "truths" about God's will, or "the plan of God." The action of God can easily become an "it" which is handed on (art. 1), a sacred deposit, a sum of religious truths which can be known "with solid certitude and with no trace of error" (art. 6 citing Vatican I). It then becomes easier to relate the other terms of the quadrilateral to the objectified concept than to the life-giving act of God. As a result, the whole emphasis comes to fall upon *what* is transmitted rather than upon the continuing word-deed of the life-giving God.[6]

2. The conception of revelation as God's action in giving life to his people calls for the use of a language that will be congenial to such a reality, words that convey a sense of ontological depth and of personal immediacy. As E. Schillebeeckx writes: "The religion of revelation is essentially a dialogue, a meeting between man and the living God. . . . The real exchange of personal relationship between God and man which grace makes possible is a partnership in which God addresses man personally and man answers God personally in faith."[7] This dialogue, of course, this medium of life-giving, engages man in community and as community. The life of this community, so far as it is God's life, is given in revelation. As C. Ernst writes: The gospel is "a reality-

in-communication, a being-manifest in Christ himself, in language and in the society in which Christ is present. . . . The Gospel is an intelligible . . . active presence of eschatological realities in human forms, a presence tied always to the definitive end-event of Christ's death and resurrection and the primary Apostolic community in which that event found its expression."[8]

The Constitution seems to utilize such a language in some articles and then to forsake it in others, without full recognition of the confusion aroused by shifting from one perspective to another. "Eternal life" becomes "a plan" (art. 2); God's presence with power to raise us up becomes "the Christian dispensation" (art. 4); "the divine treasures" become accessible to "the light of human reason" (art. 6). The process of transmission is seen as a matter by which one human generation hands on something to the next rather than a matter by which God gives life to each generation. There emerges "one deposit of faith" from which the magisterium draws "everything which it presents for belief as divinely revealed" (art. 10). The reference in this sentence to what is "divinely revealed" makes revelation and sacred tradition so nearly synonymous as to contradict the more basic and valid understandings of revelation.

3. The definition of revelation by reference to Christ as "the mediator and the fullness of all revelation" (art. 2) does not remain constitutive throughout the Constitution. The person Jesus Christ is used as affording the positive warrant of revelation but not its negative critique. If he is, in fact, the mediator of the truth and the life, then surely the apostolic picture of his work should be taken more seriously at two points.

First, more attention should be given to the configuration in his own day of our quadrilateral. In his own work, if we are to trust the records, there were sharp conflicts among divergent interpretations of revelation, of Scripture, of tradition, and of teaching authority.[9] In fact, the story of his death and resurrection would be unintelligible apart from those conflicts. It would be a mistake, to be sure, to equate the Law and the Prophets with our Scriptures, the traditions of the Pharisees with ours, the authority of the scribes and the Sanhedrin with our hierarchies. But to neglect the source and course of Jesus' conflicts with them as paradigms of later situations would also be wrong, that is, unless the doctrine of his full humanity is false. Must we not recognize that Jesus' own understanding of revelation was exhibited in the passion story as antithetical to the understanding of all other participants? If so, should we not be alert to the problematic character of all efforts to describe that revelation of which he remains the "mediator." His revelation of God as life-giver continues to transform human expectations concerning the modes by which God acts.[10]

This leads to the second point. The Constitution is silent about the "negative" aspects of that revelation which comes to us in Jesus. It says much about

God's grace but little about God's wrath.[11] His work as creator and Redeemer is stressed but not his warfare with the devil, or his jealousy in punishing the massive treacheries of his people. Revelation is described in such euphoric terms that one wonders why men so stubbornly resisted its offensive claims. The Constitution gives no hint of how the divine mystery is related to the mystery of rebellion. It recognizes, to be sure, the hiddenness of the divine purpose but it does not effectively set this hiddenness over against the manifest power and wisdom of "lords many and gods many." It does not suggest how the reality revealed in Christ is conveyed by his demand to enter into life by dying. Does not the understanding of that divine life which is given in Christ remain dependent upon the continuing folly and offensiveness of the cross?[12] If so, can we rightly grasp the relation of revelation to the quadrilateral outside the context of the conflict with cosmic powers of evil through which Jesus makes available the saving power of God? As I read the record, Jesus himself taught that God's manifestation of his wisdom, goodness and power was authenticated, at least in part, by the resistance which it prompted and overcame, as well as by the absence of confirmatory signs and the presence of contrary signs. The Constitution reflects little appreciation of this kind of "truth" and this mode of "verification." I say this, however, not simply in criticism but as a reminder that in discussions of divine revelation we should hold more firmly to the Christological criterion, and should realize the extent to which that criterion alters the character of this theological category.[13]

B. THE DESCRIPTION OF SCRIPTURE

First, let me express gratitude for the ways in which the Constitution articulates the living, dialogical character of Scripture and the responses of the Church toward Scripture. The Church hears the word of God with reverence and proclaims it with faith (art. 1). Scripture is like a mirror "in which the pilgrim Church on earth looks at God" (art. 7; a less confusing analogy might have been chosen). It is an unceasingly active and contemporaneous force, by which "God converses with the bride of his Beloved Son." Speaking through the living gospel, the Holy Spirit makes the word of God dwell abundantly in the Church for the sake of the world (art. 8). "In the sacred books, the Father who is in heaven meets his children with great love and speaks with them; and the force and power in the word of God is so great that it stands as the support and energy of the Church, the strength of faith for her sons, the food of the soul, the pure and perennial source of spiritual life" (art. 21). Therefore, the reading and study of Scripture belong in the context of liturgy, devotional reading and prayer (art. 25). Therefore, laymen, exegetes, theologians, priests, bishops—all must "grow familiar with the sacred Scriptures and be penetrated with their spirit" (art. 25; what this spirit is, is not defined;

left undefined, it creates no difficulty; any effort to define it would create difficulty).

Second, a vote of gratitude needs to be expressed for the care and clarity with which distinctions are drawn between the one "divine wellspring" and the Scripture that flows from it. The Synod found it wise to distinguish revelation from Scripture,[14] the gospel from the Gospels, the New Covenant from its verbal formulations. So, too, the utterly transcendent and mysterious purpose and will of God are never wholly identified with the words of men. Consequently, the interpreter "should carefully investigate what meaning the sacred writers really intended, and what God wanted to manifest by means of their words" (art. 12). So, too, although holding firmly to the canon as comprising a unity within which the meaning of the texts is to be correctly worked out (art. 12), the treatment rightly distinguishes the Gospels[15] from the other apostolic writings of the New Testament, and the New Testament from the Old. Also apparent is the ready recognition of the historical particularity of each writer, of the actuality of historical changes within the Bible, and of the validity of changes in interpretation since biblical times. The Fathers have assigned to exegetes an important role in contributing to this maturation in "the judgment of the Church" (art. 12).

Third, I want to observe how difficult it is to formulate doctrines about Scripture and its authority which will express both the dependence of the Church on Scripture as a whole, and which at the same time will do justice to the original motivations and intentions of specific biblical texts and authors. It is almost inevitable that any formulation, which reckons with the vastness of the biblical record and the heterogeneity of hermeneutical traditions, should collide with other formulations seeking to articulate the truth that God gives life to the Church today by speaking through the Scriptures as a whole. This collision is apparent, for example,

a) in the tendency to view the Old Testament story excessively as a preparation of "the way for the gospel" (art. 3, 15);

b) in the claim so to read the hidden motives of God as to know that he planned in advance for the secure preservation of revelation (art. 7); how he predestined the interdependence of Scripture, tradition and magisterium (art. 10); how he hid the New Testament in the Old (art. 16); and how he decided upon the salvation of the whole human race (art. 14);

c) in the assurance that God was able by acting in and through the human writers, to say "everything and only those things which He wanted" (art. 11, drawn from Leo XIII, *Providentissimus Deus*, 1893);

d) in assertions of inerrancy for the books of Scripture and their inspired authors (art. 11).

Let us glance more closely at this last assertion. It appears to be based upon three assumptions: that inerrancy is a necessary correlate of inspiration;[16] that salvation requires such a correlate; and that inerrancy has as its ultimate object "that *truth* which God wanted put into the sacred writings."

Such assumptions can, of course, be supported by citations from the Fathers, from papal encyclicals and from conciliar decrees (cf. note 32 in art. 11). But can they be supported from Scripture? Second Timothy is cited, but the text fails to establish the pivotal point. Although it claims inspiration for Scripture (i.e., the Old Testament), it does not equate inspiration with inerrancy, but simply observes the utility of Scripture in teaching, in refuting error, in disciplining and equipping the man of God. Nor does it make salvation dependent upon an inerrant Scripture. Moreover, as any one knows, the Pastoral Epistles are far from representative of New Testament perspectives. The assumed interdependence of salvation-inspiration-inerrancy does not, of course, require proof from Scripture itself, since it could conceivably be validated by sacred tradition. The word of historians and exegetes must not, however, be brushed aside too hastily. What happens to "the purity of the gospel" when we recognize that every scriptural witness to the gospel is itself a reinterpretation, which embodies an element of misinterpretation?[17] It is very difficult to apply the concept of inerrancy either to this entire, unending hermeneutical process or to one specific selected stage in the process. But the difficulty stems as well from dogmatic as from historical considerations. How can we claim that sinful men are able to receive and transmit an inerrant revelation without distortions due to their sin? The very miracle of grace would seem to require full regard for the reality of "flesh and blood."[18] Most important of all, the tradition of the inerrancy of Scripture contradicts the intrinsic character of the revelation of God's Kingdom in the passion of Christ and of the mode of salvation through sharing in that passion. Revelation, which does not come from flesh and blood, does not confer inerrant knowledge *upon* its human recipients and channels.[19] The equation of inspired Scripture and inerrant Scripture is therefore not only nonscriptural but also unscriptural. Its effect may well be to make Scripture an instrument of slavery rather than freedom (2 Cor 3).[20]

The obvious motive for asserting the inerrancy of Scripture by the Constitution is to enhance the certainty of the Church, as the basis for its acceptance and veneration of the Scriptures (art. 9). Again the question must be asked whether this is the kind of certainty that the Scriptures themselves claim and illustrate. It seems clear from the Old Testament that Israel, whether in Egypt, at Sinai, in the wilderness or in Babylon, did not have the supposed benefits of this kind of certainty. It is even clearer from the New Testament that the acuteness of the sufferings of the Messiah and of his people, during the period of the messianic woes, reflects the absence of this kind of security. The authentic biographical echoes from the struggles of the prophets, the Messiah and the apostles bespeak a quite different mood and morale. In fact, a recurrent task of God's spokesmen was to challenge and destroy Israel's reliance upon former revelations which appeared to be authenticated by Scripture. On no other terms can we make intelligible the conflicts between Jesus and his contemporaries, between the risen Lord and his churches, between the apostles and their churches, and among the apostles themselves. In sharp contrast, the Constitution seems to assure to the modern church a kind and degree of certitude that was not available within the New Testament itself.[21] Had the same assurance been accessible to the apostles and their followers, neither their sufferings nor their glory would have had such weight in authenticating their revelatory words and deeds.

Much is lost therefore by not looking within Scripture for evidence on how our quadrilateral may have been present in certain pivotal episodes as narrated therein. In what ways did veneration for Scripture become in effect the mask for self-deception? How did tradition operate, and what "controls" were effective or ineffective over it? What forms were taken by Israel's magisterium, and how did it guard, preserve and transmit the revealed word of God? To be sure, the adoption of the canon changed matters decisively, so that each element in the quadrilateral thereafter takes on a different shape. But this adoption by no means makes obsolete the analysis of paradigms drawn from the biblical epoch.[22] Such paradigms will not resolve our dilemmas, but they may free us to set those dilemmas more firmly within the context of the finality of revelation in Christ and the relativity of the Church's existence in history.[23]

In these comments on the desirability of consulting Scripture itself for alternate conceptions of the quadrilateral, I do not wish to imply that Scripture itself would provide partisan support for one or another dogmatic formulation, whether Catholic or Protestant. It is becoming clear to scholars (e.g., F. J. Leenhardt and H. Küng) that Scripture is more catholic than later partisan interpretations allow. Prof. Leenhardt discerns "the fact that Holy Scripture propounds and justifies two types of faith (i.e., Abraham's and Moses'), two spiritualities, two spiritual and theological universes," each of which presupposes, requires, and complements the other.[24] If we should proceed to look for analogous formulations of the quadrilateral within the Bible, we might well find that our greatest error is to assume that any one dogmatic definition can be adequate to cope with the revelation-reality.[25] So, too, Hans Küng has called our attention to the genuine catholicity of the New Testament. In his long study it is this catholicity which is stressed rather than infallibility; he says it is entirely Catholic to use the Bible as the ground for protest "against the un-Catholic aspects of the Catholic Church."[26] I believe it is this insight that gives Küng the courage to subject the idea of infallibility to searching examination[27] and to suggest that this notion retains its validity only as a mode of service to Christ, obedience to revelation, and standing under the Holy Spirit.[28] It is thus that study of the Scriptures can help us move toward truer perceptions of their relation to revelation, and thus to better, if also more flexible, definitions of their inspiration. I believe this would lead also to a kind of certainty which would be more akin to that of Abraham and Moses (see Leenhardt's analysis of these archetypes) than to that of the Constitution.

C. THE DESCRIPTION OF TRADITION

I am quite baffled by the treatment the Constitution gives to this category. This bafflement is due not to Protestant bias alone, but to a certain semantic elusiveness. Nowhere does the Constitution attempt to define the category. Nor does it distinguish its use of the term from the multiple modern uses of the term. It makes no clear distinction between the act of transmission, the process of traditioning, and the content of what is handed down. It discerns no significant difference between apostolic and postapostolic tradition, or between the character of tradition before and after the canonization of Scripture. It refuses to adopt the patristic practice of using the singular and plural forms of the noun to indicate, on the one hand, "the process whereby the Bible's message is continually transmitted" (tradition) and, on the other hand, "matters of liturgical usage or applied morality . . . which, though non-scriptural, are to be honoured by the faithful" (traditions).[29] It includes within the term both the strictly exegetical and hermeneutical process of elucidating the meanings of Scripture and the continuation of observances and offices which have only a tenuous relationship to apostolic practice. Finally, it gives no encouragement to the tendency to examine the connections and distinctions between the one Tradition "whose content is God's revelation and self-giving in Christ, present in the life of the Church" and the various confessional, liturgical and cultural traditions presented by Christian history.[30]

My point is this: until one can distinguish the various senses in which a word is being used, it is impossible to measure consensus or dissensus. I am quite ready to affirm the "close connection and communication between sacred tradition and sacred Scripture" (art. 9), to recognize the action of the Holy Spirit in both (art. 10), to give full weight to the presence of the oral tradition before the writing of scripture, and to agree that this tradition is effective in the salvation of souls. But is such agreement real or illusory? Does it stem from adopting a different referent for the word than is found in the Constitution? I do not know. Debate on this topic is likely to go astray unless we circumscribe the range of meanings under discussion.

Nowhere in our document is the term tradition used to refer to whatever was going on in Israel *before* the revelation in Christ. What significance attaches to this? I assume that the Council wished to limit itself to that transmissive process which is uniquely Christian. If so, the interpreter should accept that limitation. He may ask, however, two questions. Linguistically, he must ask whether the unique sense of a term is accessible without some explicit process of comparison and contrast with other senses. Theologically he may wonder whether, since revelation finds its fullness in Jesus Christ, it is wise to exclude from the circle of reference that tradition which provided his own historical milieu?[31] Does not this disjoining of tradition after Christ from tradition before Christ contradict that continuity between the Church and Israel, which is affirmed both in this Constitution and in *de ecclesia?*

Nor does this Constitution ever use the category of tradition to apply to the processes of transmission in any community other than the Christian. This would seem to exclude any component of meaning drawn from the character of human community or of the historical process as such. It avoids that clarification of terms that comes from the use of at least one analogue or antonym (in what respects this tradition is like and unlike other things commonly called tradition). Thus the Constitution by implication ignores the influence on the human traditioners within the Church of those very human factors that influenced both Old Testament and New Testament authors. Tradition thus appears to be even more tightly sealed against disturbance by historical relativities than Scripture itself.

In the Constitution there is no mention of the multiplicity of traditions within Christian history or of the multiformity of the one tradition. The task of careful discrimination between the one Tradition and other traditions is not accepted, or between traditioning as a process and tradition as deposit. I infer from this that the Council by intention avoided full involvement in the complexity of the problem, thus leaving a vast task to be accomplished by theologians in the coming decades.

The Constitution therefore presupposes the singularity and the uniqueness of tradition. Its *terminus a quo* historically viewed appears to be not Jesus but the apostles, and the apostles not as recipients but as initiators. Tradition began when the apostles handed on what they had themselves received (art. 7).[32] No *terminus ad quem* is specified for this sacred tradition; presumably the need for it will continue until the Church sees God face to face (art. 7).

This singularity of tradition requires that the Constitution utilize a very broad concept in some contexts and a very narrow concept in others. Much of the difficulty in discussing the topic stems from the alternation (or confusion?) of these two. So broad is the one concept that it seems to lack any boundaries. It includes "everything which contributes toward the holiness of life and increase in faith of the People of God." In fact it includes the transmission of all that the Church is and all that she believes (art. 8). It operates wherever God's living conversation with men becomes active, wherever the Holy Spirit empowers growth in understanding of "the realities and the words." This boundless wealth is communicated by multiple activities (preaching, teaching, example, study, observances) into "the practice and life of the believing and praying church" as the indwelling word of Christ (art. 8). So conceived, tradition becomes virtually equivalent to the uninterrupted dialogue between God and his people. It is in reference to this inclusive process that the term *living* tradition (viva traditio) seems to be preferred (art. 8, 12).

The narrower concept is more often associated with the term *sacred tradition*. In origin this flows from the oral preaching, example, and instructions of the apostles. It is the authoritative teaching of the episcopal succession (art. 7) and the truth conveyed by authorized preaching. It becomes such a deposit that it can be combined with the sacred Scripture as "one sacred deposit of the word of God, committed to the Church" (art. 10). This deposit becomes "the supreme rule of faith" (art. 21) and the "primary and perpetual foundation" of sacred theology (art. 24). Tradition in this sense is of such a nature that it can, like sacred Scripture, be accepted, venerated and guarded, and its interpretation can be "entrusted exclusively to the living teaching office of the Church" (art. 10). It is this narrower concept that enables tradition to be sufficiently distinct from the other three categories to become one component of the quadrilateral.

The advantages of the broader concept are quite obvious. It is more congenial to the conclusions of biblical theology that no single event of revelation can be formulated exclusively in the categories of conceptual speech.[33] It recognizes the validity and vitality of the empirical realities in Christian history, the actualities of growth in understanding, and the constant movement forward "toward the fullness of *divine truth*" (art. 8). It enables a clearer acknowledgment of the multiform channels and modes of transmission, many of which are not conducive to the imposition of theological or ecclesiastical controls.[34] The life and faith of the People of God are so broadly conceived that, in keeping with the spirit of the decrees on *the Church* and *on Ecumenism*, readers are entitled to include within this "living tradition" salient aspects of Orthodoxy, Anglicanism and even Protestantism. We may add that the Constitution gives important juridical status to the freedom, the spontaneity, the contemplative and spiritual aspects of the continuing dialogue with God, and thus accords a degree of primacy to the *realities* of transmissive process over the *words* by which theologians and hierarchy interpret those realities.[35]

The use of the narrower concept brings into play an opposing set of advantages. Sacred tradition can be more easily dated and limited to "this side" of the apostolic preaching. It provides opportunity and necessity for defining, not "all that the Church believes," but what is essential to such belief and what betrays it. The channels of transmission can be limited to specific institutional forms. The responsibility for final or exclusive interpretation of the rule of faith can be assigned with precision. The magisterium can maintain a juridical relation to the tradition qua sacred more easily than to the tradition qua living. The participation of the separated churches in the former can more readily be restricted. The task and the foundation of sacred theology can more readily be defined. The "one sacred deposit of faith" is for many purposes a more viable category, since it stresses *what* has been handed down more than the living process as a whole. Finally, the narrower concept is more hospitable to desires for such a discriminating definition of inspiration that the assurance of inerrancy and certitude can be established.

There are advantages, as well, in combining these two concepts of tradition under a single term. Whether it was the strategic or the theological advantages that exerted the greater strength is a matter for others to determine. One who was not engaged in the debates in Rome will more likely be impressed, however, by the disadvantages. I believe that it is a weakness theologically to make one word become a jack-of-all-trades, especially where no true analogue to this term is admitted from preapostolic or extraecclesial history. No room is allowed for any conflict between Scripture and tradition, or for conflicts among various strands of contemporary tradition. No conflict is visualized between one generation's meat and another's poison. The fact of development is recognized, but no inkling that this might entail real loss or substantial change. Genuine aberrations are simply ignored. Thus the challenges which historical developments level at the possibility of unchanging dogma do not truly enter the discussion. Nor does the theologian find much help at the crucial point—*How in precise terms* do living tradition and sacred tradition mesh into each other? How are the more dynamic processes of transmission to be related to "the one sacred deposit of faith"? Which is primary? Which qualifies the other? Should we identify tradition by its livingness or by its official dogmatic formulation? To be sure, the Constitution gives a blanket endorsement of the importance and validity of tradition. That is good. But does it clarify the critical considerations involved in the judgment of specific issues?[36] If tradition is so important, Satan will have observed that fact and shaped his strategy by it. Does the Consitution help the Church to identify and repel his deceptions? Certainly, it carries Catholic discussion well beyond the Tridentine impasse, and avoids the most dangerous traps of nineteenth-century debates. It should also carry Protestant discussion beyond untenable disjunctions between Scripture and tradition and enable us to fulfill together our shared obligation to the *paradosis tou kerygmatos*.[37] The Constitution opens the way to future work, but it does not provide conceptual terms which are sharp enough for that work. For this its category of tradition is at once too flexible and too inflexible, too inclusive and too exclusive.

D. THE TEACHING AUTHORITY

It may be, of course, that the Council was quite aware of the questions I have been raising, and that it assigned the responsibility for answering them not to a Constitution but to the continuing work of the magisterium. Can any tradition afford such certainty, and at the same time recognize its multiple conduits and forms, unless there be a teaching authority to deal with the countless tensions, both theological and practical, which are bound to appear? I think not. In this sense the Council was bound to affirm that tradition and magisterium must stand together (art. 10).

Probably most readers will expect Protestant agreement to diminish and resistance to mount as we move from revelation to Scripture to tradition to magisterium. In some respects that is true, but I believe it misses both the intent of the Council and the content of the Constitution. For the text does not itself allow us to arrange these four items in chronological sequence or on a scale of theological primacy. In fact, it resists any such arrangement by its assertion that "all together and each in its own way under the action of the one Holy Spirit contribute effectively to the salvation of souls" (art. 10). If Protestants, therefore, assume that a broader consensus exists with the Synod on revelation and Scripture, and a narrower consensus on tradition (since its differentia are not spelled out) but a dissensus on magisterium, this assumption is probably wrong, since the latter plays an essential role in defining the former. It should be noted, however, that the Constitution does distinguish the wellspring (revelation) from the sacred Scripture and sacred tradition which together flow from it. It also insists that the magisterium does not stand above "this one deposit of faith" but serves it and draws from it whatever "it presents for belief as divinely revealed" (art. 10). Thus, there is affirmed a "one-way" movement: from revelation, through the "word of God" (comprising both sacred Scripture and sacred tradition), to the magisterium, which presents the revelation to men for their faith and salvation. This sequence is of great importance, and its recognition represents a major achievement. Yet this sequence does not jeopardize the interdependence of the four stages, for the whole process stands under the authority of Christ, subject to the word of God and the action of the Holy Spirit.

Like the Conciliar concept of tradition, the concept of magisterium is *sui generis*. There is no reference to any analogy under the Old Convenant or dispensation, or within any other human community. The function of the magisterium appears to begin with the mandate from the apostles to their successors (art. 7). This, as we have seen, is the point where the tradition from the apostles begins its development, a development that signifies no diminution in divine revelation, but rather a growth in its understanding. Sacred tradition and magisterium are also alike in being sealed off from any error that might weaken the certitude of salvation. Moreover, when the question of security is uppermost, each term in the quadrilateral is defined more narrowly; when the question of "fellowship in eternal life" is uppermost, each term is defined more broadly.

Defined broadly, the magisterium embraces the total activity of the Church; defined more narrowly, it refers to the control by the hierarchy over teaching, preaching and interpretation. The apostles left bishops as their successors with authority to teach in their stead (art. 7). Apostolic preaching is continued in an unending succession of preachers who have received "the sure gift of truth" through episcopal succession (art. 8). Authentic interpretation of the word of God (Scripture and tradition) "has been entrusted *exclusively* to the living teaching office of the Church" (art. 10). This office represents the *final* court of appeal for "guarding and interpreting the word of God" (art. 12).

It is, of course, possible, with Roland Murphy, to suggest that the adverb *exclusively* in article 10 should be understood in the light of the adverb *finally* in article 12. Such an interpretation opens the way to a much broader conception of the way in which the teaching authority operates, so as to include the unending succession of preaching and teaching, along with the total life and worship, the contemplation and devout study of a believing and praying community (art. 8). The practice and profession of "the heritage of the faith" must be a single common effort on the part of "the entire holy people united with their shepherds" (art. 10). Accordingly scriptural exegetes have an important, though preparatory function. The work of translation, of theological study, of preaching, of catechetical instruction, remains, however, "under the watchful care" and requires the approval of "the shepherds of the Church" (art. 23, 25). Thus, while the living tradition and the teaching authority pervade the entire realm of the Church's activity, the final responsibility for control and definition of that tradition and authority is assigned to the episcopal office. I assume that the very promulgation of this Constitution is an example of the operation of this authority, and that it wishes to affirm both broader and narrower conceptions of its responsibility. At any rate, the document appears to contain *both* a traditionalist *and* a progressive conception of the magisterium, a fact which should enliven the future hermeneutical work.

From some standpoints, this very alternation between both conceptions will be highly conducive to the ecumenical dialogue. The broader view will provide sufficient common ground for the dialogue with non-Roman communions, while the narrower view will keep that dialogue humble and honest, unable to avoid the tougher issues. In the broader view, the whole Church exercises a genuine authority over biblical interpretation, preaching and teaching, so that we could almost substitute "Church" for "magisterium" in the quadrilateral in these terms: revelation, Scripture, tradition, *Church*. So we find important common ground, if only when each of the four categories is construed broadly. Such a construction the Constitution encourages. But it also construes each category in a more narrow sense. It is this *combination* of broad and narrow that constitutes the ecumenical problematic, for each church (not the Catholic alone) also utilizes a more exclusive understanding of the terms.

In its treatment of revelation, the Constitution thus raises the question of the relationship of magisterium to Church. It thus probes into the area of maximum tension between Catholicism and Protestantism, an area which requires frank and mutual exploration in spite of polemical hazards. Leonard Swidler is probably correct when he locates the heart of the ecumenical problem in the magisterium: "Can the Church's magisterium, under the guidance of the Holy Spirit, express truths not found in Scripture—though not contradicted by Scripture?"[38]

Because this issue will be discussed more fully in connection with the *Constitution on the Church*, I will not seek to ventilate it here, except to suggest various ways of formulating the matter. It can be formulated in terms of the relation of event to institution, of charismata to offices, of the reality of faith to the objectifications of faith, of Spirit to order, of revelation as God's deed to revelation as man's conceptualizations of that deed. I believe a better way of putting it is in terms of the relation of the Church as eschatological reality to the Church as historical reality. How are we to think of the connection between the heavenly city, the new Jerusalem, and the earthly Church, without separating or confusing the two? How are the potencies and authorities of the heavenly city revealed to the pilgrim people and shared with them? The answer of Vatican Council II in terms of the *Constitution on the Church* is this:

> The society furnished with hierarchical agencies and the Mystical Body of Christ are not to be considered as two realities. . . . Rather they form one interlocked reality which is comprised of a divine and a human element. . . . This Church, constituted and organized in the world as a society, subsists in the Catholic Church (art. 8).

The key question, then, becomes the perception and definition of the modes of coalescence and subsistence. The understanding of each category in the quadrilateral depends ultimately on such perception and definition.[39] In the broader definition given to each category by the Constitution, a mode of subsistence is described which is fully tenable. It is the narrower definition of each category (along with the interdependence of the broad and the narrow) that proves far less convincing, as judged by the central criterion of God's life-giving action in Christ.

The agenda for future study should focus therefore upon these more problematic areas. In particular, I believe the Constitution makes imperative a much more thorough analysis of two matters: the concept of inerrancy and the concept of apostolate. Let me conclude by suggesting how each of these concepts is related to each category in the quadrilateral.

I. THE CONCEPT OF INERRANCY

We have already observed the pervasive influence of the claim to inerrancy on the treatment of each basic category in the quadrilateral. Inerrancy is taken to be an essential corollary of inspiration and is necessary to that certitude which the Church must have as the ark of salvation. In dealing with revelation (cf. section A above), this pattern of convictions encourages an accent on the words rather than the deeds (cf. art. 2, 4), on the conceptualized plan of salvation rather than the life-giving fellowship with God, on the "deposit" of Jesus' teaching rather than the living presence of the crucified Lord. The mystery of revelation does not threaten certitude, but enables truths to be known "with no trace of error" (art. 6). The same pattern of convictions weights the scales against the broader conception of Scripture and in favor of the narrower formulation of "the word of God." Because God is the author of all biblical writings, and because the Holy Spirit guides their preservation and interpretation,[40] they "teach without error that truth which God wanted put into the sacred writings for the sake of our salvation" (art. 11). At every step in the development of tradition and in every decision of the magisterium, the presence of the Spirit quiets any doubt that the Church might not be led steadily toward "the fullness of divine truth" (art. 8–10). The Church hands on only what is divinely revealed, and can rely on that certainty (art. 9).

The historian will experience difficulty in adapting this picture to the actual course of Christian history, with its endless ambiguities, dilemmas, and detours. The social psychologist may well wonder how it reflects the baffling mixture of honesty and deception in every human heart and every social situation, and may be led to ask whether it springs from anxious wishful thinking or authentic trust. Such considerations are not so cogent, however, as those which stem from the character of God's self-disclosure. Because Jesus Christ is the Truth, our conceptions of the truth must be conformed to him.[41] Because he is the Messiah, our understanding of salvation must be thoroughly informed by his messianic work. Will he permit our desire for salvation to be more self-centered than this, our craving for certainty to be less vulnerable than his? Does his cross not exert its power over triumphalism in thought as well as over triumphalism in power (cf. Phil 3)? An appeal to Christ and his apostles may not invalidate all doctrines of infallibility, but it must not be prevented from playing a critical role (in Protestant no less than Catholic circles). It is by reference to the gospel that our ideas of inerrancy, whether explicit or implicit, must be tested. This at least is the direction in which some Catholic thought is moving. Gregory Baum, for instance, believes that infallibility should be limited to "only what is absolutely necessary to explain or defend the Gospel in a given situation," with full recognition that doctrinal reform and development involves "a change of heart," "a paschal dimension of death and resurrection."[42] Rosemary Ruether believes that such a renewal would shake the doctrine of inerrancy to its foundations. "We might be led to renounce the concept of inerrancy as the final fall of the Church from spirit to flesh. . . . There must be much more and deeper insecurity in the Church before a new security is gained."[43] I believe it is significant that before his candid and thorough analysis of the infallibility of the magisterium, Hans Küng deals even more thoroughly with the marks of *credibility* for the claim that ecclesiastical office is a continuation of apostolic office.[44] This point brings us to the final ecclesiological issue posed by the Constitution.

II. THE ROLE OF THE APOSTLES IN THE CHURCH

Our document reiterates the conviction that the magisterium originated when the bishops succeeded to the authority of the apostles. This makes quite decisive the understanding of the authority under which the apostles stood, the authority they exercised, and the kind of obedience they commanded. The proper definition of this authority, a task in which historians and theologians must collaborate, becomes even more determinative than agreement on how the episcopal office devolved from the apostolic office.

So, too, our document traces the rise of tradition to the work of the apostles. Tradition began when the apostles handed on to their successors the word of God which had been entrusted to them (art. 9). Because these men initiated the tradition, their own views of what they were doing should exert substantial influence on our views. Here again, historians and theologians must join in studying their relationship simultaneously to Christ and their churches, their understandings of revelation and the modes of its verification, their conception of what kind of truth they were transmitting, and how that kind of truth could be conveyed. What kind of controls over tradition did they exert? To what critical norms did they subject themselves? (A detailed examination from this standpoint of 1 Thessalonians, the Corinthian correspondence, 1 Peter, and the Pastorals would be profitable.)

Dr. Paul S. Minear

A Protestant Point of View

The same considerations apply obviously to Scripture because it was "apostles and apostolic men who . . . committed the message of salvation to writing" (art. 7). More generously than in the description of tradition, the Council recognized the "relativizing" impact of historical studies. It recognized the multiple and diverse character of apostolic testimony, the literary use of different forms of discourse, the processes of editorial selection, adaptation, and synthesis (art. 12, 13, 19). We must be grateful for this recognition, even when we observe that it does not modify the dogmatic assurance that the ultimate author of Scripture put there "everything and only those things which he wanted" (art. 11). Is this the way the apostles thought about God, in the light of his revelation in a crucified Messiah? Did they conceive of him as dealing thus with them and their writings? It would seem that a pastoral Council might have given greater weight to the ways that the apostles actually expressed their pastoral concern for their congregations, in the context of conflicts with those churches, with one another as apostles, and with the disciplining hand of God. The realistic pictures of the apostles' warfare with principalities and powers (Mk 8; Mt 24; Col 1, 2; Lk 22) "as impostors and yet true . . . as having nothing and yet possessing everything" (2 Cor 6:4–10), convey an awareness of inspiration that can play havoc with later formulations. The apostles can still tell us much about the relation to divine revelation of Scripture, tradition and teaching authority. What they tell us can convey the stamp of certainty, but it may be certainty of a different order with different modes of authentication.

I conclude, therefore, that the Constitution should stimulate a much more penetrating study of the role of the apostles, whose work constitutes a real "hinge" of history and of ecclesiology. Such study must be motivated precisely by that loyalty and veneration for sacred tradition and sacred Scripture to which the Constitution appeals (art. 9). Such study is encouraged by the broader definitions given to each category in the quadrilateral. It should adopt the criterion which is firmly established in that revelation of which the "mediator" and "fullness" is Jesus Christ himself. The revelation continues to exert its life-giving power in spite of, as well as by means of, fallible formulations concerning Scripture, tradition and magisterium.

NOTES

1. *Inspiration in the Bible* (New York: Herder, 1961) 34.
2. J. Gaffney, S.J., in *Vatican II: The Theological Dimension* (Washington: Thomist Press, 1963) 169.
3. Cf. T. Camelot, O.P., in *Vatican II: The Theological Dimension*, 195.
4. Cf. Wittgenstein's strictures on the dangers of theology's reliance on nouns, *The Blue Book* (New York: Harpers, 1965) 1ff.
5. In this respect, the Constitution endorses the excellent summary found in W. Bulst, S.J., *Revelation* (New York: Sheed and Ward, 1965) 133–142.

6. Cf. W. Bulst: "It is unfortunate that the theological manuals so often formulate revelation as God's communication to man of 'something,' 'concepts,' 'judgments,' 'doctrines,' etc." *ibid.*, 81.

7. In H. Vorgrimler, *Dogmatic vs. Biblical Theology* (Baltimore: Helicon Press, 1964) 115ff. A fuller explication of this position is given in E. Schillebeeckx, *Christ the Sacrament of Encounter with God* (New York: Sheed and Ward, 1963).

8. *Vatican II: The Theological Dimension,* 179.

9. "The matrix for the Scripture-Tradition question is there already in the life of Christ as the Gospels tell it. . . . The crisis with tradition forms an integral part of the atonement just as the part played by Judas or Caiaphas does" (James Barr, in an unpublished Ms.).

10. As an example of the avoidance of this aspect, we may note that three of the seven references to the Synoptics in the Constitution (Lk 24:27, 44; Mt 5:17) affirm the fulfillment of the Scriptures in Jesus, with no suggestion of the problematic or paradoxical character of that fulfillment. The numerous pericopes in the gospels that reflect this aspect of the revelation in Jesus are ignored.

11. Consider three gospel texts that are cited in part. In art. 17 John 12:32 is used to stress Jesus' redemptive power, but this is separated from 12:31 with its trenchant announcement of his power as Judge. In art. 19, the assurance is drawn from John 16:13 that the Spirit will lead into all truth, but the equally direct warnings of John 16:9–11 are ignored. In art. 21, the living and active power of the word of God is stressed, using Heb 4:12, but the awful warning that Hebrews intended by appealing to this "terrible, swift sword" is silenced.

12. Again citations from the gospels offer evidence of what I have in mind. In art. 16, Luke 22:20 is used to show the newness of the New Covenant; it is not used to show how, because of the blindness of the disciples, the revelation of this truth could be accomplished only by the most radical transformation on their part (Lk 22:21–34). So, too, in art. 25 "the excellent knowledge of Jesus Christ" is extolled, but not what it entails: "counting everything as loss" (Phil 3:8).

13. E.g., does Jesus himself associate revelation, inspiration, and authority with inerrancy or infallibility? If not, should our recognition of him as revealer not modify our tendency in that direction?

14. Art. 9. While the phrase "the word of God" rightly embraces a subtly complex set of referents, its use at times obscures rather than clarifies the intent of the Constitution. At least ten various referents of this phrase may be found (in art. 1, 2, 3, 8, 10, 13, 14, 17, 21, 26). The advantages of utilizing the multiplicity of connotations are obvious, since this one category unifies the four major categories (revelation, Scripture, tradition, magisterium). Of each, one can say truly in appropriate contexts that it *is* the word of God. Of each, one can say that it *contains* and that it *imparts* the word. But in doing this it is all too easy to throw a semantic smoke-screen over the critical issues because of a laudable desire to relate God's speech to all these human channels of transmission. The result may be an acceptable dogmatic formulation covering such huge entities as Scripture, but this formulation may offer little help in dealing with the assessment of the particularizations of these entities in specific words or actions.

15. It is curious that, although the special pre-eminence of the gospels is noted in art. 18, only twenty of the sixty-three explicit references to the New Testament involve the gospels, and of these twenty, thirteen are from the Gospel of John. And even in these references, the situations pictured in the gospels are not exploited for their possible contributions to the formulation of the basic questions and problems. We are not yet free of the tendencies to use the gospels for ends they did not intend and to overlook the relevance of the ends they did intend.

16. Compare K. Rahner, *Inspiration in the Bible,* 6. "For them (Catholic exegetes), inspiration signifies, in practice, the non-errancy of the Bible. This non-errancy is based upon inspiration, and constitutes, as it were, a negative norm for exegesis, but has no further meaning for the exegetes."

17. "We understand the New Testament as itself an interpretive process . . . carrying through interpretations, translations, from situation to situation, as required by circumstances. . . . Every formulation of the New Testament is really a reformulation, a translation, an interpretation" (J. M. Robinson, lecture at San Francisco, Mar. 8–11, 1965).

18. "Every time we turn . . . the biblical word of man into an infallible Word of God we resist that which we ought never to resist, i.e., the truth of the miracle that here fallible men speak the Word of God in fallible human words" (K. Barth, *Church Dogmatics* I/2, 529–30, as quoted by R. M. Brown in L. J. Swidler, *Scripture and Ecumenism* [Pittsburgh: Duquesne Univ., 1965] 26).

19. The gospel accounts of Jesus' own repudiation of omniscience, along with the pictures of Peter's errancy after his confession at Caesarea Philippi, lose their redemptive efficacy on any other terms.

20. This protest on the basis of Scripture against claims for the infallibility of Scripture will, of course, not be welcomed by Protestants who wish to use an inerrant Bible as a weapon against an

errant tradition. On the Catholic side it would modify the terms of the dilemmas implied by asserting two infallible authorities, with which Rahner wrestles so expertly, *op. cit.,* 31ff.

21. In this matter, Kierkegaard's discussion of the advantages of "the disciple at second hand" should be much more influential in our reflections on the subject at hand. Cf. *Philosophical Fragments* (Princeton: Princeton Univ., 1936) 74ff. Otherwise our assertions of secular knowledge of God's plan of salvation can easily require the rewriting of such texts as Isaiah 53:8 and Romans 11:33–36.

22. An example, not yet published, is an essay by P. W. Meyer, "Some Aspects of Tradition and the Problem of Its Control in the New Testament." Meyer illustrates the continuing shaping of those traditions that became Scripture by the story of Jesus' death. "Scripture as developing tradition is first of all the breaking of received tradition and of received theological habits, not entirely under the impact of this historical Jesus and his crucifixion—think only of the polemical and defensive pressures that play upon part of the Synoptic tradition!—but certainly also under the impact."

23. The Constitution rarely, if ever, qualifies the assertions about the Church's knowledge of the truth of revelation by any reference to the Parousia. The quadrilateral as a whole deals with *past* and *present* certainties. By contrast, the New Testament looks forward to the Parousia as essential to the confirmation, vindication and completion of revelation, the perfect understanding of Scripture, the justification of tradition, and the perfecting of communal knowledge. This is surely one of the aspects of Christian eschatology which must not be demythologized or translated into historical equivalents. Our confidence rests upon our *being known* and upon the assurance (inseparable from faith, and as difficult as faith) that we will know (1 Cor 13:8–13). To move in the direction of a different kind of security is to adopt another revelation as the ground for another eschatology.

24. F. J. Leenhardt, *Two Biblical Faiths* (Philadelphia: Westminster, 1964) 110.

25. Art. 2 of the Constitution insists upon the inner unity of deeds and words in revelation. On this ground, our question becomes this: Do not those *deeds,* because of their mysterious and miraculous character, inhibit the attribution of inerrancy to any single configuration of the *words?* Or if we start from the assertion that the divine revelation conveys treasures which transcend the understanding (art. 6), our question becomes this: How can any formulation of "the human mind" that deals with such treasures claim inerrancy?

26. Hans Küng, *Structures of the Church* (London: Nelson, 1964) 161.

27. *Ibid.,* 342–394.

28. *Ibid.,* 351.

29. Cf. J. Gaffney, *op. cit.,* 156, based on summaries of studies by Y. Congar, E. Flesseman-Van Leer and J. N. D. Kelly.

30. The value and difficulties entailed in using this last distinction, which is almost inescapable in ecumenical discussion, may be seen in P. C. Rodger & L. Vischer, *The Fourth Conference on Faith and Order* (London: SCM, 1964) 50ff.; P. S. Minear, *Faith and Order Findings* (London: SCM, 1963), report on Tradition and Traditions; *The Old and the New in the Church* (London: SCM, 1961) 12–50.

31. It may be contended (e.g., K. Rahner, *op. cit.,* 52) that there was "no infallible teaching authority" before the death of Christ, but the merit of this contention rests on the later postulate of infallibility not on the historical existence of an analogous kind of teaching authority.

32. So far as I can judge, a clear distinction between the apostolic tradition and the later tradition never becomes explicit in the Constitution. If so, this leaves entirely open the issue of the relation between these two, and theologians must continue to wrestle with it, whether along the lines argued by O. Cullmann (cf. G. A. Lindbeck, ed. *Dialogue on the Way* [Minneapolis: Augsburg, 1965] 131ff.) or the lines charted by K. Rahner (*op. cit.,* 42ff.), or still other optional paths.

33. Cf. W. Bulst, *op. cit.,* 26.

34. Once we have applied tradition to the total life of the Church, we must take seriously the reminder of C. Ernst, O.P.: "The life of any community . . . is the bearer of an indefinite complex of meanings in a far larger variety of styles of communication than are ordinarily allowed for by scholars or theologians" (*Vatican II: The Theological Dimension,* 181).

35. Tradition-as-gospel "cannot be simply identified with any of the quantities which have been historically called 'Tradition'. . . . It is quite unnecessary (apart from being in the highest degree implausible) to suppose that this living presence is capable of being itemized in quasi-creedal or catechetical forms" (C. Ernst, O.P., *op. cit.,* 180ff.).

36. The only explicit illustration which the Constitution gives of the action of the magisterium in determining the sacred tradition is the canonization of Scripture. One may conjecture as to the

probable reasons for choosing this example. Did the Fathers wish to mention an action which has the widest ecumenical appeal? Did they wish to imply that canonization established a norm which all later tradition should recognize? Or did they simply wish to avoid specifying more controversial examples?

37. This phrase which may be found in J. R. Geiselmann's important essay (in D. J. Callahan et al, *Christianity Divided*, [New York: Sheed and Ward, 1961] 55) was employed at the Montreal Faith and Order Conference during a decisive point in the discussion: "We exist as Christians by the Tradition of the Gospel testified in Scripture, transmitted in and by the Church through the power of the Holy Spirit" (*The Report*, ed. by P. C. Rodger & L. Vischer [London, 1964] 52). This non-Roman formulation of the quadrilateral (Gospel, Scripture, Tradition, Church) is strikingly parallel to those paragraphs in the Constitution that deal with the *living* tradition (art. 7, 8). In fact, future ecumenical study might profit if a group of theologians from all the major traditions would examine in precise detail these parallel documents. They would, I think, find basic agreement on J. R. Geiselmann's judgment that Scripture and Tradition are two different modes of existence within the Church of the Gospel of Christ, (*op. cit.*, 50).

38. L. J. Swidler, *Scripture and Ecumenism* (Pittsburgh: Duquesne Univ., 1965) 1.

39. I have tried to deal with this issue in greater detail in an essay in *New Testament Studies* (Jan. 1966): "Ontology and Ecclesiology in the Apocalypse."

40. The Constitution virtually ignores the scriptural stress on the extraecclesiastical work of the Spirit; on the unpredictable freedom of the Spirit to judge, to convict, to humble, to bewilder; and on the difficulties attendant on the discernment of spirits.

41. "Let the only trust that sustains us come from those words of His which shore up our pitiful weakness: 'And behold I am with you forever, even to the end of the world.'" Pope Paul VI, Address opening the second session of Vatican II.

42. *Journal of Ecumenical Studies* 2 (1965) 370, 376.

43. *Christian Century* (Sept. 22, 1965) 1154.

44. *Structures of the Church* (London: Nelson, 1964).

Question: Is there a sense in which the Roman Catholic can say that the teachings of the magisterium are subject to the judgment of Scripture, that is, must they conform to the revelation given in Scripture?

BUTLER: Put like that the answer of course is very simple. Yes, there is such a sense, and there is a statement in the *Constitution on Divine Revelation* to the effect that the teaching authority of the Church, the magisterium, "is not above the word of God, but serves it, teaching only what has been handed down, listening to it devoutly, guarding it scrupulously, and explaining it faithfully by divine commission and with the help of the Holy Spirit" (art. 10). So that undoubtedly in the mind of the Constitution the teaching authority of the Church is subject to the word of God, is subject to the judgment of the word of God. Now I take it that the real difficulty is not there. The real difficulty is *quis custodiet ipsos custodes*. It is all very well for us to say and to believe that the magisterium is subject to holy Scripture. But is there anybody who is in a position to tell the magisterium: Look, you are not practicing your subjection to holy Scripture in your teaching. That, I take it, is the heart of the whole problem of the magisterium. It is also the heart of the problem whether we can make of Christianity anything that is concrete, with definite outlines, or whether we are committed to extreme liberalism.

I think we have to admit that there is a kind of reciprocal causality between the position of Scripture in the Church and the position of the magisterium in the Church. I also suspect that it would take a very large theological treatise to work out the implications of that reciprocal causality. I've heard it said that, strictly speaking, there is no doubt that the magisterium is subject to the word of God and the word of God stands in judgment over it. But I repeat, the difficulty is who has the right, if not the magisterium, to reject in the name of sacred Scripture a certain official interpretation as being unfaithful to divine revelation. Who has the authority, the power, to do that?

I think that raises another very interesting point put in these questions to me, and that is the possible function of the laity.

> Question: *In this whole question of the interpretation and exposition of Scripture and tradition, what is the role of the charismatic gifts which lay people may have?*

BUTLER: It is very clear from the *Constitution on the Church* that we are not to suppose that, along with the other exalted gifts the hierarchy have of a sacramental kind, they have also secured a monopoly on charisms. On the contrary, we are told to recognize that the Spirit of God "bloweth where it listeth." There is no doubt, of course, that the Roman Catholic communion in the course of centuries has become a highly clericalized institution. One of the things this Council has done, less manifestly perhaps in our present document than in some of the others, was to begin to allow the laity to assume again their rightful place in the life of the Church. And I would direct my questioner to the very important section on the *sensus fidei*, the "sense of faith," in the Constitution *De Ecclesia* (art. 12), where it is made quite clear that you can attribute infallibility to the mind of the Church as a whole, not simply to the pronouncements of the magisterium.

Like so many other passages in the Council's acts, I think this too is an imperfect text because it concentrates on the infallibility of the *sensus fidei*. But we must recognize that just as the teaching authority of the Church is always teaching, but very rarely, thank God, teaching infallibly, so also the sense of faith is always giving the Church something to think about. Only under very precise conditions can we say that the sense of faith is given a special assistance that guarantees its infallibility.

> Question: *In what the Constitution says about the development of the understanding of divine revelation might there be seen a tendency, as it were, to canonize the actual process of*

*human history in the Church of God in such a way that you
not only say that the things the Church has ultimately defined
are true, but you also more or less say that the schedule or list
of the things the Church has defined gives you an adequate
picture of what the Church believes?*

BUTLER: I think that is the kind of mental attitude toward doctrinal
development that may very easily derive from a perhaps rather superficial reading of Newman's work *On the Development of Christian Doctrine.* What
has to be remembered about that book is that it was written by Newman,
when he was not a Roman Catholic, in order to clarify for himself the reasons that justified to his own mind the step he was about to take in submitting to the Roman Catholic Church. And therefore that book stresses the
divine guidance over the development of the Church's thinking and the
Church's life in general.

But one must always remember here that the only thing—on Roman Catholic principles—that we can be quite sure of is that God will not allow the
Church to make an irreparable, catastrophic mistake. I remember hearing
one of the Council Fathers, a bishop, saying very early in the course of Vatican II that the only thing we can be quite sure about with regard to an ecumenical council is that it will not issue a definition of doctrine that is false.
Short of that, any council can be a most appalling disaster in the life of the
Church. Some people think the present Council was, of course—and it didn't
give us any extra definitions of doctrine as a compensation.

But I think that it is not untrue to the spirit of the deepest thinking and
intuition of this Council to say the Council recognizes that wherever the
Church stands, phenomenologically so to speak, at a given moment, she is
expressing in her poise and even in her language at that particular moment
only a minute fraction of the totality of the divine reality which is her gift,
her mandate, for mankind. Therefore, if you read the document as a whole
(and I would like to stress very emphatically here that the documents of
Vatican Council II cannot be properly understood in isolation; each of them,
by and large, has got to be seen in the context of all the other documents),
you will see in it this tremendous sense of the necessity of getting back to the
"fons et origo," to the "caput," as St. Cyprian would have said, to the primary record of revelation. Because there you will find depths of truth and
suggestions of reality that none of your conceptual formulations have ever
succeeded in plumbing.

I have been asked in one or two of these questions about the latest Mariological definitions in view of the notion, which some Roman Catholics apparently hold, that the Scriptures contain explicitly or latently the whole
substance of the divine revelation.

It is fairly obvious that if you read the Scriptures as you read a railroad timetable, you will not find the doctrine of the Immaculate Conception on any given page of Scripture, nor the bodily Assumption of Our Lady. But I think when Newman spoke about the unplumbed depths of Scripture he was thinking about the way in which, as you get down to real biblical theology, you see once again that, as I said about the Council documents, the books of the Bible interact with one another. And I think the more the human mind meditates, in the power of the Holy Spirit's inspiration, on Genesis 2 and the infancy narratives, the more one begins to realize that, when the early Fathers spoke about Our Lady as "the second Eve," they were not being unfaithful to the biblical revelation but were getting close to its very heart. And if you take that doctrine seriously, you will find that Our Lady has her position in the total economy of the second creation analogous to the position of Eve in the total economy of the first creation, that she stands on the further side, on the supralapsarian side, so to speak, of the whole picture.

AHERN: Abbot Butler failed to point out, in answering the last question on Our Lady in Scripture, that he was touching on an area which he had richly developed for the Council, and one of the heaviest hands in the preparation of that beautiful chapter on the Blessed Virgin in the schema on the Church came from the Abbot of Downside.

> Question: It seems to me that the treatment of the Old Testament is one of the weakest parts of the Constitution. The whole Old Testament prepares one to have the mind of Christ, in your description of its message. What about the Old Testament in itself? Must we constantly seek the Christian element, the preparation for Christ? A modern understanding would also have to emphasize that even if Christ had never come, the Old Testament would remain a very important spokesman of God. I do not find sufficient emphasis on the Old Testament in its own terms.

BUTLER: This is a valid objection, a valid criticism, due I think perhaps to the literary style of the Constitution's fourth chapter on the Old Testament. I think one can realize that in the preparation of these Constitutions, time and again, those who worked on them had to move within many of the accepted phrases that have come down to them through an ancient Christian past. It was a matter, as it were, of putting new wine into old wineskins. Some of these phrases are treasured and therefore they were kept, though at times they made for a certain ambiguity and imperfection in the document. The passage to which these questioners refer is found in the fourth chapter, which reads: "The principal purpose to which the plan of the Old Testament was directed was to prepare for the coming both of Christ, the Universal Redeemer (the principal purpose) and of the Messianic kingdom, to announce this coming by prophecy, and to indicate its meaning through various types" (art. 15). This is all sacrosanct in Christian tradition. Here the thought is enlarged as though the preparation was as vast as the Old Testament itself. "The books of the Old Testament . . . reveal to all men the knowledge of God and of man and the ways in which God, just and merciful, deals with men. The books, though they also contain some things which are only incomplete and temporary, nevertheless show us true divine pedagogy. These same books, then, give expression to a lively sense of God, contain a store of sublime teachings about God, sound wisdom about human life, and wonderful treasury of prayers" (art. 15).

As you can see, this latter material is integrated into the article treating the Old Testament as a preparation for Christ. And yet, at the same time, I think if properly analyzed the perennial value of the Old Testament in itself is safeguarded. I think there are two ways of speaking of a preparation. For instance, if you have lived in Italy you know their favorite way of building; they always erect a huge scaffold and they work on the building from without, and when the building is completed the scaffold is dismantled and discarded. At the same time there is another way of preparing for the building of any kind of an edifice: you erect a steel structure that becomes the very strength of the building, a part of the building, which has a purpose of itself; certainly a part of the completed whole, it has at the same time an essential and integral value in itself. When therefore we speak of the Old Testament as a preparation, we are not speaking of it as a scaffolding that can be discarded, a scaffolding that no longer has any great worth, a scaffolding that in itself has no real meaning or impetus except in and through Christ. Rather we are speaking of the Old Testament as a preparation in the second sense: it forms an integral part of the total salvific work of God; Christ who was the first in its intention was the ultimate in its execution. And yet the whole of this, this whole fibering, this whole structuring that comes to its consummation in Christ—St. Paul calls him at once the foundation stone and the corner, the keystone—all of this in itself is valid and has its perennial dynamism. Msgr. Oesterreicher's book, *Walls Are Crumbling*, describes the spiritual odyssey of those who have lived in Jewry or who have come out of Jewry. One of them, Edith Stein, actually became a Christian, and then, of course, found the fullness of the Old Testament in the New Testament. At the same time several of those whom Msgr. Oesterreicher deals with never entered the Church, never came to accept Christ. And as he brings out so beautifully, their lives as Jews were filled with the very things here described in the Constitution. For instance, there is a true mystique in Jewry today, the piety of Jewry, its moral integrity, its strict sense of family life, its conduct of marriage (I think it has one of the most ineffable forms of marriage ethos)—all of this is the emergent from that devotion to God's word which has in itself an eternal and perennial value, although in itself it was intended to become whole and full in Christ. It could have perhaps been stated more clearly, more accurately.

Fr. Brown: I presented one of those questions, and I see the explanation. But you must admit it is not the obvious import of the words. That is one of the weaknesses of the Constitution, and that is why I could never be as enthusiastic about it as you are. One must constantly explain away the mentality of the Constitution. It is not a scriptural mentality; it is a mentality that has been directed by dogmatic concerns, as I think Professor Minear pointed out more eloquently than I could ever do it. I do not believe that these documents concerning the Old and New Testaments would have been written by an exegete in this way. They were written in view of a dogmatic concern that is extraneous to the Scriptures themselves. One could read the Old Testament and find the tremendous value there, without ever suspecting that the primary purpose of this whole book was the New Testament. I think one cannot question the explanation or the purpose, but I do think that that must be pointed out in evaluating this document. One must back into the interpretation of many of these passages.

Ahern: I wonder if it might not be needful to distinguish between the epistemological and the ontological. That ontologically God did intend the salvific history of Israel as a preparation for Christ. Epistemologically that was not recognized—at least many elements in it were not recognized. Many scholars today would hold that in inter-Testamental literature you have no clear teaching, for instance, on the suffering element of the Messiah, that even in the Messiah of the Qumran texts you are still not dealing with the personal sufferings of the Messiah. I think we can say, therefore, that the doctrine of Isaiah in the servant passages, at least in chapter 53, or again the doctrine of Zachariah, never became part of the common heritage of popular Jewish faith. It was the whole problem that the Lord faced when he came. But I think here we are in, what we might call, the epistemological; whereas the Conciliar document is more concerned with what we might call the ontological. As validation for that ontological presentation, we have the whole teaching of the New Testament, all the activity of the apostles, and the whole burden of Christian tradition, not only in the Semite world in its first century, but also all through the Greek Fathers. It is in that ontological sense the Constitution must be interpreted. From the epistemological viewpoint, yes, I would agree totally with you Father, but it is the ontological, I think, that is being guaranteed here.

Burghardt: At the risk of seeming discourteous may I first ask a question of Father Brown to clarify what he said. Is it really your contention that the Constitution would be better had it been written by an exegete, if exegetes, say, alone had written the Constitution—or is it rather your contention that exegetes should have been consulted on the level of content and presentation?

FR. BROWN: Perhaps the scriptural parts would be better if they had been written by an exegete. No, I wouldn't maintain that the whole Constitution should have been written by exegetes, and I know they were consulted. But my question is about its mentality. I thought Professor Minear brought that out, and perhaps Father Barnabas did in his answers. The ontological concern? When I read Chronicles, or Kings, I can't find this ontological concern. In other words, it is a concern that is imposed by dogmatic interest over a scriptural work. And that is the problem.

BURGHARDT: Well, my fear is that if it is written by exegetes, we run the risk of archaism. I am afraid that every document of every age has to be written in the spirit of that particular age, the way in which people think, the way in which they write. I can see an objection to the presentation in that it does not correspond to the way in which man thinks and feels, to his attitudes at this time. I can also see, as you said, that certain aspects of it, certain paragraphs, certain sentences, do not correspond to the scriptural situation. But I would find a great archaism in having the thing written by exegetes. As I say, this may not be what you are suggesting.

> Question: In what sense is God always speaking to the Church or in the Church? From the point of view of content? Yes, but if we take the word of God in the sense of an active God, does God speak anew, does he reveal anew? I should like to hear some explanation.

AHERN: I think, as Abbot Butler brought out so beautifully, God has acted in the world. The deed, the fact, is the revelation of God's self-giving, giving himself throughout the salvation history of Israel, and consummately giving himself in Christ. I think that verse from Romans sums up everything: "He who has not spared even his own Son but has delivered him for us all, how can he fail to grant us also *all* things with him?" (8:32).

In other words, Christ is the consummate fullness of God's self-revelation. The ontological gift of God, therefore, which is the saving of man by God, has been accomplished historically—the fact, the deed. Secondly, we know that these gifts of God had to be interpreted, had to be rendered epistemologically as attainable to ourselves, and that therefore there was the illumination of minds—in the Old Testament the prophets; in the New Testament the apostles—to understand this mystery. You can see it in Paul's writings, for instance. It took Paul a long time, as it did the early Church, to understand that the death of Jesus together with his resurrection constitute one unique saving mystery. There was a progressive illumination. We see true development, for instance, in Paul. Paul's doctrine of "in Christo" in Thessalonians certainly, I think, is at a stage that is not yet meeting the full attainment of his thought "in Christo," which he develops in the Captivity Epistles. There was development. In other words, God, through his Holy Spirit, was illuminating these men to understand and to proclaim what was contained in the deed of God, which is the salvation of God. This undoubtedly is something that we situate in history: the deed of God took place at a certain time. But the fundamental unfolding of the meaning of the deed through the illumination of the sacred writers and the apostles took place at a given time. And therefore that word of God is something consummated once and for all, but as Scripture keeps reiterating: that word of God contained in the word of God endures forever, *permanent in aeterno*. Accordingly, therefore, this thing which is fully meant for us is present to us, and present to us in yet a second sense. And this the Constitution keeps emphasizing. The Spirit is always with us. The Holy Spirit, who first illumined the minds of the writers and the apostles to understand the essential meaning of the gift of Christ, is constantly with us to give us also their understanding and their appreciation of it. In this we are constantly growing. So it is therefore that, when we speak of God himself communicating himself to the Church, I think it is these three things they mean: the ontological gift which is for always, the first interpretation of it by an early Church, and the continuing assistance of the Holy Spirit. He constantly illumines our minds so that we can share in the early Church's understanding and thus we ourselves be tuned in on that word of God that echoes through the stratosphere.

MINEAR: The first question given me seems to grow out of my appeal to the value of listening to Scripture itself in its witness to situations in which the writers are themselves struggling with the relationship between Scripture and tradition and authority.

> Question: Are you suggesting that the ambiguities within the
> Scripture are meant to support the developing richness of
> ambiguity in our times, rather than a negotiation of ambiguity
> into a clearer, more single view?

MINEAR: These are not clear-cut alternatives. Our every effort to enter into the situation faced by a biblical writer—the Apostle Paul in dealing with the Church at Corinth—suggests in a way an alertness, a greater alertness to that diversity of situations today and of the ambiguities reflected by those diverse situations. The more we are aware of the ambiguities in a historical period, the more we become aware of them today.

On the other hand, in every situation when a person is confronted by diversity, plurality, ambiguity and the necessity for decision, the call to faith, in that situation he must seek a clearer single view of the meaning of that confused situation in the light of God's call. So it seems to me these two things are present in every situation. There is the historical particularity which is always complex and yet immediate, and there is an interpretive freedom as a person faces that situation. But within the Bible, within the People of God, there is always the reference to God's purpose, will and word in that situation, which alone can resolve the ambiguities into decision. It seems to me, therefore, that the study of the Bible can increase the richness of ambiguity of our own day. It can also lead us in moving toward a clearer view of an unambiguous decision and in so doing make our response to God's will in this situation more open, more flexible, because we have also been listening to the scriptural passage.

The second question grows out of my feeling that the Constitution after insisting upon the unity of deed and word in the event of revelation seemed, in certain ways, to stress the words, rather than the unity of word and deed.

> Question: Isn't it equally dangerous and fatal so to separate the spirit and creed, event and word, as to separate the heavenly flesh and the earthly flesh and open the door to all kinds of noncredal spirituality?

MINEAR: Yes, it is equally dangerous. If the alternative is to stress an event that cannot be reduced to words, or a word that is abstracted completely from the event, to accept either extreme would be equally dangerous, destroying the unity of action and word in the event.

I think it might be well at this point to refer to the dialogue between Fathers Brown and Burghardt. As an exegete I would trust the dogmatician in drawing up certain statements, but it seems to me the problem here is whether in the character of the dogmatic statement one keeps his eye firmly upon this intrinsic unity of the event and the deeds, and at that point the biblical scholar might be able to give him a better sense of that unity in the historical situation. And when we do this it seems to me the event itself forces upon us the necessity of adapting our language out of the usual dogmatic modes, or out of the usual exegetical modes, into a mode of language more fitting to deal with this event in its own terms. One of the best essays that I have read in preparing for this critique was the essay by Father Ernst in Vatican II, Theological Dimensions, in which he stresses the fact that when we see this revelation reality in its fullness it forces a revision of all of the categories that we use in dealing with it—whether with revelation, Scripture, tradition or magisterium. This is a theological problem in which exegetes share with dogmaticians the need for a language that will do better justice to this intrinsic unity of word and deed without moving in the direction of a nonverbal spirituality, which can mean anything, or moving in the direction of a highly verbalized dogma, which has broken the contact with the event itself.

> *Question: Can these two terms "inerrancy" and "infallibility" be taken in a nonepistemological sense: a nonepistemological sense as something one believes in but not as a criterion for certitude.*

MINEAR: I judge epistemology here refers to a sort of assumed correspondence between the concept in the mind embodied in the word that corresponds to the object in which the reference is made. I would rather use faith as the criterion for certitude in this sense. Take the faith of Paul, as expressed in the sixth chapter of 2 Corinthians. His testimony concerning his ministry of reconciliation here is an expression of the way faith conveys its assurance, its certainty for him. It is not based upon a prior certainty of which he had been assured by someone else, but this certainty that represents his faith is in the context of great struggle—his own struggle and the struggle with the Church and with the world around him. His faith *is* his confidence. It enables him to carry out his ministry. In this sense it is a confidence we could call inerrant or infallible. But as he describes his ministry (as imposters, yet true), he is quite aware that to those who see him, who hear him speak, his very word and his very deed do not give the assurance of certainty, but rather for many produce the opposite feeling. So that what is true for Paul is recognized by him as something that is misunderstood by the others. So we get into the complex problem here of how the participation in the event of revelation communicates faith, which is its own certainty, to an individual and a congregation at church, and then how to do justice to the absoluteness of one's response to God, the unqualified commitment that is the embodiment of certainty, and how to speak of this as conveying a sense of inerrancy, of infallibility, without denying the historical particularity of this situation and the interpreting freedom of the person involved in it, which are examples of something other than a knowledge of inerrant truth.

MEDINA ESTEVEZ

DE LUBAC

MOELLER

SESSION IV

RT. REV. JORGE MEDINA ESTEVEZ
The Constitution on the Church: Lumen Gentium

CANON CHARLES MOELLER
History of Lumen Gentium's *Structure and Ideas*

REV. HENRI DE LUBAC, S.J.
Lumen Gentium *and the Fathers*

Rt. Rev. Jorge Medina Estevez

THE CONSTITUTION ON THE CHURCH: LUMEN GENTIUM

I~~T IS NOT AN EXAGGERATION~~ to state that the most important document promulgated by Vatican Council II is the dogmatic *Constitution on the Church*.[1] This statement with which I begin is justified not only by the length of the document, a length which far surpasses that of any similar doctrinal document published by previous councils, but also by the importance of the material which the document treats. So much is this the case that many of the other Conciliar documents, looking for a point of departure, have based themselves on the doctrine affirmed in the Constitution *Lumen Gentium*. To cite only a few examples: think of chapter 3, which treats of the hierarchy, and whose applications are made explicit in the *Decree Concerning the Pastoral Office of Bishops in the Church*, in the *Decree on the Ministry and Life of Priests*, and in the *Decree on Priestly Formation*; think of chapter 4, which treats of the laity, and its explicitation in the *Decree on the Apostolate of the Laity*; think of articles 16 and 17 of chapter 2, whose natural development is found in the *Decree on the Church's Missionary Activity*; think of article 15 of the same chapter, which constitutes the basis of the *Decree on Ecumenism*; think of chapter 6 concerning religious, to which are related the different propositions on religious life. This enumeration is just by way of example. It is not exhaustive. It only points out the more evident comparisons that can be made, without entering into other possible influences more difficult to trace, such as, for example, the influence upon the whole ecclesiology contained implicitly in the Introduction and first chapter of the *Constitution on the Sacred Liturgy*.

The importance of the Constitution for the life of the Church will become evident little by little as a result of the change of mentality which it will bring with it as well as of the future theological reflection on its content. We believe that this theological reflection will have a considerable influence on the gradual change of mentality, and at the same time this evolution will itself enrich theological reflection. My aims are modest. I wish to give an exposition of the steps in the formation of the Conciliar text itself. This is very important for an appreciation of the text that was finally promulgated. I am firmly convinced that it is not possible to appreciate the full value of the text of the Constitution without knowing its various points of departure as well as the criticisms leveled at it by the Fathers. My remarks will necessarily be of a general nature; only through scholarly monographs will it be possible to give a history of each doctrinal point in detail. Nor do my remarks deal with work done before the Council by the preparatory commissions and revised by the Central Preparatory Commission. The reason for this is twofold: in the first place little is known about this preparatory state and, secondly, the result of the preparatory work constitutes the real point of departure for my study.[2]

First Step: First Period of the General Congregations of the Council

Presentation of the Text

It is no secret that from the very first period different tendencies were manifest among the Council Fathers.[3] They were already implicit during the discussion of the schema on the Sacred Liturgy. They reached a peak during the debate on the schema presented under the name "The Twofold Source of Revelation." There was tension in the air (because of the discussion of the document *De Ecclesiae Unitate*)[4] when on December 1, 1962, debate began on the schema *De Ecclesia*, which had been drawn up by the preparatory theological commission and revised by the Central Commission. The schema was divided into 11 chapters: 1) On the nature of the militant Church, 2) Membership in the Church and the necessity of this for salvation, 3) The office of bishop as the highest degree of the sacrament of orders, and the priesthood in general, 4) On residential bishops, 5) The states of evangelical perfection, 6) Concerning the laity, 7) The magisterium of the Church, 8) Authority and obedience in the Church, 9) Relations between Church and state, 10) The necessity which binds the Church to evangelize all nations of the world, 11) Ecumenism.

The same booklet which contained the original schema on the Church (whose contents we have just outlined) also included another document entitled "Schema of the Dogmatic Constitution on the Blessed Virgin Mary, Mother of God and Mother of Men." It was very obvious that according to the minds of those who served on the preparatory commissions of the Council, the doctrine on the Virgin Mary would not be a part of the document on the Church, but would be a separate and exclusive constitution.

The presentation of the schema was given by Cardinal Ottaviani, who listed the merits of the document from the biblical and pastoral points of view. Nevertheless, with great realism, and with a certain bitterness, he declared that he foresaw severe criticisms forthcoming from the Fathers. Already different opinions had been formed. His fears were not unjustified. At the very moment the official schema was distributed, another text was already circulating among the Fathers. Some wanted this second text to be the basis of Conciliar discussion instead of the official text.

During the discussion of the official schema, despite the short time alloted to it,[5] the opinions of about eighty Fathers were heard. Many of them represented large sectors of opinions held by the Council. No less than ten Fathers asked for a total reworking which would be done by a mixed commission, and not just by the Theological Commission. Many other Fathers, without explicitly asking for a total rewriting of the schema, voiced such strong criticism that in the end the result was the same. Almost all of the Fathers admitted the necessity of amendments, and only very few gave a sincerely positive judgment. The facts, and the later development of the Council, have shown that the negative reaction expressed the feelings of the majority of the Council, even though these feelings were not clearly conscious at the beginning of the discussions.

CRITICISMS

What were the main criticisms? To give a detailed description would be beyond the scope of our paper. We will only present the most important ones in a general manner.[6]

a) *Criticisms of a general order.*

1. Criticisms on the structure of the schema. This was one of the general points heavily emphasized. It was a fair criticism. If the structure was defective, this was the result of failure to have one man give unity to the whole. And apart from criticizing the incoherence of the whole, there were natural unities that were broken up and scattered throughout different chapters. An evident example of this type of thing were chapters 3, 4, 7 and 8, all referring to the hierarchy.[7] In the same vein, many Fathers said that a chapter on the People of God, a biblical theme of great importance, was needed, and should be placed before the chapter on the hierarchy; it should serve as the founda-

tion for explaining the common vocation of all in whose service the hierarchy was instituted.[8] There was also a desire to place the chapter on religious right after the one on the laity, so as not to have it constitute a state of life adequately distinct from the priesthood and the lay state. Both priests and laity can be religious.

It is worth noting that as regards the structural aspect of the document, not less than four Fathers asked, even during this first stage, that the document on the Blessed Virgin Mary[9] be integrated into the document on the Church. Some of the Fathers noted the absence of eschatology[10] in the document. In effect, the official schema appeared to restrict itself to a perspective of the Church here on earth, the "militant" Church. Ultimately these first criticisms would determine the order of the actual Constitution *Lumen Gentium*.

2. Juridicism. Even though some Fathers criticized this aspect of the document with regard to specific texts, it is fair to consider this as a criticism of a general order as well. What exactly is this defect of juridicism? It more or less means a certain lack of balance by placing too much weight on institutional expressions at the expense of the doctrinal foundation on which they rest. These expressions, by the way, are not always of divine origin. Sometimes juridicism manifests itself in a certain contradiction between juridical norms and real doctrine on a particular point—an involuntary contradiction certainly, and derived perhaps from the necessary simplification that goes along with a juridical fixing of any aspect of the Church's life. Characteristic of juridicism at times is a certain complacency and smugness on the part of righteous men in the perfection of their codes of laws and morals, a smugness that leads one to consider a juridical statute as the last word on some subject, without seeing sufficiently the contingency and inevitable limits of human law. And from this flows a frequent lack of imagination, an inability to think of laws different from the existing ones, with the consequent lack of dynamism needed in any really vital phenomenon. It is quite possible that our description of juridicism is not complete, but we believe it represents the mind of the Fathers. The consequence of all this is the preponderance of men of law, and the curious situation that important positions in the doctrinal ministry of the Church are occupied not by theologians but by canon lawyers. Allow us to recall here the opinion of a professor of canon law who thought that if in mission countries it is better to have a theologian as bishop, in the established Church preference should be given to a canonist as prelate. It should be clear that these criticisms are intended in no way to deny the necessity of juridical expressions in the Church; but they must be well defined and given only the dimension which is properly theirs. The phrase in the *Constitution on the Sacred Liturgy*, "the human is directed and subordinated to the divine, the visible likewise to the invisi-

ble,"[11] expresses exactly what we have said. It also expresses the idea of one Father who was struck by the fact that the schema treated the Church more as an institution rather than a mystery, and of another Father who pointed out that in the Church power is under charity, or of a third Father who affirmed that the aspects of the external society must be considered as a means of reference to the spiritual, which is the more important and life-giving element.[12] To conclude, let us point out that no less than twenty Fathers out of the eighty who took part in the debate expressed in diverse ways their hesitations about the juridicism of the schema. And Cardinal Ottaviani foresaw this specific criticism.

3. Controverted questions. A third criticism of a general order was the one expressed by different speakers saying that the text of the official schema presumed to solve problems controverted among theologians, as opposed to the traditional procedure of past councils, when a question of suspected heterodoxy is not involved. Under this criticism come the texts referring to the concept of "member" of the Church,[13] or to the origin of episcopal jurisdiction,[14] or to the nature of the authority of bishops, in an ecumenical council.[15]

4. General Doctrine. As regards general doctrine on the Church there were also other interventions of great importance. One of these was a petition for a more explicit treatment of the relations between the Church and the poor.[16] Also a more explicit mention was sought for the existence of contingent and reformable elements in the Church.[17] The consideration of the Church as mystery and as sacrament was also the object of many interventions.[18] Another general criticism was that the schema contained very little Oriental theology and was limited to Latin theology of the last century.

b) *Criticisms on certain particular problems.*

1. When in chapter 1 it was said that the biblical figure of the "body of Christ" did not exhaust the concept of the Church,[19] this was done precisely in order to incorporate other biblical images with appropriate development. It was pointed out also that the text used the figure "body of Christ" in a manner too exclusive and one-sided, that is, in a manner relying too heavily on the external, visible and juridical aspect of the Church. The realism of the phrase as found in St. Paul was lost sight of.[20] The absolute identification of the Catholic Church with the mystical body was also the object of some criticisms.

2. There is no doubt that one of the points that aroused the most lively criticisms was the definition of "member" of the Church as it was presented in the second chapter of the schema. The definition in question was in its essence the confirmation of the theology of St. Robert Bellarmine. In brief, the schema proposed a notion extremely rigid, based above all on exterior elements, without reference to charity. It was a conception which, as one Father said, recognized the quality of member in the Catholic sinner but

denied it to the saint who was not exteriorly in full communion with the Catholic Church. It was evident that such a manner of considering the problem would arouse the opposition of the ecumenical circles.[21] Nor was it seen how this position was connected with present-day attitudes, universally accepted as the fruit of the Holy Spirit, accepted by good Pope John XXIII. The position of the text was all the more curious considering the contributions of such respectable theologians as Cardinal Journet.[22] And so it is perfectly understandable that no less than ten Fathers expressed their criticisms and hesitations in this regard, relating them frequently to the general criticism of "juridicism." Theologians in great number (such as Rahner, Schillebeeckx and Vagaggini) also proposed in written circulars their criticisms on this point, all of which were centered on an insistence that the concept "member" is an analogical concept, not a univocal one.

3. The chapters referring to the hierarchy were the objects of innumerable observations. Many Fathers considered as formally and materially deficient the exposition on the simple priesthood. The schema had only nine lines on this.[23] Criticisms were also in place as regards the total silence of the schema on the subject of the diaconate.[24] But there were still more criticisms to come. The schema seemed to ignore the theological situation of titular bishops[25] who are in reality very numerous in the Church.[26] It was affirmed that the text presented said scarcely more than Vatican I. And it was hoped that the present Council would complement the teachings of the former, especially as concerns the episcopacy, hardly treated by Vatican I. There were critical remarks concerning the negative spirit with which the schema approached the doctrine of the episcopal collegiality.[27] From the East came the criticism of the excessive separation between what was called the power of orders and the power of jurisdiction.[28] The lack of reference to Christ when the schema treated of the priestly ministry was also the object of criticism.[29] The clear absence of the sense of "service," "diaconia" or "ministry," all of which belongs to the primary spirit of the hierarchy, was also the object of numerous criticisms. No less than six Fathers pronounced themselves in this vein.[30] Finally, various voices rose up to ask for modifications in the way the schema presented the office of the pope. No one, of course, called into question the definitions of Vatican I. But what was asked for was a homogeneous complementation. For some the doctrine on the primacy should be developed more from within the context of the episcopal college.[31] For others, the office of supreme pontiff should be situated more under the aspect of the bonds of charity and unity, rather than under authority. But the latter bond was not denied. There were some who considered that the insistence on the authority of the supreme pontiff was excessive and unnecessary, although it constituted an element once and for all acquired through

an explicit proposition of faith. Others noted that in certain passages that treated of the hierarchy, it seemed to be identified with the Roman pontiff, passing over in silence the authority which belongs to bishops by divine right.[32] One Father insinuated the necessity to explain the formula *ex sese* in the definition of Vatican I,[33] a formula which has lent itself to so many interpretations prejudicious to unity among non-Catholic Christians. Also the absence of the liturgical function of the hierarchy was noted, something that was already strongly contained in the *Constitution on the Sacred Liturgy*[34]—again the objection of juridicism arose.

4. The criticisms concerning the doctrine on the laity were not too numerous, but there were some. It was remarked that the three functions of the Church (prophetic, priestly and royal) belong not only to the hierarchy but also to all the faithful; this was an important item for the future structure of the chapter on the People of God.[35] Recognition was asked for the infallibility of the people "in credendo."[36] There was an insistence on the laity not being merely passive, that they were not a body of second-class Christians, that their office cannot be supplied by the clergy, and that charisms exist in the Christian people which are ordained to the good of the whole Church.[37]

5. Chapter 8 was the object of criticism because of the unilateral vision it presented concerning obedience; it was negative and insufficiently nuanced. At the least a recognition of the nature and rights of Christian liberty was called for, without pretending thereby to deny the value and necessity of obedience.[38]

6. Chapter 9, concerning the relations of Church and state, was the object of severe criticisms. No less than five Fathers formulated these criticisms from their respective points of view. Old and worn-out controversies should no longer be brought up. Medieval theories should not be proposed as practicable for today's world. It was remarked that the principles proposed were not adequate for contemporary society, one of whose characteristics is pluralism.[39] Some Fathers proposed that in this chapter there should be a declaration on religious liberty. All these criticisms explain the disappearance of this chapter from the definitive text of the constitution *De Ecclesia*.

7. Chapter 10 on the missions was also judged to be deficient. Some Fathers insisted on the need not to give the impression that missions were just a side-line activity of the Church. It was felt necessary that missionary spirit animate the whole Constitution. Others criticized the point of view of the official schema: it concentrated too much on demanding the rights of the Church facing the state in whose territory a mission was located. The rights of the Church in this matter are sufficiently known by Catholics and are not recognized by others. It also turned out that the official text might

run the risk of bringing the missions under persecution,[40] if the text were wrongly worded. Once more it was pointed out how necessary it was in the context of actual history to have a declaration on religious liberty, from which flow as from a common source the guarantees of missionary work.

8. The chapter on ecumenism was not the object of many detailed criticisms. But the text itself was looked upon as very slightly ecumenical.[41] And it was remarked that only the Catholic Church was called "Church," a statement which seemed contradictory to the practice of important documents of the hierarchy and of the Holy See itself.[42] In reality, the *Decree on Ecumenism*, promulgated by the Fathers in the third period of the Council, reveals an unsuspected openness if one takes this chapter 11 of the original schema of the *Constitution on the Church* as the point of departure. The criticisms on this chapter dealing with ecumenism were not independent, as is evident, from the more general criticism of "juridicism."

RESULTS OF THE FIRST PERIOD

In bringing to a close our brief list of criticisms, it is possible that the reader will get the impression that the official schema lacked all value whatsoever. This would be an inaccurate impression. If the Fathers played heavily on the weak points, this was largely due to the pressure of the brief time allowed them for their speeches. They of necessity felt constrained to point out the items that needed improvement. There was no time to waste on singing the praises of the document. And there were many points that could be praised. But the future development of things showed that the Council as a whole felt itself best expressed by the Fathers who formulated the criticisms, and because of these a new redaction of the text became mandatory.

The official text had three undeniable merits. In the first place, it presented a serious basis for discussion. Secondly, it showed the maturity of the Council's becoming conscious of its own aspirations, which were not always identical with those of the preparatory commissions. Finally, it gave a series of texts and formulas which were satisfactory enough, and which were salvaged (with some retouching, of various shades of importance) to form part of the definitive version of the Constitution.

If the debate from December 1–7, 1962, was a "debate of orientation,"[43] no one failed to recognize the fundamental importance it held in the elaboratation of future texts. Without this debate the Constitution *Lumen Gentium* would be unexplainable. And this debate, as we said above, is a basic element in the evaluation and appreciation of the contents of the Constitution.

Second Step: The Work Done Between the First and Second Period of the General Congregations[44]

Two important facts framed the future work of the Council. The first was a document from the Holy Father, worded in the spirit of John XXIII, and given through the Secretary of State. It constituted a clear orientation for the Conciliar work.[45] One of its most fundamental dispositions was to decide that the official schemata must be submitted to revisison by the Conciliar commissions during the recess.[46] This was a recognition of the fact that there was no adequate agreement between the mind of the preparatory commissions and that of the Council itself. This had already been evident in the debates of the first session. Also the Holy Father's document ordered the elimination of repetitions and directed that special attention be paid to the pastoral needs of the universal Church. The concrete historical situation as well as ecumenical considerations were to be kept in view. And so the official schemata shed their attitude of "possessio iuridica."

The second fact also arose from the same document. It was the establishment of the commission to coordinate the labors of the Council. Its task was precisely to direct the works, to keep in contact with the presidents of the Conciliar commissions, and to watch over the conformity of the schemata with the aims of the Council.[47] We will not examine here the evolution of the directive organs of the Council, their complexity and their different functions. It is enough to note the appearance of the Coordinating Commission and to affirm that its influence was important at this stage of the formation of the Constitution on the Church.

The norms laid down by the Holy Father contained a delicate deference paid to the bishop: once the schemata were revised by the competent commissions, they would be sent to all the bishops of the world so that they could send in their observations.[48] In this new atmosphere the Conciliar works began anew.

ELABORATION OF THE SECOND TEXT

Immediately the Coordinating Commission introduced a first step for the reworking of the text: this was a new index of the chapters that would compose it.[49] This index contained not only the titles of the chapters but also concrete suggestions concerning the matters each one of them would treat and the manner of structuring them. We do not have the time to stop and consider these particular suggestions, but it is in place to point out the new general structure which they called for. The Constitution would be made up of four chapters: 1) On the mystery of the Church, 2) The hierarchy of the Church, and in particular the bishops, 3) The laity, 4) The states of evangelical perfection.

The Coordinating Commission still thought that it was best to keep the schema on the Blessed Virgin Mary as a separate document.

On the basis of these orientations the work began for the Commission of Faith and Morals (called by way of abbreviation: the Theological Commission) to rework the document on the Church. A new factor would play an important role within the Commission: the Fathers who were members of the Commission were authorized to call in experts whom they elected and who would act as helpers with the task at hand.

It remained to determine what would be the basis for the deliberations of the Commission. It was rather clear that if the official schema did contain quite a few profitable elements, still it did not constitute in itself an appropriate basis for discussion, because of the preceding debates. Another schema had to be proposed.

Four texts were in the running for being of service in this matter. There was a partial project done by Msgr. Pietro Parente; there was a new schema all drawn up by the German theologians; there was another schema drawn up by the French and Belgian theologians; and finally there was another one presented by Cardinal Raul Silva and various members of the hierarchy of Chile.

As is evident, it goes beyond the limits of this paper to attempt even a summary evaluation of the merits, characteristics and deficiencies of these four projects. Perhaps the incomplete character of Msgr. Parente's work was a liability; and a desire for greater clarity was against the document drawn up by the Germans, known for their heavy profundity. The text from Chile contained an original sin: it had been drawn up according to the outline of chapters contained in the first official text, and this outline had already been modified by the Coordinating Commission. But it must be said that it was sincerely admired and it did have a great influence.[50] Besides, it had another important value: it proposed in an open fashion the incorporation of the text on the Blessed Virgin Mary as part of the Constitution *De Ecclesia*.

And so there remained the Franco-Belgian text. This was the basis of the overall patient work of the Theological Commission. Again we find ourselves in the impossible situation of detailing the work which was now done. It is enough to say that at the beginning of the second period of the general congregations of the Council,[51] the Fathers had in their hands a new text of the Constitution *De Ecclesia*, and it was composed of four chapters: 1) Concerning the mystery of the Church, 2) The hierarchical constitution of the Church and especially the bishops, 3) Concerning the People of God and especially the laity, 4) The calling to sanctity in the Church.[52]

Immediately two observations arise: the theme of the People of God has now appeared explicitly in the titles, and the chapter on the states of perfection has changed its title to the calling to sanctity within the Church. But still, at the foot of the first page corresponding to the new chapter 3, a note explained that the Coordinating Commission had thought it opportune to divide chapter 3 into two parts: the first would treat "The People of God in General" and would make up chapter 2 of the whole Constitution, and the second part would treat of "The Laity" and would make up chapter 4 of the whole Constitution. The Coordinating Commission also laid to rest Conciliar dissatisfaction on another point: in the new scheme of things, before talking about the hierarchy, there was in the Constitution a text that would show with complete clarity the common heritage of all the faithful—the common heritage in which there is no difference among the laity and those who fill the hierarchical function.

And there was another new element: the change of the title in chapter 4 (which according to the new suggestion would become chapter 5). This change was not just a problem of a title but of a much more profound nature: an important wave of opinions had been heard in the Council moving in the direction of asking that the concept of the states of perfection (or of religious life,[53] as we now say) would be situated within a larger concept. This would avoid the equivocation which consists in believing that holiness is reserved to the canonical forms of life called "states of perfection according to the evangelical counsels." In this perspective it is shown that holiness is a calling for all the disciples of Christ, and that the canonical forms of the states of perfection find their place within this universal calling.

RESULTS OF THE SECOND STEP

One can only express a positive judgment for the work done between sessions. A new text, one much better ordered, more in agreement with the wishes of the Fathers, was presented for Conciliar discussion. It can be said that already the definitive structure of the Constitution was laid out, even if it had not yet arrived at its ultimate point of development. The Theological Commission had done a great deal to be faithful to the orientation debates of December, 1962. It will be said, and with reason no doubt, that the text was not perfect. However, things were now much closer to what the Fathers wanted than they were with the original official schema. Moreover, there were various papers published by Council circles distributed within the Conciliar hall, and these publications pointed out texts suitable for amendments. Thus a greater theological exactness was assured.[54]

Nevertheless, there remained some questions. The most important of these was the one referring to the possible integration of the doctrine on the

Blessed Virgin Mary into the *Constitution on the Church*. Other questions concerned the Church in heaven and eschatology.

THIRD STEP: THE SECOND PERIOD OF GENERAL CONGREGATIONS[55]

As regards the *Constitution on the Church* this period was of capital importance. During this period the Fathers discussed the text prepared during what we have termed the "second step" and the Constitution acquired its definitive structure. This is true in general terms, as will be seen further along.[56]

We will forego making an evaluation of the remarks of the Fathers during the discussion. The interventions were more than five hundred, and the typewritten text, distributed to the Fathers and to the experts of the Theological Commission, takes more than two thousand pages, without counting the discussion of chapters 7 and 8 of the promulgated text, which were discussed in the third period of general congregation.[57] In general, and attending to the prevailing lines of Conciliar opinion, it can be said that the debate accented the same orientations as the previous debate of 1962. Three points especially attracted the attention of the speakers: the People of God and the priesthood of all the faithful, the episcopal college, and the restoration of the diaconate in the Latin Church as a permanent order and without the obligation of celibacy. Another vital point for the definitive structure of the Constitution was resolved in the course of this third step: the insertion of the doctrine on the Blessed Virgin Mary in the Constitution *De Ecclesia*.

The formation of a new chapter on the People of God did not present major difficulties. The Theological Commission accepted it with grace enough.

THE DOCTRINE ON THE EPISCOPACY

The problems derived from the nature of the episcopacy were of a more complex nature. It was not easy, even after the debate, to have an exact appreciation of the feeling of Conciliar opinion; more than fifteen hundred Fathers had not spoken and so it was difficult to judge in which direction the necessary two-thirds majority was leaning. In such circumstances, Cardinal Silva and a group of about seventy bishops asked for the adoption of a practical point of order, not allowed for by the Regulations, but which was the only one able to lead to desired results. It was asked that some of the fundamental proposals on the major themes being debated be put to the Fathers in general congregation, so that the vote on the proposals would serve as a guide for the further work of the Theological Commission.[58] The redaction of the proposals was a very laborious task and kept the Council in suspension for several days: it was evident that certain areas of influence did not like such a procedure, something that became even more evident when, after the voting indicated a healthy majority, voices were still heard in the aula supporting the autonomy of the Theological Commission over against the will of the general congregation clearly indicated in the vote taken on the proposals.[59]

It is interesting to know the text of these proposals, whose passage through the Conciliar vote constituted, according to the feeling of many, one of the culminating moments of the Council, because it signified an undeniable expression of the feelings of the whole assembly.[60]

The first proposition was concerned with whether the Fathers wanted the schema prepared in such manner that it would affirm episcopal consecration as the highest degree of the sacrament of orders. Of the 2,157 Fathers who voted, 2,123 responded yes and 34 no.

The second proposal was to prepare the schema in such way as to say that every bishop legitimately consecrated and in communion with the other bishops and with the Roman pontiff (who is the head and the source of unity) is a member of the body of bishops.[61] Of the 2,154 Fathers voting, there were 2,049 affirmative votes, 104 negative and one null vote.

The third proposal aimed at preparing the schema in such manner as to say that the body or college of bishops is the successor of the college of apostles in the offices of evangelizing, sanctifying and ruling, and that this college of bishops, united to its head, the Roman pontiff, and otherwise not, possesses full and supreme power over all the Church. Of the 2,148 Fathers voting, there were 1,808 affirmative votes, 336 negative and four *iuxta modum*.

The fourth and last proposal referring to the episcopacy was that the schema be so prepared as to say that the power, referred to in the previous proposals, belongs to the episcopal college united to its head in virtue of the same divine law. Of the 2,148 Fathers who voted, 1,717 said yes, 408 no and one *iuxta modum*.

One thing was clear. The proposals brought a majority not only of the regulation two-thirds, but of 75 per cent even in the most delicate of the proposals.

As was to be supposed, the definitive redaction of the Constitution would witness to the desires of the Fathers expressed in the proposals.[62] Cardinal Silva's suggestion proved to be effective.

THE DIACONATE

The theme of the restoration of the diaconate resolved itself in principle in the same way. In effect, the fifth proposal submitted to the assembly on the same day as the four preceding ones asked if it was the will of the Fathers that the schema be so prepared that it would judge opportune the restoration of the diaconate as a distinct and permanent degree of the sacred ministry, taking into account the needs of the Church in diverse regions of the world. Note well that the proposal kept a prudent silence on the question of celibacy. But this silence was more apparent than real. The Fathers knew well enough that the restoration of a permanent diaconate bound to celibacy was utopian, and so the voting indicated their attitudes toward a noncelibate diaconate.

Of the 2,120 Fathers who voted, there were 1,588 yes, 525 no, four *iuxta modum* and three null votes. And so in this case only two votes were lacking to reach 75 per cent: the majority was more than sufficient.

THE PLACE OF THE DOCTRINE ON THE VIRGIN MARY

The problem of the insertion of a chapter on the Blessed Virgin into the Constitution was difficult to solve. The Theological Commission could not resolve this by itself, and so the question was put to the whole assembly.

The sentiment of the general congregation was not settled on this question. There were two currents of opinion. Those who fought for a separate schema spread their ideas with active propaganda. One group of experts[63] published an extended study in favor of a separate schema; they said that the insertion into the schema *De Ecclesia* gave preference to a new mentality, forgetful of the magisterium in this case. A group of the Fathers from the Malabar and Ukrainian rites distributed to the other Fathers a petition not to vote in favor of the insertion; to do so would not be understood by the Orientals. Finally, an anonymous work asked for votes against the insertion and, among others reasons, asserted that Mary was above the Church. All of these documents put together gave the global impression that to vote for insertion was to diminish the honor of the Blessed Virgin. On the other hand, to vote for a separate schema was to favor the true honor of Mary. It is understandable that such a prospect upset the Fathers. What Catholic would not be alarmed at the possibility of contributing to the decrease of honor paid to the Mother of God?

The Fathers in favor of integration did not work too hard for their position. Apart from a mimeographed sheet widely distributed and signed by Cardinal Raul Silva and Msgr. Alfredo Viola,[64] we do not know of any other document representing this group for integration. This sheet contained, in a very synthetic redaction, nine positive arguments for integration and it answered five objections against it. Its preparation was the fruit of the collaboration of theologians of various nations. Among the positive arguments there were the necessary relations between Mary and the Church, the advantage of giving the doctrine on the Virgin its proper context, the traditional sentiment of the East, the eschatological dimension of the Assumption, and so forth.

Before proceeding to the voting, two cardinals delegated by the Theological Commission gave the exposition for both sides of the question. Cardinal Franz König spoke for integration, and Cardinal Rufino Santos spoke for a separate schema.[65]

On October 29, the question was put to the Fathers of the Council if it was their will that the schema on the Blessed Virgin Mary, Mother of the Church, would be so adapted as to become chapter 6 of the schema *De Ecclesia.* The atmosphere was extremely tense. No one dared to show optimism for his own position. Finally the voting took place, and of the 2,193 Fathers voting, 1,114 favored integration, 1,074 were against, two voted *iuxta modum,* and there were three null votes. The question was decided in principle, because previously the moderator of the day had declared that since there was not a question here of doctrine, there was need only of a 50 per cent majority plus one vote. Note well that the voting resolved one other problem: the official text on the Blessed Virgin, published in the same booklet as the original text on *De Ecclesia,* must now be adapted. This work was to be done by the Theological Commission. Such adaptation was necessary because from the first moment of the presentation of the text on the Blessed Virgin Mary, and even though it was not discussed in the first period of the general congregations, there were many criticisms leveled at the official text. It was only natural to proceed to its reworking, as the insertion now required.

It seems certain that the smallest majority recorded in Vatican II in a vote taken in general congregation was a product of psychological factors and influences. This was so much the case that Cardinal Agagianian, who presided over the general congregation on the day of the voting, felt it necessary to say that whatever would have been the outcome of the voting, the Blessed Virgin Mary would have equal honor. This would have been an extraneous statement, except for the atmosphere that made it necessary.

RESULTS OF THE THIRD STEP

The third step of the development of the text on the Constitution *De Ecclesia* brought the several results. In the first place, a complementation of the text, with respect to the suggestions of the Coordinating Commission, was achieved. The text was now composed of six chapters: 1) Concerning the mystery of the Church, 2) On the People of God in general, 3) On the hierarchical constitution of the Church and especially on the episcopacy, 4) On the laity in particular, 5) On the vocation to holiness in the Church, 6) On the Blessed Virgin Mary.

In the second place, these questions were resolved in principle: the sacramentality of the episcopacy, the collegiality of the bishops and the restoration of the diaconate.

It was not possible during this session to submit to a vote any form of revised texts. The Theological Commission had to reduce more than 3,000 pages containing the propositions of the Fathers. The new redaction of the chapter on the Virgin Mary was still not finished.

It can be said that, looking at the Constitution as a whole, it was this third step which contributed most to its definitive composition. The speeches of the Fathers in the aula form a source whose study is necessary for a global appreciation of the doctrine. The scientific revision of these documents was not to be easy since three versions of them exist. There was the original, which was many times amended and augmented even with handwritten passages; there was the typewritten copy made for the use of the experts and the periti of the Theological Commission; and there was the taped recording of those documents that were actually read in the aula and not only given in writing.

Fourth Step: The Recess and the Third Period of the General Congregations[66]

It may seem strange that we group these two periods together. In reality, we are justified in considering them as a unity.

The points brought out in this step can be reduced to three: the work of amending the schema presented for debate in the preceding step, the discussion of the two final chapters of the Constitution, and the promulgation accompanied by the famous *Nota praevia*.

THE AMENDMENT OF THE TEXT

The work of revision was great and especially laborious as regards the chapter on the hierarchical constitution of the Church. The strong opposition raised in the aula concerning the doctrine of episcopal collegiality[67] was echoed and sometimes with double force in the meetings of the Theological Commission. In order to achieve the work of revision in an absolutely objective form, the subcommissions of the Theological Commission made great use of the collections of all the concrete propositions of the Fathers. It can be said that every opinion of the Fathers was sifted, considered, and then evaluated according to the intrinsic value of the doctrine of the proposition, as well as to its harmony with the general line indicated by the Council in the voting of October 30. Also the number of Fathers who supported each proposition was weighted in its favor. This was true because in the Council little by little a certain tendency became manifest of grouping together to back a certain proposition through common effort. This same tendency was later echoed in the directive organs of the Council, because these ultimately gave precedence and preference to Fathers who wished to speak in the name of a large, significant group. This was an important innovation, because during the first stages of the Council individual intervention prevailed, and from this individual procedure it was very often impossible to tell what the majority of the Council was thinking; very often the minority members made more use of the spoken word than the majority.

Among the labors of the recess special mention must be made of the redaction of the material that eventually constituted chapters 7 and 8 of the Constitution.

THE CHAPTER ON ESCHATOLOGY

Chapter 7, whose definitive title is "The Eschatological Nature of the Pilgrim Church and her Union with the Heavenly Church," resulted from the merging of diverse tendencies. Already in the discussion of 1962 some Fathers had pointed out the necessity that the Constitution should not limit itself to a partial vision of heavenly reality, considering only its transitory terrestrial aspect ("militant" aspect as the official schema put it). Other Fathers pointed out the need to insist on the eschatological nature of the Church. During the second period of general congregations (what we have called the third step), various Fathers once again insisted that a place be found for serious consideration of the saints, as an expression of the perfection of the church. Such a consideration should form part of the chapter on the calling to holiness within the Church and would be the crowning point of the Constitution. But there was another line of thought present: the Constitution ought to make a wide reference to the devotion paid the saints. This devotion, according to the opinion of some, had been lost sight of in some regions, and according to the view of others this aspect of Catholic faith had not received the development it deserved. Out of all these various anxieties chapter 7 was born. This text had many various forms. It received successive amendments and revision in the Theological Commission, and it was finally made known to the Fathers during the third period of the general congregations.[68] It was also during this period that the definitive amendments were made to this chapter. The discussion during the general congregations of 1964 modified it only slightly and introduced certain new elements, for example, the references to purgatory and to hell.[69] The very history of the text of this chapter explains a certain lack of thematic unity. It can even be said that the placing of this chapter in the total schema is a little artificial; perhaps its proper place would have been as a part of chapter 2 on the People of God.

But this place could not be given to it in the stage in which this chapter finally appeared. The chapter on the People of God was already definitively revised and ready for voting, while the chapter on eschatology had not even been discussed. And it was clear that the Fathers did not want the third session to end without promulgating the *Constitution on the Church*. Even in this case the enemy of good was the better.

THE CHAPTER ON THE BLESSED VIRGIN

Chapter 8 of the definitive text, whose theme is the doctrine on the Blessed Virgin Mary, was particularly troublesome in its elaboration. Many bishops proposed as a basis a different text from that which had appeared in the original schema. This new text was the result of collaboration of two related groups: one represented by C. Butler, Abbot President of the English Congregation of Benedictines, and the other by the bishops of Chile. The proposed text received very significant support from many sectors, but in the end it did not constitute the basis of the Conciliar text. Another approach was attempted: a special commission of bishops and periti took upon themselves the task of working out a text. But this commission did not realize any concrete results. Finally, two *periti* of the Theological Commission, Msgr. Gerard Philips and Father Carlos Balić, who held diverse tendencies on the theology of Mary, drew up a text that was revised by the Theological Commission and presented to the Council for discussion. This opened the way to a sufficiently wide approbation. During March and June, 1964, the Commission polished the text sufficiently so that it could be presented to the Fathers. The debate showed that the text was balanced and that it responded to the expectations of the Council. A deeper study reveals that the principal concerns of the Fathers were faithfully reflected in the text.

The discussion of the chapters 7 and 8 was peaceful and brief. Hence the Commission was able to give the definitive redaction to the texts and propose them to a vote in the aula.

THE DIVISION OF THE CHAPTER ON THE CALL TO SANCTITY

It is worth pointing out one more piece of background that influenced the definitive structure of the Constitution. A very large group of Fathers[70] asked that the chapter on the call to holiness be divided into two parts so that one part could be dedicated to a special chapter on the religious. This was a question of form, but with certain deep overtones. The Theological Commission left it to the Council to make the decision on this matter. In any case, the text was not to be changed. Without special discussion the Council gave its decision with a majority (but not an enthusiastic one) in favor of

the religious Fathers.[71] Thus was born chapter 6: "Concerning Religious."
At first it seemed that the desired effect of the chapter on the call to holiness would be lost completely: to show the religious life within the context of a general calling to sanctity common to all Christians. But the history of the text will serve to keep this intent in mind, and its importance cannot be denied.

THE VOTING OF THE TEXT

Finally we come to the voting on the text. We will not be detained by details. The first chapter was approved in one ballot. For the second chapter there were five ballots. The third chapter demanded forty-two separate votings. The fourth and fifth were passed on one ballot each. The sixth chapter needed two. The seventh chapter was divided into five ballots. And finally, the eighth chapter took one ballot. All the texts were approved with a substantial majority. But in the voting on collegiality and the diaconate there was major opposition.[72]

It was not yet the end. The Fathers used their right to vote *iuxta modum* on the last ballot of each chapter, and so the Commission had to study the merits of about a thousand "modi." Each one of these was studied and for each one the Commission proposed a response whose approbation was then put to the Council in general session. Only a few of the "modi" were finally admitted, those considered by the Commission as an enrichment of the approved text.[73]

It was in this stage of affairs that the problem came up concerning the *Nota praevia.* It is not possible here to trace its history. First of all because it is long and, also, because much of the history is of a highly reserved character. In fact, its study, which went on for longer than a week during which the Commission was in frequent contact with the Pope, took place without the presence of *periti.* It said that Msgr. Colombo and Father Bertrams took an active though not decisive part.[74] The text of the note was given to the Fathers before the voting on the "modi" of chapter 3, and it was published together with the official text of the Constitution. But the note itself was not the object of any vote from the Council and was not in the printed text submitted to the general congregation before the solemn vote held in the presence of the Pope. What is the meaning of the note? It is thought that its aim was to pacify the minority of Fathers who feared that the collegiality of the bishops would be a lessening of the prerogatives of the Roman pontiff. Were these fears well founded? Msgr. Parente, assessor of the Holy Office and member of the Theological Commission, affirmed in an article published in *L'Avvenire d'Italia,* January 21, 1965,[75] that the note does not say any more about the relations between Pope and bishops than the Constitution itself says. But there is still no agreement in this matter. It is clear that one side attaches great importance to the note, while the other side belittles its importance. And so it will be difficult to say exactly what is the doctrinal authority of the note, especially as long as the background history of the note is not known with complete details.

On November 19, 1964, the General Congregation voted the definitive text of the Constitution. Of the 2,145 Fathers present and voting, 2,134 voted yes, 10 voted no, and there was one null vote. On November 21, in the solemn session presided over by Pope Paul, 2,156 Fathers voted *placet*, and only five voted *non placet*. The Constitution *Lumen Gentium* thus entered into the heritage of the extraordinary acts of the magisterium of the Church.

NOTES

1. Originally published in *Teologia y Vida* 6 (1965) 187–209, given at Notre Dame with slight revision.

2. For a knowledge of the development of the Council's activity, it is most interesting to consult the four volumes published up to now by René Laurentin, a Council expert, *L'enjeu du Concile* (Paris 1963–1965). The first volume contains the preparatory antecedents, and each of the following ones corresponds to each period of the general congregation of the Council.

3. See the work of Pinera, Bishop of Temuco, in *Teologia y vida* (1964) 77.

4. This document was eventually integrated into the *Decree on Ecumenism* and into the *Decree on Eastern Catholic Churches*.

5. From 1–7, 1962, i.e., 6 general congregations.

6. For each criticism expressed by the Fathers, we shall footnote the reference to the definitive text of the Constitution. A comparison will show how the criticisms were taken into account. This will necessarily give a superficial impression. Scientific appraisal is possible only on the basis of the analysis and comparison of the texts themselves and of the stages of its evolution.

7. Almost everything concerning this matter can be found in ch. 3, and ch. 4, art. 37.

8. It forms ch. 2 of the Constitution.

9. It forms ch. 8 of the Constitution.

10. This topic is introduced in art. 5, and is more thoroughly treated in ch. 7, especially in art. 48.

11. See the *Constitution on the Sacred Liturgy*, art. 2.

12. See the Constitution, art. 8.

13. See art. 14, 15 of the Constitution *Lumen Gentium*. See also art. 3 of the *Decree on Ecumenism*, promulgated the same day. It constitutes an authorized commentary on this point.

14. See art. 21, 24 of the Constitution.

15. See art. 22 of the Constitution.

16. See *ibid*. art. 8, 41.

17. See *ibid*. art. 8 and especially the *Decree on Ecumenism*, art. 6.

18. See art. 1, 3, 5.

19. See art. 5, 6.

20. See art. 7.

21. See art. 14, 15. See also *Decree on Ecumenism*, art. 3.

22. See ch. Journet, *L'Eglise et le Verbe Incarne* 2 (Paris, 1951) 1056–1081.

23. See art. 28.

24. See art. 29.

25. See art. 21, 22, 24. The Constitution does not use the terminology "residential" and "titular" bishops, but it does consider the theological reality that these terms cover.

26. "Titular" bishops are: a large number of cardinals, high prelates of the Roman Curia, auxiliary and coadjutor bishops, normally vicars apostolic, the prelates nullius, and bishops who have renounced their residential sees. At present, they number more than a thousand.

27. See art. 22, 23 and the *Nota praevia*.

28. See art. 21, 24.

29. See art. 21 and the *Constitution on the Sacred Liturgy,* art. 7.

30. See art. 18, 24.

31. See art. 22, 23. See also the *Decree on Ecumenism,* art. 2.

32. See art. 27 and several other places in ch. 3.

33. See art. 25.

34. See art. 26. See also the *Constitution on the Sacred Liturgy,* art. 41, 42.

35. See art. 10, 12, 13, 31, 34, 35.

36. See art. 12.

37. See art. 33, 32, 12.

38. See art. 37.

39. "Plurality" or "pluralism" is understood as the fact that persons or groups of different religious convictions live together in the same political community.

40. See art. 16, 17.

41. See art. 15 and the *Decree on Ecumenism.*

42. See *Decree on Ecumenism,* ch. 3.

43. See Laurentin's *L'Enjeu du Concile. Bilan de la troisième session,* 333.

44. Technically, "Conciliar session" refers to that assembly personally presided over by the pope or his legates. They are very rare and at Vatican II were generally the opening and the closing day of a period of work. The ones held on the closing day are the most important assembly meetings since the final vote on documents and their promulgation are then taken. In popular language, however, the phrase "session" has been used to designate an approximate period of two months, corresponding to the duration of the annual activity of the Council assembly as a whole. In a still less accurate sense, the press identifies sessions and general congregations. The general congregation is the daily meeting of all the Fathers, under the presidency of a cardinal moderator. During the general congregations discussion of and voting on the schemata took place.

45. The document was called "Order of work during the time between the 1st and 2nd period of the Ecumenical Council"; it is dated Dec. 5, 1962.

46. *Ibid.* n.1.

47. *Ibid.* n.4.

48. *Ibid.* n.5.

49. These decisions were transmitted to the Theological Commission Jan. 30, 1963, by the Cardinal Secretary of State, president of the Coordinating Commission.

50. Taking part in the elaboration of that schema were José Comblin, Edigio Viganó, S.D.B., and Juan Ochagavia, professors at the University of Santiago.

51. The second period opened Sept. 30, 1963.

52. The text appeared as two booklets, each of which contained two chapters.

53. Technically, "religious life" and "state of perfection to be acquired" are not to be identified; the second phrase is broader than the first. Without insisting on the canonical classifications of life devoted to God in these states, it is worth noting, as an example, that members of secular institutes are not religious on canonical grounds; nor do they want to be. However, they belong to the category of "state of perfection." In this respect, one can consult K. Rahner's *Mission et Grace,* vol. 2, *Serviteurs du peuple de Dieu* (Tours, 1963) 173–190.

54. Of particular interest are K. Rahner's observations.

55. This period extends from Sept. 30 to Dec. 4, 1963.

56. The restriction refers to the last four chapters of the promulgated text.

57. The third period of general congregations extends from Sept. 14 to Nov. 21, 1964.

58. The Cardinal's proposal was made Oct. 8 and reiterated Oct. 22. See note 59.

59. See Edigio Viganó's article in *Teologia y Vida* 5 (1964) 15.

60. The vote on the proposals took place Oct. 30, 1963.

61. The expressions "episcopal body," "episcopal order" and "episcopal college" are traditional and are used as synonyms in the *Constitution on the Church.*

62. See art. 21, 22, 23.

63. The booklet indicated its origin in general: the Mariology consultants of the bishops of Spain.

64. Bishop of Salto, Uruguay, incumbent president of this Episcopal Conference.

65. The reports of both Cardinals were read to the assembly Oct. 24, 1963, and their texts were distributed to the Fathers. Cardinal König made express reference to Cardinal Silva's position.

66. See note 57.

67. Qualifying these oppositions as "strong" does not refer to the number of those who supported them. Among others, Msgr. Dino Staffa, Titular Archbishop of Cesarea in Palestine,

published several articles in which he rejected the doctrine of collegiality: "De Collegiali episcopatus ratione," *Divinitas* 8, and a duplicated text translated into Spanish: "Observaciones sobre los esquemas De Ecclesia and De pastorali Episcoporum nunere in Ecclesia." He also published studies on this subject in the review *Seminarium*, sponsored by the Congregation of Seminaries, the secretary of which is Msgr. Staffa. See *Seminarium* n.s. 3, 642.

68. At the beginning of the third period of general congregations, the Fathers disposed of a 220-page volume, in which the reports on the amended text and the text itself in parallel columns were contained as well as some other elements to facilitate study of the changes that had been introduced. Only with respect of the last two chapters did the two-column text not correspond to a text discussed and to a second text amended after the discussion.

69. See art. 48, 50.

70. The number exceeded 700. The initiative came from Fathers belonging to different religious families.

71. 2,210 Fathers voted. 1,505 voted for the division, that is to say, for a separate chapter devoted to religious; 698 voted against such a division. Note that before the vote the *relator* of the text, Benno Gut, Abbot Primate of the Benedictine Confederation, insistently requested the assembly to vote for the division.

72. The numerical data can be found in Laurentin, *Bilan de la troisième session*.

73. The "modi," their study and the list of those that the Commission recommended for each chapter, were contained in booklets distributed prior to the Fathers' vote.

74. See Laurentin, *Bilan de la troisième session*, 338.

75. See *La Documentation Catholique* 1443 (March 7, 1965) 415–426. Msgr. Parente gives a detailed account of the elements contained in the *Nota praevia*. He says: "All these doctrinal points are found in the text of the Constitution; the note emphasizes them, underlines them, explains them, but does not add anything substantial to the text. . . . The note remains an explanatory note, emanating from the Commission that wrote the text, and approved by the Holy Father." "The Fathers' vote did not touch upon the *note* (besides, it was not necessary) but upon the text of the Constitution" (*ibid.*, 423).

Canon Charles Moeller

HISTORY OF LUMEN GENTIUM'S STRUCTURE AND IDEAS

Anyone who would have predicted in January, 1959, that on November 22, 1964, the dogmatic Constitution *Lumen Gentium* would be promulgated, would have been considered a dreamer. And yet this Constitution is henceforth before our eyes, with its four ecclesiological axes: 1) the Church as mystery, primordial sacrament of the unity of the world in the People of God, 2) the hierarchical structures of the Church where laymen and ministers meet in the mystery of the primacy and of collegiality, 3) holiness, or the charismatic structure in the Church, and 4) the celestial fulfillment seen in an eschatological and pneumatological dimension.

Ab initio non fuit sic. I can still remember the explanations of my catechism on the Church: a perfect society, governed as a monarchy by the sovereign pontiff; I also remember the treatise on the Church mentioned by Henri de Lubac that out of 434 pages devoted only half a page to the relationship of the Church with Christ![2]

And yet, as early as 1921 R. Guardini wrote: "The twentieth century will be the century of the Church." He was right. The liturgical renewal from 1909 on; the ecumenical movement, dating from 1925, around such men as Dom Lambert Beauduin; the rediscovery of the Bible as the foundation of the theology of the Church, with exegetes like Msgr. Cerfaux; the updating of the Church's mission in virtue of its apostolic character, in a world both more diversified and more in search of unity, with men like Father

Congar—all these formed parallel currents that would converge in Vatican Council II's *De Ecclesia.*

John XXIII replied one day to a journalist who asked him what he expected of the Council: "I do not quite know." Then he led the journalist to a window, opened it and said: "At least some fresh air." Good Pope John was also one of the prophets.

It suffices to compare the schema originally proposed—with its division into eleven chapters, juxtaposed rather than ordered, with their very abstract titles—with the very clear, well-structured division of the final text and its biblical, liturgical and ecumenical titles, in order to discover that fresh air circulated freely. Nobody will be surprised that it stirred up quite a bit of dust and even caused some to sneeze.[3] The result is resolutely positive.

I. THE MYSTERY OF THE CHURCH

Whereas the schema of the preparatory commission began in the "classical" way with a study of the "Nature of the Church Militant" and then continued with one on the "Members of the Church and Its Necessity for Salvation," the text of the Constitution opens with two chapters devoted to the "Mystery" of the Church.

Some thought that there were already enough "mysteries" in Christian doctrine, and that it was useless and dangerous to add still another. Especially since quite a few people, looking at the Church from without, do not see it very clearly. To assert from the very beginning the mysterious character of the ecclesiastical institution would be to confirm them in their attitude of, to say the least, expectancy, respectful or skeptical, but definitely wait-and-see. Would it not be better to begin the exposition with "what one sees" of the Church, namely, that it is a perfect society, endowed with powers, active in the struggle against error and violence?[4]

It goes without saying that the meaning of the word "mystery," as applied to the Church, is not to emphasize her "mysterious, enigmatic" character, but quite the contrary, to assert that the Church is the great sign by which God fulfills his plan of salvation: to communicate to the human race, through baptismal faith, participation in the mystery par excellence, that of the life of the Trinity. The Constitution, then, approaches the Church from the viewpoint of the faith: it describes the Church first of all as an object of faith;[5] study of it ought to be inspired by faith and love.[6]

We should understand the term "sacrament" as applied to the Church in the prologue of the Constitution (art. 1) against the same perspective. Some had feared that the faithful would imagine there would be an eighth sacrament! This, they said, would not be very appropriate for a pastoral Council which claimed to be open to the legitimate aspirations of the apostolate. In reality, the term means that the Church is "a kind of sacrament,[7] or sign of intimate union with God, and of the unity of all mankind . . . an instrument for the achievement of such union and unity" (art. 1). In other words, the text takes up again, in a context more marked by sacramental theology, the theme of Vatican Council I on the Church as a "great sign raised up among the nations,"[8] appearing then, however, in the framework of a more apologetic epistemology of faith.

To speak of the Church as "sacrament" was to integrate into the Conciliar text two decades of ecclesiological research. The current of mystical body theology that emerged about 1925; the more recent and more localized, but no less profound, theology of sign, that is, of the Church as sign of Christ (as Christ is the "sign" of God), that developed particularly in Germany after World War II; finally the ecumenical current that discovered within the framework of the World Council of Churches the mystery of unity, at once hidden and revealed—all these meet in the first great axis of the Constitution.[9]

1. ECCLESIA DE TRINITATE

The Church is both mystery and "sacrament": she is, then, tied first of all to the primordial mystery—that of the Trinity. Thus the universal Church appears as "a people made one with the unity of the Father, the Son and the Holy Spirit" (art. 4). This quotation from Cyprian shows from the beginning the theological character of the Constitution's ecclesiology. The Latin word "de" means both "imitation" and "participation."

Oriental theologians often give a strict meaning to the term theology. For them it is the doctrine of the invisible God, One and Triune, in whose life the People of God are called to participate; they are called to "divinization."[10] The whole Church, in its unity and diversity and in its various states as pilgrim, suffering and glorious, is the efficacious sign that leads the baptized to the knowledge and love of God the Father, Son and Holy Spirit as it participates in the very life of the Trinity.[11]

There is no question of weakening the meaning by means of what Lambert Beauduin called "the atomic bomb of theology," namely, the doctrine of appropriation. From the outset, like any Conciliar document worthy of the name, the Constitution prescinds from these problems of theology and grounds itself in the liturgical and creedal formulas of tradition.[12] On the contrary, we must emphasize the ecumenical importance of this initial declaration. The Orthodox East has always insisted on these relations between ecclesiology and Trinitarian theology. Western theology often developed, with a somewhat exclusive preference, the Christological character of ecclesiology: the precise bonds between Christ and the institution he founded, the powers he conferred on his Church—all this, while remaining essential, is nonetheless only one aspect of the Church's mystery. The tradition of the undivided Church, by its insistence on the *Ecclesia de Trinitate*, integrates this Western view into a vision in which pneumatology has its place and gives to the whole an eschatological dimension reaching out toward the Father.

Furthermore, at its assembly at New Delhi in November, 1961, the World Council of Churches enlarged its doctrinal basis in a Trinitarian direction: "The World Council of Churches is a fraternal association of Churches that proclaim the Lord Jesus Christ as God and Savior according to Scripture, and together try to respond to their common vocation for the glory of the one God, Father, Son, and Holy Spirit."[13]

Finally, in the Constitution's concluding mention of the Trinity, "until all peoples of the human family . . . are gathered together in peace and harmony into the one People of God for the glory of the Most Holy and Undivided Trinity" (art. 69), the whole of ecclesiology is placed in the light of theology. Even the problem of primacy and collegiality is clarified in the light of the Trinitarian mystery.[14]

2. THE FIRST FRUITS OF THE KINGDOM

The complaint of "triumphalism," brought against the schema of the preparatory commission, made a profound impression. The word, in any case, was heard around the world, even on the lips of some theologians of the Council's minority. The insertion of a section devoted to the kingdom of God cut short the temptation to identify the Church in its present state with the kingdom of God. The Church does not inherit the kingship of Christ the Lord; "faithfully guarding His precepts of charity, humility, and self-sacrifice, [the Church] receives the mission to proclaim and to establish among all peoples the kingdom of Christ and of God. She becomes on earth the initial budding forth of that kingdom" (art. 5). Gone are the times of impatience, the Middle Ages, when the Church and the kingdom were practically identified in the "Christian Republic," and when people thought they were near the end, or on the eve of the end, of time. This vision belongs to the *piccolo mondo antico*, to the "little world of yesterday" which an unjustifiably forgotten Italian novelist, A. Fogazzaro, chose as the title for one of his novels.

3. OTHER IMAGES

To describe a reality like the Church which no one expression can capture, there are a variety of biblical images: sheepfold, field, house of God, family, temple, heavenly Jerusalem, spouse. Each of these images clarifies one aspect of the whole. The image of the mystical body must not be allowed completely to overshadow the others, for although it emphasizes profoundly the identity of the Church and Christ, it does not of itself express the face-to-face encounter between the Church and Christ, the submission and obedience the Bride owes the Spouse, the purification she constantly receives from him. Moreover, the theology of the Church as the mystical body has developed well beyond the encyclical *Mystici corporis*. The Constitution lists in a more detailed way the various aspects of this theology: a) the elements of solidarity of the members among themselves, united in the body through the sacraments;[15] b) Christ, Head of the body who stands above all the members, fills and makes his body grow through the Holy Spirit unto fullness;[16] and c) the link between this image and that of the Spouse, in order to recall that the Church is "subject to her Head."[17]

4. RELATIONSHIP BETWEEN THE VISIBLE AND SPIRITUAL CHURCH

The Constitution uses a subtle formula regarding this question, when it declares that these are not "two realities" but rather "form one interlocked reality," and that "this Church constituted and organized in the world as a society, subsists in the Catholic Church, which is governed by the successor of Peter" (art. 8). Likewise, "the Church, embracing sinners in its bosom, is at the same time holy and always in need of being purified, and incessantly pursues the path of penance and renewal" (art. 8). *Sancta simul et semper purificanda* expresses admirably the paradox of a Church that is holy in its structure and constitution and yet must purify itself constantly because of the sinners present in its bosom. Here we touch upon the ecumenical problematic that was never solved by the oversimplified distinction between the Church (holy) and its members (sinners). In the Constitution the Church herself is said to be in need of constant purification.

Moreover, the final paragraph of the first chapter recalls the Church's pilgrimage amidst shadow and light: the strength that sustains the Church is that of the "risen Lord." Thus the Church slowly presses forward "announcing the cross and death of the Lord until He comes,"[18] and the visible institution, which the Church also is, appears in the service of the mystery of God the Savior in the time between the ascension and the parousia.

5. THE PEOPLE OF GOD

The place of this theme, and of this chapter, within the framework of the mystery of the Church, not after, but before the chapter on the hierarchy, seems no doubt to be quite natural. In reality, as with Columbus and the egg, one had to think about it. The shifting of one part of former chapter three (on "The People of God and in Particular on the Laymen") to second place, before the hierarchy, was a stroke of genius; this produced the first of the Copernican revolutions which marked the elaboration of the Constitution.

The People of God does not include only those called the "faithful" who are readily distinguished from the "pastors" (as if "pastors" should not be also among the "faithful"); it includes in the unity of baptismal hope all the children of the Church, *pastors and laymen*. The sacrament of baptism is the royal gate. The most important day in the life of the pope himself, Cardinal Suenens recently remarked in an address, is not that of his consecration, but that of his baptism.

Thus chapter two of the Constitution presents the mystery of the Church, no longer in the saving plan of the Triune God and in its first realization in the life of Christ, founder of the Church which he vivifies with his Holy Spirit, but in time, *inter tempora—zwischen den Zeiten*, as the German theologians like to say. There is nothing surprising, then, that non-Catholic Christians and non-Christians are spoken of in this chapter, and that it ends on *the* mission[19] of the Church as sent into the world as witness.

Furthermore, setting this theme in its present position permitted freeing certain problems from the impasse in which they were caught. Thus the universal priesthood could be considered metaphorical, in which case it is weakened; or not metaphorical, in which case it is not very clear what distinguishes it from that of the clergy, when one envisages it solely and principally from the viewpoint of the hierarchical priesthood.[20] On the contrary, when it is considered in the theme "People of God," before any consideration of ministerial priesthood, it appears as rooted directly in Christ, linked to the sacraments of Christian initiation (baptism, confirmation, eucharist), and establishing the threefold sacerdotal, royal and prophetic dignity in which *all* Christians, lay and clerical alike, share. The ministerial priesthood then appears as a "ministry" in the exact sense of the term, that is, as a service to the People of God. No doubt in one sense the hierarchy precedes the People of God, for it constitutes the latter by means of the sacramental order;[21] yet, in another sense it presupposes the People of God and is at its service. With the same stroke the Constitution fells a widespread image of the Church, namely, the clerical pyramid with the pope at the top, then the bishops (sometimes identified with messenger boys!),[22] the priests, and finally at the base the laymen (the clientele, as Y. Congar used to say).[23]

The Christian existence of the People of God is built on this "baptismal" foundation. The *sensus fidei*, which animates it and plays such an important role in the history of the Church, is not a disposition to obey passively the teaching of the hierarchy; the *infallibilitas Ecclesia in credendo*, constantly presupposed as a basis in discussions on infallibility at Vatican Council I, is not a "passive charism."[24] Likewise, charisms are neither reserved to the hierarchy, nor limited to ancient times; they are constantly present in the life of the Church; they animate this dimension of salvation history which the ecclesiology of Vatican II recovered.[25] Should we say that this viewpoint also corresponded to the legitimate preoccupations of Protestants? No doubt the opposition sometimes established between function and charism (*Amt und Charisma*) ought not to be forced, for the powers in the Church are sacred, as we shall see later. But the distinction does exist, and it was necessary to clarify the place of charisms in the life of the People of God.

Moreover, Protestant theologians could only rejoice at the insertion of this new chapter, for in their eyes the Church as body of Christ has to be completed by the People of God aspect, which brings out the face-to-face encounter between the Church and Christ, as well as the historical dimension of salvation history that Professor Schlinck calls the Church as "People of God on the march" (*Wanderndes Gottesvolk*).[26] Professor Skydsgaard, for his part, stated that there was great progress in all this: the Constitution begins with a chapter on the Church founded by the sanctifying action of the Triune God; then comes a chapter on the People of God in which it speaks of the universal priesthood and charisms. It is only then that it takes up the hierarchy only to return afterwards to the laity. Whereas, he said in substance, statements about the hierarchy in these first four chapters are rather foreign to the Protestant mind, there are many ideas profoundly Christian (*urchristlich*).[27] Finally, the insistence of Orthodox theology on the theme of the holy people, sometimes expressed in the complex concept of *Sobornost* (already translated in 1929 as "collegiality"), found an echo in this new second chapter.[28]

It is good to recall, however, that it was not at first out of a concern for ecumenical dialogue that this modification was introduced. It was done quite simply because of the rediscovery, on the level of Conciliar expression, of one of the oldest realities of ecclesiology, from the biblical point of view.[29] The encyclical *Mystici corporis*, practically passed over in silence the theme of the People of God.[30] Even before this first renewal of ecclesiology, another took shape as early as 1939 in biblical and liturgical circles—the theme of the People of God is one of the most frequently used for the Church in the liturgy. This theme paved the way for clarification of Church unity, which is not to be confused with uniformity, but is, on the contrary, unity amidst variety, multiplicity of liturgical, spiritual, theological and canonical traditions within the same undivided faith.[31]

II. THE STRUCTURES OF THE CHURCH: HIERARCHY AND LAITY

The awareness that unity is not uniformity, but that, on the contrary, a profound unity ought to be able to integrate the legitimate diversities in a truly universal catholicity (*Ecclesia Christi circumdata varietate*)—this awareness had become almost explicit for many bishops and theologians before the opening of the Council.[32] *Missionary* anguish before a pluralist world and *ecumenical* concern for a restoration of Christian unity awakened this consciousness. In the same perspective, that of an increasingly large world, one more diversified yet more anxious to find unity, the Fathers of the Council became aware of the pastoral urgency of making the relations of periphery and center of unity easier.[33]

Moreover, the necessity of completing the work of Vatican Council I, especially as regards the role of the episcopate, seemed obvious to many bishops who were asked about this just before the opening of the first session. "We shall speak of bishops and laymen," one replied. This second group had been emphasized by the first two international congresses for the lay apostolate in 1951 and 1957. The close link between these two themes was still poorly understood. Within the framework of the *Constitution on the Church*, they were to become the subject of chapters three and four, and to clarify the structure of the Church.

These two chapters must not be separated from the others; nor should they be isolated from the context of the whole. The sort of obsession with collegiality that characterized the debates of the second session, and even more the votes of the third session, should not make us lose sight of the main lines of the ensemble. The insertion of a chapter on the laity in the dogmatic[34] *Constitution on the Church* is a theological event of considerable importance. This text, and the discussions it provoked at the Council, speaks indeed of the laity not for strictly pragmatic reasons (shortage of priests, etc.), but for strictly theological ones. The faithful have been waiting for four centuries since the Reformation, Bishop Wright was to point out, for the Catholic Church to define their place and their dignity in the Church. Today the Council offers a providential occasion for the Church to define the theological foundation of the laity's place.[35]

Before taking up the theme of collegiality, we must repeat that the laity are not "the public," "material for evangelization"; they are part of the theological structure of the Church. The Church is no more Church without the laity than it would be Church without pope and bishops.[36]

1. PRIMACY AND COLLEGIALITY

The theme of the college of bishops was introduced in two different ways into the *Constitution on the Church*: the canonical way, and the liturgical and ecumenical way.[37]

a. Canonical perspective. The teaching of the Roman theologians, particularly the one that inspired the professors of the Gregorian from 1900 on, does not ignore the theme of the *collegium episcoporum*; but it is developed solely in the canonical context, and particularly from 1917 on within the framework of canon 228, paragraph 1, concerning ecumenical councils. The college of bishops legitimately assembled in ecumenical council is endowed with the *suprema potestas* of which canon 228 speaks. Apart from this context, the question of the origin of jurisdiction (more and more explicitly associated with the pope) prevents examination of the role of the episcopal college outside a council. The theme appears, therefore, in these treatises a little like a "witnessing organ" from a period during which ecumenical councils were more frequent. After Vatican Council I, many thought there would be no more ecumenical councils. Thus, in this context, the term "college" means, directly, the *universality* of the episcopal body; it implies likewise that this universality is quite visible, for example, in the council.[38]

When Pope John XXIII called the Council, the theme of the *collegium* found its place in the first schema of December, 1962, precisely in the context of ecumenical councils; it applied only to bishops in residence and seemed to many of the Fathers to be only a sort of corollary whose presence, rather unexpected in this place, was somewhat hard to explain.[39]

b. Liturgical perspective. Meanwhile, because of liturgical studies, the sacramentality of the episcopate would be rediscovered. As early as 1946, through the publication of a study, a critical edition of the *Traditio Apostolica*, B. Botte drew attention "to the vigor and the fullness of meaning of the ordination prayers of Hippolytus; the one for episcopal consecration is especially remarkable in its brevity; the functions of the high priest of the New Covenant can nowhere else be found enumerated with such precision."[40] And in 1952, J. Lécuyer published in *Divinitas* the first results of his research on the episcopate.

The interest awakened by these first works increased at the time of the controversy raised by J. Beyer in 1955. According to him, the episcopate is only an enlarged jurisdiction in relation to the priesthood; from this point of view, there was but "one apostle," Peter and his successors. In reply, several theologians, of whom Msgr. Charue was one, stressed the sacramentality of the episcopate as the basis of the bishop's powers in his local Church. As early as 1956 Dom Olivier Rousseau published in *Irénikon* the lost letter written by the German bishops after Vatican Council I, and Dom Lambert Beauduin drew attention to the importance of this text. It affirmed that the dogma of the primacy of the pope had not made the bishops the "functionaries of the pope," and that the sovereign pontiff was not, therefore, "bishop of Breslau, Cologne, etc."[41] The same year *Irénikon* published an analysis of B. Botte, *Ordo episcoporum*. This study[42] was a real step forward, for it showed that the insistence on having several co-consecrators at a bishop's consecration was linked, not to any tutiorist concern for validity, but rather to the fact, mentioned in the *Traditio apostolica*, that episcopal consecra-

131

tion associates the bishop to the *ordo episcoporum*. The link is, therefore, affirmed between sacramentality and collegiality; but the terms *collegium* and *collegialitas* are not used; the author uses the older words, *ordo, corpus episcoporum*.

c. Ecumenical perspective. For a long time, ecumenical circles tried to find a French equivalent for the term *Sobornost* which contact with Orthodoxy had introduced in theological vocabulary in order to express organic, liturgical, and pneumatological communion of all, pastors and laity alike, in the Church, the People of God. In *Jalons pour une théologie du laïcat*, Y. Congar used the neologism *collégialité* to express in French this datum of Oriental ecclesiology.[43]

The theme appears here in another context than the canonical one in which the term *collegium* first appeared at the Council. On the one hand, there is the ecclesiology of the *Universal Church*, visibly signified by a visible organ of this universal unity, the pope, and in the case of ecumenical councils, by the episcopal college brought together by the pope; on the other, there is the *eucharistic ecclesiology* or communion of local churches. The term *collegium*, collegial communion, signifies, first of all, then, unity of faith and sacrament in the life of the Spirit, existing in the bosom of the church assembled about its priests and bishop; the brotherhood of these local churches among themselves, their union in charity, is a larger manifestation of this collegiality. Whereas in the first perspective one has to have a visible, juridical organ of this universal unity, in the second this necessity is not felt in the same way.[44]

d. Bond between sacramentality and collegiality. As early as the second session, by insisting on the liturgical rite, the text of the *De ecclesia* had pointed out this explicit bond. Thus the liturgical and ecumenical perspectives fused. This was to bring about a Copernican revolution. Gradually, the link between sacramentality and collegiality led to a radical reconstruction of the chapter: the collegial character of the episcopate was taken up immediately after the articles devoted to sacramentality and *before* those that went into detail about the bishops' *ministeria*. Thus the collegial episcopate was immediately placed in relation with the Universal Church; the college, always understood in union with its head and never without it, appeared as having solicitude for the Universal Church and formed with the pope a *subjectum quoque plenae supremae auctoritatis*.

The liturgical and ecumenical current had moved along parallel with the canonical current. The introduction of the term *collegium* in the sacramental context provoked very strong opposition from those for whom *collegium* could only endanger—at least in their eyes—papal primacy, since they understood it solely in function of juridical theories about the *exercise* of the ecumenical councils called by the pope.

e. Tradition behind *collegium*. Historical studies revealed, especially in 1964, that the term *collegium* is as traditional as the words *ordo, corpus episcoporum*.[45] It is found even in curialist theology between the Council of Trent and Vatican Council I.[46] In addition to the liturgical argument of the consecration of a bishop by a college of bishops, other reasons were enumerated in the final text (art. 22).

However, in the Constitution *Lumen gentium* the two perspectives—the sacramental ecclesiology of communion of the local churches and the canonical ecclesiology of the Universal Church—did not succeed in blending into a completely harmonious synthesis. The abstract term *collegialitas* is happily not used, only the term *collegium*. However, the final text does not gather about this term the "collegial" aspects of the relations between the hierarchy and the laity, aspects that Oriental theology stresses so strongly in its eucharistic ecclesiology of the local churches. On the other hand, although linked to the liturgical and ecumenical arguments, the term *collegium* is always taken in the strict sense, partially canonical in origin, of the *universality* of the bishops around the pope. This more juridical perspective—perfectly exact, by the way—is placed alongside others in which the term appears bound up more with the theme of organic communion. No doubt this has limited a little the influence of the pneumatological and eucharistic themes in the Constitution.

f. Primacy and collegiality. These historical considerations throw light on the meaning of the theme of the primacy and collegiality. I could not summarize it better than by giving an excerpt from a study of Msgr. Philips, whose role in the elaboration of the *Constitution on the Church* is well known.

> There is no doubt, therefore, that the episcopal function constituted from the beginning, as tradition confirms, the fullness of the sacrament of priesthood. By their consecration, bishops have received, not only the power of santification, but also the mission of teaching and guiding the flock. The Exercise of this function must always take place in communion with the successor of Peter and under his direction. The liturgical texts which have always been in use in the East and West dissipate all doubt in this regard. The episcopate is much more than a higher degree to which the lower clergy may rise; it is the fullness of which the ordinary priest receives a participation. In other words, the theology of consecration is seen in a descending line, for, in the Church everything comes from above.[47]

The *Nota praevia* changed none of these major assertions. Contrary to what some think,[48] it does not introduce a distinction between *munus* (function) and *potestas* (power), but between *munus-potestas* (which implies, therefore, much more than an obediential potency to exercise episcopal power) and *potestas ad actum expedita*, that is, "immediately apt to exercise itself." In order that there be this aptitude, "the canonical or juridical determination on the part of the hierarchical authority" must intervene.[49] Thus a validly ordained priest receives the *potestas remittendi peccata*; but he cannot exercise it before having received jurisdiction from his bishop. His *potestas*, real in virtue of ordination, then becomes a *potestas ad actum expedita*.

Having said these things we can return to the text of Msgr. Philips apropos this time of collegiality:

> Bishops form a *college* called in the oldest texts order or *corpus*, that is, a united group of which the supreme dignitary, the pope, is the unique center and head. Without the sovereign pontiff an episcopal college is unthinkable. This point of faith gave rise in the Council—the fact is well known—to animated discussions that led Council Fathers, almost to a man, to see in the union of bishops and pope the prolongation of the one between Peter and the *other* apostles. With the pope and under his high direction, they have as their task to consecrate the whole flock of Christ. This does not prevent the sovereign pontiff from exercising directly his powers without having need of episcopal authorization. Supreme power was entrusted to the successor of the prince of the apostles, but likewise to the episcopal body which, with him and under his direction, fulfills its task. The two terms are not, therefore, pope and episcopate, but pope and college of bishops of which the pope forms a part and which he directs. The powers of one do not diminish in any way those of the other, and the help of the Holy Spirit guarantees an enduring understanding. This is why the bishops are not simply "functionaries" of the pope, who addresses them as "his brothers in the episcopate." Obviously they remain subordinate to him, in such a way that no danger can threaten the unity which is built on the rock of Peter.[50]

Here again, the *Nota praevia* changed nothing in these assertions. Indeed it reminds us that the college exercises *strictly* collegial acts only on occasion, but it nonetheless confirms the permanent existence of the college. It insists on the reality of "communion," which is not an "unaccented note" following the "down beat," the juridical bond. It is an organic reality and has, moreover, been lived in the life of the Church before it was codified in law. While the text insists, as is necessary, on the primacy of the pope, it emphasizes the communion between head and members by means of the terms "and not without the consent of its head."[51] While it states that the primacy of the pope comes directly from Christ as its source, and can therefore be exercised continually and directly, two passages also point out that this exercise is *"in view of the good of the Church."*[52]

Finally, as Msgr. Philips continues, "this point of doctrine has only recently attracted the attention of theologians, but in our relations with the Orthodox it has great importance. In the East they think that Rome ignores bishops and that they can do nothing else but carry out orders from Rome.

The ecumenical importance of this most carefully weighed declaration is, therefore, evident."[53]

Once again, the final *nota bene* of the *Nota praevia* does not modify the ecumenical significance of the declaration; it even strengthens it, I would say. The text of this note specifies, in fact, that, as regards the exercise of *potestas* by the Orthodox, "the commission considered that it did not have to enter into questions of liceity and validity."[54] This is like saying that it is possible to affirm the valid, if not licit, exercise of this *potestas* among the Orthodox. It also avoids the theory, strange, to say the least, of a "convalidatio" given tacitly for centuries by the Holy See.

"Of course," Y. Congar writes, "the doctrine of collegiality will appear as balancing and complementary only with time as future events bear out. As of now it certainly corrects the one-sidedness of an ecclesiology of pure papal monarchy and situates the episcopate in the apostolicity of the Church in a way interesting to the Orthodox."[55]

2. THE LAITY

The text does not intend to define the laity in the Church in a strict sense, but only to give a concrete description. "Laymen are believers who are incorporated into Christ and thus become participants in his mission in the Church and in the world, but do not belong to the clergy or to a religious order. . . . They are to attain their salvation in an ordinary life situation and must achieve their own sanctification and that of their entourage within the framework of their profession and family."[56]

The Constitution insists on the foundation of the dignity of the laity in the People of God. Through baptism they participate in a triple dignity: sacerdotal, prophetic and royal. Their whole life in the Spirit becomes a "spiritual offering" at the same time as a prophetic witness to the Lord; moreover, by participating in the royal dignity of the baptized, the layman, by his victory over sin, merits his liberty. "And so everything belongs to him, but he belongs to Christ and ought to penetrate the whole world with the spirit of Christ. The profane world is not stunted by it but, on the contrary, infinitely uplifed. Work, technique and culture thus acquire a new interior dimension and an incalculable value in the service of humanity."[57]

In other words, it would be wrong to identify the condition of the layman with the relation "ad extra," toward the temporal world; through the threefold dignity he shares, he is *in* the Church. "It is basically incorrect to call laymen the bridge between the Church and the world: they are the Church in the world and it is *in* it not outside it that they should serve as a leaven."[58]

However, this does not mean that the world, as creation of God, loses its own consistency and is no longer more than the place, the occasion of sanctification. "There is a distinction here that we must not lose sight of, namely, between what the Church must be concerned about as a religious community and what Christians must take responsibility for as citizens of human society. The earthly city has its own principles and laws, but it would be a fatal mistake to organize society according to the principles of a laicism hostile to the Church and thus deny religious freedom and the creator's dominion."[59] In other words, on the one hand, in its own order the earthly city has a real autonomy, which might be called, at least in a vocabulary familiar to French-speaking countries, a healthy laicity; on the other hand, one must reject a *laicism* that separates and opposes, while aiming at the construction of an earthly city closed to any religious orientation.[60]

Therefore, "the Church does not preach humanism nor civilization," but she "civilizes by preaching the Gospel";[61] "authentic humanism will be the fruit of her evangelization and human civilization will be strongly stimulated by it."[62] It is along this line that the *Constitution on the Church in the Modern World* develops a few characteristics of what Y. Congar calls "Christian existence."

III. The End of the Church: Holiness

In the schema of the preparatory commission, the chapter on the "states of perfection"[63] came before the chapter on the laity.[64] Thus, they seemed to accept the "traditional" three-part division: secular clergy, religious, laity. In reality, this division is not truly a traditional one; it juxtaposes two different perspectives into one point of view: the structure *of* the Church and the structures *in* the Church. In other words, we must substitute two bipartite divisions for a single tripartite division. In this way one avoids the accusation that Protestants often make about Catholicism, that "of reserving holiness for a cast."[65] Certain Council speeches gave the impression that "religious considered this chapter (on holiness) as a sort of family heirloom."[66] Now, "the holiness of religious is ordained to the holiness of the whole Church."[67] Furthermore, the vocation to holiness is addressed to all the baptized whether they be cleric or lay, religious or simple faithful; in a sense the evangelical counsels are given to all: "Today," Msgr. Huyghe said, "we know from pastoral experience that laymen living in the world practice voluntary poverty and continence. We should lay stress on the excellence of this way of life."[68]

Thus, *religious* withdraw from the world, but do not cut themselves off from the faithful; through their consecration to God "by vows, or by other sacred bonds" (art. 44), they give special witness to the transcendence of heavenly goods. "Religious are Christians who bind themselves to the practice of evangelical counsels and, in a permanent framework, dedicate themselves totally to the service of God and of their neighbor. Most take vows in order to imitate Christ even more strictly and with an even more intense devotion. That is why, in a special way, they form part of the mystery of the Church, with great diversity in the practice of prayer, the exercise of charity, and the apostolate."[69]

If the text speaks of "vows or *other sacred bonds,*" it is because the form of the vows provided for by canon law as it is now, even if it has become customary in the West, does not cover all the varieties of religious life. The Eastern monk does not take vows, at least in the sense of Latin canon law; he does not feel any less consecrated to Christ. To limit all consideration of the religious life to the vows, such as the *De religiosis* describes them in the *Codex Juris Canonici,* is to close one's eyes to a really ecumenical perspective, that is, universal, capable of taking into account the tradition of the undivided Church. Likewise, the text mentions the eremitical life whose importance in Eastern spirituality is well known (art. 43). Finally, taking into account the existence of *secular institutes* and *societies without vows* (the commitment being made in the form of a "promise," "oath," or in some other way), chapter 6 tries to pinpoint the essential element of the religious life, and to remove it from the post-Tridentine juridical formulation. However excellent it may be, this latter must be broadened to integrate ancient as well as new forms of religious life.

With this in mind, the Council Fathers tried to bring out the ecclesiological, Christological and eschatological significance of holiness, whether in the religious life or in its innumerable manifestations among those who are not "religious" in the strict sense of the word.[70] To do this they had to avoid presenting holiness in the Church in too psychological, ascetic and moral a light, and to insist on the theological virtue of charity, place it in an ecclesial context, and show at the same time its connection with the destiny of the whole *cosmos,* which attains its eschatological destiny in holiness.

This presentation of holiness emphasizes the privileged place of the religious life in the Church (it is, one might say, "a charismatic structure" in the Church), as well as its intimate connection with the holiness of the whole People of God. Insistence on the twofold bipartite division makes it more understandable how holiness concerns everybody in the Church. The religious may be either a layman or a priest. This, we might note in passing, is the foundation of the eminent ecclesial value of the vocation of nonpriest brothers, who are not "religious" deprived of something, namely, the priesthood, but laymen publicly consecrated to God in the religious life.[71] The priest or bishop may or may not be a religious. In Eastern tradition, however, the bishop has to be at the same time a monk, in order to show in this way that he must reunite in himself the two forms of life willed by Christ, the ministerial and monastic. It remains no less true that ministerial priesthood and monastic consecration are two forms of Christian life that can be lived by one Christian but do not add up as elements arising from the same principle of division.[72] Finally, the layman may or may not be a "religious"; in either case he is called to holiness, for all the baptized must understand and live the *Beatitudes*.

The richness of chapters 5 and 6 is obvious. I believe this is the first time a Conciliar constitution on the Church has brought out so clearly the *finality of the Church*: the holiness of its members, the sanctification of the People of God and, through it, in it, the sanctification of humanity, the transfiguration of the universe. No doubt, it would have been clearer to have only one chapter on holiness divided into two parts, one on the universal vocation to sanctity and the second on the particular form of this vocation in the religious life. The true dignity as well as the close connection between the religious life and the Christian life would have been brought out more clearly. Yet one could ask whether the division into two chapters finally adopted does not allow for better enunciation of the twofold bipartite division already mentioned. With the same stroke, the internal structuring of the Constitution *Lumen gentium* began to take shape. We have already said that it would be an error to center the whole text on collegiality alone. On the contrary it seems that, important as it may be, it is only one element in a whole in which the dimension of the mystery and finality of the Church have an equal importance. In other words, the significance of collegiality is without doubt the integration of the sacramental and communion aspect with that of the visible unity of a power of universal jurisdiction; it also lays the foundation for decentralization that seems desirable on the canonical level. But, the point of collegiality becomes all the clearer when it appears as the supreme service of the People of God: the hierarchy is of the order of means; the holiness of the Church, which God calls to himself in justice, truth and charity, is of the order of finality.

IV. The Eschatological Consummation of the Church

Yves Congar's distinction between the "already" and the "not yet" as regards the Church is well known: holiness is in a sense "already" partially present; at the same time it "is not yet" completely achieved. The hierarchy, the sacramental order itself, are means for making this "not yet" an ever more real "already."[73] The two preceding chapters pointed out that the mystical Orient of the Church is holiness. They did not, however, sufficiently emphasize the tension between what was already achieved and what was not yet achieved, between the shadows, the first fruits of the eternal city, and the fullness of its manifestation. In other words, the eschatological dimension of the Church's holiness, although already present in the article on the kingdom of God (art. 17), does not sufficiently come out as a *major axis of ecclesiology*. We need not seek elsewhere for the origin of the criticism made —as early as the second session, by Eastern bishops like Msgr. Ziadé—[74] on the extremely small amount of space devoted to the Holy Spirit in the schema. As we have seen, the initial orientation of the text is Trinitarian. This immediately nuances the bearing of the criticism. It was, however, heard again during the third session; the same Msgr. Ziadé "asked for a clearer text on the eschatological role of the Holy Spirit in our vocation; Latin ecclesiology developed only in a Christological dimension, but it is still adolescent in the dimension concerning the Holy Spirit."[75] The formulation, therefore, was still too Latin.

One of the "accidents," with which the history of each council is strewn, provides an answer to this legitimate request by opening up the Constitution *Lumen gentium* more to the contributions of Eastern ecclesiology. Pope John XXIII had asked that the schema *De ecclesia* say something about the *saints in Heaven*, and entrusted this task to a special commission presided over by Cardinal Larraona.[76] "John XXIII," Cardinal Browne said, "was convinced that the doctrine of the Church would be mutilated if this part of the Church, already united to Christ and intimately united with the pilgrim Church on earth, was not treated."[77]

This new and unexpected chapter—parachuted down at the last minute, as one expert put it—was eventually inserted into the schema. On the way it was enriched precisely in the eschatological and pneumatological direction asked for by several bishops. First of all, its actual title indicated better this orientation: "The Eschatological Nature of the Pilgrim Church and Her Union with the Heavenly Church." Then, as Msgr. Hermaniuk requested, mention of "the collective eschatological expectation in the Eucharist" was inserted, and this was developed "by recalling both its community aspect as well as its aspect of joyous anticipation."[78] Also taken into account were the suggestions of Msgr. Elchinger who regretted that the text presented at the beginning of the third session spoke only of personal vocation, and at that from a purely spiritual perspective; he said the text should also "deal with the collective, cosmic, and historical aspect of our vocation; we must show that not only all humanity but all creation has a relationship with the end of time. In this way, we would establish the doctrinal principles on which schema 13, on the presence of the Church in the modern world, are to be based."[79]

The final text insists on the close connection—both in man sanctified by Christ and humanity in search of justice and of love—between the destiny of the cosmos and the accomplishment of the sanctifying mission of the Church (art. 48). This rises above the level of that "popular Platonism," which Nietzsche claimed Christianity substituted for presence in the world.

Moreover, this new chapter insists on the liturgy in which and through which "we all partake in the same love for God and neighbor, and all sing the same hymn of glory to our God" (art. 49). In the same perspective of eschatological glory begun in sacramental mystery the text would speak of the cult of the saints, particularly of the devotion to images (art. 51). It mentions in this context the Council of Trent as well as the Second Ecumenical Council of Nicaea (787). Because of the sad affair of the *Libri Carolini*, the intent of that Council was badly interpreted in the West, to such a point that the Greeks came to be suspect of idolatry.[80] By drawing attention to Nicaea, the *Constitution on the Church* is trying to reintroduce Westerners to a true understanding of the theology of holy icons, a visible means of going to the invisible. Understood in this way, devotion to images is an application of the dogma of the incarnation; thus a new steppingstone is laid for rapprochement with the ecclesiology of the Christian Orient.[81]

This community, pneumatological and eschatological ecclesiology is the result of the theological work done in biblical,[82] patristic[83] and ecumenical[84] circles during the last decades. At the same time, this work meets another line of research that investigates the ultimate meaning of man's earthly task, the significance for the kingdom of God of what nine-tenths of humanity does nine-tenths of its time.[85]

The rediscovery of these aspects of ecclesiology, as well as the unplanned but providential encounter with a Christian anthropology open to both the present problematic and biblical and patristic resources, will appear in the history of the *De ecclesia* schema of Vatican Council II as important as the Conciliar rediscovery of the collegial dimension of the Church. In the short time since the Constitution's promulgation, this has already been verified. Starting from a very Western outlook, the *Constitution on the Church* was gradually enriched with liturgical and patristic contributions influenced by the Christian East. The contribution of Maximus IV,[86] Msgr. Doumith[87] and Msgr. Ghattas—[88] to cite only the representatives of the Melchite, Maronite and Coptic churches—are not lucky accidents; future historians will view them as having progressively affected the orientation of the *De ecclesia* schema.[89]

The importance of Pope Paul VI's pilgrimage to the Holy Land should be mentioned in connection with this Oriental view of things. By means of his eyes, ears, hands and feet he concretized the "decentering" of the Church on herself and her "recentering" in Christ.[90] "The third session will not be as influenced by the last interventions of the second as by the new situations created by the pilgrimage," as H. de Lubac expressed it.[91] With good reason, B. Lambert entitled his book on the second session *De Rome à Jérusalem. Itinéraire spirituel de Vatican II*.[92] The time no doubt is not far off when the continuation of this itinerary will develop a new aspect of ecclesiology around the theme of "that Jerusalem, which is above . . ., which is our mother."[93]

Thus, centered on "renewal in view of unity," this Council, in the elaboration of the *Constitution on the Church*—no doubt the heart of Vatican II—took its orientation from the contributions of the universal tradition of the undivided Church. The words of Msgr. Parente, presenting chapter 3 to the assembly at the beginning of the third session, are valid for the whole Constitution and especially for the last two chapters: "I invite the Fathers to vote for the text; it integrates the juridical conception of the Church elaborated from the eleventh century on with the theological conception of St. Paul, St. Augustine, and the Fathers."[94] In other words, Catholic ecclesiology began once again to breathe with both lungs.

"The accident" of the chapter on the saints was to prove providential also in solving the thorny problem of the place and content of the text on the Virgin Mary.

Besides the two possibilities of composing a separate schema or inserting it as a chapter in the *Constitution on the Church*, there were two tendencies that clashed.

> In general, two positions confronted each other. Both curiously intervened in the same way regarding the pope and the Blessed Virgin. One group considered the pope as superior to and a part of the episcopal college, like the head of a body. The other considered him as superior to but apart from the college, and felt that papal primacy was diminished, run down, compromised in the other position. . . . The same thing happened when the question of the Virgin Mary came up: some saw in her an eminent and singular member of the Church, the summit of its communion with Christ; the others tended to place her in opposition to the rest of the Church, sometimes even going to the point of considering her as predestined with Christ independently of the Church and prior to it, endowed with a grace specifically different from the others.[95]

The partisans of insertion had, first of all, a concrete reason for their approach: not to separate the Virgin from the general theme of the Council. But since Marian doctrine could not be confined within the context of ecclesiology, touching as it does upon the fundamental dogma of the incarnation, Mary's role would have to be seen within the framework of Christ's redemptive work. This would not diminish the importance of the Marian theme, but it would prevent it from being developed as a foreign body. By the same token, it would provide a solid biblico-traditional and dogmatic basis for Mary's place and role in the mystery of salvation; and one would thus be able to show Mary to be the type of the Church, of which she is the first and supereminent member, of which she is the exemplar, and which she protects with her love and intercession. Moreover, one could thus bring to perfection a consideration of the Church as fulfilled in its saints, that is, in its eschatological end. Then, too, a pastoral reason recommended this insertion in the *Constitution on the Church*, for it would facilitate instruction of Catholics on faith in the incarnation and on the place of Mary in this mystery, in such a way as to direct their devotion to what is essential. Finally, obvious ecumenical reasons suggested the same solution: the Orthodox would thus again find the *Theotokos* more easily, and Protestants would see with less difficulty the foundation of Marian devotion in the testimony of Scripture and ancient tradition.[96]

On the other hand, those who opted for a separate schema claimed that insertion in the *Constitution on the Church*, especially after the chapters on laity and religious, was "a way of banishing [the Virgin], of destroying her."[97] Intense propaganda was put out to the effect that to vote for insertion was to vote against the Virgin; because of it the vote for insertion "gave rise to rather widespread feelings of guilt toward the Madonna."[98]

"This rupture of unanimity in connection with her whom the schema was pleased to call mother of unity caused a sort of consternation."[99] Some thought "that it would be better for the Council to abstain from discussing a text on the Virgin Mary."[100] As soon as the four-man commission was enlarged, "emotional elements arose; no understanding was reached, not even on the guiding principle of a new schema; the session ended in stalemate."[101]

Paul VI, however, showed the way between the opposite positions. In his discourse closing the second session, he indicated three principles of orientation: situate Mary in the Church, show that this integration is not a lowering of the Virgin to the level of the other members of the Church, and dissipate the fears of the minority by arriving at a unanimous consent on the following twofold basis—recognition of the fact that Mary belongs in the Church and yet is superior to all the other members of the Church.[102]

The "wise text," according to the words of one Council chronicler,[103] "represented not a doctrinal compromise, which would be treason to truth, but rather a middle way so as to win the unanimity of the Fathers."[104] One sees this clearly in the case of the term "Mediatrix." It seemed impossible either to suppress it, once it was introduced, or to reinforce it, for example, by isolating it and by making the whole weight of the text bear on it. On the contrary, by being inserted in the context of liturgical invocation where it is at present (art. 62), "this word reacquires the discretion and winged suppleness it had in the Eastern tradition, but no new rigidity or propaganda color that would only accentuate an uneasiness well on the road to reabsorption."[105]

Moreover, by inserting the chapter on the eschatological character of the Church *before* the one on the Virgin, the commission answered the concern of those who were scandalized to see Mary spoken of "after the laity and religious." The chapter on Mary was not only in a good place because it was the last, but also because it was inserted in the last bipartite section of the Constitution, precisely the one that accentuates the eschatological and pneumatological aspect of the mystery of the Church. Mary thus appeared within the Church and as having a supereminent place in it. In this way she was made to appear clearly as the type, the glorious icon of what the Church is progressively becoming, as the crowning of the Church, certainly not in the domain of the sacerdotal hierarchy, but in that of consummate holiness.

This eighth and last chapter of the Constitution will help to strengthen the movement to reintegrate Mariology within the sphere of ecclesiology. Without ever losing sight of the "Christotypical viewpoint of Mariology,"[106] from about 1950 on the movement to return to the sources entered, with sobriety and equilibrium, upon an "ecclesiotypical" line.[107] "Thus Mary," said Cardinal Bea as early as January, 1964, "will appear to the faithful of the twentieth century in the same light as she appeared to the Church of early times: as the most sublime member of the Church, and, at the same time, as the prototype and symbol of the grandeur and fullness of the Church."[108]

V. The Constitution in the Contemporary Theological Movement

The rapid development of ideas is striking; one can speak of a real acceleration of the *tempo* of theological discovery. "They [the Council Fathers] went from a predominantly juridical conception to the primacy of the ontology of grace, from a predominance of system to the affirmation of Christian man, and, as regards structures of authority in the People of God, they recognized better, alongside the place of the universal college of bishops the Roman monarchy, that of local organisms, and the role of the *Ecclesia*, of the Church as community."[109]

The division of the great axes into *pairs of two chapters* (mystery of the Church [1 and 2], structure of the Church [3 and 4], finality of the Church [5 and 6], consummation of the Church in eschatology [7 and 8]), the appearance of a twofold double division on the level of structures (structure of the Church: hierarchy and laity; structures *in* the Church: religious and nonreligious), finally, the double displacement of the chapters (the treatment of the People of God placed before that of the hierarchy, the chapter on religious placed after that on the laity)—all this shows the influence of earlier and contemporary theological currents.

Thus, they passed from a nontemporal, static and very juridical view of the schema to a historical, dynamic and sacramental view, one progressively more open to the contribution of pneumatology. If this contribution, like that also of eucharistic ecclesiology, with which the theme of "local Church"[110] is connected, has not sufficiently entered into the very tissue of

143

the text, it is because it was elaborated from schemas and expressions drawn principally from patristics, canon law and Western theology. What counts is the movement that animates the whole of the text, one that is very noticeable when one reads it in one sweep. The progressive opening to currents of patristic and Eastern liturgy then appears clearly. A council is a terminal point for previous theology, at the level of achievements that can muster a substantial unanimity.[111] But a council is also a starting point. The text of the *Constitution on the Church* is incredibly rich in elements that, like steppingstones, will lead to an even broader renewal of ecclesiology.[112]

If one tries to group the features of ecclesiology that stand out most in the Constitution, the resulting picture is remarkably rich: the Church as mystery and primordial sacrament; the Trinitarian starting point, the varied light of biblical images, as well as the paradox of the existence of this Universal Church in the Catholic Church; the reality of the People of God assembled in eucharistic communion around the bishop and his priests and deacons,[113] animated by charisms of the spirit, living from the mysteries of faith and called to sanctity, that is, justice and the theological virtue of charity, and hence, to divinization with joyous expectation and in union with the saints of heaven; the hierarchy as service, in the name of Christ, to this People of God, in the hierarchical communion, at once sacramental and juridical, of the apostolic college, that is, of the *ordo episcoporum*, in union with the successor of Peter, bishop of Rome, and universal pastor;[114] finally the historical perspective of a Church on pilgrimage in the desert toward the heavenly Jerusalem, supported by the strength of the risen Christ, in his Holy Spirit, holy and constantly purifying itself, a sign of hope, "until he comes."[115] All these ideas have been prepared for in the collections like *Unam Sanctam, Théologie, Quaestiones disputatae, Irénikon.* All this takes us far from the "triumphalism" so severely criticized in the first schema of 1962![116]

It is within this over-all view that we must place the debate on collegiality. Then this aspect, of which Conciliar awareness dates from the year 1960, receives its profound significance. From both the pastoral and theological viewpoint, it is situated on the level of the *ecclesiology of communion,*[117] as the famous *Preliminary Note* repeats three times.[118] One can say that this debate at Vatican II is already as famous as the debate on primacy at Vatican Council I.

From a more precise and detailed point of view the ecclesiology of the *Constituiton on the Church* is related to four theological currents.

a) It is *biblical* both because of the use of different scriptural images and because of the fact that it is an ecclesiology of the mystical body, but one which goes beyond the encyclical *Mystici corporis.*

b) It implies an *anthropology,* a vision of Christian existence, especially in chapters two and seven.

c) It is *sacramental*, before being canonical and juridical. In fact, the text insists on *baptism*, the sacrament by which a person is incorporated into Christ and, therefore, in a sense, into the Church. This opens up important perspectives from the ecumenical point of view.[119] Then the Constitution underlines the meaning of *episcopal consecration*, "the fullness of the sacrament of orders," the foundation of the three episcopal functions (*munera*) as well as of the bishop's membership in the college or *episcopal order*. Finally, this ecclesiology is sacramental because of the mention (perhaps too scattered and infrequent) of the *eucharist*; if the Church makes the eucharist, the eucharist in turn makes the Church, as Henri de Lubac wrote.[120]

d) It is *eschatological*, especially when one analyzes the text.[121] "More in the world and less of the world," Y. Congar often repeats.[122] What modern man loves to call "dialectical tension," is called more simply lights and shadows, holiness and sin, the persecutions and joys of the Church, whose pilgrim status becomes clearer as thought progresses.

Each of these four aspects is at the same time *ecumenical* through a return to the sources; each is likewise *mission-conscious* through its opening to dialogue on the part of this apostolic church *sent* into the world to announce salvation in Jesus Christ.

One day, in the course of the Council debates, Msgr. Philips described the two tendencies that share the field of theological thought. One is

> more concerned with fidelity to traditional statements and the other more pre-occupied with the extension of the message to contemporary man. . . . [The one] moves easily in the world of abstract and imperturbable ideas, with the risk of shutting oneself up in them, of confusing concepts with the mystery which surpasses them. . . . The second type of theologian . . . is convinced that his view of the truth is not the same in all its forms as the truth itself. . . . He has more sense of history, and if he considers every definition sanctioned by the Church as irreformable, he believes it, however, to be susceptible of a more profound light and of a more lucid statement.[123]

If, when it comes to individuals, the option between these tendencies "is influenced by their temperament, their education, their major pre-occupation, the particular responsibility they have, and the historical or local situation in which they are called to work,"[124] at the level of an ecumenical council these alternatives must be transcended. The ecclesiology of Vatican Council II tries to integrate the two viewpoints, at the risk of sometimes giving a text in which there is a mosaic of diverse elements. But, in a perspective hinging upon a return to the sources of the undivided Church's ecclesiology, it tries to lose nothing of the achievements of a more abstract and juridical thought.

No one comes out of a council with a feeling of complete victory or of total defeat: the suffering experienced by the most lucid at the end of the third session blended with the joy of seeing promulgated *the first Conciliar text embracing the whole mystery of the Church* shows that one was not attending something merely human. The unanimity, painfully achieved for chapter 3, especially during the last days, shows that a council is not the triumph or defeat of a school of theology, but the discovery and the proclamation of essential truths by the universal assembly of bishops for all the local churches and for all time.[125] This unanimity is, to use an expression of Cardinal Suenens, "an event of the Holy Spirit."

Thus the words of Paul VI at the end of the third session are really in place: "We can truly say that the divine presence prepared for us an hour of light; yesterday slowly ripened, today resplendent, tomorrow certainly rich with teaching, drive, and improvement for the life of the Church."[126]

NOTES

1. This contribution first appeared in the review *Collectanea Mechliniensia* (March, 1965) 105–142. With the kind permission of that review's editor, it is published here, but in a revised and updated form occasioned by the International Conference on the "Theological Issues of Vatican II," held at the University of Notre Dame.

2. *Méditations sur l'Eglise* (2nd ed. Paris, 1953) 79, note 1.

3. The plan of the schema of December, 1962 (=Text I; the final text was the fourth, not counting of course the intermediate editions prior to each rewriting), was the following: nature of the Church Militant; the members of the Church and her necessity for salvation; sacramentality of the episcopate; residential bishops (and the problem of collegiality); states of perfection (religious); laymen: their priesthood, their duties, etc.; the magisterium; authority and obedience in the Church; relations between Church and state; the proclamation of salvation throughout the earth (the missions); ecumenism (*L*, II, 118). Here are the abbreviations used:
C for *La Croix;*
DC for *Documentation Catholique;*
ICI for *Informations Catholiques Internationales;*
DCV for *Discours au Concile du Vatican*, ed. Y. Congar, H. Küng, O'Hanlon (Paris, 1964);
L, I, II, III for R. Laurentin, *L'enjeu du Concile I, II, III* (Paris: Seuil, 1963–1965);
W, I, II for A. Wenger, *Le Concile, Première Session, Le Concile, Second Session* (Paris, 1963, 1964);
L, RSPT for R. Laurentin, "La Vierge Marie au Concile," *Revue des Sciences Philosophiques et Théologiques* 47 (1964) 32–46;
B for G. M. Bessuti, "Note di Cronaca sul Concilio Vaticano II e lo Schema De B. Maria Virgine," *Marianum* 26 (1964) 1–42 (pagination of the offprint);
I for *Irénikon;*
P, I, for G. Philips, "Deux tendances dans la théologie contemporaine," *Nouvelle Revue Théologique* 85 (1963) 225–238;
P, II for G. Philips, "Le Schéma sur l'Eglise," *De Maand* 6 (1964) 330–340 (reprinted in part in DC 1434 [Oct. 18, 1964] 339–1341).

4. C, Dec. 5, 1962.

5. P, II 330–332.

6. *Ibid.,* Dec. 4, 1962.

7. It seems that ideas about the Church as the primordial sacrament mystery, People of God on the way, were introduced under the influence of German theology. But H. de Lubac already in 1953 (*Méditations sur l'Eglise*) devoted two chapters to this theme. The Council, however, did not adopt the theological theory—a very rich one, at that—about the Church as "primordial sacrament"; cf. O. Semmelroth, *Die Kirche als Ursakrament* (Frankfurt, 1953).

8. Denzinger-Schönmetzer 3014.

9. H. de Lubac, *Méditations sur l'Eglise* (2nd ed. Paris, 1953), shows the position of theology of this period, especially as regards the points of view expressed in the text. The ecclesiology of the twentieth century still awaits its historians.

10. Cf. Y. Congar, "Théologie," *DTC* 15:344.

11. The *Decree on Ecumenism*, in speaking of the elements that must be taken into account in the dialogue with the Christian East, mentions divinization as the effect of the Church's liturgical celebration (art. 15). The ecumenical aspects of grace are sketched by C. Moeller and G. Philips, *Grâce et ecumenisme*, coll. Irénikon (Chevetogne, 1957), and summarized from the viewpoint of catechesis in C. Moeller, "La grâce et la justification," in *Lumen vitae* 19 (1964) 532–544.

12. The creeds (cf. Denzinger-Shönmetzer, 1–76, for a series of texts on the creeds along with elements necessary for discovering their trinitarian structure) and liturgical texts are all "trinitarian, rising above the theological reflections that produced the theory of appropriation." T. de Regnon, *Etudes de théologie positive sur la Trinité* (4 vols. Paris, 1892–1898) is still the classic work on these questions; a new edition would be very useful. Its power of analysis, breadth and synthetic vision have not been equalled.

13. *I* 35 (1962) 19.

14. Cf. P. Haubtmann (in *Le point du Concile*, mimeographed for the Vatican press bureau, n. 3 [second session] *La journée du 30 octobre*, 7) says: "When we consider the fact that the Church, as the body of Christ, is grafted onto the life of the Trinity by reason of her communion with the mystery of the Incarnate Word, is animated by the Spirit of the Father and Son, and strains toward the Father and is caught up in the same drive of adoration, praise and love that impels the Son toward the Father in the Spirit, how could the Church not reproduce in her very make-up that which is sacramental before being juridical, divine before being human, something of the very mystery of her God, One and Triune." This view, which I think any Oriental ecclesiologist would readily accept, seems to be very enlightening on the question of the relationship between primacy and collegiality; the major difficulty of the debates was that one group of the Council read with a juridical eye (seeing a universal college over against a universal primacy, forgetting at times that, *de facto*, this universal college also involves, and necessarily so, its head the pope under pain of not being a college) assertions that also had a primarily, but not exclusively, liturgical and "communion" signification. We will try to bring this out below in section 2.

15. Art. 1–3. This point—the sacramental elements, bases of the solidarity in the mystical body—was thus a steppingstone to everything that would be detailed in ch. 2 on the People of God, ch. 3 on the hierarchical structure, and ch. 7 on the heavenly Church.

16. Art. 4–7.

17. Art. 7. In this way the ecclesiology of the encyclical *Mystici corporis* was integrated, but also surpassed in a more broadly biblical direction and more open to ecumenism (cf. J. Hamer, *L'Eglise est une communion* [Paris,1962] 11–34). See L. Cerfaux, *La théologie de l'Eglise suivant saint Paul* (Paris, 1965) 351–408.

18. Cf. 1 Cor 11:25.

19. Y. Congar often insists on this formulation, *"The"* mission, so that it will be seen right away that the whole Church is sent as "apostolic." This also avoids the danger of considering the work of evangelization as the speciality of a few (an equivocation which is too often present in the plural form "the missions"). Cf. art. 17, which quotes Mt 28:18–20, the true charter of Christ's foundation of the Church; it is identical with the Lord's sending of the apostolic college throughout the world (cf. R. Schnackenburg, *The Church in the New Testament* [New York: Herder and Herder, 1965] 135–140).

20. The first text did not avoid this dilemma: whereas the text was composed in such a way as *not* to say that this priesthood is metaphorical, the note added in this place said that this priesthood was metaphorical. Cf. *P*, II, 4. The great role played by Msgr. G. Philips at the first two congresses of the Lay Apostolate at Rome in 1951 and 1957 is well known. Cf. also his *Pour un christianisme adulte* (Tournai, 1962).

21. One should not forget, however, that baptism can be administered by a layman in case of necessity.

22. The expression is that of R. Kayser, *Inside the Council* (London, 1963) 111; he says that the American bishops did not go to the Council to give routine replies: "This would not be a rubber stamp council" (71).

23. *DCV*, 274–380; cf. *ibid.*, 47–51; *L*, III, 90–91.

24. Cf. O. Rousseau, J-J von Allmen *et al.*, *L'infaillibilité de l'Eglise* (Chevetogne, 1963), especially the study of G. Thils, 147–182.

25. *DCV*, 33–36.

26. *Deutsches Konzilspresszentrum* (Oct. 23, 1963) 6: "Diskussion des Schema De Ecclesia in evangelischer Sicht," by Prof. E. Schlinck; cf. also his "Themen des Zweiten vatikanischen Konzils in evangelischer Sicht," *Kerygma und Dogma* 9 (1963) 181–193.

27. *Deutsches Konzilspresszentrum* (Nov. 27, 1963) 2.

28. Y. Congar, *Jalons pour une théologie du laïcat* (Paris, 1953) 380–386. The term *Sobornost* was included in the last edition of the *Lexikon für Theologie und Kirche* (Freiburg, 1964) 9:842–843.

29. L. Cerfaux, *op. cit.* (note 15); R. Schnackenburg, *op. cit.* (note 16). This last study shows that, in one sense, the image of the People of God (and especially the reality) underlies all the others, even if in the New Testament it is as such rarely mentioned.

30. I refer to *Mentalité moderne et évangélisation* (Bruxelles, 1962) 329.

31. In the history of the composition of these first two chapters, one should mention, besides the role of the German theologians and bishops, the contribution of texts drawn up in Chile. Particularly striking was the international character of the teams that worked together on them.

32. Examples will be found in *Was erwarten wir vom Konzil?* special issue of *Wort und Wahrheit* 16 (1961) 594, 614, 640, 645, 699; *Fragen an das Konzil* (Freiburg, 1961) 34–44; *Qu'attendons nous du Concile?* (Paris, 1960) 45–56; "Voeux pour le Concile," *Esprit* (Dec. 1961) 795–796.

33. Cf. P. Haubtmann, *Le point du concile*, Bull. n. 3: *La journée du 30 octobre*, 7–8: "There is agreement that decentralization is today a profound need of the Church, and that it ought to be accompanied by more effective participation of particular churches in the global life of the Universal Church; in other words, that decentralization properly understood need not harm the profound unity of Catholics but reinforce it—unity not being uniformity. On the other hand, bishops feel more and more the need to "form a body," if only so that each can respond better to the most immediate pastoral needs (I do not say the most important): those that concern his own diocese. Is it not marvelous to observe that these complementary aspects of the real (*decentralization* and *federation*) correspond both, and together—I do not say identify with each other—to the second aspect of the truth of which we have just spoken, namely, that Christ founded his Church, not on one individual alone, nor on several individuals without organic and vital bonds between them, but rather on a constituted body, the apostolic college, of which Peter will ever be the head? That is why Vatican II, while wishing to be pastoral, inevitably leads to an eminently doctrinal problem. Or rather, Vatican II, in order to respond to pastoral needs, assignment given by two successive popes, sees itself obliged to engage in a *doctrinal work of depth*.

34. This term "dogmatic" is in the title: it is extremely important to note this; the *Constitution on the Church* is not a disciplinary or pastoral decree, even if it does not involve any solemn definition, *de fide divina et catholica* as at Vatican I. Cf. *Extraits des Actes du Concile* on the *Qualification théologique* at the end of this Constitution.

35. W, II, 101.

36. This recalls the famous remarks of Edouard Le Roy on the laity, "similar to the sheep of Candlemas that we shear and bless"; or the reply of Newman to a question of Bishop Ullathorne on the insistence made by some on the laity: "I do not know what the laity are, but I know that the Church would appear rather foolish without them." Bishop De Smedt also criticized, at the first session, the overly clerical character of the original text: "At the bottom the laity who are nothing or, if you wish, members of the second zone; at the top is the pope, who is everything; with Patriarch Maximus he denounced episcopolatry and papolatry." (*Études* 316 [1962] 107); *L*, II, 127; *C* (Dec. 4, 1962). One must remember that this criticism bore on the whole of the schema of 1962, for everybody agreed that, with this edition of it, the chapter on the laity was one of the best.

37. Cf. *La collégialité épiscopale. Histoire et théologie* (Paris, 1965), which gives a very enlightening over-all view and shows, at the same time, the immense field of research that awaits theologians and historians.

38. These remarks come from unpublished research of C. Troisfontaines on the teaching of *De ecclesia* in Jesuit circles which influenced the Gregorian university. Cf. also on this tie-in between "college" and ecumenical councils, H. Schauff, *De conciliis oecumenicis* (Rome, 1962).

39. *L, II*, 120.

40. B. Botte, *La Tradition Apostolique* (Paris, 1946) 24.

41. The text of this letter with the reply of Pope Pius IX, first published in *Irénikon*, reproduced in *L'épiscopat et l'Eglise universelle* (Paris, 1962) 729–736, with a study by O. Rousseau, is now printed in Denzinger-Schönmetzer (3112–3117). This simple fact shows how ideas have matured in less than ten years.

42. This study was reprinted in *Etudes sur le sacrement de l'ordre* (Paris, 1956). It suffices to consult the index of *L'épiscopat et l'Eglise universelle* (Paris, 1962) under the name of Botte in order to see in the thirty-five quotations the importance of this liturgical (and theological) study for the rediscovery of the sacramental and collegial significance of the episcopate. The liturgical movement is, as one sees, one of the most profound inspirers of theological re-evaluation; the opening of the first session with the liturgical Constitution is another of these accidents "rich" with theological and Conciliar meaning.

43. One can see in the study of O. Rousseau, "La constitution de Eclessia dans le cadre des mouvements de renouveau théologique," in *L'Eglise de Vatican II*, edited by G. Barauna (Paris, 1966), how as early as 1929 Bolton proposed in *Irénikon* translating *Sobornost* as "collegiality"; in 1951 and in the same review Y. Congar took up this translation in an article that was republished in his *Jalons*.

44. Cf. Y. Congar, in *L'épiscopat et l'Eglise universelle* (Paris, 1962) 227–261; see also his "Conclusion" in *Le Concile et les Conciles* (Chevetogne-Paris, 1959) 301ff.

45. J. Lécuyer, *Etudes sur la collégialité épiscopale* (Lyon-Le Puy, 1964).

46. G. Alberigo, *Lo sviluppo della dottrina sui poteri nella Chiesa universale* (Rome, 1964).

47. *DC* 1434 (Sept. 18, 1964) 1339–1340.

48. R. Rouquette in *Etudes* 322 (1965) 100ff. gives a series of interesting details on the *Note*. One is a bit surprised to see, however, that he seems to find there a distinction between *munus* and *potestas*, when the distinction introduced in this text is between *potestas simpliciter loquendo* and *potestas ad actum expedita*; the translation of "munus" as "function," and of "potestas" as "power" does not seem justified by the Latin text. We must not forget that this *Note*, which is no doubt authoritative, is no less introductory in the same way in which the Modi were examined by the commission for chapter 3. Besides, we should observe that the *Note* three times speaks of "communion" in positive terms; it gives an interpretation of the texts of recent popes on jurisdiction (they must be interpreted henceforth in the sense of "*determination* of powers," and therefore not in the sense of origin of this power in itself). The reaffirmation of the primacy in precise juridical terms was done in order to reply to the difficulties raised by the minority, not in order to deny what was affirmed in the text of the Constitution (cf. in number 4 of *Irénikon* [1964] the "Chronique" whose text I was able to see in page proof form, thanks to the kindness of Dom. O. Rousseau).

49. *DC* 1439 (Jan. 3, 1965) 80.

50. *Ibid.*, 1434 (Sept. 18, 1964) 1340.

51. *Ibid.*, 1439 (Jan. 3, 1965) 82.

52. *Ibid.*, 81.

53. *Ibid.*, 1434 (Sept. 18, 1964) 1340.

54. *Ibid.*, 1439 (Jan. 3, 1965) 82.

55. *ICI* 22 (Dec. 1, 1964) 5.

56. *P*, II, 7–8.

57. *P*, II, 8. The term "consecratio mundi" in this context is ambiguous. It could imply a confusion between "consecratio," in the sacral sense, and "orientation" of all human work in this world toward the kingdom. Cf. D. Chenu, "Consecratio mundi," *Nouvelle revue théologique* 96 (1964) 608–618. One should keep this remark in mind when reading the Constitution, art. 31, 36.

58. *P*, II, 8. This remark of Msgr. Philips is very important. One should note, as does he, that the title of schema 13 is not "The Church and (or before) the Modern World," but "On the Church *in* the Modern World"; there is no "face-to-face" but a "*presence in*."

59. *P*, II, 8.

60. Art. 36 and note 175. Cf. *DCV*, 274–280.

61. Pius XI wrote this to the Semaine sociale de France at Versailles in 1936; the text is in *Les conflits de civilisation* (Lyon, 1936) 461–462. This point is very important for the article on culture in the *Constitution on the Church in the Modern World*.

62. *P*, II, 9.

63. *L*, III, 87 uses the words of Cardinal Suenens in an interview about this expression. "That drives me nuts," he said literally. This expression, found in the first text, disappeared happily in the final text.

64. *L*, II, 118.

65. Msgr. Charue in *L*, III, 87.

66. *W*, II, 115.

67. *Ibid.*, 116.

68. *Ibid.*, 119. This distinction between "structure of the Church" and "structures in the

Church" was developed in the Council especially by Msgr. Charue as can be seen in W, II, 116.

69. *P*, II, 10.

70. *W*, II, 117, note 3.

71. The question raised by the nonclerical, male religious orders is very important. Integration of Eastern tradition on this point—according to which the monk is consecrated to God in an evangelical perspective that does not imply the priesthood—may clarify the question. To simplify it one could say that the West gradually "ecclesiasticized" nearly all forms of religious life in such way that a nonordained religious seems to be an exception difficult to place. On the other hand, the Orient gradually "monasticized" a series of ecclesial institutions, even the priesthood, since in Orthodoxy the bishop must be a monk; in this situation it is the addition of the priesthood to the monastic life that causes the problem (except for the small number of those monks who have to be priests in order to ensure the liturgical celebrations of the community). By speaking of "religious" in a context that goes beyond the "tripartite" division, the Constitution helps us to achieve a doctrine of "monastic," or "religious" life as being a structure in the Church, independently of whether or not a religious is a priest.

72. This point, essential in a theology of "religious life," is taken up in article 10 of the *Decree on the Appropriate Renewal of the Religious Life*, promulgated at the fourth session.

73. This distinction is frequently used by Y. Congar, for example, in *Vrai et Fausse Réforme dans l'Eglise* (Paris, 1950) 92–102.

74. *DCV*, 37–42.

75. *DC* 1433 (Oct. 4, 1964) 1239. J. R. Geiselman ("Les variations de la définition de l'Eglise chez Joh. Adam Moehler," in *L'ecclésiologie au XIXe siècle* [Paris, 1960] 141–196) shows that both forms of ecclesiology are present in the Tübingen theologian, the first under the sign of the Holy Spirit, the second under the sign of Christology. Cf. Geiselman's article, "Die Einfluss der Christologie des Konzils von Chalkedon auf die Theologie Johann Adam Moehlers," in *Chalkedon* 3 (Würzburg, 1954) 341–420.

76. *DC* 1423 (May 3, 1964) 598.

77. *Ibid.*, 1433 (Oct. 4, 1964) 1238.

78. *Ibid.*, 1240.

79. *Ibid.*, 1241.

80. The use of *adoratio* to translate the Greek term *proskynèsis* (meaning the homage rendered to sacred realities but distinguished from *latreia*, a term reserved for the worship rendered to God) made Westerners believe the Orientals were idolaters. Cf. *Lexikon für Theologie und Kirche* 7: 967–968, with the bibliography.

81. This ecclesiology is, as we know, much influenced by the mystery of Pentecost under the sign of the transfiguration. The Byzantine liturgy, for example, is a completely pedagogical celebration leading from the sensible to the spiritual, from the visible to the invisible.

82. Cf. for example, A. Frank-Duquesne, *Cosmos et Gloire* (Paris, 1927); F. X. Durrwell, *La résurrection de Jésus, mystère de salut* (Le Puy-Paris, 1954); L. Cerfaux, *Le chrétien dan la théologie paulienne* (Paris, 1962) 435–436.

83. Cf. M. Spanneut, *Le stoïcisme des Pères* (Paris, 1962) 432–434.

84. Cf. for example, *L'espérance chrétienne dans le monde d'aujourd'hui*, texts of the World Assembly of the World Council of Churches, Evanston, 1954 (Neuchâtel-Paris, 1955).

85. This problematic underlies the correspondence between Teilhard de Chardin and M. Blondel, published by Henri de Lubac, *La pensée religieuse de Pierre Teilhard de Chardin* (Paris, 1962); and by the same author: *Blondel et Teilhard de Chardin. Correspondance commentée* (Paris, 1965).

86. *DCV*, 82–87.

87. *Ibid.*, 76–78.

88. *Ibid.*, 236–239.

89. This is not complete, of course.

90. The expression is that of G. Martelet in *ICI* 224 (Sept. 15, 1964) 8.

91. *ICI* 210 (Feb. 15, 1964) 24; cf. his study in *L'Eglise de Vatican II.*

92. Paris: Ed. de Centurion, 1964. This title is a real find, indicating as it does one of the axes of *De ecclesia*'s evolution in the course of successive sessions.

93. Gal 4:26. The discourse of Msgr. Ziadé (*DCV*, 39ff.) is essential here. A series of historical studies on ecclesiology in line with the biblical theme of *Jerusalem* could be very useful. For example, while the liturgy does not speak of *Roma caelestis* it does often speak of *Urbs Jerusalem Beata* and also of the heavenly Jerusalem. Here is a subject to be studied.

94. *DC* 1434 (Oct. 18, 1964) 1338.

95. *L, RSPT,* 34.
96. *DC* 1413 (Dec. 1, 1963) 1575; the heart of Cardinal König's is reported here.
97. *L,* III, 100.
98. *L, RSPT,* 35.
99. *Ibid.,* 36; *L,* III, 101; *W,* II, 126.
100. *B,* 40.
101. *L, RSPT,* 37; *L,* III, 178–179.
102. *L, RSPT,* 37–46.
103. *ICI* 225 (Oct. 1, 1964) 10.
104. *C* (Sept. 20–21, 1964).
105. R. Laurentin, *DC* 1433 (Sept. 4, 1964) 1256.
106. *B,* 41, quoting C. Balić.
107. Cf. *B,* 38–40; but C. Balić is no doubt wrong in saying that the "ecclesiotypical" is recent.
108. *DC* 1423 (May 3, 1964) 590.
109. Y. Congar, *ICI* 224 (Sept. 15, 1964) 1.
110. In the *Constitution on the Church* (art. 23, 27) there are essential developments on these points, first of all as regards groupings of churches (including the ancient patriarchates), then what the Germans call *Altargemeinde,* that is, the presence of the "Church of God" in a sort of "intensive catholicity" in every community legitimately assembled about its bishop. Cf. also N. Afanassiev, N. Koulomzine *et al., La primauté de Pierre dans l'Eglise orthodoxe* (Neuchâtel, 1960) 9–64: "The Church which presides in love."
111. A Council is not a "victory of those in the avant-garde" of theology, but a diligent and religious search for unanimity about truths and decisions necessary to take when facing the "ecumenicity" or universality of the Church's mission.
112. The *Constitution on the Church,* no more than the decrees on ecumenism and on the liturgy ought not to be "opaque"; they ought to be transparent. In the study of O. Rousseau, quoted above in note 43, the author concludes by saying that the Constitution developed in the direction it did because it opened itself progressively to the contributions of the liturigical, patristic, biblical and ecumenical renewals. He adds that this text is not as a dam inserted in the flow of a river; it is more like a growing awareness that enables one to set up beacons to mark the further flow of the same current. The field of research open is indeed immense: communion, collegiality, role of the eucharist, the local church theme, the Jerusalem theme, and others.
113. It is good to point out that in the text of the Constitution the diaconate is not a "stage" on the way to the priesthood, but links itself on the contrary directly to the bishop; he is helped either by his priests or deacons for a series of sacerdotal or ministerial tasks. It was in this sense that the Council of Trent wanted to speak of the diaconate (cf. S. Ehses, *Conc. Trid. Acta* VI [Freiburg, 1924]601, lin. 9–34; and K. Rahner and H. Vorgimmler, *Diaconia in Christo. Über die Erneuerung des Diakonates* [Freiburg, 1962]).
114. It is important not to confuse diverse aspects of the papacy: the pope is bishop of Rome and patriarch of the West. Since the West was never but one patriarchal church, there was a risk of "telescoping" this dignity into that of the universal pastor. This latter quality, in fact and in law, is tied in with his position as bishop of Rome. He is the primate of Italy and the head of Vatican City. His title of *Pontifex Maximum* is attached to the temporal principality, while that of *Summus Pontifex* is attached to the universal pastoral function. See the remarkable discourse of Msgr. Betazzi, "La collegialité dans la tradition récente," in *DCV,* 70–75; cf. also the *Annuario Pontificio* where all these titles of the pope are mentioned. See also, in the realm of the specific use of authority where these diverse aspects are implied, the discourse of A. Ammann, "A propos des nonciatures et délégations apostoliques," in *DCV,* 149–154.
115. 1 Cor 11:26.
116. See my essay, "Le ferment des idées dans l'élaboration de la Constitution," in *L'Eglise de Vatican II* (cf. note 43), where I tried to follow the historical elaboration of the text, starting with the great currents of ideas within the Council, but linked to the theological currents from German-speaking lands (Church as mystery, sacrament, People of God), French (sacramentality-collegiality), Italian (juridical and historical studies on collegiality), Spanish (problems of pneumatology in ecclesiology, concern about the laity), English (religious liberty, and so on).
117. There is here a point of convergence between the *Constitution on the Liturgy,* the *Decree on Ecumenism* and *Lumen gentium.* The book of J. Hamer, *L'Eglise est une communion* (Paris, 1962), is the first to attempt an explanation for this view and to propose a new "definition" of the Church, integrating both the juridical and sacramental elements.
118. P. Smulders, in *Streven* (Dec. 1964), and E. Schillebeeckx, in *Kultuurleven* (Jan. 1965),

do not sufficiently emphasize this positive aspect of the Note.

119. Cardinal Bea's book *Pour l'unité des chrétiens* (Paris, 1963), is based in large part on this "baptismal ecclesiology."

120. Quoted in *DC* 1434 (Oct. 18, 1964) 1241.

121. See our study referred to above (note 116) and the study of P. Kloppenburg who will study the amendments that gradually brought the text to its present form.

122. See Y. Congar, *Pour une Église servante et pauvre* (Paris, 1963). These few paragraphs were inspired by a talk of Congar's.

123. P, I, 224, 228–229.

124. *Ibid.*, 229.

125. This does not imply, let us repeat, that the Constitution *Lumen gentium* defined dogmas in the sense that Vatican Council I did. On this point see the study of P. Betti in *L'Eglise de Vatican I*.

126. *ICI* 229 (Nov. 1, 1964) 7.

Rev. Henri de Lubac, s.j.

LUMEN GENTIUM AND THE FATHERS

I F WE COMPARE THE *Constitution on the Church*—as also the *Constitution on Divine Revelation*—with the schema submitted by the preparatory commission, the contrast between them is striking. This gives rise to an impression of novelty which has sometimes perhaps been overstressed. This is because people had failed to observe that the theology of the preparatory schemas did not reflect the actual state of theological thought in our century. In reality, the two doctrinal Constitutions of Vatican II have only consecrated a prolonged effort at reflection that had resulted in numerous publications coming from different sources and following different trends.

I. FROM THE FATHERS TO VATICAN II

Still this impression of novelty is not completely false. Neither in its doctrinal elements nor in its practical orientations could this Council be called "conservative." But here we must know how to distinguish carefully two terms which there is a strong tendency to confuse: "conservative" does not mean "traditional." In fact, it can be quite the contrary. Far from preserving them, the ecclesiological doctrine of the *Constitution on the Church* upsets a certain number of positions previously held by a school that could in more than one case regard itself as official. But this has aimed in reality at enabling us to rediscover positions more authentically founded on tradition.[1] It is evident particularly that this doctrine, in its spirit as in its letter, is in much

153

closer agreement with the teaching of the Fathers of the Church. Attention has been called to the considerable number of patristic quotations or references contained in the document. Leaving aside numerous Conciliar, canonical or liturgical texts, we can count in the eight chapters of the Constitution respectively 17, 13, 51, 3, 16, 3, 4 and 27 patristic quotations or references. In the first schema, which was very lengthy, a Melchite bishop had criticized the text for giving only five quotations from the Oriental Fathers.[2] The actual Constitution gives about forty. Naturally, not all these quotations are equally characteristic. A certain number refer only to points of detail or to incidental propositions. On the other hand, the authors of the different chapters made no attempt to unload at the bottom of their pages a whole arsenal of texts. Even had this been their desire, the working conditions confronting them habitually in the Eternal City throughout the four years of the Council would hardly have made this possible. Hence, it is not on this material and quantitative aspect that we should insist.

We must not forget that in the Church a systematization of ecclesiology is something relatively new. It was put together piece by piece, if we may use the expression, from the dawn of modern times in the West. If it could be said, as has often been throughout these last fifty years, that the twentieth century would be the century of the Church, it has been because men were already witnessing the progress of this effort at explicitation and organization, an attempt to get an objective and total grasp of a subject which the pressure of circumstances, coupled with the force of internal logic, constantly accentuated and which has precisely found expression in our Constitution.[3] Without pretending to be a complete treatise on the Church, this Constitution nevertheless presents a certain structural analogy with a treatise. Now it is evident that nothing of this kind could be expected in the age of the Fathers.[4] A certain historian of Christian doctrine was guilty of a strange lack of historical sense in being astonished at not finding in a work like the *Periarchôn* of Origen a chapter dealing specifically with the Church. Consequently, we cannot expect a perfect parallelism between the teaching of Vatican II and the explanations contained in the works of the Fathers.[5]

Does this mean that the Fathers did not have clear ideas on this reality which is the Church or that they offered on this subject only marginal, vague, scattered and purely occasional references? Not at all. The movement whereby at the end of so many centuries the Church has reached the point of being able to look at herself and to undertake a definition of herself is only a repetition of something already done. Some have felt that the Church was getting farther and farther away from the first objects of her faith, which at first occupied all her attention, in order to turn her attention to herself. They wanted to see therein evidence of a passage from transcendence to immanence, such as would characterize the evolution of human thought.[6]

In reality, under the influence of a new method, by means of a "reflex act," which is in fact "characteristic of the mentality of modern man,"[7] the Church is now coming more explicitly to what was in past ages the great object of her contemplation. If the works of the Fathers contain no special chapter on the Church, it is because for them the Church was everywhere. It was because the Church was for them the condition, the background and the aim of all Christian life. It was because they saw the Church intimately linked with all the mysteries—or rather let us say, with the entirety of the mystery of faith.

This is precisely one of the merits, the essential merit of this new *Constitution on the Church*: in a greater measure than was achieved by certain current teachings, this Constitution manifests a constant concern to tie in the truths concerning the Church with the whole body of dogmatic truth. Vatican II frequently recalled the recommendation of Vatican I. In order to penetrate as far as possible into the understanding of faith, Vatican II systematically followed one of the essential methods, which is to consider how the mysteries are linked up among themselves.

From the age of the Fathers to Vatican II, nevertheless, as is very clear, there have been many changes of emphasis or viewpoints. Certain aspects emphasized in the past no longer have any significance. Others have become more precise. Transpositions have been worked out in answer to new situations.[8] On the other hand, as is no less clear, the doctrine of the Fathers is not a monolithic block. As soon as we take up the details of individual thoughts, everything becomes infinitely diversified. Consequently we shall have to be satisfied here with a few general views, and to determine some averages in order to stress the main analogies as also the chief differences. For the rest, no matter how captivating may be the analysis of detail or how necessary it may be for historical research, this analysis, in the perspective interesting us today, would have only secondary interest.

II. The Church as a Mystery

For the *Constitution on the Church* as for the Fathers, the Church is first of all a mystery of faith: *Ecclesiae sanctae mysterium* (art. 5). In its idea as in its reality, it is a gift received from on high, one which human analysis can never completely encompass. It is superfluous to insist on anything so clear, since the fact of it imposes itself on every believer. It is equally useless to insist—although it may be helpful to call attention to the point—on this other fact that under all its aspects the mystery of the Church is not the mystery of some ideal or of some invisible reality, without palpable structure, but the mystery of a communion which, at least by reason of one of its constitutive aspects, is a visible, historical and organized society endowed with a power of government.[9] For the Church is "the visible and mystical body of Christ";[10] she is "the sacrament, sign, and instrument of union with God and of the unity of the human race" (art. 1).[11] There is not a sentence of the Constitution which, with the nuances needed in the applications,[12] does not state or at least suppose this. The ecclesiology of contemporary Catholicism can provide material for many discussions, but one must recognize that on this fundamental point it is in perfect continuity with the ecclesiology of the first Christian centuries, as Dom B. C. Butler has shown recently in his work entitled *The Idea of the Church.*

The Church is not for this reason given any less attention in her mystery. Her origin with the Trinity is explicitly recalled in one or two passages from St. Cyprian[13] (art. 4; cf. art. 39). References to the Holy Spirit are more numerous (about a dozen);[14] but the majority of them are given only in passing, more or less added on to the text. This causes no astonishment because it was not in the direction of pneumatology that Latin theology, which was by force of circumstances predominant in the Council, developed.[15] To compensate—and this is a happy heritage from the Fathers—the eucharist is insisted on, although somewhat sporadically, not merely as the source and the peak of Christian life (art. 13), but also as the interior building force of the Church (art. 3, 26, etc.).[16] If, as the Orthodox are fond of saying, the Church of Christ is a "eucharistic communion," there are solid grounds for agreement between the East and the West. Our Constitution restores strength to a doctrine that is central in our faith, a doctrine which the Latin tradition had received from the Fathers and on which it had long insisted, which St. Thomas accepted when he said that the mystical body, the Church, is the *res* of the eucharist;[17] in recent centuries it has become less prominent.

In the thought of the Fathers this eucharistic birth does not involve any real priority of the local Church in relation to the universal Church. It is very true that for them "the local, eucharistic community manifests the whole Church,"[18] but it is none the less true that they consider the churches scattered throughout the world as constituting the entire body, the one body of "the synagogues of the Church," according to the expression of Origen.[19] The Universal Church is no more a simple federation of local churches than the local church is a simple department of the Universal Church. For there is only one eucharist, as there is only one baptism and one episcopate. "There is," says St. Cyprian, "by the institution of Christ, only one Church, spread abroad in numerous members throughout the entire world."[20] At no moment did the Christians of antiquity, whether Latin or Greek, lose sight of this one Church.[21] On this point again, our Constitution is completely faithful to them.

What is less accentuated in the *Constitution on the Church* is another sort of universality which in the Fathers sometimes interferes with the notion of the visible Church. In article 2 of the Constitution there is only one explicit allusion to this point when speaking of the end of the world: "Then, as may be read in the holy Fathers, all just men from the time of Adam, from Abel, the just one, unto the last of the elect, will be gathered together with the Father in the universal Church." Far from representing a genuine infidelity, this almost complete abandonment of the theme of "the Church of the Saints," results from a concern for precision and for unification of concept, a concern which became necessary when the idea of the Church, instead of remaining universally diffused as before, became the object of a somewhat systematized reflection.

On the other hand, a still further type of universality, another kind of opening, is here given greater emphasis. Not content with affirming, along with the uninterrupted tradition of the Church that all men "are called to this Catholic unity of the People of God," the *Constitution on the Church* adds that as of this moment "there belong to it or are related to it in various ways the Catholic faithful as well as all who believe in Christ, and indeed the whole of mankind. For all men are called to salvation by the grace of God" (art. 13). These are measured expressions but also heavy with consequences, and they open a lengthy development (art. 14–17). They constitute, as we know, one of the chief novelties introduced by the Council in relation to the preparatory schema. They are the fruit of prolonged reflection, only germinal at the time of the Fathers, touching either on the salvation of non-Christians or, in a still greater degree, on the spiritual bonds mutually uniting all the baptized believing in Christ, in the factual situations created by the schisms of history.[22]

Lastly, it is hardly necessary to observe that it is in perfect continuity with the thought of the Fathers that the mystery of the Church is welded to the mystery of Christ, in keeping with the strong recommendation of the then Cardinal Montini in his intervention on December 4, 1962.[23] On this point, the first words of the Constitution are eloquent and provide the tone for what follows. Contrary to a modern method which proceeds by way of abstraction and sometimes gives the impression that the Catholic Church is setting up in herself the source of the light offered to men,[24] these opening words place us immediately in the climate which pervades the entire Constitution: "*Lumen gentium cum sit Christus. . . .*"[25]

III. The People of God

Whereas the schema submitted by the preparatory commission emphasized the idea of the Body of Christ, in line with Pius XII's encyclical *Mystici corporis*, which had itself been prepared by a particular doctrinal and spiritual movement, the *Constitution on the Church* puts more stress on the idea of the People of God.[26] It is generally admitted, and correctly so, that here we have one of the major original approaches, not only of the Constitution, but of the entire Council. To what degree can this approach be said to be patristic?

There is certainly no dearth of ancient texts describing the Church as the People of God. Similarly, in keeping with the logic of this expression, the Fathers teach the reality of a priesthood common to all the baptized. They are thus opposed to any radical and basic distinction between categories of Christians, to any favoring of one caste, as also to any insistence on the esoteric (one of the characteristics of the great "gnostic" heresy). Thus they put us on our guard even today against the dangers of any one-sided presentation in explaining the relationship between the laity and the hierarchy, between pastors and their flock.[27] It is in this spirit that St. Augustine addresses his people in one of his sermons: "For you I am a bishop and with you I am a Christian" (quoted in article 32 of chapter 4 of our Constitution). In line with this same logic, and from this viewpoint, the entire Church can be said to be sinful;[28] or, before making any distinction between the Church teaching and the Church taught, the Church will be said to believe and hope, to love her Lord and Savior and await his return.[29] Besides, the idea of the People of God makes it possible to get a better understanding of an essential characteristic of the idea of the body of Christ, in the sense that it manifests clearly the distance to be observed between the Head of the body and the other members. Lastly, it is undeniable that the concept of the Church as the People of God is everywhere basic to the dynamic, historical and "pilgrim" perspective common to the Fathers, especially the Latins.

One argument, however, appears unconvincing. During the first four or five centuries, it is sometimes said, the dominant idea of the Church was that of the People of God, and an attempt is made to prove this by arguing from the very origin of the word *Ecclesia*, which is the Greek substitute for the *Qahal Yahweh* or assembly of Yahweh of the Bible. The observation is correct,[30] but it does not follow therefrom that every time the Fathers used the word *Ecclesia* they were referring primarily to this origin and consequently to this special significance of the term.

Nevertheless, whenever there is question in Christian antiquity of the Church as the People of God, the reference is to the People of the Old Testament. As St. Paul had done, so the Fathers present the Church as "a spiritual Israel," "the genuine race of Israel," heir to the prophecies and the promises.[31] This is a major application of their doctrine, one with countless developments and ramifications, on the relationships of Old and New Testaments. Our Constitution does not fail to recall this (art. 9). Nevertheless it devotes less attention to this idea, and perhaps in the passage from one Testament to the other, from one people to the other, it puts more emphasis on continuity than on transformation. The tone is not at all the same as the one most frequently used in the Fathers. Without doubt the Christians of old willingly called the biblical believers of old "our Fathers and our ancestors." But after the example of St. Paul they were not less aware of a relationship of opposition between the two Testaments, since the Spirit of Christ had renewed everything, transfigured everything and "spiritualized" everything.[32]

On the other hand, with the Fathers as later in the Middle Ages, within the framework of this doctrine of the twofold Testament, biblical images suggested in profusion many varied aspects of ecclesial reality. By their very exuberance and diversity, these images became almost a "game," thus emphasizing their extreme complexity.[33] Our Constitution does not fail to recall this, and this reminder is most valuable for purposes of future study.[34] But the Constitution understands that, especially in a text which is to be authoritative, our age demands a more sober style, and for this reason the Constitution makes a more careful choice of such images. This was normal, even necessary, granted the Council's intention to set up a body of doctrine as organic as possible. If the Constitution's choice of images is such as to please Reformation Christians,[35] it may arouse, certainly not a contradiction, but a little concern among some of the Orthodox, who fear that less emphasis is thereby placed on the interior and divine aspects of the Church, descending from on high and animated by the Spirit.[36] But it is important here to call attention to the place occupied by this chapter on the People of God, a place which, as we know, was not discovered all at once. Although it comes before the chapter on the hierarchy (and this explains the characteristics we have pointed out), it is preceded by the chapter on the mystery of the Church. Thus the proper balance is established.

The choice of images by the Constitution is not exclusive. More particularly, although it has no special chapter on the motherhood of the Church, the title of mother is nevertheless attributed to the Church in several passages.[37] We shall come back to this point in our discussion of the final chapter. Nevertheless, we must recognize that this title enjoyed greater consistency and awoke more precise echoes in the texts of the Fathers. We have only to think, for example, of the letter of the Christians of Vienne or of Lyons, or of the inscription on the baptistry of St. John Lateran's, or of the commentaries on the vision of the woman giving birth in the Apocalypse, or of many sermons on baptism. Recall Irenaeus, too, in what he says of the life-giving faith with which the Church alone, more fruitful than the Synagogue of old, nourishes her children.[38] Hippolytus states that "the Church never ceases to bring forth the *Logos*, Man and God, from her heart."[39]

Origen expresses the hope that his listeners may "be the joy of their Mother the Church," but fears that she might, on the contrary, have to "bring forth more children in sadness and pain."[40] Tertullian sings the praises of her whom he calls "our Lady Mother the Church," "the true Mother of the living."[41] Cyprian lays down the celebrated principle that "no man can have God for his father unless he first has the Church for his mother."[42] Cyril of Jerusalem teaches the catechumens that "Catholic Church" is the proper name of this Holy Mother of us all.[43] Optatus, Augustine, Fulgentius and Caesarius give testimony of their affection for the *Catholica Mater*.[44]

The Constitution appropriately quotes those texts of Scripture which are the basis for this title (art. 6) and refers to them in more than one passage. And yet the Constitution's usual viewpoint is different. The idea of the People of God generally dominates the chapters on the hierarchy, whose ministerial priesthood is at the service of the people at large; on the laity who constitute the most numerous portion of this people; and likewise on religious. When mention is made of holiness, the text certainly does not forget that the Church is a sanctifying Mother, but greater attention is paid to the vocation of all the members of the People to become holy. In a word there is less description of the mother than of the children, less of the house than of those who dwell therein, less of the voice summoning men to assemble in Christ (*convocatio*) than of the result of this assembly (*congregatio*). Nevertheless we should observe that this is a question only of proportion and nuance, and that between these two aspects there is no yawning abyss. The distinction between the idea of the People of God and the idea of the Church as a Mother is not complete, as is well demonstrated by the investigation carried out by Karl Delahaye on the first three centuries and which is explained by Yves Congar in his preface to this work.[45] The *Ecclesia Mater* is not only the hierarchical Church; every holy soul begets the *Logos* and contributes to begetting him in those around it.[46]

In the rich but scattered treasury of patristic writings, nothing essential was neglected. Nevertheless a choice had to be made, the choice of a unifying element. Terminology corresponding to a given aspect of reality was privileged. This was, we repeat, indispensable from the moment that the Council, without intending to provide a complete treatise, wished to offer a body of teaching that would be both well organized and adapted to the needs of the times. It was likewise this concern for adaptation which caused the introduction of a few new developments that really add nothing substantial to existing doctrine. The chief of these elements is the chapter on the laity, composed "because of the special circumstances of our age" (art. 30).[47] Hence, it is not surprising that the only two patristic quotations in this chapter, one from Augustine and the other from the *Epistle to Diognetus*, really refer to all Christians.

IV. Eschatological Perspective

One of the elements that might be called new in relation to the classical teaching of recent centuries is the eschatological perspective of the Constitution.

The seventh chapter of the Constitution explains "the eschatological nature (*indoles*) of the pilgrim Church."[48] But, in fact, throughout the entire Constitution the Church is considered in this fashion, from a viewpoint at once collective and dynamic. The Church is the People of God en route to a great common goal. Coming from God's universal plan of salvation, the Church has as her mission to realize this plan by uniting all men in Christ. Assuredly nothing is more traditional, but this tradition was not rediscovered without some suffering,[49] and it could not simply be found without taking into account a new element.

In effect, in proportion as the Church continued, her thoughts were increasingly directed to those of her members who had disappeared. She looked upon them as forming the "Church triumphant" or the "Church suffering," whereas she herself on earth was the "Church militant." This explains why an important part of this seventh chapter treats of the union of the Church here below with the "Church in Heaven." This part is evidently less patristic, and its title is not patristic at all. When Origen wrote in book 4 of the *Periarchôn*, "We must attach ourselves to the rule of the heavenly Church of Jesus Christ, according to the succession of the apostles,"[50] it is clear that for him the "heavenly Church" was identical with the Church living on earth, historical and visible. It was the same when Zeno of Verona described for the newly baptized "this heavenly Mother who gives birth to you in joy and liberty."[51] Irenaeus likewise recognized in the Church of today, founded by Christ and his apostles, the "heavenly Jerusalem" of which the ancient earthly Jerusalem had been a preparation and a figure,[52] and Hilary of Poitiers shared this view when he alluded to the heavenly Jerusalem in comparing the mystical body of Christ to a city: "By means of our participation in his flesh we are residents of this city."[53] Another mode of speech, presupposing another conception, has prevailed today and the chapter we are considering still shows traces of this in the words: "Celebrating the Eucharistic sacrifice, therefore, we are most closely united to the worshiping Church in heaven" (art. 50).

Nevertheless, this relatively new consideration of the bonds that exist or are established between two Churches, or between two parts of the Church, the one on earth and the other in heaven—a consideration which was not entirely unknown to the age of the Fathers[54]— does not de-emphasize the dynamism that impels the Church toward her eternal goal: "The Church, 'like a pilgrim . . . , presses forward . . . ,' announcing the cross and death of the Lord until He comes . . . until through the cross she arrives at the light which knows no setting" (art. 8, 9). This was already expressed by Cyprian when he proclaimed his hope in the definitive victory of the Church fulfilled in the hereafter.[55] Thus also Gregory the Great compares the Church to a city: "This city, namely, the holy Church, which is to reign in heaven, still struggles here on earth."[56] In these words, Gregory only repeated the explanations given by Augustine at the beginning of his great work *The City of God*, although in this work the word "church" does not appear.[57] By means of these terms, Cyprian, Gregory and the others designated the Church actually visible here below, suffering or on pilgrimage, and in this our Constitution is in perfect harmony with their viewpoint.

In other words, consideration of personal eschatology that had little by little introduced the present duality of the Church on earth and the Church in heaven united in "the bonds linking the whole mystical body" (art. 50) —a duality which has been retained in the seventh chapter of our Constitution—has not suppressed the idea of collective eschatology that shows the People of God as being guided, from generation to generation, toward the heavenly Jerusalem and already mystically united with it. More precisely, this collective march is defined as a march toward unity, since the People of God, already assembled from the moment when the gospel was first preached, has received the mission to unite the entire human race. The most significant text in this connection is found, not in chapter 7, but in chapter 2, article 9: "This messianic people, although it does not actually include all men, and may more than once look like a small flock, is nonetheless a lasting and sure seed of unity, hope, and salvation for the whole human race." Article 1 had already expressed the same idea, as we observed earlier, when presenting the Church at the outset as "the sacrament or sign of intimate union with God, and of the unity of all mankind, . . . an instrument for the achievement of such union and unity." These affirmations find their completion in the reference to the final end found in article 36 of chapter 4: "To Him [Christ] all things are made subject until He subjects Himself and all created things to the Father, that God may be all in all."

Historical progress to the final unity of men in Christ and consummation of the universe in God—this twofold characteristic reproduces faithfully the eschatological thought of the Fathers; the first of these was perhaps emphasized more by the Latins, who were more sensitive to the evolution of history,[58] and the second by the Greeks, whose mentality was more cosmic.[59] This final unity and consummation presuppose a passage, in the footsteps of Christ, through death and radical transfiguration. This is the thought set forth at the end of the chapter on the universal call to sanctity where the warning of the Apostle is quoted: "Let those who make use of this world not get bogged down in it, for the structure of this world is passing away" (art. 42). This is repeated in the chapter consecrated to the religious state, which "foretells the resurrected state and the glory of the heavenly kingdom" (art. 44). Chapter 7 develops the same thought. Beginning with the introductory sentence it proclaims the heavenly and transcendent character of this universal consummation: "The Church . . . will attain her full perfection only in the glory of heaven. Then will come the time of the restoration of all things. Then the whole human race as well as the entire world, which is intimately related to man and achieves its purpose through him, will be perfectly re-established in Christ" (art. 48).

We must rejoice that patristic and traditional thought has been so officially resurrected in the *Constitution on the Church*. This is the final consecration of theological effort in our century, an effort which may have been stimulated and in some way made necessary by a general state of mind, but which was nonetheless to revivify what, since the very beginning, was at the very heart of Catholic tradition and so well preserved by the liturgy.

In this connection we might point out in passing a slight transposition of thought in the use made of an old literary form. The last sentence of chapter 2 (art. 17) states: "In this way the Church simultaneously prays and labors in order that the entire world may become the People of God, the Body of the Lord, and the Temple of the Holy Spirit." With the modification demanded by the text, this passage reproduces a liturgical prayer from the *Gelasian Sacramentary*: ". . . grant that, into the sons of Abraham and into the dignity of Israel the fullness of the entire world may pass."[60] This prayer is still used in the Roman liturgy for the Easter Vigil.

The fact remains that the option in favor of the People of God as the basic concept for the study of the Church coupled with the actual juxtaposition of the two churches or of the two parts of one Church—the earthly church, to which we belong, and the heavenly church, composed of the elect who have entered their "homeland"—was bound to result in a certain narrowing of patristic horizons. "You have come," says the Epistle to the Hebrews (12:22), "to Mount Sion, the city of the living God, the heavenly Jerusalem." Our Fathers meditated on these words in faith. The Church that gave birth to them in the waters of baptism, this earthly and visible Church, was thus for them at the same time "the heavenly Church," "the heavenly Jerusalem, our Mother." "Let us dwell now in the Church, the heavenly Jerusalem," Augustine was to say, "in order not to be rejected for eternity."[61] And again: "The present Church is the kingdom of Christ and the Kingdom of Heaven."[62] In this synthetic view of the mystery, the Church is identified with Christ, her Spouse, who is himself the kingdom—"self-kingdom," according to the admirable expression of Origen. This viewpoint is in harmony with the most profound logic of Christian eschatology, and apart from this logic it would risk leading to many abuses in thought and action. The kingdom of God is to come, but "without waiting for history to run its course" it has already, "in a mysterious anticipation, made its appearance inside history." Since the coming of Christ and his resurrection "timelessness is already present inside time." Such is the most mysterious aspect of the Church, the one whereby she identifies herself with Christ, just as Christ is identical with the kingdom. There is no question of imagining a kind of indefinite middle-point between the "not yet" and the "already there." There is no question of a threshold to be only half crossed. In one sense, for the People of God considered as advancing through the obscurity of the world, the situation is completely the "not yet"; but in another sense, inseparable from the first, for the Church as descended from on high and as indwelt by Christ and his Spirit, it is completely "already there."[63]

The choice of the first of these two perspectives (without excluding complementary indications) made it impossible to reproduce exactly certain expressions of the Fathers. This would have encouraged confusion and would have led to the reproach that under its visible aspect the Church was being substituted for the kingdom and its hierarchy for God. This choice involved still another consequence. To the question whether the Church exists for the world or the world for the Church, this choice left only one answer possible, namely, the Church is for the world. (We should point out immediately that these two conflicting answers are only apparently contradictory; the question is one of perspective. The word "Church" is no more univocal than the word "world.") Insofar as she is visible and temporal, the Church is destined to disappear. She is a "sign and sacrament" and signs and sacraments will be absorbed into the reality they announce.[64] She is a means, a necessary means, a divine means, but temporary like any other means. This is what impelled Pius XI to declare one day: "Men have not been created for the Church, but the Church is created for men—*for us men and for our salvation.*"[65]

On the part of all the Church's members, and particularly on the part of its hierarchy, this viewpoint demands an attitude of humble service, after the example of the attitude adopted by the Word in his incarnation, coming "not to be ministered to, but to minister." The *Constitution on the Church* insists very happily on this point (art. 5, 8), echoing the words of Paul VI[66] and thus preparing for the development and the practical application made by the *Constitution on the Church in the Modern World.* On this point too our Constitution could have fallen back on patristic precedents. It was Origen, for example, who said: "He who is summoned to be a bishop is not called to be a prince, but is invited to the service of the entire Church."[67] And again, turning his attention to all men, he insisted: "The bishop must be the servant of all by his humility, in order to render service to all in the things touching on salvation. This is the commandment given to us by the Word of God."[68]

On the other hand, however, and without prejudice to this humble service of which he gave a heroic example, it was in the name of a more complete and more profound understanding of this mystery and in conformity with the other aspect of patristic teaching that Abbé Jules Monchanin could deplore the ravages of a trend of thought "which makes the world the reason for the Church and no longer the Church the reason for the world."[69] In the last century Dom Gréa echoed this same teaching and this same universal vision when he wrote at the beginning of his recently re-edited treatise on *The Church and her Divine Constitution:*[70] "The Catholic Church is the beginning of and the reason for all things." And the second-century writer Hermes said substantially the same in the second vision of his *Pastor:* the Church is like a woman grown old "because she was created first before all things; it was for her that the world was made"[71]—for her, that is to say, to be taken up, saved and transfigured in her. The Church, declared Origen, is "the cosmos of the cosmos." And before him Clement of Alexandria had said: "Just as the will of God is an act and is called the world, thus his intention is the salvation of men and that is called the Church."[72] *Mundus reconciliatus, Ecclesia.*[73]

V. The Church and the Virgin Mary

On the subject of the People of God, and again when discussing eschatology, we alluded to the title "Mother" which in several instances the Constitution attributes to the Church but which it did not use as a principle of synthesis. We now found this title once more in connection with the final chapter on "The Role of the Blessed Virgin Mary in the Mystery of Christ and the Church."

There was much discussion in the Council itself before deciding to include these pages on the Virgin Mary in the *Constitution on the Church.* Contrary to what has often been said, let us make clear that this was the original idea of the preparatory doctrinal commission.[74] The separation of this chapter from the schema on the Church was effected by the commission only at a later date, after it had become clear that the chapter in question was notably longer than the others and formed a brief summary of Marian theology (no longer entirely true in its present version). In any case, the decision to consider the Virgin Mary in relationship to the Church, a decision which had been suggested by Paul VI,[75] not only provided a fitting conclusion to the entire Constitution but was also the most effective means for bringing this chapter in line with the thought of the Fathers, without prejudicing further development. It also provided an opportunity to consider the Church herself as "spouse" and "virginal mother," a theme very specially dear to the Fathers.

Unless we are mistaken, the Church as spouse is mentioned briefly four times in this Constitution (art. 6, 7, 9, 39). This theme is dwarfed by the Council's treatment of the People of God, just as it was formerly, in the theology of recent times, by that of the mystical body. On the contrary, like the other two, it is eminently patristic as well as scriptural. "The Fathers see a mysterious parallel between the birth of the first woman and the birth of the Church."[76] The analogy of the body itself often led them, as it did St. Paul, to the analogy of the spouse. According to Origen,[77] "Christ and the Church are no longer two beings, but only one flesh, for it is said to the Spouse: 'You are the members of Christ.'" And Hilary wrote: "The Church is the Body of Christ and the mystery of Adam and Eve is a prophecy concerning Christ and the Church." Numerous texts of this kind appear throughout the whole of the patristic age and in different circumstances, beginning with the Second Epistle of Clement of Rome (in reality a very ancient sermon) and up to St. Augustine and his followers.[78] All the espousals mentioned in the Bible are interpreted in this sense.[79] We know that from the time of the first commentators (Hippolytus and Origen) the Canticle of Canticles was understood as the bridal hymn of Christ and his Church.

Now this Spouse is a mother and a virgin. Our last chapter explains this in articles 63 and 64, developing the analogy of the Church and of the Virgin Mary. Giving birth to a new and immortal life by her preaching and baptism in children conceived of the Holy Spirit, the Church keeps intact and pure for her Spouse the fidelity she vowed to him. A note in the text here refers to St. Ambrose and St. Augustine. Such references could be multiplied.

As for the explicit parallelism between Mary and the Church, Msgr. Gerard Philips wrote in 1963 that this theme "arose in contemporary theology in a manner as unexpected as it was spectacular." But this was not the result of any arbitrary or passing fancy. "Far from remaining on the periphery of Christian doctrine," it is "one of the major characteristics of Catholic thought."[80] This theme is also patristic.[81] Thus we understand why the Council wished to retain it. Nevertheless, as Msgr. Philips again observed, "Mary is not the prototype of hierarchical power in the Church but the model of spiritual receptivity before the influence" of divine grace.[82] This can be understood in two ways, or rather this involves two kinds of consequences; both of them are made explicit in our chapter, and both of them are based on the thought of the Fathers.

In the first place, the virginal motherhood of Mary, the fruit of this spiritual receptivity, is the prototype of the motherhood of the Church in regard to Christians. "For in the mystery of the Church, herself rightly called mother and virgin, the Blessed Virgin Mary stands out in eminent and singular fashion as exemplar virginity and motherhood." This statement from article 63 is developed in the following articles. Ambrose is the first one to take it up explicitly. Before him Justin and Irenaeus had seen the new Eve in the Virgin of the annunciation. Tertullian and Methodius had pointed to the Church, the true mother of the living, as coming forth from the wound of the dead Christ on the cross, just as the first Eve had come forth from the side of the sleeping Adam.[83] Bringing these two themes together, Ambrose described Mary as *typus Ecclesiae*,[84] and Augustine followed him.[86]

Under the first aspect of the analogy, Mary is the figure of the Church as a sanctifying mother.[86] But the Church is also the sanctified People of God or in the process of being sanctified. This is the second aspect which the *Constitution on the Church*, given its main perspective, certainly could not neglect. In fact, we find it explained in article 68: "In the bodily and spiritual glory which she possesses in heaven the Mother of Jesus continues in this present world as the image and first flowering of the Church as she is to be perfected in the world to come. Likewise, Mary shines forth on earth, until the day of the Lord shall come, as a sign of sure hope and solace for the pilgrim People of God." The *Constitution on the Sacred Liturgy* (art. 103) had already stated that in Mary the Church "holds up and admires the most excellent fruit of the redemption, and joyfully contemplates, as in a faultless model, that which she herself wholly desires and hopes to be."

In a word, under this second aspect, Mary, full of grace and the prototype of all perfection, is the eschatological image of the Church and of the entire People of God. Beginning with the Middle Ages, especially in Marian commentaries on the Canticle of Canticles, the analogy was often exploited in this sense. By anticipation Mary stands out alone as the perfect Church, the perfected community of the faithful.[87] Thus in the mystery of the assumption this theme finds its full development.[88] It was natural that the proclamation of the dogma by Pius XII should have restored this theme to new favor.[89] Nevertheless, it was not completely foreign to Christian antiquity. Ambrose had referred to it more than once,[90] applying the general principle on which Origen had based his explanation of the Canticle of Canticles, namely, the symbolization of the Church and of the faithful soul or, if one prefers, their "mysterious interpenetration."[91] If the Church, after the example of Mary, conceives of the Holy Spirit and brings forth Christ in his members by giving them faith and baptism, then every Christian soul which, after the example of Mary and the Church, heeds, receives and guards chastely the Word of God, also brings forth Christ. *Ecclesia in sanctis*, *Virgo Mater*.

But this final chapter of the *Constitution on the Church* is not satisfied with merely explaining the analogy existing between the Church and Mary.

167

It completes its explanation by indicating the place occupied by Mary in the Church as "the pre-eminent and altogether singular member" (art. 53). On this point there has been much discussion, somewhat purposeless and often one-sided; participants on both sides have failed to examine the text of either the Pope or the Council. On the one hand, in effect, the Constitution itself affirms Mary's spiritual motherhood, not only in relation to each one of us but also in relation to the Church herself: "Taught by the Holy Spirit, the Catholic Church honors her with filial affection and piety as a most beloved Mother" (art. 53).[92] Later the Constitution states further that, as "mother of Christ and mother of men," Mary "occupies a place in the Church which is the highest after Christ and yet very close to us" (art. 54).[93] This is exactly what Paul VI said he was hoping for in his closing discourse for the second session of the Council on December 4, 1963; it goes even farther.[94] On the other hand, every time Paul VI wanted to honor the Virgin Mary with the title "Mother of the Church," as he had often expressed the desire to do, he did so with a series of precise, cautious expressions that are perfectly in line with the teaching of the Council.[95] Particularly, his closing discourse at the third session on November 21, 1964, "insistently manifests his intention to tie up his proclamation with the actual text of the Constitution."[96]

The fact of the matter is that here we are actually on ground that is basically traditional. However, if the expression "Mother of the Church" were to be used alone and without explanation, it would be less in keeping with tradition. The first authors to use this expression explicitly associate, as Paul VI did, the two terms "Mother" and "Daughter." This was the mind of Berengaudus in the eighth century, in his commentary on the Apocalypse: "Mary is the Mother of the Church because she gave birth to him who is its Head; she is a daughter of the Church because she is a member of it, its most august member."[97] For the preceding period we find only a few pertinent texts. Up until recent years the only one which could be quoted was this passage from St. Augustine's *De Virginitate*: "Mary is not the spiritual Mother of our Head; spiritually she was rather born of him; but she is truly the Mother of his members, which we are."[98] Antoine Wenger has provided another text, drawn from the most ancient account of the "Dormition" of Mary, which he discovered in a Syriac manuscript dating from the end of the fifth century. In this text Mary addresses herself to Christ, to the whole Christ, Head and body, saying to him: "You are the fullness. I begot you as first-born and all those who hope in you."[99]

It should be noted, finally, that both the Pope and the Council insisted on remaining in the direct line of the tradition of the Fathers, as also of Scripture, as regards the unique mediation of Christ and service of God (art. 60, 64, 67).[100]

In conclusion let us return to the matter of typology. The bonds of mystical analogy between the Church and Mary are no less clearly perceived in our day than they were in the time of Ambrose and Augustine. By explaining these bonds and letting them clarify the doctrine on the Church as well as on the Virgin Mary, Vatican II consecrated with its authority something that wells up from the depths of the Catholic conscience. Scholars and the historians of dogma and of piety were not the only ones to study the testimony of tradition[101] on the subject of these mysterious bonds, but, in a manner altogether independent, this testimony has been brought to light and revivified by some of the most eminent, original and yet dissimilar Catholic thinkers writing today.[102]

In *Le Coeur du Monde*, by Hans Urs von Balthasar, Jesus says to the Church: "Mysteriously, your image tends to fuse with that of my virginal Mother. She is one woman, but in you she becomes the Universal Mother."[103] And in *La prière contemplative* by the same author, Mary, "the archetype of the Church," is contemplated at length as the archetype of Christian contemplation. As the "place of the incarnation of the Word," she strengthens us against both the danger of considering the Word as something exterior (whereas it is "the deepest mystery in the center of ourselves") and the similar danger of confusing the Word with our own word "with a wisdom available according to our own whims." In Mary, the faithful soul, the Church, "expressed perfectly that 'yes' which is the origin and the substance of all Christian contemplation."[104]

With his deliberately straightforward brusqueness, Paul Claudel wrote one day to a correspondent of his: "For me, the Blessed Virgin is the same thing as the holy Church, and I have never learned to distinguish the one from the other." What he wanted to say was that he had learned rather to unite them indissolubly. He had learned by personal experience when, on a certain Christmas eve in Notre Dame Cathedral, during the singing of the Magnificat, the entire faith of the Church had taken hold of him. Since that time he often returned to the old cathedral to continue his "theology course," and his teacher was, as he tells us, "the Blessed Virgin herself with great patience and majesty." With his face glued to the choir grilles, he "watched the Church live" and by means of this spectacle, that leaves the minds of so many others in a state of listless boredom, he suddenly understood everything and everything took life in him. For, as he explained later, "What Paul told me, what Augustine showed me, the bread which Gregory broke for me with the antiphon and the response—the eyes of Mary were there looking down on me to explain it all to me." The "motherly and reassuring majesty" that enveloped him was at one and the same time the Church's and Mary's. Without making further distinctions, he had only to find his support in this twofold and unique Mother "who pours everything into his heart silently and who brings into one sole focus all the contradictory lines."[105]

It is still this same lack of distinction, or rather the same mystical identification, which finds expression in another man whose spiritual orientation appears quite different from that of the two earlier ones; his name was often spoken at the Council with less right than we evoke it here—Pierre Teilhard de Chardin. This poem of his, written during World War I, describes the ascending phases of the "Eternal Feminine" who, under the figure of biblical (and liturgical) Wisdom, addresses herself to men:

> From the beginning was I created, . . . And unto the world of the future I shall not cease to be. . . .
> . . . God I attracted to myself long before you.
> Long before Man had measured the extent of his power and guessed the meaning of my attraction, the Lord had already conceived me in my entirety in his wisdom, and I had won his heart.
> Do you think that without the attraction of my Purity to seduce him, he would ever have come down, in the flesh, into the midst of Creation?
> Love alone is capable of moving being.
> God, then, in order to go out of himself, had first to open up before his steps a path of desire, and diffuse before himself a perfume of beauty.
> It is then that he made me rise, as a luminous cloud, over the abyss—between the Earth and himself—to come into me in order to dwell among you.
> Now do you understand the secret of your emotion when I draw near to you?
> . . . Placed between God and Earth, as an area of common attraction, I cause them to come to one another, passionately.
> . . . Until there takes place in me the meeting in which the generation and the plenitude of Christ are fulfilled, across the centuries.
> I am the Church, spouse of Jesus.
> I am the Virgin Mary, mother of all men.[106]

To this threefold witness, finally, we add that of another precursor, Abbé Jules Monchanin. In a few meaty phrases, in a meditation on *La Vierge aux Indes*, Abbé Monchanin linked up the twofold typology that the Constitution *Lumen Gentium* was to make its own with the theme retained also by this final chapter, namely, of the motherhood of Mary in relation to the Church, a theme which he expanded to the point of cosmic motherhood:

> Mary is the fullness of the Virgin and of the Woman, of the Mother. Virgin always and *usque in aeternum*. Everything virginal in the world before her announced her coming and everything virginal after her found fulfillment in her. Is not unicity of love the essence of virginity? She was a perfect woman, receptive of God, made fruitful for God and with God. Mother of the Word Incarnate—her giving birth is comparable to the very generation of the Word by the Father rather than to the giving birth of other women: *prius concepit mente*—and then of the Church, of Humanity, of the World; Cosmic Mother, universal Mediatrix, initiator of renunciation and dispenser of the joy which does not pass,

Providence Heights -4/25/66
Intro: We do the difficult
immediately; the impossible
takes a bit more than 8 min.
1) **Purpose:** Not to state the
theological advances of the
meeting (there were really
none), but to indicate the
weaknesses that made such a
advances impossible.
II) The weknesses
A) **Organizational**
  1) **Read papers** - no mimeo
  cuts down discussion
  2) **Too many participants:**
  You can have too much of
  ravioli, freedom in con-
  creto, classes, experts.
  No one fully developes his
  ideas
  3) **Too many topics of dis-**
  cussion - the Council documents.   Like discuss
  everything knowable and a
  few others
  4) **Imposed topics:** Ruins
  creativity

REV. HENRI DE LUBAC, S.J.
Lumen Gentium and the Fathers

he God who became a changing being; Christ-bearer e Spirit who dwells in her in his fullness and whose st whom she continues to bring forth, these two r, she summons the Church to the secret of the

r, reflection of the Principle, of the Mediator, of the the daughter of Abraham will be . . . the arouser Trinity, as the prototype of the Church and of its s a call to the Father whose fatherhood she shares m she brings forth to kenosis and change, to the tes to Creation from her own superabundance.[107]

NOTES

e de la deuxième session (Paris, 1964) 37, note 3, observes ere called innovators used more judiciously arguments from his address opening the second session Sept. 29, 1963, said: ims is not a turning upside down of the Church's present al and worthy of veneration in her tradition. It is, rather, an of what is decrepit or defective so that it can find its true

John of Acre, Dec. 6, 1962. [2nd ed. Paris, 1953) 9–21. ican II, edited by G. Baraúna (Paris, 1966); G. Bardy, La concile de Nicée (Paris, 1947) 7–8; C. Butler, The Idea of the Church (Baltimore, 1962) 85: "The [ancient] councils did not recognize any need to give similar dogmatic expression to the Church's convictions about her own nature."

5. Read Paul VI's words opening the second session: "There can be no doubt whatever of the Church's desire, need and duty to give a more thorough definition of herself. . . . It should not come as a surprise that, after twenty centuries . . . there is still need to enunciate a more precise definition of the true, profound and complete notion of the Church."

6. Cf. my preface to the work edited by G. Baraúna (see note 4).

7. Paul VI, Ecclesiam suam 30.

8. Thus, for example, the theme "Church of the Jews, Church of the Gentiles" naturally withered. On the contrary, juridical clarifications about the hierarchy took on great significance. More recently, there arose a concern to distinguish the many possible degrees in which one can belong to the Church.

9. Cf. Butler, op. cit., 83–86.

10. Paul VI, in his address opening the second session.

11. "Ursakrament," insisted Cardinal Frings of Cologne; "primordial sacrament," suggested Msgr. Guano of Leghorn. When Origen says that we must beware of letting ourselves be seduced by heretical teachings and thus dare to diminish the mystery of the Church, he is clearly not speaking of a Church that is merely visible (Selecta in Job 20, 15; PG 12:1036).

12. Thus in art. 8: "This church, constituted and organized in the world as a society, subsists in the Catholic Church."

13. One could also cite Tertullian, De baptismo 6; De pudicitia 21.

14. Art. 4, 9, 11–13, 15, 17, 48, 50.

15. Msgr. Ignatius Ziadé, Maronite Archbishop of Beirut, said at the second session that "the period of the Church in the history of salvation is called the economy of the Spirit by the Fathers." Again, at the third session he maintained that, "while the Latin Church had greatly developed her Christology, she was still an adolescent in pneumatology." On the very same day, Abbot Butler expressed regret over the Council's silence on the Holy Spirit—mentioned only once and at that, he said, "in a calamitous way."

16. See also art. 7, 11, 13, 28, 34, 50. The Fourth Council of the Lateran, in its decree of Nov. 30, 1215, no. 1, says: "There is only one church . . . in which Christ himself is at once

both priest and victim." This brief statement hardly suffices to speak, with R. Foreville (*Latran I, II, III, et Latran IV* [1965] 282), of "the eucharistic character of the church," and of an "ecclesiology of communion."

17. *Summa Theol. III*, 73, 2 and 3; etc.

18. O. Clément, *L'Eglise orthodoxe* (Paris, 1965) 7. Cf. the intervention of Msgr. E. Schick, Auxiliary Bishop of Fulda, at the second session, on the importance of the local church: "Each one is the real actualization of the entire Universal Church."

19. *In Matt.* 13, 24.

20. *Epist.* 55, 24, 2. Cf. Origen, *In Genesim hom.* 12, 3. Regarding the primacy of the Universal Church, see C. Butler, *op. cit.*, 97.

21. Cf. G. Bardy, *En lisant les Pères* (Paris, 1933) 103.

22. The interventions of Cardinals Liénart and Frings in December, 1962, and Cardinal Lercaro on Oct. 3, 1963, in the discussion of ch. 1, were decisive in this direction. Already in his address opening the second session (Sept. 29, 1963), Paul VI spoke of the "separated brothers who are also called to belong fully to the Church."

23. And again as Paul VI opened the second session, he referred to the mosaic, at the Basilica of St. Paul outside the walls, in which Honorius III (representing the whole Church) is shown "tiny and prostrate, kissing the feet of a Christ of gigantic proportions blessing the assembly." Cf. H. de Lubac, "Paul VI, pélerinage en Terre Sainte," *Christus* (January, 1964).

24. Cf. Paul VI's discourse Sept. 14, 1964: "The Church must not close in on herself in an attitude of complacency, forgetting, on the one hand, Christ from whom she receives everything and to whom she owes everything, and on the other hand, the humanity which she is committed to serve . . . she is not an opaque screen between him and the world."

25. See also the beginning of Paul VI's first encyclical, *Ecclesiam suam*. Cf. H. de Lubac, "Paul VI vu à travers *Ecclesiam suam*," *Choisir* (April, 1965).

26. This was proposed by Cardinal Frings already in December, 1962, and in this he was simply echoing a German doctrinal movement. Msgr. Garrone, Archbishop of Toulouse, was one of the chief architects of this chapter. One should note that these two principal images were somewhat fused in art. 9: "That messianic people has for its head Christ. . . ."

27. Some modern documents are not free of this fault. Cf. R. Laurentin, *L'enjeu du Concile IV. Bilan de la troisième session* (Paris, 1965) 115–116.

28. Cf. Origen, *In Cant. comm.* 4. Msgr. S. Laszlo, Bishop of Eisenstadt, Austria, spoke during the second session about sin in the Church of God.

29. Innumerable texts. Likewise in the *Constitution on Divine Revelation* (art. 10) the Council speaks first of the relationship of Scripture and tradition to the whole Church before it clarifies the role of the magisterium.

30. See my *Méditations sur l'Eglise* (2nd ed. Paris, 1953) 48–49; *Catholicisme* (Paris, 1965) 40.

31. Thus Justin Martyr, *Dialogus cum Tryphone* 11, 5.

32. Would it be excessive to see in this chapter the fruit of a fortunate biblical movement, but one that has not as yet explored in depth the traditional teaching regarding the relationship between the two Testaments, of which the *Constitution on Divine Revelation* reminds us in a few words?

33. On the meaning of these images, which are more than mere "illustration," see K. Delahaye, *Ecclesia Mater chez les Pères des trois premiers siècles* (Paris, 1964) 35–53.

34. Y. de Montcheuil makes this point in his *Aspects de l'Eglise* (Paris, 1949) 19–22.

35. Cf. P. Meinhold, a Lutheran, who says: "Calling the Church the People of God with all its consequences may facilitate understanding among separated Christians" (G. Baraúna, *L'Eglise de Vatican II* [1965]). Y. Congar regards this chapter as "one of the most promising" (*ibid.*).

36. Cf. A. Scrima, *ibid.*, 1194. O. Clément (*L'Eglise orthodoxe* [Paris, 1965] 65) describes the Church directly as the body of Christ, "an organism whose head is in the heavens." The *Constitution on the Church* (art. 9) says the same: "That messianic people has for its head Christ . . . who now, having won a name which is above all names, reigns in glory in heaven."

37. Art. 6, 14, 42, 63.

38. *Demonstratio* 94.

39. *De Antichristo* 61. Also Methodius on "mater semper in partu."

40. Cf. J. Plumpe, *Mater Ecclesia* (Washington, 1943) 69–80.

41. *Ad martyres* 1; *De anima* 10.

42. *De catholicae ecclesial unitate* 6, 23; *Epist.* 74, 7: "ut habere quis possit Deum patrem, habeat antea ecclesiam matrem."

43. *Catech.* 18, 26.

44. See texts in P. Battifol, *Le catholicisme de s. Augustin* (5th ed. Paris, 1929) 270–274.

45. See note 33.

46. See the last pages of my *Exégèse médiévale* 4 (Paris, 1964).

47. The *relator* was Bishop J. Wright, of Pittsburgh. "Many bishops complained that the schema did not provide a theology of the laity without ever themselves contributing the elements of a clear doctrine" (A. Wenger, *Vatican II, Chronique de le deuxième session* 102–103)—in other words, all the essential doctrine that should be put in a chapter on the People of God.

48. This was discussed for only two days: Sept. 15–16, 1964.

49. Again on Sept. 30, 1963, Cardinal Frings deplored the absence of an eschatological perspective in the new schema.

50. 4, 2; Koetschau 308. Origen also speaks of "the Church of the first-born" or of "the first-born of the heavenly Church," understanding by that the members of the Church "whose names are inscribed in heaven" (*In Lucam Hom.* 7, 8; *In Rom.* 8, 5). This is quite close to our modern terminology.

51. *Adlocutiones paschales* 1.

52. *Adv. Haereses* 5, 35, 2.

53. *In Matt.* 4, 12; *PL* 9:935. Augustine, *In psalm.* 148, 4; *PL* 37:1940—the Church is the heavenly Jerusalem "in mysterio."

54. Cf. Augustine, *Enchiridion* 15, 56: "Ecclesia . . . quae tota hic accipienda est, non solum ex parte quae peregrinatur in terris . . . verum etiam ex illa quae in caelis semper ex quo condita est cohaesit Deo. . . . Haec in sanctis angelis beata persistit et suae parti peregrinanti sicut oportet opitulantur." But one can see the difference. (See *ibid.*, 29, 110, on prayer for the deceased.)

55. Cf. Butler, *op. cit.*, 89.

56. *In Ezech.* 2, hom. 1, 5; *PL* 76:338.

57. *De civitate Dei*, praef.: "Gloriossimam civitatem Dei, sive in hoc temporum cursu, cum inter impios peregrinantur ex fide vivens, sive in illa stabilitate sedis aeternae, quam nunc expectat per patientiam, etc."

58. It is not a question of a purely temporal history either in the Fathers or in our Constitution.

59. Cf. W. Visser't Hooft, *La royauté de Jésus-Christ* (Geneva, 1948) 44: "By means of the notion of the cosmic significance of Christ's victory Orthodoxy contributed to the enrichment of Western theology."

60. Ed. H. A. Wilson (Oxford, 1894) 82–83.

61. *In psalm.* 124, 4.

62. *Sermo* 105.

63. Cf. Augustine, *In Ioann tract.* 81, 4; *PL* 35:1842—"What we want because we live in Christ is one thing, what we want because we still live in this world is quite another."

64. Cf. *Méditations sur l'Eglise*, 56–63.

65. Discourse to Lenten preachers in Rome, Feb. 28, 1927.

66. Address opening the third session: "The Church is not an end unto herself." In December, 1962, Msgr. Huyghe criticized the first schema in these words: "The Church is described as a power. . . . Such a spirit . . . was not Christ's. In the Church founded by Christ, what does authority mean but service to others?"

67. *In Cant. comm.* 3.

68. *In Matt. comm.* 16, 8.

69. *Ermites du Saccidananda* (Tournai, 1956) 22.

70. Paris, 1965.

71. Vision 2, 4 (3rd tableau). Cf. 2 *Clem.* 14, 1, on "the spiritual Church created before the sun and the moon."

72. *Pedagogus* 1, 6, 27. For St. Ambrose, all the world is contained in the bosom of the Church: *In psalm.* 118 sermo 12, 25.

73. Augustine, *Sermo* 16, 8; *PL* 38:588.

74. The subcommittee preparing the schema on the Church decided at its first meeting November 26, 1960, to compose a provisional text including a chapter on Mary. See historical details in R. Laurentin, *La vierge au Concile* (Paris, 1965).

75. Address opening the second session. The insertion was requested by Cardinals Frings and Silva and Msgr. Garrone; Cardinal König pleaded the cause, and it was decided by a weak majority (1,114 against 1,074) on Oct. 29, 1963.

76. O. Casel, *Le mystère de l'Eglise, union de Dieu et des hommes* (Tours-Paris, 1965) 55. Cf. S. Tromp, *Ecclesia Sponsa, Virgo, Mater* (Rome, 1937).

77. *In Matt. comm.* 14, 17. Cf. *In Cant. hom.* 1, 7.

78. Cf. M. Agterberg, "*L'Ecclesia virgo* et la *virginitas mentis* des fidèles dans la pensée de s. Augustin," *Augustiniana* 9 (1959) 221–276.

79. At the beginning of this century one author put it: "In order to remove the smell of scandal from the Old Testament facts about the prophets, Christian exegesis turned their marriages into mysteries" (G. Oger, *Les Pères apostoliques* I, *Doctrine des apôtres* [Paris, 1907] xcix).

80. In *Maria* 7 (1964) 365–366.

81. In an article entitled "Marie, mère et type de l'Eglise" (*Osservatore Romano*, Feb. 7, 1964), C. Balić wrote: "All who love the freedom manifested at the Council are sure that complete freedom will be allowed to theologians to follow the traditional Christological path or the more recent ecclesiological one." The only thing is that the opposition between "traditional" and "more recent" is hardly exact.

82. Art. cit. (note 79) 367.

83. Tertullian, *De anima* 43; *PL* 2:723. Methodius, *The Banquet* 3, 8; 8, 8.

84. In *Lucam* 2, 7; *PL* 15:1555. Cf. Philips, art. cit. (note 79) 368.

85. In *Ioann.* tract. 13, 12; *PL* 35:1499. Sermo 191, 192; *PL* 38:1010, 1012–1013.

86. Cf. *Méditations sur l'Eglise*, 279–293. In a public audience May 27, 1964, Paul VI said: "[Mary is] the ideal figure of the Church, as St. Ambrose and, after him, St. Augustine say . . . . We find in Mary all the riches the Church represents, possesses, and dispenses. In Mary we have above all the virginal Mother of Christ, in the Church the virginal mother of Christians. . . . The Virgin's prerogatives are shared with the Church."

87. Cf. *Méditations sur l'Eglise*, 293–305.

88. Thus Serlon de Savigny in *Maria* 7 (1964) 390, 438.

89. The Orthodox know this: thus W. Losski, *Essai sur la théologie mystique de l'Orient* (Paris, 1944) 190.

90. Cf. Philips, art. cit., 381. Cf. In *Lucam* 2, 26; *PL* 15:1642. This was quoted by Paul VI (Laurentin, *La vierge au Concile*, 48).

91. K. Delahaye, op. cit. (note 33) 192.

92. Cf. Paul VI, address at St. Mary Major's, Oct. 11, 1963: "Bring it to be, O Mary, that the Church . . . in defining herself will recognize you for her mother, her eminent daughter and sister, her incomparable model, her joy and hope."

93. Doubtless it is to this sole text that Wenger refers when he writes: "The Council calls Mary mother of the faithful. . . . The pope goes much further" (*Chronique de la troisième session* [Paris, 1965] 112–113.)

94. For he did not say that he wanted the Council to give this title to Mary. "We hope that . . . the Council . . . will acknowledge the place, by far the most excellent, that Mary occupies in the Church . . . so that we will be able to honor her with the title *Mater Ecclesiae*."

95. In the audience Nov. 18, 1964, he said: "Mary has a unique position. She is a member of the Church; she too was redeemed by Christ and is our sister. However, precisely because of her election as Mother of the Reedemer and because she represents humanity perfectly and in a unique way, she can rightly be called in a moral and typical sense Mother of all men, especially our Mother, Mother of all the redeemed, of all believers, Mother of the Church, Mother of all the faithful." And at the Angelus on Nov. 22, 1964, he added that as "Mother full of charity," she is to be venerated by "all believers, by all of us, not only as isolated persons, but also as a community."

96. R. Laurentin, op. cit. (note 88) 40. "We proclaim the Most Blessed Mary Mother of the Church, that is, of all the People of God, of the faithful as well as of the pastors, who call her the most loving Mother."

97. In *Apoc.* 12, 14; *PL* 17:960. Cf. Bruno of Segni, In *psalm.* 44: Mary is "the lady of the whole Church" and "daughter of the Church" (*PL* 164:421, 857–858; 165:1021).

98. *De virginitate* 6; *PL* 40:399.

99. "In this text in which allusion is made to Eph 4:13, Mary asserts her spiritual maternity over all who hope in her Son. . . . This text, which enjoys no doctrinal authority, equivalently affirms Mary to be Mother of the Church" (Wenger, op. cit. [note 92] 124–125).

100. In this vein, Paul VI, on Nov. 21, 1964, said: "We wish especially brought out the fact that Mary, humble servant of the Lord, stands entirely in a relative position to God and to Christ, our unique Mediator and Redeemer."

101. Bibliography in Philips, *Maria* 7 (1964) 418–419.

102. For a Protestant witness, see M. Thurian, *Marie Mère du Seigneur, Figure de l'Eglise* (Taizé, 1962).

103. Trans. by R. Givord, 219.

104. Trans. by R. Givord, 25–26, 73–74, 101–113.
105. *L'Epée et le Miroir*, 198–203. Cf. my *Méditations sur l'Eglise*, 292–293, 321–324.
106. Pierre Teilhard de Chardin, *Ecrits du temps de la guerre* (Paris, 1965) 261.
107. In *Dieu Vivant* 3 (1945) 47–48.

Question: What is the present status of the Nota praevia?
What indication is there that the Nota praevia was not promulgated by the Council. Should it be taken into consideration by theologians in the explanation of chapter 3?

MEDINA: As I have suggested it, the problem of the Nota praevia is not
very clear. The historical background of this note, a very important element
in order to appreciate its content, is not yet fully known. At any rate, one
must say that the authority of the Nota praevia is very great indeed. One
could not afford to ignore it in an explanation of chapter 3 of the Constitution on the Church. However, one should add that Nota praevia is not a
Conciliar document in the same way as the Constitution Lumen Gentium.
It was pointed out that it was not put to the vote. It was simply announced
by higher authority that it was an element of interpretation of the chapter.
Therefore this Nota has great authority and must be taken into consideration
in the explanation, and I believe one can find in it some valuable points
not found in the text itself, for example, the brief piece on the condition of
ecclesiastical powers in the East and on the nature of the canonical determination in the appointment of bishops by the sovereign pontiff.

BUTLER: Could one perhaps point out that in interpreting a Conciliar document the text itself has primacy over all other considerations. It is not even of primary importance for the interpretation of the text to know what the Commission that composed it intended. Primary consideration is what the text itself says. And it remains true that the *Nota praevia* is not a Conciliar text.

> *Question: You have spoken of the primordial sacrament. This term designates the theological interpretation of Semmelroth, Rahner and Schillebeeckx, but the Council did not go so far as to accept this interpretation pertaining more to the tract on the sacraments than to ecclesiology. Furthermore, the Council did not use the expression primordial sacrament.*

MOELLER: I thank Father Congar for this question; it allows me to clarify a point that I left somewhat ambiguous. The Council did not use the expression primordial sacrament *Ursakrament*, because a council never adopts, as such, a theological theory or interpretation. And I am very happy to have the opportunity to recall this. However, there does exist this theological theory of the Church as the primordial sacrament, foundation of all the sacraments' efficacy because she is filled with Christ. It was precisely the German school that emphasized this aspect of the sacraments. And I believe, in passing, that historically it was the influence of certain German theologians in the episcopal conference at Fulda in 1963 that contributed toward the introduction of the theme of the Church as a sacrament. But the word "primordial" does not appear in the Constitution, and I am very happy that Father Congar has reminded us of this.

Furthermore, Father de Lubac as early as 1953 in his book, *Méditations sur l'Eglise*, devoted two chapters to the Church as mystery, and this book is at the basis of Semmelroth's book, *Die Kirche als Ursakrament*, published in 1964.

There is a second line of thought, and that is the Church as sacrament, taking the term "sacrament" in the sense of "mysterium," in the sense of the sign of the mystery, and bound up, as we said, with the Trinitarian life communicated through and by the Church. If Father Congar wants to insist, I would be very happy to hear him.

CONGAR: No. I was somewhat surprised that you did not develop further the idea of Church as sacrament. You have just barely touched on this subject. For my part, I believe that the Council takes the term in the second sense you have mentioned. *Ursakrament* is a theory of tract on the sacraments; but it is much more—it brings out the idea of the historical sign of grace, the historical form that grace takes in the world.

177

*Question: Canon Moeller said that there cannot be an iden-
tification between the mystical body and the Church. What
kind of identification does he mean? Is there any identification
at all? Please explain further the sense of the expression "subsists in." Is it used in a theological context, i.e., regarding
other doctrines that might clarify its meaning there?*

Moeller: In the first place, this idea of the Church, the mystical body,
this whole reality of the mystery of the Church which subsists in the visible
Church, must not be analyzed independently from the context. For example,
when one asks if "there is any identification at all," I do not think one can
say either yes or no. Because in one sense, the visible Church is identified
with Christ; in another sense, she is not identified with Christ. Therefore,
one should never lose sight of the context in which the Constitution speaks
of the Church as the body of Christ and also of the bride and where it
speaks of various other biblical images (art. 6–8). While originally this
article (6) on the various biblical images was only like a list appended to
the article treating of the Church as the body of Christ, it was later given a
fuller development, which is rather significant. Therefore, in order to answer
the question put to me, the problem is posed in terms of identification and
nonidentification as well as in terms of communion. Let me insist here on
one point. I have spoken about the Church as bride, about the possibility
it provides of ecumenical dialogue, and about how it brings out the face-to-
face encounter between the Church and Christ. I did not emphasize this,
but it goes without saying: the very notion, the very reality of marriage
signifies indissolubility in distinction, not separation.

And this leads me to a second complementary answer to the double question. Take a look at the context in a more narrow sense, the article itself
where we have the expression "subsists in." It is important to observe that
article 8 where we find "subsists in" starts with the mention of Christ. It is
completely Christological. It is in this sense that we must understand the
whole first paragraph, and the first paragraph of article 8 explains in what
sense one speaks of "subsists in" in the second paragraph. In the first paragraph the Church is presented in the context of Christ's incarnation. "Christ,
the one Mediator, established and ceaselessly sustains here on earth His
holy Church, the community of faith, hope and charity, as a visible structure." Thus the fundamental theme is stated. "Through her He communicates truth and grace to all. But the society furnished with hierarchical
agencies and the Mystical Body of Christ are not to be considered as two
realities, nor are the visible assembly and the spiritual community, nor the
earthly Church and the Church enriched with heavenly things. Rather they
form one interlocked reality which is comprised of a divine and a human

element." This is very important: when it speaks of two aspects of one reality, it doesn't say that they form two things, but one complex, interlocked reality. When it speaks of the human and divine elements, it points out the analogy with the incarnation. "For this reason, by an excellent analogy, this reality is compared to the mystery of the Incarnate Word." And here the Latin text is more cautious than the translation I just read: *non dissimili modo*. This means "pretty nearly in the same way." For one should show what light the analogy with the incarnation sheds on the distinction as well as on the unity between the visible and invisible in the Church, and at the same time the distinction and unity in Christ. And here in the text we read: "Just as the assumed nature inseparably united to the divine Word serves Him as the living instrument of salvation, so, in a similar way, does the communal structure of the Church serve Christ's Spirit, who vivifies it by way of building up the body." There is here a comparison very well known to the ancient tradition of the Council of Chalcedon. It is presented in a context which is more Western than Eastern, but in this context one can answer the question which was asked. I would say that the expression "subsists in" does not come directly from the vocabulary of the incarnation; it could not be used in that sense. But it must be understood in a general comparison with this mystery of incarnation.

WOLF: I would like to ask whether the concept of baptism as admitting to membership in the Church has some sort of theological relationship with the use of the word "subsist"?

MOELLER: No, no. Historically speaking, in the work of the commission it has not at all this objective in mind. One chose between "est" which was in the original version, or "adest" or "inest," and the expression "subsists in"; this last was retained as the formula that expresses two aspects at the same time: the indissolubility of the union, the same complex reality, and yet a certain distinction.

STRANSKY: I think what Professor Wolf was getting at was perhaps not understood by Canon Moeller. This is perhaps *the* most important one-word change in Vatican Council II—subsists *in*. The reason officially given was that de *facto* there does exist outside the visible boundaries of the Catholic Church *elementa bona sanctificationis*. I think this is a crucial issue for a theology of the Christian divisions, the relationship not only of individuals, but of non-Roman Catholic Christian communities, to the Roman Catholic Church, and vice versa. Much of it is based, I think, on this distinction between *est* and *subsistit in*. In fact, we do not have all of the Christian elements of sanctification existing within the Catholic Church. And what does this mean when we talk about where *is*, not subsists but where *is* the one, holy, catholic and apostolic Church professed by the creed.

MOELLER: I thank Father Stransky for this assistance. I did not fully understand the question put to me in this way. You are quite correct, because what in the paragraph follows the expression "subsists in" says exactly what you just said. Since there are elements of sanctification that exist in a way outside of this visible structure, to use the expression of the text itself, the expression "subsists in" was retained. But it is not linked to the theology of baptism, as such. But I am very grateful for your assistance, because, ecumenically speaking, this is fundamental, and we find it in the text.

CONGAR: What I want to say has already been partly said by Father Stransky. It appears to me that Canon Moeller has explained "subsists in" as if it were a question of the mystical body and union of Christ, whereas it is essentially a matter of the Church as a society. And it seems to me that the intention of "subsists in," as was said at the Council, is not to unchurch the other churches, not to disqualify other churches as churches. That is why this expression was repeated, at least by way of the allusion, at the beginning of the *Declaration on Religious Freedom*.

BUTLER: Father Congar said nearly all that I wish to say. I could perhaps add that Paul Evdokinoff in his book on Orthodoxy, giving the Orthodox position with regard to the identification of the Church (and I hope I am quoting him correctly), says that while it is possible to say where the Church is (and for him the answer to that question is, of course, in the Orthodox communion; a Roman Catholic will give a different answer), it is not so easy to say where the Church is not. I think the use of "subsists" here takes account of that curious situation.

> Question: Could you amplify further the distinction between
> the Church as the community of sinners and the Church as
> the sinful community?

MOELLER: I'll say first that I did not use the expression. I merely wanted to comment on the phrase *ecclesia sancta simul ac semper purificanda*. I insisted on the fact that in order to solve the problem it is not sufficient to appeal to the distinction between the Church as such and the members who are (I don't know exactly what they are) outside or vis-à-vis the Church, because they are not fully members of the Church. I simply wanted to insist on that fact. For a further explanation of this phrase I would refer you to the conclusion to Msgr. Philips' paper.

> Question: It has been said that for the Fathers the Church
> is the "we" of Christians; consequently ecclesiology encom-
> passes anthropology. What about Lumen Gentium from that
> particular point of view?

DE LUBAC: This view was not the object of any explicit topic in *Lumen Gentium* but it is evident that for a Christian any light shed on the Church is, in many respects directly or indirectly, a light on man, and consequently an anthropology. But I believe that *Lumen Gentium*, without knowing it itself, left to the pastoral *Constitution on the Church in the Modern World* the task of developing a few elements of anthropology in relation to the Church. It is more in the first part of the *Constitution on the Church in the Modern World* that we shall find a more explicit connection between Christian anthropology and ecclesiology. From a study of the Church in *Lumen Gentium*, or in patristic thought, we see that even when Christians were conscious of being nothing, of being a wretched and poor flock, people without any direct influence on the march of events, they always had a universal vision of salvation. This can be seen already in the New Testament and in almost all the texts of Christian antiquity. Deeply anchored in Christian revelation are the individual, interior as well as the universal diminsions of salvation. However, I do not find anything explicit in *Lumen Gentium* about the question Fr. Congar asked. At least, I can't recall anything.

> *Question:* When do you think Christian thought made the transition from the idea that the Church on earth is the Heavenly Church to the distinction between the two Churches, Militant and Triumphant?

DE LUBAC: Fortunately Fr. Congar himself gives the reply. He is more of a historian than I and is better acquainted with the texts than I, and he says here: "I believe it is about 1140." Of course, in such matters one cannot give an exact date or even a century. One can certainly determine the first time an expression, a distinction appears, but these expressions and distinctions arose only after the development of thought that already more or less contained them. At any rate, I believe it is toward the middle of the Middle Ages. But once again I do not think that it prevented true, genuine theologians, or even the spiritual Christian, from retaining a very lively idea of the unity of the Church, or the unity between the Church on earth and the Church in heaven. Even when Christians—in an earlier period, by the way —made a distinction between the body born of the Virgin, the Eucharistic Body and the body of the Church, they still believed that there was one body of Christ and one single Savior. And so to draw a clear-cut distinction here between the Churches doesn't prevent us from viewing the Church as one whole. But this can be dangerous, namely, to distinguish too sharply. After distinguishing one must unite. And here the Fathers are good counselors to us all. Do you have anything to add, Father Congar?

CONGAR: No. My date of 1140 comes precisely from a study of expres-sions. From the patristic expression *ecclesia cuius pars peregrinatur* (it is the Heavenly Church of which one part is still *in via*) we come to a distinction between *ecclesia militans* and *ecclesia triumphans*.

Question: Whether the new concept, or rather the new picture of the Church that emerges from Vatican II, the Church in the modern world, is in agreement with the views of the Fathers?

De Lubac: It is evident that since the situations are somewhat different, the nuances too are somewhat different. I believe, however, that one can find very interesting points of agreement that are very far-reaching. I am thinking now of that famous text of the Epistle to Diognetus, in which the author is conscious of the fact that Christians who have not yet hung their sign out on the street, so to speak, who have not organized themselves into a society that attracts the attention of all men, or who have certainly no power, no temporal power—that these Christians are the soul of the world. I think this is one of the powerful ideas regarding the Church in the world, as it emerges from the texts of Vatican II, especially from the pastoral Constitution on the Church in the Modern World, if one wants to understand it well. And as you know, the Epistle to Diognetus is quoted in chapter 4 on the laity in Lumen Gentium (art. 38). It is quoted in connection with the laity, but it could be quoted in reference to all Christians. There is here an agreement between the thought of the Epistle to Diognetus and the thought of Vatican II. And this is not a marginal view; it is one of the fundamental ideas.

Cooke: It seems to me, Father, that you have, fairly early in the patristic period, the influence of the Platonic point of view, in which the world is something rather to be escaped from than to be involved in. I wonder if there is not a change of viewpoint now, as represented in Vatican II, a reorientation of the Church's thought to a more realistic acceptance of the material world.

De Lubac: I do not think that we should exaggerate. On the one hand, we find what is called a cosmic viewpoint among the Fathers, even the most Platonist. And on the other hand, if today we believe that the Church must insert herself in the world, this is because she must become the soul of the world and lead it eventually to its end; it must pass through death to transfiguration. Therefore, the two viewpoints are much closer than is brought out in antitheses that are, I think, a little too fictitious. Let's take a contemporary author, whose thoughts I do not want to discuss here, but who is like a symbol of cosmic thinking in a theology that takes terrestrial realities, human things, into account. The thought of Teilhard de Chardin is entirely eschatological. He laid tremendous stress on the total death and transfiguration of the cosmos and consequently on the necessary detachment with which the Christian must act within the world as he gives himself with genuine passion to human work. Human work is good, first of all, because creation comes from God, but also because it is a necessary condition for parousia. We need complete detachment from all the external particular forms of everything in the world. And so, he has quite a Platonic vocabulary; he speaks of flight, of escape, of running away from this world. And for him the greatest misfortune would be to remain imprisoned within this cosmos. His vocabulary is more Platonic than some of the contemporaries of Plato. That is why I don't think there is such an opposition. There would be an opposition, if we thought that the service rendered by the Church to the world is only to help the affairs of the world along without any eschatological perspective. That would indeed be a distortion of what the Council teaches us.

BURGHARDT: Père de Lubac, my question goes, I think, to the root of why the Council goes back so much to patristic thought, and secondarily why you find it important to give a paper on the relationship between *Lumen Gentium* and patristic thought. My question would come down to this. Is the Church just going back, has the Church rediscovered remarkable ideas, fruitful ideas, that have been lost somewhat in the course of the centuries between the patristic age and ours? Or are we in an evolution, a development of doctrine where these ideas are germinally present in the patristic era and are just coming to a flowering in the Council?

DE LUBAC: Every time the Church inquires about her own faith, and about her thought, about her theology, she instinctively turns back to the Fathers. She calls them "Fathers," not only because they are ancient writers, but because she finds in them a kind of paternity and, consequently, an element that we can call permanent, eternal. However, this should not lead us to believe that in the years that have just passed, especially in the work done before the Council and by the Council, there has been a remarkable discovery of the study of the past along with a discarding of what happened in the last few centuries. Not at all. May I perhaps give you a concrete example? I recall that in my youth as a student I heard it said that the previous generation had neglected the Fathers, but we were going through a patristic renewal. I heard it again after World War I and still again after World War II. In other words, there is a kind of perpetual resurrection, perpetual rediscovery of the Fathers. But perhaps it has become more apparent now after Vatican II. The theologians of any century who now come to the fore the most—a Möhler, a Newman, for instance—were essentially patristic. And their entire doctrine was based on the Fathers. And the great editions of the Fathers, the reading of the Fathers, in our great seventeenth-century France, were extremely popular. At the end of the fifteenth century there was a great renaissance of the Fathers, as compared with the fourteenth and the beginning of the fifteenth century when they suffered a slight decline. St. Thomas Aquinas himself in the thirteenth century said that he would give the whole city of Paris to have a better manuscript of St. John Chrysostom.

Was it a question of rediscovering an ancient element or of a development? I think that by giving a few examples I have shown that the Council, on the basis of the patristic thought (and in a sense rediscovering it), has nevertheless set forth new harmonies because there are new situations at present. Because it wanted, for the first time, to set up an official text of doctrine on the Church, and to bring to it some light, some logic, some unity, Vatican II was obliged to make a choice in its perspective, not in its doctrines, of course, but in its perspective. And hence, while using concepts and notions that are found in the Fathers of the Church, Vatican II has put its own mark on them, it chose from among them, it put a certain inflection on them.

CONGAR

LINDBECK

COLOMBO

SESSION V

RT. REV. GERARD PHILIPS
The Church: Mystery and Sacrament

REV. YVES M. J. CONGAR, O.P.
The People of God

MOST REV. CARLO COLOMBO
The Hierarchical Structure of the Church

DR. GEORGE A. LINDBECK
A Protestant Point of View

Rt. Rev. Gerard Philips

THE CHURCH: MYSTERY AND SACRAMENT

T HESE FEW PAGES ARE INTENDED to describe the spirit in which we should read and understand the first chapter of the *Constitution on the Church*. Without being a commentary properly so-called, they will, we hope, clarify the doctrinal exposition as from within by pointing out its main lines in order to shed the greatest possible light on the mystery.

CHRISTOCENTRISM

From the beginning, the *Constitution on the Church* explicitly adopts a Christocentric perspective, one which runs like a golden thread throughout the whole treatment. The Church has a profound conviction that the light of the nations does not radiate from her but from her divine Founder; however, she also knows that the radiance reflecting from her countenance reaches out to all humanity and bathes it in the ineffable brightness that emanates from God alone. St. Paul affirms this in his famous text on the transforming glory of the Lord (2 Cor 3:18).

The Church transmits this light to men by preaching the good news to every creature, a limitless perspective set by the immense horizons of the gospel itself and necessarily implied in the *universality of the redemptive mission* of Christ. As reduced in her resources as one can imagine, the Church is nonetheless sent to all men without restriction, although she will never achieve her mission until the end of time. The impetus received orients all her dynamism toward totality of mankind in an effort that cannot let up for a single instant. This is the very reason for the Christian community's life and gives it an awareness of bearing a responsibility that transcends boundaries and frontiers. Thus the Council shows unequivocally that it is not pursuing a policy of power or human prestige; the unique end, the only motive, is the glory of the Lord.

SACRAMENT

That is why the Church is aware of being the *sacrament* of the encounter with God. The wider meaning given here to the word "sacrament" is hard for certain Christians to assimilate, even though contemporary theologians are trying to re-evaluate this authentic patristic conception. While taking care to explain the exact meaning of this expression, the Council does not hesitate to make it its own. It defines it as the *sign* and the *instrument* by which God raises men to intimacy with him and thus realizes, in the bosom of his eternal Being, the total unification of the human race.

Sign and instrument do not constitute two separate entities; it is through the symbol itself that divine action works. As opposed to "new" peoples who have remained much more receptive to the suprasensible, outlined rather than clearly defined by symbols, our intellectualism has made us almost impervious to any sacred symbolism; happily a reaction against this narrow rationalism is appearing. If the creature always exists in relation to his Creator (without which, according to the standard mythical expression, the creature would be cast into nothingness), the outpouring of the divine we are speaking of here "signifies" an inconceivable degree of intimacy, by this very fact placing the unity of the human race on an infinitely superior level.

Nor are sign and instrument separate *things*. Christ alone is the fundamental sacrament; the Church is a sacrament only by association with him. By means of sign language one person speaks to another and initiates by his word an interpersonal encounter. In the sacrament, the word joined to the gesture becomes the visible word (*verbum visibile*), according to the forceful expression of St. Augustine, because addressed to men—spirits incarnated in matter. The sign ensures a participation in a higher life. Hence it is quite rightly called an *instrument*, since it shows itself a bearer of divine efficiency. But let not the somewhat material resonance of the term "instrument" deceive us. It is really a communion on the spiritual plane, even if it is established between men, therefore between bodies animated by spirit.

It is, therefore, quite natural to see the Fathers, following Scripture (cf. 1 Tm 3:16), greet Christ the Redeemer with the title of *sacrament* or *mystery* (a simple transcription of the Greek equivalent). "Mystery" is the divine decree by which the Father realizes his salvific will in Christ, at the same time that he reveals it through the mesh of a temporal reality that retains all its transparency. St. Augustine wrote: "The mystery [or sacrament] of God is nothing else than Christ."[1] And Pope Leo the Great insisted that "all the saints—even those who lived before the time of our Lord—are justified by this faith and became the body of Christ by this sacrament."[2] Thus we see the title *sacrament* lean almost imperceptibly toward the Church, which permits St. Augustine to declare: "The Church of the baptized is the *mystery* of the saving ark."[3] St. Cyprian is even more categorical: "The Church is the indivisible *sacrament of unity*."[4] Relying on these explicit witnesses of Scripture and the Fathers, Henri de Lubac has a perfect right to say that the Church "is here below the sacrament of Jesus Christ as Jesus Christ is himself for us, in his humanity, the sacrament of God."[5]

Of course, for the faithful the term evokes above all the seven rites that transmit grace, the list of which the Council of Trent solemnly proclaimed.[6] But these sacred signs can be understood only as different means that permit the saving institution par excellence, the Church, to sanctify the Christian in the various phases of his life. A valid theology of the seven sacraments always presupposes this relation to the sacramentality of the Church. The efficacy of the sacred symbols leads us to ineffable communion with God, and through it, to true union with others, and not the reverse. Like every sacrament, the Church comes from God. If this were not so, the whole process would remain on the level of a sterile effort of man to achieve his redemption by himself, the formidable temptation of modern times. Actually, without this perspective, the mystical body simply ceases to be intelligible, whether in itself or in its universal mission.

The Church is then the sacrament of union with God and, thereby, of the mutual union of believers in the same élan of love toward him. Thus, it has value as a sign for the whole human race. It is not her role, it is true, to work directly toward universal peace; the task of building a peaceful planetary order belongs to the nations. But for the achievement of this ideal the unity of the Church is for all men a perpetual invitation, a living example, a source of unfailing energy.

The problem of the Church, the principal lines of which become gradually clearer from the end of medieval Christianity, is seen in its totality by the Reformation and by the Council of Trent. It is now no longer a matter of "what the Church proposes for our belief," but of *the Church herself*, of what she "is" for the believer. From this flows her mission—and hence her right and even duty—of handing on the good news. In our time, attacking a specific point of Catholic doctrine is largely outdated, and heresies of this type appear as anachronisms. Modern man is radical; rather than waste his energies on a particular dogma, he rejects with disdain the very notion of dogma.

It is not by chance that the dogmatic *Constitution on the Church* gradually took on the importance of a keystone for Vatican Council II; all the rest, indeed, was determined by it. The apologetic character of the ecclesial controversy was not misunderstood, but was singularly surpassed. The Council sees the Church, as the symbol presents her to us, that is, as the *object* of the act of *faith*, as holder and propagator of holiness under the impulse of the Spirit. In its *Constitution on Faith* Vatican Council I proposed the Church as an argument of credibility and designated her by means of an expression that has since become famous: "She is the standard raised up before the nations."[7] Now the faithful penetrate the Holy of Holies of the Church in order to encounter Christ, the author and apogee of unity not only among Christians but among all men.

MYSTERY

As a rule, theological treatises rarely emphasize the relations between the Church and the Holy Trinity—the fundamental mystery, not only of theology but also of the whole Christian life. How many Catholics look upon the Trinity as an untouchable dogma, one having little relation to their concrete existence. This impenetrable mystery seems to them a formidable rock of majesty, but it has also the immovable coldness of a rock; it radiates no warmth of life. On the contrary, revelation teaches us to know the divine Persons precisely in their salvific activities. Hence the *Constitution on the Church* could not have been given a better beginning than this reminder of the plan of salvation which the eternal Father designed for us and which he achieves through the incarnation of his Son and the mission of the Holy Spirit.

It is solely by the word of God that the Church could come to know this economy of salvation decreed by God, and in the first place *by Scripture*. The gospels rarely speak of "the Church," but almost always of the "kingdom"; this fact deserves the greatest attention, especially in the numerous parables that begin: "The kingdom of God is like a field, a house, a flock, a wife, and so on." These same figures are found as well in many places in the epistles. St. Paul develops one of them into an extended allegory, that of the body of Christ or of a body whose head is Christ. In the present state of ecclesiology the schema had to consider carefully these diverse images.

All we have just said describes the Church as having very mysterious features. From another point of view she appears as a visible society which is not her double, but rather her epiphany in the world. Post-Tridentine theology often takes as the starting point of its speculations the definition of the

190

Church as a perfect society, as visible, Bellarmine would say, as the republic of Venice. A historian would hardly say that the origins of the Most Serene go back to a decree of the eternal Father; yet the Bible does say this for the Church, and it is striking to note to what degree the Council accepts this point of view. The *Constitution on the Church* begins not with a definition, but with the affirmation of a fact of "history" (of sacred history, obviously). For the faith, the economy of salvation willed by God is at the very basis of the Church, and anyone who wishes to describe her development should begin with the foundation before worrying about the roof or the decoration of the facade. Every Christian should make this evangelical "reconversion" for himself and change completely the poles of his perspective. He will then see that, far from constraining him to walk on his head, this attitude will put him on his feet again.

In a sense the New Testament identifies the Church with Christ; in another, it opposes her to him. The Constitution underlines this twofold process of identification and opposition, especially when it seeks to examine thoroughly the parallelism between the Incarnate Word and the ecclesiastical community. Its first chapter ends with a vision of the final episode in which unity will attain its fullness and the depths of its mystery will shine in all its splendor.

The Final Stage

At the time of the glorious *Eschaton* the Church will then be seen to embrace all the elect without distinction. There will then no longer be any "anonymous Christians," saved by the grace of Christ but without any visible contact with him here on earth. Assumed into the Church of the blessed, each of the elect will see his Savior and pay homage to him.

The Church, then, is here understood in the broadest sense, which, in fine, comes down to being her only exact meaning. In this world her stature is still so imperfect that she achieves only partially her own definition. This is what explains her painful striving toward the final state: she must still become (completely) what she already is now (in an incomplete but very real way). That is why the Constitution abstained from considering this broader meaning before the end of its declaration, in order to view it then in the light of eschatological fulfillment. Meanwhile, the Fathers often speak of the Church "from Abel, the just one, to the last of the elect."

How should we understand this teaching of tradition? The answer is a delicate one. In the eyes of those whose witness we have just invoked, the "body" to which the just living under the Old Covenant already belong, or even before it, is indeed the visible and hierarchical Church founded by Christ and propagated under the inspiration of the Holy Spirit through the preaching of the Apostles. They know no other Church than this one. But for the faithful there are several ways of belonging to her. The most important of all is *communion with Christ the Savior*, origin of all life and source of all grace. As Mediator transcending time and space he established an organism for the purpose of procuring the means of salvation for all it can reach, but to it also belong all the elect who are prevented by circumstances of time and place from receiving the sacraments of the New Law. These too will be saved by faith in the humanity of Christ or, as the Bible says, "in his body." Into this body he assumes all who welcome him; he leads them to the eternal Church by means of a process that, in many cases, completely escapes our vision here below.

But to reject knowingly this *Church-as-visible-sacrament* is to reject at the same time Christ as Mediator; it is to cut oneself off from the "body" of the Lord on all levels. For the Lord himself willed this concrete form of incorporation and placed it in time and space in order that, to the extent of their possibilities, and therefore at least in their hearts, all men hasten to join it.

In other words, the fact that, according to the Fathers, the body of Christ exercises its saving action beyond the limits of time and space in no way contradicts the other fact that, to lead men to God in a truly human way, he subjected himself to the limitations of time and space. Conversely, the foundation of a Church as an institution of salvation channeling and dispensing grace in no way prevents this countless crowd, deprived of all visible contact with the hierarchical Christian society, from entering the communion of saints. They too are bound to the Church, for her reality extends to the infinite; she too transcends time and space and completes herself by emerging in full eternity.

The Council stresses this "totalizing" aspect of the Church so strongly, without thereby dissolving her features in an ethereal vagueness, because our times are the first truly to realize the incredible number of generations that lived before Christ or the enormous number of contemporary masses that have never heard of him. How many of these will be found in the triumphant Universal Church. This is the secret of the last day.

CHURCH AND TRINITY

The prologue of the Constitution ends with a compact and concise reminder of the theme *Ecclesia de Trinitate*, the Church as fruit of the Holy Trinity. The quotation is taken from St. Cyprian: "The Church is the unified people that participates in the unity of the Father, the Son and the Holy Spirit." For this holy doctor, the phrase does not have the value of a "definition" of the Church, but it illustrates a text on the prayer that establishes her unity, the Lord's Prayer.[8]

The neat play on words of the original is practically untranslatable. "De unitate . . . plebs adunata." The Latin preposition *de* evokes both the idea of imitation and that of participation; it is "starting" from this unity among the divine Hypostases that "the unification" of the people spreads. By becoming unified the people participate in another Unity, so that according to St. Cyprian, the unity of the Church can in no way be understood without that of the Trinity.

May Catholics, if only at the reminder of their baptism included in the least sign of the cross, never lose sight of this profound symbiosis: Trinity-Church! The Roman Creed underlines this association by an ingenious comparison of terms: *Credo in Spiritum Sanctum, sanctam ecclesiam*. The words *Sanctum-sanctam* suggest eloquently the Church one and Catholic, sanctified by the Spirit who is holy.

One can only rejoice in noting that, in its declaration of principle at the congress in New Delhi in 1961, the World Council of Churches insisted on this explicit reference to the Trinity: "The love of the Father and of the Son in the unity of the Holy Spirit is the source and end of this unity which God, Father, Son and Holy Spirit, willed among all men and in all creation. We believe that we participate in this unity in the bosom of the Church of Jesus Christ who was before all things and through whom everything subsists. In him alone, destined by the Father to be the Head of the body, the Church possesses this true unity which the gift of the Holy Spirit revealed on the day of Pentecost."

Professor Sittler of Chicago, a member of the United Lutheran Church of America, makes this judicious commentary: "By recognizing the indestructible bonds that unite Jesus Christ to the Church, we are necessarily led to confess the Holy Trinity . . . foundation of the Church." It would be interesting to follow his whole exposition step by step and to compare it with the first part of the *Constitution on the Church*. We shall not follow Professor Sittler to the point of reproaching the Catholic Church for having, since St. Augustine, dug an abyss between creation and grace; let us hope that a true dialogue will shed full light on this divergence. We are not losing sight of the fact that the Trinitarian profession in question was admitted only after having aroused objections from several Protestant groups. The declaration of New Delhi remains remarkable, nonetheless, and to such a point that one could, as Fr. Le Guillou has pointed out, give it the same title the Fathers of Vatican Council II gave to the first chapter of their principal Constitution: "The Mystery of the Church."[9]

May I point out the urgent obligation incumbent on Catholics to place the Conciliar vision of the "Church-mystery-of-faith" within the reach of the average layman. On this point, even our theology textbooks need a thorough revision. Before achieving that, we must expend considerable effort with perfect docility to the promptings of the Holy Spirit.

The Visible and Spiritual Church

Only with the eyes of faith can one see the Church as she is described in the first chapter of the *Constitution on the Church*. This chapter also speaks of functions that go to make up an organ one can see with human eyes. It is from this latter viewpoint that the unbelievers "see" the Church and that her enemies can persecute her. To recognize the Church as the house of God, as body and bride of Christ, is beyond their capacity. Perhaps we are not sufficiently aware of the fact that these considerations likewise rise above the intellectual capacity of Catholics; for them, too, it is faith, and faith alone, that reveals this mystery to them. In general, they receive it with joy, though they are often less enthusiastic about accepting ecclesiastical institutions and their leaders such as they see them with their own eyes. Even though they may complain about authority, they do not fail to exalt the Church of the Spirit, as they imagine her idealized features in eternal mansions. More than one sect has succumbed to this Illuminist temptation.

This is what the Council teaches. The Church as a mystery has truly appeared on earth in a concrete and tangible form, and she remains present here for if she did not we could not speak of a "mystery." For mystery, according to the New Testament, is God's plan of salvation as he revealed it in this world through transparent veils. This revealing in our time lifts only in part the veil from the hidden reality. But this does not mean that the result is two different realities, still less, that they are opposed to each other. At the most, one can speak of two situations of one same reality or of two elements that form a complex whole. It is too evident that the two designations, *mystical body* and *ecclesiastical organization,* do not have the same evocative force. They both express in effect, a special aspect of the same institution of Christ. It is not possible to transpose every qualification of one concept to the other, or of one image to the other, without adding to it delicate nuances, just as one cannot purely and simply identify the allegory of the body and that of the bride.

The fundamental unity of the living Church is affirmed in the Conciliar text in three different ways; it is not possible to divorce concepts grouped in pairs:

> hierachical society—mystical body of Christ
> visible assembly—spiritual community
> earthly Church—the Church enriched with heavenly things.

The two descriptions in each group are not, for all that, said to be identical;

194

we are facing a complex reality that is indivisible but is nonetheless composed of a human and divine element.

The *Constitution on the Church*, for its part, reveals in this unique whole a certain diversity of aspects and, what is more, an organic structure. Human and divine elements, if one may so speak, are linked together interiorly. Merely juxtaposed, they would not form a unity. However, we are in the presence of an indissoluble union that one can quite properly compare to the mystery of the incarnation of the Word. The humanity of Jesus is the *conjoined instrument* of his divinity.

"In a similar way" (non dissimili modo), the Constitution says with great care (art. 8), the social organization of the Church is at the service of the Spirit for the edification of the body (cf. Eph 4:16). The Church, then, does not form a hypostatic union between the baptized and the Holy Spirit, but a most profound and efficacious union that issues in redeeming actions.

The structural union of the Church and the Spirit is of prime importance for theological explanation. The Church is the *sign* of the presence of the Holy Spirit and who accomplishes, in and through her, the salvation of the elect. To be at once sign and cause of grace, constitutes the very essence of the *sacrament* or *mystery*: visible sign of the invisible power. We are still, and always will be, face to face with the Church, sacrament or mystery.

Conclusion

At the end of the first chapter, the Constitution uses a text of St. Augustine[10] to describe the arduous ascent of the Church, persecuted and consoled, fortified by the living hope of the dead and risen Lord's return. Consolation comes from God, persecution comes from the world, says St. Augustine. The Church encounters within and without the trials and difficulties over which she must triumph. Since the enemy is always on the prowl within the walls, even if only secretly, it will never do to build a rampart around the Church and let her be enclosed within her fortress—a prey to the fever of siege—and forgetful of her duty of bringing the message openly to the world.

She will only conquer stubborn difficulties with charity and patience of the Spirit. Let us reread carefully the following sentence, for it may well be the most important in the whole chapter. Thus the Church "*shows forth in the world the mystery of the Lord in a faithful though shadowed way*, until at the last it will be revealed in total splendor" (art. 10).

The weaknesses, the difficulties, yes the inadequacies of the Church as an earthly society, are not chimerical but real. Nor is the victory of Christ's Church over all these difficulties fictitious but very real—at least for him and in him who believes.

By comparing the Constitution's last sentence with the teaching of Vatican Council I on the Church as holy and infinitely sanctifying—attributes cited as guarantees of her truth and which make of her, as the text says, "a standard raised up before the nations"[11]—we can see not only a fundamental resemblance but also a remarkable change of tone. In the *Constitution on the Church* human triumph nowhere comes through. Let us recognize, however, that Vatican Council I refers also to "the supernatural power of God" (*ex superna virtute*), in order to make the faith triumph. Vatican Council II offers a realistic theological clarification of the doctrine that Vatican Council I had treated primarily according to apologetic principles. Precisely because the Church, though composed of weak men, produces unquestionable fruits of holiness, we can conclude in the spirit of faith: here God accomplishes his work; light from above shines through the shadows.

In this way, the Church becomes *object* of our faith, a continuation of the mystery of the Holy Trinity and of redemptive incarnation—as the beginning of the first chapter shows us. Here we are fully in a dogmatic theology at once of the cross and of the transfiguration, because it brings back everything to the central mystery of Christ, the Son of the saving God.

NOTES

1. *Epist.* 187, 11; *PL* 33:845.
2. *Sermo* 30, 7; *PL* 54:234. Cf. *Sermo* 32, 1; *PL* 54:314.
3. *De bapt. contra Donatistas* 28, 39; *PL* 43:196.
4. *Epist.* 52, 21; *PL* 3:787.
5. *Méditation sur l'Eglise* (Paris, 1953) 157ff.
6. Denzinger-Schönmetzer 1601.
7. *Ibid.*, 3013ff.
8. *De oratione Dominica* 23; *PL* 4:553. Cf. M. Réveilland, *St. Cyprien, l'Oraison dominicale* (Paris, 1964).
9. "Le Conseil Oecuménique et la recherche de l'unité," *Vers l'Unité chrítienne* 15 (1962) 53–58.
10. *De civitate Dei* 18, 51, 2; *PL* 41:614.
11. Denzinger-Schönmetzer 3013ff.

Rev. Yves M. J. Congar, O.P.

THE PEOPLE OF GOD

THE DRAFT OF THE *Constitution on the Church*, drawn up by the preparatory theological commission before the opening of the Council, included, among its eleven chapters one, number 6, entitled *De laicis*. The discussion of this draft as a whole, at the beginning of December, 1962, led the Council's Theological Commission to propose a schema in four chapters, the third of which was entitled "Of the People of God, Especially of the Laity." The term "People of God" did not have here its full biblical meaning. It was taken rather in the sense of "people of the Church," and from a still somewhat juridical point of view. When the text was discussed however, starting October 15, 1963, the situation had already changed. On a motion of the Coordinating Commission,[1] the Theological Commission had already agreed to divide this chapter into two parts and to allocate the contents to a separate chapter on the People of God and a chapter on the laity. The People of God chapter took its place between chapter 1, on the mystery of the Church, in which the Church is linked to her divine causes, and the chapter devoted to the hierarchy. We believe that this decision was one of the most important made, and that chapter 2 on the People of God, as it was finally drawn up and voted by the assembly (September 17, 1964), has the greatest promise for the theological, pastoral and ecumenical future of ecclesiology.

The initial idea behind a chapter devoted to the People of God and for putting it in this particular place—that is to say, between the mystery of the

Church and the hierarchy—was to follow the proper method of describing first what is common to several categories before considering what is peculiar to each one: the generic before the specific. It is for this reason that we have a treatise on the virtues in general or (and this is more debatable) on the sacraments in general before the treatises devoted to each of the virtues or to each of the sacraments. Likewise, before speaking of the hierarchy, of the laity and of religious, it was fitting to state what was common to all. But the significance of this step was to extend well beyond its interest from the viewpoint of method! Indeed, what is common to all is nothing less than Christian existence. Under these conditions, the Council committed itself not only to giving at least a quick look at what a Christian man is, but to recognizing the priority and even the primacy of the ontology of grace, which makes a man Christian, over organizational structures and hierarchical positions.

As regards the first point, the chapter on the People of God has some very valuable elements; it does not sketch out a Christian anthropology. As a matter of fact, this was not the ideal place to do it. The Christian man is considered here only insofar as he is a member of God's People. The Council, I might add, ran into anthropology in many of the paths it entered upon: People of God, apostolate of the laymen, religious liberty, Christian education, the Church in the modern world, etc. It was in the *Constitution on the Church in the Modern World* that the Council studied the question more closely, without, however, taking up all the aspects of modern man or using all the resources of biblical tradition. Its vision remained too static. In our chapter man is seen in his natural state, at one and the same time threatened by evil, yet capable of bringing something to the kingdom of God (cf. art. 13, 16, 17); according to his new birth through the water of the Holy Spirit he is a *consecrated* being, both priest and prophet. He becomes personally involved in a spiritual worship and is the subject of Christian liturgical action. He knows the meaning of faith thanks to which, from the viewpoint of its unity, totality, and unanimity, the People of God cannot fail in their faith.[2] This prerogative is linked to the anointing of the Holy Spirit, which is the action by which God raises and nourishes faith in the hearts of those who understand the word of truth coming from Christ.[3] We are far from the words of George Tyrrell, who said that according to Catholic doctrine the Church or the body of the faithful could only be called infallible "because it possessed an infallible pope, somewhat as though a flock of sheep united with its shepherd could be called intelligent."[4] We are far from the formula which Möhler used in 1823 to sum up the ecclesiology he had received from the rational theology of the eighteenth century: "God created the hierarchy and thus he provided more than sufficiently for the needs of the Church until the end of the world."[5] The Council recognized the place of the magisterium from which the faithful receive the objective determination of their faith, but one of its characteristic theological steps was to attribute again to God as to their subject operations that create the People of God and bring about salvation.[6] This is emphasized by rather notable statements about the charisms or spiritual gifts parceled out by the Holy Spirit within the Church for the common good (art. 12). This is not the only place in the Constitution where the Church is seen as an "event" constantly giving existence to the "institution."

We shall see that this People of God is *de iure* coextensive with humanity. However, it exists in a concrete and visible form through a positive initiative of God. However, it can only be truly a people if it has a certain structure. A people is more than a collection of individuals without any organic links with one another—in the same way that a tree is more than a certain quantity of wood cut and piled up: it has a structure, roots, a trunk, branches and leaves. A house is more than tons of stone heaped in a pile; it has a structure determined by its end. Thus, a people is a stable and structured group, united for the purpose of attaining the same good. Hence, in article 9 of chapter 2 we find these expressions of great depth and immense significance: "It has pleased God, however, to make men holy and save them not merely as individuals without any mutual bond, but by making them into a single people, a people which acknowledges Him in truth and serves Him in holiness. . . . That messianic people has for its head Christ. . . . The heritage of this people are the dignity and freedom of the sons of God, in whose hearts the Holy Spirit dwells as in His temple. Its law is the new commandment to love as Christ loved us. Its goal is the kingdom of God."

In proposing chapter 2 on the People of God, the Council also committed itself, as we have said, to recognize the priority and even the primacy of the ontology of grace, which makes a man Christian, over organizational structures and hierarchical positions. It is a fact that we are emerging from a predominantly juridical view of the Church. It had been necessary, in order to meet the denials or misunderstandings of Protestants, to affirm the visibility of the Church and of its hierarchical structure, and, therefore, also its nature as a juridical society. Too often this was all that was spoken of. The Church seemed entirely to consist of this. The Church was the clergy, or even the pope; the faithful were hardly more than the object over which the clergy exercised authority and concern. In the past the categories used when speaking of the Church were those of society, power and hierarchy. Hence the strong juridical bent of ecclesiology generally taught until the contemporary ecclesiological renewal.[7] We can speak of juridicism, and it is juridicism, when primacy is given to juridical structures and rules—however necessary and good they may be in their own order—rather than to the ultimate realities of life.

Vatican II has eliminated juridicism in more than one way. In particular, the Council gave a sacramental ontological foundation to the powers of the hierarchy (the episcopate) and to the apostolic mission itself (priesthood, apostolate of the laity). One of its most decisive steps in this direction was the chapter on the People of God and the place assigned it between the explanation of the mystery of the Church (the Church linked to its divine causes) and the chapter devoted to the hierarchical constitution of the Church. This meant that the most profound value is not what makes the Church a society, "societas inequalis, hierarchica," but what makes it a community through the participation of a great number of people in the same goods of divine life. Hence, the first value is not organization, mediatorial functions, or authority, but the Christian life itself and being a disciple. All this was evident to one who reads Holy Scripture, the Fathers of the Church, even the medieval and great scholastic theologians.[8] The Council went back to this tradition. That is also why it often presented the greatness of the hierarchy as one of service: a service of the sovereign action of God, of his word, a service to men and the world for their salvation, a service of the lasting greatness of holiness. The sublimity of hierarchical functions consists in their ordination to service. What nobler thing can one do than to make men disciples of the gospel?

The notion "People of God" has its own rich meaning which comes from the Old Testament. The Council's text does not develop all its aspects but they are necessarily connoted. One cannot reintroduce such a rich category in ecclesiology without certain consequences. With it comes the idea of election and of calling or convocation; by this very fact it invites us to bring our tract on the Church into accord with those on predestination and grace. The biblical idea of election is always that of setting someone aside to carry out a plan in the world. It involves the notion of consecration: the People of God is consecrated to know God, and to praise him, but also to be his witness. It is not set apart in order to remain separated, but rather to serve God in the fulfillment of his universal plan of salvation. It is dedicated to an action, to serve the dynamism of a mission.

The notion "People of God" has still other uses. To our mind there are two principal ones.

TO POINT UP AND SITUATE THE HISTORICITY OF THE CHURCH

The Church was first shown (ch. 1) to be dependent on its divine causes and even, through the mission of the divine Persons, on the mystery of God himself. But the Church is made up of men and placed in the world; chapter 1 ends with a long article (8) in which the Church is shown as being both visible and spiritual, pursuing here below the way of humility and service inaugurated by Christ in his redemptive incarnation. Chapter 2 on the People of God then emphasizes the historical quality of the Church: "in historiam hominum intrat." One of the purposes of the chapter formally expressed in the *Relatio* is to show the Church taking shape in human history. Article 9 broadly sketches this entry into history. Shall we use here the expression "history of salvation"? The text does not. Beautiful though it may be, it has something ambiguous about it. In effect, the history of salvation starts with the beginnings of humanity (cf. Gn 3:15). Today it is thought that this takes us back perhaps a million years before Christ or even before Abraham, father and first link of God's People in its visible and public historical reality. Salvation was there, and hence, in ways and in a mode that theologians must strive to define, there was faith and charity, grace and the presence of Christ during the ten thousand centuries that preceded the eighteen centuries reaching from Abraham to Jesus. "If Christ is the center of history, he cannot be absent from any moment of history" (F. Ravaisson). Should we call the People of God the sum total of all the individuals saved, even apart from positive and public revelation. The Council does not. It prefers the expression, dear to St. Gregory, of *ecclesia universalis*, which includes all the elect from Abel to the very last.[9] With Holy Scripture and the whole of tradition the Council reserves the title People of God for this structured reality which is bound to positive revelation and to the Covenant. The history outlined here is therefore that of revelation rather than of salvation. The People of God, in its existence and structures as a people, are those who know God and serve him in a holy way.

It begins with the election of Israel. Because of this election, and because of the Fathers in whom it was first made, the Jewish people are always dear to God, "for God does not repent of the gifts He makes nor of the calls He issues" (Rom 11:28–29), our text says (art. 16). Had the Council followed more deliberately the idea of this "concrete and historical theology centered on the history of salvation," of which the Holy Father spoke on October 17, 1963, when he took up the words of Professor E. K. Skydsgaard, it could have inserted here a theology of the relations between the Jewish people and the Church, and perhaps even the declaration on the Jews which was finally included in that on non-Christian religions. But there were other specific difficulties involved in that and, in any case, the exposé of the history of God's People in chapter 2, remained in the form of a simple sketch.

If there is a history of salvation broader than the history of revelation with which the People of God begins, it is a secret history about which we could mumble but a few syllables. What role is played in it by the other non-revealed religions, the non-Judeo-Christian religions? The Council did not really take up this point either here or in the declaration *Nostra aetate* on non-Christian religions, or in the *Decree on the Church's Missionary Activity.* The question raises very complicated problems, and a valid approach to

201

them supposes not only theological elaborations but studies on the religions involved, studies which are far from having reached the necessary maturity. The Council could not enter an area that has hardly been cleared. In the above-mentioned documents, however, the Council asserts that everything good and true can be considered as a preparation for the gospel and should be assumed, not destroyed, in passing through the necessary purifications.[10] It cannot be said that it canonizes an *Erfüllungstheologie*, but it is rather in this sense that it orients us.

The People of God, in its historical, public and concrete form, is identified with the Church. It is the historical form that the divine Covenant takes just as the Church, insofar as she is an institution, is the visible, historical and public form of grace. Whoever speaks of historicity speaks of the involvement of man and his liberty which is exercised in the world and time. The need to search and the possibility of falling immediately follow. One cannot attribute these weaknesses to the Church, if one considers her as the immaculate spouse of Christ insofar as she is entirely from Christ.[11] The category "People of God" helps us correctly to think and situate the weaknesses of the concrete Church in the world and her need for continual renewal and reform: "so that in the weakness of the flesh she may not waver from perfect fidelity, but remain a bride worthy of her Lord; that moved by the Holy Spirit she may never cease to renew herself, until through the cross she arrives at the light that knows no setting."[12] We can understand why Dom Anscar Vonier, after having written a book on the Holy Church, *The Spirit and the Bride*,[13] felt the need to publish *The People of God*,[14] in which he brought out the human and historical aspect of this Church.

This aspect is, moreover, not only a source of imperfection. If going beyond the mere juridical point of view (the institution) allowed the Council to reaffirm the anthropological value of a Church *composed of men*, this led it not only to recognize the reality of the imperfections, but also to propose a positive theology of catholicity. This indeed has not only a transcendent source from above, that is to say, the fullness of Christ; it likewise has a source in humanity. It is the point of encounter between what is for man in Christ and what is for Christ in man. The Council proposes (art. 13) a theology of the property of catholicity which, to our mind, has not yet received the attention it deserves. In effect, it anticipates certain developments of Oriental theology; it contains several precious hints toward a theology of the Church as communion and for a theology of particular churches.[15] If the People of God is not an inorganic mass but on the contrary a people structured in the very thing that makes it the People of God (it is this, our text says, whether because of the distinction between simple faithful and ordained ministers, whether by reason of the states of life) neither is it an undifferentiated mass on the part of its human components. It is itself composed of diverse historical *peoples*, each of which brings its own resources: *Volkerkirche*.

TO EXPRESS UNIVERSALITY AND THE DYNAMISM
THAT IMPELS THE CHURCH TO ATTAIN IT

Article 13 on catholicity begins with the statement that "All men are called to belong to the new People of God," and ends by developing it: "All men are called to be part of this catholic unity of the People of God, a unity which is harbinger of the universal peace it promotes. And there belong to it, or are related to it in various ways, the Catholic faithful as well as all who believe in Christ, and indeed the whole of mankind. For all men are called to salvation by the grace of God." The succeeding articles take up each of these broad categories: Catholics, non-Catholic Christians, non-Christians; and they are brought to a conclusion in an article on the missionary character of the Church. No distinction is made *here* (art. 17) between ecumenism and the missions, or between simple dialogue and kerygma. The Council merely states the goal toward which the whole effort of the Church tends; "In this way the Church simultaneously prays and labors in order that the entire world may become the People of God, the body of the Lord, and the temple of the Holy Spirit." The People of God which is formally and fully such is impelled by its internal dynamism to attach or unite to itself all men who either already belong to it in some way or are destined for it. We would like to emphasize here two points: the way the document speaks of "Others" and the dynamism of God's People.

Chapter 2 of the schema drawn up by the preparatory theological commission was entitled "The Members of the Church and the Necessity of the Church for Salvation." The material in this chapter became the second part of our chapter on God's People, but it underwent a serious transformation. The preparatory commission's chapter reflected directly the teaching of Pius XII's encyclical *Mystici corporis* in that it reaffirmed two things: the rigorous identity between mystical body and the Roman Catholic Church, and consquently the idea that the Catholics alone are members of the mystical body, the non-Catholics being spoken of only as "ordered" to it.

But on these two points Vatican II goes beyond the encyclical. Firstly, it does not purely and simply identify the mystical body with the Roman Church: it does not approach the notion of the body of Christ first from the societal or corporative viewpoint, but under that of the personal mystical identification with Christ as a consequence of which all those who are thus regenerated form a single body (art. 7). Then, speaking no longer in terms of mystical body, but in terms of the Church founded by Christ, the Council says that "this Church . . . subsists in the Catholic Church, which is governed by the successor of Peter and by the bishops in communion with that successor" (art. 8), and it acknowledges that some elements properly belonging to *this* Church founded by Christ are found among the others.

Secondly, the Council does not employ the term "members." It avoided it intentionally because it caused endless discussions. Instead of raising the question of member which can have only a yes-or-no answer, the Council used a more subtle vocabulary. The encyclical *Mystici corporis* recognized only two terms: "member" (reserved to Catholics) and "ordered to" (applied indifferently to pagans of good faith and to non-Catholic Christians). The Council used three terms.

For Catholics (art. 14) it uses the expression "to be incorporated." For *full* incorporation it requires not only external loyalty to the visible institution but that people have the Spirit of Christ. This is a most important point on which the very fate of the definition of the Church in its essence depends. The Church is not a pure society adequately definable *ab externis*. Once more juridicism is left behind.

Regarding non-Catholic Christians the Council formally avoids the expression "ordinari ad," nor does it speak of belonging in (implicit) desire, *voto*; it uses the word *coniunctam* "to be united." The idea is that of real but imperfect communion by means of one or other of the elements that make up the goods of the Covenant entrusted to God's People, the totality of which is required in order that there be complete or pure and simple communion, but some of which are missing among our separated brethren. The basic idea, left half implied, is that all the baptized are members of God's People, but some of them, raised in a dissident church or ecclesiastical community, do not enjoy all the goods of the Covenant and do not have full communion with the body of the Church in which the Church of Christ and the Apostles exists. The Council expresses itself in terms of perfect or imperfect communion within a radical belonging to the same body or people by baptism. The decree *Unitatis redintegratio* on ecumenism takes up and develops this theology.

Finally, where non-Christians are concerned, the Council speaks of an ordering or relation to the People of God: among some by means of positive elements depending on the Covenant, the Jews, and—at least according to the material content of biblical faith—the Moslems; among others by means of the personal orientation of their lives and because of the necessary aids to salvation given them by God. Among all of them there exists at least this objective bond consisting in the fact that they are called to salvation, that they belong to a saved humanity whose existential situation is modified by this very fact. Karl Rahner thinks that this is sufficient to justify extending the expression "People of God" to all humanity.[16] Scriptural usage as well as liturgical and patristic tradition do not justify this way of speaking, but the Council neither adopted nor rejected it.

This absolute universalism of God's plan to gather men into a People of sons who, as the *Decree on the Church's Missionary Activity* (art. 7) states, can say "Our Father" as with one voice, gives rise to the correlative vocation of the People of God, in the explicit and formal sense, that is, the Church, to radiate and to extend itself to the ends of the world. This vocation is expressed in diverse ways: "populus messianicus" (twice in art. 9), "habet pro fine Regnum Dei . . . dilatandum" (*ibid.*), "germen unitatis, spei et salutis" (*ibid.*); the People of God is used by Christ "as an instrument for the redemption of all, and is sent forth into the whole world as the light of the world and the salt of the earth" (*ibid.*), "that for each and all she may be the visible sacrament of this saving unity" (*ibid.*); "it spreads abroad a living witness" (art. 12); "this People, while remaining one and unique, is to be spread throughout the whole world" (art. 13). To this list should be added what formally pertains to the missions at the end of article 16 and in all of article 17. With great regret, but because of the necessity of being brief, I leave aside what concerns missionary activity properly so-called; this international conference did not put that on the program.

There remain two great themes to discuss: the Church (the People of God) is the sacrament of salvation; the People of God is the messianic people.

The theme of the Church as sacrament of salvation frequently comes up in the *Constitution on the Church*.[17] It means that the Church is the historic and visible form which God's will for the salvation of men takes. What is interesting here is that the theme is applied to the Church *insofar as it is the People of God*. It is not, therefore, solely a question of the institution, of the ensemble of objective means of grace. It is the People of God that transmits through the world the offer of grace and of the Covenant; it is the community of Christians united to their pastors that is the sign and the instrument of the "dialogue of salvation,"[18] a dialogue which transpires within the framework of the People of God through the use of the objective means of salvation, in the first place, the sacraments in the classic sense of the word. The Council does not go any further in the clarification of this notion which, in the Council's mind, is related more to the economy of salvation than of sacramentary theology.

The expression "messianic people" appears twice in article 9 and twice in the other Conciliar documents; it is new in the texts of the magisterium. It is quite in place if the new People of God is the People and the body of Christ, for "Christ"—we risk forgetting it by force of habit—means "Messiah." One can readily see that the expression has a powerful dynamism. It presupposes a plan of salvation that is going to be realized, a plan seen and proclaimed by the prophets; the Messiah, the messianic people are bearers of a message that inspires hope about the collective destiny of men: they bring the promise of salvation. Among the prophets, in the gospels (the significance of so many "signs" and cures), and in apostolic writings, this salvation is not purely individual and "religious": it is total. It is a whole exegesis, a whole discreetly demythologized theology of salvation that one should bring up here. But in the *Constitution on the Church*, the Council insists on these elements: unity, peace, hope, greater justice and order.[19] This is splendid; we believe that this corresponds to reality. But how can we make it credible to men? How can we be equal to such claim—with such a mission and grace? Is the Church—and with it other Christians who belong basically to the People of God—effectively a source of peace and unity for the world, the hope of a better order? This Council tried to give a positive answer in the *Pastoral Constitution on the Church in the Modern World*. Others will describe its significance this week. Personally, I regret that this great document did not return more unreservedly to the categories "People of God" and "Messianic people."

NOTES

1. No document provides exact knowledge of the work and influence of the Coordinating Commission. This influence, in several cases, seems to have been decisive. It seems that, in the one that interests us here, the initiative came from the Germans: on the other hand, the text took into account several suggestions from Santiago, Chile. The succeeding steps of the Council, which we summarize briefly, were such that the idea and over-all structure of the chapter on the People of God were never really discussed at the Council.

2. "In credendo falli nequit." See G. Thils, *L'infaillibilité du peuple chrétien "in credendo."* Notes de théologie posttridentine, Bibl. Ephem. Theol. Lovan. 21 (Paris and Louvain, 1963). Where it is a question of over-all life of the People of God, we would rather speak of indefectibility than of infallibility: the latter applies to acts; the former applies to the whole of life in which there may be some darkness, even faults, but which, finally and on the whole, is preserved from error.

3. Cf. art. 12: quotation from 1 Jn 2:20, 27; one could add 2 Cor 1:21–22, compared with Eph 1:13. Cf. I. de la Potterie, "L'onction du chrétien par la foi," in *La vie selon l'Esprit, condition du chrétien*, Unam sanctam 55 (Paris, 1965) 107–167.

4. *Suis-je catholique?* (Paris, 1909) 91; French translation of *Medievalism*.

5. *Theolog. Quartalsch.* (1823) 497.

6. Cf. for example, the way in which the Kingdom of God is spoken of in art. 9: "Habet tandem pro fine Regnum Dei *ab ipso Deo* in terris inchoatum, ulterius dilatandum, donec in fine saeculorum *ab Ipso etiam* consummetur."

7. On this trend of thought, see S. Jáki, *Les tendances nouvelles de l'Ecclésiologie* (Rome, 1957) and my *Sainte Eglise*, Unam sanctam 41 (Paris, 1963).

8. Affirmations like "omnis praelatio cessabit" are constantly found among them: *Glossa ordinaria* in 1 Cor 15:24 (*PL* 113:547). S. Thomas certainly tells us how he views the economy of values in *Summa Theol.* I–II, 106, 1 and 2; *Q. disp. de spirit. creat.* 8, ad 11.

9. Art. 2 with reference to St. Gregory, *Hom. in Evang.* 19, 1 (*PL* 76:1143 B); S. Augustin, *Sermo* 341, 11 (*PL* 39:1499 ss); St. John Damascene, *Adv. Iconoclast.* 11 (*PG* 96:1357). Cf. my *Ecclesia ab Abel*, in *Abhandlungen über Theol. u. Kirche*. Festschr. K. Adam (Düsseldorf, 1952) 79–108.

10. *Constitution on the Church* 16 and 17; *Decree on the Church's Missionary Activity* 3, 8, 9; *Declaration on the Relationship of the Church to Non-Christian Religions* 2.

11. See *Sainte Eglise* (note 7) 131–154; "L'Eglise est sainte," *Angelicum* 42 (1965) 273–298.

12. Art. 9, end. Because the Council rediscovered—for the first time we believe in a text of

the magisterium—the eschatological meaning of all God's work, it could begin again to speak of the Church dialectically: holy and imperfect, celestial and terrestrial, and so forth. A completely juridical consideration is easily static and had, in fact, abandoned this dialectical view through which, however, one takes into account so many features of the Church which are found at the heart of New Testament statements.

13. (London, 1935).
14. (London, 1937).
15. One finds others either in ch. 3 of *Lumen gentium* or in ch. 3 of the decree *Ad gentes.*
16. Cf. *Schriften zur Theologie* 2:84f.; French translation: *Ecrits théol.* 2 (Paris: 1960) 101ff.
17. Cf. "L'Eglise sacrement universel du salut," *Eglise vivante* 17 (1965) 339–355.
18. Expression of the encyclical *Ecclesiam suam, AAS* 56 (1964) 641–642.
19. See "L'Eglise, germe d'unité et d'espérance pour tout le genre humain," *Chicago Studies* (1965).

Most Rev. Carlo Colombo

THE HIERARCHICAL STRUCTURE OF THE CHURCH

B<small>Y WAY OF INTRODUCTION</small>, let me indicate the precise theme of my talk and then indicate the point of view followed in drafting my speech.

The *hierarchical* structure of the Church has a twofold meaning. It indicates, first of all, that according to traditional Catholic doctrine, reaffirmed by Vatican Council II, the pilgrim Church, the People of God, whom by his grace he unifies and builds up in the Holy Spirit into the mystical body of Christ the Lord, is not composed of members equal in every respect. It implies rather a hierarchy, men who, by special gift of Jesus Christ, are institutionally endowed with spiritual powers exceeding those of other members. There arises then the problem of the relationship between the faithful and the members of the hierarchy: not primarily the juridical relationship of authority and dependence, but rather the relationship of specific cooperation of the two categories in the life and mission of the whole Church.

The second meaning of the theme "hierarchical structure of the Church" concerns the *internal* structure of the hierarchy. Since it is composed of diverse members and organs, each with different powers or competence (hierarchy of order and jurisdiction with their subdivisions), there arises the problem of mutual relationship between these members and organs in the Church's complex yet unified life.

In a word, the theme is then: the hierarchy in relation to the other members of the People of God, the internal relations of the organs and members of the hierarchy and their specific function within the People of God. Special attention will be given to the relationship between the episcopate and papal primacy.

The scope of my talk is not to develop a personal doctrine, but rather to explain with some clarity the theological thinking of Vatican Council II as manifested in the Constitution *Lumen Gentium*, which we must consider as the most complete expression of Catholic doctrine to date.

I do not propose to justify such a doctrine with the usual exegetical, historical and theological arguments. We all know too well that it is one of the fundamental points in the interpretation of the teachings of Christ that divides Christians. We also know that a profound personal conviction on these basic points cannot be had except through long meditation and study.

However, we are convinced that a precise understanding of each other's point of view is an indispensable requirement for fruitful dialogue. My intent is then to make known the Catholic point of view as manifested in Vatican Council II.

I. The Hierarchy as Sacramental Sign of Christ's Action

In order to understand Catholic doctrine it is necessary never to lose sight of the fundamental concept used by the Council to define the Church— *sacramentum salutis* (art. 1, 9, 48).

The sacramental constitution of the Church is a general category affecting the Church's whole life and all her aspects: in each and every one of her aspects the Church is *sacramentum, seu signum, seu instrumentum* of Christ's salvific action among men. The whole Church is the sacrament of salvation for all humanity, and in the Church the individual faithful with their gifts —pastors, religious, married people—are a sacrament, sign and instrument of the action of Christ, the Savior. Note the expression *sacramentum, seu signum et instrumentum*. The Catholic concept of sacrament includes not only a function significative of Christ's action, but also a causal function bringing about active, dependent, and instrumental cooperation in respect to Christ's salvific action. Christ uses the Church for the salvation of mankind. The same sacramental significance is acquired by the individual aspects of the Church's manifold mission, each with its proper function: Christ signifies through each of them a particular salvific action that he performs.

It is not necessary here to justify this Catholic concept of sacramental sign, which is analogically applied to the various aspects of the Church's life. It is enough to have called attention to it in order to emphasize the need to keep it ever present in our minds for a precise understanding of the place and function of the hierarchy within the People of God.

The study of the hierarchy then becomes a search for its specific characteristic as a "sacramental sign" within the complex of sacramental signs of which the whole life of the Church is composed. The Constitution gives an answer to this query in article 21, where it states: "From the tradition which is expressed especially in liturgical books and in the practice of the Church both of the East and of the West, it is clear that, by means of the imposition of hands and the words of consecration, the grace of the Holy Spirit is so conferred, and the sacred character so impressed, that bishops in an eminent and visible way, undertake Christ's own role as Teacher, Shepherd, and High Priest, and that they act in His person." (See also article 10, where it states that "the ministerial priest, by the sacred power he enjoys, molds and rules the priestly people. Acting in the person of Christ, he brings about the Eucharistic Sacrifice, and offers it to God in the name of all the people"; and article 11: "those of the faithful who are consecrated by holy orders are appointed to feed the Church in Christ's name with the Word and grace of God"; and finally article 27: "Bishops govern the particular churches entrusted to them as vicars and ambassadors of Christ. This they do by their counsel, exhortations, and example, as well, indeed, as by their authority and sacred power . . . which they personally exercise in Christ's name.")

There are three consequences that flow from this teaching.

a) Those upon whom sacred orders are conferred by sacramental ordination represent visibly before the other faithful, and each in his own rank, Christ the Teacher, Shepherd and High Priest. In the fulfillment of the duties assigned to them by their visible mission they are signs of Christ's presence and action in the community.

b) They not only signify Christ's action, but they also transmit it. By means of their human world and action the salvific action of Christ the Teacher, Priest and Shepherd is exercised in the Christian community for the building up of the whole body as well as of the individual members in faith, charity and obedience to him. They are efficacious signs of Christ's salvific action.

c) This is accomplished, not because of special human merits on the part of the members of the hierarchy, but in virtue of an interior transformation of their spiritual being, which is appropriated by Jesus Christ as sign and instrument of his presence and action in the community. Sacramental ordination is not a simple human act of a juridical nature, but a transforming action of Christ who chooses and consecrates his representatives and endows them with his sanctifying Spirit.

The members of the hierarchy, therefore, are not primarily representatives of the People of God nor do they receive from them the authority and power behind their actions. They are, first of all, representatives and legates of Christ from whom they receive what distinguishes them from their brothers, and to whom they will render an account of their mission. In this light is to be understood the importance attributed to the doctrine on the sacramental value of episcopal consecration and to its sacramental effects, not only of sanctification but of teaching and governing as well. This doctrine transforms the concept of authority from a primarily juridical one to a sacramental one, and clearly emphasizes the primacy of Christ's action in the exercise of the magisterium and pastoral government.

The consequences of this doctrine are the efficacy of the action of the hierarchy and its relative independence of the community. The efficacy, which is dependent upon the presence of Christ's action in it, makes the hierarchy the ordinary instrument used by Christ for the education of the community in faith and the spirit of Christianity. The faithful experience indistinctly the mysterious presence of the divine Teacher and Shepherd in the words and actions of their legitimate shepherds; the faithful know that they are different from the others because of a particular relation to Christ; and according to the measure of their faith, they transfer to their shepherds a share of their docility, faith and love for Christ. In this sense and for this reason the spiritual action of the hierarchy becomes truly the "pattern to the flock" (1 Pt 5:3) far superior to the personal value of its members.

In the supernatural order of causality there is, therefore, a true precedence and independence of the hierarchy in regard to the community. However, one must hasten to add that, under a certain aspect, even the hierarchy is an expression of the life of the community. Since those that Christ selects or uses for his action are human instruments, he respects their personality and all the manifold circumstances and influences that contribute in forming it and are merged in the spiritual life of the community. Furthermore, Christ's action in choosing his representatives is not limited to the decisive moment of sacramental consecration, but he prepares from afar the subjects that sacramentally will become his legates; he usually prepares them not by means of extraordinary action but through the normal vicissitudes of the spiritual life of the Christian community. Finally, it is a basic Catholic doctrine that the whole Church, having achieved the plenitude of revelation in Christ, lives today the faith and the spiritual tradition transmitted by the apostles and faithfully preserved by the entire community, under the guidance of the teachers and pastors who are the representatives and interpreters of Christ, Teacher and Shepherd.

Thus the faith and morals (I do not mean individual pedagogical applications) that the hierarchy instills in the faithful are not a personal invention or gift. It is the faith that the members of the hierarchy received from the Church and in which they were formed from infancy throughout all their life; it is the Christian spirit that through various ways has molded their spirit, which, having reached its full maturity, suggests or imposes new applications coherent with the spiritual tradition received.

In this sense the origin of the teaching and action of the hierarchy truly depends upon the faith and life of the community. What is said in article 25 about definitions of the magisterium must be proportionately applied also to the entire activity of the hierarchy. The hierarchy is the sacramental sign of the faith and Christian life of the community. Not only in an instrumental causal sense but also in a demonstrative one.

II. THE STRUCTURE OF THE HIERARCHY

Now we must examine the structure of that "sacramental sign" which manifests and actuates in the Church the salvific action of Christ, Teacher, Shepherd and High Priest. Since this aspect of the sacramental mission of the Church is found on a visible plane wherein the Christian community assumes the form of an organized society, we can speak of a hierarchical constitution of the Church by analogy with civil societies. In addition, because it is our task to examine how Catholic doctrine, as expressed in the Constitution *Lumen Gentium*, interprets the thought and the teaching of Jesus Christ, we can rightly speak of the "divine constitution" of the Church according to Catholic doctrine.

The problems to be examined are many; however, let us direct our attention to three of them since they have, more than others, engaged the thought of the Council Fathers or have received more light from the Constitution's teaching: the relationship between episcopal consecration and episcopal authority, the mission and authority of the episcopal body or college, the relationship between the episcopal college and the Roman pontiff.

As can be seen, we do not intend to examine all the degrees of the hierarchy, not even the priesthood and the diaconate about which also the Constitution has made valuable comments (see art. 28–29). But this doctrine does not raise particular difficulties. The entire patristic and liturgical tradition, both in the East and West, conceives the episcopate as the full sacramental sign of Christ's power and authority, the priesthood and diaconate as two subordinate and limited sacramental participations in this plenitude. The differences in degree of participation, which are on occasion found in various traditions or during the course of history, are rather minor problems that belong to the Church's power of economy in sacramental matters.

Who in the Church possesses this power of economy to interpret with authority the conditions wherein the salvific action of Christ will be realized? The first answer that comes to the mind of those who know the history of the Church's first millennium, when various liturgical-sacramental and disciplinary traditions were formed without disrupting the unity of the Church, is the episcopacy, namely, the communion of bishops.

EPISCOPAL CONSECRATION, EPISCOPAL COMMUNION, EPISCOPAL AUTHORITY

The fundamental thought of the Constitution about the origin of episcopal authority is expressed in the following sentence: "Episcopal consecration, together with the office of sanctifying, confers the offices of teaching and of governing. These, however, of their very nature, can be exercised only in hierarchical communion with the head and the members of the college" (art. 21; see also art. 22).

There are two conditions required for a disciple of Christ to be able to receive and exercise the full function of sacramental sign of Christ's salvific action: episcopal consecration and communion with the other members of the episcopal community which, with the bishop of Rome divinely constituted as its head, is a hierarchical communion.

Episcopal consecration, with the real transformation it accomplishes, is the supernatural basis indispensable for the subject to become a sacramental sign of the action of Christ. The actions performed by the bishop are not purely human actions but, to a certain degree, theandric ones, since Christ himself acts through him. For this reason they require a new and real basis. Episcopal consecration is what radically distinguishes authority in the Church from any purely juridical authority and introduces it into the mysterious order of Christ's re-creating salvific action.

Episcopal consecration, however, does not suffice: the tradition of the Church has never conceived of bishops, however rooted in Christ, as totally autonomous but as members of a communion. This communion as a whole has received the mission, authority and the guarantee of divine assistance to preserve and transmit faithfully the doctrine of Christ, to preserve intact and administer fruitfully the immense patrimony of the means of grace left by Christ to the Church, and to interpret authoritatively his thought and will when new problems arise from Christianity's confrontation with human life that varies through the centuries. The strongest proof of the need for this episcopal communion and of its authority is found in the painful occurrences of schisms and heresies. Those bishops who lived independently and separated themselves from the tradition of faith and discipline, preserved and transmitted by the communion of bishops, were not recognized as legitimate representatives of Christ, though, being consecrated, they were still capable of performing some sacred actions.

Episcopal authority comes sacramentally from Jesus Christ but must be recognized and, as it were, legitimated before the faithful by the episcopal communion. The concrete methods for verification or legitimation have been various throughout history, but the principle of canonical mission remains constant even in its various manifestations (see art. 24).

The essential and unique position that Catholic tradition attributes to the bishop of Rome makes communion with him the fundamental principle of communion with the entire episcopal Body: *cum omnibus orthodoxis atque catholicae et apostolicae fidei cultoribus.* Besides, it explains the historical fact that the verification of membership in the episcopal communion, and consequently of the full legitimacy of episcopal authority, was progressively more and more accomplished through a personal act of the Roman pontiff; as head and foundation of the episcopal college, he was seen to be the essential condition for verification of membership in the college.

THE UNIVERSAL AUTHORITY OF THE EPISCOPAL BODY

The constantly recognized necessity of belonging to the episcopal communion for a consecrated bishop to exercise his function of sacramental sign of Christ's authority, while being accepted by all and particularly by his faithful, confirms in a most outstanding manner that individual bishops do not possess supreme authority in the Church: above them is placed the episcopal communion with the bishop of Rome as its head.

The whole doctrine of episcopal communion and the need to belong to it is based on this traditional principle that is also the foundation of the doctrine and authority of the ecumenical councils: in matters of faith, of sacramental discipline, of canonical discipline of morals or of the organization and life of the Church, the supreme authority to which Christ has promised his perennial particular assistance and the permanent gift of his Spirit, is the episcopal body. This principle applies whether the episcopal body be united in council or acts in common throughout the world, according to the needs of the times. Above the body of bishops forming a community, there is but Jesus Christ; all together they are truly vicars and legates of Christ, mediators between him and the Christian community.

The authority of the episcopal body, being supreme and binding on all, is necessarily universal, and every bishop in communion with the body participates in it. Being supreme, it is also necessarily full: there is no problem that cannot be presented to it or on which it has no competence, when we are dealing with matters of fidelity to Jesus Christ, to his teachings, to his spirit, to his will, and to the permanent necessity of his salvific action for all mankind.

The Constitution *Lumen Gentium* has accurately chosen these words to express the authority of the episcopal College: "The order of bishops is the successor to the college of the apostles in teaching authority and pastoral rule, or, rather, in the episcopal order the apostolic body continues without a break. Together with its head, the Roman Pontiff, and never without this Head, the episcopal order is the subject of supreme and full power over the universal Church" (art. 22). The identical terms used by Vatican Council I to express the supreme authority of the Roman pontiff are repeated in this Constitution: he has over the Church "full, supreme and universal power. And he can always exercise this power freely" (art. 22).

The last sentence clarifies a difference. The episcopal body (which includes necessarily the Roman pontiff) and the latter even by himself possess equal powers in regard to amplitude or universality, intensity or fullness of content, the supreme degree. It is the same fullness of Christ's power that is expressed through the common exercise or the personal exercise of the sacramental sign. For this reason their exercise may be interchangeable and may vary in frequency and manner during the course of history.

But the personal exercise is more readily activated, being always free. The common exercise depends instead, by its very nature, upon the will of the head, the Roman pontiff: "This power, however, can be exercised only with the consent of the Roman Pontiff" (art. 22).

Some have lamented that these qualifications were progressively introduced in the text of the Constitution, and have characterized them as a return to Roman legalism as opposed to the spirit of communion which should have inspired the chapter on epicsopacy. We have to understand the religious meaning of these points; we are dealing with sacramental signs of Christ's salvific action in the Church and with the normal and highest expression of his action in the community as such. Just as for the seven sacraments, the constant tradition of the Church is to exercise particular care in specifying the characteristics of the sacramental sign, so that these gifts of God not be wasted because of man's inertness, and so that, on the other hand, we poor men may possess some certitude of encountering this salvific action of the Lord. Thus the specification of the sacramental sign in this case serves one sole purpose: to guarantee through the sign, performed according to his will, the encounter with his Person and his action of Teacher, High Priest and supreme Shepherd of our actions and of the entire community.

THE EPISCOPAL COMMUNION AND THE ROMAN PONTIFF

The juridical relations underlining the equality and difference between the common authority of the episcopal body and the personal authority of the bishop of Rome, successor of Peter as universal shepherd, are necessary to clarify the structure of the sacramental sign, but they express neither the entire nor the most profound meaning of it.

As already stated, the common authority of bishops is, according to Catholic doctrine, an authority of a hierarchical communion; it can neither exist nor act without the active presence of the bishop of Rome. It is not, therefore, an authority that can be opposed to the authority that the Roman pontiff can exercise personally as successor of Peter. At the human and visible summit of the Church, there is no possibility of conflict or division between the two forms in which the presence of the Lord's salvific action in the Church is realized; Christ is not divided, nor can he be.

Over and above the juridical problem, we must emphasize what unifies and what distinguishes, in the internal and supernatural order, the action of the episcopal body and the personal action of the Roman pontiff in the execution of the task entrusted by Christ to the apostles and their successors. In a certain sense we can say that the Roman pontiff is the interpreter and the expression of the common thought of the episcopal body, just as this body is witness and interpreter of the faith of the entire Christian community and of the Christian spirit lived by all the faithful. The doctrine which the Roman pontiff presents to the whole Church, and which he interprets whenever new problems demand solutions, is not a personal doctrine. It is the teaching of Christ given to the apostles and transmitted by them to the Church; it is the teaching that the entire episcopal body in communion with the bishop of Rome has faithfully preserved, authentically interpreted, and coherently developed to the present day, through the special supernatural assistance of Christ and his Spirit. The Roman pontiff could not teach anything that is not already contained, at least in an implicit form, in the apostolic tradition that the episcopal body transmits and guarantees. The same must be said about the sacramental discipline and the essential conditions for the true Christian spirit and the realization of the evangelical precepts, since the author of the sacraments and supreme Shepherd of souls is Jesus Christ, as manifested to the apostles and by them transmitted to the Church through their successors. For this reason and in this sense, the Constitution clearly states: "When either the Roman Pontiff or the body of bishops together with him defines a judgment, they pronounce it in accord with revelation itself. All are obliged to maintain and be ruled by this revelation, which, as written or preserved by tradition, is transmitted in its entirety through the legitimate succession of bishops and especially through the care of the Roman Pontiff himself. Under the guiding light of the Spirit of truth, revelation is religiously preserved and faithfully expounded in the Church" (art. 25).

There is also another relationship between the Roman pontiff and the other members of the episcopal body. We mentioned at the beginning that the whole visible Church is a sacramental sign of the Lord's salvific action, on different levels and in various manners. It is not only a symbol of Christ's inner action, but also a means or instrument of his presence and action in the community. For this precise reason, individual bishops not only become witnesses before their faithful of the common faith, but also build up the faith and supernatural life of the community by means of their authority as representatives of legates and vicars of Christ, Teacher, Shepherd and High Priest (see art. 21, 27).

Catholic tradition, by basing itself on the word of the Lord ever more clearly understood (Mt 16:17–20; Lk 22:32; Jn 21:15–17), has attributed to the bishop of Rome, as successor of Peter, the same function of sacramental sign of the action of Christ in regard to other bishops and to the whole Church, as was recognized by Vatican Council II for the entire episcopal body. The bishop of Rome is not simply expression or sign of the common faith of the episcopal body, but is also instrumental cause of it, established and used by Christ. The Lord avails himself of the bishop of Rome while respecting his human liberty, but at the same time he illuminates, directs and supernaturally assists him by means of the Holy Spirit, so that he be constantly the foundation of the whole Church, he who confirms his brothers in the faith, the shepherd of the whole flock, faithful and pastors and the representative of the Supreme Shepherd.

This is the teaching of Vatican Council I, which the Second Vatican Council has reaffirmed and made its own (it could not have done otherwise), while more clearly illustrating it. The promise of infallibility that Christ made to the Church, and to the body of bishops as its instrument (the ecumenical councils are testimony of this principle), involves the successor of Peter, who, when speaking *ex cathedra*, is the primary human instrument the Lord uses: "For then the Roman Pontiff is not pronouncing judgment as a private person. Rather, as the supreme teacher of the universal Church as one in whom the charism of the infallibility of the Church herself is individually present, he is expounding or defending a doctrine of Catholic faith" (art. 25).

As can be seen, the Catholic doctrine on the relationship between the Roman pontiff and the episcopal body, as well as on the relationship between the hierarchy and faithful is totally illumined by the sacramental understanding of the Church and by faith in the active, constant and variously distributed presence of the Holy Spirit. It is he who interiorly unites the pope and the bishops. "This [episcopal] college insofar as it is composed of many, expresses the variety and universality of the People of God, but insofar as it is assembled under one head, it expresses the unity of the flock of Christ. In it the bishops, faithfully recognizing the primacy and pre-eminence of their head, exercise their own authority for the good of their own faithful, and indeed of the whole Church, with the Holy Spirit constantly strengthening its organic structure and inner harmony" (art. 22). It is he who unites the faithful to the hierarchy in the life of faith: "To the resulting definitions [by the Roman pontiff or the entire episcopal body] the assent of the Church can never be wanting, on account of the activity of that same Holy Spirit, whereby the whole flock of Christ is preserved and progresses in unity of faith" (art. 25).

One is the Lord of the Church, of whom men are only "vicars" on different levels and with different functions and competence. One is the Spirit that vivifies and unifies the members and subjects them to the Head, Jesus Christ, in obedience to faith and the obligation of the Christian life. Men, on any level, are only "signs" in which we can recognize with certainty the presence of his action: sacramental signs. Because of this the Church is the body of Christ built up in the Spirit, not the body of bishops, not even of Peter.

Dr. George A. Lindbeck

A PROTESTANT POINT OF VIEW

IN DEALING WITH VATICAN COUNCIL II's *Constitution on the Church*, I should like to make two main points: first, it is a highly ambiguous document, perhaps particularly to non-Catholic readers; second, it does nevertheless represent a watershed in the history of the Roman Catholic Church that is likely to have consequences beyond the present possibility of our imagining. This is true, not only because the Council intended it to be its most important pronouncement, and not only because this is by far the fullest dogmatic statement on the nature of the church that has ever been formulated by any Christian body, but also because of the intrinsic merits it possesses despite its ambiguities.

As I mentioned, the ambiguities of the Constitution are perhaps particularly apparent to non-Catholics. Indeed, the equivocations which they are inclined to discover will probably seem fantastic to Roman Catholics. Nevertheless, the difficulties they have in interpreting the text are real for them, and Catholics as well as non-Catholics should try to become clear as to what they are if ecumenical discussions of the document are to be profitable.

My own awareness of these difficulties has been greatly heightened by reading critical expositions with which I sharply disagree, but which, nevertheless, are in a sense thoroughly cogent.[1] These have convinced me that the Constitution can indeed be understood in radically different ways by honest and competent scholars.

This is particularly true if it is read in abstraction from its historical context, and if one seeks to see how it *could*, and not only how it *should* be understood. A Protestant is more likely to do this than a Catholic. The Catholic will normally be much more aware of the past official and unofficial positions of his Church and, further, he will naturally attempt to find definite guidance and directives in the text rather than start with an effort to find the variety of possible meanings.

The basic reason why the document is open to fundamentally different interpretations is that it is a compromise. We are all aware to some degree why this is so.[2] The present text represents a radical departure from the initial draft that was prepared before the Council began and was, in effect, rejected by the bishops because it seemed to them an overly rigid and massive expression of traditional *Romanitas*. The substitute draft was also subjected to extensive revisions, partly as a result of Conciliar discussions, with the result that the text we now have represents an enormous advance over anything that most bishops or theologians would have thought possible before the Council began. Yet, it is still very much a compromise document. Not only theologians, but also bishops speaking in the Council, have made proposals far beyond it. Even many Catholics, not to mention Protestants, think of it as falling short at many points of the best contemporary Roman Catholic thinking about the Church.

To say that the Constitution is a compromise is not, of course, to criticize it. Any official *prise de position*, ecclesiastical or nonecclesiastical, must try to rally a consensus out of varied groups: to satisfy, or at least be tolerable, to conservatives as well as progressives. However, a compromise, by its very nature, tends to be an amalgam of diverse elements which can be interpreted in widely different ways.

I would like to illustrate—without any pretense at completeness—the possible diversity of interpretations by distinguishing, in a crudely schematic way, between three concepts or images of the church and two theological world views that are present in the Constitution, and then cite four points at which this creates difficulties for the non-Catholic reader. In the theologically basic initial chapters, the Church is described, first, as the mystery of salvation, which is best summed up perhaps in the Pauline image of the body of Christ, and, second, as the pilgrim People of God. Then, in the third chapter, which is generally considered the most important of all because it officially introduces for the first time the notion of episcopal collegiality, the traditional post-Tridentine view of the Church as primarily the divine institution of salvation often seems to be dominant.

Related to the tension between these three views of the Church, there is another between two different theological pictures of the world in which the Church exists. The first is popularly caricatured these days as a "two-story" view of the universe in which there is a relatively static, perpendicular contrast between two sharply different levels of created reality, an immaterial and timeless heaven above, and the realm of temporality and matter beneath. The other is the more biblical one emphasizing the eschatological history of salvation. One might say that, in general, the view of the Church as divine and changeless institution fits most naturally into the static, two-story picture of the world; the concept of the pilgrim People of God, in contrast, has its natural locus in an eschatological history of salvation; while the Church as the mystical body of Christ is an inherently ambiguous image that can be developed in either a more historical framework, as is done in this document, or in a static one.

The mere presence of these various views of the Church and the world does not, of course, imply equivocation. They are not, at least not *prima facie*, mutually exclusive and so can presumably be combined into coherent and consistent wholes. They serve simply as models or patterns of thought by means of which theologians attempt to organize what might, in fact, be very much the same set of doctrinal affirmations and beliefs. Thus, for example, all Roman Catholic theologians, no matter what their image or concept of the Church, would find a place within it for papal infallibility. Similarly, the use of one of these images does not require that the others be rejected. If one starts with the notion of the People of God, for example, it is clearly proper to go on and discuss the institutional structures appropriate to this People and also those aspects of its life that led St. Paul to describe it as the body of Christ.

However—and this is where the difficulty arises—a relatively coherent doctrine of the Church requires that one or another of the fundamental motifs be made systematically central, because otherwise there will be unresolved conflicts between different possible lines of interpretation. The understanding of people, institution and mystical body differ considerably, for example, depending on which of these models constitutes the starting point and therefore supplies the basic hermeneutical framework and principles in terms of which the whole corpus of ecclesiological affirmations is organized. Similarly, a particular affirmation, such as infallibility, will acquire notably different connotations and implications depending on which of these three models governs thinking about the Church.

Now, from this perspective, the problem with the Constitution is that it makes no clear decisions regarding the priorities of these various views of the Church and the world. It tends simply to juxtapose them without specifying their interrelationships. Consequently, an opponent of change, for example, is left free by the text itself to continue to think of the Church as primarily the divinely instituted ecclesiastical organization (at least when dealing with the hierarchy), and thereby largely, even if not entirely, naturalize the fresh approaches in the document. Conversely, another reader might argue that the notion of the pilgrim People of God is hermeneutically normative with the result that, in a sense quite justifiably, he makes the whole Constitution into a clarion call for renewal. This is not a criticism. It was presumably necessary at this juncture in Roman Catholic history to leave both alternatives open. But this does create difficulties of interpretation.

Among the many places where the Protestant reader is likely to sense these difficulties, I shall mention, somewhat at random, the last two chapters, the concept of collegiality in the third chapter, and the tension between the mystical body and the People of God ecclesiologies in the first two chapters.

The last chapters of the Constitution are a good place to begin because the tension between what I have called the two theological world views is particularly evident in them.

Thus chapter 7, which deals with eschatology and the saints, starts by using the biblical categories of salvation history, of *Heilsgeschichte*, which now, after eighteen hundred years of relative neglect, are once again being revived among Catholics as well as Protestants. It speaks in terms of the contrast between the New and the Old Aeons, and between the present "period between the times" and the full manifestation at the end of the ages of the kingdom of God which has begun in Christ when, as the text puts it, "the human race as well as the entire world, . . . will be perfectly re-established" (art. 48). Then, with drastic abruptness, it shifts to the classical perspective in which the horizontal-temporal contrast between the new and the old is replaced by the ontological-vertical distinction between higher and lower realities, between heaven above and earth beneath, between the celestial and terrestrial Church. The hope for cosmic redemption, for the restoration of the world as a whole, appropriate to the first outlook, is replaced by the traditional concentration, which has been characteristic of both Catholics and Protestants, on salvation as the escape of individual souls from earth into transcendence (art. 48), and this is then followed by a carefully guarded, but still wholly traditional exposition of the Catholic doctrines of the invocation of the saints and the communion of those below with the saints on high (art. 49–51). I do not mean that the two sections logically contradict each other. Actually biblical language is consistently used even in the paragraph that is most classically individualistic in its import (art. 48, end). However, the reader is puzzled as to the interrelationships, and it is quite clear that a traditionalist and a modern disciple of Teilhard de Chardin would both feel justified in reading the text in their two very different ways.

A similar uneasy juxtaposition of two approaches is evident also in the next chapter on the Blessed Virgin. The over-all expository structure is the newer one of the history of salvation in which the Virgin Mary is, above all, the "handmaid of the Lord" whose free assent in obedience, faith and love to become the mother of Lord (art. 56) makes her the pre-eminent member of the Church and its type and exemplar (art. 53). This pattern of exposition suggests an emphasis not wholly dissimilar to, for example, Luther's *Magnificat*, but into it is introduced, without any indication of the logical relations, much of the language and conceptuality of the Mariology that developed in the classical two-story framework and that presents the Virgin in isolation from the Church as the divine mother who is the queen of the universe (art. 59). Once again, I am not suggesting that these two streams of thought cannot in some fashion be harmonized, but only that there is no clear indication of how this is to be done, of which has theological primacy and should therefore provide the fundamental rules of interpretation. As a result, the so-called Marian maximalists and their more biblically and patristically minded critics can both read the chapter pretty much as they wish, and a certain kind of Protestant is left totally unsatisfied. He is happy that the maximalist surge in progress up until 1950 has not been pushed farther, but he sees no evidence in the text itself that it might not once again regain impetus, and his anxieties are further heightened by that attribution of the title *Mater ecclesiae* to Mary at the end of the Council's third session.[3] For reasons that will later be discussed, I myself do not share these fears, but they must be mentioned in any Protestant discussion of *De Ecclesia* together with an explanation of why even an attentive reading of the eighth chapter does not dispel them.

However, the point where the uncertainties of the non-Catholic become greatest is in reference to the treatment of the episcopacy and of collegiality in the third chapter. It is true that most of the published Protestant comments so far have been favorable, but I have the impression that this is largely a reflection of Catholic enthusiasm, and that those who give the text an independent reading are often more reserved.

In speaking of these reservations, I am not thinking now of the Protestant impression that the use of Scripture in this section is more irresponsible than anywhere else in the Constitution except in the chapter on the Virgin.[4] After all, the exegesis contained in an ecclesiastical pronouncement such as this does not have the same authority in Catholic eyes as does the doctrinal content, and so we may expect that Catholic biblical scholars will soon undertake the task of exposing its questionable character.

Nor am I thinking now of the special problems created by the peculiar rhetoric of this section. As we know, the resistance of those who feared that papal primacy would be endangered by any emphasis on bishops was so tenacious that everything possible was done to reassure them. This was done so successfully that the non-Catholic reader can easily be deceived into supposing that nothing has changed. He is all too likely to end by remembering chiefly that "the college or body of bishops has no authority unless it is simultaneously conceived of in terms of its head, the Roman Pontiff . . . and without any lessening of his power of primacy over all, pastors as well as faithful" (art. 22), and his suspicions of *immobilisme* will in all probability be reinforced by the notoriously ambiguous *Nota explicativa praevia*.[5]

However, these difficulties are only preliminary. On further study, even a non-Catholic can see easily enough that the affirmation of the fundamentally collegial structure of the hierarchy does make a profound difference. He sees that the present highly centralized and unilaterally monarchical pattern of Church government, while remaining juridically completely legitimate in Roman Catholic eyes, has in effect been declared to be, from the theological point of view, a kind of abnormal, emergency structure which it would be desirable and normal to replace by more autonomy on local levels and greater cooperation on the higher ones. Yet, even after this is said, the non-Catholic is puzzled. He finds no clear indication of how far these principles extend, and what, therefore, are the limits of the changes implicitly recommended or allowed by the Constitution.

The outsider develops one opinion when he reads this chapter by itself, and quite another when he interprets it in the light of other parts of the Constitution. By itself, chapter three seems to come straight out of a static, two-story world view. It seems to say that the episcopacy and papacy—without, of course, actually asserting this—were established by Christ when he was here on earth in pretty much their present form. Further, Peter and the other apostles seem to have a certain kind of both logical and temporal priority to the rest of the Church (art. 19). The results are, first, that the principle of collegiality seems to be restricted—though this, fortunately, is not actually stated—to the bishops alone, and, second, that the Church as the body of Christ and the People of God is somehow secondary, a kind of product of the ecclesiastical institution. It is easy to see from this why one Greek Orthodox commentator has expressed the fear that *De Ecclesia* has simply compounded the mistake of Vatican Council I. It raises, he suggests, the episcopacy to the level of the pope, rather than reintegrating the whole hierarchy, bishops and pope together, into the People of God.[6]

However, this impression is changed when one makes, not this chapter, but the first two chapters, the systematic center of the Constitution. If one focuses on the Church as the People of God which is also the body of Christ, the spirit-filled community in which, as the fourth chapter on the laity suggests, even the lowliest member has the right and the responsibility to make his voice heard (art. 39), then it becomes natural to think of the entire company of Christians, and not simply the hierarchy, as collegially structured. It becomes natural to think, as Bishop Edelby suggested in Rome, that Christ first calls, not apostles, but "believers to whom the preaching of the gospel rightly belongs, then gives them apostles, and finally chooses a head of the apostolic college so that this college will remain united."[7] It becomes possible to suppose that the relation of collegiality, rather than strict subordination, that the Council has declared to exist between bishops and pope extends by analogy to the relation between bishops, priests and deacons and also to that between the laity and their pastors. A vast expansion of what a Protestant tends, rightly or wrongly, to speak of as democracy becomes conceivable at all levels in the Roman Catholic Church.[8]

From this point of view, chapter three becomes, not a restrictive and final declaration about the collegiality of the church, but simply a first step. However, there is nothing in the actual words of the Constitution to invite such an interpretation, even though it is not forbidden. Once again, the simple juxtaposition of different approaches has left room both for those who wish to believe that almost nothing has happened and those who think that a radical structural transformation has been authorized.

The final uncertainty I would like to mention concerns the relation between the Church as the mystery of salvation and the mystical body, on the one hand, and the eschatological pilgrim people on the other. The tension here is more subtle than those we have previously sketched because, for one thing, both views are clearly biblical and, further, they are both developed within the context of an eschatological history of salvation. Many Protestants will find themselves, not only agreeing with most of what is said in these chapters, but even admiring certain passages, such as those dealing with biblical images and with the Church's imitation of Christ, as constituting something of a high-water mark among official statements of the doctrine of the Church, whether Catholic or non-Catholic.

Yet these same Protestants find themselves regretting that the image of the People of God is not clearly given systematic primacy. Those passages in which it is dominant seem to them to strike exactly the right notes. For example, "the Church, embracing sinners in her bosom, is at the same time holy and always in need of being purified, and incessantly pursues the way of penance and renewal. . . . [She] 'like a pilgrim . . . presses forward . . .' announcing the cross and death of the Lord until He comes . . . to show forth in the world the mystery of its Lord in a faithful though shadowed way" (art. 8). The Protestant would like to be sure of the centrality of such a description of the Church as a thoroughly historical and human community, simultaneously holy and sinful, differentiated from other peoples by its explicit, though sometimes dim, witness to Christ. If these affirmations are hermeneutically decisive, then some of the other language that seems to threaten the proper distance between Christ and the Church can be given acceptable interpretations. One can then agree that, in a sense, "by her relationship with Christ, the Church is a kind of sacrament or sign of intimate union with God, and of the unity of all mankind" (art. 1). One can agree that it is to some degree comparable to the Incarnate Lord because it is "one interlocked reality which is comprised of a divine and a human element" (art. 8). One can even grant that it is "the initial budding forth of that kingdom" of God on earth (art. 5). This becomes possible, because, on the hypothesis we are considering, it would be clearly understood that the Church is sacrament and beginning of the kingdom, not as a kind of continuation of the incarnation (as would be implied if the mystical body concept is made exclusively central), but as witness to the Lord who alone is fully the sacrament of unity and the beginning of the kingdom. Further, it would become possible to think of certain omissions as, so to speak, temporary. It would be possible to expect that Catholics, pushed by the inner logic of what is said about the pilgrim People, would see that the Constitution needs to be supplemented by greater emphasis on the possibilities of tragic unfaithfulness on the part of the Church in history and on the fact that the coming kingdom stands over against the People of God, not only as fulfillment, but also as judgment. Such views have already been advocated, not only by theologians, but in part by some bishops speaking in Council.[9] Thus Catholics could read the Constitution in this way without giving up any of their distinctive doctrines.

However, there is no indication in the text itself that this will happen. It remains possible to take as normative those expressions which are susceptible of a triumphalist interpretation and thereby neutralize the significance of precisely those other phrases which a Protestant finds most encouraging.

We have said enough, perhaps more than enough, about the ambiguities that some Protestants see in the *Constitution on the Church*. As was said at the beginning, a Catholic may well regard them, at least in part, as fantastically farfetched. What our analysis disregards, he might say, is the concrete historical setting of the document. By looking at it in isolation, in a kind of hermetically sealed exegetical vacuum, we have failed to emphasize how radically new this Constitution is in comparison with what has gone before. We have overlooked its dynamic thrust, which is not in the least ambiguous but, rather, decisively points away from the past into a quite unprecedented future.

There can be no quarrel with this critique. It is quite true that what we have so far said fails to do justice to the freshness of this Constitution. Thus the biblical-eschatological framework of salvation history is much more dominant than we have indicated. While the classic two-story outlook is not excluded, it has, nevertheless, receded to an astonishing extent: the language of the medieval distinction between the natural and the supernatural, for example, is entirely absent, not only from this Constitution, but from all the Council's documents. New also is the description of the Church as the People of God, the insertion of Mariology into the doctrine of the church, and the affirmation of collegiality. Familiar themes are treated in fresh ways so that, for example, the presentation of the doctrine of the mystical body is quite different from that in Pius XII's 1943 encyclical *Mystici corporis*. Some of the most unprecedented aspects we have not even mentioned, for instance, the stress on the laity and the priesthood of all believers (art. 10); the explanation of the religious life in such way as to, in principle, answer the objections of the Reformation to monasticism (art. 40, 41, 44); the amazing openness to God's saving work among non-Christians, including atheists, (art. 16); and above all, the ecumenical attitude to other Christian bodies which becomes possible because Christ's Church is not narrowly identified with the Roman Catholic communion but is rather said to "subsist" in it (art. 8; cf. art. 15).

Yet even after due note is taken of all these facts, many Protestants are still not convinced that *De Ecclesia* will be interpreted in what is called a "progressive" direction. The main source of their anxieties, it seems, is the memory of how major doctrinal pronouncements have influenced the Roman Church in the past. They have been ceaselessly repeated in such way that the thinking of Catholics has been molded into a kind of replica of them. They have been used as a set of premises for theological deductions in the manner of what has come to be known as "Denzinger theology." They have served as great dams thrown across the surging torrents of advancing thought, which has thus been forced to pile up and spread out into often stagnant pools of attempted systematizations. This is what tended to happen four hundred years ago after the Tridentine decrees on justification, the sacraments, and Scripture and tradition. It happened again less than a hundred years ago after Vatican Council I's pronouncement on the papacy. What guarantee is there that it will not occur once more after this Council's *Constitution on the Church?*

Obviously a Protestant cannot regard such a prospect with enthusiasm. If this Constitution operates as a conclusion, not a transition, if Catholic thinking and attitudes are stamped into a kind of simulacrum of its compromises and ambiguities, then the last state, while no doubt better than the first, will not be much better. Catholics will then continue to be trained to think and feel about a wide range of topics, but especially about ecclesiastical authority in general and the bishops and pope in particular, in a way that not only Protestants and Orthodox, but even some of the most impressive contemporary Roman Catholic voices, would describe as unbiblical and sub-Christian. There are better ways, better Catholic ways, of discussing many topics than those which the Constitution uses, but if this becomes a fixed norm, these will be excluded and wither away.

Clearly a great many Roman Catholics do not think this will happen. They believe that the Constitution will be a transition, not a conclusion, an open door and signpost to the future, not a ceiling or prison for reflection. Their confidence, as far as an outsider can determine, comes from the conviction that the modern historical awareness of the time-conditioned character of all human utterances, including ecclesiastical ones, has now become so pervasive that it will never again be possible to treat dogmatic pronouncements as if they were permanently adequate expressions of eternal truth. What might be called a "decision theory" of doctrinal development seems to be replacing not only the classical deductive ones, but even the organic growth theories which derive from Cardinal Newman. According to this, as I understand it, the Church, as the pilgrim People traveling through history, finds herself from time to time at the parting of the ways and needs to choose which path to take. Once a dogmatic choice is made with the help of the Holy Spirit, there is, so the Roman Catholic believes, no possibility of reversing it. The dogmatic decision is, to use the traditional language, irreformable, and the Church is forever committed to pursuing that road into the future. But along that road, new alternatives requiring new decisions are constantly encountered, so that what the Church says about herself and its faith in times to come may go far beyond, even while not contradicting, what it has said in the past.[10]

Reinforcing the belief that this is the way the Constitution will function is the fact that the council itself has insisted that it is pastoral in character, not dogmatic. This means, I take it, that even in its dogmatic constitutions it intended, not so much to bind the future as to give guidance in the present. This implies, to change the metaphor, that De Ecclesia is not to be viewed as a barrier to further ecclesiological developments, but as a series of sluice gates channeling those developments in certain directions without, however, rigidly determining their future course.

If this is true, then it is possible to make some predictions, even though necessarily tentative and speculative ones, regarding the ultimate consequences of this Constitution for Roman Catholicism's understanding of itself and of its relations to other churches and the world. My own guess is that it is to the eschatological view of the world and to the theme of the pilgrim People of God that the future belongs. These categories have a competitive advantage, not only because they are supported by much in recent biblical scholarship, but also because they provide points of contact with modern views of the universe as a unified developmental-historical process and of the Church as affected by, even if not totally subject to, the same sociological and historical factors which condition other human communities.

In conclusion, let us pause for a moment and try to think concretely of what this world picture and this image of the Church entail. They take quite seriously the biblical vision of a heaven and earth moving toward their final transformation, not abolition, in the kingdom of God. Within this context, the Church is viewed, not fundamentally as an institution hovering between heaven and earth, mediating grace to individuals, but as the eschatological pilgrim People—the community that preserves at least some memory, however faulty it may sometimes be, of God's promises, of the promises summed up in Jesus Christ, and that hopes for their fulfillment.

Two of the consequences following from this are of special importance for our purposes. First, the mission of the Church is radically reconceived. It can no longer be thought of as representing some kind of quasi monopoly of the divine action, for God is working out his redemptive purposes through all the processes of nature and history and in human lives everywhere. The task of Christians, therefore, is not primarily that of rescuing individual souls from hell, nor even of converting the world, but rather that of witnessing, that of serving the world by reminding it in all that they are, say, and do of God's purposes, of the true future of humanity which is Jesus Christ. Christians do this, not exclusively by their individual lives and actions, but more fundamentally by being a communion of faith, love and peace, by being a sign, however imperfect, of the kingdom which is to come.

The second consequence is that, within this perspective, it becomes obvious that Christians must be reconciled among themselves, and by their communal action, reconcilers in the world if they are to be credible and persuasive witnesses. This clearly makes ecumenism central to the purpose of the Church in a way that it is not in traditional views of the mission of the Church, whether Catholic or Protestant, which have centered on the salvation of individuals out of the world at the expense of the coming redemption of the world itself. It becomes clear that even preliminary steps toward unity are important. While the goal is the full reconciliation of the churches, and ultimately of mankind, everything which can be done to increase communication and cooperation, and among Christians, common worship and witness, is fundamental to the Church's nature as a sign and source of the eschatological unity of the divided world. In this last sentence, you will recognize, I am paraphrasing the Council's *Constitution on the Church* (art. 1).

We could go on and speak of this ecumenical vision at length, about how, for it, unity has nothing to do with uniformity. Indeed, diversity within the Church is necessary, because a church which is homogeneous, which does not reconcile groups of different races, cultures, classes, liturgies, spiritualities and even theologies, is not an effective sign or agent of reconciliation. This, by the way, is a point that is stated clearly, even if not with all the consequences a Protestant would draw, in the *Constitution on the Church* as well as in the *Decree on Ecumenism*.

Now it is quite impossible to predict, I suppose, how powerful will be the influence of this concept, vision, or, if you will, image of the Church. However, anyone who thinks back over the course of Christian history will remember that the development of theological ideas, even on a rarified level, can have profound practical effects. Roman authoritarianism and rigidity, as well as Protestant amorphousness, were both responses to concrete historical circumstances, but they would never have developed in the form they did without the support and direction given by theologians. Similarly, the ecumenical and missionary renewals the churches are now trying to undertake are responses to contemporary historical developments, but they will not become really effective, they will not become matters of systematic, enduring and powerful policy, unless they are supported by a new theological vision of the Church itself which is both persuasive in terms of the peculiarly but genuinely rational norms that theologians use, and which also, in its homiletical and devotional versions, catches the imagination and fires the emotions. If this happens, it is conceivable that the future of the ecumenical movement, the renewal of the Church and even the overtly Christian contribution to the shaping of the future of our planet might be considerably greater, perhaps even in our lifetimes, than I for one would have thought possible four years ago before anyone anticipated this *Constitution on the Church*. I do not predict that this will happen, but I have enough hopes so that I find myself praying for it.

NOTES

1. An example of this is K. G. Steck, "Lumen Gentium? Zum Verständnis der 'Constitutio dogmatica de ecclesia,'" *Materialdienst des Konfessionskundlichen Instituts* (Bensheim) 16 (1965) 85–90.

2. A Protestant account of the background of the Constitution is to be found in G. Lindbeck (ed.), *Dialogue on the Way* (Minneapolis: Augsburg, 1965), especially in chs. 2, 3 and 7.

3. For a judicious comment on this, see R. Laurentin, *The Question of Mary* (New York: Holt, Rinehart and Winston, 1965) 138–140.

4. O. Cullmann comments on these exegetical failings in *Dialogue on the Way*, 139–140. Article 19 is the exegetically most questionable part of ch. 3 of the Constitution.

5. For a Protestant comment on this *Nota*, see P. Meinhold, " 'De Ecclesia' du point de vue luthérien," *Irénikon* 38 (1965) 317–319.

6. "It is an attempt to complete but not to correct the formula of Vatican I by extending the idea of divine right by analogy also to the bishops" (Nikos Nissiotis, "The Main Ecclesiological Problems of Vatican II," *Journal of Ecumenical Studies* 2 [1965] 35).

7. *Informations catholiques internationales* (Nov. 15, 1963) 14.

8. Perhaps the theologically most developed study of the possibilities is H. Küng's *Structures of the Church* (New York: Nelson, 1964). His thesis is that "the Church is *in essence* the ecumenical council by divine convocation" (16).

9. E.g., Bishops Pangrazio of Italy and Laszlo of Austria, *Council Speeches of Vatican II*, eds.: Küng, Congar and O'Hanlon (Glen Rock, N. J.: Paulist Press, 1964) 189–192 and 44–48 respectively.

10. This "decision theory" of doctrinal development has not been explicitly formulated, as far as I know, by any Roman Catholic theologians, though it seems to me that it is implied by the attitudes that many of them adopt toward dogma, and is even to a certain extent overtly suggested by such statements as the following: "perhaps the day will come when it will be fully recognized that although the term 'infallibility' does indeed express the binding force of the formulations of faith, it does not indicate their fragmentary character. With this in mind perhaps a concept will then be found which, better than the term 'infallibility,' will present in an encompassing and balanced manner the strict binding force of decrees and at the same time their profoundly incomplete character" (H. Küng in *Journal of Ecumenical Studies* 1 [1964] 111).

SESSION V   DISCUSSION

*Question: You have said that the anthropology of the Council
has remained static. Explain this opinion.*

CONGAR: In short, the Council's anthropology is based only on the idea
of the image of God in man. But it seems to me there are other values in
Holy Scripture. In particular there is the whole idea of man's search for
truth, power and justice, that takes the form of the three functions of prophecy, kingship and priesthood; these symbolize somewhat the whole realm
of human endeavor. That is why I said the Council's anthropology was
too static.

*Question: Can we integrate the two notions of the People of
God and the body of Christ? In other words, to formulate a
eucharistic ecclesiology intrinsic to the People of God?*

CONGAR: These two notions, People of God and body of Christ, each
have their own intrinsic value, and the notion of People of God is preliminary to that of the body of Christ. The People of God says: *congregatio
fidelium*, assembly of believers. This assembly of the faithful brings about
or does the eucharist (*Populus Dei facit eucharistiam*). And then the

231

eucharist makes the body of Christ; the eucharist molds the People of God into the body of Christ, which in turn introduces new values: identity with Christ, the Holy Spirit as soul of the people, etc. It is clear that here eucharistic ecclesiology has its full place.

> Question: To what extent do non-Catholic Christians enter into this People of God? In what way are the Jewish people included in this notion of People of God?

CONGAR: I believe that the essential notion adopted by the Council is that of communion, full communion or partial communion. I think that the Jewish people are still the People of God in the sense that God's choice is definitive. But the Jewish people do not have the benefits of the New Alliance, i.e., all the goods that are constitutive of the People of God as the body of Christ with the Holy Spirit as the very soul of this People of God.

> Question: Is the Synagogue still a means of salvation?

CONGAR: It is impossible to answer definitively yes or no, because the answer depends on the aspect. One can say yes, in the sense that the Synagogue has as its internal constitutive principle some real goods of the Alliance, primarily the Word of God. But one would also have to answer no, in the sense that it does not have as constitutive principle, the fullness of the goods of the Alliance, particularly the eucharist, which is the very sacrament of the New and Eternal Alliance. This approach of the Council—imperfect but real communion—also explains the situation of other Christian faiths and churches in relation to the Catholic Church in which subsists the Church of Christ and the apostles. Here, without any doubt, the idea of *vestigia ecclesiae* keeps its value, and this should not be interpreted in the sense of the "poor remains," but in a more dynamic fashion. These churches incorporate a number of goods of the Alliance—word of God, certain sacraments (in the Orthodox Church, all the sacraments)—and therefore the People of God are not only *de facto*, but *quo ad institutionem*, as regards the ecclesial institution itself. Therefore it is against this perspective of full or partial communion in the goods of the Alliance that one must consider the Council's theology.

> Question: You have insisted, Bishop Colombo, upon the fact that the unity and function of the episcopal college is based on the presence of Christ and his Spirit which make the episcopate a sacramental sign. Why is the presence of Christ and his Spirit among the Orthodox bishops not a sufficient basis of communion with Roman Catholic bishops?

COLOMBO: Any answer, it appears to me, must take into account the whole tradition of the Church, which has always required, over and above the presence of a sacramental reality as basis for communion, also an external expression and manifestation of communion. This manifestation consists in the acceptance of a gift present in the total community of bishops and of the gift present in the successor of St. Peter. These two things have always been considered as necessary: the sacramental basis and communion in this gift. Where the second aspect is lacking there is no real communion; there is a reality of internal and spiritual communion. And this explains—and as Father Congar said—why we must emphasize more the very real elements of the Church which exist in communities that have a true and real episcopate. But this does not suffice for the realization of that total communion which allows the fullness of expression by means of the supreme sign of communion, the eucharist.

> Question: *How can the doctrine on the hierarchy, as expressed in ch. 3 of* Lumen Gentium *open the door to reunion between the Roman and Orthodox episcopates? Can this doctrine influence the process of reunion between Rome and the East?*

COLOMBO: Without doubt this doctrine that expresses a more complete conception of the reality of the episcopate, one more conformed to the tradition of the East and West, will help toward developing mutual understanding and a fuller acknowledgment of the positive values in each other. I am convinced of this. However, in order to achieve complete unity, it is necessary to be in communion not only with the gift diffused throughout the episcopal body, but also with the personal gift existing in the successor of Peter.

> Question: *I am extremely surprised to see Dr. Lindbeck, a Protestant, criticize a text of the Council because it does not attempt to systematize the different images or concepts of the Church found in Scripture or tradition. I had always thought that the tendency to do so was most characteristic of all kinds of shallow scholasticism. Nothing, in my opinion, could be more unscriptural than to reduce, for an example, the views of St. Paul on the Church, to such a one-sided, purely rational kind of theology that Dr. Lindbeck seems to think to be not only the ideal but the only acceptable one.*

LINDBECK: This illustrates the danger of abbreviating. In the complete text of my manuscript I make it very clear that I am not criticizing the Constitution because of its ambiguities. I say that the Constitution as any official *prise de position*, ecclesiastical or nonecclesiastical, must try to rally a consensus out of varied groups: to satisfy, or at least be tolerable to, conservatives as well as progressives. However, a compromise by its very nature tends to be an amalgam of diverse elements which can be interpreted in widely different ways. The remainder of my analysis of these ambiguities was simply that there are ambiguities in the document, with the consequent result that it can be interpreted in widely different ways. I think we have already seen, in the distinctions that have been given today, illustrations of the fact that it can be interpreted in widely different ways.

I am not recommending that an ecclesiastical document be an expression of a systematic theology. However, it must also be added, that in order to avoid drastic ambiguities, one must indicate logical interrelationships between different themes, different concepts, different images of the Church. To show interrelationships, to organize things, is not the same thing, I would suppose, as deductive Scholasticism. There are many different ways of ordering material that are not deductive Scholasticism. I myself would be just as strongly opposed to any attempt to develop an ecclesiology which was deductive in its structure, even though I think it must be systematic.

DR. BROWN: I would like to address a question to Father Congar. Bishop Colombo's speed would seem to suggest that the hierarchy is the basic fact in the structure of the Church, and I wonder how this is to be related to the decision, described in your talk, to reverse the orders of chapters 2 and 3 of *De Ecclesia*, thereby giving precedence to the notion of People of God and then, and only then, speaking of hierarchy? I am not yet clear as to how these two points of view are to be combined.

CONGAR: Well, I have spoken essentially from the viewpoint of hierarchy of values, and not from the viewpoint of the genesis of the Church. It is certain that from the angle of the hierarchy of values, the Christian ontology of People of God is higher, and this is the finality of the hierarchy itself. From the viewpoint of the genesis of the Church, Jesus first chose the disciples, choosing from among them a few apostles, and then the apostles preached. And thus the hierarchy *makes* the People of God either through preaching the word or through the celebration of the sacraments. I do believe that there is an interrelationship between hierarchy and the People of God. In any case, from the viewpoint of hierarchy of values, personal holiness is the objective of all; everything is directed to it.

BURGHARDT: My remarks really have to do with Dr. Lindbeck's paper, and are meant more as reassurance then anything else. I think you can be reasonably sure that there will no longer be any significant amount of "Denzinger-theology," or stagnant pools of attempted systematizations. The reasons, I think, are basically two. One, our students; and second, the theologians. The students, whether in seminary or college, simply will not stand for it. They do not listen, and they read. The contemporary Catholic student demands a theology that is biblical, historical, ecumenical, eschatological, personal. If he does not get it in your classroom, he simply tunes you out. Secondly, the Catholic theologian of today who is listened to is precisely the man who combines this approach to theology, and I mean not only the Rahners and the Congars and the deLubacs, but those of us who operate on lower levels. I think a good example of this is in the field you mentioned, Mariology. It is true that you can find indications of "Queen of the Universe" in isolation in the text, but it will not make any difference. For Mariology fifteen years ago began to develop in a different direction, with an attempt to put the so-called prerogatives and privileges in the context of the mystery of Christ and the Church, precisely the way the Council entitled this particular chapter. Mariology, if it is to survive, if it is to be a genuine theological discipline, must always preserve that fruitful tension between Christ and the Church, between the mystical Christ and the physical Christ. And if, as I say, they already began to do that fifteen years before the Council began, it has mushroomed, snowballed, since then. It is because of this background that the Council could speak about Mariology the way it does. The other things in there will have no significant effect in Catholic theology of the future.

LINDBECK: I would like to make one comment. The purpose of this paper is to urge on Catholics the necessity of explaining the documents to Protestants. I agree wholeheartedly with what you say about the future. The place of these documents in history, the place of the Council in history, reassures me too that these will be open doors to the future rather than prisons for reflection. I am morally sure of this. But the plausibility of this interpretation of the Council is undermined when Catholics do not explain to the Protestants that the documents can, when they are read on the level of bare *explication de texte*, in a hermeneutically sealed vacuum, which is the way a Protestant tends to read documents, be interpreted in very different ways.

MOELLER: It is not a question I have, but an illustration of the problem of collegiality. It is helpful to study the story of the introduction of this topic into the text of *Lumen Gentium*. This theme was first introduced into the schema with a more juridical bent. It was seen only from the viewpoint of collegiality expressed in ecumenical councils, and some passages of the definitive text still cast in the same context. A second influence came to bear on the Council's treatment of collegiality, however, and that was the liturgical viewpoint encouraged by studies on the sacramentality of the episcopate that began about 1946 exemplified by the work of scholars like Bernard Botte, O.S.B. By the end of the first Conciliar session a union of these two approaches was achieved. Ecumenical studies were a third source of influence on the evolution of the Constitution. In 1929 a monk of Chevetogne published an article in which he translated the famous word "sobornost" in Russian theology as *collegialité*. This translation was taken up by Father Congar in 1953, if I am not mistaken. I think this point is of interest for the dialogue with our Orthodox brethren.

It seems to me that it is very fortunate that it was not possible for the Constitution to achieve too systematic a presentation of all that. Why? Because we now have three approaches to the same topic. In this direction we may be able to find dialogue with our Orthodox brethren more possible. They are quite puzzled by the first approach, the juridical one, yet the presentation is not juridical because in the famous *Nota praevia* this communion aspect is a very important point.

OUTLER: If I understood Bishop Colombo clearly and rightly, he made a very stark distinction between the hierarchy and the faithful in the question of power, authority and ministerial office. Now I want to raise the question whether this sharp and almost mutually exclusive distinction, if I understood it rightly so, can be harmonized with the notion of the People of God as sharing power, authority and the exercise of ministerial office? Can this distinction be harmonized with chapter 4 of *Lumen Gentium* in which the laity is understood as having a genuine ministry derived, not, I thought, from their dependence upon the hierarchy, but from their office as baptized and confirmed Christians, from their having an apostolate, and their being defined as the Church in the world. These strike me as being in some real sense discordant. And I should like to understand how we might think of their being harmonized, if they can be.

COLOMBO: In the People of God there is a diversity of charisms. The priests have their own, the laity have theirs, and the religious have theirs. All the charisms are necessary for the vitality and realization of the mission of the Church. But as the charisms vary it is necessary that there be mutual influences. In the People of God we have all experienced the fact that our personal faith has been influenced by the faith of the most humble: parents, friends, teachers. But there is another influence that derives from the ministry consecrated by Jesus Christ himself, and which is a charism of a very specific nature, a charism transmitted through the episcopate as such. I do not believe that there is any opposition here.

CONGAR

DE LUBAC

HÄRING

SESSION VI

Rev. Yves M. J. Congar, o.p.
The Laity

Rev. Bernard Häring, c.ss.r.
Holiness in the Church

Rev. Henri de Lubac, s.j.
Meditation on the Church

Rev. Yves M. J. Congar, O.P.

THE LAITY

As THE COUNCIL DURING ITS SECOND SESSION tried to elaborate a doctrine of the episcopate, it was said: Vatican I was the Council of the papacy, Vatican II will be the Council of the episcopacy; will we have to wait for Vatican III to have one for the laity? We do not need to wait for Vatican III. The Council was a council of the laity. From the second session on, not only were there lay auditors of both sexes who were heard, and who collaborated effectively on several commissions, but the Council gave the laity an important place in its teaching. We should note carefully under what conditions.

In several documents it assigns them a role in the apostolate of the Church: the decree *Ad gentes* on the missions (art. 21 and 41), the decree *Christus Dominus* on the pastoral office of the bishops (art. 17), the decree *Apostolicam actuositatem* on the apostolate of the laity, which is supplemented by the pastoral *Constitution on the Church in the Modern World*. If the Council had done only this, it might have been interested in the laity only for their usefulness, even were it apostolic. But it did better than this: the very existence of these documents, and especially of the *Decree on the Apostolate of the Laity* enabled the Council Fathers to speak of the laity in a more internal way, from the angle of their relation to the mystery of the Church itself and with its internal activity, that is, in the dogmatic Constitution *Lumen gentium*.

It is a noteworthy fact that all the successive schemata that led to *Lumen gentium*—beginning with the one produced by the preparatory theological commission—had a chapter on the laity. This did not result only from a practical allocation of matters to be treated. It was due to progress in our understanding of the Church, henceforth indisputable: one cannot treat the Church doctrinally without speaking of the laity—and in a Christian way. The Constitution *Lumen gentium* does so indeed on two occasions: in chapter 2 on the People of God (we have already spoken of it) and in chapter 4, which is devoted to explaining what properly concerns the laity. There they are clearly seen as in the Church. They do not enter the picture only because of the relation of the Church *ad extra*, as a sort of prolongation or appendix; much less do they appear as a simple *object* of the action of the clergy who alone would really and truly form the Church. The Fathers at the Council dropped completely this perspective in which the Church was something that belonged to the clergy while the laity were simply their clients. The laity are, in their place, the Church; they are the People of God.

The American bishops—I am not saying this because I am speaking here, but because it is true—were the most zealous in emphasizing the novelty and the meaning of the council's approach. Bishop Wright, of Pittsburgh, remarked that the faithful have been waiting four centuries for the Catholic Church to define seriously their place and their dignity in the Church. Bishop Primeau, of Manchester, demanded a just share of initiative and freedom for a laity now become adult (October, 1963). This has now been done. We can say that on the theological level, and already on the pastoral level, the situation is profoundly different from the mentality that explains how the *Kirchenlexikon* treated the laymen in 1891 when it simply printed the term as "*Laie. Siehe Clerus*" (8:1323). At that time the layman was rather generally "defined," so-to-speak, in a negative way, as one who was neither cleric nor monk.

This definition could be valid on two conditions: 1) that one speak first of all in a very positive way of the People of God and of Christian existence, so that the "neither cleric nor monk," in avoiding a particular situation, leave intact all that is positive in the pure and simple Christian condition—in this sense we can say that the layman does not need to be defined, but the cleric and the monk do; 2) that one does not make of cleric, monk and layman three distinct classes, of similar ecclesiological importance, although of very unequal dignity. This was often done during the Middle Ages with the well-known division of Christian society, or even of the Ecclesia, into three *ordines*.[1] This stems from a sociological, not a theological, point of view. In reality, this threefold distinction, found for example in the *Controversies* of Bellarmine, a practical one that comes up again even in the *Constitution on the Church*, proceeds from the application of two different categories of distinction (this is precisely the point of view of the *Constitution on the*

Church: see art. 13, 44). On the one hand, there is a distinction in structure arising from the social organization which the Lord himself willed for his Church and, therefore, from the Lord's own institution or gift—a distinction between ordained ministers and faithful. On the other hand, a distinction within these structures arises from human response and differentiates Christians according to their state of life: secular and religious.[2]

To be quite frank, apart from this way of doing it, it is very difficult to define the laity positively, perhaps even impossible. I tried to do it in my book, *Lay People in The Church,*[3] but in a rather descriptive way and from an anthropological point of view. The layman, I said, is the Christian who does not hold back from involvement in the temporal order as such in order to serve God, but serves God in and through such involvement. Any idea of defining the layman in terms of the temporal as object of his action was far from our mind, as can be seen in the 447 pages of the above-mentioned book. It was only a question of the conditions in which he renders his service to God. We prefer, however, the expression of Karl Rahner, because it translates our thought more exactly: the layman, he says, is one whose Christian being and Christian responsibilities are determined by his native insertion in the life or fabric of the world.[4]

The Council did not wish to commit itself to a definition of the layman. It was satisfied with giving a description that was both positive and negative or exclusive: "The term laity is here understood to mean all the faithful except those in holy orders and those in a religious state sanctioned by the Church. These faithful are by baptism made one body with Christ and are established among the People of God. They are in their own way made sharers in the priestly, prophetic and kingly functions of Christ. They carry out their own part in the mission of the whole Christian people with respect to the Church and the world" (*Lumen Gentium* 31). It is a long sentence in Latin; our English translator has broken it up into several sentences, but it forms a whole which must be taken in its unity and which one should speak, if it were possible, in one breath.

The first thing to notice is that the layman is described as a consecrated being and, by this very fact, committed to a mission. One of the most characteristic steps taken, perhaps the most characteristic of the whole Council, consisted in rediscovering and affirming the link between consecration and mission. This is profoundly biblical. In the Bible one was chosen and set apart or consecrated *for* something. The People of God are chosen and consecrated to announce the wonders of God. This link between consecration and mission is at the root of what the Council says about the episcopate and priesthood (I would like to illustrate this if I had the time). We find it again as regards laymen, that is to say, Christians *sine addito*. In the *Constitution on the Church* as well as in the *Decree on the Apostolate of the Laity*—the

241

latter document speaks on several occasions of the right and duty of the apostolate (art. 3, 25)—the apostolate is based, not on a reality of the juridical order, but in the supernatural ontology which makes a person a Christian, namely, in Christian existence itself. Here as there, the basis of the right and the duty of the apostolate is membership in the body of Christ, the vitality and dynamism proper to this body into which the Christian is inserted and nourished by the sacraments of Christian initiation (baptism, confirmation, the eucharist).[5] This was already the teaching of Pius XII. This clearly supposes that there is no Christian initiation, no catechesis without an Apostolic orientation (*Decree on the Apostolate of the Laity* 30). Thus, the true title to apostolate consists in one's belonging to a body of which Christ is the head and internal principle of life through his Spirit, and as such participating in the mission of Christ. The fundamental title of apostolate is not therefore a mandate given by the hierarchy. The term "mandate" does not even appear in the *Constitution on the Church*. It does figure in the Decree *on the Apostolate of the Laity* (art. 20 and 24) but discreetly and in regard to a well-defined reality which, as far as the apostolate of the laity is concerned, appears as a part not as a whole: when the bishops take charge of an organization or apostolic movement and associate it with the pursuit of their own apostolic mission. This is what is called in France *Action catholique* in the strict sense of the word, but the categories and terms used vary from country to country. The Council employed them only with the greatest care and with an awareness of their relative character. From beginning to end, the Council restored the priority and primacy of the ontology of grace over juridical structures. We have already seen this as regards the People of God. One could show that this was also true of the episcopate, even of ecumenism itself, based on the unicity and identity of Christian baptism. The apostolate of the whole Church is based on her being the body of Christ because of which she participates in his mission.

In fact, the *Constitution on the Church* speaks in terms of participation in this mission (art. 30, 31, 33). The *Decree on the Apostolate of the Laity* starts with the same idea (art. 2) and then immediately specifies the content of this mission: to spread the kingdom of Christ and to procure thereby the salvation of man and the glory of God; it then indicates two ways in which this mission is to be carried out: spreading the knowledge of Christ and of His grace, and the penetration of the temporal order in a Christian way (art. 2, 5). These two points are further explained in articles 6 and 7.

But before this, the Decree already identified the carrying out of this mission with the apostolate by saying that all the activity by which the mystical body tends to achieve the goal of this mission is called the "apostolate" (art. 2). It therefore gave to "apostolate" an extremely broad content and intentionally avoided canonizing the distinction, widely enough known and

242

used by Pope Pius XII, between apostolate in the strict sense and apostolate in a broad sense.

This identification of the apostolate with complete participation in executing the mission of the Church taken in all its fullness can be justified from papal texts.[6] However, various studies have brought out more clearly the importance of mandate and of being sent *by* someone, which seems essential to the apostolate.[7] It is true that "mission" and "apostolate" mean the same, whether one starts from the Latin or from the Greek. However, "mission" lends itself better than "apostolate" to designate the content, while "apostolate," because of its connection with the twelve apostles, seems to refer to the formal sending of them by Christ who was himself sent by the Father. The extension of the terms "apostolate" and "apostolic" beyond a reference to the apostles, even to signifying every activity of Christian zeal, is a relatively recent fact.[8] It is used widely today, but people tend to forget the importance of the being sent *by* someone and consider only the content and goal of the action.

During the Council's discussion of missionary activity, several Fathers asked that mission be considered as belonging to the whole People of God as such, and not primarily to the hierarchy, that is to say, to the episcopal body headed by the pope, which succeeds the college of apostles headed by St. Peter. They based their argument on the order followed by the sequence of chapters 2 and 3 of the *Constitution on the Church*. The Conciliar Commission replied that there was not an exact parity here. *Lumen gentium* emphasized the priority and primacy of Christian dignity and existence over juridical structure. Here it is a question of mission. Now, one cannot deny that it was given to the apostles by a definite mandate recorded by all the gospels.[9] Nor can one deny that all of the disciples, the whole Church, were also sent. That is why the *Decree on the Apostolate of the Laity* (art. 5) shows how the apostles bore a twofold character: they were both the seed of the new People of God and the beginning of the hierarchy. It distinguishes, therefore, two titles of mission: the mandate given to the apostles which the hierarchy inherits, and the responsibility of communicating the life received inherent in the fact of membership in the People of God or in the mystical body.

We have already emphasized the fact that in the dogmatic *Constitution on the Church* the Council avoided treating laymen only from the viewpoint of their apostolate. It fully satisfied the general desire of having a broad exposition of the ontology and dignity of the Christian, of Christian existence. It did this within the framework, adopted in several of its documents, of the three offices or functions one sees at work in the history of the People of God and which were brought to perfection in Jesus Christ. We shall take them up in the order in which they appear in chapter 4 on the laity: priesthood, prophecy and kingship. This distinction into the three offices was first systematized in Calvinist theology. It is abundantly attested to by Scripture, the Fathers of the Church, the great scholastics and the liturgy.[10] The application made of it to a Christian *sine addito*, the layman, is very remarkable. It considers him as a consecrated being, fully a member of the Church, having a share in all the vital acts of the holy City of God, the Church.[11] On the level of Christian existence or dignity, and even from the viewpoint of what they bring to the building up of the body of Christ, all Christians are equal. Article 32 of the *Constitution on the Church* affirms this with great emphasis.

The New Testament idea of spiritual sacrifice had been restored in the last fifteen years, not only by exegetes but also theologians.[12] It is the offering to God of our whole life, of our persons such as they are, along with their internal and external activity (cf. Rom 12:1). For the Christian everything is matter for personal sacrifice, and for this each one is himself the irreplaceable priest—everything, that is, except sin. Seen in this way, the limits and distinction between the so-called sacred and profane disappear. Everything one offers up is sacred; the only thing that is profane is what one profanes by sin. Our leisure, even conjugal relations (not only family life) are matter for spiritual sacrifice. The *Constitution on the Church* adopts and expressly consecrates this view of things (art. 34). In complete accord with what was said above in articles 10 and 28, and in the *Constitution on the Sacred Liturgy* (art. 48), as well as in the *Decree on the Ministry and Life of Priests* (art. 2, 5), it adds that the personal priesthood of self-offering finds its fulfillment in liturgy when the baptized unite their self-offering to that of Jesus Christ corporately through the ministry of ordained priests in the celebration of the eucharist. The true subject of this celebration is not the priest alone but the *ecclesia* through him—or the priest insofar as he is a minister of the *ecclesia*.

Thus a profound unity between one's personal life and the communal liturgical act is achieved, between what each one does and what the ordained priest does for all and with all. The personal and spiritual priesthood of the Christian, which already has a liturgical value, is not confused with the public priesthood of ordained ministers, which is given by another sacrament. However, the Council refused to characterize the common priesthood as simply "metaphorical." It is spiritual but real; spiritual means something altogether different from "moral."

That all this was proclaimed in a solemn document of the extraordinary magisterium represents a sensational recovery on the part of the contemporary Church. To my mind we are far from having drawn all the consequences or fruits, either at the level of the spirituality of the faithful—if we may use this expression—or at that of a still imperfect theology of the liturgy, of the real subject of liturgical action, of the true nature of Christian cult.

What is said in article 35 of the *Constitution on the Church* on the participation of the laity in the prophetic function of Christ is no less remarkable. A century ago these declarations would have been called Protestant. Now they are there; they are supported by other passages, whether from the same document (art. 12 on the meaning of faith and charisms), or from the dogmatic *Constitution on Divine Revelation* (art. 10 on the whole People of God as guardian and propagator of the apostolic tradition), or from the *Decree on the Apostolate of the Laity* (art. 6 on witness; art. 11 on the family as the place where faith is preserved and transmitted, and so forth), or from the *Decree on the Ministry and Life of Priests* (art. 2 with the citation from Ap 19:10). The repeated mention of charisms in these diverse texts is quite noteworthy. Oftentimes, very important themes are barely mentioned in these texts—a little like an area about to undergo urbanization where a number of avenues, which will be lengthened in the future, are barely outlined. This seems to us to be the case with what is suggested in the *Constitution on the Church* (art. 35) about the struggle against the "Powers" by means of a simple citation of Eph 6:12. This theme touches on the spiritual kingship of the Christian.

This kingship is also priestly. In the patristic tradition it is usually explained and developed in the sense of spiritual liberty and of the paschal ideal, of a mastery of our covetousness and passions. In this sense, one is king of what one can bring and offer to God: spiritual kingship is priestly. The *Constitution on the Church* (art. 36) does not overlook these themes, but it does not give much attention to them. It develops rather the aspect of Christians' cooperation with the royal action by which Christ subjects all things to himself. The reason for this difference between the Fathers and the Council is perhaps that formerly the task of Christianizing the civil and political temporal order was left to the prince; today the temporal appears to be much larger than the political, for it includes the social and cultural, scientific research, ideologies, opinion, collective structures and the means of communication—and it depends on all the citizens of the human city. The themes of spiritual kingship are still valid, and personally I regret that they are not sufficiently developed. They could be, in view of the new knowledge we have gained about man. But one will encounter a certain amount of dissatisfaction if they are presented only in a purely moral, individual and interior direction along the lines of the *Imitation of Christ* or of Port Royal. It should also be shown that work along the social and even economic lines of the temporal order makes it possible for a greater number of men to acquire moral control and a deeper spiritual life. We must show and achieve the unity of the twofold exercise of Christian kingship.

These observations bring us to a new theme contained in the Council's documents and especially in the *Constitution on the Church*. Let us emphasize again the fact that the Council in no way reduced the laity to being the long arm of the "Church"—I use the expression here to mean the hierarchy—in the temporal order. On the contrary, it wanted to describe them first of all as members of the Holy Church "set apart," as they say, and as active in the spiritual domain whether in the liturgy, the apostolate or charity. However, it is still true—and it is stated in all the decrees—that lay Christians, in the Council's sense of the word, are by their very situation in a position to act on the temporal and, as the *Constitution on the Church* says, to sanctify it from within, so to speak (art. 31). Although the priest has to help sanctify the temporal order by his own ministry, the sanctification of the temporal order depends in a special way on the laity insofar as the temporal order itself must be directed, as regards its own structures, in a Christian way and toward God.[13] Thus the area touched on by the Council is enormous. We shall come back to it during the week. I would simply like to make here three important points.

1) The basic category "People of God" is of great significance in a new approach to these questions, and I am surprised that it appears so little in the pastoral *Constitution on the Church in the Modern World* and in the *Decree on the Apostolate of the Laity*. In the older view of things, in which "Church" meant primarily the hierarchy and the institution, this Church was seen as something other than the world, as confronting it, as over it. It sent missionaries into the world. Seen as the People of God surely the Church does not receive its constitutive principles from the world, but the Church is in the world and participates in its movement (such is the Church of the *Constitution on the Church in the Modern World*)—the faithful are not so much sent to it as find themselves in it and form part of it. They are simply asked to be Christians in all that they are!

2) The Council did not wish to treat formally the question of the relations between Church and state. The *De Ecclesia* of the preparatory commission included a chapter on this question, but the Council formally excluded it from its consideration. However, it could not avoid touching it. In reality, the decrees of the Council—I have in mind especially, but not exclusively, the *Constitution on the Church in the Modern World* and the *Declaration on Religious Freedom*—make little sense from any other perspective than a frank recognition of the laicity of temporal things. Of course, the word "laicity" has many meanings. Taken in the sense defined by the *Constitution on the Church* (art. 36) it should be proscribed. But the same text and others in the *Decree on the Apostolate of the Laity* (art. 7), or in the *Constitution on the Church in the Modern World* (art. 36), frankly recognize the autonomy of the temporal. René Laurentin has written, in connection with the schema on the apostolate of the laity: "The first dominant idea of

the schema is the recognition of the normal lay character of the modern world."[14]

3) It follows then that the "consecration of the world," which the *Constitution on the Church* (art. 34) discreetly mentions,[15] cannot be considered as a consecration of the sacral type given by a liturgical act. It is merely the sanctification of the temporal order, not only in the respect shown its structures, laws and relative autonomy—such "respect" would be a rather negative value—but in the promotion and service of its structures and movement. Once more this supposes a decisive exorcising of the deceptive distinction between the so-called profane and sacred. This distinction was clearly denounced in other, more concrete words at the Council.[16] The task has been started well; the *Constitution on the Church in the Modern World* represents a step forward. But we must push to the complete assumption of "the religion of man" into the Religion of God, in the sense in which Pope Paul VI spoke in his unforgettable address of December 7, 1965. The perspectives opened up by this address are basically those of the pastoral *Constitution on the Church in the Modern World*. We must carry on and extend the movement of the Council in this direction. This will also involve some anthropological work.

We would like to raise one final point which has been touched upon by several Conciliar documents,[17] namely, the relations between laity and hierarchy. They obviously contain classical statements—always true, by the way—on the subordination of the laity to pastors. But a certain number of new emphases keep reappearing. There is, first of all, the insistence on community of life and on dignity in the order of Christian existence, then the correlative and profound theme of hierarchy as service; the acknowledgment of the existence of charisms among all the faithful, and for the priest the duty of taking them into consideration, which affords a rather new pneumatological view of the Church.

The Church of Vatican II has emerged from the fortress of the Counter-Reformation and of a certain defensive mentality in which nothing must enter the citadel without being duly checked and carefully sifted. The Church claims there is something for her to learn from the world (*Constitution on the Church in the Modern World* 44); contact with the laity can refresh the spirit of pastors (*Decree on the Apostolate of the Laity* 10). They should, then, listen willingly to the laity and allow them a considerable amount of freedom and initiative. The creation of a diocesan pastoral council in which laymen, though chosen by the bishop, will have their place[19] is envisaged. There should be established in Rome a Secretariat for the apostolate of the laity (*Decree on the Apostolate of the Laity* 26). Cardinal Heenan predicted that it would be headed for failure, if it were modeled on the already existing services of the Curia, and if a goodly number of competent laymen were not made members of it.[20]

All this is excellent and a good omen. Nonetheless we must recognize that we are very far from attaining not only what concerns the operation and structures of Vatican II's Church, but, more seriously, we are still very far from having the necessary theological concepts. It will take time for the idea underlying the People of God to find its full explicitation. Do we even have the indispensable historical and exegetical studies for that? The idea of collegiality was limited at the Council to the level of ecclesiastical structures; it had reappeared much too recently to have aroused much reflection on its profound roots and its place in Christian ontology as such (even now this has been barely outlined).[21] Canon Ch. Moeller very wisely remarks: "The final text of *Lumen gentium* does not gather about this term [collegium] the 'collegial' aspects of the relations between the hierarchy and the laity, aspects that Oriental theology stresses so strongly in its eucharistic ecclesiology of the local churches"[22]—not only Oriental theology but Protestant (Lutheran as well as Calvinist) theology of ministries. There is unquestionably here a whole area for our ecclesiology and pastoral organization to recover. Everything the decrees of the Council say is excellent, but they lack a bit of ontological depth. There is still much to be done. To follow it up means to go forward along the lines opened up by the Council which consistently looked at juridical relations in the light and on the level of the ontology of communion and of the sacramental foundation of the Church.

NOTES

1. See my chapter "Les laics et l'ecclésiologie des "ordines" chez les théologiens des XIe et XIIe siècles," *I laici nella "Societas christiana" dei secoli XI et XII* (Milan, 1966).

2. On this matter, see my article "Laie, Laienstand," *Lexicon f. Theol. u. Kirche*, 6 (2nd edit. 1961) 733ff.; G. Martelet, *Sainteté de l'Eglise et Vie religieuse* (Toulouse, 1965).

3. (Westminster, Md.: Newman, 1957); French edition: *Jalons pour une théologie du laicat*, Unam Sanctam, 23 (Paris, 1953).

4. *Über das Laienapostolat*," an article reproduced in *Schriften zur Theologie* 2 (Einsiedeln: Benziger, 1955) 339–373; in French as "L'Apostolat des laics," *Nouvelle Revue théologique* 78 (1956) 5–32.

5. Cf. *Constitution on the Church* 33; *Decree on the Apostolate of the Laity* 1–3. Cf. also the *Decree on the Church's Missionary Activity* 5, 21, 36.

6. See, for example, the speech of Pius XII of Oct. 14, 1951; his exhortation of Dec. 8, 1947, to the young members of Roman Catholic Action; his sermon of Jan. 25, 1950, to the Italian bishops. Apostolate means to lead men to Christ and to his reign.

7. See particularly L. M. Dewailly, *Envoyés du Père* (Paris, 2nd ed. 1960); A. Seumois, *Apostolat. Structure théologique*, Urbaniana, N.S. 1 (Rome, 1961); F. Klostermann, *Das christliche Apostolat* (Innsbruck, 1962).

8. See L. M. Dewailly, "Note sur l'histoire de l'adjectif Apostolique, *Mélanges de Science religieuse* (1948) 141–152; H. Holstein, "L'évolution du mot apostolique au cours de l'histoire de l'Eglise," *L'Apostolat*, Probl. de la Religieuse d'aujourd'hui (Paris, 1957) 41–62; F. Klostermann, op. cit., 93–172.

9. Mt 28:18–29; Mk 16:14–16; Lk 24:44–48; Jn 21:19–23; Acts 1:8.

10. See J. Fuchs, *Magisterium, Ministerium, Regimen. Vom Ursprung einer ekklesiologischen Trilogie* (Bonn, 1941); my *Jalons* (note 3) with bibliography.

11. Commenting on Eph 2:19, St. Thomas Aquinas notes that the Church is both a family and a city: a family if one considers the relations between its members and their head who is God the Father; a city if one considers the status of the members who participate in the same "actibus praecipuis," in the highest activities and in the same common good. There are no islands in the Church, no proletariat: all have full citizenship.

12. For exegesis: Ph. Seidensticker, *Lebendiges Opfer* (Rom 12, 1). *Ein Beitrag zur Theologie des Apostels Paulus* (Munster, 1954). For theology see my *Jalons* (note 3) and "Structure du sacerdoce chrétien," *Maison-Dieu* 27 (1951) 51–85; reprinted in *Sainte Eglise* (Paris, 1963) 239–274.

13. Cf. *Constitution on the Church* 31, 33, 36; *Decree on the Apostolate of the Laity* 7; *Constitution on the Church in the Modern World* 43.

14. *L'enjeu du Concile* 3: *Bilan de la deuxième session* (Paris, 1964) 89.

15. See the illuminating pages of M.-D Chenu, "Consecratio mundi," *Nouvelle Revue theologique* 96 (1964) 608–618 and in the collection edited by P. G. Baraúna, *L'Eglise de Vatican II*.

16. For example by Msgr. Sani (Indonesia) who was "surprised that the cooperation of the layman with God's plan seemed to be presented as something over and above 'their burdens and functions in the world' (praeter sua officia et munera). . . . it is not alongside of but in the very fulfillment of his daily duty that the layman is an apostle. If not, we are in full dualism." (R. Laurentin, *L'enjeu du Concile* 4: *Bilan de la troisième session* [Paris, 1965] 124–125.) The *Decree of the Apostolate of the Laity* overcame this dualism well; cf. art. 4.

17. *Constitution on the Church* 32, 37; *Decree on the Apostolate of the Laity* 10, 24–26; *Decree on the Ministry and Life of Priests* 3, 6, 9; *Constitution on the Church in the Modern World* 43; even the *Constitution on Divine Revelation* 10, 25.

18. *Constitution on the Church* 12, 35; *Decree on the Apostolate of the Laity* 3; *Decree on the Ministry and Life of Priests* 9.

19. *Decree on the Bishops' Pastoral Office in the Church* 27; *Decree on the Church's Missionary Activity* 30; *Decree on the Apostolate of the Laity* 26.

20. Cf. Laurentin, op. cit., 122.

21. See however, J. Ratzinger, "The Pastoral Implications of Episcopal Collegiality," *The Church and Mankind*, Concilium vol. 1 (Glen Rock, 1965) 39–67.

22. Ch. Moeller, History of *Lumen Gentium's* Structure and Ideas," in this volume, p. 133.

Rev. Bernard Häring, C.Ss.R.

HOLINESS IN THE CHURCH

C HAPTER 5 OF THE *Constitution on the Church* may be considered as a key to the right understanding of the whole Council, namely, that it is a Council of spiritual renewal. This chapter may also be seen as a response to some dangerous tendencies in the Church and a positive response to what had already come to life in the Church through the biblical and liturgical renewal. Pope John explained in his first talk after his election that he saw his pontificate above all as a call to all the clergy and the whole People of God to become "a perfect people for the Lord."

As to the history of this chapter, it should not be overlooked that some, especially the preparatory commission for the religious life, showed a tendency to make perfection or holiness some kind of monopoly of religious; for instance, they originally asserted that those who wish to become perfect freely choose the state of perfection or evangelical counsels, whereas the others live only under prescripts and laws. Such tendencies were judged by our separate brethren as seemingly betraying two sets of moral standards: one for those who freely choose to go fully the way of perfection; still another for those living only under the law. It is clear, however, that at the very heart of the moral teaching of the New Testament stands St. Paul's reminder: "You are not under law but under grace" (Rom 6:14). This he says of all Christians. They are not under a mere external regime of law; they all are called to the holiness of the People of God by means of a spontaneous response to God's gifts.

250

We must also realize the nature of the Church would be changed profoundly, if only a small part of her membership were actually to be called to holiness, or if holiness were really possible in one state of life only. The implications of the Church's very essence and existence, then, had to be brought out by means of this chapter on the universal call to holiness. The Church is holy by reason of her being called by the Holy One of Israel. Being called to be holy, what does this mean?

God Alone is Holy

When we speak of the holiness of the People of God, we must always keep in mind the fundamental truth: "You alone are holy . . . , O Jesus Christ, . . . with the Holy Spirit in the glory of God the Father." If there is any holiness in the Church, it comes from the One who is the Holy God. Holiness in man is above all loving worship of the One who alone is holy. This is the meaning of the life of Jesus Christ: his whole life is a loving worshiping of his heavenly Father and a glorification of him through his love for his brethren. As the Constitution says, "Christ, The Son of God who, with the Father and the Spirit is praised as being 'alone holy,' loved the Church as His bride, delivering Himself up for her. This He did that He might sanctify her. He united her to Himself as His own body and enriched her with the gift of the Holy Spirit for God's Glory" (art. 39).

In this introductory text of chapter 5, Christ's activity is placed alongside the mystery of the Holy Trinity. Christ accomplishes the sanctification of the Church by giving himself in a love that is boundless. We should remember here the words of the Lord's priestly prayer, "For them do I sanctify myself, that they may be sanctified in truth" (Jn 17:19). On Christ rests the fullness of the Spirit who anoints and sends him for the salvation of the poor. In Christianity holiness is more than good ethical conduct, but at the same time it is not something besides its ethical content; it is but the perfect synthesis of adoring love and fraternal love. Christ consecrates himself to be sacrificed and that means to make his whole life one of praise of the Father through his redeeming love for his brethren. His manner of consecrating himself to the work of redemption, the sanctifying of his own for the human race, manifests the ultimate mystery, "All things that are mine are thine and thine are mine" (Jn 17:10). He who comes from the Father and reveals the boundless depth of his love returns to the Father by way of self-sacrificing love for his own.

Holiness in man must fundamentally be understood as *a gift coming from God* who reveals the glory of his triune love by making man a sharer in his own love, in his own freedom, in his own goodness. Hence, human holiness of necessity means giving back to God the honor he has in himself. This understanding of the entire Christian life in terms of worship is especially emphasized in the *Constitution on the Sacred Liturgy*. It is taken up again and developed with even greater clarity in chapter 2 of the *Constitution on the Church*, especially in articles 10 and 11, as well as in chapter 4 on *"The Laity,"* particularly in articles 34 to 36. Already in these two places the accent falls on the universality of the call to holiness. Christ has sanctified himself making himself a sacrifice for his entire people. Therefore the whole People of God is a "priestly people." Chapter 5 follows as a matter of course from the sanctification of the Church through the self-sacrificing love of Christ and the giving of the Holy Spirit. "In the Church, everyone, whether belonging to the hierarchy or being cared for by it, is called to holiness, according to the saying of the Apostle: 'For this is the will of God, your sanctification'" (art. 39).

The obligation of leading a holy life in the service of one's brethren for the glory of God comes above all from the fact that holiness is a gift. From this it follows that nobody should ever frustrate or render unfruitful the sanctifying and freely bestowed operations of God. Article 39 accordingly speaks of "the fruits of grace that the Spirit produces in the faithful," by which the holiness of the Church is unceasingly manifested. Article 40 continues this theme with reference to the sanctifying operations of God in the sacraments: "By God's gifts they must hold on to and complete in their lives this holiness which they have received."

The holiness of the whole Church and of every individual Christian has to be understood in the light of the sacraments and, therefore, finally in the light of the paschal mystery. There we see Christ responding to the love of the Father: "A body thou hast fitted for me. . . . Behold I come to do thy will" (Heb 10:5, 7; cf. Ps 39:7–9). He is totally given to the Father as a response of gratitude for what he is and is, therefore, accepted as a holocaust for his brethren. Surrendering himself totally to the Father through this worshiping love, Christ redeems man from the sin of Adam and his followers. This sin is the refusal to render total worship to God. Chapters 3 and 4 of Genesis, as well as chapter 1 of the Epistle to the Romans, show that the misery of sin with all its perversions falls upon mankind when Adam, the prototype and the forefather of all sinners, refused to receive everything as a gift of God and to return it to God. He wished to have his freedom and his wisdom as his own; he did not adore God, and the consequence is that this same attitude separates men from one another. Adam began by accusing his wife: "It was the woman," said he to God, "the woman, whom thou gavest me to be my companion" (Gn 3:12). It was also out of the refusal to be a worshiper that arose the sin of Cain who murdered his brother. In the same vein Lamech, in disregard for the dignity of woman, takes two wives and threatens them with words of violence.

Worshiping Love and Redeeming Love

Christ is the prototype of those who worship the Father in spirit and truth. His act of worship, his sacrifice, is at one and the same time the manifestation of the full extent of his love for the Father and of the Father's love for the whole of mankind. Christ redeems us through an act of worship. His worship of the heavenly Father is the witness of fraternal redeeming love. But at the same time, it follows that there can only be a full act of worship in a love that makes our brethren free, that embraces all. In view of Christ, to worship the heavenly Father fully means (as chapter 15:5–6 of the Epistle to the Romans puts it) to glorify the Father with one mouth through oneness of heart.

Holiness in the Church expresses itself in terms of a reverential encounter with others, and finally with the Father in Heaven. Love of God is not possible without love for one's neighbor; biblical theology confirms this. In love of God and neighbor man also finds his true self. In religious morality, there is no question of mere self-perfection, or of a slavish subjection to impersonal laws: everything becomes a personal relationship with the personal God who encounters us in Jesus Christ. Everything that happens to us takes on a new wealth and beauty, a much higher degree of seriousness: in particular is this true of the moral law, which becomes a personal call to an unselfish love of benevolence. Whether or not we obey it, it is a matter of a personal relationship with our best friend, our creator and Redeemer. A moral theology that is purely abstract and impersonal, or purely legal, makes for infantilism. The following of Christ educates one to personal maturity in community. The community must also remain a worshiping community if the relationship of members of the community is to remain reverential, respectful, unselfish.

It is self-evident that such a moral message of interpersonal relations is not relativism. The three Divine Persons who are and express themselves in their relation to one another are opposed to a relativism without content as the absolute of personal being and intercommunion. Man finds his stability and essence only in God's creative and redeeming word and work. He apprehends his true being in a word that in due time becomes a deed: it has to be a *true* deed and word insofar as it is responsive word. There is no so-called objective morality in the sense that its starting point is mere abstract cold principles that express nothing of the actuality of the person and of personal relationship. There is, however, a truly objective morality, or one grounded in reality, insofar as in all its principles it considers above all the person in the rectitude of his relations with God, with his neighbor, with the community, with all created things and events, to all of which he is related in the word of God.

This must be clearly stated against certain tendencies of a so-called *situational ethics* which claims that apart from love there is no objective reality or law, and seems to assert that this love could legitimately express itself in a discontinuity of opposed contents. Personal relationships, or a personal relation which is based on the outgoing quality of one person to another, must show that love is faithful, witnessing to the continuity of the word of God. Love guarantees true continuity through growth in depth. True love has its order, its structure, its truth. But this truth cannot be found or be expressed if we forget about the persons who are involved—if we fail to pursue the building up of personal relationships between God and man, between man and man, and between community and community.

THE LAW OF THE SPIRIT

Nothing is perhaps more indicative of the nature of the *Constitution on the Church* as its constant pneumatology. All the Church's activity, all the gifts of grace, are presented throughout in the light of the Holy Spirit's operation. Almost without exception, every article of this long document presents the doctrine about the Church according to its relationship to the Holy Spirit. He "was sent on the day of Pentecost in order that He might forever sanctify the Church, and thus all believers and would have access to the Father through Christ in the one Spirit. He is . . . the fountain of water springing up to eternal life" (art. 4). To him are attributed, most of all, the gifts of unity and love in an all-embracing solidarity (e.g.: articles 7, 12, 15, 17, 22). The Holy Spirit vivifies and rules the Church through the variety of gifts and ministries. In fact, it is precisely through the manifold character of his gifts and callings that he creates authentic unity (art. 32).

The leading idea of chapter 2 on the People of God is that sanctification and salvation in community are the purpose of God's salvific plan in choosing the Israelite people. Then in full continuity with the prophets (Jer 31:31–34), the law written by the Holy Spirit in the hearts and minds of men is described as the sign of the new and eternal covenant (art. 9).

The universal call to holiness is very heavily accentuated in chapter 3 on the laity. The variety of gifts and commissions can in no way prejudice holiness in unity and love precisely because this variety of gifts and commissions is the work of one and the same Spirit (art. 32). Thus he unites and sanctifies the Church. Article 34 explains that it is through the Holy Spirit that Christ, the supreme and eternal priest, gives us a share in his priesthood and urges us on to every good and perfect word.

It is important to notice how the doctrine of chapter 5 concerning our common vocation to holiness is basically linked to the workings of the Holy Spirit. For the New Covenant's moral teaching, it does not suffice to speak now on the great mystery, reality, and commandment of love and then on the grace of the Holy Spirit. Everything must be seen in the light of "the law of the Spirit" who gives us a Christ-like life and sets us free from the law of sin (Rom 8:2). Like the Epistles of St. Paul, the *Constitution on the Church* should serve as an example to the theologian and pastor. The moral message of the New Covenant is always and in everything the good tidings of the loving God who has poured out his love in our heart through his Holy Spirit.

Article 39, introducing the entire chapter on the universal call to holiness, is as pneumatological as it is Christocentric. Holiness is seen from the viewpoint of the gifts of the Holy Spirit who makes us sharers of Christ's mission and life. But we must not think of these exclusively in terms of the classic schema, the seven gifts of the Holy Spirit. The viewpoint is rather that of the sanctifying will of God. All holiness must be understood as the "fruits of grace that the Holy Spirit produces in the faithful." If in this context a freely chosen life according to the evangelical counsels is said to provide a kind of pattern of holiness, that is not to be understood as if lay spirituality were a mere stereotype of cloister spirituality. Article 40 teaches that it is the Holy Spirit who moves the conscience of the faithful from within to love of God and neighbor, bringing about in us that love which is the fullness of the New Law. Love and other fundamental Christian attitudes are to be taken here not so much as a commandment imposed upon man, but as of the "harvest of the Spirit of sanctification." This demands a deeper commitment of greater urgency than the external understanding of a mere commandment.

The variety of God's gifts revealing his sovereignty and love are also a factor essential to the understanding of the characteristics of the different forms of life and ministry in the Church. Everyone participates in the life of Christ in a unique way under the impulse of the Holy Spirit. Evidently, there are precious special gifts of the Holy Spirit (one of them, celibacy for the kingdom of God). These special gifts are an urgent call to those on whom they are bestowed to become witnesses to the universal vocation to holiness. In this great perspective, the life of the evangelical counsels does not separate Christians into two classes: it dedicates one group totally to the service of all, helping them to understand ever better their common call to holiness and their different tasks and charisms.

The fact that the *Constitution on the Church* so consistently expounds the Christian life and the vocation to holiness in the light of the operations of the Holy Spirit not only closes the door against the constant temptation to a Pelagian or semi-Pelagian way of thinking, but is also a rampart against legalism that seeks to insure men and institutions by means of mere legal supervision and the reduction of all forms of life to dead uniformity and immobility.

Consequently, a genuine formation of Christians and in particular that of tomorrow's priests is something that will bring to maturity the freedom of the sons of God, which grows constantly in the context of the "kairos": the time of favor, the time prepared for by God through the internal call of grace and through the particular situation in which one finds himself. It is not possible simply to work out a full Christian perspective according to a preconceived plan of life. Christian life remains constantly subject to the challenge of the Holy Spirit's gifts, to the present needs of one's neighbor, in view of a person's real potentialities. Such a life means courage in the spirit of Christian adventure, a constant deepening and assimilation of the significance of events in the light of eschatological hope.

Many will anxiously ask if this is not to leave the door open to lawless situation ethics. It is a question that must be faced. Those who hitherto have not been able to see their way between a legal uniformity and an ethics without content make life extremely poor and hinder creative generosity. On the other hand, a situation ethics hostile to all law misunderstands the true meaning of "the law of the Spirit who gives us life in Christ Jesus." It speaks about love and freedom as though they were no more than doing one's own will. But we simply may not react in a legalistic way, for legalism is at the very root of situation ethics. The Christian is, in fact, not under a regime of law but under grace (Rom 6:14). Christian existentialism means leaving one's own selfishness aside in a total surrender of one's self to the guidance of God's grace, doing the true good "here and now" possible. Living under the law of faith is the real triumph over a situation ethics hostile to law and is at the same time the positive establishment of the magnificent order "imposed" by love and grace.

The chapter on the universal call to holiness, especially the fact that this doctrine permeates the whole *Constitution on the Church*, opens new horizons for the renewal of Christian morality. The Church's moral message will more visibly be a preaching of the good news and an appeal to a constant vigilance. It will be more clearly seen as a unified view in the light of the great *mystery* of love. It will help to educate Christians to face their responsibility in the world of today.

I understand the anxiety of those who fear that this perspective will diminish the number of vocations to the priesthood and religious life. But my own deep conviction is that only such a view of the law of the Spirit can prepare Christians for the great variety of roles within the Church's work for the salvation of the world. It will prepare Christians always to face up to the questions "What is the loving will of God here and now? Where can I best serve the common good, the building up of the mystical body of Christ?" Only a perspective that perceives the full value of the Holy Spirit's operation can prepare for particular vocations without diminishing appreciation for the common vocation to holiness. It is precisely faith in the universal vocation to holiness through the Holy Spirit that develops a variety of spiritualities expressing the unity of the People of God and the special mission of priests, religious, and the laity in their different states of life. Variety will always become one in seeking the common good. Gift of the Holy Spirit who distributes the charisms with divine largesse, charity is the bond of unity in variety, opening man's heart to his neighbors, in humble watchfulness for the signs of the time. It also guarantees true continuity in spiritual growth.

On this earth, however, holiness in human beings demands *constant conversion*—renewal of mind, heart and will—of persons and communities, in order to render glory to God who alone is absolutely faithful and holy.

Rev. Henri de Lubac, s.j.

MEDITATION ON THE CHURCH

I<small>T MIGHT BE GOOD FOR US TONIGHT</small> to interrupt for a moment our analyses, exegesis, theories and discussions, in short, all the work of a reasoning and probing theology, to pause together in a contemplative gaze on the object of our common study—a gaze that is closer to what an ancient and venerable tradition used to call "theology." It can be good for us, perhaps even necessary, if it is true that the *alpha* and *omega* of our study are summed up in the word "mystery"—*De ecclesiae mysterio*. But by way of introducing ourselves to it, let us begin, if you do not mind, with a more modest step. Before considering the mystery of the Church, let us meditate on the paradox of it.

What a paradoxical reality, indeed, this Church is with all its contrasting aspects! How many irreducible images history presents us with! In her nearly twenty centuries, how many changes have occurred in her attitudes, how many strange developments, how many metamorphoses! Even today, and despite the new conditions of a world that is tending to become standardized, what a distance, sometimes what an abyss—not to speak of the divisions resulting from the ruptures—between the Christian communities of the various countries, in their mentality, in their manner of living and viewing their faith! Moreover, at the same time and place, does it not happen that we see groups or individuals, each claiming with so much fervor to belong to the Church, each claiming an equal fidelity to her—and yet opposing others in almost everything, to such a point that a good observer could recently say

258

that profession of the Catholic faith, far from being a principle of unity, seemed rather to be a principle of division.

The Church . . . but when I myself look for her, where will I find her? Of what features is her face composed? All these disparate elements that belong to her, can they even form a face? Yes, I believe they can; she is a *complexio oppositorum*. But after all, must I not first recognize that this clash of opposites hides from me the unity of the *complexio*? Does this come only from the successive angles under which I observe her? Is it not in herself that these incompatible things subsist? I am told that she is holy, yet I see her full of sinners. I am told that her mission is to tear man away from his earthy cares, to remind him of his eternal vocation, yet I see her constantly preoccupied with the things of the earth and of time, as if she wished us to live here forever. I am assured that she is universal, as open as divine intelligence and charity, and yet I notice very often that her members, through some sort of necessity, huddle together timidly in closed groups—as human beings do everywhere. She is hailed as immutable, alone stable and above the whirlpools of history, and then, suddenly, under our very eyes, she upsets many of the faithful by the suddenness of her renewals.

Yes, paradox of the Church. This is not vain rhetoric. Paradox of a Church made for a paradoxical humanity, and sometimes only too well does she adapt herself to it. She takes on its characteristics with all their complexities and inconsistencies, with the endless contradictions that are in man. We can point to this phenomenon in every century, and specialists in criticism and pamphleteering—alas, a proliferating race—do it with glee. In the very first generations, when she hardly extended beyond the limits of the old Jerusalem, the Church already reflected the features, the miseries, of our common humanity.

Let us try to focus our attention. Let us try to pierce the thick layers of her profile. Let us shake off the illusion of quantity that always hides the essential, for the essential is never in large numbers, or in first impressions. Then shall we discover the paradox peculiar to the Church, and this paradox will lead us to her mystery.

She is both human and divine, given from above, and come from below. Those who belong to her resist, with all the weight of a burdened and wounded nature, the Life with which she tries to permeate them. She is turned toward the past, meditating on a memorial which she knows contains what will never be surpassed; and, at the same time, she looks to the future and rejoices in the hope of an ineffable fulfillment that suffers not even a glimpse. Called, in her present form, to disappear completely like the face of this world, she is destined, in her very essence, to remain whole from the day her innermost being is disclosed. Varied and multiform, she is nonetheless one with the most active and the most demanding unity. She is a people, a huge anonymous crowd, and yet—what other expression is there—the most personal Being. Catholic, that is, universal, she wants her members to be open to all, yet she is only fully herself when she withdraws to the intimacy of her interior life in the silence of adoration. She is both humble and majestic. She claims to assimilate every culture and ennoble its every value; at the same time, she sees herself the home of little ones, the poor, the simple, miserable multitude. Not for a moment does she pause—for this would mean her death, and she is immortal—in contemplating him who is at once the crucified and the resurrected, the Man of suffering and the Lord of glory, the Victim of the world and its Savior, at once her bleeding Spouse and her triumphant Master, the Heart wide-open and ever infinitely secret, from whom she received her existence, from whom she draws at every moment of her history the Life she yearns to share with all.

How can I encompass and understand this Church? The more I try to come to terms with her, the more I put aside the erroneous ideas about her, the more her profound truth bursts before my eyes—the less I know how to define her. Should I ask her own definition of herself, she speaks to me with a profusion of images drawn from her ancient Bible, which are not, I know very well, simple pedagogical illustrations, but rather allusions to a reality that will always remain blurred at its center for my natural intelligence. Yes, even after she answers me as she has never done before, with a special effort of logical and precise clarity in this Constitution *Lumen gentium*, when I begin to meditate about her I plunge into a mystery whose obscurity lingers on.

My eyes, however, have not deceived me. They revealed something to me, prior to any reflection and confirmed by every reflection. This something I can sum up in a word, the simplest, the most childlike, the first of all words: the Church is my mother. Yes, the Church, the whole Church: that of the past generations which handed on her life to me, her teachings, her example, her mores, her love; and that of today, the whole Church, not only the official Church, or the teaching Church or, as we still say, the hierarchical Church, the Church that holds the keys the Lord entrusted to her, but, more broadly, more simply, "the living Church"—the Church that works and prays, acts and meditates, remembers and searches; the Church that believes, hopes, loves; that in the thousand and one situations of existence weaves visible and invisible links among its members; the Church of the humble, those near to Christ, a sort of secret army recruited from everywhere, enduring even during periods of decadence, dedicating itself and sacrificing itself, with no idea of revolt or reform, climbing unceasingly the slope that is our wounded nature, a silent witness that the gospel is always fruitful and that the kingdom is already among us. Yet more, the whole Church without distinction, this enormous flock, the Christian people so many of whom are so little conscious of the royal priesthood that is theirs, and of the fraternal community they form among themselves. Nonetheless in this community I find my support, my strength, my joy. This Church, she is my mother. It was at my earthly mother's knees that I first learned to know her. At each stage of my life, amid events and situations too numerous to analyze, I came to recognize her better. Her experience, she tells me, permits her to grow, in the course of centuries, in her perception of the truth revealed to her. And my own experience, my modest experience, it too, I can say to her, has permitted me to grow, in the course of my brief years, in the perception of what she is for me as for each of her faithful and in understanding her motherhood. This word "mother," the most childlike, the first one we learn—it is still the one that best sums up the knowledge acquired by an adult, by one who has known to some extent what men are, and what is in man.

The Church is my mother because she gave me Life. She is my mother because she does not cease to sustain me and, however little I lend myself to it, to deepen my knowledge of that Life. And if within me that Life is still fragile and weak, I have contemplated it outside of myself in the strength and sureness and purity of its welling up. I have seen it, I have touched it, without any doubt, and I can assure everyone of it. Just as she is everything in any sacrament, so the Church is complete in any saint. For here is the wonder: if my eyes were not always aware of it, it was because I did not know how to look. I could not see at first sight the rarest, the most unexpected and the most disconcerting beauty, because it is the most unimaginable to man: not the human perfection achieved, about which I could dream, not the wisdom fulfilled, but a strange and supernatural beauty that opened up to me unknown lands and left me completely bewildered as I answered I know not what hitherto hidden call—a beauty which, even if its radiance had never shone but through one single being, would be a witness in favor of its Source: a saint. The whole Church passes into a saint. This is what the ancients called the mystery of the *anima ecclesiastica*, two worn-out words, and hence untranslatable today, but expressing a reality of which the history of the Church gives many examples, and of which our own generation is not deprived.

Happy are those who learned from their mothers in early childhood to regard the Church as a mother! Happy, yes, happier are they whose experience, whatever it may have been, has strengthened them in this first insight! Happy are they who were one day struck, and who are so more and more, by the incredible newness, the incredible richness, and the incredible depth of the Life imparted by this mother!

This is the incredible newness spoken of by St. Ireneus when he said of Jesus Christ: "Omnem novitatem attulit, semetipsum afferens." This is richness of salvation promised in Jesus Christ, which St. Paul said he had the mission of announcing to all men (Eph 2:77; cf. 1:18). This is depth revealed by the Spirit of Christ who searches the deep things of God (1 Cor 2:10). In a word, the Church is our mother because she gives Christ to us. She gives birth to the Christ in us. She begets in us the life of Christ. She tells us as St. Paul told his dear Corinthians: "In Christ Jesus through the gospel did I beget you" (1 Cor 4:15). In her maternal function, she is the "glorious and spotless" spouse (Eph 5:27) that the God-man brought forth from his pierced heart to unite to himself "in the ecstacy of the Cross" and to make forever fruitful. (That is why her mystery, as one of the principal speakers at the Council reminded us, will always be linked to the mystery of the cross.)

Once this is seen, and I mean really seen, it will no longer be necessary to exorcise appearances in order to contemplate and love the Church as a mother. It will no longer be necessary to regain the freshness or simplicity of the first age. The Church, even today, gives me Jesus. And that is everything. What would I know of Him, what link would reach from him to me without her? Do those who disown her know that they owe him to her, if they receive Jesus? "Who will separate us from the charity of Christ? Who will separate us from the love of God that is in Jesus Christ?" The Apostle knew very well that no created force could do it. There must still be a living bond, a new Jacob's ladder, to assure across the centuries a pathway from him to us. "For millions and millions of believers (taken from among the most intelligent of men)," as someone has written, "Christ, ever since he came into the world, has never failed after each crisis in history, to re-emerge more present, more urgent, more overpowering than ever." And we believe indeed with Paul that no crisis of history will ever cut us off from him. But this certainty comes to us precisely from the Church. Jesus is living for us. But without his Church's visible continuity, in what quicksand would be lost, doubtless not his memory or his name, but his living influence, the action of his gospel and faith in his divine Person? If the first Christian community, in the fervor of its faith and love, had not been the bearer of the Spirit who brought forth the evangelists; if from generation to generation this community had not maintained substantial identity as it handed down the cult of the Lord; if in time of need churchmen had not risen, great doctors, fearless leaders or humble witnesses, to maintain in all its rigor and simplicity the letter of unalterable dogma (such as good Pope Zephyrinus in the third century, unlearned in things metaphysical, and was caught between the subtle, contradictory speculations of the followers of Hippolytus and those of Noëtus; and there have been many others since); if the great councils had not fixed once and for all Christological orthodoxy—what would Christ be for us today? And what would humanity be, deprived of Christ?

Whether it is aware of it or not, humanity needs him. Painfully emerging from the cosmos of which it was born, the human mind, an irreversible force, needs the irreversible Victory of Christ in order to fulfill its divine destiny.

Humanity must become the body of Christ in order to enter into God with him. It is adopted by the Father in Jesus the Son. It is by receiving his Life and following him as a model that it will be purified and transfigured. It "must take on the form of Christ." Such is the plan of God, this mystery hidden from ancient generations, which the Son who was with the Father revealed to us "in the fullness of time." Now it is through the Church, in the bosom of the Church, that God's plan is to be realized. The Spirit of Christ has placed in her a "unique divinizing power." She is the sacrament of Christ, the channel through which the light and strength of his gospel comes to us. She is, in our history, the axis around which the great mystical gathering must assemble. The Jerusalem of the Hebrews was only the insignificant capital of a small nation, perpetually at the mercy of powerful empires that encircled her. The Church today, a new Jerusalem, may well appear to be very small and weak, her growth quite compromised, her means of action somewhat ridiculous, even her witness often hidden. She is subjected to the assault of powerful forces, brutal or insidious depending on the century, forces of the flesh and forces of the spirit, that at times seem about to smother her, or to undermine and distintegrate her. Spiritual heir of the ancient city, the true Jerusalem, she is nonetheless "the privileged central axis," the axis of progress and of assimilation; about her eventually must gravitate everything that one day is to be transformed, saved, eternalized. To her applies the prophecy of the Psalmist:

> Glorious things are said of you,
>> O city of God!
> I will number Egypt and Babylon
>> among those who know Me;
> See, Philistia, Tyr, and the people of Ethiopia,
>> these were born therein.
> And they shall say of Sion: "One and all were born in her,
>> the Most High himself has established her."
> The Lord writes in the book of the peoples:
>> "It is there that they were born!"

Ps. 86:3–6.

The more our humanity grows, the more it is transformed, the more the Church too must renew herself. From her ancient, jealously guarded treasure she knows how to draw new things. But her relationship with Jesus Christ does not change. Her power to bring forth new children does not weaken. Far from falling back in fear, she leaves herself open, generous and naked, hospitable and serene. The more her tasks as a mother seem not only enormous but impossible and discouraging, the more she trusts her Spouse. Her children do not all understand her: some are dismayed or are scandalized;

others, who live too little according to her Spirit, believe that the time has come to introduce into all things "their own novel or subversive criteria." Under such circumstances, those who acknowledge her as mother ought to be more attached to her than ever, more anxious than ever to be renewed, as St. Paul says, by a spiritual transformation of their own mind (cf. Eph 4:23), in order to fulfill their mission with humble and active patience. For she is the hope of the world.

Now this Holy Church is sometimes also abandoned by those who, blind to her gifts, have received everything from her. Again, it also happens—and our own times show this—that she is ridiculed by those she continues to nourish. A wind bearing bitter criticism, worldwide and without reason, sometimes turns men's minds from her and poisons their hearts. It is a parching, sterilizing wind, destructive, hostile to the breath of the Spirit. When I look upon the humiliated face of my mother at such a time as that, I shall love her more than ever. Without becoming involved in counter-criticism I can show that I love her even when she is enslaved. And at the very hour when some are hypnotized by those features that make her face look old, love will make me discover in her, and with how much more truth, the hidden forces and the silent activity that give her a perpetual youth, "the great things that are born within her heart and will contagiously convert the earth."

It is an effort of unusual magnitude that she asks today of us all, an effort that corresponds to the needs of an age of change. And if this is generously given, it will indeed spell for her "a second springtime." But I must understand the conditions for this. Openness and renewal—these two words that sum up the whole program for such an effort can be misunderstood. The openness that is expected of me will be an expression of my being deeply rooted in the essential. The renewal I must promote will be an exercise of fidelity. "Only an authentic Christianity is a force of salvation for the world." Woe to me if under the pretext of openness and renewal, I begin to adore, as Newman used to say, some vague and pretentious creations of my mind instead of adoring God the Son eternally living in his Church; if I place my trust in novelties that are all too human, whose momentary warmth is already no more than that of a corpse, destined soon to disappear; if I choose to draw up alone my own *Credo*, for good or for ill, from the deep wells of truth, instead of relying on the wisdom and purity with which the Spouse has permanently endowed his Bride! May I always understand that only my attachment to her tradition, which is not a burden but a source of strength, will be at the root of bold and fruitful innovations!

To shore up these thoughts, in closing, I will call upon two witnesses; I will appeal to them as intercessors.

"We receive the Spirit of God," the great St. Augustine tells me, "if we love the Church. We are united by charity, if we are happy to bear the name of Catholic and profess that Faith." Few men have had the intellectual genius and strong personality of an Augustine. Few men, if indeed any, were as he, an explorer of subjectivity to such a point that he actually molded Western humanity for many centuries. Few men in the Church, on the other hand, have suffered as much as he for having encountered in her "the form of a slave." But no individual greatness, no interior life, have any value, if they become obstacles to the Gift of God that comes to man through the Church. He came to understand this better and better. He likewise understood that no suffering could be stronger than the bond of Catholic unity. Any personal ambition that threatens this unity cannot but be sacrilegious; it can only spring from a "false lover of the Bride," for the true friend of the spouse watches jealously over the Bride's incorruptibility. As he sees it, neither the greatest learning nor the most profound wisdom is sufficient, but rather the greatest obedience and the deepest humility. Augustine keeps repeating it; he preaches unity tirelessly, a unity that prevails over every divisive force, a unity that is love and in which love has the last word. Such a show of basic concern for the unity of the Church and her interior life will seem cramping only to one who has not understood the universality of the God-Man: "The Church is the precisely fixed horizon of the redemption wrought by Christ just as Christ is for us the horizon of God" (H. Urs von Balthasar).

From among my fathers in the faith, I shall choose a second intercessor, quite different from St. Augustine the genius; he is a man very close to us, the one we call "good pope John." He was not a reformer, not an ideologist; he was neither disdainful of the past nor always inclined to criticize. He was a good priest with a "lively and simple" faith, leading a traditional way of life, a man of classical piety. He liked to refer to those he imitated as "these good old priests of Bergamo of former days, whose memory is blessed." He enjoyed reading the *Imitation of Jesus Christ* and the *Moralia* of St. Gregory. He loved the Virgin Mary and meditated with her when saying the rosary. By means of moderate asceticism he preserved and with the help of retreats he nourished the call he had received "toward an intimate union with God." Although he was open to all who, in his words, "leave intact the sacred deposit of faith" and do not deviate from "the true mind of the Church," he was nevertheless suspicious of all "pretense and quest for self-assertion," and kept on his guard against "the mortal enemy who corrupts all that we do." Love for and fidelity to the Church guided his life. Thus does he appear in the *Journal of a Soul*, a charming book published after his death. Such was the man who was able, at a crucial moment and by "sudden impulse," to guide the bark of Peter "toward new ways of feeling, willing and acting." Good pope John never changed; he never abandoned his simplicity or lost his equilibrium, but continued to dwell peacefully "on the quiet and safe sea of God's will." One day, attracted by its fidelity, the Spirit descended upon this humble existence—the true Spirit of God, the sole Inspirer of authentic renewal. A great prophetic breath awakened the whole Church, so to speak, and overflowed. As the good Pope, without having sought it, found the way to the heart of modern men, it became evident to the world that the Church was once again alive.

CONGAR: I'm asked a question regarding my definition of the laity, a definition in which I had included the commitment to the work of the world. The questioner tells me, however, that the priest is committed in the work of the world, too. There are married priests, there are priests who teach science, and there are even priest-workers and therefore there is an involvement in the work of the world. That is true; however, one cannot build a theology on exceptions. This is what was done by Ockham, but this is somewhat nominalist. It may happen that priests act as laymen. But the service of God proper to the priest is determined, not by his native situation in the world, but by the mission given him by the Church, insofar as the Church is something else than the world. Thus the priest-worker does not really act as a priest, unless he is sent. It is the Church that determines this situation. I believe that in this definition the essential thing, something underscored by Rahner, is that the layman is one whose service to God is determined by his human commitment as such, whereas the priest's service is determined by the Church as distinct from the world itself.

FRANSEN: Could you not say that the priest remains at the same time one of the faithful? And as one of the faithful he keeps his responsibilities with regard to the world?

CONGAR: Well, that is true. Of course, he is still one of the faithful, and in particular he must offer his personal sacrifice, do penance, pray as any one of the faithful. But I believe that as far as service is concerned, the totality is assumed within the priestly ministry and, as far as I am concerned, the priest should not normally do the work of the world; he should not vote, he should not serve in the army, he should not have a temporal *metier*, because he is entirely dedicated to the service of the kingdom of God.

SHEPHERD: I did not ask that particular question but one similar to it. I do raise the question in view of the very fine development in Father Congar's paper, which I heartily share, about the removal of the distinction between the sacred and the profane. I wonder whether this definition of the laity does not re-establish this distinction in a very bad way. The clergy also, it seems to me, are born in and belong to the life of the world in the same way as the laymen. We have the problem in my own communion where when we refer to holy orders we mean only the clergy, as if the baptized laity were unholy. It seems to me that this attempt to define the laity simply in terms of the world, as over against the clergy, raises a very false and dangerous distinction.

CONGAR: For me this distinction between the laity and the clergy does not in any way resemble the distinction between the profane and the holy. I stated that I should like to exclude this distinction. For the Christian nothing is profane except what he himself profanes through sin. There are, however, degrees of consecration. Father Häring spoke a while ago about the sanctity of the relgious life. Clearly the religious life is nothing more than baptism, but it is a new degree, a new form, within the baptismal consecration itself. Thus for me the lay Christian is entirely sacred, and it is remarkable how St. Peter in his first epistle applies to all the faithful practically all the terms used by the Old Testament in reference to the levites: a kind of priestly spirituality of the laity itself.

FLOROVSKY: It seems to me that Father Congar has defined the position of the laity in the Church more from a sociological viewpoint rather than from the ecclesiological point of view. The laity is an order in the Church and must be defined according to purely ecclesiological traits. On the other hand, as Father Fransen said, the laity is practically the same thing as the faithful. That is the initial, primary position of a Christian. When one is baptized he becomes a member of the faithful, or a member of the *laos theou*. Father Congar defines the position of the layman from the viewpoint of his relation to the world, but *laos theou* is not defined in terms of the world but in function of his relationship to God.

CONGAR: I may have given this impression to Father Florovsky, but it is not at all the feeling I had regarding my own exposition. It seems to me that in my own explanation, which attempted to translate what the Council said, the layman is defined according to his relation to God, as consecrated, as a priest, as having charisms, the *sensus fidei*; all this goes far beyond defining him according to his relationship to the world. But perhaps the impression I left was something else. I accept the expression "order," but I don't see what light it sheds on the question. In any case, in the Western Middle Ages this question of *ordo*, gave rise to a very sociological interpretation which I do not believe interests us any longer.

BUTLER: I should like to suggest that this question of the definition of the laity is a completely false problem. There is no definition of laity. There is a definition of a Christian. We have a definition of a priest or of a minister in holy orders. There is no third definition of the laity. A member of the laity is very simply a Christian.

CONGAR: I thought I said as much: the Christian *sine addito*, as I say very frequently.

MOELLER: My question is about Father Häring's talk. I was very much interested in his lecture. I would like not so much to ask a question, but to give to the assembly some details that may be useful for the solution of this problem that we are discussing now about laity, bishops and priests.

It seems to me that the distinction between chapter 5 and chapter 6 has some theological significance. We must not think that the so-called traditional division between priest, religious (in the canonical sense of the word) and layman is a traditional one. It is not a traditional one, because it gives the impression of being a division into three orders. On the contrary, you know that in the first elaboration of this part of the Constitution it was planned to present things in this order: the priesthood (hierarchy, bishops, pope, priests), religious, and then the laity. The division was fortunately changed, because we have there not a division into three parts but a twofold division. The first one is hierarchy and laity, the structure of the Church, and then we have a distinction between the Christian who is not a religious (in the canonical sense of the word) and one who is. We have there two kinds of distinction, two different theological principles: for one set it is the structure of the Church as such through priesthood and laity; for the other it is the way in which each baptized Christian concretely approaches the goal of holiness.

And so if we underline this theological significance of the division into chapters 3–4 on the one hand, and chapters 5–6 on the other, it is because it brings to light an ecumenical approach to the problem. I think that in the Eastern tradition the monastic life—*soli Deo placere desiderans*—was seen as coming as immediately from Christ as the priesthood. In this way one can understand why the state of a religious who is not a priest is not the state of a religious *deprived of something which is very important*; on the contrary, the state of a religious without the priesthood is a complete

269

consecration to God. It seems to me that this point is very important, because some religious undergo a crisis due to this misunderstanding, for example, brothers who are not priests sometimes get the impression that they are not completely religious men. That is completely untrue, because it is quite clear that the monastic life as such is a complete one.

And one last remark along the same line of thinking: it seems to me that in Eastern tradition the theology of the ecclesiastical hierarchy was a bit monasticized; in Western tradition, on the contrary, it was the monastic life, the religious life if you will, that was a bit ecclesiasticized. The religious life in Western tradition has been so ecclesiasticized that it is very difficult to understand the significance of religious consecration to God without the priesthood.

HÄRING: I would not deny any of Canon Moeller's points, but personally I am not happy with this chapter on religious. I am not happy, because the religious superiors just wanted to have their own chapter, which does not express well their concern for vocations, and so on. They were not concerned with seeing the whole as a whole. It was a good structure beginning as it did with the whole mystical body and the People of God. This was a very great and very important move. There was also good emphasis put on the variety of charisms. After that it was logical to speak about the Church's ministries, namely, that of bishops, priests, deacons, and the others who have a special function in the Church without receiving a special sacramental consecration. Then it would have been normal to indicate the function of the other parts of the Church, namely, the laity, their charisms, their contribution to the Church. And finally to bring out once more what unites all, what brings all together in the Church, namely, their common vocation to sanctity and thus their belonging to the communion of saints. This would have been a perfect structure.

The structure still remains in thought. But in my eyes it would have been much better if the religious would have been satisfied to have been put within this chapter on how all Christians strive together to achieve the holiness of the one Church. Already in chapter 5 there is mention of the great charity of priests, how they contribute to those in the apostolate. This would have been the perfect place to explain the charisms of religious consecrated to God, not as separated from others, not as living under another law of perfection in comparison with others. It would have perfectly shown how they are within this charismatic approach of the whole Church, are consecrated by the Church, live from the gifts of God and then help others.

McGRATH: Having worked on these chapters, I would feel that this chapter on religious is particularly weak under one aspect, and I ask Father Häring's opinion on this. It seems that much has been done to remove from the description, and to a certain extent from the definition of religious, canonical aspects that are rather external—religious life being defined in the past canonically in terms of the solemnity of the vows, or the fact that the vows are externally professed. And now it is somewhat centered in the notion of state of perfection. And yet the state of perfection itself receives many times a rather legalistic description. I think a very necessary first task has been done in restoring to the religious life, not a canonical description, but a theological sense of consecration. However, I believe that this has not been sufficiently developed, particularly in terms of the rest of the theology in this Constitution. This is a certain lacuna that must be filled in by theological thinking in this period of crisis in the readjustment of the religious life. I would like to have Father Häring's opinion on that.

HÄRING: I would return once more to one of the keys of my talk, namely, everything has to be considered from the viewpoint of God's gifts, of the Holy Spirit, who through the variety of his gifts builds up the richness, the oneness of the mystical body with its many functions. Instead of beginning with the state of perfection, a concept greatly removed from the Council, the real starting point is from the one who calls them to oneness, calls them to their special ministry, gives them their special charism, their special witness. Hence, the important question is to what is God calling me. Hence the only theologically pertinent question: Is this the contribution toward the building up of the mystical body that God expects of me because of his gifts? Did he prepare me for this? Are these the needs of the People of God? So it is the variety of the charisms. This approach avoids danger- ous claims about a state of perfection. We still heard at the Council some speeches about this unbelievable distinction: bishops belong to the *status perfectionis acquisitae*; religious belong to the *status perfectionis acquirendae*; priests belong to holy orders under canonical law; and all others are under only minimal laws. This is the most deleterious approach possible.

CONGAR: There are a lot of questions I have received that stem from the same problem. I am asked in what sense the whole People of God can be called vicar of Christ, and then why should bishops and the pope be special vicars. Or I am told if the chapter on the People of God is what I said it is, why did not the chapter on the laity follow immediately, why do the laity not have more part in the administration and direction of the Church. I am asked if laymen have a prophetic mission, why and how does the hierarchy determine the range of freedom conceded to them. Finally I am asked, with vehemence, what will be the role of women in the Church, and whether the woman is always a diminished being for the Church, an irra- tional being, only half-human some claim, or whether she should not be admitted to the functions of the priesthood. I believe that all these questions, while being quite different, stem from the same point, that is, the distinction between the order or level of personal life and the order of the public functions.

In the Church there are two distinct participations in the priestly, royal and prophetic dignity of Christ. There is a participation on the level of personal dignity, and on that level a woman is exactly like a man, and frequently much better; a layman exactly like a priest, and sometimes better. But then there is the level of public function: a participation in the priesthood, prophecy and royalty as authority—a participation in Christ's quality as head, a participation on the level of public function. This is where the difference is made in Church between laity and hierarchy, and this is where the difficulty of ordination of women comes up. This is not an invention of canon law or of the Roman Catholic or Orthodox Church, but it seems to derive from revelation itself. We have the well-known text of St. Paul. We have the example of Christ himself, and then of the apostles when Judas had to be replaced and the question of a female substitute was not even raised in the apostolic college. There may, therefore, be an element here of divine institution, certainly an apostolic institution. I would not dare affirm absolutely that it is of divine institution, but I am close to thinking so. I believe that it is a matter of fitness, for it seems that a man represents Christ better as head. This does not at all mean that Christ's sex is all that important, but rather that according to the whole of revelation from the beginning of Genesis (through the gospels, I believe) to St. Paul the function of public authority is better represented by man than by woman. Some will say there were women who were queens, judges. That's true. But should one settle Church matters on the basis of sociological and human developments. That's a problem.

Let me add two things. First of all, on the plane of personal charisms and gifts, not only is there an absolute equality, but frequently woman overruns man. Mary is above St. John the Baptist, despite the fact that we have here the two most perfect types of humanity. Secondly, not only is there a distinction between personal life and public function, but between the two you have the whole order of ministries, not only the ministries instituted as sacraments, strictly sacerdotal or episcopal ministries, but also those stemming from charisms sanctioned by a consecration of the Church. There is the ministry of teaching, a ministry to the sick, of liturgical action, of Catholic action, of missions, and so on. These are true ministries. We should restore to our ecclesiology this notion of ministry, which in fact has been too monopolized by the priesthood of the ordained. I would have no objection to seeing these ministries consecrated by liturgical ceremonies and eventually by the imposition of hands, which is a polivalent ceremony and could perfectly apply here despite the fact that it is not so traditional, if one considers the *Apostolic Tradition* of St. Hippolytus.

HÄRING: I am in full agreement of the perspective of Father Congar. I am not, however, so inclined to assert that it is of divine revelation and apostolic teaching. St. Paul gave many prescriptions and much advice to women, for instance, to be veiled if they appear in public. But these are not eternal commandments. The whole Bible must be read as history of salvation. God acted on his people always within the structures already at hand. Many Christians justified slavery because in the Holy Bible slavery was not rejected as an institution. For such a long time it was asserted that women have no right at all to speak publicly in church. It was something revolutionary when Pius XII admonished the women of Italy to take the most active part possible in public life in order to save Italy from communism. But if this can be done in such an extreme situation, then it is evident that they can speak in the assembly.

It was a need of earlier times; sociologically women did not have positions of leadership in society. It was absolutely impossible. It would have been a stumbling block for all, not only because of that terrible anthropology of Aristotle (who indeed asserted that the soul of woman is in between the soul of man and animal) but because it was indeed the way God acted historically. In this historical context no consideration at all was given to women. Then very early the institution of widows and then deaconesses was considered by the Church to be a high consecration. At that time distinctions were not yet made between order and a way of life. I believe that it would be possible to ordain women as deaconesses at the present moment. I would advise my women theologian friends not to lay claim on the episcopate or papacy yet, but to prepare the way for women to be ordained deaconesses. And if they pass the test of humbly fulfilling such a holy order in the Church, then future theological thinking on the history of salvation may clear the way for further steps.

LITTELL: I would like to raise a point concerning the *Decree on the Apostolate of the Laity*. For one thing, it is easier to get at for a Protestant, particularly a free churchman, than the articles on the role of the hierarchy as defined in the *Constitution on the Church*. And also it appeals to all men and women of good will; it reaches out a hand to take hold of. The thing which struck me in Father Congar's paper was not only that, but also the emphasis on *laicité*, on the secular order. There was the beginning of an emphasis there on the integrity of the created order in its own terms apart from a field to be worked by Christians. But I wonder if we could have some word as to how consistently this is carried out in the Decree, because in the section on associations, for instance, the statement is made that "associations

273

are not ends unto themselves; rather they should serve to fulfill the Church's mission to the world," and then "conformity to the goals of the Church" is commended (art. 19). This still leaves the lingering question whether the created order is only affirmed as the place where the Christians are to go forth and missionize, so to speak, or whether there is a breakthrough which recognizes the integrity and purpose of God, though frequently hidden, in the process of secularization itself perhaps in the modern world. To be specific—and it has very practical implications—are Christians in a great public or state university there to try to draw that institution back into the pattern of the monastic or cathedral schools out of which the modern *universitas magistrorum et scholarum* emerged, or are they there to help that institution to be a true republic of learning, a model city that serves the world? This seems to be to me the origin of much of the crisis which not only Catholic but also Protestant universities are now going through, namely, that we still have in our midst this lingering thought that we go out occasionally from the fortress to engage in sorties, so to speak, or as it was once put, scalping expeditions. But we don't really take the secular order seriously—not of course the world as the dying age now, but the world as the created order where Christ also is working, sometimes before the Church ever gets there, and where he leads us, where he goes before us. My question is: To what extent are we moving, perhaps, toward a hardheaded and courageous attitude to *laïcité*.

CONGAR: For Catholics who participate in a university that is not confessionally Catholic, there are, first of all, historical questions that arise. One cannot move from one situation to another within a few weeks; there are historical questions that may weigh upon the matter for some years. In addition, whenever one speaks of education the Church considers that her maternal function of teaching the faith is committed, and therefore she is quite cautious. I note, however, that the *Declaration on Christian Education* had its title changed; it was *on Schools* and then became *on Education*. The Declaration insists on universal education rather than on schools.

But you have raised a problem on a much wider scale. The Council has nowhere spoken formally of a passage from a world of sacral Christianity to one of prophetic Christianity, but this is its spirit from one end to another. I said before that the *Constitution on the Church in the Modern World* and, above all, the *Declaration on Religious Freedom* are hardly understandable apart from this perspective. For the rest, the chapter on the laity in *Lumen Gentium* distinguishes clearly between the work of the Church as such and temporal works which enjoy their autonomy at their particular level, because one has moved from a juridical consideration to an ontological one. In a juridical consideration the Church considers that she must have authority over temporal matters; things are conceived as subordinate one to

another. From this point of view, the Church intervenes by way of commandment, by "the jurisdiction of Church over the city," to use the expression of Cardinal Journet. However, in a more ontological perspective it is
more a question of Christian witness in the world already penetrated by the
presence and grace of God. It is more an influence than an action of power.

This has its repercussions in the notion of *consecratio mundi*, to which
I alluded a while ago. The word appears in *Lumen Gentium* as a verb:
the world *is consecrated* to God. Here it is not a question of removing certain elements from the world to consecrate them by means of a liturgical
form, as was the case in the Middle Ages, with fraternities, with ceremonies,
and so on. What is intended is the Christian use that Christians make of
a world where nothing is profane as long as it is used in a spirit of faith
and charity.

Higgins: I think it would be in order to put the *Decree on the Apostolate of the Laity* in some perspective. The point has been made more than
once during the last days that it is inadvisable to discuss any Council document in isolation from others. I think this is particularly true of the one on
the laity. It is one of the weaker of the sixteen. It has many good points, but
it was begun before the *Constitution on the Church* was drafted. It was to
have included what we now know as schema 13, but schema 13 was separated from it, and as a result it was prepared too early in the Council to
benefit from the theological insights of *De Ecclesia* and from the anthropology, if you will, of schema 13.

Hence, if it is going to be considered a Conciliar document and therefore
in the light of the entire Council, it must be read in conjunction with
schema 13 or the *Constitution on the Church in the Modern World*. In
that latter document you will find, I think, a much clearer statement, a much
more explicit and refined statement, on the legitimate autonomy of temporal
institutions. There are several very forceful, and from my point of view, and
I would think from your point of view too, Dr. Littell, quite adequate statements on the complete, legitimate autonomy of temporal institutions, and
an explicit warning to Christians, to Catholics especially, not to infringe
on that autonomy as a rationalization of the Christian apostolate. But really
my specific point, and the only point for which I asked for the floor, was
to suggest that the *Declaration on the Apostolate of the Laity* is a weak
document, primarily because it was drafted too early in the Council and did
not benefit from the theology that later developed from the experience with
schema 13.

Ahern: Father Häring, the answer to my question is, I think, obvious,
but at the same time I think it has to be spelled out in order to avoid ambiguity and misunderstanding. In speaking of the vocation of all Christians
to sanctity and following St. Augustine and St. Paul, you emphasize very

much the predominance of love, the law of the spirit, the absence of law, and that we live by grace. This is all very true. Yet at the same time our Catholic people are constantly confronted with a whole battery of laws, laws of God, laws of the church, precepts of superiors. Hence there is something of an antinomy in their thinking when we so emphasize love, because immediately they are conscious only of the law. How then practically is this antinomy to be resolved? We can't be on the one hand antinomian and on the other hand Pelagian. How then, Father, when you speak of this great wholeness of love, do you reconcile it with this whole battery of laws which our people have to live by?

HÄRING: I think this is a most important question. Let us take a look at the theological justification for law. First, as against the tendencies of the new situational ethics according to which love can express itself in total discontinuity (today in this way, tomorrow in a totally opposite way), it must be seen how much Christians must try to perceive the order of love, the *ordo amoris*. Love is a true word, a true message, that must always receive its continuity from the very word of God, from the very love of God. A situational ethic that does not acknowledge any content in love is wrong. The true content of love must be found; everything isn't an exception.

Secondly, we must see the necessity of human laws, which in the best Thomistic tradition express a response to the signs of the time. The People of God as a whole has to consider the signs of the time, and then authority must guarantee unity of action. Another aspect of law is also important: our pilgrimage from a very imperfect condition to a better one. In heaven there will be no law; there we will find only the absolute power of love, to be loved and to love. Here below we pray that God's "will may be done on earth as it is in heaven"—though the power of love is already here on earth, so is the power of sin. That is only common Christian theology. Reformed theologians also develop law insofar as it keeps us humble and aware of our state of sin, that we are sinners. To some extent law is necessary in view of our sinfulness and in order to provide the minimum guarantee of a common response to the signs of the time. But these laws must then be explained by spiritual men without omitting the virtue of *epikaia*, namely, that one must try to understand the meaning of laws and to act upon laws in a spiritual way, making the necessary adjustments to new needs and integrating them into the whole law.

The whole Christian life must be conceived as a continuous conversion, a conversion from the understanding of law as the minimal requirement to the mature realization that the Sermon on the Mount is our true law. "Be ye perfect as your heavenly Father is perfect." "Love each other as I have loved you."

The growth in Christian life is shown by the shift of accent from those laws that set limits to those that indicate direction. It is very dangerous in our preaching and in the teaching of moral theology in seminaries to put the emphasis one-sidedly on those laws indicating minimum requirement. This would not be so bad if moral instruction were only for confessors, and if confessors were not, first and foremost, proclaimers of the words of peace and reconciliation but merely such who meted out judgment in anticipation of the final judgment of Christ. A renewal of the sacrament of confession would help to do away with many of these minimalist distinctions.

Lastly, I think this whole battery of laws must be seen sociologically. Legalism arose, at least partially, because of the structure of the society; it was a closed society, an absolutist one, the whole of life was controlled, and the Church, going along with this sociological fact, gave priests the chief control in the sacrament of penance, as they had been given control in almost every other way. But things have changed; we are now living in an open society, a pluralistic society. It is evident that only a man with great sense of responsibility, with deep insight into the order of love, and into the content of true love, with a great sense of solidarity and with great maturity can stand.

CALLAHAN: Father Congar, do you feel that anywhere in the Conciliar documents there is imposed upon the hierarchy an obligation to consult the laity in matters of doctrine?

CONGAR: You know that this word "consulting" was the object of a whole explanation on the part of Newman in a rather famous article. It has several senses, the juridical one and the ontological value of communion. It is certain that the bishops have no new revelation and that they must simply teach the faith of the Church. In the *Constitution on Divine Revelation* it is said clearly of the hierarchy that "pie audit" (it listens piously, religiously). Therefore, there is no doubt but that the bishops must listen to the *ecclesia*, not that they are juridically subordinated, but they are in an obligatory position of communion. Now on a disciplinary level, in terms of decisions to be taken for the direction of the Church, the Council has instituted a pastoral council in which laymen are to figure. And this council has been established in a number of dioceses, although the decree of application has not yet been promulgated. Hence, we are moving unquestionably toward a more active participation of the laity in the life of the Church and their assumption of responsibility for the life of the Church. This will have to be done progressively in order to be vital and not artificial or purely mechanical, and it must find its juridical forms. But it is essential that it find its theology, which will be the theology of communion and the People of God. Much work remains to be done on this.

STRANSKY: I think the question was very good, but I find difficulty with the answer, Father Congar, which is usually the answer given. If we take charisms in the Church seriously, I cannot see why the institutional aspect of the Church is not obliged by the very nature of the Church, the fullness of the Church with its charismatic element, to consult. Furthermore, it is not only a matter of charisms; it is a matter of the prophetic witness stemming from baptism and confirmation. I think that there is an obligation, perhaps not a legal statement about it, but an obligation arising out of the very nature of what the Church is in time and in the world to consult in order to achieve this unification of which Father Häring speaks—this unity in action to discover the signs of the times. That means also that it has to be structured.

CONGAR: It is clear that when we had a merely juridical notion of the Church, such considerations did not have their place in ecclesiology. But the moment one accepts a Christian-ontological notion of the Church, one of communion, the Church seen as the People of God living by the Holy Spirit, it is clear that these considerations have their place in ecclesiology. But at the same time they can hardly be formulated in terms of juridical obligations, in terms of juridical structure. It is somewhat analogous to the relations between the episcopate and the papacy in the episcopal college. If we try to define this in purely juridical terms, we will not arrive at the whole truth. And this is where I differ with Father Bertrams. He is a canonist, whereas the thing must be considered on the ontological level of communion. There is a lot of work here to be done by jurists. One must show that there are other sources of obligation besides legal obligations, and that communion and love are sources of obligation, of strict obligations, but not legal obligations. I believe there is quite an area, practically new, for Catholic reflection.

SISTER ANN IDA: Actually my question has already been answered, but I can't resist making a few remarks. It is rather a comfort to women in the Church today to realize that the Church, which for so long has been building a theology of women on social and historical events and has not been too interested in the metaphysics of human nature, is at long last turning to a consideration of the role of women in the Church and in society. I think the explanation given that theology has been built on social and historical events is a healthy indication that it has at long last been realized. I think that very often in the past the Church thought she was explaining the nature of women and not the situation of women in Western civilization.

Another point I would like to make is in regard to religious orders, and this is simply underlining the question I was originally going to ask. It seems to me that as the Church is building the bridge to the world and telling us that the place of the Christian is in the world, religious orders, which have always represented or reflected the relation of the Church to the world themselves, must move into the world. And therefore your description of laymen, and the description of Father Rahner which was accepted, as one who is born in and belongs to the life or events of the world, equally refers to religious today who belong to the world and are born to it but are not at home in it. The distinction is rather in the pilgrim aspect, it seems to me, that of being in or belonging to the world. So in the distinction that you make I'd like to ask where between priest and layman would you put the religious.

CONGAR: It is clear that the distinction between the Church and the world appears today more difficult than in former days, because we have better considered things in their reality. The Church and the world do the same thing: help mankind succeed. But they do it with different resources coming from different sources: the world starting from the energy of history, the Church from the energy of Christ. This latter is a new fact, a divine, free initiative, one that is new but nonetheless enters history and is not foreign to history. Therefore, it is true that we see less well today, than ten or twenty years ago, the distinction between the Church and the world. In my opinion the important idea always to keep in mind is that the Church is not simply the spiritual movement of the world coming from down up, as the crest of a wave is transported by the movement of the wave. But the Church comes from above, by a divine initiative, positive and original, or if you will, as one would say in law, an institution of positive divine law. Therefore, there are certain realities in the world that are not determined by natural situations of the world, but stem from this initiative of God. And this is the case of the priesthood. It is in that sense that I repeated Rahner's definition; it clarifies the one I gave.

Now the religious life has another logical starting point. Here it is not a question of something stemming from a divine initiative, except for a vocation, but it is rather the answer that man gives. Certain men and certain women, in order to serve God better, do not wish to go through the means of the world, the family, the mundane profession, political involvement, and so on, but desire merely to organize their life from beginning to end from God's point of view. What really makes for the great difference between the religious life and life in the world is that *everything* in the religious life, even sleep and food, is directly regulated by the service of God, ideally speaking of course. I think this is where we find the main, concrete difference between the two.

SISTER ANN IDA: Might I say that I think that is a pre-Council approach to religious life, namely, that we are better, that we are doing things better, because of the way we are doing them. It seems to me that as a result of the Council what we are doing is living differently, but we are not in a higher state of perfection of a better life because we are so doing.

HÄRING: I think that Father Congar is constructing a spirituality of priesthood and laity in view of the actual situation. It is a legitimate function of theology to consider what they are now and what is the Christian spirit, and understanding, behind what they are doing. But in this good theology I fear one danger: that we take as given the actual separation and division of the states of life. It was said already that in Sacred Scripture we do not have a laity. Christ, although he was already the high priest, even if not in public life, was a man living in an earthly condition and sanctifying that earthly condition as a carpenter. He remained in the secular conditions of that People of God, of that special culture, even when he undertook his public ministry. I feel too that the example of St. Paul will once again and increasingly enjoy favor in the Church, namely, that one preaches the gospel while remaining in the situation of a worker.

There has been a tremendous historical development regarding religious. For a long time religious women were understood only as those living behind high walls, having no contact with the outside. When St. Vincent tried to draw them into activity, there was a great outcry of indignation and scandal among so many theologians and bishops. Religious women consecrated to God must not be brought into ordinary conditions of life. When we see the change that has actually taken place, we can understand better the importance of secular institutes. Without undermining other forms of the religious life, we can see that they are fully dedicated to living the evangelical counsels while remaining in the total conditions of human life. Some of these dedicated people do not even want to be known as belonging to a secular institute or as having vows; they just wish to live as all other Christians, giving the Christian witness without the external signs of a special state of life, to show how one should live as a Christian in his condition of life, how one tries to consecrate himself to God.

So we can see the danger there is in giving a theological interpretation, as St. Paul did, to the situation of women in a patriarchal society. There is always a danger that such a misunderstanding be given an eternal, abstract, theological quality that immobilizes future historical events.

LADY JACKSON: I would like to make one little point. Could we take this question on the role of women beyond whether or not they are going to be consecrated in the Church or have any particular office in the Church? Frankly, I don't know that that is something that concerns them very deeply at the moment. I think one of the troubles is that, unlike their fellow men in the Church, there is quite considerable doubt about their role in the world. I think we need a theology for the life of women, married women—perhaps particularly married women—in the world, that will do away with some of the difficulties that Father Rahner reminded us of, namely, that we only very recently got souls. Therefore, a general consideration by theologians of what it means exactly to be a female human being is perhaps one of the important tasks of the Church. Because I would have you know that, on balance, the influence of the Church at its more official levels is not thrown exactly on the side of this reconsideration happening. Although one does not want to insist that 50 per cent of the human race receives undue attention, we would, nonetheless, like to feel that theologians were thinking about us—in the words of Mary Wollstone-craft—"in the grand light of human creatures." Men don't have any problems of becoming creatures; they know they are. But there is a problem here. Perhaps a little illustration here would help: Father Rahner mentioned with what vehemence the question was put. Was it all that vehement? I can't see that it was. It raised a series of questions. But, of course, if we raise questions we tend to be thought vehement. I don't myself feel that this is entirely irrelevant. I think that we would like to be considered as human beings, and this is a theological point.

McGRATH: I think the vehemence, Lady Jackson, is accentuated by the exclamation marks, and so on.

CONGAR: Just one word. I'm in full agreement that we need to consider better woman and her role in Church. Her role is very real, but with regard to explicit things that could be said about it, it has not emerged sufficiently. I am quite in agreement, however, with what you said, but I would like to make one slight observation. In the commission for schema 13 on which I worked, there were several women who spoke. Let me assure you that they spoke, and they were listened to. At one point we wanted to express the specific role of a woman. They are the ones who said: "No. Say simply that woman has a role *sui generis*, that she is a being *sui generis*. But don't say anymore. It is enough at the present time. It is quite certain that it is merely the beginning." At the Council there were female auditors, but their role was not very great. They intervened in commissions, but they did not play a decisive role. But I am quite in agreement that here there is a big gap in Catholic theology and in the practice of the Church, despite the fact that 50 per cent of the Church's members are women. ·

LADY JACKSON: It would be a tremendous help to women in the Church if men and theologians were to take this up, because owing to our status the fact that women have to speak for women is always embarrassing and a bit silly. Why should we have to do it? I think it is difficult for us to speak entirely objectively about such a subject, and yet the Church should be able to. So I would plead specially that men and theologians help us in this.

DR. BROWN: This is an over-all question about the criterion for interpreting Council documents of the sort we have been studying. I will make it a discussion only to the point of trying to clarify the question. It is prompted in part by the brief comment made by Abbot Butler to the effect that "one need not know the mind of the commission in order to interpret the document; all one needs is the text itself."

I have been proceeding on very different terms during and since Vatican II, and if I am in error I want to be made aware of the magnitude of my error. It seems to me quite indispensable to know as much as possible about the history of the composition of the texts, what were the interventions that helped to mold them, what phrases were introduced or excised in early or later drafts, and so forth. In other words, within a given text it becomes helpful to know as much as possible of the history and background of the text in order to know which parts of it to take with greatest seriousness. That is one factor.

The other factor upon which I would appreciate some comment from Roman Catholics present is the degree to which the meaning of the documents we are studying is in a sense not yet determined and will be determined by the use that the Roman Catholic Church will make of them in the future. It seems to me that what happens in subsequent discussion of the documents, which parts will be highlighted within the discussions of the Church, in the writings of other documents, and so forth, will also play a large part in determining what the document comes to mean. Certain parts will be highlighted in discussion and may become the normative portions of the documents, thus indicating the direction in which the documents will take the Church in the next few years. Hence, the meaning may be focused partly by what the Roman Catholic theologians make of the documents, possibly even in part by the attention called to them in ecumenical discussions in which separated brethren will also be involved. For example, if attention focuses in the future on such terms as "People of God" and a "pilgrim people" rather than on such terms as the "Mystical Body," that fact itself may be determinative for the meaning that *ecclesia* will have in the future of the Church. I am interested then in reactions from some of the Roman Catholics as to whether this way of approaching the Council documents is too subjective or perhaps even too Protestant, or whether this is a kind of legitimate way in which to interpret the texts.

FRANSEN: I must say that I am personally interested in the study of the ecclesiastical documents. Our Roman Catholic commentaries on the Council documents are still in their infancy, and I think, first of all, that it would be very dangerous to interpret a document without any study of the preparatory discussions that led to the definitions and the documents of the Council. I think it is a further question of simple human psychology. If you read the text not knowing anything about its origin, about its real motives, about its real intentions, then there is a very serious danger that you would interpret those documents according to your own vision, your own terminology, to your own problematics. So I always try in articles and talks to insist upon the primary necessity of studying the historical genesis of any text of the Church. There are a few other points I would like to make, but I think it would make a whole talk in itself.

I think we have to elaborate in the next years a real methodology for interpreting the texts of the magisterium. For instance, to give only one example, there is a very important difference between a negative statement and a positive statement. A *negative* statement is in itself a condemnation. Such a statement is in itself always univocal, because then the Church takes an error or a heresy, or what she thinks somebody was thinking, a historical opinion of a certain group or person, let us say, and she says this is not according to the tradition of the Church, not according to the revelation. But a *positive* statement in a Church document cannot be univocal; it must be necessarily analogous, because a positive statement on the content of revelation supposes such a richness, such a depth of divine reality that the Church can only give a few directions, draw out a few general implications, but not bind our mind to specific ideas. To give a very brief example, in the discussions with the Pelagians there is a very short formula: *"non imitatione set generatione."* *"Non imitatione"*—that is the opinion of Pelagius, namely, that Adam harmed human nature only by this bad example. That is a very univocal, historically determined opinion. But when the Church says *"generatione,"* there we have a real theological reflection, and I think that in the centuries since the Council of Carthage we have come to see that the real intent of *"generatione"* is only to defend human solidarity in original sin.

I think a whole methodology really needs to be elaborated for the interpretation of Church documents. Today we are still in infancy; we have no methodology. When you examine writings, you see they are merely quoting documents of the Church. But that is completely insufficient.

HÄRING: From the very philosophy or theology of the word, we must know how a commission was challenged, what was the problem presented to them, how it was presented, and then how the commission intended to respond. A word is meaningless if it is not related to the persons who spoke; a word is never absolutely fixed. Modern philosophers and theologians explain how important it is to locate the word in the interpersonal dialogue. But it is true that when those in authority wish to make a restrictive commandment or explanation, sometimes God prevents them from expressing their full repressive attitude. And in the case of laws, of restrictive attitudes, we are not obliged to more than authorities were capable of expressing in the words as such. If the words do not express more, and if the real spirit of obedience, respect and responsibility does not invite us as Christians to do more, then we have no further obligation. But the words themselves deliver their full message and intent only if you know who responded to whom, and what was the problem. This is true of all human speech and must, therefore, be true even for the human speech dealing with salvation. It cannot be outside the world; it must remain with the realm of human word.

Houtart: I think it is extremely important not only to judge the Conciliar texts now, but also to try to evaluate the future of those texts, along the line Dr. Lindbeck took in his paper, along the line of dynamic theological thinking. As he said, there are examples of some councils we have not followed. I think, however, that we are now living in another world, a world of communications and pluralistic societies that tend to develop different values. In this kind of world theological thinking will have more of a chance to develop.

Higgins: I think I understand the import of Dr. Brown's question, and I sympathize with the sentiments behind it. At the same time I have a certain fear that for a pastoral Council there is an excessive preoccupation with the interpretation of texts; I would have thought this was more appropriate to an earlier type of council. Many of the texts, it seems to me, are written in such an explicitly informal pastoral style, that I can conceive of grave difficulties arising if we try to judge them according to the categories of earlier theological quarrels or discussions about the value of each word. That is particularly true I think of the *Constitution on the Church in the Modern World* and the *Decree on the Apostolate of the Laity*. I don't think these documents were ever meant to be theological documents in the sense that we earlier conceived of conciliar documents, in which each word was subject to some kind of explicit, objective permanent evaluation of its merits. I am talking off the top of my head here, and I will be glad to make tracks if anyone thinks I should. But I'm a little disturbed at the seriousness which several of the Protestant observers have attached to this question of interpretation of documents, for it seems to me that they were quite deliberately meant to be more pastoral in tone than dogmatic.

Fransen: Well, Msgr. Higgins, I don't think that earlier councils were so strict in the promulgation of their documents. For instance, the Council of Trent in what was called the "Introduction to the Canons" gave only a very general view of the opinion of the Church at that moment. Even in the canons those council Fathers worked very hard to arrive at a very sharp formulation, but with the intention of condemning only a particular Lutheran position without touching on any of the many Catholic positions current in the Church. So even the old councils were more broad-minded than what we have thought.

Moeller: We must be very attentive to the different modes of speech. The dogmatic Constitutions, such as *Lumen Gentium* and *Dei Verbum* are different in this respect from the pastoral Constitutions like *Gaudium et Spes* and the declarations and decrees. It is quite evident that for *Lumen*

Gentium, for example, we must study the text in a more accurate way than for other documents. Furthermore, we must always begin with the objective divisions of the text as they were proposed, discussed and promulgated. The analysis of the text is not to be done in an arbitrary way: it is not a question of its being dynamic or not dynamic. The first thing to do, it seems to me at least, is to know what was the meaning of the members of the commission or subcommittee and of the Fathers when they voted these things. To do that we must carefully read the reports made before the discussion or before the promulgation.

Let us take only two examples. The first is article 51 of *Gaudium et Spes*. It is said that the moral aspect of any procedure for regulating the number of children does not depend solely on subjective criteria, but must be determined by objective standards based on the *natura* of the human person and his acts. In order to know the exact meaning of this word *natura* we must read the official *relatio*, and there we will find that this word includes not only the biological order of things in this matter, but also the manner according to which man lives. You can know that only by reading the report.

The other example comes from the famous statement on the Jews. To discover why the word "deicide" was dropped from article 4, we must consult the draft between the third and the fourth sessions. Fortunately, the explanation was published in *L'Avvenire d'Italia*, and there we read that words like "deicide," "Christ-killer" and "God-killer" must be completely reprobated and suppressed in Christian language. It is very important to know that, for then you know it is clearly excluded by the text. It is no longer possible to speak of the Jewish people as a deicide people.

These two examples bring out concretely what I want to say. We are not left to an arbitrary interpretation of the text. On the contrary, for a correct understanding of this Council it is necessary to have accurate studies made about the meaning of the text as it is and as it was promulgated. One of the most important things to be done now, I think, is to publish a line-for-line commentary of *Lumen Gentium*.

Lastly, it is certainly true that the way in which the Council's texts will be applied in the concrete life of the Church is very important. But it is simply impossible to apply the texts in a way that would contradict the meaning of the text and the way it was promulgated. This does not mean in any sense that we must refuse to take a dynamic approach. I am not saying in the least that these texts are the ultimate goal of theology for all time. On the contrary, they are a starting point. And we must vigorously stress that Vatican II never canonized any theological school as such; the Council was always above theological schools as such. Hence, it is possible to foresee quite a lot of future development, always taking the text and its history as the starting point.

STRANSKY: I am surprised at Monsignor Higgins' talking of casual writing. I don't like to think that for four years we were casually writing forty-one lines on the Jewish question. I think a distinction that ought to be made here is that the Council is not the Church and that all of the theological charisms in the Church are not absorbed by the Council. Secondly, our task right now is to see not only the harmonies of the texts, but also their disharmonies. I am thinking especially of the relationships of the great ecumenical problem right now, the relation between the mission of the Church and the service that the Church renders, for instance. I think that what is important right now in ecumenical work is to apply what Oscar Cullmann called perhaps the most significant phrase of all the Council documents, the statement about the hierarchy of values in the *Decree on Ecumenism*. This is very important, not only for the internal thought life of our Church but for the whole Christian family. We will have to stand above all sixteen documents, see the harmonies and disharmonies and then determine the hierarchy of values.

My last point is that a Council is an act of the Church and the very method that was used in this Council was a reflection on the experience of the Church. It wasn't a reflection about an abstract Church in an abstract world; it was the experience of this Church in this world. Therefore, I think the options we are going to take in the future will determine our understanding of Vatican II. And some of these options are going to be shaped by how seriously we take ecumenical dialogue and by how seriously we are reading the signs of the times. Just as the times shaped the atmosphere in which the Conciliar process was set, so the interpretation of Vatican II in the life of the Church will be determined by the signs of the times and how alert we are to what the Spirit is telling us through those signs.

HIGGINS: I didn't mean to imply that the writing was casual, although at times it was. It wasn't quite as casual as some of the *relationes*. I would hate to put as much faith in the *relatio* on the Jewish problem as Canon Moeller does. But I refer precisely to the last point that you made. There is an infinity of statements in the Council documents which I do not think were ever meant to come close to even dogmatic statements, let alone definitions. There are thousands of contingent statements in the documents, on which I think it would be, at best, a waste of time to look for anything like a permanent objective theological note. Let me give you just a few trivial examples from the *Constitution on the Church in the Modern World*.

Some American bishops, notably Archbishop O'Boyle, and some bishops from other countries insisted quite emphatically that in the document on the Church in the modern world something of some length and vigor should be said about the problem of race relations throughout the world. *De facto* the document touches upon the subject in a few sentences, if not just in a few words. Now are we to conclude from that that the Council attached little importance to race relations, or are we to conclude that this was a document which came out, as others have said, perhaps a year too soon, perhaps ten years too soon, which had to be hurried through, which could not include everything that needed to be said? If we begin to weigh the mind of the Council and the mind of the Church with regard to the importance at this pastoral level of contingent problems, I think we are going to go down a blind alley.

Take the celebrated dispute in the commission on the lay apostolate over the subject of Catholic Action. I don't think anyone has to be a soothsayer to understand that the issue wound up in a compromise, a compromise that was necessitated by widely divergent sociological experiences of people from varying cultures, with the preponderance of the people who happened to be in possession at the time, namely, people from the Latin countries. I would hate to see theologians spend too much time trying to attach anything like a theological note to what the Council says about the value of Catholic Action, because it would be a great test of my faith if their decision went the wrong way.

TUCCI: Certainly that was not casually written. I think we made at least twenty different drafts, and the last one was a real compromise. A little commission was selected, having two people representing the Latin world, two other people representing the rest of the world, with somebody presiding, and we prepared that compromise. But George, even if we are not able to distinguish the values, we have to study the history of the text on Catholic Action to discover the real significance of the text. So practically, I think it is very important to study all the various stages of a text in order to know the meaning attached to the words, the importance of the magisterium in that special text.

DUNNE: There is mention of infallibility in one of the documents, the one on the hierarchy. The question has arisen how we are to interpret the whole thing on the Church, whether to give the weight to the People of God or the institutional aspects. Perhaps as a test case we could take the matter of infallibility. How far can this thing be pushed in the direction of the People of God notion? By that I would mean not that this perhaps would be the intended sense in the Council. But would it be theologically possible in view of the Council definitions on infallibility to say that infallibility is not an actual criterion for certitude, but that rather it is something pertaining to the object of faith? To believe in infallibility, or inerrancy, is to believe in the truth, the reliability of the word of God, in its written form or its proclaimed form. But perhaps it doesn't mean that I can use this to determine that such and such a thing is infallible and such and such another thing is not infallible. In brief, the question is: Can infallibility be taken in nonepistemological sense?

HÄRING: This is one of the most important questions, and here allow me to show that I am just an old-fashioned theologian whenever there seems to be a need of being old-fashioned. There is an infallibility in the Church according to which the Holy Spirit protects her and assists her in a very special way. This means that the Church finds a sufficient instrument in human language to protect and to proclaim the truth of salvation in such a way that men of good will can with Christian humility safely accept it. It is not a mathematic infallibility, but the infallibility that guarantees us that the Church in all the things necessary for salvation, the things revealed by God for man's salvation, presents us with the truth in such a way that she cannot lead us astray, that she leads us toward the real understanding of saving truth. This does not exclude the need for the Church to rephrase the truth. On the contrary, she must do so, because in different epochs the truths of faith are not understood in the same way, due to different questions and problems. This is not relativism; it is simply the Church relating to real men; she gives these fundamental questions in which divine revelation is at stake a direction in actual situations and thus protects men and helps them along the way of salvation. Her teaching is never perfect, because the perfection of truth is God himself, while human truth is always only an approximation.

The same question arises regarding the infallibility of Holy Scripture. Now in the light of the *Constitution on Divine Revelation* we see that such infallibility is not a guarantee that this or that happened, e.g., that the cock crowed a second or third time. That is not a truth of salvation. But where truths of salvation in the Old or New Testament are concerned, we are led step by step to a deeper understanding of the way of salvation, and are thus guaranteed and protected against going astray. It is always in the direction of a fuller understanding, but that does not mean that the Church has the fullest understanding at all times. Only in the course of time and after much effort does she come to a full understanding. When the Church makes use of final authority, declaring this or that on *absolute decision*, then we are obliged by faith to hold it, for then we are sure that she protects the essential understanding of the truth of salvation.

Hence, I think there is infallibility, but an infallibility as on earth, one that always leaves the way open for spiritual growth. The whole Church is also open to be led by the Holy Spirit to a greater, more unified view, toward placing her emphasis on this or that aspect as man's salvation needs protection. There is still objective truth, but objective truth as possessed in an earthly way, not a heavenly way.

FRANSEN: I fully agree with Father Häring, if really we understand this growth, this direction toward truth, because truth is God himself; the Church is leading us toward God. But I think there is one question that Dr. Brown raised and was not answered. When we have established the historical meaning of a text, is then everything finished? I don't think so. If we really accept sincerely and honestly this ontological communion which was spoken of so frequently today, then I think we have to accept a very interesting, important and valid tradition of the Eastern Churches, namely, the *sobornost*, the agreement of the Church as a whole. As an example, we have the creed recited at Mass on Sunday. It is said to be the creed of the Council of Constantinople. In the beginning at least, the Council of Constantinople was not an ecumenical council; it became an ecumenical council afterwards. But it is very probable that this creed was not written at the Council of Constantinople. Nevertheless it is *the* most important creed of Christianity. In the liturgies of all the churches—Catholic, Orthodox and Protestant—this creed has always been accepted as one of the most fundamental expressions of Christian faith. This century-old acceptance by the Church *as a whole* has an importance and gives a special value to a certain document.

AHERN

MEDINA ESTEVEZ

SESSION VII

REV. BARNABAS AHERN, C.P.
The Eschatological Dimensions of the Church

RT. REV. JORGE MEDINA ESTEVEZ
The Blessed Virgin

Rev. Barnabas Ahern, C.P.

THE ESCHATOLOGICAL DIMENSIONS OF THE CHURCH

Some may think that the title of this paper promises a commentary on chapter 7 of the *Constitution on the Church*. By happy chance, however, the title suggests larger vistas. The very word "dimensions" signifies not only an upward thrust to the heights, but also depth and length and breadth. The phrase "eschatological dimensions" opens up a vision of fullness: the Church charged with momentum impelling it upwards and, at the same time, rich to its very depths with heavenly life; the Church reaching out to the length and breadth of all creation so that one day, when the end comes, God may be all and in all.

This vision, though, does not appear fully in a precise section of the Conciliar corpus. It is glimpsed momentarily in the opening sentence of chapter 7:

> The Church, to which we are called in Christ Jesus, and in which we acquire sanctity through the grace of God, will attain her full perfection only in the glory of heaven. Then will come the time of the restoration of all things (Acts 3:21). Then the human race as well as the entire world, which is intimately related to man and achieves its purpose through him, will be perfectly re-established in Christ (art. 48).

Unfortunately, however, only half of the theme enunciated in this opening sentence is developed in the ensuing chapter. The treatment in chapter 7 envisages only man, his future destiny and his present spiritual participation in it: this chapter describes only the height and depth of the Church's eschatological dimensions. The vast expanse of length and breadth must be

293

painted into the picture with the deft strokes of the *Constitution on the Church in the Modern World*. The thought of the Council Fathers on eschatology, therefore, comes to us as a composite picture, their full teaching must be gleaned from several parts of the Conciliar corpus.

This divided presentation may lead to misunderstanding. Too many people will read only one Constitution and overlook another; and even those who do read the whole Conciliar documentary may fail to synthesize its complementary teachings. Whatever regret one feels, however, cannot compare with the joy and gratitude all of us experienced in knowing that a true and full eschatology at long last emerged from Conciliar discussion.

It is somewhat embarrassing and yet amusing to recall that the first schema on the Church contained almost nothing on the heavenly vocation of the Church. When Bishop Volk of Mainz first read the schema, he instantly asked the pertinent question "Wohin denn gehen wir?" To him the schema seemed to be so concerned with the life of the Church upon earth that it had almost nothing to say about the Church's destiny. God's pilgrims were furiously on the march; but the schema had them marching a treadmill. Happily, Bishop Volk acted promptly; two days later on the Council floor he expressed his consternation and, with charged voice, uttered the heartfelt request of many of the bishops that a chapter be added to the schema under the title "The Eschatological Nature of the Pilgrim Church and Her Union with the Heavenly Church." Pope John XXIII recognized the merit of Bishop Volk's intervention and he himself warmly seconded his words.

Msgr. Gallagher describes the emergent chapter as "one of the most original and inspiring in the entire Constitution."[1] Inspiring, certainly; the chapter is so rich that it cannot be merely read but must be pondered prayerfully. But original, no; because every thread of the texture is drawn from Scripture, the chapter simply affirms the truths of revelation as the Church has always understood them. In substance it presents the Church as always moving forward to a heavenly home and as already sharing on the march some of the joy and fulfillment of the endtime. Any Catholic child who has studied the catechism will recognize in this chapter a familiar medley of the truths he has learned: the end of the world, resurrection and heaven, purgatory, the communion of saints, prayer for the dead and prayer to those who are already with God. Even the most unlettered Catholic will find nothing new here.

At the same time, however, the Council Fathers have presented the age-old familiar doctrines with special attention to perspective and proportion. Popular Catholic thinking always needs instruction to save it from exaggeration and faulty emphases. Non-Catholics, too, I believe, will be impressed by

---

[1] W. M. Abbott, ed., *The Documents of Vatican II* (New York: America Press, 1966) 78, note 223.

the manner in which the contents of this chapter accord with the contents and the perspectives of the biblical *donnée*. The most noteworthy feature of this chapter is its fidelity to Scripture in contents, perspective and even in phraseology. It will be of interest to indicate the main correlations between the teaching of Scripture and the contents of this chapter.

1. Christ in the mystery of his own resurrection is seen as the model, the cause and the very substance of the Church's heavenly vocation. Whatever the Church attains in the eschatological age will be only in him and through him.

2. It is the whole Church of regenerated mankind that will enter upon heavenly life. The earlier chapters of the *Constitution on the Church* have made crystal clear that God has created a "people" for his glory. There is no place for atomistic individualism in the economy of God's plan. Christian life and Christian fulfillment at the endtime have an essentially *social* character. The Father's glory will be perfect only when his *whole* family closely knit together in love come to him led by his Son and their Brother, Christ Jesus.

3. The very fact that Christ, the loving Brother of this family, has already reached the Father's home spells strength and comfort for the Church still on the march. Faithful to his own promise, he has not left his brothers orphans. He shares with them his own Spirit, who is at once pledge and foretaste of final inheritance (cf. Eph 1:14). For the Church upon earth, therefore, life is rich with a "jetztschon" and a "jetztnoch": "Now already" it possesses, through the indwelling Holy Spirit, an experienced anticipation of heavenly life, while "now still" it awaits the perfect consummation of the endtime.

4. The very fact that the Church is a family, owing all that it has to Christ, means that it must cherish with love those members of the family who have already joined him in the bosom of the Father, and that it must honor him by praising the work he has accomplished in those who have already completed their course. Far from detracting from the glory of Christ, the unique Mediator, veneration of those who are fully in Christ Jesus is but the full-blown radiance of him who has become for us "God-given wisdom, justification, sanctification and redemption" (1 Cor 1:30).

Chapter 7, therefore, has been written with an eye to instruction and to ecumenical rapport. In judging it one must remember that, because it belongs to an official Conciliar Constitution, its purpose is to put forth clearly and correctly the truths in which the Catholic firmly believes. Many theologians could have said more and would gladly have translated the figurative language of biblical revelation into the preferred thought patterns of their own theological system. Theologians will necessarily ask the burning questions "How" and "In what way?" Such speculation is the metier of the theologian.

But the principal task engrossing the minds of the Council Fathers in preparing a dogmatic constitution is quite different. Their concern was always the single query "What is the certain teaching of revelation?"

The real weakness of this chapter, therefore, is not its lack of theological speculation, but rather its incompleteness. Many reading this chapter will be confirmed in the "spiritualist" anthropology of so much of Catholic thinking. They will see the teleology of God's plan as relative to man alone and to man as almost foreign to matter and to the world. They will continue to think of the "last day" as a cosmic reproduction of Nagasaki and Hiroshima. For too long a time the figurative language of St. Paul in Thessalonians and 1 Corinthians 15 has been interpreted literally and has been so absolutized as to exclude all the other teleological elements that God has revealed in the Scriptures. For many the last day is seen as something apart from every day which preceded it. God in his heavens will utter a magic abracadabra: thunder will roar, lightning will flash, hurling balls of fire will smite to crisp cinder, bones will rattle, flesh will come—and, lo and behold, we shall be with the Lord. No wonder, good Bishop Robinson, that much criticized pioneer, wrote his *Honest to God!*

Chapter 7 does nothing to eliminate these faulty notions—"when I was a boy I thought as a boy." It presents the eschatology of the Church only in its dimensions of height and depth—the upward lift of the Church to heavenly life with God and the continuing share in the spiritual riches of heaven which the Church upon earth experiences in the very depths of her being.

Happily, however, the *Constitution on the Church* is only one document in the Conciliar corpus. Its deficiency is wonderously complemented in the opening chapters of the *Constitution on the Church in the Modern World*. Here the eschatological dimensions of height and depth are filled out with those of length and breadth.

Only a spirit of deceitful and blatant triumphalism would suggest that the mutual relation between these two parts was deliberate and purposeful. The fact is that, just as the schema on the Church originally had nothing on eschatology in height and depth, so the *Constitution on the Church in the Modern World* originally had nothing on eschatology in length and breadth.

The latter schema when it first came to the study of the Council Fathers showed a very brave effort to explain why the Church must be concerned with the world and involved in its problems. It reminded me of the brave effort of St. Celestine V to act as pope, a real tour de force which held him in Rome for only five months until, almost beside himself, he fled back to his hermit's cell. It takes more than good will to cope with the world. Only truth and sureness of vision can fiber the Church for that contact, and in the first schema truth and vision were lacking.

The Christian was encouraged to live and work in the world, but he was also warned again and again to beware of contamination. A strict dichotomy was drawn between "spiritual" and "material," between "sacred" and "secular." One gathered the impression that life upon earth was only a testing place. Man was to live "migrans ut transiturus"; for those who prefer the vernacular, man was to live out of his suitcase, always ready to bang it shut at a moment's notice to move on to the heavenly country, his only true home. The greatest encouragement to take real part in secular life was drawn from the fact that life in the world offers many opportunities for the practice of those Christian virtues with which a man works out his eternal salvation: justice, charity, industry, truth and meekness.

I am afraid that in this oversimplification I am sketching only a caricature of the first schema presented to the Council. The significant fact, however, is this: the authors of the schema had not taken cognizance of the unity of God's plan; they had failed to take into account the truth of revelation that the world was made for man and shares in his teleology. Unfortunately, all through the ages much of Christian thinking has been plagued by the unresolved dichotomy of "spirit" and "matter," "soul" and "body," "man" and "the world," "the world of flesh" and "the world of spirit."

Historically there is a reason for the problem. When God first revealed his plan he spoke to men with a Semite mentality, to men with an almost intuitive sense of the perfect unity of man as a "body-person" and of the intimate bond between man and all creation. The Hebrew of the Scriptures could not think of life or of its rewards except in terms of his whole self, his whole people and his whole world. These things were all of a piece: when man sinned his whole self was caught up in the distortion, his fellows were hurt by it and his world, little or big, suffered. When man lived for God, the whole world became a halcyon abode. Man lived in the world as part of it. What God had joined together no one dreamed of separating. In modern terms, the world was rich with the sacramentalism of the life of the people of God. This mentality obviously affected the whole biblical vocabulary. "Spirit" and "Flesh" were seen not as two parts of man but as the whole man under divergent aspects. "Life" and "Death" were not merely biological phenomena; they were experiences of the whole man and were deeply colored with social and theological connotations.

When revelation passed from the Semite to the West it underwent a process of translation which at once enriched, refined and clarified it but also exposed it to the misunderstandings that can come from shifted perspectives. The corpus of patristic tradition has truly conserved and has deepened men's appreciation of the contents of the biblical *donnée*. At the same time, however, Western philosophy with its system of distinctions made it difficult for lesser minds to keep intact the sublime sense of unity that dominates Hebrew thought. "Soul" was often set in opposition to "body," and man to the world.

A species of dichotomy, symbolized by such phrases as "flesh" and "spirit," "the city of God" and "the city of evil," appeared frequently in later spiritual literature. Undoubtedly there were reasons for these distinctions; and when understood in the full context of Christian thought, they expressed truths that are rooted in revelation itself. Only too often, however, these concepts were not seen in right focus, for they were not presented within the range of full perspective. This resulted in distortion and faulty emphases that have often marred the spiritual writings of the past few centuries. Unfortunately, the mentality set forth in this literature provided the background for the first draft of the *Constitution on the Church in the Modern World.*

Cardinal Meyer of Chicago was the first to point out in his Council intervention the inherent weakness in this myopic attitude. To him it was unthinkable that the Church and Christian people could really work in the world unless they were illumined by a full picture of God's eschatological plan. In his Conciliar intervention he described briefly the world's teleology as Scripture presents it. The world was made for man and man was to "dominate" it. He was so to perfect the world by his own labor, so to master all its secrets and to develop all its latent powers, that one day this world could become the choice abode of the family of God whom Christ himself would re-establish in perfect unity and love. Cardinal Meyer emphasized the biblical theme of the "new heavens and the new earth." He drew on the clear teaching of St. Paul who represents the present world as "groaning in travail while it awaits redemption" (cf. Rom 8:22). He pointed out that the kingdom which Christ will turn over to the Father is both the world of man and the world of things, that "God may be all and in all" (cf. 1 Cor 15:28).

The very day that Cardinal Meyer made his memorable intervention Bishop Charrue of Namur touched upon the same theme. Both prelates pointed out the schema's faulty opposition between sacred and secular, material and spiritual. For them the schema labored under an almost Manichean pessimism. Their final verdict was a pointed one: the schema has missed an essential element in the beautiful plan of God who created the world for man and who intended man to perfect the world that it might share in his own destiny.

The cogent argumentation of these two prelates could not be overlooked. The first part of the schema was completely redrafted. Especially in chapter 3 it is made crystal clear that the eschatological dimensions of the Church reach to the length and breadth of the whole world. First, the Constitution affirms the intimate bond between man and the world around him:

Throughout the course of the centuries, men have labored to better the circumstances of their lives through a monumental amount of individual and collective effort. To believers, this point is settled: considered in itself, such human activity accords with God's will. For man, created to God's image, received a mandate to subject to himself the earth and all that it contains . . . , a mandate to relate himself and the totality of things to Him who was to be acknowledged as the Lord and Creator of all (art. 34).

But let there be no mistake. The labor and toil upon earth is not the hermit's detached weaving and unweaving of baskets as something to occupy him while he prepares to take his flight, as a disembodied spirit, to another and better world. Man's perfecting of the world is his own wholehearted share in fulfilling the divine will that man himself prepare the world which is to be his abode with God forever.

For after we have obeyed the Lord, and in His Spirit nurtured on earth the values of human dignity, brotherhood and freedom, and indeed all the good fruits of our nature and enterprise, *we will find them again*, but freed of stain, burnished and transfigured. This will be so when Christ hands over to the Father a kingdom eternal and universal: "a kingdom of truth and life, of holiness and grace, of justice, love, and peace" (art. 39, italics ours).

What will be the finishing touch that God himself will provide, the Council wisely leaves unsaid. Here we deal with mystery; and no Council Father made boast of the charism of prophecy. Instead, the Constitution pleads nescience: "We do not know the time for the consummation of the earth and of humanity. Nor do we know how all things will be transformed" (art. 39).

But the day and the hour and the manner of the final consummation are really of little importance. What really matters is the tremendous truth affirmed by the Council that all worthwhile human activity is part of the creative plan of God and of the redemptive ministry of Christ who died that he might re-establish all things and might transform them into the perfect eschatological kingdom of his Father. The whole world—the heavens and the earth, the vast oceans and the verdant fields, the tangled bush of Africa and the trampled streets of New York, men of all colors and of all backgrounds— all that God has made is alive with an *élan to God*.

Man is the agent who must make this momentum real. God has laid upon him the command to "dominate" the world. Every technical advance, therefore, all cultural progress, all effort at humanistic development, every project to make life more livable, to provide men with the comfort, security and the material goods necessary for a happy and full human life, every thrust into outer space, every scientific discovery, every talent developed and every career fostered, rightly ordered marches for civil rights and conscientious efforts to secure the unionization of our southwestern migrant workers—all this fits perfectly into God's plan that man himself should prepare the eternal abode of God's family.

These eschatological dimensions of length and breadth must be the Church's concern, for they are as much part of God's plan as the dimensions of height and depth. The Church cannot be indifferent to human progress. In preaching Christ she must present him as the Savior of all things. Even more, she must act in accord with her conviction that his presence in the community of men must bring salvation to the whole man and to his whole milieu. While on earth Christ did not only forgive sin and save "souls." His messianic mercy touched everything human, he strengthened withered limbs, gave sight to the blind and raised the dead; he fed the hungry, showed mercy to the outcast, defended the downtrodden and comforted the sorrowing. To continue this saving work of Christ's messianism is at once the privilege and responsibility of the Church in which he lives.

This element of the Church's mission is brought to the fore in the *Decree on the Church's Missionary Activity*. After pointing out that the saving plan of God "applies first of all to persons, but holds also for the various goods of this world" (art. 8), the decree emphasizes the totality of the Church's role: "Missionary activity is nothing else and nothing less than a manifestation or epiphany of God's will, and the fulfillment of that will in the world and in world history" (art. 9).

At the same time, however, the Church must be even more concerned with conserving the dimensions of height and depth in God's eschatological plan. Human progress and material development belong to a sphere where human autonomy can reject the control of God's plan. Men can become so concerned with life on the horizontal plane of this world that they refuse to look upward and to follow the vertical thrust of God's plan. This means a deliberate thwarting of the very teleology that God has designed for all the things he has created. Thus, only too often in the past, "creation has been made subject to vanity not by its own choice but by the will of him who made it subject" (Rom 8:20), wayward man who does not look to God and who does not honor the beautiful will of him who made all things for himself.

As Robert McAfee Brown has remarked, the greatest challenge the Church faces today is the task of wise, practical and tireless activity to ensure this vertical thrust in the world of human progress. If only men do their part and if only the Church fulfills her role, then God's plan will be realized in its full dimensions of height and depth, length and breadth. Then one day the eschatological consummation will come and the word of the psalmist will be fulfilled in the world which God has created and which man, through the power of Christ's Spirit, has perfected: "In his temple all say 'Glory'" (Ps 28:9).

Rt. Rev. Jorge Medina Estevez

THE BLESSED VIRGIN

F IRST, I WOULD LIKE TO APOLOGIZE for daring to present this theme. As you know, this lecture was offered to Msgr. G. Philips, whose twofold competence as mariologist and as main author of chapter 8 of the Constitution *Lumen Gentium*, would have insured a lucid and very authoritative exposition. Unfortunately, the excessive work imposed on him by the Council activities were seriously detrimental to his health, and the physicians did not allow him to come to Notre Dame. My taking his place does not mean that I am a specialist, but is probably due to the fact that I was closely connected with the elaboration of this important chapter of the Constitution.

It is obvious that this exposition cannot plumb the depths of the subject. Its purpose is rather to present an overview so far as is possible. Two appendices are added. One affords an inventory-outline of the Conciliar documents, the greater part of which has not yet been published and will be the basis of a series of monographs; but, in any case, we will indicate where they can be found. The second appendix is a small bibliography, not a mariological bibliography, but a list of works that are important because of their close relationship to the Conciliar document.

1. THE PRE-CONCILIAR SITUATION OF MARIAN DOCTRINE

It is extremely difficult to make a diagnosis on this point that would be not only objective but also generally accepted. From the very beginning we have

301

to take into account a factor of experience: we are at a sensitive moment of contemporary Catholic theology.

Whether we like it or not, a very simple terminology helps pigeonhole positions: we hear of "maximalists" and "minimalists."[1] Such terminology stirred up more or less violent opposition. Whoever is accused of being a "maximalist" is exposed to the criticism that casts doubt on the theological rigor of his presentation; whoever is classified as "minimalist" feels reproached for having little generosity and love toward the Blessed Virgin, or even suspected of an "irenism" seeking union with other Christians even at the price of sacrificing doctrine. The studies of Alois Müller,[2] Laurentin,[3] and Roschini,[4] cited in the bibliography, illustrate this situation.

This schematization is projected into a number of areas, a few of which we can point out, without pretending to exhaust the list, for example, the "fundamental principle" of mariology,[5] the so-called Christo-typical or ecclesio-typical tendencies in reference to Mary,[6] the concept of the liturgical cult of Mary,[7] terminology concerning the function of Mary,[8] deduction of the Virgin's privileges, emphasis on her "function" or her "greatness," the highlighting of what brings Mary close to us or, on the contrary, of what gives her a transcendent position, emphasis on the absolute transcendence of God, or on Mary's peculiar condition among creatures. Should we give in to the impulse to enrich the glorious titles of the Mother of God, or should we maintain a sober exposition of her role in the plan of salvation, safeguarding thus the homogeneity of theology as a whole?[9]

Here we have to note another aspect of this complex situation. Certain more or less frequent tendencies among mariologists have been regarded as manifesting a certain independence and even detachment from the rest of theology,[10] as well as from the scriptural foundations of mariology.

From the viewpoint of popular piety toward Mary, we also notice a certain diversity, a diversity that not only enjoys a variety of local expression and accent, but that also entrains special ways of living out other realities of the Church's life. Also to be noted is the greater or lesser degree of affectivity implied by this piety.

All these aspects, so summarily enumerated, show why the Catholic doctrine about Mary gave rise to a peculiar situation: despite fundamental accord, the marked differences of opinion gave the superficial observer the impression of a radical disagreement. It even went so far that the press, or better, certain areas of the press gave the impression that the Fathers of the Council were divided in this respect into "pro-Marianists" and "anti-Marianists." We all know the deplorable reaction that such information caused among the faithful.

This explains why the Council had such difficulty in formulating a text on these matters. Almost all Conciliar texts had to go through the sieve of more or less divergent opinions. However, currents of opinion did not manifest the same intensity in all matters. Chapter 8 of the dogmatic Constitution *Lumen Gentium* represents one of the more important cases of Conciliar dialectic, in addition to chapter 3 of the same Constitution, the *Declaration on the Relationship of the Church to Non-Christian Religions* and the *Declaration on Religious Freedom*. The *Dogmatic Constitution on Revelation* also belongs to this group of documents, especially in its initial phase.

It would be unrealistic to say that the Conciliar document on the Blessed Virgin has already produced a synthesis of the various tendencies, but we can say that it does provide a basis for such synthesis.

2. Historical Exposition of the Formation of the Text[11]

A. first phase: from the preparatory work to the beginning of 1963

In the first half of 1962 a text was already elaborated by the preparatory theological commission. Destined merely to form a part of the schema on the Church, it later on became a separate schema. It was presented to and revised by the Central Commission and then distributed to the Fathers on November 23, 1962, and was printed in the same fascicle in which was presented the first schema of the *Constitution on the Church*.[12] During the first debate on the schema *De Ecclesia*,[13] which can be considered as an orientation debate, no less than four Fathers pleaded for the reintegration of the schema on the Blessed Virgin into the schema on the Church, and Cardinal Suenens and Cardinal Montini expressed their opinion already at this time in favor of the title "Mother of the Church."[14]

B. second phase: 1963

At the beginning of February, 1963, Cardinal Raul Silva presented the Commission on Doctrine with a multigraphed brochure having the title "Annotationes generales in Schema Constitutionis De Ecclesia."[15] In this brochure, proposed by a group of Chilean bishops, Marian doctrine formed the last chapter "*ut summa totius De Ecclesia Constitutionis*."[16] It presented a new text whose purpose was to correct certain defects, as it said, of the official schema. It manifested an ecumenical and pastoral concern, made ample use of sacred Scripture, used more realistic language, and was more cautious in referring to controversial questions.[17] This text was the point of departure in dispelling anxiety about the composition of a new text.[18]

303

During the second phase of the Council[19] the work became more intense. Two points had to be decided: first, whether it should or should not be integrated into the schema on the Church, and second, how the text itself should be formulated. Both points developed in a relatively parallel way, although the first was decided before the second.

Integration. During the second debate on the schema *De Ecclesia*, Cardinal Frings, Msgr. Gargitter, Msgr. Garrone (in the name of several French bishops), Msgr. Elchinger and Msgr. Mendez Arceo advocated integration. Against it were Cardinals Arriba and Castro.[20] Cardinal Silva said on this occasion:

> We greatly desire that Marian doctrine itself be inserted into the schema *De Ecclesia*. For in our countries of Latin America piety toward and veneration of the most holy Mother of God often enough take on forms that do not have enough of a connection with the mystery of Christ and his Church. We think it is of great importance and general interest, from both the ecumenical and pastoral viewpoints, that Marian doctrine does not appear as a sort of independent theological overgrowth, but takes its place in the whole complex of the message of salvation. Both the doctrinal exposé on the Church and that on the Blessed Virgin will gain in richness.[21]

The problem was posed and was not solved in the Commission but was deferred to the aula. The Theological Commission had two cardinals explain to the Fathers the reasons for both positions; Cardinal Rufino Santos advocated a separate schema and Cardinal Franz König argued for integrating.[22] The matter was to be resolved by vote on October 29. An active propaganda developed to demonstrate to the Fathers the advantages and disadvantages of the one or other solution;[23] the written declarations against insertion emphasized that in their judgment such integration would give less honor to the Mother of God. The result of the vote, which took place in an atmosphere of tension, was a very small majority in favor of insertion: 1,114 in favor, 1,074 against. The vote solved in principle the second point: the original official schema was to be amended in view of integration, and the Theological Commission was to carry out this work.

Toward a New Text. From the beginning of the second session, various efforts were made to edit an appropriate text. Abbot C. Butler presented one;[24] Cardinal Silva presented another—a corrected re-edition of his earlier one.[25] Finally, both authors came to an agreement on a third text, which was also presented to the Council authorities.[26] The Cardinal proposed an interesting prospectus as a *desideratum* for a Marian text:

1. the use of scriptural texts pertinent to Marian doctrine;
2. the eschatological sense that so beautifully stands out in the dogma of the Assumption;

3. a pastoral character so that the teaching given the faithful on the Blessed Virgin helps them to see the intimate relation of Marian doctrine with Christ and the Church;
4. the admirable fulfillment in Mary's life of the spirit of the beatitudes;
5. a doctrine at once solid and in conformity with the Church's tradition, one that would easily rally the support of Catholic theologians;
6. an exposition of doctrine that, without detracting from or obscuring the truth, avoids new dogmatic definitions and opinions that are not common.[27]

None of these texts was adopted as basis. A special commission formed by Cardinals Santos and König and by S.S.E.E. Doumith, the Maronite, and Msgr. Théas, Bishop of Lourdes, tried to reach an agreement on a project that was to be presented to the representatives of the episcopal conferences, but this agreement did not mature sufficiently. The matter was finally given to two theologians representing the conflicting groups: C. Balić,[28] supporter of the old official text, and Msgr. Philips who was to be the author of the text that was definitively submitted to the Fathers.

C. THIRD PHASE: 1964

Five successive redactions, worked out by Msgr. Philips and submitted to Father Balić, were amalgamated into a textual plan, which the Theological Commission examined in March, 1964.[29] The corrections proposed by the Fathers were examined by the editor, and in June the Commission examined the text again, this time more carefully. Once more corrected, the text was distributed to the Fathers in the volume that contained the amended text of the first six chapters *De Ecclesia*.[30] But there was an important difference: while these six chapters had already been discussed and were ready for vote, chapters 7 and 8 were merely in the phase of a text ready for discussion. On September 16 and 17, at the very beginning of the third session of the Council, the text was discussed. The Fathers were conscious of the difficulty of the issue, and, although the opposed tendencies were expressed, it was clear that it could not be pushed to extremes. The schema, the best among the possible ones, represented, according to Cardinal Frings, a compromise in which each one had to yield somewhat in order to arrive at a general approbation. The Commission examined the "postulata" of the Fathers and a new "Textus emendatus" was distributed as a basis for voting.[31] After that the Commission examined the "modi" and proposed to the aula the result of its deliberations.[32] After the last modifications, introduced by way of "modi," had been approved in General Congregation, the text was promulgated November 21, 1964.[33]

3. The Main Lines of the Conciliar Text

A. A BALANCED TEXT

It is hardly necessary to justify this characteristic of balance after what has been said about the pre-Conciliar situation. Although this did not seem necessary in regard to other themes, the Council made it clear in this case that it did not intend to decide problems not yet sufficiently clarified. And it added that the opinions about Mary freely proposed by the schools maintained their rights.[34] These were very prudent statements that receive their full significance in the light of the original official text, which, in the judgment of some theologians, committed itself to positions of different schools.[35] Equilibrium demanded a sobriety of statement, and progress was clearly manifested in this respect from the first text. Thus a Father could rightly say:

> The exposition of this chapter's doctrine wisely seeks to propose those things which are clearly traditional, avoiding new definitions, without obscuring or lessening what undoubtedly belongs to Catholic doctrine. . . . Since, however, the exposition of Catholic doctrine can use formulations somewhat diverse—without affecting its substantial identity—in both Oriental and Latin Churches, it seems absolutely necessary that, in proposing doctrine concerning the Blessed Virgin Mary, we employ such expressions as can be accepted by all as their own.[36]

In passing we may note that the few interventions of Oriental Fathers were generally positive, although reticent on the title "Mediatrix." The equilibrium of the text leads to an important conclusion that will be taken up when we speak about the Marian cult.

B. RETURN TO SOURCES

It is not possible here to make a detailed study of this aspect of the text, but a simple reading of it shows how the declarations were based on biblical and patristic doctrine. In the successive redactions of the text an objective presentation of the sources had always been intended without attempting to use a certain text out of its context or in an accommodated sense. This is the reason, for example, for the use of the abreviation "cf." for numerous biblical quotations that are not used in a literal sense or in a less than rigorously literal sense.[37] This effort to go back to the sources prompted discretion in the use of papal texts. Not that the Council would forget or, even worse, deny or contradict the papal magisterium, but as a matter of fact it is not always easy to discern the literal character of the various documents, all the more since the Roman pontiffs exercise various functions as, for instance, that of primate of Italy, patriarch of the West, and primate of the

Universal Church. These juridically different levels are reflected in a certain way in the actions of popes. It is also necessary to distinguish between an affirmation found in an explicitly doctrinal document and one expressed in a document oriented more directly to piety. A papal declaration does not always exclude legitimate differences among Catholics, above all if it does not represent a constant.[38] Although the text of the Vatican II does not comprise an exposition of the whole of Marian doctrine,[39] we can nevertheless say that nothing has been forgotten as to what constitutes the common patrimony of those living in the Catholic community.[40]

C. CHRISTOLOGICAL REFERENCE

The pastoral nature of Vatican II's activity imposed this characteristic on its Marian doctrine. It did so, not only out of ecumenical considerations, but in order to provide orientation to the movement of Christian life within the Catholic Church herself. Sometimes certain imperfections and even deviations originate in what is *not* said rather than in an explicit affirmation of erroneous propositions.[41] It is the absence of an element that causes the loss of the equilibrium of the whole. For this reason the Council reinforced various points of doctrine that tend to maintain the equilibrium necessary for a right understanding of faith, as for instance, the doctrine affirming the redemption of Mary,[42] the affirmation of the unique mediation of Christ,[43] and the direct union of the faithful with the Lord.[44]

Mary does not come between Christ and us, but she uses her power of intercession to establish a closer union between the head and the members of the mystical body, a union that is realized in an immediate, not in a mediate, way. For the same reason the Council advises the ministers of the word of God to see to it that the gifts and privileges of the Most Holy Virgin are always referred to Christ, the source of all truth, holiness and piety.[45] In full consonance with this characteristic of the Conciliar document are the words of Pope Paul VI's address closing the third Conciliar session: "We wish above all that this fact be shown in full light: that Mary, humble servant of the Lord, is completely oriented and related to God and to Jesus Christ, our only Mediator and Savior."[46] And the papal legate at the Congress of Santo Domingo said that "the only way to recognize an authentic piety and love for the Mother of God is a close examination of the degree to which this piety leads to the Lord."[47] This orientation of the Conciliar text fulfills the desire of those Fathers who wanted to see Christians have a greater homogeneity between their manifestations of devotion to the Mother of God and their participation in liturgical and sacramental life, the center and highpoint of all Church life.[48]

D. RELATIONSHIP TO THE CHURCH

Not only because of its inclusion in the *Constitution on the Church*, but because of the very nature of the things, this text had to preserve a relationship to the Church. This relationship can be seen on two different planes: Mary as a type of the Church, and Mary as exercising a maternal role in the Church.

In the typological aspect, the Council points out that the Church has reached its perfection in Mary, while the faithful still struggle with sin.[49] This typology of the Virgin in regard to the Church is observed not only in regard to Mary as a perfect model of faith, hope and charity, but is realized in the fact that the present state of Mary in heaven constitutes a sign of the future state of the Church.[50]

This "ecclesial" typology leads to the second aspect of Mary's relationship to the Church. Very often we find in the Conciliar text expressions that emphasize the maternal role of Mary within the Church,[51] affirmations that conclude that she "is our mother in the order of grace." This motherhood consists in the influence Mary exercises on the attainment of the new life to which the members of the body of Christ are called.[52] This influence is twofold: on the one hand, it manifests itself in her divine maternity in regard to Christ, first-born of many brothers, and, on the other hand, in her multiple intercession, because of which she finds a place in the present economy of the dispensation of heavenly gifts.[53] However, this influence does not arise out of necessity but out of divine benevolence and the superabundance of Christ's merits; it rests on his mediation, depends totally on it and receives all its power from it.[54]

The Council does not define more specifically the scope of Mary's maternal role since it expressly seeks to abstain from deciding matters disputed by schools of theology.

E. THE CULT OF THE VIRGIN

We know that the cult of Mary takes on varied characteristics within the Catholic Church, within a constant tradition of honoring the Mother of God. In regard to this cult, the Council limits itself to general guidelines that are, in large part, but consequences of what has hitherto been said. After establishing the fact of this cult, the Council immediately points out the difference between the cult of Mary and of God, a difference that is essential.[55] This is important, both from the ecumenical viewpoint in order to eliminate misunderstandings, and also from the pastoral viewpoint in order to impress on the faithful that every cult must be definitely oriented to the Highest.

Orthodox forms of Marian piety hold that "in honoring the mother, the Son, for whom all things have been created (cf. Col 1:15–16) and in whom the eternal Father desired that 'all his fullness should dwell' (Col 1:19), should be properly known, loved, glorified and his commandments observed."[56] The Council insists on the pre-eminence of the liturgical cult of Mary, which again accentuates Mary's relationship to Christ and the Trinity, for the liturgy is the highest expression of the piety of the Church, without interfering with the traditional, extraliturgical devotions.[57] Besides recommending a balance in preaching that is equidistant from "false superlatives" and "exaggerated narrowness," the Council insists on carefully avoiding "anything in word or deed that can lead the separated brethren and other persons into error about true doctrine in this matter."[58] The Council Fathers close with a warning against sentimentalism and vain credulity by emphasizing that true devotion consists in understanding Mary's greatness through true faith, in filial love and in the imitation of her virtues.[59] Whoever reads this part of the Conciliar text cannot but think that the Council takes into consideration that there are, here and there, chapters of devotion to Mary that call for attention and need correction and reorientation.

F. ECUMENICAL SIGNIFICANCE

The ecumenical value of the Marian text is rooted precisely in the synthesis of the characteristics stated above. It is precisely its balance, its return to the sources, its situating of Mary in a Christological and ecclesial context, the direction it gives to the cult—all these make for better understanding and dialogue. Moreover, the very integration of Marian doctrine within the *Constitution on the Church* is of ecumenical importance, since it tries to locate a matter of difficulty for Protestants within a more accessible context. What the *Decree on Ecumenism* desires regarding the order or hierarchy of the truths that constitute the Church's teaching[60] has been observed in chapter 8 of the *Constitution on the Church*, and thus the latter tries to give solid foundation for pastoral preaching and popular piety by providing a greater penetration of the mysteries and not a simple material extension and multiplication of titles.[61] Two criteria may serve to evaluate the ecumenical resonance of the text. From the Anglican side, Professor de Waal says:

> I cannot end without saying a few words about the chapter consecrated to the Blessed Virgin Mary. Its balance deserves, in great part, our admiration for combining as it does an insistence on the unique mediation of Jesus Christ with the affirmation that Our Lady is the sign that within the Church all the People of God are called to participate in his redemptive work.[62]

A Lutheran theologian, Professor Mainhold, says:

> One may say that the incorporation of this mariological doctrine within the
> *Constitution on the Church*, requested by a large number of Council Fathers, is
> progress. Kind attention is thus paid to all non-Catholic Churches, which would
> have been particularly offended by a new mariological treatment given in
> isolation.[63]

We can say that the express citation of texts of sacred Scripture that makes
for difficulty from the viewpoint of the theology of the Mother of God,[64]
as well as the explanation of the meaning of the latest Marian dogmas, are
not slight contributions to the field of ecumenism.[65]

4. Some Mariological Problems in the Light of Vatican II

A. MATER ECCLESIAE

We know that there was rather considerable commotion in the Council over
the expediency or inexpediency of the use of this title in regard to Mary.
Without intending absolute exactitude, we can say that there were many
Fathers who urged the use of this title as well as many who were against it.
It is well known that the Theological Commission, while giving ample place
to the idea of Mary's maternal role in the Church,[66] did not want to use
explicitly the title "Mater Ecclesiae," perhaps in order to avoid occasion-
ing less correct interpretations that unnecessarily prejudice the cause of
ecumenism.

The Holy Father considered it opportune merely to proclaim this title,
and he did so in the public session of November 21, 1964. The declaration
is placed in that part of the Conciliar document which strongly emphasizes
the maternal role of the Virgin. The proclamation of Paul VI calls Mary
"Mater Ecclesiae, hoc est totius populi Christiani, tam fidelium quam Pas-
torum" (i.e., of the whole Christian people, both of the faithful and of pastors), a precision very apt for understanding the meaning of the word
"Church" in this document and for eliminating equivocations: Mary's
motherhood refers to persons and not to the institutional elements of the
Church. Her maternity belongs to the order of personal grace and not to
the order of the institution of the means of grace. Another very valuable precision springs from the discourse of the Pope: Mary is very near to us; like
us, she is a daughter of Adam and is therefore also our sister because of our
common human nature.[67]

B. MEDIATRIX

For about forty years there has been in the Church a considerable development of studies concerning Mary's mediation. But the subject never reached maturity, and there exist among Catholics serious divergencies in this respect. Hence, there was clearly felt at the Council a whole current that did not look favorably on the use of expressions and titles for Mary, that are proper to Jesus Christ. There was a fear that the Christian people might not perceive the difference in content of these expressions in the one or the other case. There were also the theological problems given rise to by the extension of this mediation ("mediatrix omnium gratiarum") and the manner of exercising such mediation.[68]

The promulgated text is much more cautious than the original official text. It says nothing about universal mediation, nor does it determine its content. Whenever it uses the title it does so together with others and with two explanations: first, that it is to be understood in such a way that nothing can increase or diminish the dignity and efficacy of Christ, the unique mediator; that consequently such mediation is by way of participation in the divine goods in a way that it cannot be placed on the same level as Christ's mediation or become one with it. The example of the priesthood and participation in priesthood offers an analogy.[69]

C. CO-REDEMPTION

Neither the original nor the final text uses this term. The reason is twofold: first, an all too easy equivocation which could result, and, second, the fundamental theological divergencies that exist in regard to the explanation of the content of this expression. The Constitution *Lumen Gentium* does not favor any particular position in this respect. It speaks in general terms about cooperation in the act of salvation and was very careful to avoid every expression that could be interpreted as favoring a given position. The unquestionable content of Mary's cooperation is expressed by the Council in terms of "motherhood in the order of grace."[70]

Besides the preceding three great themes, the Council was confronted with divergent opinions about the following points: (a) Mary's consciousness of her Son's divinity at the time of the Annunciation, (b) the meaning of the expression "virginitas in partu," and (c) the death of Mary.

It is a fact that there are controverted opinions about these three points—which does not mean that all of them are of the same value.[71]

The Conciliar text does not solve these controversies; the opinions retain the status which they had before the Council. It is deserving of mention that, as has been said in the report about the first project,[72] some hoped to settle these discussions by way of the magisterium. But this did not happen. The texts and words were so chosen as to leave the problems as they were. This can be inferred not only from the text itself but from certain concrete propositions made by the Fathers. But the prudent reserve of the Council in these matters has not the value of a judgment, as if it attributed the same value to opposing opinions in these matters: very simply, "manent in suo jure."

In conclusion it seems fitting to quote the words of Paul VI on the occasion of the promulgation of the Constitution:

> For the first time—and we may say it with profound emotion—an ecumenical council has endeavored to present in a sort of vast synthesis what Catholic doctrine teaches on the place to be attributed to the Blessed Virgin Mary in the mystery of Christ. This clearly is in accord with charge given to this Council: to show forth the face of the Church, with which the Mother of God is intimately united, and of which she is, as one author says so well, "the most important part, the best part, the principal part, the most chosen part."[73]

APPENDIX 1

The Conciliar documentation on the doctrine of chapter 8 of *Lumen Gentium* is very ample. We shall try to give a list; there will, of course, be lacunae.

1962:
1. Printed text of the primitive project submitted to the Central Preparatory Commission for approval.
2. Printed text approved by the Central Commission, distributed to the Fathers Nov. 23, 1962, in the gray fascicle "Series, secunda. De Ecclesia et de Beata Maria Virgine."

1963:
1. Multicopied fascicle presented by Cardinal Silva, Archbishop of Santiago, Chile, entitled "Annotationes generales in schema Constitutionis De Ecclesia," pp. 84–88. It is found in the archives of the Theological Commission and numerous private archives. Note that in this fascicle the Marian chapter is already incorporated into the Constitution. This was written in February, 1963.
2. September to October, 1963. Text by Abbot Butler, O.S.B., presented with many signatures to the moderators of the Council, found in private archives.
3. Same period. New version of Cardinal Silva's text, presented with many signatures to the moderators. May be found in private archives.
4. October, 1963. Combined text of Cardinal Silva and Abbot Butler, presented to the moderators and sent to the Theological Commission. To be found in Conciliar and private archives.
5. Oct. 24, 1963. *Relationes* of Cardinals Santos and König in favor of a separate schema or one integrated into *De Ecclesia* respectively. The fascicle also contains the "quaesitum" which was to be submitted to a vote Oct. 29.
6. Nov. 16, 1963. Study by C. Balić on the possibilities of using the 1962 printed text (cf. above 1962, 2) with the corrections suggested by the German and Scandinavian Conferences. In Conciliar and private archives.
7. There were in this period at least four written pieces of propaganda about insertion or noninsertion of the Marian schema into the Constitution De Ecclesia. There were three against insertion: one anonymously printed, a second multicopied by N. Garcia Garces,

C.M.F., Marcelino Llamera, O.P., and Bernardo Monsegú, C.P., the mariology consultants of the Spanish bishops, and a third signed and multicopied by five Malabar and Ukrainian bishops. The one in favor of insertion was signed and multicopied by Cardinal Silva and Msgr. Alfredo Viola, president of the Episcopal Conference of Uruguay. To be found in private archives.

1964: 1. March. Multicopied text, distributed to members of the Theological Commission, composed by Msgr. Philips and C. Balić. Archives of the Commission and of the Fathers who were its members. This text was later printed in a gray fascicle for the use of the Fathers of the Commission.

2. June. Multicopied text, a correction of the preceding, approved with additional corrections by the Commission in this month's meetings.

3. July. A two-column text printed in a green brochure: "Schema Constitutionis De Ecclesia," pp. 197–218. The first column contains the March text and the already corrected one of June. *It is worthy of note that up to this time there had not been any discussion by the Council on the text prepared by the Commission.*

4. Sept. 16. *Relatio* of presentation of the text for Conciliar discussion. Printed text distributed to the Fathers.

5. Sept. 16 and 17. Addresses by the Fathers in the aula on the previous "textus emendatus." The text of the speeches and of the written comments comprise 264 multicopied pages. To be found in the Conciliar archives and those of the Fathers and *Periti* of the Commission.

6. October. Green fascicle "Textus emendatus capitis VIII Constitutionis De Ecclesia et relationes," distributed to the Council Fathers. The first column reproduces the "textus emendatus" of the large July brochure which is now called "prior"; the second column gives the text modified by the Commission according to Conciliar discussion, called now the "textus emendatus."

7. November. "Modi. Caput VIII de Beata Maria Virgine Deipara in mysterio Christi et ecclesiae." A gray text printed and distributed to the Fathers. It contains the "modi" proposed in the voting of the chapter and the reply of the Commission which were submitted Nov. 18 for approval in the aula.

8. November. "Schema Constitutionis dogmaticae De Ecclesia, de qua agetur in Sessione publica diei 21 Nov. 1964." A gray fascicle distributed to the Fathers with the text of the Constitution which was voted on the date indicated.

9. November. "Constitutio dogmatica De Ecclesia." Yellow fascicle distributed to the Fathers with the approved and promulgated text.

APPENDIX 2

This selected list is not a Marian bibliography but rather a presentation of texts whose relationship with the Conciliar text is rather close.

1. R. Laurentin, *La vierge au Concile* (Paris: Lethielleux, 1965). This is the first published commentary on the Conciliar text.

2. *Idem, Court traité de théologie mariale,* 4th ed. (Paris: Lethielleux, 1959).

3. *Idem, La question mariale* (Paris: Seuil, 1963). A work important for appreciating the diverse tendencies in the Council milieu.

4. *Idem, Bilan du Concile,* vols. 1, 2 and 3 (Paris: Seuil, 1963–1965). A very useful work for getting an orderly and composite view of the Council's work.

5. A. Müller, "Problemas y perspectivas de la mariología actual," in *Panorama de la Teología actual* (ed. Guadarrama, 1961), a translation of the original German, *Fragen der Theologie Heute* (Einsiedeln: Benziger, 1957).

6. G. Roschini, *La cosidetta questione mariana* (Roma: pro manuscripto, 1964). This printed work replies to the observations of Laurentin (n.3 above) and Müller (n.5 above).

7. C. Balić, *La Beata Vergine Maria, Madre di Dio, nel mistero di Cristo e della Chiesa.* A manuscript of the Constitution *Lumen Gentium.*

8. Cardinal R. Silva, "Discurso de clausura del IV Congreso Mariológico de Santo Domingo." Closing speech given by the Cardinal Legate March 22, 1965. Spanish text in *Teología y Vida* 6, 2; French text in *Documentation Catholique* 1446 (April 18, 1965) 699–711.

NOTES

1. Employed also in the "Praenotanda" of the original official text. Cf. Appendix 1, 1962, 2, p. 100.

2. Cf. Appendix 2, n. 5.

3. Cf. *ibid.*, n. 3.

4. Cf. *ibid.*, n. 6.

5. Cf. *ibid.*, n. 5., p. 388 (ed. Guadarrama.)

6. Reference was made to these orientations in the official presentation of the text to the Fathers (cf. Appendix 1, 1964, 4) stating "Christotypica et Ecclesiotypica interpretatio se invicem nullo modo excludunt, sed complent."

7. Cf. Appendix 2, n. 3., p. 71.

8. *Ibid.*, 78.

9. *Ibid.*, 76ff. Cf. also the comments expressed in the multicopied text of the Spanish mariologists referred to in Appendix 1, 1963, 7.

10. Conciliar speech by Cardinal Raul Silva, in the name of more than forty Fathers made Oct. 1, 1963.

11. Cf. Appendix 2, n. 1, pp. 8–50.

12. Cf. Appendix 1, 1962, 2.

13. It took place between Dec. 1–7, 1962.

14. K. Rahner wrote some multicopied notes on this first text. Later, German-speaking Fathers and the Conference of Scandinavian Bishops presented numerous notes on and emendations to the original text; these were based in part on Rahner's notes. The presentation by these Fathers, notable for its theological clarity, requested integration in *De Ecclesia*. These multicopied documents exist in numerous private archives of Conciliar Fathers. Patriarch Maximus IV also made some observations on the text.

15. Cf. Appendix 1, 1963, 1.

16. *Ibid.*, 84.

17. *Ibid.*, 87.

18. In fact, Rahner and the German and Scandinavian bishops considered rather the idea of amending the original official text.

19. This period of General Congregations lasted from Sept. 30 until Dec. 4, 1963.

20. Cf. Appendix 2, n. 1, p. 12.

21. Cf. note 10.

22. Cf. Appendix 1, 1963, 5.

23. Cf. *ibid.*, 7.

24. Cf. *ibid.*, 2.

25. Cf. *ibid.*, 3.

26. Cf. *ibid.*, 4.

27. Letter of Cardinal Silva to the moderators of the Council presenting the text. There are multicopied copies in private archives.

28. Carlo Balić, president of the International Marian Academy, was, in the words of Laurentin, the principal author of the original text; cf. Appendix 2, n. 1, p. 21.

29. Cf. *ibid.*

30. Cf. Appendix 1, 1964, 3.

31. Cf. *ibid.*, 6.

32. Cf. *ibid.*, 7.

33. Cf. *ibid.*, 8 and 9.

34. Cf. *Lumen Gentium* 54. Henceforth the Constitution will be referred to with the abbreviation *LG*.

35. Cf. note 14.

36. Speech by Cardinal Silva in the name of forty-four Council Fathers, given in the General Congregation, Sept. 16, 1964.

37. Cf. *LG*, especially 55–58.

38. Consider, for example, the title "co-redemptress" used with some frequency by Pius XI but not by his successors.

39. Cf. *LG* 54.

40. Cf. the *Relatio* given by Msgr. Roy: "Concilium vero, secundum universalem suam methodum, in controversias inter catholics theologos non intrat, sed ubique placita fundamentalia doctrinae catholicae fidelibus exponit, circa quam omnes Patres consordant, ut exinde tum

praedicatio pastoralis solide fulciatur, tum pietas populi christiani enixe foveatur" (Appendix 1, 1964, 4).

41. Cf. the observations of O. Semmelroth, *Le sens des sacrements* (Brussels: Pensée Catholique, 1963) 13ff.

42. Cf. *LG* 53: "Redeemed in an especially sublime manner by reason of the merits of her son."

43. Cf. *ibid.*, 60: "We have but one Mediator, as we know from the words of the Apostle. . . . The maternal duty of Mary toward men in no way obscures or diminishes this unique mediation of Christ, but rather shows its power." Cf. also *LG* 62.

44. Cf. *LG* 60: "For all the saving influences of the Blessed Virgin. . . . in no way . . . impede the immediate union of the faithful with Christ. Rather they foster it."

45. Cf. *LG* 67.

46. Cf. *L'Osservatore Romano*, Nov. 22, 1964.

47. Cf. *Theología y Vida* 6,2, p. 91.

48. Cf. *Constitution on the Sacred Liturgy* 7, 10 and 103.

49. Cf. *LG* 65.

50. Cf. *LG* 68.

51. Cf. *LG* 53: "mother of the members of Christ"; *LG* 54: "mother of men, particularly of the faithful"; *LG* 61: "mother to us in the order of grace"; *LG* 62: "This maternity of Mary in the order of grace . . . . will last without interruption."

52. Cf. *LG* 63: "In their (the faithful's) birth and development she cooperates with maternal love."

53. Cf. *LG* 62.

54. Cf. *LG* 60.

55. Cf. *LG* 66. This expression seemed more exact than that of "infinite distance" proposed by some Fathers. The term *hyperdulia* was not used because the Orientals do not use it.

56. Cf. *LG* 66.

57. Cf. *LG* 67.

58. *Ibid.*

59. *Ibid.*

60. Cf. *Decree on Ecumenism* 13.

61. Cf. Appendix 1, 1964, 4.

62. Cf. *Irénikon* 38 (1965) 308.

63. Cf. *ibid.*, 324ff.

64. Cf. *LG* 57 and 58.

65. Cf. *LG* 56, regarding the Immaculate Conception; *LG* 59, regarding the Assumption.

66. Cf. notes 51 and 52.

67. Cf. note 46.

68. About 250 Fathers were unfavorably disposed to the use of the term "mediatrix"; a slightly larger number accepted the title, although some Fathers suggested that it would be better not to use it in an exclusive form, i.e., speaking of it, rather, along with other titles. This latter suggestion was followed by the Commission.

69. Cf. *LG* 60 and 62.

70. Cf. note 51.

71. Cf. Appendix 2, n. 1, p. 85ff. Concerning the sense of "virginitas in partu" see the article by K. Rahner under this same title in "*Schiften der Theologie* 4 (Einsiedeln: Benziger, 1964) 173–205. On this theme there is an observation by the German Fathers (cf. note 14). Note that the first official text used the expression "corporalem integritatem Matris in ipsomet partu incorruptam atque illibatam manere." The promulgated text, employing traditional expressions, says: "Filium suum [ostendit], qui virginalem eius interitatem mon minuit sed sacravit." Regarding the death of Mary, the Conciliar text uses precisely the same formula as the definition of the dogma of the Assumption (cf. *LG* 59), which does not solve the problem by way of the magisterium.

72. Cf. Appendix 1, 1962, 2, p. 100.

73. Cf. note 46. Rupert, *In Apoc.* 1, 7, 12.

AHERN: Before I begin answering the questions, I would like to ask Abbot Butler of Downside to make public the wonderful observation he just gave me before the lecture.

BUTLER: I want to say that I think the subject-matter of Father Ahern's paper is perhaps the most important of all the things we shall discuss this week. For, in my opinion, the eschatological dimensions of the gospel take us to the very heart of the whole theological problem of our day. We have all learned that one must take the Bible on its own terms, and in order to give an exegesis of it one has to understand the mentality that operates in the Bible. We have learned from great men like Oscar Cullman that the Hebrews thought in historical categories. Now it seems to me that as one contemplates the eschatological moment in the Jewish-Christian teaching, one appreciates that, if I may put it like this, eschatology stands to history as in the Greek systems of thought metaphysics stands to physics. On that analogy I rather like to talk, not about eschatology, but about "metachronics." "Metachronics" stands to history as metaphysics stands to physics. It is the ultimate dimension of thought, apprehension and understanding when you approach reality in historical categories. Now if there is any truth in what I am saying, one sees at once the extreme importance of the fact that we have in Christianity a realized eschatology. In other words, Christianity —the gospel—offers us, not history on one side and "metachronics" on the other as two unrelated, completely discontinuous phenomena, but history shot through with the richness, values, of "metachronics." And secondly, it occurs to me that, while the patristic and medieval effort to express Christianity in the thought-categories of Greek philosophy was entirely legitimate and immensely enriching for the Church, nevertheless in the end those categories are inadequate for the gospel; we must find our way back—and it is not very easy for us who are the heirs of Greece and Rome—to the primary historical categories.

Now what is exciting for the Church at the present moment is that we are living in an age of the human story in which the historical and durational categories of thought are regaining, even independently of our own efforts, a central place in human thinking. While the Council itself was concerned, not with baptizing a theology, but with presenting doctrine, nevertheless a large part of the drama of the actual Council was the clash between the Greco-Roman, ultimately philosophical, and the more biblical, historical and contemporary approach to the same set of data.

By way of conclusion, I would like to say that I do not conceive our being faced here with an ultimate either/or. If we wish to accept the historical approach, we need not, therefore, finally reject the philosophical approach. What I think we are aiming at, and what it may not be the good fortune of our generation to achieve, is some kind of a higher synthesis in which both those elements are given their due place. But I feel perfectly certain that the historical categories have got to be given the prior place.

AHERN: First there are two corrections of the material I presented which I think are very important. Father Congar pointed out that he thought the cosmic aspect of eschatology is a little more amply expressed in chapter 7 of the *Constitution on the Church* than had I allowed for. I checked on the paragraph to which Father Congar referred, and there are allusions in it. I would like to call them steppingstones for what comes later in the Constitution. But they are there.

Father Congar also pointed out that the lack of completeness observable in chapter 7 can be explained by the history of the text's formation. He also indicated that in the first draft, prepared by Cardinal Larraona, there was reference only to the saints.

Father Congar also referred me to article 8 of the *Decree on the Church's Missionary Activity*, in which it is pointed out that the very spread of Christianity brings with it this forward-moving development:

Now, since he who does not believe is already judged, the words of Christ are at one and the same time words of judgment and of grace, of death and of life. For it is only by putting to death what is old that we are able to come to a newness of life. This fact applies first of all to persons, but it holds also for the various goods of this world, which bear the mark both of man's sin and of God's blessing; for "all have sinned and have need of the glory of God." By himself and by his own power, no one is freed from sin or raised above himself, or completely rid of his sickness or his solitude or his servitude. On the contrary, all stand in need of Christ, their Model, their Mentor, their Liberator, their Savior, their Source of Life.

In other words, when Christ comes the whole of man is changed. That fearful body-soul dichotomy under which we labor explains why we have never appreciated the miracles of our Lord, why we look on them as deeds that a veterinarian could have performed, curing an injured limb, giving sight to eyes, hearing to the deaf. We see them only as physical things and miss the whole point of the miracle, namely, that it was a complete giving of himself to this person. It was a messianic manifestation; it touched the whole man. And hence, when he gave sight to the eye, it was not only that the man could see physically, but that the man could see the goodness of God in a new way. When he gave health to a limb, it was not only that a man could walk, but that he could take giant strides. It was the *whole man* that he was saving. Notice the *whole man*. I have emphasized the spiritual element in this, but conversely, the whole man was physically changed by his coming to that life. So it is with the Church; the Church is Christ. And when the Church comes, Christ comes. With his whole messianic ministry he has to touch and change not only what is spirit, but to touch and to change the whole thing, the whole man, and the whole city, and the whole world. And this is beautifully brought out in the *Decree on the Church's Missionary Activity*, where this whole cosmological involvement in the salvation of Christ is to the fore.

> Question: *The Constitution begins by remarking that the human race will be perfectly re-established in Christ. Does this not burst on universalism. In other words, can we ask is the Council teaching that all will be saved, and if so, is this faithful to the entire witness of Scripture and tradition?*

AHERN: It is true that the expression "human race" is used, but I think it can well be interpreted as merely a generic reference and must be qualified by the whole context of the chapter. In the material that follows it is made very clear that mankind will be saved, but that mankind will be those who are living in Christ, for it is possible that we can fail. We are warned by the Council not to be like the wicked and the slothful servant. Therefore, the full possibility of failure is certainly indicated in the chapter, so that I do not think the chapter can be said to be teaching a universalism of salvation for all men. It is a matter of a man cooperating with God's grace, saving himself through his own will.

> Question: In the New Testament eschatological thinking is inseparable from the warfare between God and Satan. Considering this, can one claim that fidelity to Scripture in content and perspective dominates this chapter, when the chapter makes almost no reference to this warfare? In the New Testament Satan attacks the Messiah most vigorously. He attacks Peter, the other apostles. The Church must carry on this warfare to the end.

AHERN: It is true that the warfare is not mentioned in this chapter, and I think with reason. When one comes to the eschatological doctrine of the New Testament, we are faced with the fact that here eschatology is presented in the thought-patterns and imagery of Hebrew thought. Hebrew thought always deals in quasi-poetic forms. A Hebrew will always, as it were, concretize and personalize. If there is any area, therefore, of New Testament thinking which has to go through a process of demythologizing, I think it is this area of the warfare idea in the New Testament. There are certain univocal constants. Always before the end there must be tribulation, the polipsis. Before the end there must be temptation, pyrosmos. It is all capsulized in the synoptic presentation of the agony in the garden: Christ about to enter upon messianic glory must go through his temptation, must go through his tribulation. This is a constant all through the Hebrew writing. And yet this is all the way through human life; it is all the way through history. When we come to look at the thing theologically, we have to face the fact that the personal evil spirit is evil; he knows neither more or less of evil. His will is always to evil; he is always working to do evil. When therefore we speak, as it were, of great output of evil, theologically we know that, demythologizing this concept, what we really mean is that men will let this constant power of evil become stronger than ever before through their own wills. Hence, to have preserved here the thought-patterns coming from the apocalyptic literature that dominates New Testament thinking on this might have led to the actual missing of what is the cardinal point in all of our dealings with God along this pilgrim path, and what will be the cardinal point in the last age, namely, that we ourselves, with our own wills, are the ones who make that evil which is univocally constant, the evil that is in the personalized spirit, something now more dynamically powerful than ever before. I think wisely, therefore, the responsibility is pressed upon ourselves. There is no denial of the reality of the spirit of evil, no denial of his activity. There is rather an emphasis on the fact that that activity becomes real in

319

the world only insofar as human persons, who dominate their own lives, have made that evil a reality.

GREMILLION: The other day Father de Lubac cited Teilhard de Chardin. I am curious to have some sort of assessment of Teilhard de Chardin from this distinguished group.

AHERN: Father, when we were on schema 13, the day came when Bishop Weber of Strasbourg rose at the Council and said: "How can we prepare a schema on the Church in the modern world if we are not even speaking the language of the modern world?" Then he went on to say that in his diocese he had many agnostics and atheists, who, after having read Teilhard de Chardin, came to him and said: "Now for the first time we understand what you Catholics are talking about." The whole aula burst into applause, and following upon Weber there were at least five encomiums on Teilhard de Chardin. Certainly, Father, I think that in this whole eschatological dimension of length and breadth the thinking of Teilhard de Chardin was certainly influential.

DE LUBAC: I believe that Father Teilhard de Chardin would have been very happy indeed to hear the paper which Father Ahern delivered. If Tielhard had wished to give a synthesis of his seeing things from an eschatological point of view, he would have added a second point and insisted very much on the necessary transfiguration, the passage through death and transfiguration to the image of Christ, who died and rose, which must mark eschatology. And that is what I asked Father Ahern—if he did not think it a good idea some day to develop this theme.

This is in direct relation, not only with what is at the very heart of Christian dogma, that is, the mystery of Christ, dead and risen, but this also has tremendous importance from a spiritual point of view. Father Teilhard de Chardin insisted on saying that the more man is interested in matters of this world, the more impassioned he is in favor of the work of the world, the more he must do this work in a spirit of profound detachment, remaining indefinitely detached from all particular visible forms. All this is but the figure of a passing world; it is a condition—not a cause but a condition—of the day of the Lord, of the parousia, a world that in all its visible, specific, earthly forms must disappear entirely. This is the principle he used to renew the expression of the traditional doctrine of the gospel and the Church on Christian detachment.

He had always wanted to join an impassioned interest in this world with a detachment as total as possible from everything specific, visible, restricted in the forms of this world. At every stage of his life he spoke of this, but there are few texts that show his idea on this subject, an exchange of letters with the philosopher, Maurice Blondel, that lasted only a month (December, 1919). I just edited them, with a few annotations in a small brochure published by Beauchesne in Paris—*Maurice Blondel et Teilhard de Chardin: Correspondance Annotée*. I believe that central to the correspondence is this point that ran through all of his life. It is certain that when some people make use of Teilhard de Chardin's ideas for a love of the world and for a spirituality of action, they do not say anything erroneous, but they understand him too incompletely; in the end this falsifies things.

To take this from a different angle, you know that he has produced a spiritual work called the *Milieu divin*. He himself says that he wanted to put into this work what he tried to live, pray and teach in the various retreats he preached. At the end of his life he said that from the spiritual and religious point of view this work still described well his last thoughts. This small book has three parts. In the first part he takes up the Christian who wants really to follow Christ and seeks Christian perfection. The first part concerns the divinization of activities, very important but only a first step. If we stop here we have not grasped his whole idea.

The second part deals with the divinization of passivities. And this is where he shows that what are habitually called the passive virtues in a pejorative sense in some devotional works and literature critical of Christian thought, are activity par excellence, if they are received in a Christian spirit. He indicates how this activity par excellence is the total passivity summarized in the fact of death. He also shows that the death of Christ, accepted out of loving obedience to his father and love for man, is the supreme activity, the great active power that leads the world toward its end.

In the third part he says that it is because of this divinization of passivities one can reach the divine milieu, the real place, of which the visible, temporal world is but the wrong side. Hence, the love of the world he speaks of is not love of the world such as it is today. He says that the most frightful thing for man would be to think that he will be left in the conditions of this world. He calls this the horror of being trapped in the cosmic ball. The way out of this cosmic ball is the transfiguration of this cosmos. One can still think of this cosmos, but there are all sorts of gradated, analogous meanings. Teilhard de Chardin's idea was very close to what Father Butler reminded us of a few moments ago, and that is why—it appears paradoxical at first—Teilhard de Chardin's thought has been compared to biblical thought. It is very true that he thinks according to the double category of history, or better perhaps cosmic evolution around which history turns, for all cosmic evolution in his mind emerges in a dynamic anthropology and then in "metahistory," eschatology. His thought is entirely eschatological. But to fully grasp his thought one must see to what extent he considers everything must be transfigured by means of this passage through death. And this is what dictates our spiritual attitude in our action in the world.

AHERN: Canon Moeller gave me a question, but I feel that he will answer it much better than I will, since it has a very important ecumenical overtone. Would you kindly develop it a little bit?

Moeller: I was only saying that it seems to me that this chapter 7 has a liturgical aspect: the very close relations between the earthly and the heavenly liturgies, the cult of the saints, and the veneration of images (a quotation of the Second Council of Nicaea). I think this aspect of the chapter is very important for giving a more complete view of the eschatological dimensions of which you spoke so well. From this viewpoint the remarks made by Father de Lubac about Teilhard de Chardin are completely relevant, for it seems to me that we must show quite clearly that the Church's liturgical activity is in some sense a beginning of the transfiguration of this world. We have today a great love for this world, but this world as being transfigured more and more through eschatological consummation.

I think we also have there an ecumenical approach, because it seems that our Eastern Orthodox brethren are very much interested in stressing the cosmological signification of the liturgical activity of the Church. I cited the Second Council of Nicaea because it was very badly misunderstood in Western tradition due to the *Libri Carolini*; this Council was quoted in chapter 7 in order to prepare in the West a better understanding of the Eastern tradition of the cult of icons.

Romanides: As a patriotic Greek I would want to come to the defense of my Greek patristic tradition. Father Ahern mentioned a certain type of metaphysics of the Greek philosophical tradition which is supposed to have come into the Greek patristic tradition. Father Butler made some references to the same subject. I would simply like to point out that of all the Christian traditions that I know of the Greek patristic tradition is the only one which officially has condemned as a heresy Plato's doctrine of ideas. And in the Greek fathers you have an emphasis on the fact that this world is unique in itself; it is not a copy of anything else. And the dimensions of change and motion are essential to the creature. Immutability is a characteristic only of God, and that doesn't mean that God doesn't move; it simply means that God transcends the category of creaturely motion. I would quote as an example probably the one Father of the Church who is considered the most Platonic of the Platonic Fathers, St. Dionysius the Areopagite. Speaking about God, he uses the Aristotelian category of the unmoved mover, but then adds "but moved" also, you see. Then when he is speaking about the distinction between love and eros he speaks, of course, about man's eros for God, but then he turns around and slaps the Platonist right in the face by speaking about God's eros for men. I think this is very important. Now when he deals with the whole question of perfection, he does not do so in terms of the doctrine of happiness that you find somewhat in Plato and sometimes in an Aristotelian type of theology. Rather he is thinking of human perfection in terms of the transformation of man's happiness seeking love into a love that does not seek its own. This, I think, brings in a full appreciation of the dimensions of history. So that I would disagree with Father Butler in speaking of history and metachronics. I would speak about history and metachronic history, because history has its eternal dimension: perfection never comes to an end; it goes on even in the realm of eternity.

BURGHARDT: I would like to add briefly to what Father Romanides said. I feel that at one point in his talk Father Barnabas does what I objected to in another context. He simplifies to the point of distorting. When one speaks of the contribution of the Greek world as "to refine and clarify while marring and impoverishing," this simplifies to the point of distortion. As Father Romanides has suggested, the contribution of Greek patristics has been not primarily to clarify or even to refine but to enrich. So that in a doctrine such as the image of God in man, for example, you have a deepening understanding of what Scripture only suggests. I am not saying that they got it out of Scripture, because I don't quite know what it means for something to be in Scripture. However, what they do is to give a deepening understanding of the original revelation, without which our theology would be impoverished. Therefore, I think what has been done here is to identify unjustifiably Greek philosophy with Greek Christian thought. They are not the same thing.

OUTLER: Two brief comments. Our discussion of eschatology illustrates the fact that this chapter in the *Constitution on the Church* is more of a charter than a Constitution, because a great many of the notions that have been developed here in the last hour and a half are clearly permissible but not required by any part of the text of this chapter. Father Ahern and the commentators have illustrated the extent to which the chapter has to be supplemented in order to suggest the richness of eschatological thought in the contemporary period.

My other thought is that, in spite of all of the emphases upon the relation between eschatology and this world, we still are missing, it seems to me, one of the really crucial conceptions of realized and present eschatology. And that is with respect to the interpenetration in daily life of the experience of life and death, of the psychological and psychotherapeutic dimensions of the understanding that the eschatological dimension is not the "sweet by and by," not metachronic and not transcendent, but genuinely here and now, imminent, enabling the Christian to live in the moment of suffering and frustration, deprivation, on the way to death, in this life, here and now, today—in the sense that the in-time is not down yonder nor up above, but here within the actual textures of the power of grace and of the redemptive force of God's love suffusing the temporal textures of chronological existence.

AHERN: Dr. Outler, I am very grateful for that. Actually Dr. Quanbeck

323

brought that up immediately before the question period. He also pointed out that when the chapter speaks of eschatology, it sees it in too much of a static light, that it doesn't see it nearly enough as something dynamic in the here and now. I think we have to realize that when we deal with the sources of revelation you have at once the thinking of St. Paul in Thessalonians, where the *in Christo* is of the future (the whole historical background prompted him to see it in that light), but as you move through the Pauline corpus into the captivity epistles, for instance, eschatology has become a realized thing. Hence, this whole dynamic process of death and life, to which Père de Lubac referred, is going on here and now. As Père de Lubac was speaking of the form of the cosmos, all I could think of was the form of Christ in Philippians (2:6ff.). The form of his humanness was transformed through the power of love. Once more the form of divinity came through the love that prompted death leading to resurrection. So even here and now we are caught up in this dying and in this living.

It is imperative also to remark that today the doctrine of the Apocalypse is no longer seen as referring to the static in time (end-time). John does not know dichotomies and demarcations in time elements. For John the revelation, the apocalypse, is something of the here and now, because John is concerned with the ontological; we might call it the reality of the life of God here and now bursting in upon the world. If this chapter were to be rewritten it would have to have this very thing that you are talking about, namely, the eschatological tension with which we are caught up in the here and now. When I spoke with Dr. Minear, he said that this emphasis on the struggle between the demon and God in the end-time has to be seen in its essential univocal constant, the thing going on always. Here and now we are going through this eschatological tension. I think this is the whole reason why the scene of the agony in the garden, for the Christian community, was presented in this way. Their preachers were saying to them: "Watch and pray because you are going to enter into temptation." They saw in the agony in the garden the very thing they were living through and the thing they had to live by, the very thing that Our Lord himself was doing.

FLOROVSKY: One cannot but welcome the recovery of the eschatological dimension, both of the Christian message and of the Christian life. But I am afraid that the growing concern with the cosmic dimension of revelation distorts a bit the true perspective which we find in the Bible. I have the impression that in modern discussion of these matters there is a tendency to subordinate man to cosmos. It is true that the cosmos has been freshly rediscovered. But there is now a tendency to interpret the destiny of man in the context of the cosmos, instead of discussing the destiny of the cosmos from the perspective of man. And this is what I stumble over in the poetic production of Père Teilhard de Chardin. Man is the center, and this centrality and cruciality of man has been re-emphasized by the incarnation of the Son of God. Cosmic categories are subordinate to human or anthropological categories. But there is always a danger that we will miss this, and this explains, I think, the influence the concept of evolution has acquired over the minds of theologians. I don't find much about evolution in the Holy Writ. Evolution comes from Greek philosophy, and I am astonished to see that the very people who reject biblical ideas sometimes protect themselves by pretending that their ideas are biblical. Evolution is not a biblical idea.

Furthermore, when we speak about a new heaven and a new earth, we must remember that the Bible's revelation of eschatology includes also the last judgment and discrimination. Therefore, to say that the concept of transfiguration is the cardinal theological concept of the Christian message is wrong. The crucial point in the Christian message is the message of discrimination: there will be sorrow and tribulation at the end. This will be true not only because evil grows, but because the judge is coming. While judgment is a biblical idea, the notions of transfiguration and universal salvation do not come from the Bible; they come from philosophy. But I find that many people think that discrimination is not in the Bible; they wind up interpreting biblical texts in such a way that universal salvation is presented as the only thing compatible with the love of God. It is conformed neither to the spirit nor to the letter of the Bible. The Scriptures suggest that God's design may be not fulfilled, and this possible failure of God's creation is in the Bible as it is in the tradition. Just because it is suggested that God wants all people to be saved, we must not forget that there is this possibility that not all will be saved and therefore God's desire for universal salvation will be not fulfilled. This must be taken seriously. It is not philosophical speculation; it is in the Bible.

HESCHEL: I should get a dispensation first, because what I am going to say will probably be heresy to many. My justification is that I think heresy is the spice of faith. It is the spice of faith because I would like to say a word about biblical thinking.

The greatest challenge, I believe, for all of us today is to rediscover the essential categories of biblical thinking. We are attached to the Bible, but we think like pagans. Now I have no doubt about the great contributions of clarification and methodology that we derive from Greek philosophy. But the Bible represents a sort of philosophy, only it is forgotten and wasted upon us. I need that heresy because I am not sure of my faith. No one in the Bible is quite sure of his own faith. If you study the words of Ezra, you will see that he wasn't sure that he had perfect faith. So we are all seeking.

What is the suggestion? I am not sure that doctrine is going to save me. The question I ask myself daily is: Will Abraham feel at home in my life? The question I ask is not doctrinal. What I ask myself is: When I write an essay or a book will Jeremiah understand my language? It is to my distress that a great many books in theology, which may be highly intelligible to students today, would be unintelligible to the ancient Hebrews or the contemporaries of Jesus. Now to give an example, because this is mentioned and referred to by Professor Florovsky, to me it is heresy in a very deep sense to say that men belong to the cosmos. Of course, they don't; men belong to God alone. The earth isn't our mother, and the cosmos isn't our origin. The earth is our sister, not our mother. We shouldn't accept the beautiful poetry that seeks to establish a sort of unity of natural mysticism with biblical thinking, because nature is seen in the Bible in a different way.

Deep in our hearts we know that there is only one way, to me at least as a Jew, and that is the guidance of the Bible. The Bible is holiness in the form of words. The presence of God is in the Bible, not only in the forest. And there we find that even Moses had to hide his face when he thought that he saw God, because he was afraid to see the face of God. I am afraid this is not always quite understood in Christian thinking. Often doctrine claims to see God or to express God, but this articulation is certainly not infallible. From many of these pronouncements I get the impression that theologians know so much—when in truth we know so little, except to be humble. The claim of trick formulations to make things clear and distinct is dangerous, for ultimately things are mysterious. All we have are allusions.

I again have to ask for a dispensation, but speaking as a devoted friend of yours, I heard some very great and beautiful statements, and they all are Christ-centered. But where is God? Don't you think too much Christology could be a screen, a dangerous screen, between the God of Abraham and ourselves? I had hoped that a new awareness of the ultimateness and sovereignty and pathos of the creator of heaven and earth would come to the fore. After all, whom did Jesus himself worship? And what was the Holy Scripture for him? My prayer is for a new realization of what is ultimately real, namely, God and his presence. While his presence is found on many levels of experience, let us not forget his transcendence.

Littell: I would like to follow immediately on what Rabbi Heschel has said and lay hold of that portion of Father Ahern's paper that moved me most: the reference to the redemption of the created order, and not to salvation of the Church alone. After all, the kingdom that is to come is not just the last period of Church history; it is also as it were the penultimate period of the history of the world. This would suggest then that a minute of this conference might well be spent in response to Father Schlitzer's original question: What shall we mark out for our future task? Someone has suggested that Vatican Council I was the pope's council, Vatican II the bishop's council, and the third the council of the laity. If this is to be true in any sense, then the theological task in preparation for that council is the development of an adequate theology of the created order. One thing we have noted in the *Declaration on Religious Freedom*, as magnificent as it is in many respects, is that it stakes out the freedom of the Christian conscience but leaves rather suspended the freedom of secular government to be just government, limited creaturely and without sacral pretensions. The thing which we noted in the *Decree on the Apostolate of the Laity* is that it still leaves somewhat suspended something which I am glad to see answered in the *Constitution on the Church in the Modern World* and in the *Decree on the Church's Missionary Activity*, namely, the integrity of vocations in the secular order. If this be true, then pointing in the same direction as Rabbi Heschel, I would suggest that it is the creationist dimension of the theological task that aims Godward and also aims us to our next years of work before Vatican III.

Question: In what circumstances was this title Maria, Mater ecclesiae *born?*

MEDINA: I must say that it was Paul VI, when he was still Archbishop of Milan in 1962, who proposed this during the first session of the Council. However, the commission, in working over the text, wished to avoid the title itself because it is open to misunderstanding, particularly with regard to the activity of Christ in the Church. There is no doubt, of course, that there is a maternal role within the Church and that the Church herself has a maternal role. Mary's very belonging to the Church, then, entrains understandably a maternal role. At the end of article 65 of the Constitution there are a few lines added on the relations between Mary and the apostolate to the effect that she be considered as an example of maternal love, for this maternal love is a *Christian* quality, a quality of the Christian community. Hence, the idea itself of Mary as mother of the Church is well-founded.

When the concrete title was discussed, various trends of opinion were manifested in the Council. The Polish bishops insisted on having such a statement. Documents were sent to the bishops throughout the world in an attempt to gather supporting signatures and thus prepare a dossier for the pope on the problem of *Maria, Mater ecclesiae*. These sheets were somewhat curious. They contained three points all in one package: *Mater ecclesiae*, a strengthening of the pontifical authority with respect to collegiality, and a tribute to the Roman Curia. In any case it shows that there was a certain group, perhaps 500 bishops or so, who wanted this title.

Question: What is the authority of the title?

MEDINA: A title does not have dogmatic authority of itself. What could be discussed is the dogmatic authority of the title's content. Then the answer would be the same as the one I have already given during my talk, when I said that the Catholic Church recognized in Mary a double maternal role: one with respect to Christ the head of the Church, and a second with respect to the individual Christian because of her intercessory activity, her charity.

> *Question: How can one, without a fantastic paradox, that is, without seeing a contradiction in the terms themselves, accept this title redemptrix (art. 62) when one considers the sole mediatorial function of Christ?*

MEDINA: The text does not say *redemptrix* but *mediatrix*. But theologians have tried to solve this difficulty by way of explanation. I should like to take, for example, creation. This is the problem of the being of God. God is being, of course, and after creation one can see that beings are much more numerous. Yet being is no richer; there is no greater richness of being after creation than before, because the whole richness of being is concentrated in God. Now in our question Christ's mediation is the central and sole fact. It resists absolutely any mathematical addition; it cannot be added to. But there is a difference between addition and participation; participation is quite different from an addition. We Catholics say that the hierarchical priesthood is a participation in the priesthood of Christ, yet it remains true that Christ is sole priest of the New Alliance. It is from the same perspective, I believe, that one should understand Mary as mediatrix. I believe that every Christian is a mediator. I believe that our Protestant brethren will accept the statement that a man who preaches the word of God is a mediator, that his is a work of mediation. Mediation may be explained one way or another, but there is a mediation. Therefore, since God's freedom is enormous, an essential freedom, one can see how God may communicate a mediation of greater richness, of greater extension, than that of a priest preaching the gospel, or of a Christian who spreads God's kingdom around him.

FR. BROWN: I think that Father Medina has clarified one aspect of the question, but I wonder if there isn't a sort of existential aspect that we might bring out here. I suspect that both of those questions on the titles—and I suppose there could be one on the co-redemptrix title as well, even though it is not used—reflect a fear that perhaps under those titles there is more of a personal Mariology being subtly introduced. I think your explanation has somewhat answered that. But I think that the real answer lies in the thrust of Catholic thought today. Just as Father Burghardt mentioned that there are certain things that will not happen, not because they are in the documents of the Council, but simply because they are impossible in the present thrust of Catholic life, so I really cannot conceive that there will be further Mariological obstacles raised in Catholic thought. After all Catholic thought responds to a Catholic life situation, and if we are sincerely interested in the ecumenical movement (not out of minimalist tendency or a tendency to conform) then we must recognize that the whole Christian consciousness must be taken into consideration. And if we are seriously to accept the Protestant, and to some extent even here on this question the orthodox understanding of Christian reality, it really would be a contradiction in terms for us in any way to press the Mariological situation further. I don't know whether I have expressed a view that all would share, but I do think there is a certain amount of truth to that. In the life situation of the Church after Vatican II, I can't conceive that any of these titles is going to be pressed to introduce really new Mariology into the Church.

McGRATH: I would just say very briefly, I think it is very good to accentuate what Msgr. Medina brought out in his paper and which is very clearly expressed by Father Laurentin in *La question mariale*. There was a tendency during the last decades before the Council for the theology of the Blessed Virgin to grow off by itself as a separate discipline, too isolated from scriptural, patristic and other theological foundations. I think the Council, by the effort that was there achieved of bringing the Marian question into the perspective of the Church, and by the efforts achieved in the Theological Commission of bringing together the two tendencies, has perhaps applied a *sanatio in radice* and saved us from any continuance of this tendency.

There is also another aspect that I believe is important. In this area more than any other there has been a tendency for piety to lead theology, rather than vice versa. This was evident in the discussion as to whether or not the section on the Blessed Virgin would be included in the Constitution. I remember, and all those who were present at the Council will remember, that on the day that we were to take the vote one Eastern Catholic bishop was standing on the steps of St. Peter's handing out to us as we entered (afterwards it was forbidden but at that point it was still done) handbills that stated that to vote against a separate constitution for the Blessed Virgin was to play down our love for the Blessed Virgin. Actually, it turned out that most of his Eastern colleagues did not agree with him, but since we could not distinguish very well between one and the other, the impression carried that the Eastern bishops wanted this done. In fact, I spoke with several bishops who really felt that this was a question of devotion to the Blessed Virgin that was measured by the fact that she should have her separate document. And so here emotion and piety sometimes colored discussions that should have been much more clearly theological.

Question: How could you illustrate the doctrine of tradition, because tradition plays an important part in Mariology?

MEDINA: I remember an observation of Father de Lubac when the famous vote was taken on the famous *modi* regarding the relation between Scripture and tradition. "The Church comes to a real knowledge of all the articles of faith only through tradition and with tradition." He went on to say, "I don't know whether the Church could come to certainty of a single dogma in the absence of tradition." I remember from my theological studies how very difficult it is to prove a dogma *exclusively* through Scripture. Therefore, when we are confronted with a development that at first glance appears to be somewhat remote from the text of the Scriptures, tradition, i.e., the Christian life animated by the Holy Spirit, plays a considerable part. However, this is not a tradition that is exactly located outside of Scripture, but rather one that shows the whole richness that is to be found in Scripture.

Let us take a look at the problem of assumption. This is not affirmed in Scripture in the same way as it is in the dogmatic declaration of Pius XII. But there is a whole series of biblical data that helps one to understand why the Catholic faith has accepted the assumption as revealed by God. I do not want to discuss the theology of the assumption, but only to point out that there is the problem of victory over sin, the victory of Christ that involved the resurrection of Christ. It is against that background that you have to view the assumption of the Virgin. Then you have a number of anticipations in Scripture, for example, the episode of Elias who was taken away in fire by the Lord. There are the saints who arose from the dead on the day of Christ's death; this was a manifestation of the Lord's victory over death and sin. The transfiguration of Christ was in a sense an anticipation of his resurrection and ascension. It is within this context that one has to view the Catholic doctrine of the corporeal assumption of the Virgin. It is an eschatological manifestation of the final destiny of man that is realized by way of typology, or real anticipation in one person, because theology is not a matter of abstraction but is based on *concrete* data revealed by the Lord. Therefore, the assumption for us Catholics—and I fully appreciate the difficulty of the Protestants on this point—is to be seen within the framework of God's economy of victory over death and sin, an economy of prophetic anticipation of the final fate of the People of God, and within the framework of an economy of transfiguration, that is to say, the realization within a concrete person of what in the abstract is our final destiny.

MINUS: I wonder if Msgr. Medina would comment on the dogma of the assumption in relation to the statement in the *Decree on Ecumenism* about the hierarchy of truths. Would you join these two issues for us please?

MEDINA: I remember that a Council Father stated that there is a scale of values in the Christian faith. One cannot compare, for example, the assumption of the Virgin with the resurrection of Christ, nor the hierarchy with the Trinity—that is obvious—even if the hierarchy, in a certain sense, is a sort of a prolongation, a manifestation of the missions of the Trinity;

even if the Virgin's assumption is the accomplishment in a concrete creature of the resurrection of Christ. I think that integral Catholic truth cannot fail to accept defined dogmatic data; it is unthinkable. One can only situate these data, give new explanations, show their coherence with other more fundamental truths, and in this way arrive little by little at a common understanding. Sometimes, I must admit, among Catholics certain Marian dogmas are understood in such a fashion by the masses and some preachers that they run the risk of having no meaning whatever in the life of the Church, in the plan of salvation; at times it looks like an inexplicable display of trying to demonstrate all of the possibilities of divine omnipotence. But really that is a rather erroneous procedure. When Catholic faith—and I speak as a Catholic, of course—shows us an exceptional fact, one does not have the right to separate this fact from the plan for salvation.

STRANSKY

TANENBAUM

SESSION VIII

Rev. Thomas F. Stransky, c.s.p.
The Declaration on Non-Christian Religions

Rabbi Marc H. Tanenbaum
A Jewish Viewpoint

Rev. Thomas F. Stransky, C.S.P.

THE DECLARATION ON NON-CHRISTIAN RELIGIONS

FOR A ROMAN CATHOLIC, when his Church is in a state of Council, a point is reached at which the torrent of history seems to pause and, for a passing instant, to crystallize God's working through the density of historical circumstances and events of human beings wounded by sin and weakness yet gifted by the graces of the redemption.[1] The Council itself becomes a *locus theologicus*, even though the theologian who has experienced the Council finds it impossible fully to explicate either to himself or to others that penetrating experience, and even though he cannot and dare not accurately evaluate the precise historical context of the Council, or all of its consequences, direct or indirect, obvious or hidden. Nevertheless, the theologian has experienced the specific milieux, or self-created *genius loci* that has conditioned the dynamic development of a dialogue by which insights and judgments are formed, modified or finalized in Conciliar decrees. He became quite aware that the Holy Spirit's active presence in the Council does not bypass those laws, methods, processes and problems that go to make up the natural operations of collective knowing and judgment, but rather *by* and *in* these very causalities, beginning with the language, the mental climates, collective experiences, openness to religious *and* political public opinion, technical analysis of theologians, the imperceptible and sometimes impassioned give-and-take that occurs both inside and outside the Council aula, both during the sessions in Rome and during the interim periods.

335

I could elaborate on this at length, with clarifications and examples, but this is not the place. What I would like to emphasize, however, is that the experience of the Conciliar process at Vatican II became a daily, humbling awareness, that although no council of the Roman Church can be a complete failure, neither is a council assured of a complete success. This solemn, most authoritative action of the magisterium does not, in every decree, always formulate in the clearest and most efficacious way everything of which the Church has need at its stage of history. (Often the non-Catholic, Christian or non-Christian, seems to expect more perfection from a Council than the Catholic dares to hope for). Through the experience of Vatican II the theologian sees more clearly, and believes more deeply, that the Church is a pilgrim Church, which stands under the word and therefore is daily judged by it, and advances only from a knowledge more or less exact of its historical situation, from an understanding more or less penetrating of its mission, and from a response more or less faithful to that mission.

And if I may reflect publicly on my own participation in Vatican II, I would say that in the genesis of no document have I experienced more deeply the interaction of God's design and the concrete historical process, the dynamism of progress yet not perfectly a successful one, the holy step forward which closes a period of history yet opens one to a less definite future, than in the development and final form of the shortest of the Conciliar documents, the *Declaration of the Relationship of the Church to Non-Christian Religions.*

THE HISTORY OF THE DECLARATION

The history itself is fascinating, shaped at times by elating and clearly positive events, at times by exasperating elusive or tragically depressing ones. Many of the details have appeared in magazine articles and Council *bilans*. They have been embarrassingly accurate or ridiculously inaccurate. Other details rest in the archives of the Christian Unity Secretariat, of the Vatican Secretariat of State, of chanceries, apostolic nunciatures and embassies, or remain, in calm frustration, in the private diaries of many of us.

Let us trace briefly this history. In July, 1960, Pope John XXIII commissioned the newly created Secretariat for Promoting Christian Unity to draft a Conciliar statement—its format undetermined—that would improve Christian attitudes towards the Jews.[2] The short (42 lines) statement entered into open Conciliar debate during the second session, when the Fathers gave their general impressions of the whole schema. *De Oecumenismo,* of which the Jewish draft formed the fourth of five chapters.[3] The statement (70 lines) returned to the floor, by itself and on its own merits, at the beginning of the third session.[4] Redrafting was called for, and here began the crystallization of an intra-Conciliar process that proved to be one of the most positive results of Vatican II. By the third session there had developed a threefold (although not exclusive) awareness and explicit consciousness:

1) It was becoming clear that the Roman Catholic Church is no longer a Mediterranean church, as it was in the first eight councils; no more a West-European church, as it appeared during the Middle Ages; nor a South-European church as it seemed at the Council of Trent; and no more a world-wide church governed by European bishops, as it was at Vatican I. Vatican II became the first council in which Europe—if we think of Europe as reaching into the Levant—had not the predominant voice. With one-fifth of the episcopate coming from Latin America and over one-third from the churches of Asia, Africa and Oceania, and with a surprisingly articulate unanimity among these bishops, the first two sessions marked the transition of the Church from a European basis to a world-wide one. For the first time in its history, the Church had to face up to the full implications of its catholicity.

2) At the same time as the bishops were realizing that the Roman Catholic Church is *de facto* a world-wide Church, they became conscious that the Church, as the whole of the Christian family, is facing a new historical situation in which committed Christians are becoming more and more a minority religious community in relation to the rest of the world. Most Christian churches had occupied a majority position within Western, European culture, and where they had existed as a minority—Asia, Africa, yes, Latin America—they had operated blindly on principles drawn from their majority status in the West. But the West itself has been witnessing indifferentism and practical atheism—organized or, more often, "anonymous"—resulting in the subtle apostasy of large numbers. Since World War II the churches in Asia, Africa and Latin America have steadily become autonomous, and, as their nations have gained independence, the churches have been under increasing pressure to become indigenous, with the result that they have been forced to accept the minority status in full measure. The result is a new situation. Instead of occupying a massive, majority position in the West, from which Christian Churches reach out to "occupy" the rest of the world, they are a minority throughout the whole world. The world-wide Church is not coterminus with humanity; the area of the visible Church and the area of effective salvation do not coincide at this moment in the history of salvation.

3) Through the Conciliar process there developed an existential concern for people as people, whether within or without the Roman Church, whether Christian or not. Dialogue becomes more than a cliché, and by dialogue I mean every relation with another as an "other," in which we accept to receive from the "other" in order that we ourselves may grow religiously, and thus grow together with others.

This threefold consciousness (which, by the way, gripped Pope Paul as he wrestled with himself in the writing of *Ecclesiam suam* during the summer preceding the third session) can be seen in the episcopal reflexes and explicit interventions on most of the schemata, and it is very clear in their reactions to the draft on the Jews in the second, and especially at the beginning of the third session.

The variety of questions and suggestions led to a clear and insistent request: the world-wide Church, conscious that it is the one and only authentic revelation of the one and living God, is likewise conscious that the majority of the religiously committed people in the world do not live from the Judaeo-Christian tradition. What of the exploding East, the home of the oldest religions, shaping and shaped by corresponding cultures? In fact, the "Jewish problem" is, in many ways, a Western, near-Eastern one. Deepened and corrected though our attitudes must be in the relation of the Christian to the offspring of Abraham, it would be scandalous if Vatican II narrowed its vision of dialogue to other Christians and to Jews.[5]

The only Conciliar organ on whom this pressure was put, and the only document in which the objections could be met, was the Christian Unity Secretariat and its proposed Declaration on the Jews. (In fact, the 1963 Declaration had been entitled, "The Relation of Catholics to Non-Christians, and especially to the Jews." But there was only polite, introductory reference, in two lines, to "conversing and cooperating with non-Christians, who nevertheless worship God, or at least with good will, try to follow their conscience in carrying out the moral law situated in human nature." The brief reference only gave leverage to the bishops' complaints: "Two lines to two-thirds of the world!") Pope Paul set up the Secretariat for Non-Christians between the second and third sessions (May 23, 1964), but this Secretariat avowed that it would not enter into Conciliar matters, whether the question of non-Christian observers or the problem of a charter-statement. The Unity Secretariat was reluctant at first with the assignment. The theme was not within its competency of drafting and judging. And, above all, the unique character of the Jewish-Christian relation in salvation history might be lost sight of, and the treatment of the specific pastoral problem of anti-Semitism and its roots that had to be spelled out might not harmonize with the over-all style of the enlarged document and, therefore, would have to be weakened. Nevertheless, aware of the difficulties, the Unity Secretariat drafted non-Secretariat experts and began the new work—a Declaration in five chapters: introduction, various religions (primitive, Hinduism, Buddhism, etc.), the Moslem religion, the Jewish religion, the condemnation of every kind of discrimination. The new format returned to the Council Fathers for their vote on November 18, 1964.

Frankly, I think that the Western religious and secular press has underestimated the pressure of the Council Fathers to enlarge the scope of the Declaration to include all non-Christian religions, perhaps because this press underestimated the legitimate problem and concern. The enlargement was more than a "trick" to save the Jews or a softening embossment of the specific treatment of the Jews. Nevertheless, the additional chapters did help to gain the support of formerly indifferent bishops, especially from Africa and Asia, and this indirectly helped the Jewish statement, now a chapter *within* the Declaration. The enlargement protected the Jewish theme, and its opponents as well as its supporters knew it. The gem was so embedded into the draft that it could not be removed without crudely disfiguring the whole setting.

The Problematic in the Declaration

religious experience: religion and the religions

The Declaration observes that in our time, the human race is "being drawn closer together, and the ties between various peoples are being multiplied" (art. 1). This process of unification is not merely the result of human activity but it unfolds God's saving plan for mankind. "For all people comprise a single community, and have a single origin, since God made the whole human race of men dwell over the entire face of the earth. One also is their final goal: God. His providence, His manifestations of goodness, and His saving designs extend to all men against the day when the elect will be united in the Holy City ablaze with the splendor of God, where the nations will walk in His light" (*ibid.*).

This objective unity of origin, pilgrimage and ultimate destiny is reflected in the universal quest for "answers to the profound riddles of the human condition." "What is man? What is the meaning and the purpose of our life? What is goodness and what is sin? What gives rise to our sorrows and to what intent? Where lies the path to true happiness? What is the truth about death, judgment, and retribution beyond the grave? What finally, is that ultimate and unutterable mystery which engulfs our being, and whence do we take our rise, and whither our journey leads us?" (*ibid.*).

The experience of man before these questions is a faith-experience, and faith is experienced as a whole and cannot be experienced in any other way. (Are we not appreciating this in the Christian dialogue? We may seem to agree on a creedal proposition, but that very agreement is conditioned and limited by the rest of the system to which we adhere, and by the way of life we lead. As a result, perspectives differ, emphases vary, and even the apparent agreement is caught up in the net of disagreement about other things. If this is true in comparisons between different Christian confessions, how much more, for example, in comparing the Christian and Buddhist "libera-tations"!) But the existential search is made not by individuals, isolated in their options. The method of the Declaration is to recognize, evaluate and respect *faith-communities*, whose collective life has taken, and is developing, options of thought and responsible action before the mystery of human existence. It constantly uses expressions like "Ad religiones," "a religionibus," "de religionibus," "religiones vero," "In Hinduismo," "in Buddhismo," "de religione islamica."

But to understand even the context of the basic religious responses of religions to basic questions, one has to expose oneself to each religion as a whole, and understand that each is an expression of a collective reaction to the total human situation. Is the reaction adequate to that situation? Or are there certain areas that are disregarded or ignored? What needs of the human spirit does this religion meet, what legitimate needs are ignored or denied? Is it related to community peace and harmony? Does it point to a liberation from, and a fulfillment beyond, the limits of time and space?[6]

Such an evaluation cannot be based merely on a comparison of ideas, by detaching theories or doctrines of thought and action from the living experi-ence that has given rise to them. Such method, important though it may be, reveals very little of the living fabric of religion.

In the Declaration the Church does not claim to have yet experienced the dialogue with the non-Christian religions, but it is trying to reflect on the fact of their existence and to give "deeper study to her relationships" with them (art. 1).

The Church is plunged into a reverence of God's grace-filled workings among all men, everywhere, at all times. It respects, not only tolerates, all men outside the Church's walls who, seeking the ultimate reality, raise their hearts to the living God, even though they do not always know his name. The Catholic Church rejects nothing that is true and holy in them (art. 2), for there are "treasures that a bountiful God has distributed among the nations of the earth" (*Decree on the Missionary Activity of the Church*, 11). The Church recommends that Catholics converse and collaborate with the followers of other religions in order to "acknowledge, preserve and promote the spiritual and moral goods found among these men" (*Declaration*, 2). The Declaration offers a positive method of dialogue, based upon "what human beings have in common and to what promotes fellowship among them" (art. 1).

This positive methodological approach (which Cardinal Bea insisted upon in the official *relatio*) is an extraordinary step, and one can easily wager that not just a single chapter but the all-embracing character of the entire docu-ment is the sign by which future scholars will mark its commanding import in conciliar history. Nevertheless, the Declaration, understood along with the other documents, has not answered but only presented anew old theological questions.

The sincere faith-experience of an individual non-Christian is salvific, based on a search for God as expressed by the striving by deeds to do his will as it is known through the dictates of the conscience (*Constitution on the Church*, 16; *Decree on the Missionary Activity of the Church*, 7; *Constitution on the Church in the Modern World*, 16). He is ordained (*ordinatur*) to the Church (*Constitution on the Church*, 16). What we have called the "unbeliever" or "non-Christian" is saved insofar as he is a believer by a salvific faith that is already, in some way, both Christian and ecclesial.

But how salvific is the collective faith-experience, that is, how do the other religions enter into the designs of a saving God? The *Constitution on the Church* does not treat other religions *ex professo*, although it does refer to the patristic theme of divine pedagogy in the preparation for the gospel (art. 16; cf. *Decree on the Missionary Activity of the Church*, 3). It speaks of the good that "lies latent in the religious practices and cultures of diverse peoples" (art. 17; cf. *Decree on the Missionary Activity of the Church*, 9, 11, 21). The Declaration, on the other hand, is the only Conciliar document which treats in principle religions as such, and the "*vera et sancta*," "*modi agendi et vivendi*," "*praecepta et doctrina*," "*bona spiritualia et moralia . . . in his religionibus.*"[7]

If the fact is so stated, then the assertion that God saves the individual non-Christian *despite* his community-faith is untenable. This assertion is made because of a judgment on religion itself: there is only *the* religion, the supernatural revelation, which, in the person of Jesus Christ, gives to the Christian religion an absolute and exclusive character; all other "religions," so the assertion continues, are based on the natural knowledge of God, and develop naturally in teaching, cult and practice.

But cannot the explanation of religions be found *within* the history of salvation, precisely because of Christ, the exclusive source of salvation, and because of his Church, "*sacramentum salutis*" (*Decree on the Missionary Activity of the Church*, 3), who because of her relationship with Christ is "the sacrament or sign of intimate union with God, and of the unity of all mankind . . . an instrument for the achievement of such union and unity" (*Constitution on the Church*, 1)? Are not the other religions salvific in and *through* themselves, because in some way they incarnate the sufficient beginnings ("*incepta religiosa*," *Decree on the Missionary Activity of the Church*, 3) of a religious response to the revelation in Christ? Are the other religions implicitly Christic and ecclesial, tending upwards toward their explicit fulfillment in the Church of Christ, even though they are also burdened with the downward push toward destruction?[8]

The Church is "the messianic people" who, although they do not include all men, stand as the symbolic representative of all (cf. *Constitution on the Church*, 9). The Church becomes in history what she is: the "incarnate sign" of Christ's presence among all peoples, doing sacramentally among each people what he has already done once and for all in his historical presence among some men. And the mission of the Church is to go out, not to a vacuum, but to where both Christ and his Church already are, but in weak and threatened sacramental signs. "Through her work, whatever good is in the minds and hearts of men, whatever good lies latent in the religious practices and cultures of diverse peoples, is not only saved from destruction, but is also healed, ennobled and perfected unto the glory of God, the confusion of the devil and the happiness of man" (*Constitution on the Church*, 17). But the Christian faith is a historic faith, an absolute religion but appearing at a specific historical moment. The "objective legitimacy" of another religion ceases when it meets the Christian religion in a *historical* and *authentic* confrontation. But what is the minimum for such a confrontation, and at what moment can we say this confrontation has taken place? Is it simultaneous for all religions?[9]

These are real questions, and the recent attempts to answer them are only faint beginnings.[10] Just as the theology of ecumenism is developing from a reflection on the *fact* of only one Church divided within itself, so now we are witnessing a reflection on the *fact* of no other name but his can save, no other sacrament but his Church, and a plurality of vital, now resurgent religions? What is God saying to us through these facts?

GLOBAL UNITY THROUGH SECULARIZATION

It is true that the whole of mankind is being brought into the fact and into the *consciousness* of sharing a single history, but this unification is not primarily in terms of a common religion, not even of common religious questions, but in terms of a common pattern of civilization marked by secular development: in short, global unification through global secularization. By secularization I mean "the acceptance of a way of living in which one concentrates on problems as they come up, in terms of their bearing on immediate human welfare, and without being controlled by ultimate metaphysical or religious beliefs about the nature and destiny of man" (L. Newbigen). The world is existing qua world, as a legitimate secular society.

In the non-Western world, the new order, even if it is beyond the present one, is accessible within history, whether that new order be defined in terms of the victory of the proletariat, of national independence, of the welfare state, of technical equality with the West—a new messianic order in which man is freed from hunger, want, anxiety.

This direction of world history has been set within the context of old Western civilization. We cannot pursue the theme here—the relation between Western scientific civilization and the Christian faith, technology as the agent of Christianity—except to say that it seems naively arrogant to assert that the technology of the West sufficiently represents the world obligations of Christian faith or fulfilled them in the best contemporary form. We do see that the Christian mission from the West did help to produce a revolution in non-Western society, but failed to show the relevance of Christian faith to it. The missions did help to introduce a technical urban culture in Africa and Asia, but did little to reflect on how these peoples could live from Christian faith in this new society. If Christian preaching brought a new conception of man, rooted in his dignity as a free responsible person, it little regarded what political structures could give new expression to the new understanding of state, citizen and nation.

In any case, the world religions are involved in this global secularization, and in the encouraged dialogue with them, the problematic in the *Constitution on the Church in the Modern World* seems to be far more important than the list of positive values given in the Declaration.

For there is indeed a renaissance of these religions and an effort to restate the fundamentals of their faiths in order to respond to the revolutionary situation brought about by modern science and technology, Western liberalism, the communist idealogy, and, not the least, the missionary work of Christian churches. These religions are now trying to find an adequate dynamic of faith for the modern Asian man, to evolve a new secularism with religious motivation by loosening the bond between culture and religion. Moreover, they are becoming strong missionary faiths, claiming, as do Buddhism and Hinduism, to have a more adequate basis for universality than the Christian religion.

In short, global unification through global secularization is becoming the operative stimulus for the positive resurgence of the other religions, as it is for the Christian renewal. Is it not this stimulus that helped create the strong Conciliar statement in which the Church exhorts her children "prudently and lovingly, through dialogue and collaboration with the followers of other religions, and in witness of Christian faith and life, [to] acknowledge, preserve, and promote the spiritual and moral goods found among these men, as well as the values in their society and culture" (art. 2).

Comments on Article Four: Judaism

1. addressed primarily to roman catholics

At no time did the drafters naively presuppose that the brief treatment would please all Jews. The variety of religious commitments among the Jews, the built-in varied, often conflicting "histories" of their various religious and/or secular communities made us aware that some Jews would not be happy

343

with whatever was stated, indeed that some would object to the very fact that a Christian council would take up the subject. But the subject is necessary, and urgently so, for the Roman Catholic *conscience.* Furthermore, it would be an understandable insult to the Jews if the Council wrote a document for them, as if the Church had condescended to tell our brothers of Abraham that Catholics have magnanimously decided to stop maltreating them by word and act and would start applying also to them the Christian law of universal love.

The document is for Catholics, and thus in itself is a humble admission —and confession—that the Church still has need, in the 1960's, of an evaluation of her positive relationship to the Jews and must condemn anti-Semitism in all forms. Phrases and qualifications had to be introduced—or omitted—in the final text, and these have changed the document from one of a fresh, bold proclamation of the Church to that of a nuanced, forceful argument within the Church. The shift was regretfully thought necessary— for Roman Catholics.

There are three excellent examples of this change of tone and purpose in the clarifications inserted in order to destroy the culpability" charge against the Jews. The opponents to previous drafts had been worried that the Council, as a "technique" for better relations, deliberately side-stepped biblical facts. Perhaps this opposition was a blessing. By its protest it was clear that the anti-Jewish tone of so much of past Christian catechesis and preaching was derived from certain false theological presuppositions, and these, in turn, were based on an interpretation of biblical facts. What the drafting commission judged necessary in the text was a clear statement of historical, biblical facts but an equally clear denial of the false theological conclusions: a) granted that some Jews rejected the gospel (preached by many who "sprang from the Jewish people"), nevertheless "the Jews still remain most dear to God because of the Fathers"; b) granted that Jewish authorities "pressed for the death of Jesus," nevertheless "what happened in His passion cannot be blamed upon all the Jews then living, without distinction, nor upon the Jews of today"; c) granted that the Church believes herself to be the new People of God, nevertheless the Jews should not be "presented as repudiated or cursed by God." Some, I know, would have greatly preferred not to mention these "granted's," but I wonder if the omission would not have kept clouded the force of the theological conclusions, and thus help to continue anti-Jewish bias.

2. POSITIVE PEDAGOGICAL PURPOSE

True, "applied culpability" is explicitly rejected, and must never be used in Christian teaching. True, the article strongly deplores hatred, persecutions, manifestations of anti-Semitism directed against Jews at any time by anyone. These two points are necessary, but it would be a serious pedagogical mistake to concentrate on them. There is little hope of changing reflexes and attitudes with lists of "do's" and "don't's."

The primary purpose of this article is not to forbid Catholics to despise, scorn, hate, persecute Jews, but to instruct Catholics on why they should, and how they can, understand, respect and love Jews, and collaborate with them in fraternal dialogue.

a) The interest of the Christian Church in the Jewish people is not due simply to today's *de facto* condition of religious pluralism. The Church's concern is based on its search into its own mystery; "it recalls the spiritual bond linking the people of the New Covenant with Abraham's stock."

b) The Church is not a totally new beginning in God's plan of salvation. The beginnings of her faith and her election are found already in the patriarchs, Moses and the prophets. The divine promises are fulfilled, not abrogated, with the coming of Jesus. Through him, God's salvific design for all mankind—first given to the Chosen People—is confirmed and extended through the Church to the entire world.

c) The story of salvation took place within the the Jewish people. Jesus, Mary, the apostles, the early disciples were as much members of that people as the enemies of Jesus. The Jews are God-bearers, our special brothers. The Gentiles are but wild shoots grafted onto the well-cultivated olive tree, which is the Jewish people (cf. Rom 11:17–24).

d) The Jews remain most dear to God. Their election stands, for God does not repent of the gifts He makes or of the call He issues. No human decision can break this bond (cf. Rom 11:28–29).

e) The sins of all men are responsible for Jesus's free acceptance of his passion and death. The cross is the sign of God's all-embracing love, not a whipping post for any class of men.

3. ALL THEOLOGICAL QUESTIONS NOT ANSWERED; AREAS OF REFLECTION SUGGESTED[11]

a) The salvation of the Church is "mysteriously foreshadowed (*mystice praesignari*) by the Chosen People's exodus from the land of bondage." From that paschal event, mysteriously prefigured, can one derive principles for the salvation not only of the Jews of the Old Testament but also of those who today continue to live within the framework of the Mosaic Law? Furthermore, in this typological theology is the Jewish people not only representative of humanity but also of the Church itself in its spiritual destiny?

b) The Church "received the revelation of the Old Testament through the [Israelite] people." But the revelation of the Old Testament continues to be salvific in the Church in the measure that the Church *de facto* continues to "draw sustenance from the root of that good olive tree" (Rom 11:17–24). And in the measure that the Church does not. . .?

c) Christ "reconciled Jew and Gentile, making them both one in Himself (cf. Eph 2:14–16)." But this reconciliation which is *already* realized at its *source* is *not yet accomplished* in history. The theology of history in Romans (9–11) is a dialectical relationship of Jews and Gentiles, both bound to a common destiny. What is the eschatological destiny of the Jews in relation to the nature of their permanent election (the nature of that permanency, the value of the irrevocable gifts of God, and thus the value of the Jews in themselves), and to the incomplete, wounded universality of the Church (Eph 2) as long as the "proto-schism" is not healed? What is the nature of that *common* messianic and eschatological hope between Jews and Christians, even though there are profound differences about the forms of the realization of the event?

d) The statement that "the Church is the new People of God" in no way closes discussion on the Jews' being in some way *of* this new People. Nor does the text—as was clearly brought out in the drafting meetings—rule out the opinion of those few theologians (e.g. P. Demann) who hold that a radical schism has divided the People of God on earth into the Church and Israel. Is the schism within the Church or, rather, within Israel?

e) Nothing is to be taught or preached that is "out of harmony with the truth of the gospel (*cum veritate evangelica non congruat*)." What is the difference between ideological anti-Semitism and the polemic of the evangelists, especially of Matthew and John, whose texts tend to excuse the disciples and to accuse more and more Jews in excluding more and more Romans? Who are "the Jews" whom the evangelists accuse, and whom do they represent? In other words, what is the typology of "the Jews" in John?

f) To what extent is ideological anti-Semitism a heresy? What is the nature of the specific guilt of Christians (and of the Church) for much of their past treatment of Jews?

These all are *problems*, to be sure, but no matter how explicit future explanations may be, they will only heighten what can never be understood through the dark glass of faith—the *Mystery* of Israel.

NOTES

1. "The main events, the decisive moments, the most characteristic and formative manifestations, the most painful and the most victorious dramas in the Church's life have been in its councils," John Baptist Cardinal Montini, "The Council in the Life of the Church," *The Mind of Paul VI*, ed. James Walsh, S.J. (Milwaukee: Bruce, 1964) 258. Also cf. Eugene M. Burke, C.S.P., "The General Council in the Teaching of the Church," *The General Council*, ed. William A. McDonald (Washington, D.C.: The Catholic University of America, 1962) 2–3.

2. The Secretariat approved the first rough draft in its plenary session of November, 1961. The

one-page statement had four main points: 1) the roots of the Church are found in the Old Testament; 2) Christ our peace and reconciliation has united both Jew and Gentile; 3) the Jews are not "*maledicti*"; they remain "*carissimi propter patres*"; 4) racism is a grave danger in our times, and a special danger is anti-Semitism because it directly attacks Jesus of the house of David.

3. As separate documents of the Secretariat, both *De libertate religiosa* and *De Iudaeis* ran into trouble in the meetings of the central preparatory commission. The liberty draft was seen to be almost, if not, contradictory to ch. 9 of the *De Ecclesia* schema, "De relatione inter Ecclesiam et Statum." Since the entire *De Ecclesia* would have priority of discussion in the first session, *De libertate religiosa* was sidetracked. The schema on the Jews, by a decision of the Secretariat of State, was not even discussed, as planned, in the June, 1962, meeting of the central preparatory commission. A few days prior to this meeting, the Israeli radio, to the surprise of the Vatican and especially to the Unity Secretariat, announced vaguely that a former member of the Israeli Ministry of Education would attend the first session of Vatican II as an "observer" of the World Jewish Congress. Arab political action was swift. Thus Cardinal Bea reported to the Council Fathers in November, 1963: "The discussion (in the central preparatory meeting) was omitted not because of the ideas or doctrine expressed in the schema, but only because of certain unhappy political conditions at that time" (cf. *Council Speeches*, ed. H. Küng, Y. Congar, D. O'Hanlon [New York: Paulist Press, 1964] 254). After the experience of the first session it had become obvious that the forest of preparatory drafts would have to be whittled down to a manageable number. A vote of the first session ensured that a new draft on ecumenism would see future Conciliar debate. Through a complicated maneuver between the first and second sessions, the Secretariat managed to attach to the new ecumenism decree both the Jewish and the religious liberty drafts as chapters 4 and 5, in order that all three subjects would eventually be debated. The Secretariat, on the whole, was in favor of detaching the last two chapters and of treating them as separate documents *after* an initial Conciliar vote of approval of the entire five-chaptered *De Oecumenismo* as a basis of future elaboration.

4. The Secretariat's tactic only half-succeeded in the second session. After the general discussion on all five chapters, the secretary general announced a division of the important, initial vote: an immediate vote on the first three chapters, a "later" vote on the last two. The "later," it turned out, would be the third session for the Jewish theme, the fourth for the religious liberty schema. And at the beginning of the third session the Council Fathers faced a weakened Jewish text that was admittedly not exactly that composed by the Unity Secretariat.

5. Although most of the opposition to a restricted declaration is found in the written interventions, the opinion was voiced in the aula during the second session (November 19–21, 1963) by J. M. Bueno y Monreal (Seville) and P. Doi (Tokyo), and most explicitly and forcefully by F. Da Veiga Coutinho, the Coadjutor of Belgium (India); during the third session's discussion (September 28–29, 1964): again by Bueno y Monreal, and F. König (Vienna), Y. Plumey (Garoua, Cameroon), L. Satoshi Nagae (Urawa, Japan), S. Hoa Nguyen-van-Hien (Dalat, Vietnam), P. Sfair (Maronite), J. Parecattil (Ernakulam, India); J. Attipetty (Verapoly, India), J. Gahamanyi (Butaré, Ruanda) in the name of eighty Fathers.

6. Cf. Stephen Neill, *Christian Faith and Other Faiths* (London: Oxford Press, 1961) 5.

7. The *Constitution on Divine Revelation* alludes to the God of supreme love "carefully planning and preparing the salvation of the whole human race" (art. 14), and giving "men an enduring witness to Himself in created realities . . . in order to give eternal life to all those who perseveringly do good in search of salvation" (art. 3).

Ecclesiologists have only recently studied the role of "churches and ecclesial communities" within the divided Christian family. But from the beginning of Christian times apologists have tried to ascertain the value and signification of non-Christian religions. Yet even here, the polemic— not always negative—focused more on an analysis of the doctrines, customs and rites of these religions than on an evaluation of a non-Christian religion as such. Cf. Gustave Thils, *Propos et Problèmes de la théologie des religions non chrétiennes* (Tournai: Casterman, 1966) 33–37. Even the postive *praeparatio evangelica* approach within one stream of patristic thought was strained in the evaluation of *post Christum* religions. The only *post Christum* religion with which Christianity had to deal for nearly a millennium was Islam. But because Islam itself claimed to be the fulfillment of all the prophecies of salvation, including those of Jesus, Christians, in turn, interpreted the Islamic advance as the fulfillment of those plagues and afflictions which John in the Apocalypse had prophesied for the final sifting of the Church. In fact, through this polemic with Islam, Christian theologians shaped their principles with regard to other religions uncovered by the discoveries. Cf. Ernest Benz, "Ideas for a Theology of Religion," in *The Theology of the Christian Mission*, ed. Gerald A. Anderson (New York: McGraw-Hill, 1961) 138–139.

8. The *Decree on the Missionary Activity of the Church* describes the dialectic: "Whatever truth and grace are to be found among the nations, as a sort of secret presence of God, this activity frees from all taint of evil and restores to Christ its maker, who overthrows the devil's domain and wards off the manifold malice of vice" (art. 9). This last clause was added in the final draft to avoid "undue optimism."

9. All the world religions have influenced one another wherever they have come in contact. What is still needed are careful studies on the influence of Christianity on the further developments of non-Christian religions either directly or indirectly, as through its influence on Islam which, in turn, influenced new religious forms, e.g., in Hinduism or in Sikhism.

10. E.g., Eugene Hillman, C.S. Sp., *The Church as Mission* (New York: Herder and Herder, 1965). Stephen Neill, *op. cit.*; Raymond Panikkar, *Religione e religioni* (Brescia, 1964) and *The Unknown Christ of Hinduism* (London: Darton, Longman and Todd, 1964); Karl Rahner, S.J., "Grundzüge einer katholisch dogmatischen Interpretation der nicht-christlichen Religionen," in *Pluralismus, Toleranz und Christenheit* (Nuremberg, 1961) 55–74; Luigi Salerno, O.P., *La Chiesa e le Religioni non cristiane* (Napoli: Ed. Dominicane, 1966); Edward Schillebeeckx, O.P., "The Church and Mankind," *Concilium* 1 (Glen Rock, N. J.: Paulist Press, 1964). Gustave Thils, *op. cit.*

11. One of the best commentaries so far to appear is J. P. Lichtenberg, O.P., "Contenu et portée de la Déclaration conciliaire sur les Juifs," *Nouvelle Revue Théologique* 88 (1966) 225–248.

Rabbi Marc H. Tanenbaum

A JEWISH VIEWPOINT

I<small>T SHOULD BE SAID</small> at the very outset that there is considerable confusion in the use of the term "ecumenical," confusion both within Christendom, as well as confusion between Christianity and Judaism. In its strictest technical sense, the term "ecumenical" applies to relationships among Christians —Catholics, Protestants and Eastern Orthodox; and the ground of ecumenism is the shared Christology which is particular to Christendom. In this sense it is, therefore, a misnomer and a misapplication of the term "ecumenism" to apply it to relations between Christians and Jews. One can apply it, of course, to Christian-Jewish relations in its broadest, most generic sense; but in its authentic theological meaning it is a term specifically applicable to relations within Christendom. In this application, it deals with the activities of Cardinal Bea's Secretariat relating to the reunion of the "separated brethren." Yet having said that, at the same time one cannot really explore or exhaust the full meaning of what ecumenism means in its ultimate reaches without its application to relations between Christians and Jews, since the Hebrew Bible is the foundation of all monotheism. But for reasons of clarity, it is probably wise and prudential that we use the term "interreligious relationships" to describe the relations between Christianity and Judaism and between Christians and the Jewish people.

It is appropriate, I think, to ask why it is that "the Jewish declaration," introduced at the second session of Vatican II, November, 1963, and promulgated October 28, 1965, has elicited such widespread universal attention.

As Cardinal Bea said in his *relatio* September 25, at the time of his introduction of the "Jewish declaration,"

> I can only begin with the fact that this Declaration certainly must be counted among the matters in which public opinion has shown the greatest concern. Scarcely any other schema has been written up so much and so widely in periodicals. . . . Many will judge the Council good or bad by its approval or disapproval of the Declaration.

This decree has engaged the concern and the attention of 2,300 Council Fathers in Rome over a period of three years. It has involved the attention of the Protestant and Eastern Orthodox observers. Why is the issue of the relationship of Christianity to Judaism and the practical relations between Christians and Jews on a daily level of such central significance? Why has it attracted such widespread attention?

It is my thesis that the issue of relations between Christians and Jews has reached the point of ripeness, of maturation, in a way that can be seen analogously in terms of the ripeness and the fullness which relations between the Negro and white societies have reached. The moment of crisis, or the moment of truth, in relations between Negro and white are being tested and resolved to the degree to which we overcome the contradictions between our professions of love, charity and justice and our practices which have often stood in flagrant opposition to our pious verbalizations. In the process of being confronted by Negroes with a challenge to our moral claims, and our negative attitudes and behavior toward them, we have begun to find it necessary to face truthfully the fact that we have been dealing with Negroes in the main as abstractions, as mythic perceptions, but not as real people, not as persons who have a human dignity that demands a certain response from us as brothers. One of the facts that has become very clear to us is that we have evaded our moral duties to the Negro by substituting a series of myths for genuine confrontation. These myths have buffered us from encountering the reality of the Negro. As we dig beneath the surface of our attitudes and feelings in all the issues of the civil rights struggle, we find that in each instance we have developed a mythology that has crippled us from coming to grips with realities. Thus, we have told ourselves, literally for 350 years, that the Negroes are illiterate; the Negroes have weak family life; the Negroes are lazy and unreliable, and, perhaps the most diabolic myth of all, the Negroes have a bad odor.

We have told ourselves that the Negroes are illiterate, refusing to face up to the fact that by the year 1830, every state in the South had passed a law proscribing Negroes from learning to read or write because of the fear that literate, educated Negroes would rise up in rebellion against their white masters, the plantation barons. And so now we justify our segregation in schools by saying the Negro never learned to read or write; he is illiterate and therefore he cannot have equal education opportunities. We have broken up Negro families, used Negro women for breeding purposes, sold them "down the river" to the plantations of Louisiana, destroyed the foundations of Negro family life, and now we use this as an excuse for saying that Negroes cannot live next door to us because of their family habits. We have prevented Negroes from getting certain forms of employment and we have justified this by saying that they are lazy, shiftless, unreliable. Then we have kept Negroes away from public accommodations because of their supposed "bad odor." But as Gunnar Myrdal said in *The American Dilemma*,[1] "This has never prevented us from using Negroes as porters or as people who run our houses for us as maids."

Now in many ways the mythology, the unreality, the capacity to abstract human relationships and to empty them of solid human meaning and feeling, finds its analogy in the relations between Christians and Jews. What we have begun to confront in the relationships between Christianity and Judaism and between Christendom and Jewry is the fact that there is a fundamental ambivalence historically and theologically within Christian teaching and within Christian social practice that has never been confronted before in any serious and systematic way in the past nineteen hundred years of the Christian-Jewish encounter. Just as the social revolution of the Negroes today has caused us to confront the race issue in a way that we cannot escape, so certain revolutionary facts of the twentieth century have made the Christian-Jewish confrontation inescapable.

I believe that the Nazi holocaust and all that that has meant for the Christian conscience, as well as the tremendous needs of a new world of the twentieth century in which Christians and Jews together find themselves increasingly a minority in relation to a non-white, non-Judeo-Christian world, are compelling us to confront the deep realities of the relationship between Christians and Jews. Fundamentally, Christianity has never made up its mind as to where it stands in terms of its common patrimony with Judaism and its daily attitudes and relationships and behavior toward Jews. We find as we look into the history of the Christian-Jewish encounter for the greater part of the past two millennia that there have been teachings and episodes betokening the greatest of mutual respect and esteem between Christians and Jews. Thus, we find St. Athanasius, one of the early Church Fathers at the beginning of the fourth century, who said that "the Jews are the great school of the knowledge of God and the spiritual life of all mankind." St. Jerome, who lived in the fifth century and who spent forty years in Pales-

[1] (New York: Harper and Row, 1962).

tine where in Caesarea with Jewish scholars and biblical authorities he studied the Holy Scriptures and the Masoretic traditions—and from whom he obtained insights on which be based his translation of the Scriptures into the Vulgate—declared that "the Jews were divinely preserved for a purpose worthy of God."

This side of the affirmative attitude of the Church toward the Jews reflected the tradition of St. Paul in Romans 9 to 11, which speaks of Christians being engrafted onto the olive tree of Israel (11:17) planted by God. This tradition also found expression in positive behavior of popes even in the Middle Ages. Thus Callixtus II issued a bull in 1120 beginning with the words "Sicut Judaeis" in which he strongly condemned the forced baptism of Jews, acts of violence against their lives and property, and the desecration of synagogues and Jewish cemeteries. Gregory IX issued the bull "Etsi Judeorum" in 1233 in which he demanded that the Jews in Christian countries should be treated with the same humanity as that with which Christians desire to be treated in heathen lands.

Side by side with that tradition there existed a tradition of hostility and contempt which the late French historian, Professor Jules Isaac, has written about in his various studies. This tradition was perhaps most explicitly embodied in the eight sermons of St. John Chrysostom, who in the year 387 spoke from the pulpits of the city of Antioch to the first congregations of early Gentiles who became Christians, saying:

> I know that a great number of the faithful have for the Jews a certain respect and hold their ceremonies in reverence. This provokes me to eradicate completely such a disastrous opinion. I have already brought forward that the synagogue is worth no more than the theatre . . . it is a place of prostitution. It is a den of thieves and a hiding place of wild animals . . . not simply of animals but of impure beasts . . . God has abandoned them. What hope of salvation have they left?
>
> They say that they too worship God but this is not so. None of the Jews, not one of them is a worshiper of God. . . . Since they have disowned the Father, crucified the Son and rejected the Spirit's help, who would dare to assert that the synagogue is not a home of demons! God is not worshiped there. It is simply a house of idolatry. . . . The Jews live for their bellies, they crave for the goods of this world. In shamelessness and greed they surpass even pigs and goats. . . . The Jews are possessed by demons, they are handed over to impure spirits. . . . Instead of greeting them and addressing them as much as a word, you should turn away from them as from a pest and a plague of the human race.

Now, if one enters into the historic background and the context within which St. John Chrysostom made these remarks, perhaps one can understand a little better—one can explain if not excuse—what led St. John Chrysostom to make these anti-Jewish remarks. It may be useful to take a moment to observe that the Church in the first four centuries of this era was struggling for its existence as an autonomous, independent faith community. In the minds of the Roman Empire the early Christians represented another Jewish sect. Judaism was the *religio licita* (a favored religion), and for early Christians to achieve any status, including the right to conduct Christian ceremonials, they had to come as Jews to achieve recognition from the Romans.[2] And so the early Church Fathers found it necessary to separate Christians from the Jews. The early Christians felt very close to Jews; observed their Sabbath on the Jewish Sabbath, their Easter on the Jewish Passover. At the time of the Council of Elvira (ca. 300) many Christians in Spain thought the Jews had a special charism as the People of God and therefore invited them to bless their fields so that they would be fruitful. To separate Christians from their associations with Judaism, to create a sense of autonomy and independence for Christianity, apparently in the wisdom of the early Church Fathers it became necessary to embark on a drastic effort to break the bonds between church and synagogue and to give Christians a consciousness of difference from the Jews. In the process of this disidentification, however, the pattern of anti-Jewish attitudes and of anti-Jewish behavior became so entrenched, that by the time the Church became the established religion of the Roman empire, these attitudes were reflected increasingly in ecclesiastical legislation. These laws subsequently led to the establishment of ghettoes, the forcing of Jews to wear yellow hats and badges, and in general, this legislation reduced Jews to the status of pariahs throughout the Roman empire. As the Church became the major institution integrating the whole of medieval society, the perception of the Jew within medieval Christendom became the perception of the Jew within Western culture and civilization.

Lest one think that these attitudes are mainly of academic or historic interest, one needs to confront the following facts. A prominent Catholic educator has recently traveled around this country to various Christian seminaries and universities, to speak of the new understanding between Christians and Jews. As she sought to elaborate her thesis of the historical and theological factors which helped shape the conception of the Jew in the Western world, she received many questions from students at the end of her lectures. These are some of the questions that were asked of her by students in Catholic and Protestant seminaries and universities, and also on some secular campuses:

> If the Jewish people did not kill Christ, who did?
> You said that the high priest and the elders and not the Jewish people had a share of responsibility in Jesus' condemnation. That is not true. The gospel says that the people clamored for his death.

[2] See James Parkes, *The Conflict of the Church and the Synagogue* (London: Soncino Press, 1934).

I am a Catholic and I know what I have been taught when I went to catechism; and that is that the Jews killed Christ. That is what my Church teaches.
I don't like it. I have several friends who are Jewish, but what can I do? I have
to believe my Church.

Don't you think that in this country we are antagonistic to Jews because they
are too successful in business?

Why are all Jews rich?

Why are the Jews better than anyone else in business?

I have heard it said that Hitler had to do what he did because the Jews held
all the money in Germany.

The St. Louis University study, in its examination of Catholic parochial
school textbooks, found that there are echoes and resonances of this tradition
of contempt in materials used even to this day. Thus, for example, to cite
some of the teachings which have an unerring echo from the teachings of
St. John Chrysostom, it is written in some of the religious textbooks studied
by Sister Rose Albert:

The Jews wanted to disgrace Christ by having him die on the cross.

Show us that the Jews did not want Pilate to try Christ but to give permission for his death.

When did the Jews decide to kill Christ.

The Jews as a nation refused to accept Christ and since that time they have
been wandering on the earth without a temple or a sacrifice and without the
Messias.

The findings of the Yale University Divinity School study, published in
book form as *Faith and Prejudice* by Dr. Bernhard E. Olson, have revealed
analogous results in some of the denominational textbooks used in Protestantism. There have been significant revisions, as well as improved portrayals
of Jews and Judaism, in Catholic and Protestant teaching materials since the
publication of the St. Louis and Yale studies. Nevertheless, there is still a
heavy residuum from the polemical histories of the past in far too many
textbooks, and above all, in sermons, religious radio broadcasts, Seminary
Manuals, Bible commentaries, liturgical missals, catechisms, passion plays,
and in fact in the daily attitudes of many professing Christians.

These studies, which are of interest, I think, to people who have professional religious and educational responsibilities, do not begin, however, to
make us aware of the consequence of these generations of teachings in terms
of the impact they have had on the attitudes toward Jews in Western society
and culture. These views which began in a theological and religious matrix
have penetrated into the marrow of Western civilization and continue to
influence the Western world's attitudes toward the Jews to this very moment.

When you go home to your studies, if you will open any unabridged dictionary and look up the definition of a Jew, you will find the following:

Webster's Universal Dictionary:[3]
"Jew—to cheat in trade; as to Jew one out of a horse. To practice cheating in trade; as, he is said to Jew. To Jew down."
Funk and Wagnalls:
"Jew—(slang) to get the better of in a bargain; overreach: referring to the proverbial keenness of Jewish traders."
Merriam Webster:
"Jew—adjective, Jewish, usually taken to be offensive."
"Jew—verb, to cheat by sharp business practice, usually taken to be offensive."
"Jew—noun, a person believed to drive a hard bargain."

Contrast this with the dictionary's definition of "Christian":

Webster's Universal Dictionary:
"Christian—colloquial, a decent, civilized, or presentable person, characteristic of Christian people, kindly."

If one looks at the general social reality in terms of the way the Jew is perceived by and large (with significant changes in recent years growing out of our greater contact with each other), one finds, for example, a striking double standard in the evaluation of the behavior of the Christian and the Jew in the world of commerce. When a Jewish business man is successful in a given business or industry, in the parlor rooms and in the bars where the "man-to-man talk" is made (and all of us have heard this enough to know that it is true and not a figment of one's imagination), one hears the "explanation": "Well, he's a Jew." There's something sharp, there's something cunning about his practices. It is the Jewishness of the man which leads to his success. But if a Christian or a Gentile is engaged in the same industry, using virtually the same business practices, achieves the same kind of success, then in the American mythos this is the result of "Yankee ingenuity." This is living out the Horatio Alger myth of rags to riches in American life. It is a consequence of living out the "Puritan ethic."

One must confront ultimately how as recently as the past twenty-five years in a country—which, when it vaunted its great values and its great moral traditions, spoke of itself as a country of ancient Christian culture, which was in fact the seat of the Holy Roman Empire for almost a millennium beginning with Charlemagne—it was possible for millions of Christians to sit by as spectators while millions of human beings, who were their brothers and sisters, the sons of Abraham according to the flesh, were carted out to their death in the most brutal, inhuman, uncivilized ways. And one must confront as one of the terrible facts of the history of this period the conversation that took place between Adolf Hitler and two bishops in April,

---

[3] See Jacob Chinitz, "Jews and Judaism in the Dictionary," *Reconstructionist Magazine* (June, 1963).

1933, when they began raising questions about the German policy toward the Jews and Hitler said to them, as reported in the book, *Hitler's Table-Talk*, that he was simply completing what Christian teaching and preaching had been saying about the Jews for the better part of 1,900 years. "You should turn away from them as a pest and a plague of the human race," said St. John Chrysostom, and 1,500 years later thousands of his disciples implemented his teachings, literally.

One must compel oneself to face these hard facts in our own time because there is a tendency to want to evade the reality of this problem, since in America both for Christians and Jews anti-Semitism is not much more than a social nuisance. It is not a serious problem of human deprivation, of human discomfort, or a clear and present danger. But to this very day in the city of Buenos Aires, for example, where 400,000 Jews live, Jewish merchants are packing guns into their business places, synagogues are being stored with armaments because in the past three or four years the Neo-Fascist, ultra-nationalist movement called the *TACUARA*, consisting entirely of young, well-to-do Catholic students, have been tramping through the streets of Buenos Aires spraying machine gun fire at synagogues and throwing bombs into Jewish businesses. In June, 1963, the *TACUARA* apprehended a Jewish girl, Graciela Sirota, as she came home from the university in the evening, kidnapped her and carved a swastika in her breast. The chaplain of this *TACUARA* movement is a Father Julio de Meinvielle, who has written a book called *The Mystery of the Jew in History*. Father Meinvielle has claimed that he bases his "ministry" to these students in the *TACUARA* movement on the fact that the tradition of St. John Chrysostom's views toward the Jews and Judaism and those who have repeated that tradition, represent *the* authentic view of the Church toward the Jewish people and to Judaism.

Within the past four to five years all of us have lived through what in fact may be the most revolutionary period in the history of the Christian-Jewish encounter over the past two millennia. As in race relations, the churches have begun to seek to reconcile the ambivalences and the contradictions between theology and history. The Catholic Church, through Vatican Council II's approval of a declaration dealing with Catholic-Jewish relations, the World Council of Churches, in its very forthright resolution at New Delhi in December, 1961, and American Catholic and Protestant bodies have all contributed dramatically to the powerful assault against anti-Semitism. Their wide-ranging programs of textbook and curriculum revision, teacher training, seminary education, retreats and adult education have been confronting increasingly the issues of responsible portrayal of Jews and Judaism.

If nothing else came out of Vatican Council II other than what took place in Rome on September 28 and 29, 1964, the Council more than justified its existence in terms of Jewish interests. On Friday, September 25, 1964, Cardinal Bea arose in the aula of St. Peter's Basilica to read his *relatio* to the "Jewish Declaration." After indicating the importance of this decree to the life of the Church, the importance of the Church's understanding of her true relationship to Israel, to the Bible, to the Jewish people, ancient and present (an understanding upon which is founded the whole future and prospect of the biblical, liturgical and theological renewals of the Church), Cardinal Bea declared before 2,300 Council Fathers, "There are many historical instances from various nations which cannot be denied. In these instances this belief concerning the culpability of the Jewish people as such has led Christians to consider and to call the Jews with whom they live the deicide people, reprobated and cursed by God and therefore to look down upon them and indeed to persecute them." Then he described what he thought was authentic Church teaching about the role of the Jews in the passion and the mystery of the relationship between Christians and Jews. The moment of truth, as those of us who were privileged to be in Rome were able to observe, occurred on those two days when thirty-five cardinals and bishops from twenty-two countries arose on the floor of St. Peter's, and one after another, in terms more powerful and more committed than had ever been heard before, called upon the Catholic Church to condemn anti-Semitism as a sin against the conscience of the church. Thirty-one of the cardinals and bishops from every major continent of the world took positions regarding Catholic attitudes in relation to the Jewish people, Judaism, the role of Israel in salvation history, the synagogue and its continued relevance, conversion, anti-Semitism—positions that have never been heard before in 1,900 years of Catholic-Jewish history, positions articulated with such friendship, indeed, fraternal love, as to make clear that a profound turning point had taken place in our lifetime.

Cardinal Cushing, the first of the American hierarchy to speak out on the declaration on the Jews, called for a denial by the Council of the culpability of the Jews as a people for the death of Jesus. "Rejection of Jesus by the Jewish people is a mystery and is to serve to instruct us not to inflate us," Cardinal Cushing said.[4] He declared that the Catholic Church cannot judge the ancient judges of the Jews, as that is for God to do. At the same time, the Cardinal said Christians must be aware of the universal guilt of all men who by sinning crucified and are crucifying Christ.

The late Cardinal Meyer of Chicago stated that "it is not enough for the Church to deplore any injustices against the Jewish people. It must

---

[4] These paraphrases of the interventions of the Council Fathers are based on the press reports issued by the Press Service of the National Catholic Welfare Conference and also on the summaries printed in the *Herder Correspondence*. The publication of the full texts of the interventions would be a valuable contribution, in my judgment, to a fuller understanding of the historic implications of the Council's actions for the future of Catholic-Jewish relations.

also point out the close relationship of the Church with the Jews." Cardinal Meyer pointed out that St. Thomas Aquinas taught that the Jews were not guilty of deicide.

Cardinal Ritter of St. Louis said that the declaration would repair injustices of past centuries. He said that it is often assumed that God abandoned the Jews, and the Jews were rightly to be accused of condemnation of Jesus. Now he said an opportunity had been offered to remedy these errors and to remove these injustices. Referring to the passage that spoke of the "reunion" of the Jews with the Church, Cardinal Ritter said it sounds as if the Church envisions conversion of the Jewish people. He pointed out that the text did not speak of the Moslems, Hindus and Protestants in the same respect. Therefore he suggested that the final text find less offensive wording and include a paragraph expressing the biblical hope of the union of all men at the end of days.

Cardinal Leger of Canada called the declaration a necessary act of the Church's renewal.

Cardinal Lercaro of Bologna suggested that the declaration emphasize biblical discussions with the Jews. He said the Jewish people should not be regarded as having value only in the past. But the heritage of Israel, the institution of the eucharist within the Jewish paschal cycle, the relation between the Passover meal and the Mass, the common fatherhood of Abraham—all these should be emphasized in the declaration, Cardinal Lercaro said, in order to give witness in a pastoral way and to foster piety. He added that the Jews of today should not be called an accursed or deicide people, but rather that we should recognize that all of us "have strayed like sheep."

Archbishop Pocock of Canada said that the Church must acquit the Jewish people of all false accusations made in the past through the abuse of truth and charity.

Bishop Stephen A. Leven of Texas, in rejecting the ancient deicide charge against the Jews, declared:

> Fathers of the Council, we are not dealing here with some philosophical entity but with a word of infamy and execration which was invented by Christians and used to blame and persecute the Jews. For so many centuries, and even in our own, Christians have hurled this word against Jews, and because of it they have justified every kind of horrible excess and even their slaughter and destruction. It is not up to us to make a declaration about something philosophical but to reprobate and damn a word which has furnished so many occasions of persecution through the centuries. We must tear this word out of the Christian vocabulary so that it may never again be used against the Jews.

During those two days of debate in Rome and in the final text that was promulgated by Paul VI on October 28, 1965, the Catholic Church took a great and historic leap forward in reconciling this ambivalence, affirming on the highest levels of its teaching authority the indebtedness of Christianity and the Christians to Judaism and the Jewish people, the rejection of anti-Semitism and an unprecedented call for fraternal dialogue between Christians and Jews. Later in this paper I should like to discuss the Declaration that was promulgated and both the Jewish and Catholic reactions to it.

There is a larger dimension to what took place in Rome at Vatican Council II that should be of as great significance to the Jewish people as the Jewish Declaration itself. The clue to that larger signficance is suggested by the letter that Pope Paul VI sent to Cardinal Tisserant, dean of the Council presidency, on November 9, 1965. In that letter, Paul VI announced that Vatican Council II would end on December 8, "on the same date on which in 1869, there was solemnly inaugurated the first Vatican Ecumenical Council." The Pope then said that "our Council can well be considered under many aspects a worthy counterpart" of Vatican Council I. Before this audience, I need not belabor the point of how great an advance, indeed a revolution, Vatican Council II represents in contrast to Vatican Council I. As you well know, most objective, impartial historians have described Vatican Council I as that which marked the decisive victory of ultramontanism. The foundation stones of Vatican Council I were based on the encyclical *Quanta Cura* and the accompanying *Syllabus of Errors* issued by Pius IX in 1864.[5] J. B. Bury, regius professor of modern history at Cambridge, in his study *The History of the Papacy in the 19th Century* summarizes the contents of the encyclical and the *Syllabus* in this way:

> The leading ideas which are associated closely with modern progress are described as *monstrosa opinionum portenta*, and those who propagate them are designated as slaves of corruption who design to demolish society, *civilis societatis fundamenta convellere*. . . .
>
> He [Pius IX] begins his comments on this doctrine (of toleration) by quoting with approval a passage from *Mirari Vos* of his predecessor, where liberty of conscience and the right of each man to practise his own religion are described as *deliramentum*. Such liberty, says Pius, citing St. Augustine, is *libertas perditionis*.

[5] Whether the *Syllabus* possessed dogmatic character is a subject of controversy which Prof. Bury discusses at some length. He cites critics, such as M. Dupanloup and others, who sought to minimize its binding import, but concludes from evidence contained in letters of Cardinal Antonelli "that the *Syllabus* was intended to have dogmatic value . . . on the subject of modern errors." Similarly, there is a deep divergence of views regarding ultramontanism itself. Paul Droulers, S.J., for example, writing in the *Journal of World History*, characterizes the "ultramontanist" movement as one "impelled by the desire for greater purity and fervor" and constituted a "voluntary renunciation of local ecclesiastical particularism. It held up the pope, the head and center of the Church, as the visible source of Catholic vitality, while steadily consolidating his practical authority." Looking at the same set of "facts," the Lutheran church historian, Rudolph Sohm, in his book, *Kirchengeschichte im Grundriss*, characterized ultramontanism as "the intolerant doctrinal Catholicism which with its lust for power demands once more the complete subjection of the individual, of the world itself, to the supreme authority of the Church."

Professor Bury concludes (p. 6) that "the general drift of the argument [of the encyclical] is: liberty, toleration, secularism, and democracy are closely bound together, and what they mean is materialism."

Wrapped up in religious phraseology, Bury adds, the encyclical "is really a political document, setting forth an ideal of civilization and declaring principles of political import."

> The positive principles which it asserts by means of condemning their negations may be summed up thus: The State must recognize a particular religion as regnant, and submit to its influence, and this religion must be Catholic; the power of the State must be at its disposal, and all who do not conform to its requirements must be compelled or punished. The duty of governments is to protect the Church, and freedom of conscience and cult is madness. Not the popular will, but religion, that is the papal authority, is the basis of civil society, otherwise it will sink into materialism. The Church is superior to the State, and therefore the State has no right to dictate to her, and has no power over religious orders. The family and the education of children belong to the Church, not to the state. The Pope can decree and prescribe what he chooses, without the State's permission, and his authority is not limited to doctrines and morals (p. 8).

The Episcopalian scholar, the Rev. Dr. Frederick Grant, in his introduction to Professor Bury's study, described the mentality of Vatican Council I and of Pius IX as that which held that "the best safeguard of the Christian faith" against liberalism and modernism was to convert the Catholic Church into "a Maginot line of impenetrable defense." In the face of a series of shocks beginning with the Reformation in the sixteenth century and climaxed by the French Revolution in the eighteenth century, the Church became preoccupied with her own self-preservation and was relatively indifferent to the fate of those who were non-Catholic. This virtual obsession with the preservation of herself and her institutions made it possible for the Church to enter into concordats with the blackest forces of reaction, a tradition which led to tragic consequences in the twentieth century.[6]

As one reads the texts of the sixteen declarations promulgated by Vatican II and compares these with both the spirit as well as the rhetoric of the documents of Vatican Council I, there is no conclusion possible other than that the Catholic Church has undergone a revolution in terms of not only her self-perception but in her attitudes toward non-Catholics and her own responsibility for the welfare of other people. Nowhere is this new attitude of con-

---

[6] Paul Droulers, S.J., writing on *Roman Catholicism in the 19th Century World*, states, "The diplomacy of the Court of Rome . . . was adapted to meet the varying circumstances of the individual countries, striving to obtain the fullest possible measure of civil liberty for the celebration of worship and the exercise of spiritual government. . . . The Bull *Sollicitudo Ecclesiarium.* of August 7, 1831, contains an explicit reminder that in the cause of religion the Holy See will negotiate with any duly constituted government, though this does not imply recognition of its legitimacy before the law (293).

cern for others, involvement in their fate and destiny more clearly reflected than in the *Constitution on the Church in the Modern World*, the *Declaration on Religious Freedom*, the *Decree on Ecumenism*, and the *Declaration on the Relationship of the Church to Non-Christian Religions*.

No person of good will can fail to be moved by these words contained in the *Constitution on the Church in the Modern World*:

> The joys and the hopes, the griefs and the anxieties of the men of this age, especially those who are poor or in any way afflicted, these are the joys and the hopes, the griefs and the anxieties of the followers of Christ. Indeed, nothing genuinely human fails to raise an echo in their hearts. For theirs is a community composed of men (art. 1).
>
> In our times a special obligation binds us to make ourselves the neighbor of every person without exception, and of actively helping him when he comes across our path, whether he be an old person abandoned by all, a foreign laborer unjustly looked down upon, a child born of an unlawful union and wrongly suffering for a sin he did not commit, or a hungry person (art. 27).
>
> Respect and love ought to be extended also to those who think or act differently than we do in social, political and even religious matters (art. 28).

This emergence from behind something of a Maginot line and the joining of a dialogue with the world was dramatically ratified as much for non-Catholics as for Catholics in the brilliant address of Pope Paul VI before the United Nations at the end of last year. The Pope renounced for the Catholic Church any pretense to temporal power and then declared, "We make our own voice of the poor, the disinherited, the suffering, to those who hunger and thirst for justice, for the dignity of life, for freedom, for well being and progress." Pope Paul VI gave Catholic support to "the pluralism of states" and to "coexistence" between peoples. He said to the United Nations: "Your vocation is to make brothers not only of some but of all peoples." He then ratified "the formula of equality" saying: "Let no one inasmuch as he is a member of your union be superior to the others; never one above the other." The Pope then decried that "pride" which "disrupts brotherhood." Noting that the United Nations proclaims "the fundamental rights and duties of man, his dignity, his freedom—and above all, his religious freedom," the Pope declared that "the life of man is sacred; no one may dare offend it."

I believe that I speak the mind of most informed Jewish observers when I say that if this mentality had been normative for the popes, the Vatican and the Catholic and Protestant masses over the past one hundred years, the incredible phenomenon of hundreds of thousands of so-called devout Christians becoming accomplices or passive spectators to the cruel slaughter of millions of men, women and children who happened to be born Jews—or Gypsies—would not have been possible. The pragmatic significance of this newly articulated humanitarian mentality has given birth, I have no doubt, to the magnificent involvement of priests, nuns and Catholic laymen who, together with ministers and rabbis, marched together through the streets of Selma, Alabama, or in the March on Washington as a powerful renunciation of that mentality which echoed in traumatic silence less than twenty-five years ago in the cities of ancient Christian culture of Germany and Austria. The Pope cried out "No more war, war never again!" and moved the world when he pleaded. Vatican Council II has proclaimed to the whole of the human family "No more indifference, indifference and silence no more!" as long as the dignity of a single human being is offended or is exploited.

The promulgation of the *Declaration on the Relationship of the Church to Non-Christians* on October 28, 1965, received a mixed reaction in the Jewish community. As a commonplace pun has it, "Where there are two Jews, there are three opinions"—which is a Jewish self-critical way of describing the deep-seated democracy and pluralism that exists in Jewish life. The Jewish reaction ranged across a broad spectrum. There were those who opposed the Declaration and, in fact, who resented it. There were those who were indifferent to it. There were those, including myself, who welcomed the Declaration as an important contribution to improve the future relations between Catholics and Jews. In my study of the Jewish responses, I became aware of how decisive a role mass media played in influencing relations between groups. A substantial segment of the Jewish community reacted not to the content of the Declaration, as much as to the headlines which reported *about* the Declaration. The day following the promulgation, newspaper headlines throughout this country and, in fact, throughout the world, carried such statements as "Vatican Council Exonerates Jews for Death of Christ"; "Catholic Church Absolves Jews of Crucifixion." The so-called Jewish man-in-the-street naturally responded to such presumptive formulations with resentment, if not worse. No Jew in my acquaintance has ever felt guilty for the death of Jesus. Therefore, no Jew ever felt in need of absolution. But it was the newspapers and the radio and television commentators who used those words. The text of the Declaration itself does not use "absolve" or "exonerate" even once. This is not to impute bad motives or incompetence to the mass media. The problem of reducing to headlines a complex historical and theological problem is one that I am glad I did not have to face. But again, the fact that such headlines and such radio and television reports were dinned around the world for days both prior to and following the promulgation, led almost inevitably to a negative reaction of so many Jewish people.

A more substantive consideration is the fact that the Vatican Council, for whatever reasons, "backed and filled" over this declaration for some four years. And to many Jews it was as though the Jewish people were being subjected to a trial over this period of time. When you add to that the fact that a number of unfortunate episodes took place during those four years (including the insulting articles and speeches by Bishop Carli of Segni, who said, in fact, the Jews and Judaism today are collectively responsible for the crucifixion and stand under God's reprobation because of it), then one has another insight into how the Jewish patience wore thin. Overriding all, however, was the absence in the Declaration of any note of contrition or repentance for the incredible sufferings and persecutions Jews have undergone in the Christian West. The Church's various declarations asked forgiveness from the Protestants, the Eastern Orthodox, from the Moslems, but not from the Jews. Many Jews, especially those who lived through the Nazi holocaust, asked with great passion, "How many more millions of our brothers and sisters will need to be slaughtered before any word of contrition or repentance is heard in the seats of ancient Christian glory?"

The Jews who are indifferent to the Vatican Council's action believe that it was too little and too late. Within this group there is a strong feeling that the Catholic bishops in Germany and perhaps Pius XII himself could have spoken out decisively, unambiguously at a time when it would have meant something of profound importance to the Jewish people. That did not happen in terms adequate to the need and, therefore, the loss of confidence in the present usefulness of the Vatican statement is widespread among this group. In the perspective of history this group has also been aware that up until the time of the Enlightenment and the French Revolution the Church contributed to the disenfranchisement of the Jewish people of the Western world and much worse. This group looks to the secular powers of the world for its political and civic salvation. In the view of this group history has outdistanced the Christian community, and such statements are only pleasant rhetoric and are really of no significant effect in terms of the security or fate of the Jewish people in the Twentieth Century.

In the view of the third group the text of the final version of the Declaration that was adopted represented a compromise document compared to the text that was introduced at the close of the third session and which received an overwhelming majority vote of the Council Fathers. The earlier version was warmer, more generous, and less severe: it dealt explicitly with the "deicide" concept which became something of a symbolic test of good will. In that perspective, the failure of the Council to enact the majority will of the Fathers of 1964 was a disappointment. But in the view of this group, seen in the perspective of 1900 years of Christian-Jewish history, this Declaration represents an incredible achievement.

As important as the Declaration itself is, the commitment of Catholic Church authorities and institutions to translate the guidelines in this document into reality in the lives of 550 million Catholics throughout the world was of even greater importance. That commitment was given decisive expression when the American Catholic hierarchy designated a special subcommission on Catholic-Jewish relations charged with the responsibility of implementing the objectives of the Declaration throughout every level of Catholic culture and society. The determined action of the Vatican shortly after the Declaration was promulgated which put an end to the veneration of Simon of Trent—that ritual blood libel episode which since the fifteenth century has been celebrated by annual procession through the streets of Trent, repeating an insult to the whole of the Jewish people—was another impressive demonstration of the commitment of the Catholic Church to express in deeds its new attitude of respect and esteem for the Jewish people. The instruction given by Cardinal Döpfner of Munich to the organizers of the Oberammergau Passion Play to revise the text so that all anti-Jewish references are removed is another earnest of the Catholic Church's commitment to the uprooting of the sources of anti-Semitism.

In the face of the agonizing history that many of the people of the cross had wrought in the transformation of the Jews into a cross among the peoples, there should not be too great bafflement or wonder over some of the skepticism of a number of the Jewish people in this country and abroad as to the real meaning of the Vatican Council Declaration to them and their children. As long as Father Julio de Meinviele of Buenos Aires is allowed by the Catholic hierarchy to serve as chaplain to a group of young Catholic Fascists, who ruthlessly exploit anti-Semitism for their economic and political purposes; as long as hostile references to the Jewish people, Judaism and the synagogue continue to appear in Catholic textbooks, missals, liturgical commentaries, theological dictionaries and sermons, a great many Jews will continue to view the Vatican Council Declaration as a vain and even hypocritical show. Having worked closely with members of the Catholic community both here and abroad, especially in the fields of religious history and religious education, I am deeply persuaded that a vast and irreversible tide of self-purification and self-correction with regard to the portrayal of Jews and Judaism in the teaching process of the Catholic Church—nor should the Protestants be slighted—is under way and that the fruits of this process are already in evidence. That is not to overlook the hard reality that a great deal more needs to be done before the last weeds of anti-Jewish teaching and anti-Jewish poison are removed. But in my judgment, no Jew has a right to belittle the great advances that have been made already. I am persuaded that we are now going through a period of transition which will find both Jews and Catholics fumbling and stumbling as they seek to find appropriate new modes of relating to each other in a growing climate of mutual tolerance and esteem.

A Jewish Viewpoint

During the course of the deliberations of Vatican Council II in connection with the "Jewish Declaration," the contradictory and at times confused views expressed with regard to the inclusion or elimination of a passage in the third version of the text relating the question of the conversion of the Jews brought into sharp focus the fact that the Catholic Church has done very little serious thinking about the place of Jews and Judaism in the divine economy. That episode alone underscored the need for Catholic theologians and scholars to develop a theology of Israel and the synagogue in salvation history that has some correspondence with the historic realities of the present-day living Jewish people. At the same time, the bewildering and bewildered response of many Jews to Vatican Council II, whose attitudes toward present-day Christians are based on old-world memories of Christians as persecutors, threw into sharp relief the critical need for Jews to develop a theology of Christians and Christianity that is consonant with the realities of an emerging "new Christian" society that is struggling in unparalleled fashion to uproot anti-Semitism and to restore her traditions to biblical modes of thought and practice.

At the heart of Christianity's problem of what to make of the Jew is the Christian's immense ignorance, if not illiteracy, regarding Judaism. If the Jews were supposed to have committed deicide against Jesus, then a great many Christians in fact have committed homicide against him. They have killed Jesus as a Jew and as a man. The weapon was ignorance of Jesus' Jewishness. But Jesus' life, his preaching, his teaching, his vision of the kingdom of God, the very ground of his messianism cannot be accurately or profoundly understood apart from his background in the synagogue, his life of worship and observance as a Jew, and his education with the Pharisaic rabbis of the first century. Indeed, the New Testament itself cannot be fully comprehended as other than a Jewish book, written almost entirely by Jews for Jews, and in the Jewish mode of exegesis, known as *Hagaddah*. Long passages of the New Testament are, indeed, actually nothing less than new and different exegesis of the Jewish Bible, the difference being determined by the belief in the divinity of Jesus, which stands in opposition to the uncompromising monotheism of Judaism.

The significance of this Christian amnesia regarding the Jewishness of the origins of Christianity is that the Christians who live in this ignorance are expressing the Marcionite heresy. Further, God bestowed promises upon the Jews and chastised them with curses, in order that they might repent. But a certain tradition of Christian teaching appropriated the promises for "the new Israel" and imposed upon the "old Israel" the left-over curses. In this way, many Christians found it possible to cease to identify religiously with Judaism and, worse, perceived the Torah and Judaism as "stagnant" and "desiccated." From this conviction it was but a short step to the belief that the Church "superseded" Israel—despite St. Paul's admonition in Romans that God's call and promises to the Jews are irrevocable.

When one adds to this ignorance of first-century Judaism the even greater lack of knowledge about post-biblical Judaism, the ground of misunderstanding becomes an abyss. To most Christians, Judaism came to an abrupt end with the close of the canon of the Hebrew Scripture. But Judaism did not come to an end with the Old Testament. Just as a non-Catholic does an injustice to Catholicism by failing to take into account the significance of tradition, Church teaching and canon law, in addition to Sacred Scripture, so do non-Jews distort Judaism by failing to recognize that modern Judaism is the product of a long and rich development of postbiblical thought, devotion and piety that the great rabbis and sages of the Jewish people developed over the past 1,500 years. In the absence of that knowledge, the Christian pedagogues' continued use of the stereotypes of "Pharisees" for hypocritical post-biblical Jews, the false antimony of Judaism as a religion of law and justice versus Christianity as a religion of love, mercy and compassion will only serve to perpetuate bias and know-nothingism in religion.

In this perspective, it has now become very clear that there are at least three major and decisive areas of scholarship that must be vigorously pursued by Catholic and other Christian scholars if the call of Vatican Council II for "biblical and theological studies" is to be translated into "mutual understanding and respect." These are, first, critical commentaries and interpretations of the New Testament that will remove any possibility for bigots to exploit certain expressions in the gospels for anti-Semitic purposes. An excellent example of such studies is to be found in the essay "Anti-Semitism and the Gospel," by Dominic M. Crossan, O.S.M., which appeared in a recent issue of *Theological Studies*. In that essay Crossan wrote that "the often-repeated statement that the Jews rejected Jesus and had him crucified is historically untenable and must, therefore, be removed completely from our thinking and our writing, our teaching, preaching, and liturgy."

The second area is that of historical studies. If one reads Church histories and Jewish histories of the same events, it is as though Christians and Jews are being educated in different universes of discourse. A Christian historian, for example, Philip Hughes, writes of the Crusades of the eleventh and twelfth centuries as holy war to free Jerusalem. "Never before had Europe known such a vast and successful propaganda as the preaching of the First Crusade, and its success is a most eloquent proof of the reality of the new reform papacy's hold on the average man and of its popularity with him," wrote Hughes in his *A Popular History of the Catholic Church*. To Jewish historians the Crusades "becomes a gory story of pillaging Jewish settlements, killing Jewish people, looting Jewish wealth. Such serious restrictive legislation as the humiliating garb, ritual-murder charges, Host desecration libels, and confinement of the ghetto were not the heritage of the Dark Ages but the heritage of the Crusades."[7]

As Edward Flannery, author of *The Anguish of the Jews* has written, "most Christians have torn out of their history books the pages that Jews have memorized." The time has come, perhaps, for a proposal to be made for Christian and Jewish historians to join together in writing a common history of the Jewish-Christian encounter which will fill in the blank pages.

The third area of much-needed scholarship is that of theological studies in Jewish-Christian relations. Unless and until Christian scholars and people develop theological conceptions regarding Judaism and the synagogue that reflect in some way the vital reality of the existence of present-day Judaism, very little else of significance in Jewish-Christian relations will be possible. Gregory Baum has begun to point the way:

> The apostle tells us, that the Jews of the Synagogue remain dear to God for the sake of the fathers (cf. Rom 11:28). Their election stands. Why? Because God is faithful, his gifts and call are irrevocable (Rom 11:29). His election cannot ultimately be undone by human decision against it. This scriptural theme is invoked in the conciliar text.
>
> What does this mean for the understanding of the Jews of our day? Giving this Pauline theme its weakest possible meaning, it asserts that God continues to be present and to address Jewish believers in their synagogue services. The testimonies of God's mercy in the past as celebrated in the synagogue worship remain a way of divine action, for "his gifts and call are irrevocable." We have here the answer to a question crucial to the Jewish-Christian dialogue. What is the present synagogue worship before God? Is the Christian forced to regard present Jewish worship as an empty form, as words and gestures without meaning? Or is he able to acknowledge in Jewish worship the presence of the living God? The conciliar text answers this question by its adoption and use of the Pauline theme. God remains present in his gifts to Israel.[8]

[7] Max Dimont, *Jews, God and History* (New York: Simon and Schuster, 1962).
[8] Gregory Baum in *Ecumenist* (May-June, 1965).

367

FR. BROWN: I have a question for Father Stransky, a question concerning the statement that although the Church is the new People of God, the Jews should not be presented as repudiated or cursed by God. Later in your talk you say although the Church is the People of God, this in no way closes discussion on the Jews' being in some way of this new People. I presume this means in some way, of the Church. Outside of that possibility, if you abstract from their relationship to the Church in some mystical way, can the Jews still be called in the Christian understanding the People of God?

STRANSKY: In the official *relatio* the point was that the People of God, Israel, is not in the same position now as before. That we can claim is sure. Exactly what the difference is, what is lost, is open for theological reflection. To talk of losing something, does not mean that Israel does not have a reality in itself. And even using that word "lose" may be a little hard. All that we know is that the position of the Jewish people after the coming of Christ is not the same as it was.

CALLAHAN: I don't want to put you in a difficult position, but I was caught by the fact that you mentioned that qualifications had to be introduced or omitted in the final text, and these have changed the doctrine from one of bold proclamation to that of forceful argument. I would like your opinion on what the significance of this change was. I myself harbor the horrible feeling that though the Church made tremendous progress here, it would still be capable of drawing back from the boldest possible proclamation of what it believes out of concern for internal problems of the Church, that is to say, it would compromise its own convictions for the sake of peace, for the sake of political situations, and so forth. What, in other words, is the significance of this change, in your opinion?

STRANSKY: First of all, I think the main pressure for those changes was not of a political kind at all. They were the three changes that I meant. The political obstacle was settled between the second and third sessions, rather than between the third and fourth. The critical opposition wasn't to whether or not we used "subsistit in" or "sit" or "nevertheless" or anything. The fact is the changes were made because of a conservative—if you want to use that word—theological school still within the Church. I mentioned these three "granteds" that were put in, that did irritate, legitimately, some of the Jewish commentators. As I stated, what had to be done, not because of external pressure, but just because of the problem itself, was to make it very clear that you can accept the biblical fact but deny the theological conclusion. That is in all of this. We accept the fact that some Jews rejected the gospel, but we don't say this; we accept the fact that some Jewish authorities pressed for the death of Christ, but we don't include this; we accept the fact that the Church believes herself to be the new People of God, but we don't accept this. Perhaps we should have been even more explicit and have listed ten more "granteds," which would have made it worse as a bold proclamation. But I am wondering whether or not that bold proclamation we wished for would have been hypocritical.

BURGHARDT: May I address a few sentences, if I may, to Rabbi Tanenbaum, and perhaps some preliminary to my remarks?

I think you know from our great meeting at Woodstock how deeply impressed I am by your data, your facts, your message. And I might add that only last week I added a bit of fuel to your particular fire, at the Jewish-Christian Institute in Boston, by documenting the early Christian attitude toward "the Jews" on three levels: 1) that "the Jews" in the eyes of the early Christians were responsible for the death of Christ; 2) that "the Jews" were rejected by God; 3) that Jews in significant measure and numbers were responsible for much of early Christian persecution—a good bit of bad theology and bad history all involved in several centuries. So much for the preliminary notes.

I would suggest, in fact insist, that the brief summary of Vatican I and of Pius IX's documents as you gave it simplifies the facts so dreadfully that history suffers rather badly. Obviously yours is a summary statement, and

369

therefore there is no attempt at documentation. But there doesn't seem to be any effort to situate categories like freedom of conscience, democracy, the modern state, etc., in their historical context. I would suggest that the choice of Rudolf Sohm as a quotable historian on an institutional Church is not awfully happy. I would suggest that the pioneering research of men like John Courtney Murray on the political philosophy of nineteenth-century Catholicism, specifically Pius IX, does not seem to have had sufficient impact on the Jewish understanding of nineteenth-century Catholicism. Now I simply bring this up because I do not believe that this aspect of your presentation is necessary for your admirable and defensible thesis. Quite the contrary, I would say that this apparent lack of understanding of Vatican I and Pius IX, for whom I hold no great grief, this apparent lack of initimate understanding of what they were about, would hinder rather than help your presentation of Jewish-Christian relations in the past, and certainly do not help for an understanding between Jew and Christian in the present. I do not mean to sound harsh and hope I have not.

TANENBAUM: Father Burghardt, I must confess that, in dealing with the passage, I asked myself whether I should have developed it at the length I did; it turned out apparently to be too brief in its present form. It suffers from a kind of flattening out of the history of that period, and I am very much conscious of it. In fact, in other speeches that I make to Jewish audiences I try to state the other side of the case, which is the case that you are making, namely, that I believe that in many ways one of the problems we inherit today, as we confront each other over issues such as the separation of Church and state, is almost a paranoid Jewish response in terms of what Jews take to be an intention to create a sacral society, and at the same time an insensitivity on the Christian side as to what a sacral society and its overt meanings have for Jews. And part of the reason for that is that as Jews read their history books on the French Revolution, and to them it was the cause, the source, of their emancipation for the first time in 1700 years, it was the Enlightenment, it was Deism, the *Aufklärung* that gave them political and civic equality for the first time. For the Catholic Church the French Revolution was as great a trauma and almost of as great a magnitude as the Nazi holocaust was for the Jews. One can read Father Hughes on that chapter and come away instructed in terms of what it meant for the destruction of all the major centers of Catholic education, the rapings, the murder of nuns and priests, especially in France, the brutality against half of the French clergy, and the disestablishment of the Church. I am aware of all that. The problem was how to treat that adequately. I recognize that there is an imbalance and perhaps in the final text that can be taken care of.

FULLER: This is to Father Stransky. Actually I have three questions. You say that: "All other religions are based on a natural knowledge of God. . . .

No other name but his can save. . . . The sincere faith experience of an individual non-Christian is salvific." Now there appears to me to be a prima facie inconsistency in these statements which could be removed only by a Barthian denial of the natural knowledge of God or by a denial of the third proposition I quoted, namely, "the sincere faith experience of an individual non-Christian is salvific." Could the essential truth of all three statements, however, be retained by the substitution for the concept of a natural knowledge of God by one of general revelation through the pre-incarnate Logos, thus preserving the *Solo Christo* which you assert so strongly? Maybe it is only that I don't understand what a Roman Catholic theologian means when he speaks about the natural knowledge of God.

STRANSKY: Father, I think it was my English rather than my opinion. I said "this assertion is made," and I mean the assertion that God saves the individual non-Christian despite his community faith. When I say, "this assertion is made," I do not mean it is my assertion; this assertion has been made. But I think the problem has been in the past that we have just talked about *the* supernatural religion and *the* natural religions: *the* one supernatural religion, and *the* natural religions. And that is what I would reject. I think that there is no such thing as a natural religion or a natural faith. It is precisely not to get involved in, or to deny, let us say, a very strict Barthian thesis that the statement was put in that the saving faith of an individual is in some way Christic and ecclesial. I would hold this to be true also of the community. In these communities there is something Christic and ecclesial. They are not just natural; they partake of the one sacrament, the Church.

FULLER: You accept then the concept of general revelation in this context?

STRANSKY: No, I wouldn't accept that.

DR. BROWN: I would like to address a question to Father Stransky, but I would also be pleased if Rabbi Tanenbaum wanted to comment on it. This has to do with the placing of the statement on the Jews and the theological implications of this. As I recall, the statement was originally in *De Oecumenismo*, and it was put there for strategic reason: to get in on the floor. But it seems to me upon reflection that perhaps there are theological issues for its being placed there also; the whole question of Judaism and ecumenism is raised by this. Its present position in the *Declaration on the Relationship of the Church to Non-Christian Religions* seems to suggest that Judaism is simply one among a number of other world religions that do not happen to be Christian. Its position within *De Oecumenismo* at least suggested that Judaism stands in a unique relationship to Christian faith among other world religions. It seems to me that the unique relationship between Christian and Jew is a very important part of the dimension of relationship between the two faiths today, and even though that is not symbolized by the location of the present statement, I wonder if the purposes of our theological encounter would better have been served if it had been left in *De Oecumenismo*.

STRANSKY: First as to the fact, it was placed in *De Oecumenismo* both for theological and pastoral, practical reasons. The practical reason was to get it on the floor. But when it was only half-way in, they detached it. The statement on the Jews, then, was left all by itself. Then a great deal of pressure to enlarge the statement to include other religions. Well, we couldn't put it back into *De Oecumenismo*; it was already off. We were very conscious of making a distinction between Judaism and other religions. If you read the text of article 4, you see the difference being brought out by the phrase "As this sacred Synod searches into the mystery of the Church. . . ." There is a difference of content to show that there is a difference of relationship. It hasn't been spelled out clearly enough though. But I do think that many of the reactions that I find, for instance even in Rabbi Tanenbaum's talk, are not my reactions to the Jewish people. These are the reactions that any non-Christian has, in a way, at not being regarded as a person or his church as a religious community. Thus we have an added problem now, precisely by looking at the non-Jewish religious communities in order to find out where they are in the plan of salvation, we double the specific problem of the relationship of Israel to our Church.

Now for theological reasons, right from the beginning the whole theology of the proto-schism, the relationship of the Old and the New and what that means, and the prophetic element that calls us constantly, the very prophetic presence of the Jewish people in the world—all these things make *De Oecumenismo* the ideal place for the statement on the Jews. I agree. But in fact it didn't happen, but not for theological reasons.

TANENBAUM: I would want to respond somewhat facetiously, by saying that if this group believes it has complications in terms of the Catholic Ecumenical Council, it would be itself equally intrigued if there had been a Jewish Ecumenical Council facing the problem of the relationship of Christians and Christianity to Jews and Judaism. And the range of positions might not have been very different from that which is being discussed here today. It would have been a body of Jewish opinion seeking to stake out a theological relationship in which the common bonds, the common monotheism, the common traditions of spirituality would have been affirmed. There would have been a range of opinion at the opposite end of the spectrum reflecting perhaps the Jewish curia desirous of joining forces with something of a Marcionite tendency in your camp in order to break or minimize the bonds. Quite obviously there are great risks on both sides. I am not altogether sure that we have as yet a complete understanding of the ultimate meaning of placing the relationship of the Church and Christians to Judaism and Jews in the context of non-Christian religions.

HESCHEL: This is an exceedingly complex subject to talk about, this Declaration. I cannot do justice to it in a few moments. But let me make a few general remarks.

To me as a friend, as a person who prayed for great achievements at the Council, I feel that greater things could have been accomplished in this document. Why did I have such an expectation? Because from experience, encounters and dialogues I discovered a very great movement; yes, I witnessed a miracle: there came Pope John. He tried to open the windows, and he certainly opened them fast. And an outpouring of grace and greatness was witnessed. What I expected, then, was a document, unconditional, without ambiguities, just full of love and reverence—the kind of love and reverence the gospel stands for. This isn't an unconditional document. It is however an important document. It is important as a milestone, but it is not the climax, because the movement is greater than the Council. It is quite clear that there are in this document some very beautiful statements which will contribute to greater understanding. And there is no doubt about that. But somehow I speak out of silence, almost out of stillness; I think my longing was greater than the document, and I am a little sad that the document did not come up to the greatness of the moment.

However, I would like to point out one thing that is of greatest significance to me in this document. The omission of any reference to conversion of the Jews in the Declaration must be regarded as a step of great historic importance, a new and indispensable preamble to a relationship of mutual esteem between Christians and Jews. I should like to express it bluntly and sharply: there is a deep suspicion on the part of a great many simple Jews that the Church still has in mind that there is only one way for the Jews, and that is conversion. This is a theological problem for the Church, I understand. But the problem was, I believe, advanced considerably in this document. For this reason it contains, I believe, a great statement. It is an attempt to understand this whole issue in terms of eschatology; what will happen at the end of days no one knows. Here I find a shift of emphasis, a new understanding of the problem of the Jews in relation to the Church, one which, may I say, is even missing in good Protestant denominations. In this respect the Catholic Church has taken a step far beyond the boldness of most Protestant Churches. I remind you also that Pope Paul revised the prayer in the Good Friday liturgy which used to be entitled "For the Conversion of the Jews." It is now entitled "For the Jews." This undoubtedly testifies, I believe, to a new awareness of the permanent preciousness and holiness of the existence of the Jews as Jews.

And finally one other word as a friend, as a person who prays for the spiritual health and integrity of Christians, I am particularly delighted with the new emphasis upon the study of the Hebrew Bible. I think the renewal of biblical studies encouraged by the document on Scripture is to me, as a Jew, of equal importance. All I would like to see is that the world should open its mind and heart to the words of the prophets, and then there will be no need for documents on Jews or others.

If you would permit me to speak another two minutes, I would like to suggest that the statement on the Jews calls for dialogue. What divides us, what unites us? Now we disagree in law, in creed, in commitments that lie at the very heart of our religious existence. We say "no" to one another in some doctrines essential and sacred to us. What unites us? Our being accountable to God, our being objects of God's concern, precious in his eyes. Our conceptions of what ails us may be different, but the anxiety is the same. The language, the imagination, the concretization of our hopes are different, but embarrassment is the same and so is the sigh, the sorrow. And the necessity to obey? We may disagree about the ways of achieving fear and trembling, but the fear and trembling are the same. The demands are different, but the consciences are the same and so is arrogance, iniquity. The proclamations are different, the callousness the same. And so is the challenge we face in many moments of spiritual agony. Above all while dogmas, while forms of worship are divergent, God is the same. What unites us? A commitment to the Hebrew Bible as Holy Scripture, faith in the creator, the God of Abraham, commitment to many of his commandments, the justice and mercy, a sense of contrition, sensitivity to the sanctity of life, to the involvement of God in history, to the conviction that without the holy the good will be defeated, and the prayer that history may not end before the end of days, and so much more. Maybe then it may come very soon when the Hebrew Bible will be called the Hebrew Bible—without the adjective "old."

STRANSKY

SESSION IX

REV. THOMAS F. STRANSKY, C.S.P.
The Decree on Ecumenism

Rev. Thomas F. Stransky, C.S.P.

THE DECREE ON ECUMENISM

THROUGH THE CONCILIAR *Decree on Ecumenism* the Roman Catholic Church acknowledges not only the fact of Christian separations and the scandal caused by them, but also the ecumenical movement, into which the Church has willed to enter. In this sense, the Decree is more than a text; it is an act. And insofar as ecumenism is not a specialty within the Church but a dimension of every expression of its life that reveals "an increase of fidelity to its own calling" (art. 6), the general concern for continual renewal at all levels on the Church's life and in the interior evangelical life of each Roman Catholic is the over-all Conciliar ecumenical act.[1]

The present situation—the Roman Catholic Church in the ecumenical movement—is causing far more problems in the life of all the Christian churches than the prior state of the Roman Catholic Church *and* the movement: the very size and organizational apparatus of the Roman Catholic Church; the holy irritation of renewal caused to the "reformed and reformable" churches by the "unreformed and irreformable" Roman Church; the new initiatives of the Roman Seè toward the whole of Orthodoxy, which is not prepared psychologically, and perhaps theologically, to evaluate both the motives and the actions; the appearance of "ecumenical romantics" or an enthusiasm without depth that could easily die before it can change into deep commitment with enthusiasm; the creation of confusion without clear explanation, or without even the necessary time to change old psychological reflexes according to fresh theological insights; the entire new setting for "ecumenical structures" within the Roman Catholic Church, within other churches, and between themselves, for effective institutional action (e.g., the Roman Curia—not just the Unity Secretariat—and episcopal conferences; bilateral vis-à-vis Conciliar cooperation in study and actions; membership in local, national, and in world councils of churches); the determining of *immediate priorities* in theological collaboration among faculties of theology; and so forth.

All these problems caused by the entrance of the Roman Catholic Church into the ecumenical movement presuppose that through Vatican Council II this Church has revealed enough of its own self-understanding in relation to other Christians and their communions that these others feel there can be true dialogue. Do the Catholic principles of ecumenism legitimately flow from Roman Catholic ecclesiology; and if so, can the key concept of dialogue be preserved: *par cum pari* (on equal footing)? We are not restricting the formula to methodological attitudes: the elimination of self-justification, to speak and to propose, to hear and to receive, in order that together we can enter more deeply into the will of God for his one, holy, catholic and apostolic Church. Dialogue is between Christians, and, more fundamentally, between Christian communions. The questions are 1) how does the Roman Catholic Church regard other Christians as Christians; what is the relationship of other Christians to the Church of Christ; 2) how does the Roman Catholic Church regard the communities in which these Christians live; how and to what degree is the reality of the one, holy, catholic and apostolic Church to be found outside the clearly defined walls of the Roman Catholic Church; what is the relationship of other Christian communions to the Church of Christ; 3) how Rome-centered are the Roman Catholic principles of ecumenism?[2]

These problems are beginning to come into proper focus because of the ecclesiological distinction upon which the vision of the Church in the *Constitution on the Church* and the *Decree on Ecumenism* is based. The mystery of the Church is primarily and at its deepest level an *internal communion* in faith, hope and charity of those who live out their fellowship with one another and with Christ, his Holy Spirit, and God the Father. But it is also an *external, visible institution* of means which beget, bring about and manifest this communion: the preaching of the gospel or written word of God, the administering of the sacraments, and the governing of the flock. These are means which come from Christ and lead back to him. Through them the internal communion of his people is expressed and perfected in the confession of the one faith, in the common celebration of divine worship, and in fraternal harmony of ministries. "But the society furnished with hierarchical agencies and the Mystical Body of Christ are not to be considered as two realities, nor are the visible assembly and the spiritual community, nor the earthly Church and the Church enriched with heavenly things" (*Constitution on the Church* 8; *Decree on Ecumenism* 2–3). On the contrary, this internal communion of the faithful, this institution of means to beget and bring about this communion, this visible expression of the communicable favors Christ received from the Father in the Spirit for his people form "one complex reality"—the one, holy, catholic, and apostolic Church, the sacrament of God's love in the world, "a sign lifted up among the nations" (Is 11:12). This Church "*subsists in* the Catholic Church, which is governed by the successor of Peter and by the bishops in union with that successor" (*Constitution on the Church* 8). The Roman Catholic Church is the "all-embracing means of salvation"; only through it can the fullness of the means of salvation be found (*Decree on Ecumenism* 3). But this pilgrim Church has seen in its history an ebb and flow in the dynamic possession, assimilation and manifestation of its divine gifts. The members have failed to live them out with all fervor (art. 4). The Church itself has found in its history deficiencies in moral conduct, in her discipline and laws, even in the formulation of her teachings (art. 6). Her witness to God's care for his world is not perfect, and thus the growth of God's kingdom is retarded (art. 4).

INDIVIDUAL NON-ROMAN CATHOLIC CHRISTIANS

The Council asserts that the Christian message preached outside the Roman Catholic Church and the sacraments received beyond her visible borders do mediate the new life of Christ and communicate the Holy Spirit to those who cling to the message and the sacraments in faith. By the sacrament of baptism, "man becomes truly incorporated into the crucified and glorified Christ and is reborn to a sharing of the divine life" (art. 22). All the baptized have a right to be called Christian (art. 3). Together we share the same Lord and the same Spirit. To the other Christians also the Spirit "gives His gifts and graces, and is thereby operative among them with His sanctifying power" (*Constitution on the Church* 15).

The Latin text of article 15 in the *Constitution on the Church* uses the word *coniungere* to express the relationship to the Catholic Church of those baptized "who do not profess the faith in its entirety (*integram fidem*) or (*vel*) do not preserve the unity of communion with the successor of Peter." The Church in many ways "is linked" (*Ecclesiam coniunctam*) with them. By baptism "they are united with Christ" (*coniunguntur*). "In some real way they are joined with us in the Holy Spirit" (*vera quaedam in Spiritu Sancto coniunctio*).[3] On the other hand, the *Decree on Ecumenism* prefers as its key concept not the body-image but the richer and more patristic notion of *communio*: the common possession of *sacra* and the unity created by this possession. The Decree speaks of the "marvelous communion of the faithful" brought about by the Spirit in the sharing of the gifts of Christ (art. 2). And insofar as other Christians share those visible and interior *elementa et bona*, "which together go to build up and give life to the Church herself," they are in communion with the Church; insofar as they do not, they are in imperfect communion (art. 3). If this is stated, then the community of grace and fellowship among all believers reborn in baptism and the sharing of the Holy Spirit—a *communio baptismalis*—is more extensive than what is circumscribed by the visible boundaries of the Roman Catholic Church.[4] If one analyzes the body-image concepts (*incorporari*) in both the *Constitution on the Church* and the *Decree on Ecumenism*, one will find it very difficult to claim that Vatican II does not assert, at least implicitly, that all the baptized faithful are members of the Church, though they have different degrees of membership. The nervous avoidance of an explicit statement was due to the closeness of the Council to Pius XII's *Mystici Corporis* and to the debate on how to interpret it.[5]

In conclusion, all baptized Christians are in full or less full communion with each other in the one Church, full or less full members of the one Church.

THE OTHER CHRISTIAN COMMUNIONS

If the Council acknowledges that our brothers who believe in Christ and are baptized in him are members of the same family of Christ, it also recognizes that the communions possess and use, in varying degrees, those holy means that communicate to their faithful a share in the life of Christ and the guidance of the Spirit. They preach the gospel, they celebrate holy baptism, they carry out liturgical actions, they give apostolic witness in extending God's kingdom, and in his name they give service to suffering humanity. These elements or endowments of sanctification and truth—Christian life and the Christian means to foster that life—come from Christ and lead back to him. They belong by right to the one Church of Christ, for together they go to build up and give life to the Church herself. Yet they can and do exist outside the visible boundaries of the Roman Catholic Church (art. 3). Thus, for the non-Roman Catholic Christian, the process of sharing in the new life of Christ takes place within his own communion and by means of it. True, these communities as such may be, in varying degrees, defective because they lack the fullness of means and "are not blessed with that unity which Jesus Christ wished to bestow on all those whom He has regenerated and vivified into one body and newness of life," but they still have "significance and importance in the mystery of salvation," for the Spirit of Christ uses them as *"media salutis."* But these means of salvation "derive their efficacy from the very fullness of grace and truth entrusted to the Catholic Church" (art. 3).[6]

In conclusion, there is a real relationship of these other communions to the Church of Christ. They are "Churches and Ecclesial Communities," but separated from full communion with the Roman Catholic Church. This means that there still remain degrees of communion, though imperfect.

THEOLOGICAL QUESTIONS

These assertions of Vatican II with regard to individual non-Roman Christians and their communions provide new questions for theological reflection.[7] There are ambiguities, to be sure, especially concerning "churches and ecclesial communities,"[8] but the ambiguities are similar to, at times identical with, the ambiguities in the ecclesiological thinking within non-Roman circles. The more general problem is the relationship of the churches to the one, holy, catholic and apostolic Church, between the churches and the Church.[9] The specific problem for the Roman Catholic arises from the acknowledgment that the Roman Catholic Church, and it alone, is the all-embracing means of salvation, but, in fact, "some, even very many of the most significant elements or endowments which go to build up and give life to the Catholic Church" exist outside that Church's visible boundaries.

According to the official report of the Theological Commission, the fact that "many elements of sanctification are to be found outside the visible confines (*extra compaginem*) of the Catholic Church" was the reason for what may be the most significant one-word change of the Council. The "one interlocked reality," which is the one, holy, catholic and apostolic Church of Christ, *is* not the Catholic Church (1964 draft), but "subsists · in" it (*Constitution on the Church* 8). In what way is the Church of Christ realized and embodied in the Catholic Church? As the only *institutionally* perfect realization of Church? If the church-building elements belong by right to the one Church of Christ, then the question is: since other Christian communions *de facto* possess these means in varying degrees, what is their status *within* the mystery of the *one* Church of Christ? And if they possess these means which by their very nature "build up and give life to the Church itself" (*Decree on Ecumenism* 3), then is there not a partial, incipient existence of the *one* Church outside the juridically defined boundaries of that community that acknowledges the authority of the body of bishops in communion with the successor of Peter? If these non-Catholic communions are "separated from full communion with the Catholic Church" (art. 3), there still remain various degrees of communion. Is there not, then, a basic communion *within* the *one* Church of Christ between the perfect institutional realization of it (the Roman Catholic Church) and its imperfect realizations?

Some theologians have suggested that the relationship of non-Roman communions to the Roman Catholic Church is based on the degree to which the others resemble *ecclesiae particulares*.[10] In fact, this was the predominant thought of the Unity Secretariat in its drafting of the *Decree on Ecumenism*.

Particular churches are living cells, each of which contains the whole living mystery of the one body of Christ. Each community can rightly be called *Ecclesia* (cf. 1 Cor 1:2; 2 Cor 1:1). Through the bishop and his priests' preaching the gospel, celebrating the eucharist and guiding the apostolic witnessing of the people, Christ's action as prophet, priest and king becomes effective in the local community. Above all, by celebrating the eucharist (which includes the breaking of the word), the particular church builds up the whole Church, makes present the whole Church in all her fullness, and expresses most deeply the unity of the particular community and the unity of the whole Church (*Constitution on the Sacred Liturgy* 4, 6, 10; *Constitution on the Church* 8, 32, 33).

The structure of the individual community remains incomplete if, under the bishop, it does not live in communion with the other bishops of the different churches, with and under the bishop of Rome. The Church of Christ, then, is a communion of local churches, through which the Universal Church and each particular church achieve their growth in perfect harmony, each being open to the needs of others ("solicitude of all the churches") and each sharing its own goods with others.

The Decree, following a long tradition in Roman documents, does not hesitate to designate the Eastern churches separated from the Roman Catholic See as "churches," not only because of the common heritage of spirituality and liturgy, of discipline and theology, but above all because of the episcopal structure. Through the celebration of the eucharistic mystery in each of these churches, presided over by their bishops, the Universal Church of God is expressed, built up, and grows in stature (art. 15; cf. *Constitution on the Church* 26). Nevertheless, they are separated from "full ecclesiastical communion" with the Roman Catholic Church because they are separated from the See of Rome. The Decree leaves it to future theological reflection to determine, if possible, the extent and depth of the wound that this separation inflicts both on these local churches and on the Roman Catholic Church.

The Decree, however, hesitates to call all the non-Roman communions of the West "churches" and settles for "churches and ecclesial communities" without designating into which category fall specific communions.[11] (Is a communion without the sacramental succession of the episcopacy and thus without the "genuine and total reality of the Eucharistic mystery" [art. 22] an *ecclesia?* The Decree, it should be added, did not settle the question of Anglican orders). In any case, all of these communions have an ecclesial, supernatural character. They are communities that look to Christ as the source and center of their entire church life (art. 20). They announce the word of God (art. 21), celebrate the baptismal liturgy (art. 22), and extend the kingdom of God in the world (art. 23). Even if the Catholic Church does not acknowledge their eucharistic celebrations in its fullness, it does respect their setting forth the eucharistic signs by commemorating the death and resurrection of Jesus, by expressing life in communion with Christ, and by keeping alive hope in the glorious return of the Lord. But whatever, according to Catholic belief, their sacramental shortcomings may be, God uses these communions as merciful instruments in building up and saving his chosen people.

The *Decree on Ecumenism* does not evaluate the *total* reality of the other communions, but it does "grade" them *qua* institutions of means according to the institutional elements which they share with the Catholic Church, "in which the fullness of the means of salvation" can be found.

According to the Unity Secretariat's official treatment of proposed amendments, "fullness of means" should not be understood in a merely quantitative sense. "The fullness of truth and grace means more than a numerical completeness of the deposit of faith and the means of salvation. The fullness indicates a transition to the qualitative order; it means perfection and an integral wholeness that admit of neither more or less. Only the 'fullness' guarantees the coherence of the whole and the importance of its individual parts. For this reason the Decree does not understand the relation of Protestantism to Catholicism simply in a quantitative way."[12] This strong statement, along with the insistence that the one, holy, catholic and apostolic Church subsists in the Roman Catholic Church as its institutionally perfect and unique realization, rules out an ecclesiology that would claim that Christ's Church is made up of the sum of several Christian Churches here on earth or that the Roman Catholic Church is the best of "particular churches" because it has the most of means.

The Decree does appreciate the *qualitative* development of institutional means wherever they exist. Like the Roman Catholic Church, each of the other communions is *primarily* an internal fellowship with one another in and with Christ. Both dimensions—community of fellowship and institution of means—form a whole, and as a whole is answerable to Christ and must ever answer to him. Since Christ is the power of salvation and the Spirit moves where he wills (e.g., the charisms in other churches, including their prophetic charism vis-à-vis the Roman Catholic Church!), the institutional *possession* of means does not guarantee the perfect assimilation and manifestation of these means, nor does this mere possession guarantee its absolute conformity to the image of Christ being formed in its members. When the Roman Church regards itself as the measure of ecclesiastical fidelity, it still recognizes the need for the continual renewal of these means—*ecclesia est semper reformanda* (art. 6)—and the continual renewal of heart and mind in faith and loving service (art. 7). But the Church dares not and cannot judge the interior fidelity of its members, and for all the more reason, that of members of other communions. If the Church stands under the word, it is daily judged by it.

Furthermore, the Decree acknowledges, explicity for the Orthodox churches, unfortunately only implicitly for the other churches and ecclesial communities, that non-Roman communions have developed and manifested qualitatively church-building and saving means in ways not found in the Roman Catholic Church. Thus not only by the existence of means outside the visible boundaries of the Roman Church but also by their "outside," communal, qualitative development, the "fullness" in the Roman Church is impaired by reason of the separations; it is prevented "from effecting the fullness of catholicity proper to her" (art. 4). The Church "finds it more difficult to express in actual life her full catholicity in all its aspects" (*ibid.*). The Latin nuance of the opening two words of the Decree, *unitatis redintegratio*, suggests that perfect unity is not to be found in the actual life of any one church; only the union of all Christians in the one renewed Church is necessary before this "perfect" unity can be said to exist.

Nevertheless, insofar as the Roman Catholic identifies his Church with the one and only Church of Christ, he is localizing the visible witness to unity in Christ in a way that no other Christian does. This is why others see in the mind of the Roman Church "a tension between a Christologically-centered and a Rome-centered ecumenism."[13] They see the Roman Catholic not so much "seeking" unity as offering only his Church as the inescapable locus. "Home is Rome!"

The impulse of Vatican II is beginning to break down the image of "return" and "surrender" to the static Roman Church. Although the Catholic Church has in no way abandoned its belief in its unique position among Christian communions it is insisting on its own constant reformability. And much of the future renewal will depend on the proper incarnation of the proper "hierarchy of values" in Christian living as well as Christian teaching.[14] It is quite rash for a Roman Catholic to predict what either "home" or "Rome" will be like. I would only add that I cannot see that in a truly reformed Christian communion "Rome" will be the most important designate of the Catholic Church.[15]

CONCLUSION

Ecumenism means that all Christians make a *common* effort to foster whatever gifts God has given to the *whole* Christian family, whether these gifts be within the external confines of one's church or not. The very gifts of Christ in his Spirit, which unite us to the Trinity and to each other, are dynamic. By the living out of these gifts and by common reflection on that experience, we uncover our sources of agreement, and together push on to ever greater unity. The imagery is not one of "return" or "surrender" but one of forward movement, first upwards toward Christ in his will for a divided Christian family, then across toward other communions, "moving as far as each can do without sacrificing its integrity, but nevertheless moving out at certain risk, the risk of realizing that an encounter is going to take place, and that in an encounter into which two partners genuinely enter, neither partner emerges from the encounter precisely as he was beforehand."[16]

In this sense the dialogue is a *par cum pari* relationship between the churches. And by churches I do not mean triumphalistically described abstractions but the living churches: their concrete structures, international, nation-wide, city-wide, parish-wide; their concrete hierarchies and laity; their concrete life of worship, preaching, ministerial formation, lay education, married life, neighborhood and world involvement; their *de facto* resolve to hear the word of God in fidelity to Christ, and in fidelity to his world to hear God speaking through the men and events of these times. Dialogue is between the churches, and the purpose of dialogue is to help one another renew our churches in their concrete theological and pastoral life. Why? The continuing pressure of the gospel is insisting that ecumenism means unity for mission through church renewal: the obligation to draw all Christians together through the renewal of the churches into one Church always in renewal, and the obligation of the whole Church to preach the whole gospel to the whole world, as sacramental servant to both that gospel and that world.

NOTES

1. As is already evident from Conciliar commentaries, the evaluation of this act depends on the principles used for the interpretation of any church document: 1) a document is seen above all as an act in the dynamic historical development of a church, and *then* is compared with the historical life of the other churches; or a document is judged above all as a static set of *ideas* with immediate comparision with the ideas of other churches and traditions; 2) the importance of the act is judged by its *terminus a quo* (an historical approach) or by its undetermined *terminus ad quem* (a cautious or naive, true or false prophecy).

2. In this paper I am confining myself to these three questions. Lengthy commentaries have already been published which cover the whole range of ecumenical assertion, insights and pastoral guidelines in the Decree: Walter M. Abbott, S.J., *Decree on Ecumenism* (New York: The America Press, 1965); Augustine Cardinal Bea, *Commento al decreto conciliare sull'ecumenismo* (Roma: Città Nuova, 1965); Giovanni Cereti, *Commento al decreto sull'ecumenismo* (Torino: Borla,

1966); Werner Becker, "Das Konzilsdekret 'De Oecumenismo'," *Una Sancta* 2–3 (1965) 83–100; Y. M. Congar, O.P., *Introduction au décret sur l'oecuménisme* (Paris: Centurion, 1965); C. J. Dumont, O.P., and R. Beaupère, O.P., "Le Décret conciliaire sur l'Oecuménisme," the entire issue of *Istina* (Oct.–Dec., 1964) 353–544; Adalberto M. Franquesa, O.S.B., *Decreto sobre el Ecumenismo* (Barcelona: Ed. Estela, 1965); Heinrich Fries, "Das Konzil und die Einheit der Christen," *Catholica* 2 (1965) 83–107; Lorenz Cardinal Jaeger, *A Stand on Ecumenism: the Council's Decree*, trans. Hilda Graef (London: Geoffrey Chapman, 1965); Bernard Leeming, S.J., *The Vatican Council and Christian Unity* (London: Darton, Longman and Todd, 1966); John F. Long, S.J., "East and West in the Decree on Ecumenism," *Unitas* (Eng. ed., Jan., 1965) 1–16; Miguel Nicolau, S.J., *Decreto sobre el Ecumenismo* (Madrid: Apostolado de la Prensa, 1965); *L'Oecuménisme: Texte, notes et commentaires par une équipe de laïcs et de prêtres* (Paris: Mame, 1965); Edmund Schlink, "The Decree on Ecumenism" in *Dialogue on the Way*, ed. George Lindbeck (Minneapolis: Augsburg, 1965) 186–230; Thomas F. Stransky, C.S.P., *The Decree on Ecumenism* (Glen Rock: Paulist Press, 1965); *idem*, "The Decree on Ecumenism: An Analysis," *One in Christ* (Jan., 1966) 5–26; *idem*, "The Decree on Ecumenism: an Interview with Fr. Stransky," *Clergy Review* (Jan., 1966) 3–26; Gustave Thils, "Le Décret sur l'oecuménisme," *Nouvelle Revue Théologique* (March, 1965) 225–244; Maurice Villain, S.M., "The Debate About the Decree on Ecumenism," in *Concilium* vol. 2 (Glen Rock: Paulist Press, 1966); Valdo Vinay, "La Chiesa romana e la Christianità non romana nei documenti del Concilio Vaticano II," *Protestantesimo* (1965) 129–151; Stefano Virgulin, *L'Ecumenismo del Concilio* (Milano: Ancora, 1965); "Comments on the Decree on Ecumenism" by Oscar Cullman, Robert McAfee Brown, Paul Evdokimov, J. Russell Chandran, Hébert Roux, Oliver Tomkins and José Miguez Bonino, *The Ecumenical Review* (April·1965) 93–112.

3. Abbot B. C. Butler judges that this paragraph in *De Ecclesia* "is full of good will, but this good will, strangely, is not supported by theology." The Abbot of Downside continues: "It is deplorable that the Constitution does not give maximum importance to the strongest of all bonds, the unity in the Holy Spirit who is the true principle of unifying love, and does not present a theology of baptism and of the baptismal character. One can also observe that in fact it does not in any way advert to the bonds which exist between the Catholic Church and organized groups in which individual non-Catholics live their religion. The point of view adopted has been almost exclusively individualistic." B. C. Butler, O.S.B., "Rapporto tra i cristiani non cattolici e la Chiesa," in *La Chiesa del Vaticano II*, ed. G. Baraúna, O.F.M. (Florence: Vallecchi, 1965) 658.

4. By its exclusive concentration on initial baptismal bonds Vatican II did not face up to an evaluation of one who indeed professes in word and act the Christian faith but a) by conviction does not accept the sacrament of baptism (e.g., the Quakers), or b) by "accident" is not properly baptized according to the present Roman Catholic understanding of the requirements for *valid* baptism.

5. Cf. Thomas F. Stransky, *Decree on Ecumenism*, 23–24. B. C. Butler, *op. cit.*, 662. G. Philips, "Deux tendances dans la théologie contemporaine," *Nouvelle Revue Théologique* (March, 1963) 231–232.

6. It was Paul VI who added "Catholic" to the text prior to the final vote on the Decree.

7. With these Conciliar assertions it is difficult to find any *theological* reason to prevent the full membership of the Roman Catholic Church in the World Council of Churches. For the present the difficulties seem to be pastoral (proper preparedness in all the constituents of the World Council of Churches and in the Roman Catholic Church) and organizational.

8. "To be sure, the phrase 'churches and ecclesial communities' is still equivocal, and more precision will be needed in the future to discern just how and to what degree the reality of the *ecclesia* is acknowledged by the Roman Catholic Church to be present outside its own clearly defined walls" (Robert McAfee Brown, *art. cit.*, 96). "The expression 'the non-Roman Catholic Churches and ecclesial Communities' is not defined doctrinally. Its meaning is merely implied, although a precise definition of it is essential for a dialogue if it is to be really frank" (Paul Evdokimov, *art. cit.*, 98).

9. Although Vatican II treats of the relation of other communions to the Roman Catholic Church, it wisely avoids the issue of the relation of other communions among themselves. Indeed, this does require theological reflection, but as is obvious from the discussions of Orthodox, Anglican and Protestant theologians on the ecclesiological significance of councils of churches, further study will be unproductive *until* questions about the ecclesiology of denominations are clarified. Cf. *The Ecclesiological Significance of Councils of Churches* (New York: The National Council of Churches, 1963).

10. The most provocative author is Gregory Baum, O.S.A., to whom I am greatly indebted for my own reflections. Cf. his "What Are the Other Churches?" *The Ecumenist* (Nov.–Dec., 1963)

1–4; "The Ecclesial Reality of the Other Churches," in *Concilium*, vol. 4 (Glen Rock: Paulist Press, 1965) 62–86. The best pre-Vatican II summary of various positions, cf. Emilien Lamirande, O.M.I., "La signification ecclésiologique des communautés dissidentes et la doctrine des 'vestigia ecclesiae': Panorama théologique des vingt-cing dernières années," *Istina* (Jan.–March, 1964) 25–58; Ulrich Valeske, *Votum Ecclesiae* (München: Cladius, 1962).

11. Another reason for the hesitation: what theological criteria does one use to "circumscribe the boundaries" of a Protestant communion? Protestant thought itself is questioning. For example, is there a Lutheran World Church? "If so, where is this phenomenon? What constitutes the Lutheran Church? The Lutheran confessions? But the confessions say that only the word and sacraments constitute the Church. Is the Lutheran Church perhaps the sum of all its parts: The Church of Finland, the Church of Saxony, the Lutheran-Missouri Synod, etc.? Or perhaps the only true Church is the local congregation and all the rest is machinery developed to assist the local congregation? Thus, the problem is not simple" (E. Clifford Nelson, "The One Church and the Lutheran Churches," *Proceedings of the Fourth Assembly of the Lutheran World Federation* [Berlin and Hamburg: Lutherisches Verlagshaus, 1965] 279).

12. Lorenz Cardinal Jaeger, *op. cit.*, 82–83.

13. José Míguez Bonino, *art. cit.*, 111.

14. Oscar Cullman regards the passage in art. 11 concerning the order of hierarchy of truths in Catholic doctrine as "the most revolutionary to be found, not only in the Schema *de oecumenismo* but in any of the schemas of the present Council" (*art. cit.*, 94).

15. The Roman Catholic does believe that the "papal principle" is a fundamental principle of Christ's Church, although he is uncertain of how it will develop in our understanding and will express itself in history. "It is to be hoped that, while remaining faithful to its own understanding of the truth, the Roman Catholic Church will not bracket this question out of discussion as 'non-negotiable,' and that the other churches will not entrench themselves behind a declamatory rejection of the 'claims' of Rome and refuse to come to grips with the basic question which these claims pose" (José Míguez Bonino, *art. cit.*, 112).

16. Robert McAfee Brown, "Problems in a Theology of Ecumenism," *Proceedings of the Twentieth Annual Convention of the Catholic Theological Society of America* (Yonkers, N. Y.: St. Joseph's Seminary, 1966) 99.

387

STRANSKY: Analyzing the approach that the documents use to the Church's institutional means, we see that we have to avoid giving the impression that these are just quantitative·means. They are in the state of separation. On either side there have been different developments, and I think some of those developments are due to historical factors. That does not mean that these are accidental to the development; there is enrichment of the very use of the Bible, not just in how it's read, but how it's lived among fundamentalist groups, let us say, that have according to the *Decree on Ecumenism* very few means. We cannot judge what the total effect of this is in God's way, the way his Spirit blows.

A small fundamentalist group, as a little community in a Roman Catholic country, for example, may be being blessed by God far more than the institutional Church with all of the means. As for the Church's development in totality, another church can develop aspects that the Roman Catholic Church, with all its ecclesiastical completion, so to speak, has not fulfilled so well. Certainly the role of the laity in the Protestant Churches has been a great development of awareness of the prophetic function of the layman, the ministerial function of laymen, than the Roman tradition. Although I think Protestants today are getting a little triumphalistic about that, because

388

they themselves are facing the problem of clericalism and also of waking up a laity. And so I say we are concerned with the common problems of renewal.

This is one of the weaknesses I see in evaluating churches according to the scale of quantitative elements. Just because an element is outside does not mean it loses all its development or its richness; nor is it true that just because an element is inside it is fully developed. And there is no hope for ecumenism, unless we see the whole dimension of the plenitude and catholicity of the one, universal, apostolic Church trying to unfold, adapt, assimilate and manifest these means.

Another questioner says that the *Decree on Ecumenism* was a break with an unbroken tradition of papal teaching on the subject from Benedict XV to Pius XII with no significant exceptions. It stands off at 180° angle to *Mortalium Animos*, 1928. The questioner probably wants to know how many degrees before you break the chain.

Placing these documents in their historical context, I think that there was understandable bad judgment. I think Vatican Council II began with the death of Pius IX. If you take Vatican Council II as the crystallization of a renewal process, you can see the definite line to that already beginning with Leo XIII, in different strands and different stresses, in the various movements in the Church, some of which progressed more quickly than others. On reading those documents we see that there was bad judgment, but understandable in that there was no association with the other churches.

VON ROHR: May I comment on the matter of means. I was very much moved by the portion in your paper where you made the distinction between internal communion and external means, and the relation of internal communion to faith in Christ and life in Christ. One thing that strikes me in this kind of discussion is that sometimes the doctrine of means gets imposed upon those for whom it is not quite as desirable as it might be for others. Now you took note of the fact that there are some Protestant groups who do not accept baptism, for example. (I think you mentioned Quakers); these are left out of consideration. In another way others are left out, namely, some who have a valid baptism in the eyes of the Roman Catholic Church but who do not interpret this baptism in the manner in which it is interpreted in Roman Catholicism. They thus find themselves a little bit embarrassed, I think, by seeing that they are a part of the body of Christ by means of a baptismal bond, when in reality it would seem from their own perspective and experience that there is a more significant bond that relates them to the body of Christ, namely, the bond of faith in Christ. In their eyes this makes them hopefully a part of the internal communion, even though in the eyes of the Roman Church and other churches they may be lacking some of the external means. My comment is simply to point that out, and then also perhaps to make the query as to whether or not there is in the offing a fuller exploration of the role of faith as a uniting ground in Christian life and Christian experience, wholly apart from the means of grace.

STRANSKY: Yes, I am very aware of the weakness of our theology about the nonbaptized Christian. If interior fidelity or interior communion is the primary element of the Church and one is living this Christian faith, then certainly that is not insignificant. I think much of the question concerns the fact that a person is not merely an individual, just as the sacrament of baptism itself is not only for an individual, aimed at getting *him* somewhere; it is also the basis of the whole sacramental structure of the Church as a community and as a sacrament in the world. So I don't want to give the impression of speaking only about the individual and what is good for *him* in the Church. Much of the problem also rests in his relationship to the community, or the communion, and to its sacramental signs.

I think your second question is very important, the analysis of what we mean by separation in faith, or the dynamism of the act of faith, especially when faith does not terminate in doctrinal statements, but in the person, the total commitment of the person to Christ. There may be a different understanding of what the implications are of this full commitment to Christ and his mystery in the world. I think an exploration is definitely going on now in Roman Catholic theology, especially in the catechetical movement, of the richness of faith itself as distinguished from the doctrinal formulation of it.

OUTLER: I should like to come back to the question of the relationship of the *Decree on Ecumenism* to previous papal teachings. It is one thing to describe these as instances of bad judgment and to give an historical explanation of why the judgment was bad. It is another thing to draw the consequences of this rather long and consistent record of bad judgments, according to this theory, a consistent bad judgment with respect to a major topic in the Christian Church and its internal life. In the theory of the papal magisterium I would ask (a) is bad judgment there calculated, like a baseball batter's average would be, higher or lower according to historical circumstances; and (b) can you draw a proper inference from these instances of bad judgment as to the dynamism that goes into the correction of bad papal judgments when they have been made. Who corrects which papal judgment with what authority after they have been judged by whom to have been bad?

STRANSKY: Well, at times we do appear to be going through a kind of mental gymnastics, with certain papal statements. Father Burke was just mentioning last night the need to demythologize papal statements, in the sense of trying to see them in their context and to discover just what was being said and where the real problems lay. I think that we are oversimplifying it right now, because we do not have a method of evaluating papal statements. That too is part of the renewal of the Church. We have been giving just as much attention to what the pope may say on a Sunday afternoon in a sermon in a Roman suburb as to what he says at the end of the Council. I think we have to be very realistic about evaluating papal statements. This is not a question of infallibility, but of papal statements.

AHERN: Father Stransky, with regard to your previous emphasis on faith as the binding power in our union with God, I am wondering if it isn't imperative that in all of this we keep in mind the whole historical background of baptism. Faith would be enough if we were angels, if we were disembodied spirits. But we are whole persons, and therefore the whole man has to be committed, to some kind of psychosomatic rite. It's that same old question as to whether or not Paul was justified by his faith at the gate of Damascus, or whether Paul was justified by his baptism three days later. I don't think Paul ever even dreamed of any dichotomy. He couldn't think of an interior act which did not really and truly have to take in the whole man, the body, the person. Although we certainly do know that faith in itself unites to God, nevertheless that same faith does require, by the very fact of our own anthropology, that there be a consecration through something psychosomatic, through baptism.

COOKE: I wonder, Father Stransky, if there isn't another dimension to this. I know it has bothered me that oftentimes a greater sense of community in faith is felt with those who do not have the same sort of denominational community link that I have. I wonder if perhaps we aren't going to have to start thinking about different elements of Christian community—not, of course, in any way to destroy the community allegiances that we have in churches. With regard to this whole question of judging positions and working toward clarifications and so on, I wonder whether one of the things that isn't operating within the Catholic Church and across church lines is the developing consensus or community of Christian theological opinion, and whether this isn't really a very important normative element in what is taking place now in the whole ecumenical development? I wonder if I can get your reaction to that.

STRANSKY: I have thought a lot about that myself. One of the weaknesses in thinking today, in the Decree itself, is the role of the councils, the Council of Churches, intra-ecclesiastical forms and community life. One of the main reasons why it is difficult to find an answer on the part of others, say, is that there isn't any other Church that has really investigated its relations to other churches. This is a problem, in other words, of trying to find anything like a decree on ecumenism in any other church. The point you brought up is, I think, going to become more and more of a crisis problem in the Church, if we regard ecumenism not so much as staring at each other as looking to Christ for the needs of the world. And we are going to find many more blurred distinctions in community life as well as in faith life,

391

than we have right now. As the churches grow together, one has to expect that there is going to be more blurredness, and that we are going to have communities of faith running across church lines.

COOKE: I'm not exactly talking about blurring lines. As a matter of fact I'm not very much in favor of that. I think it is a question of keeping our positions as clear as we can and clarifying them when they tend to become blurred. What bothers me is that oftentimes one who is a Roman Catholic will find a greater identification in his Christian faith with many who are not Roman Catholics than he will with many Roman Catholics who do not understand his position and who hold, for practical purposes, let us say, something that, from our point of view, is well-nigh heretical. I think in a sense we have two conflicting principles of Christian identification and community. The one is structural and identifiable in a sensible fashion; the other one, the real community in faith, I think, is an important element of the ecumenical dimension.

STRANSKY: I think that is where your blurred lines are going to be coming from, and you will clarify the blurred lines, not eliminate them.

HÄRING: To the question what is more important faith or sacrament, I think St. Thomas Aquinas gives a very short and clear response. He says that man is saved through faith and the sacrament of faith, but more fundamentally through faith. But then he explains that it is not only through the sacraments of faith that faith finds its expression in the whole of life. He does not make the distinction, faith here and means there; sacraments are for him more than means. It is very modern language he uses when he calls sacraments signs, solemn profession of faith. That is the way Christ wished us to express the fundamental commitment of faith. He himself produces faith.

To the other question of Dr. Outler, I think that as Catholics and Christians we find the fundamental response in Galatians. Peter was wrong and Paul used his prophetic office to tell him so. In many cases we can explain that the popes gave the best possible directive at that moment; things were not clear enough to do otherwise. But in other questions we may have failed to use the prophetic gift in the Church, the prophetic courage that is still compatible with full reverence for the teaching and pastoral office of the successor of St. Peter. It is letting authority down, when we do not use the prophetic gifts God gives us in full submission, in full charity, but also in full frankness. So I think that there could be a change in this and other matters. God never fails to provide prophetic men who speak out freely, who show that they are of the right spirit, and are able to convince authority. If it sometimes comes late it may be that there was undue stress put on structural office and not enough help and collaboration on the part of those in authority.

392

HAY: I think this Decree is one upon which a Protestant viewpoint would have been very appropriate. I shan't take much time but there is at least one thing I must say. When one reads this document one is impressed by the familiarity of some of it. Father Stransky lays every stress upon identifying the Church by the criteria of the preaching of the word, the celebration of the sacraments, and the exercise of discipline. This is just terribly, terribly familiar to the reformed theologian, and of course to a Lutheran. It is rather remarkable, I think, that in asking the question where the true Church is to be found, the Fathers at the Council got the same answer as Luther and Calvin got. This is most welcome, indeed.

May I pass on now to the next point which is even more important. That in hitting upon these marks of the Church, as they were called, they find an answer to the question of schism. They refused on this basis to unchurch anybody. They said that a church is more or less pure according as the word is more or less purely preached and rightly heard, and the sacraments are more or less rightly administered according to the institution of Christ—and some people, like John Knox, like to add the matter of discipline.

Now this fact that there can be more or less purity in these matters saves their charity. They didn't unchurch anybody, though regrettably we were unchurched by Rome. What I do feel lies very strongly in my heart to say at this moment. As I am here, a Presbyterian guest of a Roman Catholic University, it would be most unfortunate if I did not stand up and thank God that now the door is opening; that Rome has now said a thing that she can never go back on. I don't quite know how many of these *vestigia ecclesiae* we are going to be allowed to be in possession of in Presbyterianism, but it is obvious that we have some of them. And when you open a door, even though it be an indefinable chink, an awful lot of light can come through, and much more charity. And I therefore want to express my very grateful appreciation for the fact that this quite marvelous event has happened, that we are no longer to regard ourselves as completely unchurched. Furthermore, the marvelous charity with which we are being received is an even more splendid manifestation of this fact.

MEYENDORFF: I would like to make a very brief comment on this issue of *communicatio in sacris* and focus the issue. It seems to me that the main criticism that we Orthodox have on the issue is the separation—I think consciously made on the part of the Fathers of Vatican II—between sacramental validity and sacramental life and faith. It seems to me that the remark of Father Stransky about this hierarchy of values and which comes first, Christ or Peter, sort of focuses the problem. Because, if Christ and Peter are in any sense opposed to each other, it means that there is something wrong, either with Christ or with Peter. There is then, on the one hand, Peter as the symbol of the communion in the magisterium as understood by the Roman

Church, the institutional Church as understood by Roman Catholic brethren, and, on the other hand, the sacramental reality that exists outside of it. It seems to me that since sacramental communion implies a full communion in faith, this commitment, this full commitment of Christians, can be made only in the Church of God. Now can you make a commitment of that sort in a community which you do not see as being *the* Church of God? This seems to me the problem.

LINDBECK: It seems to me that it's probably necessary under a circumstance such as this to make the point that it's not simply that the Catholic Church is now becoming enlightened and arriving at the position where other Christian communions, at least some of them, have been for a long time in regards to ecumenism. I myself belong to a tradition that contains in its confessional writings the assertion that the papacy is the Antichrist. The clergy of this communion, in their ordination vows, still assert that they believe that the confessional writings are in basic harmony with Scripture. This doesn't mean that they commit themselves to this particular proposition but do nevertheless commit themselves to a body of writings that contains this proposition.

Everybody is aware of the fact that for centuries now Protestantism has looked at Rome as that Christian body which has publicly committed itself to a position that comes closer to blasphemy than any other Christian body has done, comes closer to absolutizing the finite. The problem that is raised for Protestants by this *Decree on Ecumenism*, it seems to me, is whether in fact we can seriously say that we believe that the Roman Catholic communion as an organized body is a church that at one very fundamental point is not in error to a greater degree than other Christian communions. The traditional Protestant tradition is that at one fundamental point the Roman Catholic Church is in error in a way that no other Christian communion is. This kind of talk is very uncommon in ecumenical circles. It is the sort of thing that has been avoided in the World Council circles, where many Protestant groups tend to have a somewhat similar, though not equally severe, set of questions regarding the Orthodox. But it is not very politic to discuss this in World Council circles normally. I am not proposing that there are no answers; as a matter of fact, most Protestants here would have very quick answers to the questions I've raised. All I'm saying is that realism demands that we constantly be aware of the fact that as communions, as communities vis-à-vis Rome, we are at least as condemnatory and remain as condemnatory among the mass of the people as Catholic attitudes have ever been toward Protestant Churches.

SITTLER

McGRATH

MOELLER

SESSION X

Most Rev. Mark G. McGrath, c.s.c.
The Constitution on the Church in the Modern World

Canon Charles Moeller
Man, the Church and Society

Dr. Joseph Sittler
A Protestant Point of View

Most Rev. Mark G. McGrath, c.s.c.

THE CONSTITUTION ON THE CHURCH
IN THE MODERN WORLD

T HIS IS THE LONGEST DOCUMENT by far that any Council has ever produced. Of itself that is a dubious merit, especially for those who over the course of three years had to rework the entire document time and time again. It is also the most original document of this Council, not merely by quantitative criterion, but because it is the first time a Council has so directly and assiduously addressed itself to the whole broad question of the Church and the temporal order.

Yet the originality of this Constitution is that of the Council itself. No other document is more typical of Vatican Council II. The fact that neither this nor any document resembling it was to be found among the nearly four score drafts drawn up before the Council for the consideration of the Council Fathers is in itself a measure and a sign of what happened within the Council. The very thrust of the Council, toward an *aggiornamento* of the Church in today's world, made this document necessary. This was not obvious at the beginning, but it became increasingly so. As Archbishop Garrone, the final *relator* charged with presenting the Constitution to the Fathers for their approbation, so aptly put it, this Constitution "is at the very heart of the Council. One could say that it is the only schema formally willed by John XXIII," that is in what he desired of the Council, although as a text it was not put together until well into the Council. "It is the prolongation of the *Constitution on the Church*, and it represents an endeavor to place the

Church in dialogue with the world, truthfully and realistically. In *Lumen Gentium* the Church readied herself so that she could talk to the world. It will become increasingly obvious that between *Lumen Gentium* and this Constitution there is a passage from preparing for action to the action itself."

The purpose of this first talk is to describe the conception and birth of this singular document—out of the very heart of Vatican Council II.

It was a difficult birth—given the nature of the infant. Work on the document, even when officially ordered, got under way slowly. Time and again its aims and methods were subjected to doubt and debate: Whom is the Council addressing in this document? From what standpoint—revelation? Natural law? Should specific questions be treated or merely general doctrine? Almost down to the last few days of harried labor many doubted that the document would ever see the Conciliar light of day.

First Stage: Emergence of the Idea

Anyone willing to do so can find many of the preoccupations of this Constitution reflected in the schemata prepared by the pre-Conciliar commissions.[1] Yet there they were parts of other separate treatises, written to teach, to exhort or sometimes to condemn, not yet caught up in the spirit and the driving purpose that was to unify vision of the Council and give birth to the Constitution on *The Church in the Modern World*.

Words and events of the first session from October 7 to December 8, 1962, set this spirit and began to clarify this vision: the inaugural discourse of Pope John XXIII, especially his insistence that we had not come together to condemn errors or to repeat old doctrines, but with optimism for the world we live in to offer it every service a renewed Church could provide; the election of the Council's commission members, delayed three days so that candidates could be presented by each separate hierarchy, thus assuring on the commissions the continued representation of the Church's preoccupations in every corner of the world; the open and cordial message to the entire world approved by all the Council Fathers as they were about to begin their first debates; the renewed vision of the Church and of the People of God, united in his word and his worship, which led to the pastoral conclusions favoring variety and adaptability in the external forms of the liturgy to facilitate a fuller participation of the People of God in the liturgy of the word and of sacrifice and sacrament; the anxiety throughout the debate on the

---

[1] Cf. the pre-Conciliar or preparatory doctrinal commission's (Commissio de doctrina fidei et morum) schemata entitled: *De ordine morali, De matrimonio et familia, De ordine sociali* and *De communitate gentium;* the schemata of the preparatory commission on the discipline of the clergy and the Christian people (*De disciplina cleri et populi christiani*) entitled: *De cura animarum* and *De Communismo;* and that of the commission on the apostolate of the faithful (*De apostolatu fidelium*), entitled *De apostolatu laicorum.*

double source of revelation to be faithful to the developed sciences of scriptural hermeneutics and its ancillary studies; in this and in other matters, the anxiety to avoid all positions unnecessarily offensive to other Christians, understanding their viewpoints, expressing our own as intelligibly as possible to them and stressing more what unites us than what divides, according to the norms of ecumenical dialogue as set forth in the rousing speech given on the Council floor by Bishop de Smedt of Bruges; the innumerable conferences by bishops and theologians given all over the Holy City; the formal and informal discussions that multiplied in the religious houses and hotels of Rome among all concerned; the work groups preparing studies on the Church of the poor, aid to the underdeveloped nations, marriage and other palpitating themes—all brought to clear expression by the speeches of Cardinal Suenens, Cardinal Lercaro and the then Cardinal Montini in the closing days of the first session (1962), insisting that the Council should thenceforth center its attention upon the double theme of the Church and the Church in relation to the world.

SECOND STAGE: PREPARATION OF A SCHEMA FOR COUNCIL DEBATE

Pope John instituted a Coordinating Commission, composed of seven cardinals, which shortly after the close of the first session reduced the more than seventy pre-Conciliar schemata to seventeen, the first of which was *De Ecclesia* (On the Church) and the last *De presentia Activa Ecclesiae in Mundo* (On the Active Presence of the Church in the World). This latter document, called then and for a time schema 17, was to be drawn up by a mixed commission, made up of the Doctrinal Commission and the Commission on the Lay Apostolate. Cardinal Suenens, as a member of the Coordinating Commission, was named *relator* of the schema by his colleagues and charged with getting it under way. He communicated to the responsible mixed commission an outline of what was expected of them. Drawing upon some of the pre-Conciliar schemata wherever possible, a new schema was to be prepared consisting of six chapters: the first was on the admirable vocation of man in its full human and Christian meaning; then five specific chapters were to follow dealing respectively with: person and personal rights, marriage and the family, culture and its spread, the socio-economic order and the community of nations and peace.

The work on schema 17 got under way slowly. The Doctrinal Commission was brought to Rome at the end of January; the members received the outlines of the new schema, described above. But almost all their time was consumed on another task, a difficult and trying one, the writing of a new schema on divine revelation, working with the Secretariat for Christian Unity, to replace the pre-Conciliar schema on the double source of revelation, which had not been accepted by the Council. Only toward the end of the three-week Commission session was time found to meet with the Commission on the Lay Apostolate, to divide the members of the mixed commission (twenty-four from each side, in principle, though not all were in Rome) into mixed subcommittees, composed of a few members from each commission, to begin the consideration of each of the six proposed chapters of the new schema. Some of the theologians attached to the pre-Conciliar commissions had already prepared drafts of a few of the five latter and more specific chapters. These were not very successful. Some of them retained too much of the text-bookish, moralistic and somewhat negative tone that had characterized the pre-Conciliar schemata from which they were drawn. Each subcommittee agreed on some guidelines for the matter charged to it, put its trust in a few theologians whom they chose to work out the next drafts, and there the matter was left.

In May, 1963, the commissions were in Rome once more. By now the Doctrinal Commission had finished most of its work on the *Constitution on Divine Revelation*, but was hard at work on the draft of the *Constitution on the Church*, which had been begun in its new form in January, so that once more but little time, the final days, could be dedicated to schema 17. Nonetheless, the subcommittees worked hard. On Friday, May 31, as the last of them turned in their new drafts, Pope John XXIII entered upon his death agony. The world watched and prayed with him until his death three days later. All was in suspense.

Little was heard of schema 17 at the time the Council was reconvened under Pope Paul VI. In his inaugural discourse for the second session he did not mention it, though very significantly he spelled out the four ends of the Council: meditation on the Church, renewal of the Church, the ecumenical effort and the throwing out of a bridge from the Church to the world. This colorful expression was to be quoted often in later discussions, emphasizing as it did the chasm that had opened so broadly in modern times between the Church and the world, and the Church's desire to bridge it.

During the protracted discussion of the second session, which concentrated largely on the *Constitution on the Church*, little was heard of schema 17. Finally, in late November a plenary session of the mixed commission (now increased to sixty members, thirty on each commission), assisted by over fifty theologians and other experts, met to take stock of the situation. The members had been informed that the Coordinating Commission (which had since been replaced in its authority by a larger body called the Council of Presidency, including the twelve presidents, the four moderators and the members of the Secretariat of the Council) had decided that the draft of the document as completed in May was not yet mature enough for discussion on the Council floor. The first chapter, "The Admirable Vocation of Man," was found particularly wanting. Cardinal Suenens had been charged with preparing a new draft of this chapter. He had called together in Belgium a small number of European theologians for this purpose, and their draft for the chapter was presented to the members of the commission. It was markedly dogmatic in its approach.

There ensued a lively debate between those who contended that a truly Conciliar approach to social questions must be theological in the proper sense of proceeding from data of revelation to doctrinal conclusions, and the other school, arguing ardently from the profound impact caused in the world by the two great social encyclicals of Pope John XXIII (*Mater et Magistra* and *Pacem in Terris*) that any document meant to speak to the modern world must begin from a consideration of the world's problems and speak to men in language and with arguments that they can understand and accept. The lengthy and somewhat confused debate, complicated by the unwieldy number of participants, threatened an impasse. But a practical decision was taken: a small steering committee (called a central mixed subcommittee) was elected, composed of three members from each commission, to put a new draft together, utilizing the older ones but trying to keep in mind the criticisms expressed by members of the mixed commission. Those elected were Bishop Schroeffer (Germany), Bishop Ancel (France) and Bishop McGrath (Panama) of the Doctrinal Commission; and Bishop Guano (Italy), Bishop Hengsbach (Germany) and Bishop Menager (France) of the Commission on the Lay Apostolate. Since five of the six elected members were from Europe, the six requested the Cardinal presidents of the Mixed Commission, Cardinal Ottaviani and Cardinal Cento, that Bishop Wright of the United States and Bishop Blomjous of Africa be added to their number to assure a broader perspective. This was done. The members then chose Bishop Guano as their president and invited Father Bernard Häring, C.S.R., to act as secretary.

It was agreed by the mixed commission that the first or "doctrinal" chapter would be developed more at length, to which a final chapter would be added indicating briefly the chief problem areas that had been written up before in chapters 2 to 6 (person, marriage, and so forth). These chapters would be published separately as appendices (the famous *adnexa*), under the responsibility of the mixed commission. They would not constitute a Conciliar document, since they would not be debated or voted upon on the floor of the Council, but rather a highly official commentary on the Conciliar document. This well-intentioned proposal reflected the lingering unwillingness of the commission members to plunge the Council into the debate of many temporal issues that seemed too passing, too contingent to become the object of a Conciliar document meant to stand for the ages. Also many were concerned with the time element. The debate and vote on so many particular issues could be almost interminable. But there was uneasiness about the *adnexa* from the beginning. The commission, in its majority, felt that they were necessary for the proper understanding of the document and therefore should be published simultaneously with it. Yet what authority would they really have? The Council Fathers were to express their concern that their document would be commented upon by *adnexa* over which they would have no control. The colorful phrase of Cardinal Heenan made the headlines: *Timeo peritos adnexa ferentes* ("I fear the experts bearing *adnexa*"). Furthermore, the Council Fathers did plunge into the discussion of the particular issues, and by the second appearance of the schema for discussion on the Council floor at the beginning of the fourth session, the *adnexa* were back into the text of the schema as separate chapters. What this meant most significantly was that the Council had gotten over the novelty of the whole idea and had committed itself to discussing at some length in a Conciliar document many questions at once temporal and transitory.

The steering committee met twice briefly in Rome before the end of the second session and decided upon the main lines of the work to be done. A handful of theologians were chosen who, under the direction of Bishop Guano, as president, and Father Bernard Häring, as secretary, were to prepare the new draft.

At the end of January, 1964, in Zurich, Switzerland, this small group went over the new text. What they worked out and approved was to undergo much more revision; yet the basic content, method, address and style began to emerge with greater clarity and conviction.

This draft was sent to the members of the mixed commission, already augmented to sixty by the election of six new members to each of the two commissions (Doctrinal and the Lay Apostolate), and to the experts of each of these commissions. In March, amidst other occupations, time was found for two plenary sessions of the mixed commission to hear and comment on the new text. The steering committee took the spoken (and written) observations of the commission members and theologians as the basis for a new revision. This was presented anew to the mixed plenary commission in three days of concentrated debate in early June. Only two of the *adnexa* were discussed, and not at length. The main attention was spent upon the schema itself, which, duly approved by a quasi unanimity (the *quasi* is important), was sent to the Coordinating Commission of the Council, which approved it for distribution to the Council Fathers and discussion on the floor at the third session of the Council.

Thus ends the second stage. The mixed commission had been charged with preparing a text along certain given lines. It had done so, according to its own lights. Once this text was given to the Council Fathers and was discussed by them, the role of the commission changed. From then on it was to revise and improve the text not by its own lights, but according to the suggestions and directives most representative of the expressed opinions of the Council Fathers.

It is very interesting to note that from January, 1963, until June, 1964, when a text was approved for Council debate, both the commissions (Doctrinal and Lay Apostolate) were busy on other tasks that were more pressing and that most of their members considered to be far more important. The organization of the Council proved defective in that it permitted such a heavy concentration of work to devolve upon a few commissions, notably the Doctrinal, while some others had little or nothing to do once their schemata were either suppressed or gravely foreshortened in the sweeping decisions taken in January, 1963. This situation hampered the work on schema 13. But undeniably there was another factor at work, to which I have already alluded. Many, especially on the Doctrinal Commission, found it hard to take this new document very seriously. Compared to the great dogmatic *Constitutions on the Church* and *on Revelation*, this new schema seemed to be very light fare indeed. The fact that the title given the schema was changed with almost every new revision left it almost *innominatus* (without a name). It was referred to for a time as schema 17; and then, when the list of Conciliar schemata was again reduced, it became the thirteenth, still the last. It was disparagingly referred to as "illud famosum schema XIII," "that extraordinary schema 13." Some of the Orientals thought it purely social preoccuption if not, perhaps, a bit of socialism. Some of the members of the Doctrinal Commission, most of whom were former professors of Scripture or theology, as well as some of their theologians, could only come with difficulty to accept this "social" document as truly Conciliar. For a few of them, of course, its new approach to today's problems and its effort to illuminate these problems precisely, rather than repeat older expositions of theology on the various areas treated, went against the grain. All in all, it took the pressure of debate on the Council floor, to which was quickly added the mounting interest of the press and of the listening world, to give this Constitution its due importance in the full perspective of the Council.

Third Stage: Council Debate and Revision

A. During the Third Session

The text as proposed to the Council contained a brief prologue, which stated very simply the Church's identification with the "joys and sorrows" of the world and the Council's desire to speak to her faithful and all who would listen about the "signs of the times," and what we should understand from them and therefore try to do for the welfare of men in our day. The first three chapters treated the doctrinal presentation of the full vocation of man, the Church of God committed to the service of men and the manner in which Christians should bear themselves in the world. Then came the indication of key contemporary problems in chapter 4 and a brief exhortatory conclusion.

Even before the schema came up for debate on the floor, the steering committee, augmented by the invitation of other members and theologians from both commissions, had several meetings to consider the written observations that had already come in from a good number of bishops, episcopal conferences and *periti*. A mimeographed note was given out to the Council Fathers to indicate a few changes the steering committee itself suggested on the basis of these observations. These concerned principally doctrinal clarifications and an effort to avoid a presentation of the world and its problems that would be excessively European or even Western. Two special subcommittees were set up immediately. Each met frequently during the following weeks. One was to analyze the biblical and doctrinal concepts underlying the entire schema. It was agreed that the schema was not a strictly doctrinal exposé, but it was felt that the notions of "Church," "world," and the like, as well as the biblical references and a series of doctrinal points needed more careful analysis. The other subcommittee was to study the notion of "the signs of the times," a term used in the document in imitation of John XXIII, and the description of these "signs," to be sure that this would reflect with sufficient universality the situation of the entire world and not merely its Western part. The spadework done by these two subcommittees during this third session contributed notably to the later emendations of the text. Archbishop Garrone, who headed the so-called doctrinal subcommittee, continued later as *relator* charged with the whole doctrinal section of the schema, and, upon the illness of Bishop Guano, as *relator* of the entire schema for the final session of the Council. The subcommittee on the "signs of the times," or, as it was later called, "on the universal outlook of the schema," held meetings with bishops and experts from each of the various major sectors of the Church and compiled their observations into a small volume, which helped the commission members in all further revisions of the text. This led to the inclusion of more bishops from the underdeveloped areas and communist nations on the steering committee and eventually to the composition of the expository introduction to the Constitution with all that it came to signify for the tone and the method employed throughout the document.

Bishop Guano's presentation of the text to the Council Fathers stressed the urgent necessity of this schema as the Council's effort to bridge the gap of mutual ignorance, diffidence, indifference or apparent hostility often evident between the Church and the world of the modern age. Referring to the will of Pope John and Pope Paul (as expressed in his recent encyclical *Ecclesiam Suam* and in the discourse with which he opened this third session of the Council) he urged this schema as the vehicle and the sign of the new dialogue with the world.

The Council approved the schema in general with a more than sufficient plurality, but not before fifty-two speakers had worked it over quite thoroughly. Their speeches as well as the many written observations sent in set the stage for the next revision. There were 830 pages of observations sent in by the Council Fathers. Style was a first observation; the Latin of the text was castigated. This highlighted a problem. Generally, first drafts of the texts had been done in French. The Latin translations were not always good renditions of the sense or even good Latin. Toward the end of the work in March, 1965, it was insisted that all first drafts be done in Latin; and after much debate the rule was set and held that in every instance clarity of expression, often through the use of modernized terms, was to be preferred over classical correctness. Cardinal Bea's insistence in both sessions, 1964 and 1965, helped determine this rule.

Biblical references were found to be often imprecise. Many pointed out incoherencies and repetitions throughout the text. (In fact the individual chapters had been done by separate subcommittees without sufficient time for their proper correlation.) The speakers often referred to the *adnexa*, a fact which encouraged their reintroduction into the text itself. Many stressed once more the need for a more universal description of the world, with stronger emphasis on hunger and other human needs in the underdeveloped areas. The problem of address came up time and again. To whom is the Council speaking—to Catholics directly, and only secondarily to other men, or to all men? (Eventually it was decided to change over to an address directed to all men.) In what manner did the document speak—from the basis of natural law or from a Christian view of things? (Eventually a mixed method would result: a presentation of the real order and state of things, fully comprehensible by all men, and thereupon a reflection on these matters in the light of the gospel.)

The most fundamental of all the criticisms was directed at the manner in which the life of the Church and of Christians in the world was presented. Not only were the terms "Church" and "world" found to be used unclearly and ambiguously. Cardinals Meyer, Doepfner and other bishops also pointed out the lack of a unified vision more profoundly biblical in its roots and in its expression, which resulted in a false dualism and gave to the entire text a heavily moralistic tone, lacking the teleological dynamism of creation.

There were other matters insisted upon: that atheism be treated more completely under its various forms, that the vocation of man in the world be more fully spelled out, and so on. In short, the Council Fathers were plunging into the heart of the schema, feeling its purpose, finding it yet immature, but on the whole guiding it and wishing it "Godspeed."

Bishop Guano spoke once more, just before the affirmative vote on the schema, expressed the thanks of the mixed commission for the excellent criticisms given, summed them up, answered some and promised that they would all guide the next revision. The steering committee went to work again (November 17 to 20). It made several important proposals, which were accepted by the plenary mixed commission:

1. Besides the eight original members of the steering committee, elected at the close of the second session (November 29, 1963), eight others were elected at this time (November 16, 1964), and five others from India, Japan, Africa, Poland and the Near East were drafted from outside the mixed commission, as well as one from Italy and one from Spain who had spoken well on the Constitution, in order to provide a bigger working team and an expanded vision for the growing work of the steering committee.

2. Six *periti* were chosen to form a team of writers for further drafting and editing. Father Haubtmann of Paris would be the initial composer, Father Häring continued as secretary, while Msgr. Philips, now freed from the work on *Lumen Gentium*, would serve as the final supervisor of the text. Fathers Tucci, Hirschmann and Moeller completed the team. It would work under the authority of the steering committee and specifically of its president, Bishop Guano, and of Bishop Ancel, recently elected vice-president.

3. A general description of the world, later to be called an expository introduction, would be put together. This became the task of the subcommittee on "the signs of the times," under Bishop McGrath, largely made up of the bishops from the so-called Third World (the orient, Africa, Latin America), ably assisted by Father Houtart and other *periti*. This subcommittee was also to submit its criticisms of the entire text as to the validity of its observations for the non-European world.

4. The *adnexa* were to be substantially incorporated into the text.

Thus the text took on a new form: a brief prologue, the expository introduction, a first part made up of the doctrinal chapters, a second part composed of the reincorporated *adnexa* in place of the previous resumé of them in one sole chapter and the conclusion.

B. JANUARY TO SEPTEMBER, 1965

By the end of January the new team of writers put together a draft of the prologue, expository introduction (based on a proposition of the subcommittee "on the signs of the times") and the first or doctrinal part (based on the previous text and the observations of the Council Fathers which had been duly studied and classified).

From January 31 to February 6, twenty-nine Council Fathers (the full steering committee and a few other Fathers specially invited), thirty-eight *perii* and about twenty lay men and women auditors and invited experts worked in the town of Ariccia, near Rome, in an atmosphere of prayer and dedicated labor, which marked a decisive step forward for schema thirteen. The task was not easy. At this point the commission was still entitled to revise freely. Yet it had to use the text proposed to the Council Fathers in the third session as the basis of its work, and all revisions had to go along the lines indicated by a consensus of the Fathers who had expressed their points of view. The work was done first in small subcommittees, one for each part: the expository introduction, the doctrinal chapters, the specific chapters to be built out of the *adnexa*. Soon it became evident that the specific chapter on person and personal rights, the first chapter of the second part, could well be suppressed and its contents brought into the first chapter of the first part where the vocation of man was now centered on the concept of person, under the title "On the Vocation of the Human Person." In the chapter on marriage, the candescent question of birth control was to be spoken of only in general terms, leaving all questions of methods licitly to be employed to the special papal commission studying these matters. A draft of a new chapter, "Political Life," was drawn up to fill a lacuna that had become obvious in the second part. A late arrival, this chapter never would reach maturity or say very much. The chapters on marriage, culture, the economic and social order and on the community of nations and peace retained their original orientations as found in the *adnexa*, but were deepened and perfected. Little had been said, relatively, on these chapters during the third session, since the *adnexa* were not directly under discussion then. But it was enough to guide the work and especially to forewarn about the points of major concern. The chapter on the community of nations and peace was much expanded so as to build up a positive, dynamic presentation of peace in terms of social and international justice and collaboration, while in the treatment on war the delicate question of total war advanced considerably toward a formulation at once Christian and realistic.

It is here that one may bring in the question of how adequately competent experts in all these areas were consulted by the commission. Lay auditors had been consulted from the beginning, as in a special session held with a group of them as early as April, 1963 on this schema. Yet most of these auditors, and other laymen who took part in the discussions during 1963 and 1964, were Catholic apostolic leaders of broad culture and intimate knowledge of the Church, without however qualifying as experts in the areas of science, technology, communication media, culture, economics, politics and the arts of war that were touched upon by the schema. There were exceptions, but not enough. The lack was made up by a number of clerical experts in the social sciences (Fathers Lebret, Calvez, Houtart, and others), by the consultations many commission members carried out with outstanding experts in their own countries or continents, and by other consultations solicited and obtained from experts by correspondence. But more was needed. Ariccia was a breakthrough. The presence of laymen, more of them specifically competent in one or other area touched upon by the schema, was more comforting. This effort was intensified throughout 1965. Yet the obvious lack of communication between the Council and the world's outstanding lay experts in the secular arts and sciences was a serious problem throughout the history of schema 13. One can hope that the Constitution itself, now published, by its very insistence on this point, will overcome this situation, so typical of the chasm between the Church and the world that it would span.

The most difficult work at Ariccia devolved upon the large subcommittee directed by Archbishop Garrone and charged with the whole doctrinal part. Most of the criticism of the third session had hit at this part. The exposition had to be more centered on man, avoiding a dualist nature and super-nature view, and searching for a biblical vision that would still embrace natural values and indeed be so presented as to speak to men in terms of the life and society they live in today. A new order of chapters evolved: the vocation of the human person, the community of men, the meaning of human striving in the universe and the role of the Church in the world today. Here, at last, began to evolve in more coherent form and for the first time in any Conciliar document, a biblical Catholic synthesis of the meaning of Christian man and Christian society on earth and in time striving toward eternity. It was more than a set of moral laws for the individual, or a code of Christian social teaching for a here-and-now society. But it was still immature. Not only did the authors wish to avoid any partial so-called theology of history which would be that of one school or some few theologians, but also they recognized the still imperfect state of thinking in the Church on these vast problems, so acutely posed in our times.

Much effort was expended, as yet with little success, in setting forth the various forms of modern atheism in a manner that would reveal, rather than condemn the inadequacy of any concept of man cut off from God, the source and ultimate meaning of his and of all existence.

The Ariccia text was presented, discussed and approved during the following week in laborious and tedious sessions of the plenary mixed commission. It became evident that once more there were serious problems of incoherencies and repetitions between the various chapters, prepared by separate subcommittees and not yet properly integrated into one whole.

The mixed commission had hoped to schedule another plenary session for June or July so that the team of authors, working under Bishop Guano, would have ample time to iron out the many difficulties discovered and the many alterations proposed in the meeting that ended in February. But the Council's Coordinating Commission decreed otherwise. Since the Council

408

session of 1965 was to be the last, all the documents had to be edited and sent to the Council Fathers by May. Thus the plenary mixed commission found itself once more in sesssion in Rome from March 29 to April 6, confronted by a text not yet fully corrected and edited in its Latin form according to the suggestions made in February. Working once more beyond all accustomed hours, the commission read through and evaluated the now quite lengthy text and left to the team writers the task of incorporating all the changes it had approved. As one *peritus* remarked, those who worked on schema 13, for three full years were so constantly pressed that it was always as though all had to be done in a day.

On May 11 the schema was approved by the Council's Coordinating Commission and sent to the Council Fathers with the indication that unlike most Conciliar texts this one would be submitted again to discussion on the Council floor.

C. THE FOURTH SESSION OF THE COUNCIL, SEPTEMBER TO DECEMBER 1965

The mood of many on the steering committee at the start of the fourth and last session of the Council was not optimistic regarding schema 13. They felt all had been done that was genuinely possible. Yet the difficulties inherent in this most novel Council document, plus the delays occasioned by other labors, had not permitted them to perfect a document such as they would have wished to have in hand at this late hour. Basically it was good, what was wanted, what was urgently needed. But it was immature—not yet coherent in its total vision, rough in many of its details. They would have desired yet another year—of maturation, of discussion, of study, of final editing.

None could suspect how much they would have to work in that final session or how much they would accomplish in months of unbroken labor. The criticisms of the Council Fathers guided them; the swelling interest of the press and a world public sustained them; the decisive favor of Paul VI encouraged them; and quite literally the Spirit of God carried them through incredible months of hurried days and nights until the final public proclamation of the Pastoral *Constitution on the Church in the Modern World* on December 7, 1965. It is not a perfect text, but far more mature, coherent and to its purpose than they could have expected when the fourth session got under way.

The schedule of this last stage is interesting. The discussion of schema 13 began on September 24 and went on for two weeks. As the discourses and other written observations poured into the secretariat, they were broken down on file cards dealing with each part. Each subcommittee had a week to rewrite its section according to the new observations; for a week the plenary mixed commission read through and approved or altered the revised texts according to the express mind of the Council; and then the team of authors, working with the bishop head of each subcommittee under the over-all direction of Archbishop Garrone, now definitely in charge due to the prolonged illness of Bishop Guano, composed the new text. It reached the floor again at the beginning of November. This time it was not discussed, but voted, part by part. It was approved in several days' voting. But the Council Fathers appended to their approval over 20,000 *modi* or suggested alterations. Even though many of these were repeated, there were still thousands of individual changes proposed. These had to be classified. Then each subcommittee studied the *modi* pertaining to its parts and altered the text whenever the *modus* proposed did not change the sense of the text substantially, since all the chapters of the text had been approved by the Council, but rather bettered it by clarification or further precision. The modified texts were then read before the entire mixed commission and approved part by part and in their entirety in the closing days of November. When the final text was voted through in the early days of December it represented somewhat of a miracle. This, the longest text in Conciliar history, had been rewritten once in its entirety and then once more modified in hundreds of minor points, all within the short space of October and November.

At each presentation of the text on the Council floor, in September and in October, the *relatores* for the introduction, the doctrinal part and the second or applied part had explained the method, content and purpose of the schema. The significance of the expository introduction became more clear: to approach concretely the world in which we live with all its characteristics of change, so notably due to the scientific and technological revolutions of modern times, and the deep and extensive effects of these changes upon society and man himself, not least of all in his sense of values, his concept of the universe and his search for or indifference to the answers to the fundamental questions of life and human destiny. This empirical approach marked the novelty of the schema. In each chapter of the second part, before sketching the Christian view of one or other of the key areas of life's problems today, a similar descriptive introduction to the situation was spelled out. Even the doctrinal part views man and society in the concrete reality in which he lives today. This is more than a *captatio benevolentiae*, a good beginning for dialogue; it is a frank pursuit of the proper values of the things and structures and situations of which the life of man is made, values which are theirs of themselves, and which must be understood to be lived and to be offered to God through the men who live them together in their striving for him. It is also a clear statement that doctrinal and moral judgments of life must be true to life and its conditions. It is above all a statement, however imperfect, of the meaning of our every effort for a better world today as a preparation for the heavenly world to come.

It is to be noted that the descriptive introduction is of set purpose objective, even phenomenological. Throughout, it centers its observations on the human person alone and in society as effecting change and affected by the changes described. At the insistence of Cardinal Doepfner, Bishop Volk and others, two significant improvements were worked into the closing paragraphs of the final edition: first, an indication of the division existing within the heart of each man and its projection upon society, expressed in a paraphrase of St. Paul, Romans 7; and secondly, a carry-over from the anthropological view, so common today, to the unity of man in Christ, the new creature, changing and unchanged through the centuries. These passages were meant to introduce directly the doctrinal considerations of the first part.

If we remember what the first or doctrinal part is trying to do, we can understand better the difficulties inherent in its composition. Canon Moeller will explain them. I will simply mention the changes. Atheism is discussed more in length, still in the positive context of a fuller concept of man. The condemnation of communism or of Marxist atheism requested by a minority was rejected by the Commission because: 1) it would have changed the positive tone of the text as approved by the great majority; 2) it would have required the condemnation of other forms of atheism as well; 3) it is too complicated a question: the object of the condemnation would need to have been very precisely described in order that the Council would not appear to be condemning economic theories or other aspects of Marxism not necessarily condemnable or atheistic.

The more fundamental questions of the first chapter deal with the paradoxical situation of man, made in God's image, yet sinful, immortal yet tantalized by the spectre of death. These aspects and the fuller centering of anthropology in Christ were the most telling suggestions of the Council Fathers. Chapter 3 is the doctrinal heart of the entire schema: the vision of faith on the meaning of time for eternity—a scriptural Christian response to the interrogation posed by the very title of the Constitution. Why are we interested in human progress? What is the intrinsic concern? The final text is clearer, more precise, has certainly helped to clarify our thought and urge it.

Since the chapters of the second part were not discussed during the third session, when they were but humble *adnexa*, many individual alterations were proposed on the floor during the fourth session. Yet the work of the subcommittees proved to be competent. The chapters were improved but not substantially altered. One must remark, nevertheless, that the real progress of these chapters is not so much in their content, mostly expressed in modern Catholic social teaching; or in the synthesis, the putting together of all these points; or even in the fact that the Council would concern itself so urgently with these affairs. It is rather in the approach. The empirical description of the given situation, initiated by the descriptive introduction, is carried on at

411

the start of each new chapter. Does the theological vision of the first part also dominate the moralism of the second? I would say very imperfectly. There is a contrast between the parts in this respect that augurs radically new approaches in our moral theology.

The title of the Constitution reflects its timeliness. It is a question of the *Church in the Modern World*—not merely the modern world of recent centuries but the modern world of *today*, the world in which we live here and now, at this moment. The qualification given the document, that of *Pastoral Constitution*, decided after long consideration, bears out its purpose and nature. Fundamentally it is doctrinal, a Constitution, both in the doctrinal part, so called, and in the applications of doctrine to our present situation. But it is in purpose pastoral, directed to action, the action of Christians, in the mind and spirit of Christ, for the service of the world, in dialogue and cooperation with all men of good will.

The conclusion of the Constitution bears repeated reading. It is an exhortation to Christians to act for all men, in truth and charity, and an invitation to all men to dialogue and to common effort for a better world. But it is more than that. It admits to the imperfection of the Constitution itself—an imperfection due to the diversity of problems about the world that no single document can pretend to exhaust and to the continual appearance of new situations and to new problems; an imperfection whose remedy lies in the continuation and application of this dialogue by Christians the world around, under the guidance of their pastors, with all men.

The Constitution calls for this dialogue to go on—in the manner begun.

Canon Charles Moeller

MAN, THE CHURCH AND SOCIETY

I AM GOING TO LIMIT MYSELF to enumerating the essential points of the first part and to try bringing out the theological structure present in the text. I will do it very briefly because the discussion yesterday morning of Barnabas Ahern's paper brought us to the heart of the problem.

I. THE CHURCH AND THE WORLD

My first point is that the fundamental underlying image of the Church in schema 13 is that of the People of God; I say "underlying" because in fact it does not appear very readily. At the time of the last revision of the text during the fourth session, the Fathers wished to avoid giving the impression of a chosen people separated from the rest of men, by insisting too much on the words "People of God." That is why the first article speaks of the community of believers. The central image of the Church in this text is that of the People of God present in a world of diaspora, in a pluralistic world, in the world of today. The word "world" was defined in the final edition and was largely the work of German-speaking experts. In a single phrase we are told that the world it speaks of is that of men, one which is the theater of the successes and disasters (clades—a very strong Latin word). Believers know that this very world was created by God, that it was spoiled and corrupted by sin and is under the power of the evil spirit, that it was redeemed, transfigured by Christ and called to its fulfillment.

This second article, in the minds of those who drew it up, was supposed to dominate the whole schema. Each time that the word "world" is used, one must think of this paradoxical reality of the world of men which we love, which we wish to improve, and of this wounded world under the power of the evil spirit but redeemed by Christ.

II. The Church and the Human Vocation

"What is man," exclaims the Psalmist, "that thou art mindful of him; or the son of man, that thou art concerned about him? And thou hast made him a little less than the angels; thou hast crowned him with glory and honor, thou hast given him power over the works of thy hands; thou hast placed all things under his feet" (Ps 8:5–7). These words sum up the fundamental intention of the pastoral *Constitution on the Church in the Modern World*. The Church is also at the service of men.

It was indeed a doctrine on man, an anthropology, that the Council wanted to outline. "One of the most important tasks," Charles du Bos wrote, is to write a new "treatise on the soul."[1] No doubt. But a more urgent need, and a much greater one, invites us to sketch out, first of all, a treatise on man.

Schema 13 wishes, in fact, to present man in the concrete, "with flesh and bones," one who in his bodily condition sums up the physical universe, and is rooted in space and time, which the Bible teaches were created by God, the place of a history having meaning, for it is open to hope. Here we are, then, suddenly beyond that dualism which practically separated soul from body. Without ever mentioning Nietzsche, the Constitution goes beyond that "Platonism for the people"[2] which the German philosopher saw in Christianity.

Hence it is not first of all the individual man, isolated in his library, or taking refuge in the "serene temples"[3] of wisdom, that is presented, but man in the world, the human person, the community of men, man in the universe. The first three chapters of part I revolve around these three theological truths.

Man was created in the image of God. Some say that this expression is obscure for the contemporary mind. One has only to look to the first chapter of Genesis to discover the fundamental meaning of this theme: "Man was created in the image of God." That means that he is called to dominate the world, to bring it under subjection, to make it human. Of course, being created in the image of God also means man's intelligence, liberty and conscience. In a time too much given to utilitarianism, it is good to insist on the importance of disinterested research, on contemplation. This does not prevent the power that man exercises on the universe from being rooted in his divine vocation. Who does not see the light this throws on the scientific work by which humanity tries to construct a "better world"?[4]

I have just spoken of humanity; it is to the community of men that this task has devolved. Man, created in the image of God, is "man and woman"; at the very heart of what God willed in creating him there is this relationship, this original communion; there is "more than one" that founds social life on dialogue, fraternity and love. It is together that men exercise this activity in the universe. "The question that interests me," Teilhard de Chardin told Maurice Blondel in 1917, "is to know whether what nine-tenths of humanity does during nine-tenths of its time, namely, building the earthly city, has any meaning in relation to the kingdom of God."[5] Schema 13 tries to recall a few principles used by theology to reply to this crucial question.

We will discover here a second theological idea, that of the *Servant of Yahweh* such as it appears in Isaiah 53. Looking more closely at the theme "Image of God," we discovered a first outline of the royal dignity of man. Later we discovered more deeply hidden in it the community of men, and especially man and woman.

Here, in the light of a more profound revelation, we read an even more secret, fundamental sign, that of the *obedience of the Servant of God*. Because Christ, the new Adam, perfect image of God, was obedient unto death, he was exalted above every name and was made Lord of the universe. He is then the new Adam but also *Eschatos Anaer*, the man of eschatological times.

But this human creature fell into sin. The French philosopher, Albert Garaudy, in connection with schema 13 as finally drawn up, spoke of the "grisaille of sin" with which "a first and much more optimistic text was sprinkled and soon covered."[6] Alas, egoism, hatred, violence are horribly visible realities. The text of the Constitution insists that the disorders existing in the world are not only due to "technical defects," to accidental errors in organization, but are rooted more deeply in an inclination to evil which splits man within himself. This is what sin is, the fundamental disorder that human remedies can never completely heal.

No doubt, this does not mean that one can always rely passively on God in struggling against evil and suffering. Rather it simply means that human hope ought to be based on Christian hope; as a sort of "future memory,"[7] it knows that God, through our efforts, while supporting them and transfiguring them, will manifest the city of peace and light, will reveal "new heavens and a new earth . . . wherein dwells justice."[8]

Thus, the center of gravity of this doctrine on man is Jesus Christ. He is the New Adam, that is, the perfect man of the consummation. The reality of his condition as man is not absorbed by his condition as Son of God; it is, on the contrary, safeguarded, founded and consecrated. It is because Christ obeyed his Father that He conquered sin and therefore death. Thus through his lordship and domination over the forces of evil, he showed the full meaning of salvation; by his death he conquered death, the liturgy tells us. And who is saved? It is the whole man, one with his human brothers and responsible for the universe which he must humanize. It is in communion with all men in Christ, in the Church, the People of God, that the community of men finds its ultimate meaning. It is in his victory over death that the universe participates mysteriously in redemption.

There is a third biblical theme present in schema 13, that of the *Word Creator and Light*. The universe was created by the Word. "All things were made through him," St. John says in the prologue of his Gospel. The Word remains close to his creation; he is present there in a veiled way even before his incarnation, as St. Irenaeus said. In the universe, then, there are realities that, without being as yet visibly touched by the visible extension of the Church, are perhaps mysteriously inhabited by the Word as Light.

Here is a principle that allows us to see meaning in all those human activities untouched by the Christian world. One can no longer call them profane; we must go beyond this distinction. To the extent that they are just and good—of this God alone is judge—human activities are illumined by the Word. Perhaps we might even see there a steppingstone of recent theology to the *universal* history of salvation.

"The Church of the Council," Pope Paul VI said in his closing address, "has been concerned not just with herself and with her relationships of union with God, but with man—man as he really is today. . . . It might be said that all this and everything else we might say about the human values of the Council have diverted the attention of the Church in Council to the trend of modern culture, centered on humanity. We would not say diverted but rather directed. . . . To love man, we say, not as a means, but as the first step toward the final and transcendent goal, which is the basis and cause of all love. And so this Council can be summed up in its ultimate religious meaning, which is none other than a friendly and urgent appeal to humanity to rediscover in fraternal love the God 'to withdraw from whom is to fall, to turn to whom is to rise again, to remain in whom is to be secure . . . to return to whom is to be reborn, in whom to dwell is to live' ".[9]

III. THE CHURCH AND ATHEISM

We have just quoted St. Augustine, "to return to God is to be reborn."[10] "An outstanding cause of human dignity lies in man's call to communion with God" (art. 19). How is it, then, "that so many of our contemporaries fail to see this intimate and vital link with God, and sometimes even reject it," to such a point that "atheism must be considered one of the most serious problems of our times" (art. 19).

We all know that this question aroused the interest of almost all the Council Fathers; it was among the most debated issues. And schema 13 devotes three sections to it. A subcommittee was, incidentally, responsible for drawing them up.

Rather than condemn, the text invites us to try to know the diverse forms of atheism and to understand their origin. Negative atheists, for example, believe it impossible to prove the existence of God or, at least, to know anything for certain about it. George Duhamel and Martin du Gard would belong to this category. Some of them would prefer to explain everything by means of the exact sciences; one thinks of Jean Rostand. Others would much rather affirm man than deny God; the philosopher Maurice Merleau-Ponty seems to think this way. Others still, atheists like Albert Camus, protest vigorously against both the moral and physical evil that fill the world. Still others, impressed by an authentic sense of man's power over the world, are less easily brought to appreciate the reality of pilgrimage toward God. Finally others, like some of Françoise Sagan's characters, "never think of God."[11]

Needless to say, the names I have just mentioned are not in the text of the Constitution; they are given here as examples of the different forms of atheism.

The Constitution goes on to analyze systematic atheism; this is what one might call "positive atheism." Sartre asserts that "atheism is humanism," in the sense that God's nonexistence is a condition for the reality of man and his involvement in the earthly city.[12] This harks back to Malraux's famous commentary on one of Nietzsche's sentences, "God is dead, therefore man is born."[13] What characterizes this widespread form of atheism is an instinctive distrust of any religious faith, for it would of itself imply an attempted evasion of, or flight from, the realities of this world in which men are hungry and thirsty, cold and sick. Man should be the "*sole* artisan and creator of his own history"[14] and of that of humanity so that his energies will be truly applied to the concrete realities of society and history. As schema 13 says, this form of atheism is often propagated and imposed by political regimes of our time; to this end they use the pressure tactics known and described by sociology.

It is important to repeat: the Council refused to hurl anathemas. The very enumeration of the diverse forms of unbelief, such as they have summarized them, suffices to show that the Council Fathers' purpose was to understand and discover the causes of atheism, both those that arise from the condition of profane or religious society and those that are occasioned by the fundamental experiences of such and such a man. The Council even refused to refer explicitly to Marxism and communism, for these terms, having so many meanings in which philosophical, economic, political and sociological elements are mixed with religious elements, could be misunderstood. In particular, people might not clearly realize the unique but definitely religious intention behind Conciliar statements on this subject.

What the text outlines is rather the essence of the Church's attitude toward atheism. Without doubt, she cannot avoid reproving the error of atheism, for it contradicts reason and the common experience of humanity. But, above all, she wishes to uncover the profound causes of unbelief in order to study them seriously. But this study emphasizes the fact that hope of celestial reward in no way diminishes the importance of earthly tasks; on the contrary, it affords new motivation for applying oneself to them. Besides, the Church asserts that without divine foundation human dignity is wounded, and the enigmas of life and death, of guilt and of sorrow, are left without an answer.

Man himself remains an unresolved question, one obscurely perceived, but more clearly in the major events of life. Does not the success of a book like Robinson's *Honest to God* show, in a paradoxical way, the profound and eternal relevance of the question of God?

However that may be, the remedy for atheism is a proper explanation of Christian doctrine as well as the integrity of the Church's life and members. The Church must be constantly renewed and purified; the riches of the Christian faith must appear more clearly, particularly in the realm of practical aid and effective charity which the present world so sorely needs, for two out of three men do not even have the vital minimum. The text of the Constitution does not hesitate to say that believers also have their share of responsibility for contemporary disbelief, for sometimes their way of explaining their faith hides rather than manifests clearly its true meaning. If the truth of St. Irenaeus' words, "The glory of God is the living man," were to appear more clearly in the life of Christians, their witness would be more evident and the road easier.

It is obvious that we have here a new way of approaching the problem. The Church of Vatican II has resolutely set out on the road of dialogue. The Holy Father wished moreover to exemplify this new approach by creating a Secretariat for Non-Believers. "For" and not "against," as Cardinal König, its first president, put it. Doubtless it is too soon to be specific about the purpose and the activities of this Secretariat, but one task it will unquestionably have will be to awaken all missionary organizations to this immense problem. The Council has shown that it is no longer possible to regard it as a corollary of pastoral activity but, on the contrary, as a major fact of our day it must be studied in preparation for preaching or any proclamation of the truths of salvation. In other words, reflection on atheism could shed a new light on Augustine's words: "You made us for yourself, O Lord, and our hearts are restless until they rest in You."[15]

418

IV. THE CHURCH AND CULTURE

The second part of the *Constitution on the Church in the Modern World* takes up a few more urgent problems, such as the dignity of marriage and of the family, economic and social life, political life, peace and war. Among these problems, that of culture is one of the most important. Chapter 2 of part II is devoted to it.

For a long time now, culture has been identified with leisurely activities that make man "more human." "Not so long ago only lawyers were considered to be really cultivated," Jacques Leclercq used to say rather ironically.[16] Culture was judged to be the ability to quote appropriately from learned books.

Now, culture is that, but it is much more than that. A man who is not cultivated is not a man at all, but a sort of animal in a forest. Once again, the "good savage" does not exist, any more than the Emile of Jean-Jacques Rousseau. Culture belongs to the essence of the human person. It is not something superfluous that one can do without; it leads to true and full humanity. It includes, therefore, the means for cultivating the land, improving social and political institutions as well as artistic expression of man's great experiences. It has, therefore, a sociological and ethnological aspect; it is realized in history and enjoys great diversity.

I hope you will forgive these somewhat pedantic words. They bring us to the heart of the problem raised by the new forms of life—science, critical judgment, psychological discoveries, industrialization, urbanization—which give culture its constantly changing character. Man becomes aware, moreover, of the fact that he is the author of his own culture; for the first time humanity can act on a planetary scale. For example, he realizes he is capable of ending the specter of misery and hunger. This is a "new humanism," marked with a sense of responsibility for one's brothers—yes, for history.

By the same token, a new series of problems arise: a conflict between universal cultural exchanges and the traditional wisdom of a people—this is the drama of Africa; a conflict between the new, particularly the scientific, culture and the so-called classical forms of culture—this is the problem of the humanities; a conflict between an inevitable specialization and a no less necessary synthesis—this is the problem of the universities; a conflict between the increase of cultural riches and the destitution of a whole part of the world—this is the question posed by one-third of the world; a conflict between the legitimate autonomy of culture and the religious attitude of self-surrender —this is one of the keys to the problem of atheism.

The Constitution does not claim to answer all of these questions; it only recalls a few principles that are necessary for the true progress of culture. The text reminds us, for example, that the obligation of seeking the things of heaven does not diminish but increases the importance of Christians' collabo-rating in the construction of a better world. In doing so, man fulfills indeed the divine order of bringing the earth into submission and of perfecting creation. At the same time, he fulfills Christ's great commandment of devot-ing oneself to one's brothers. Moreover, by the study of history, philosophy and the sciences, and through the fine arts, the human family can be enlight-ened with a reflection of eternal wisdom and even be better disposed to welcome the divine Word, present in the world, even before the incarnation. If there is, therefore, in the development of culture—for example, on the level of the physical sciences—a danger of seeing in them the sole criterion of truth, in the same scientific research done in common with patience, objectivity and forgetfulness of oneself, there are also values that can be a "preparation for the gospel," values informed, enlightened and transfigured by the charity of God.

Moreover, the bonds between the gospel and culture are many. The diverse forms of culture have always been an essential instrument in preaching the gospel. The Council reminds us that the Church is not bound indissolubly to any form of culture, but can and ought to assume them, penetrate them with her light, and in turn she receives from them the "multiple splendor" of a varied diffusion on the level of language. Moreover, mutual respect for each one of the activities is necessary. On the one hand, the Church, by announcing the gospel, "civilizes while evangelizing"; on the other, she recognizes the proper meaning of culture and sees it not just as a means of her apostolate. From this point of view the Council, relying on the texts of Vatican I, explicitly asserts the autonomy of cultural activities, in their order, and especially the sciences (art. 59).

On all this the Constitution notes some tasks that are more urgent at present (art. 60). The right of all to culture must be recognized, not only in a theoretical way—by declarations—but in a practical way. The impor-tance of this point for one-third of the world as also for rural masses and for woman in the world will escape no one. The Council explicitly mentions these points.

Then, the need of the education for an integral culture is underlined, especially when with increasing specialization the notion of "general cul-ture" or the ideal of "the universal man" becomes more and more problem-atic. Once again, the family is seen as the cradle and first school of culture, but it is helped in its task by the multiplication of new means of communi-cation. "In the phonograph record and photographic reproduction, the arts of space and in time (architecture, sculpture, painting, on the one hand, and music, on the other) have found their printing press," as Malraux used to say. "This fact is as important as the discovery of the printing press by Gutenberg in 1454."[17] One might also mention paperbacks, travel and tourism, and sports.

Finally, we must repeat, the relations between the Church and culture have never been idyllic. One has only to remember the case of Galileo. However, even these difficulties can and should promote a more profound diffusion of the Church; they raise new questions that require new research on the part of theologians. (Think, for example, of the problems raised by psychoanalysis.) They invite theologians to revitalize their language, according to the wish expressed by Pope John XXIII in his inaugural address to the Council. Finally, they help the faithful to purify and grow in their faith. Art too can also help enliven the language of the Church.

It is to be hoped, then, that the faithful's "religious practice and morality can keep pace with their secular culture (art. 62). The Council desires that the efforts of all who study theology be marked both by a more profound knowledge of revealed truth and by a closer tie with the contemporary world of culture.

This chapter too, then, shows well that the Church, in the pastoral *Constitution on the Church in the Modern World*, does not want to present herself as "confronting" the world, but as being "in the modern world." She wishes to be less "of" the world and more "in" the world.[18]

NOTES

1. Charles Du Bos, *Approximations* (Paris, 1965) 1419.
2. This aphorism of Nietzsche sums up the essence of his criticism of Christianity.
3. "Templa serena"; the expression comes from Lucretius, *De natura rerum*, 1–10.
4. An allusion to the movement "per un mundo migliore" as well as to the present human effort to create a more human situation for all.
5. This is the heart of the correspondence published by H. de Lubac, *Maurice Blondel et Teilhard de Chardin. Correspondance annotée* (Paris, 1965).
6. "Bilan du Concile," *Le Monde* (Dec. 19, 1965); see also A. Garaudy, *De l'anathème au dialogue* (Paris, 1965).
7. The expression is of G. Marcel. Cf. C. Moeller, "Religion et littérature," in *Comparative Literature Studies* (1965), 331.
8. 2 Pt 3:13; cf. *Constitution on the Church in the Modern World*, art. 39.
9. Discourse of Pope Paul VI, Dec. 7, 1965; NCWC Documentary Service, Dec. 23, 1965.
10. *Solil.*, 1, 1, 3; PL 32:870.
11. Cf. C. Moeller, *L'homme moderne devant le salut* (Paris, 1965) introduction.
12. J. Lacroix, *Le sens de l'athéisme moderne* (Tournai, 1958) 55–66.
13. A. Malraux's *La tentation de l'Occident* (Paris, 1926) is centered on this idea.
14. *Constitution on the Church in the Modern World*, art. 20.
15. *Confessions*, 1, 1; PL 32:661.
16. This comes from a conversation.
17. A Malraux, *Les voix du silence* (Paris, 1955) part I: "Le Musée imaginaire."
18. The expression comes from Yves Congar's *Pour une Eglise servante et pauvre* (Paris, 1964).

Dr. Joseph Sittler

A PROTESTANT POINT OF VIEW

U<small>NTIL QUITE RECENTLY</small> there has been a tradition in literary criticism that may be called the *genetic*. Its procedure in text-analysis was to bring to the description and assessment of a particular text whatever extrinsic facts might help explain its occurrence and its message. Such facts were commonly these: other texts, historical and contemporary, of the same *genre*; the personal career and literary relationships of the writer; the demonstrated influences—artistic, cultural, social—that are reflected in the text. In some instances close attention was paid to concrete biographical data in the confidence that parental relationships, love-life, and what our fathers called "scenes of early childhood" might cast a decisive light upon the work in question.

Within our lifetime this mode of criticism has been succeeded by another. On principle the *new criticism* eliminates attention to anything other than the text itself. The authenticity of a work must be evidenced by the stuff of the text. The text is regarded as a self-contained, integral work of art, a concrete statement. Any critic who derives his canons of criticism from material extrinsic to the text itself is firmly excluded from the club of the new critics.

This little essay about literary criticism is but preface to my consideration of the pastoral *Constitution on the Church in the Modern World*, in order that what I am about to say may be understood from within the limitations that actually define my way of reading it, I have simply sat down before the

422

ninety-two pages as nakedly open to its argument as a mortal can manage. What a mortal Protestant, aged sixty-one, and a professor of theology at that, can manage in such an effort is somewhat short of the angelical objectivity that one intends. One intends to divest himself of presuppositions about proper starting-point in theology, the number and balance of elements in the Christian tradition that refract his vision and influence his judgment, the particular interests and accents that are at the moment forward in his mind as he lives in both the Church and in the modern world.

This intention, however admirable, is severely qualified in the process of study. So what one is left with is whatever justice survives the operation of the stated qualifications. And in my own instance, something more—an almost complete innocence as regards the internal history of Vatican Council II. I was not an observer at the Council, have not immersed myself in the rich, personal-episodic literature of reminiscence and comment that has, in a steady stream, poured from it. Of the history of the genesis, development, various stages of formation and reformulation of schema 13 I have no knowledge at all. From such a background then, I want to organize my comments about this Constitution. This may be done in several extended paragraphs.

THE REPORTORIAL AMPLITUDE OF THE STATEMENT

I have long enough been a member of several commissions of the World Council of Churches, as over the years that body has struggled with a comparable body of data, to imagine how this document was actually produced. From many parts of the world, articulated by many classes of persons, bundles of raw fact are laid before a commission and each claims due place in whatever descriptive effort emerges. A drafting committee must then search for general types among multitudinous problems, a general tonality amidst many cries of pain, a general description of predicaments that are wildly various. The order in the presentation is gained by a decision as to priority among the general. Indeed this ordering activity must go further and ask if out of an ever so rich a recital of woe and anxiety there is a common motif.

A remarkable similarity obtains between the two great ecumenical efforts both as regards the precise specification of those forces that constitute the modernity of contemporary men and nations and as regards the central motif: it is the threat to the very identity and dignity of the human person.

In this document those threats are specified, the dynamism of them whereby an *imbalance* is perceived as threat is described, and the resultant damage to man in the human community is addressed with understanding and freighted with a pastoral concern that is rich in pathos and at times eloquent with the anger of true charity.

The theologically sensitive reader is particularly struck by the term used to summarize, in articles 8 to 10, the basic fault from which these ills proceed, a corrective to which is presumably to control the later constructive theological teaching. The term used is *imbalance*. While, to be sure, the term can be used as a referent to that proposed order whereby the God-relationship known as righteousness is acknowledged to have been fractured into disorder, the subsequent argument invites the mind to find the intention of the term less in misdirection of the moral will than in failures of right reason after the model of classical anthropology. So that, just as specification of fault determines what description might be salvatory, a theological issue is raised right at the outset.

One must ask if the imbalances so sharply designated in article 8 can be adequately addressed from the position taken. Is it possible that the actuality of man as unfolded within the intersection of forces unknown to older times can be confronted at sufficient depth by so serene an admonition? Indeed the document itself in the soaring final article of the Introduction seems to me to put this very question, although in an indirect way. In that paragraph Christ is spoken out as the power who "can through the Holy Spirit offer man the light and the strength to measure up to his supreme destiny" (art. 10). And significantly, it is not the *balance* in the obedience of Christ but his immolation, "who died and was raised up for us all," which is proposed as redemptive. For He is "the key, the focal point and the goal of man, as well as of all human history." This terminology, so recollective of the problems of men in their total natural and historical involvement, is resonant with visions deep-folded in patristic anthropology and presently explicit in contemporary Christological studies, Roman and other. One wonders, therefore, if *imbalance* is not too cool a word for analysis in depth and for the indication of a redemption which shall be as universal in scope as the actual environment of the damnation it encounters.

ANALYSIS OF THE SCIENTIFIC METHOD IN THE FORMATION OF THE MODERN MIND

In article 5 of the Introduction, it is recognized that "spiritual agitation and the changing conditions of life are part of a deeper and broader revolution." This revolution is rightly described as including. areas of discourse other than mathematics and the physical sciences. The problematic of *the historical* as a mode of man's being in the world is so lightly touched upon, that one is led to equate that problem with the more obvious references to "dominion over the past by means of historical knowledge" and the fact that "history itself speeds along on so rapid a course that an individual person can scarcely keep abreast of it."

My question at this point is a twofold one. First, is the problem of the historical in its full force and peril to faith adequately stated in that description? The question has only to be raised to suggest a negative answer. When Sören Kierkegaard asked "is a historical point of departure possible for an eternal consciousness; how can such a point of departure have any other than a mere historical interest; is it possible to base an eternal blessedness upon historical knowledge," he blasted open a problem that had been gathering pressure ever since the Enlightenment. This question today torments both Roman and non-Roman thought, constitutes the profoundest anguish of modernity as it weighs the Christian gospel, and is the awesome but promising context for our common reopening of the meaning of tradition.

If that is true, then the inclusion of the rubric of *history* under the generality of science, while correct as regards the *methods* of historical research, is not proper or sufficient to specify the historical as a theological problem.

My second question arises out of the same article of the Constitution. It is acknowledged that "intellectual formation is ever increasingly based on the mathematical and natural sciences and on those dealing with man himself"—and technology is stated to stem from these sciences and to be of mounting importance. However, as the document unfolds when the "spiritual agitation" alluded to is fully specified, it is the shock of *technology* that occupies the foreground, and the "intellectual formation" remains in the background.

That this should be true of a document addressed to the common life is understandable and was perhaps tactically necessary. Men must be spoken to where the agitation is a fact of instant awareness, but as one goes on to press theologically through the holes this document punches, one becomes aware that even the term "intellectual formation" does not take the measures of the soul of modernity. What is involved is rather a total dubiety about the real, and a sense of the end of those promises that the Englightenment held out. For by a strange irony, the very scientific enterprise that has so deeply shaped modernity now falters in its confidence that it can fulfill such promises. The very structure and process of the world recedes from the penetration of the scientific gaze so that correspondences between human thought and actuality are questioned in fact and, more importantly, in principle. The modern intellectual is thus characterized by what may be termed the pathos of intellection, and the sardonic as a total mood displaces the pilgrim gallantry of an earlier generation.

This is a problem which need not even be envisioned by those who investigate the differences among the several Christian communities. But for the penetration of this problem and proper address to it, the resources of our several traditions in their older form are only modestly sufficient. Indeed it may be that an attack upon this problem may draw us together as we confront a novel phase of human development, and in that common effort we may be granted a measure of unity beyond anything we have thus far envisioned.

SOCIAL ANTHROPOLOGY

Just as Father Godfrey Diekmann remarked, in his commentary about the liturgy, that he felt its doctrine on the Church a sound and deeply biblical one, but added that its force was not matched by a sufficiently sensitive social anthropology—so of this Constitution the same question must be asked. The many-sided analysis of the man who inhabits this world, and particularly the urban, corporate man whose life is lived as a functionary within complicated technological procedures, is not accompanied by a sufficiently perceptive theological proposal.

If one were to reduce this feeling of disquiet to a theological proposition, he might affirm that the doctrine of grace remains trapped within the rubric of redemption, while at the same time the joys, hopes, griefs and anxieties that evoke the document are most sharply delineated under the rubric of creation. Put in another way this disquiet would read: the interrelationships of men with the neighbor, with nature, and within history, all of which are in tumult, are described in pathetic detail; but theological facts and energies appropriate to them remain conceptually and terminologically traditional. This is the more surprising in that other Constitutions of the Council do grope toward such doctrinal development as might be congruent with contemporary experience and language. That moving edge of development is most frail precisely in this document whose data would seem most urgently to require it.

The theological problem here suggested is by no means more pressing upon Roman Catholic theologians than upon others. Along the entire Christian intellectual front there is pressure to give a too compactly soteriological center an orbit of force and meaning that shall be of the same magnitude as the operational world in which man lives, works, investigates, reflects, hopes. While, to be sure, this document firmly places a modern theological program squarely in the middle of men's involvements and predicaments, this movement in itself, though a tribute to sensitivity and to charity, cannot develop what is called for. What is required is nothing short of a doctrine of grace elaborated as fully under the article of God the Creator as a doctrine of grace has been historically developed under the article of God the Redeemer.

That the framers of this Constitution beheld the lure and the necessity of a development along such lines is indicated by the moving last paragraph of the Introduction. In that paragraph, it is stated:

> The Church believes that Christ, who died and was raised up for all, can through His Spirit offer man the light and the strength to measure up to his supreme

destiny. Nor has any other name under heaven been given to man by which it is fitting for him to be saved. She likewise holds that in her most benign Lord and Master can be found the key, the focal point, and the goal of all human history.

One observes, however, that the precision of the anthropological-social analysis in that paragraph is stated in terms that owe more to scholastic ways of thought than to biblical acuity about sin, pride, grace and freedom or to contemporary language in which man confesses where he hurts and what it is that hurts him. The concept of imbalance again invites the mind to suppose that "imbalance . . . between the conditions of collective existence and the requisites of personal thought" (art. 8) is adequately met by mere restoration of balance. The shocks of personal loss of being and brutal deprivation, which are so marked a feature of our time, would suggest a quite new theological development, a doctrine of grace related afresh to the dynamics of man's transaction with nature. The socializing of the personal and the personalizing of the social is the task we face, and the "imbalance" we lament may be but the anguished phase whereby we are made aware of a calling and the availability of a grace for which "balance" is an insufficiently evocative term.

By the divine righteousness man is made free in faith to act in love. This freedom is man's obedient trust in the creator, taking up the commission to administer the world in the freedom of the heir who has come of age (Gal 4). The usual translation of the biblical term is to *subdue* the earth, but the facts of our times suggest that in this instance the command of God must be understood in relation to those instruments of man's devising whereby world-subjection now confronts us in the new, terrifying and wondrous new obedience of world-administration. If Christian theology does not take responsibility for the way in which the transformation of nature into the historically changeable artificial form of human society by means of technological civilization is to be judged and administered, it disavows the peculiar task of theology in our time.

As I conclude this brief essay of response to and gratitude for this *Constitution on the Church in the Modern World*, I am dismayingly aware that I have failed to do what my topic directed—to articulate a Protestant point of view! I cannot find anything Protestant in what I have written. If, however, the separated brethren in your company forget in the heat of discussion their separation and do not self-consciously speak out of it, things perhaps have gone farther than we had supposed.

427

McGrath: The first thing I would like to do is to make reference to some of the points raised in Dr. Sittler's talk. I am very interested in many of the points that he brings up, because they are precisely the ones that we discussed for over two years. And as was stated by Father Stransky in another connection, we always have to remember that a council document is just that: it is the reflection of all the council Fathers' thinking. They have arrived at a synthesis that is as far as possible homogeneous, but not always so. In this document, as in others, there are contrasts. I think I pointed out one that is striking to me, and that is that many sections of the second part are very traditionally casuistic in their approach to problems and not much illuminated by the type of thinking that went into the first part. This is not so much the case with the chapters on culture and marriage, because there was more doctrinal application and discussion in them. I think this is important.

Dr. Sittler concentrated largely in his observations on the descriptive introduction, which is precisely the area in which I most worked, along with Father Houtart and a few others. I would say that, in the question of history, for instance, there was no attempt in the descriptive introduction to do more than very rapidly present some of the impressions of our surrounding world, certainly no attempt to get into an interpretation of history, or any theological explanation of a Christian's sense of history. This was really the role and purpose of the doctrinal part. And in setting up the problem every effort was insistently made that it be objective, phenomenological and as little interpretative as possible.

The reference that Dr. Sittler makes concerning a lack of intellectual participation in change is most interesting, because after the first draft had been drawn up and discussed there were several criticisms along these lines. Change was presented as though it were entirely the result of scientific attitudes and technological applications in which the element of thought, the personal element, the human element, was left very much in the background. This criticism was made on many occasions; as a result various phrases were included in the descriptive introduction (e.g., changes initiated by men's intelligence and creative energies in turn affect men) and in later articles (e.g., reference to the problem faced by man today to arrive at a new synthesis of his conception of the universe, and so forth).

Dr. Sittler also said something to the effect that in the Constitution theological facts and energies appropriate to them remain conceptually and terminologically traditional. As I pointed out, I believe this is true for much of the second part; I do not think it is as true for the first part, which was reworked over and over again by our special commission. A very serious effort was made to present a theology suitable in these contexts, but this was difficult to do for the simple reason that this is a new area of development for modern Catholic theologians. However, there really was, I think, throughout this experience much evidence of advance in thinking. The bishops along with the *periti* were forced to think; there was great advance. And a formulation resulted which very conscientiously does not state more than can be stated, representing the clear thinking of the Church at this time and leaving future developments for the future.

HOUTART: The word "imbalance" was used in a purely sociological sense, in a descriptive way, just to avoid theological language. And I must say we had to fight again and again to avoid putting theological language in this descriptive part of the Constitution. It was precisely because of our desire to avoid making any kind of moral judgment in the description that we used words like "imbalance." I think this was very important, but it certainly did not appeal to all the theologians. I remember hearing a very good theologian-bishop remark, "Well, it seems that this text has been written by a sociologist, not by a human being." I really think it was a matter of methodology, but I agree that this is not followed up in the text with an adequate theology.

Question: Canon Moeller, you expressed the important point
that a multiplicity of human personality, culture, etc., is
needed to image-forth God. What are the implications of this
regarding religious pluralism and related questions of heresy?

MOELLER: I cannot see it as a question of heresy. But I do think it is
quite true that a multiplicity of human personality and culture is able to
make the image of God more manifest. One condition is very important,
however, namely, that this culture would be baptized by the Christian way
of thinking. What are the implications of this for religious pluralism? It
seems to me there is a very simple theological principle, a bit paradoxical
perhaps. The Church must indeed proclaim Christ as the unique Redeemer,
but this Christ whom the Church must proclaim is at the same time the
reconciliation of all good that is in the world. And just this morning in my
paper I said that it is not only the Risen Christ but the Logos too who is
mysteriously present in the world. From this point of view, I think it is possible to assume all that is good in older religious traditions, baptizing them
in Jesus Christ.

Question: In the light of what we know about the history of
life before man emerged, was created, can we any longer say
that man would have been immune from bodily death except
for his sin?

MOELLER: It is a difficult question, and I must say that I am unable to
answer it alone. Article 18 speaks of "that bodily death from which man
would have been immune had he not sinned." In this text we avoid taking
a position on the biological, paleontological problem; it says only that
without sin man would have been without ordination to death. This does
not affirm any theory about natural immortality or natural mortality.

DR. BROWN: My question focuses on an over-all problem growing out
of the text as a whole and the use that we are to make of it together, since
this document is addressed to the separated brethren as well. I realize and
applaud the importance of the affirmative stand the document takes toward
the modern world and feel that this is most necessary, both theologically and
apologetically at the present time. But I wonder if there may not be a
danger in this approach as we now proceed to work it out together, a danger
that I sense in some Protestant treatments of the same theme, namely, the
danger of coming to a too uncritical affirmation of the secular. Even in the
redeemed world sin persists, and in our understandable concern to relate
creatively to the movements of modern culture, we must not be blinded to
demonic forces that are also at work within them. I relate this also to the
remarkable statement Father Ahern made of an affirmation of the secular

order, introducing the qualification that not all that men do or propose in the technological order, for example, can or should be the object of approval. Our exploration of space, for example, needs to be undertaken at the expense of failing to feed starving people, and so forth. Do we not, therefore, need an approach to the modern world, which, now that we have adopted this affirmative stance, will proceed in a clearer way than the Council document or its Protestant counterparts do to indicate that a prophetic note of judgment must also be present both in our analysis of the Church's relation to the modern world and in our analysis of the modern world itself.

CONGAR: I would like to put a question here to our Orthodox friends. Canon Moeller spoke about the presence of the Word of God everywhere in the world since the beginning of history, human history, cosmic history. I think that presence could be expressed in terms of the presence of wisdom. And as a matter of fact, all these Christological statements in St. Paul are probably taken from sapiential literature. I should like to ask some Orthodox theologian if he could tell us briefly what is the relationship of this theme to the very important Orthodox theology about wisdom.

FLOROVSKY: May I start from my own point of view? It will be easier then to come to the question. I was wondering about the meaning of the term *aggiornamento*. It is quite appropriate because the question under discussion is the Church in the modern world. The word itself implies the problem, possibility, or necessity of a certain adjustment *ad tempus*. But the term is ambiguous; it may mean two completely different, even incompatible, things. On the one hand, *aggiornamento* can mean simply that one has to be realistic and relate everything he is doing to the real situation. It would be dangerous for the Church for one to imagine that he lives in a good old world which doesn't exist and behave accordingly. On the other hand, *aggiornamento* means adjustment, and it may involve compromises. The critical problem must first be raised and pursued very carefully: just where is adjustment justified; where does it mean betrayal.

Now one cannot speak about the modern world as a block. The big problem of the modern world and especially of modern man is just who is this modern man. I recall a caustic remark by one of my Presbyterian friends in Scotland expressing the conviction that modern man has not made up his mind and that therefore one cannot speak of modern man because he does not exist. There are modern confusion, modern moods, modern cares and modern demands. The difficulty of the problem is augmented by the fact that many people claim they are modern while others are not. I would claim that I am a modern man, because I do not think the same way as my father and grew in a world different from the world of my parents, trying to learn as much as I could. What was regarded in me as rather strange forty years ago makes me a contemporary to my own situation now.

431

I am a bit distressed by one thing. Of course, I am a historian by profession, and a Christian by profession. And therefore I am a man of tradition. While we are thinking about the modern world and speaking about the Church in the modern world, we must not forget that the modern world is a result of a tragic development in the past. Recently I was a bit perplexed when, in my graduate seminar on the Fathers, two Catholic priests (not the Protestant boys) asked why we were going to study those antiquated things? They want to be up to date, you see!

MEYENDORF: Since we have been challenged by Father Congar, I would like to answer this question about wisdom. It seems to me that the answer to your question has to be looked for in the over-all Christian understanding of sapiential literature, which is actually very close to the theology of the Logos developed in the Constitution as well as in Canon Moeller's comments. While the contemporary contributions to this question on the Orthodox side can be useful as a contribution to or as a conclusion of this tradition of the Logos (the presence of God in the order of creation, wisdom), they have to be treated critically because they also represent nineteenth-century German idealism. This latter, of course, is more questionable as a contribution to Christian tradition than the Logos theology of the Fathers. But this is, of course, such a very big question. It can't be treated in a very brief way.

CONGAR: I asked the question because it is a question. I think the wisdom of God is his plan of creation. Christ is the plan of God that summarizes the totality of God's plan for all creation.

MOELLER: My paper was exclusively theological, and consciously so. My intention was to indicate which theological points were a fundamental part of the Constitution. These points can serve as a theological foundation for discussing anthropology. Regarding Dr. Brown's question on secularization, I think we must admit that the Christian of these times is a new one, a modern one and a very important one. While taking all the data of modern anthropological studies into consideration, we can still avoid an excessively modern presentation by starting out with these theological truths: man as the image of God, Christ the Lord, and the presence of the Logos in the creation as wisdom, and so on.

And I would say almost the same thing as Dr. Florovsky. Perhaps this theological conference should have allotted time for a paper about this descriptive part on modern man. Although I spoke only about the theological principles, it may well be such stress on the description of modern man would have been more important. I do not think that the description of modern man as it appears in the Constitution is as superficial as it seems. While it stresses the positive side of modern man, at the same time it also stresses very strongly the paradoxical aspect. At any rate, we must never forget that we have here a document that is, not a final goal, but a starting point.

AHERN: In regard to Dr. Brown's observation on the need for pointing out abuse or misuse in secular activity, I wonder if article 37 does not adequately point out that human activity is infected by sin.

McGRATH: One more word along the line of Dr. Brown's question. In January, 1965, Father Stransky took several of us to Geneva, where we had the pleasure of meeting many people at the World Council of Churches headquarters. I remember one of the points that came out very clearly was that the World Council was also preparing a document along these lines, and there was a common concern of an overidentification of the spread of the kingdom of God with progress in modern technological terms. This concern was also in evidence during the fourth session of the Council and was influential in having inserted into the text of the Constitution many additions that bring out the paradoxical situation of man in society much more clearly. To speak in concrete, pastoral terms, one can take an area like Latin America where the Church is certainly placing itself on the side of social progress, and many are even using terms like social revolution. There is a very grave danger of many inhuman, not to say anti-Christian, elements of hate and misuse of violence and development of internal conflicts, and simply opportunism, which would spoil the whole Christian concept and approach to the situation. So I would agree heartily with what you say; I just wanted to indicate that there was a serious attempt, particularly in the last session, to bring this into the text. Even during the Conciliar debates we heard opposing reactions: one asked if it was not too optimistic; another questioned whether it was not too pessimistic. I think different persons find different tones.

HYSLOP: I do not have a copy of your address, Dr. Sittler, but I think I remember accurately. You said total dubiety about the real is the true fact of modernity; an attack on this problem may draw us together. Is that approximately correct? In any case, if you didn't say it, I think you think it. Would you elaborate that just a bit? It seems to me that for those of us who are deeply involved in the ecumenical movement, this is the precise point we are missing. Our own younger generation—my own children—are for me very active evidence of this, because very little that I say to them carries any authority at all; the whole structure upon which everything I say is based in question for them. And yet they are most positive young people engaged in the most positive kind of social action in the world today.

SITTLER: The section you quote comes from the paragraph in which I am trying to make the point that that phrase of the Constitution "intellectual formation" is not a sufficiently ample phrase wherewith to designate all things whereby the world view of this generation is actually being formed. That levels other than, perhaps deeper than, mere intellectual formation constitute the self-formation of the responding person, living in the world.

433

It is interesting that you should talk about the young people, because when Father Congar asked me this morning in a private conversation how I happened to get interested in the expansion of Christological doctrine in the particular way I did, and asked whether it was from this or that theological starting point, I had to say that I came to it simply from the same starting point he was talking about, namely, by listening to what students are saying and finding out that their train is moving in one direction, while mine is calmly moving in another, and trying to understand why. I have sometimes used the incident that happened in the classroom to make this point. It is so dramatic that I think I might use it here.

A student interrupted a lecture I was making one day on the pre-Nicene options for the Christological solution, by saying: "But look, how can *anything mean if everything doesn't.*" The longer I reflected upon the eloquence of that uncalculated outburst the more profound it got. I was intensely involved in what I was proposing to him as a meaningful act of the faith of the Church, and he, from morning paper to television, knows that people are riding around among the galaxies, as it were, and unless there is a Christology whose magnitude is somehow congruent with the magnitudes of his experiential world, unless this *anything* (Jesus Christ) can somehow have a magnitude of possible meaning that is identical with the magnitude of his personal experience as reflected in the world, then nothing will have very much meaning. It is out of that kind of barefoot-boy reflections that one begins to open new questions about what perhaps hitherto unadministered strands in the Church's Christological inheritance must be opened toward the particular kind of question this generation is asking.

Noonan: In your paper Dr. Sittler, you pointed with what seemed to me great insight to a serious area of weakness in the Constitution, its ignoring of the problematic of the historical as a mode of man's being in the world. Now I suppose that remark could be developed with ontological implications or epistemological ones, but just in terms of the methodology of theology, I wonder if you would agree with me that in general a greater sensitivity for the tasks of history is required of Catholic theologians if we are to have, as you suggest, the possibility of a common reopening of the meaning of tradition?

Sittler: Yes, I would agree with you, but I find it a point hard to make even to myself, because Catholic theology is drenched in history. Their competence in history, that is, as they share knowledgeable grasp of the sequence and richness of historical fact, because of your education procedures and other things in your life as Christian worshipers, generally exceeds that of the Protestant. Catholic training is profoundly, rigorously, monotonously and sometimes painfully historical. So that to say they do not attend to history is on the one side nonsense. But what I meant to say was that the traffic between investigation of the historical emergence of the community and the witnessing literature of that community, on the one hand, and those in the Church who have the vocation to define doctrinal matters—this traffic seems not to be so incessant, so open, so embarrassing as it constantly is among Protestant theologians. You see, I as a systematic theologian have always got to keep in a kind of messed up, unsystematic, embarrassing conversation with the biblical theologians. And the biblical scholars are always reminding me of the importance of my omissions as a doctrinal theologian, for all the arrogance of my formulations. Now this makes being a non-Roman Catholic theologian a highly risky and nervous business. But it does mean that you are excruciatingly conscious all the time of the problematic of the historic. So that when the Constitution points to history under the general rubric of scientific method, it tends to specify that in the historical science which applies mostly to the refinement of method, of dealing with documents and manuscripts, and cross-checking and all that. You don't answer the problem of the historical simply by learning more about history. The more you learn about it the more clearly you put the problem, you see. That is why I used Soren Kierkegaard's statement: how can a historical event become the point of departure for eternal blessedness? This is an undismissable, tormenting and most creative question, as I see it. It seems to me that Catholic theologians are not dealing with that question at the point where it addresses the common life at least; they are not dealing with it, if I may modestly say so, as I think Protestant theologians have been stuck with it and forced to deal with it.

COOKE: Actually my question was along the same lines as Dr. Noonan's, but I would like to push it further. What struck me in your presentation was the possibilities not only of listening to the historian as a Catholic theologian, but the need, both in Catholic theology and Catholic faith, or Christian theology and Christian faith in general, to take cognizance of Christianity as a historical type of being, that is to say, that the Church exists in history, exists historically, in that one is forced to a constant acceptance of the ongoing and progressive nature. How do we take account of that sort of constant changing element in the very being we are dealing with, and of which we are a part?

SITTLER: I wish I knew. I don't know, Father Cooke. I know that we can neither dismiss this nor in our present state of our knowledge solve it. I don't know.

GREMILLION: To go back to your student and to Dr. Hyslop's children, the committed ones, and the social apostolate. The Church is a community. Our Lord says he will make himself present when we assemble in his name. To what extent in your concept of the Church do the committed Christians in the community of service become the Church in the world? I don't mean that human beings create the Church (it is the Holy Spirit who does that), but to the extent that this ripens into love. Does this beget this *koinonia* which is the Church? And then, to what extent is *this* the proclaiming of the gospel today?

SITTLER: I would make a modified yes as my answer to both. It seems to me this may be the place of the effective presence of the Church in the world. This may be the hand the Church holds out to the need of the world, or the intonation of the voice of the Church as concerned with the cry of the world. It is not *the* Church in the world, but it is a form of the presence of Church in the world. Now I would define Church, in terms of the Constitution on the Church, speaking out of my own confession, as being where the word of God is preached, the sacraments administered according to the directions of Christ. I would not give this up for any coffee house, you see. This does not create Church, of course. But on the other hand, who knows what are the exterior limits of the possibilities of presence of Church in the world. And this, I think, is what is of importance in what is happening up and down the streets of cities this day. And we are trying to investigate without *a priori* judgments, where and how and among whom that presence may announce itself, and the certification of that presence is not our business. It will be self-certified by the rejoinder it evokes, by the sanctity it creates.

CONGAR: Once or twice in your paper you criticize the Constitution because its answers to some questions are not given in the framework of the notion of redemption. But my problem is that there are many notions of redemption. That is a theological topic very difficult to define. Do you think that there are some notions of redemption, for instance that of Irenaeus and perhaps others too, that could give a clearer and broader answer to the questions put by the Constitution?

SITTLER: Yes, sir, I think so. At least in Protestant Christianity we have tended to connect the notion of redemption to the theological rubric of soteriology. I think you are suggesting that the biblical notion of redemption does not begin with the Savior, but precedes it, transcends it and is not capturable within it, although it is not separable from it either. And Irenaeus is, I think, the Father who is most instructive at this point, because he does not do this. Think of that remarkable verse in Romans (8:22–23) where the whole creation groans in travail waiting for the redemption whose occasion is somehow related to the sons of God.

HÄRING

TUCCI

SESSION XI

REV. BERNARD HÄRING, C.Ss.R.
Marriage and the Family

REV. ROBERTO TUCCI, S.J.
Political Life
Culture

Rev. Bernard Häring, C.Ss.R.

MARRIAGE AND THE FAMILY

I<small>T IS MOST IMPORTANT</small> to see why the crucial questions on marriage and the family are treated in the *Pastoral Constitution on the Church in the Modern World*. Some traditionalists say that here we are faced only with pastoral perspectives and that we have to seek the doctrine exclusively in earlier documents of the magisterium. But they forget the words of Pope John at the very beginning of the Council where he made clear that the whole teaching office of the Church is pastoral. It is one of the most important developments of Christian doctrine that in Vatican Council II there was a greater awareness and consciousness that all doctrine has to be understood as a ministry for salvation. It was also better understood that moral teaching as a guideline for life must look not only to abstract principles but above all to persons and to their context: the world, the environment in which these persons have to live. One of the most striking exhortations of this chapter is that the faithful should learn to distinguish carefully the abiding, "eternal realities from their changing expressions" and so to use to the full the present opportunities (art. 52). Christians never will mold the world if they do not pay attention to the signs of the times. Christian presence in the world is only possible if Christians are at the same time inbued with the spirit of the gospel and are men of their time. Pope John expressed it in his most simple way, saying: "Never forget that the Church is not a museum." The title *Church in the Modern World* must be related to the Greek word *kairos*. This means that we see in our time, above all, the opportunities prepared by God. We see it as "a time of favor." "Days will be simply bad," only if we do not recognize the signs of the time and do not use the present opportunities to the full.

The great changes of the modern world have produced very difficult questions and problems concerning marriage and the family. Yet, at the same time, the profound changes in modern society better reveal the true character of marriage and the family in one way or another (art. 47).

Redeemed and Redeeming Love

The chapter mentions as one of the positive signs of our time the fact that "many men of our own age also highly regard true love between husband and wife as it manifests itself in a variety of ways depending on the worthy customs of various peoples and times" (art. 49). In earlier ages the various secondary functions of marriage and above all the married couple's membership in the larger patriarchial family including several generations and couples could hide the very essence of the marriage, namely, the covenant of love. In a time when the heads of two families decided on the marriage partner of their son or daughter, they made a family or marriage contract, which was an economic and social affair. Out of this custom arose the great emphasis on the marriage contract. Thus the word "contract" came into the Church's language. But in our own time it is no longer a question of a contract between two families. Social, cultural development shows that consent in a covenant of mutual giving is the essential thing. This permitted the Council to move away from this "contract" language. The Council sees marriage as a covenant patterned after the covenant between Christ and the Church. No Christian would dare to call that a contract. In the face of strong pressure from those who followed older thought patterns, the Council commission refused to use the word "contract." One of the reasons is that "contract" in the modern understanding means that the people involved can decide on the content of the contract. Another reason is that the contract in the modern understanding means a mutual agreement which regulates impersonal rights and duties. Marriage, under the influence of the contract idea, was then also understood in Canon Law as a contract in which two people grant to one another the right to certain acts, namely, "to those acts which are capable to procreate new life."

It must be recognized, however, that theological thinking even during past centuries never forgot that marriage is more than a contract. Alfonsus de Liguori in the mid-eighteenth century wrote: "Three ends may be reckoned in marriage: intrinsic essential ends, intrinsic accidental ends, and extrinsic accidental ends. The intrinsic essential ends are two, namely, the mutual gift of husband and wife and the indissoluble bond of marriage. The intrinsic accidental ends are likewise two, namely, the procreation of offspring and the remedying of concupiscence. Extrinsic accidental ends can be manifold" (*Theologia moralis* 4, 2, n. 882).

Once it is understood that marriage is a covenant of love, its relationship to the covenant between Christ and the Church becomes more evident. The Constitution shows that married love is a way of salvation made possible only through the active presence of the Redeemer.

> Christ the Lord abundantly blessed this many-faceted love, welling up as it does from the fountain of divine love and structured as it is on the model of His union with the Church. For as God of old made Himself present to His people through a covenant of love and fidelity, so now the Savior of men and the Spouse of the Church comes into the lives of married Christians through the sacrament of matrimony. He abides with them thereafter so that, just as He loved the Church and handed Himself over on her behalf, the spouses may love each other with perpetual fidelity through mutual self-bestowal (art. 48).

It is evident that the sacramentality of marriage cannot be understood in any magic way. It is the constant action of Christ upon the mutual love of the spouses. He purifies it; he appeals to the spouses mutually to bestow on each other such a love that will help them to understand ever better his own redeeming love. The two spouses are cooperators with the Redeemer. The sacramental reality urges them to give each other an experience of love that will bring them the intuition: "How blissful must be the love of God!" The imperfections in their love requiring forbearance also remind them not to adore each other as idols, but to set out together on the way toward the One who is the Tremendous Lover.

It is most evident that the Council does not see this sacramentality as something alongside conjugal (and parental) love, nor is it attached to a mere contract. The love-covenant itself is the means of salvation through the loving presence and help of Christ. "By virtue of this sacrament, as spouses fulfill their conjugal and family obligations, they are penetrated with the spirit of Christ. This spirit suffuses their whole lives with faith, hope, and charity. Thus they increasingly advance their own perfection, as well as their mutual sanctification, and hence contribute jointly to the glory of God" (art. 48). Here once more it becomes evident that their mutual love has a redeeming quality only if it is linked to the glory of God, if together they are adorers of God, the fount of all love. But they do so only if they truly love each other.

A Fuller Understanding of Conjugal Love

We must be grateful to those men in the Council who repeatedly presented a viewpoint which not seldom in earlier centuries obscured the understanding of marriage as a sacrament. Spiritualistic streams of thought did not see how married love in its sexual expression could be related to a sacrament. They explained that the sacrament pertains only to the spiritual friendship of the spouses, while sexual life is only a remedy of concupiscence. Against this kind of thinking the Council of Trent had already explained that the sacrament "sanctifies the natural love" of the married people. The text of Vatican Council II's Constitution allows no room for an erroneous spiritualism that excludes the typical marital experience from the realm of sacramentality, namely, from the realm of an encounter with Christ's redeeming love. The typical expressions of married love are both fully personal and total, being expressions of the body and the mind. "This love is an eminently human one since it is directed from one person to another through an affection of the will. It involves the good of the whole person. Therefore it can enrich the expressions of the body and mind with a unique dignity, ennobling these expressions as special ingredients and signs of the friendship distinctive of marriage. . . . This love is uniquely expressed and perfected through the marital act. The actions within marriage by which the couple are united intimately and chastely are noble and worthy ones. Expressed in a manner which is truly human, these actions promote the mutual self-giving by which spouses enrich each other with a joyful and thankful will" (art. 49).

From this deeper and fuller understanding of love it follows that self-denial, self-control, or asceticism is not something imposed as from without. It is rather the very nature of married love that imposes on the spouses the constant effort to purify their love. The dignity of married love itself is the chief norm of conjugal chastity. It can easily be understood, then, that self-denial must never destroy mutual affection, must never endanger the indissoluble bond.

LOVE AND PARENTHOOD

Catholic moralists have for years used a hopeless vocabulary to discuss the relationship between love and procreation, namely, the vocabulary of primary and secondary ends. On one side it was asserted that married love is fundamental, of prime importance, and *therefore* procreation must be something of minor or secondary importance. On the other side, it was clearly seen that the fact of being a cooperator with God's creative love cannot be something of secondary value. But from this some drew the wrong and dangerous conclusion that therefore married love is of minor importance, or a secondary end. Taking the historical documents out of context, they gravely misunderstood them. For instance, when St. Thomas asserted that procreation is the primary goal of marriage and married love a secondary one, by "primary goal" he meant what man "has in common with all the other animals" and by "secondary" what is on the higher, specifically human level. So "primary" by no means meant the higher goal, and "secondary" the lower one. For modern anthropology it is most evident that human procreation is not on the level of animals. It is an act in which the spouses cooperate with the loving creator. They should do so with full awareness of their responsibility —but also with full consciousness of the exigencies of true mutual love.

Already in the dogmatic *Constitution on the Church* a new approach showed, better than the distinction between primary and secondary ends, what the relationship between conjugal love and fertility really is. It is in the light of the mystery of the Church that this approach becomes most convincing. Nobody will invoke a distinction between what is primary and secondary in the calling of the Church, namely, between the love of the Church for Christ and the Church's apostolic zeal and love. Nobody would dare to admonish the Church to love Christ less in order to achieve more in her apostolic tasks. The Church is the mother of all living. She is fruitful in her apostolate in the measure that she responds to the love of her heavenly bridegroom. So it is with marriage, and this becomes evermore visible in the changing situation of our world. The more married people love each other with a true love that necessarily includes affection too, the more they will desire children in order to have them as sharers in their mutual love. As God creates man with no other motive but his abundant love in order to make them sharers in his own blissful love, so in modern society the spouses will desire children only if they are united by a deep, typically conjugal love.

In past ages, many economical, cultural and social motives spurred them on to have children, even if their love was weak or dead. This is no longer the case in modern society wherein parents gain no economic profit from a large family, but rather have to make enormous sacrifices to prepare their children for a fully personal and social life in modern culture. A great, tender and increasingly unselfish conjugal love disposes the spouses to show generosity to achieve the full fruitfulness of their marriage. And this includes the harmony which is necessary for the education of the children. The Council teaches the principle of responsible parenthood in article 50, in spite of the loud warning of Cardinal Ottaviani that by so doing the Church would also have to change her doctrine on infallibility. He thought that the goal of procreation implied blind reliance on divine providence. But this had never been the doctrine—and certainly not the infallible doctrine—of the Church. St. Thomas Aquinas, in fact, explained that man relying on divine providence must be himself "a small providence." The Council says clearly that people must not only be cooperators with the love of God the creator, but are also, "so to speak, the interpreters of that love." It is a higher way of participation in divine providence if man in the light of faith uses his intelligence in order to understand the loving will of God.

Responsible parenthood is not the same as "a planned parenthood" with cold human reckoning. It is a response to God's loving will in view of the total reality that reveals the true possibilities prepared by divine providence. It is further a response of the spouses to each other. It is the result of a loving respectful dialogue. It is responsibility for the children they already have and the children they wish to have.

The doctrine on responsible parenthood is most decisive for the whole understanding of Christian morality. The Church of Vatican Council II is convinced that the person and the small community should bear the proper responsibility, and that it should not be handed over to others. It is said with emphasis that the spouses themselves must decide. Before God and with responsibility for Church and society must they decide how many children they wish, and at what time they wish, to have them, as far as it is within their "providence." This doctrine excludes the notion that a confessor must make all the decisions, instead of allowing the penitent to follow his own upright conscience. Responsible parenthood also excludes the interference of public authority in the most intimate decisions of the spouses (art. 87). The last chapter of the *Constitution on the Church in the Modern World* does not deny the responsibility of the public authorities in population problems. But their chief responsibility is to contribute to the development of the personal responsibility of the spouses and all other persons involved in this problem.

Open Recognition of a Grave Problem

The full recognition of the responsible transmission of life and of the great importance of expressions of tender affection and mutual giving pose the problem of how to harmonize these two exigencies in their circumstances in which the procreation of a child would clearly be against the principle of responsibility.

Following the example of frankness with which St. Paul (1 Cor 7:5ff.) recognized that a long-lasting abstinence could produce grave temptations and dangers, the Council also fully expresses its concern when rigorists easily declare, "There is a good solution for all these problems, namely, total abstinence during all the years in which a new pregnancy is not desirable." The Council realizes that "couples find themselves in circumstances where at least temporarily the size of their families should not be increased. As a result, the faithful exercise of love and the full intimacy of their lives are hard to maintain. But where the intimacy of married life is broken off, it is not rare for its faithfulness to be imperiled and its quality of fruitfulness ruined. For then the upbringing of the children and the courage to accept new ones are both endangered" (art. 51).

It is a characteristic of the spirit of Vatican Council II that it dares to acknowledge frankly the existence of the problem and the fact that at the moment no satisfactory solution is at hand. This is only one case in point of the general statement made in article 43: "Let the layman not imagine that his pastors are always such experts, that to every problem which arises, however complicated, they can readily give him a concrete solution." The Council appeals to married people and to those skilled in modern sciences, "notably the medical, biological, social, and psychological," to pool their efforts in order "to explain more thoroughly the various conditions favoring the proper regulation of births" (art. 52).

One who realizes how new the situation of the marriage in modern times is will not blame the Church if she is slow in putting out new pastoral guidelines. It cannot be a question of changing the fundamental principles of doctrine, but only of seeking a new way of protecting the same values which the Church tried to protect by means of her earlier teaching in this matter under totally different conditions of life. It must clearly be stated that the Council did not fully resolve the problem of how to harmonize the needs of conjugal love and the responsible transmission of life. As footnote 14 (of the Latin text; n.173 in Abbott) explains, it is precisely the task of a papal commission to continue the studies on "population, family, and birth, in order that, after it fulfills its function, the Supreme Pontiff may pass judgment." But the Council has given some fundamental guidelines or principles for future study. The chief principles are the following.

"The Church issues the reminder that a true contradiction cannot exist between the divine laws pertaining to the transmission of life and those pertaining to authentic conjugal love" (art. 51). If therefore the solutions given by moralists do not fully recognize the needs of authentic conjugal love, this indicates an absolute necessity to rethink the whole matter. The Council does not assert that the Church knows fully all the divine laws, but rather urges that all possible efforts be made in order to know them better.

The Church warns against subjectivism in this matter. "When there is question of harmonizing conjugal love with the responsible transmission of life, the moral aspect of any procedure does not depend solely on sincere intentions or on an evaluation of motives. It must be determined by objective standards. These, based on the nature of the human person and his acts, preserve the full sense of mutual self-giving and human procreation in the context of true love" (art. 51). This text gives a most precious orientation as to how Catholics should understand natural law, namely, as the nature of the human person, and the actions of the person insofar as they are personal expressions of love and openness to God's creative will. The conjugal act is a word and must be a true word, namely, it must express the mutual self-giving of the spouses. This does not mean that every conjugal act must

445

have a procreative quality; this cannot be asserted in view of the biological sciences of today. But it is clearly indicated that besides the communicative good the procreative good must also be considered, namely, there must be a constant endeavor on the part of the married couple to preserve and foster "the context of true love" for human procreation. The Theological Commission explained in its responses that this does not mean the physical expression is thereby made meaningless, for it is one part of the reality which must be integrated into a full appreciation of the different values that are at stake in view of the hierarchy and the urgency of values that must be protected.

The Council reminds us further that the sons and daughters of the Church "may not undertake methods of regulating procreation which are found blameworthy by the teaching authority of the Church in its unfolding of the divine law" (art. 51).

In my opinion two firm principles follow from the above quotations. First it cannot be said that a method of birth regulation is blameworthy because it does regulate birth or hinder a new pregnancy effectively. But neither are all methods good just because the necessity of birth regulation is evident to an upright conscience. No method is good if it destroys "the full sense of mutual self-giving," or if it spoils "the context of true love" in which human procreation should happen.

It is highly encouraging to see pastors of the Church and moralists recognize that they are not competent to pass judgment on the various methods without the help of experts in modern sciences and married couples who are taught by their virtue and experience. Hence no pressure should be brought to bear on the Supreme Pontiff to come out as soon as possible with a final solution. He is above all dedicated to safeguarding truth; and until truth shines forth, he cannot use his teaching authority. But the Pope can still give the best possible pastoral directives that correspond to our present state of knowledge and research without locking the doors against future development. And such development cannot be expected to be drastic, except in the eyes of those who unduly have overemphasized the very secondary and minor aspects of the whole problem.

Rev. Roberto Tucci, S.J.

POLITICAL LIFE

After having dealt with the problems of culture and of the economic and social order, the *Constitution on the Church in the Modern World* turns to the problems of political life. It starts from two phenomena of contemporary public life. On the one hand, contemporary man now has the power to institute "a political-juridical order in which personal rights can gain better protection" (art. 73), especially the right of political and religious liberty; on the other hand, many people feel the desire to assume greater responsibilities in the organization of the life of the political community. The Church recognizes the right to this aspiration and this effort but at the same time confirms the nature and scope of the political community, because only an effort that corresponds to its nature and aim can make possible the political community's endeavor to advance the human person.

Thus, after having indicated that the political community arises from the awareness that without a greater community families and groups cannot establish a life capable of responding to the needs of human nature, it states that the end of the political community is the common good (art. 74), defined in the encyclical *Mater et Magistra* as "the sum of those social conditions which allow, and favor in human beings, in families and associations, the fullest pursuit of their perfection" (par. 65). The political authority, born out of the necessity of directing the energies of diverse men toward the common good, must be exercised with the pursuit of the common good in view and within the ambience of moral law. At this point the Constitution warns: "Where public authority oversteps its competence and oppresses the people, these people should nevertheless obey to the extent that the objective common good demands. Still it is lawful for them to defend their own rights and those of their fellow citizens against any abuse of this authority, provided that in so doing they observe the limits imposed by the natural law and the gospel" (art. 74).

How is the life of a political community supposed to unfold? Above all it is necessary to think of creating "political-juridical structures" that will be the better able to afford all "citizens the chance to participate freely and actively in establishing the constitutional bases of a political community, governing the state, determining the scope and purpose of various institutions, and choosing leaders" (art. 75). Here we touch upon the greatest problem of contemporary political life, the problem of an authentic democracy that will be one not only in name but in fact. Also necessary is "a positive system of law . . . which should establish a division of governmental roles and institutions and, at the same time, an effective and independent system for the protection of rights" (art. 75). In addition, although the intervention of the state is today becoming more frequent on account of the increasing complexity of modern problems, it must not deprive families and intermediate institutions of their legitimate action. It therefore "harms humanity when government takes on totalitarian or dictatorial forms injurious to the rights of persons or social groups" (art. 75). Finally, there is a recommendation to political parties to advance the common good and never allow personal interest to take over.

Then the Constitution goes on to examine the relations between the political community and the Church. It states, above all, that the Church must in no way be confused with the political community or bound to any political system, adding that "in their proper spheres the political community and the Church are mutually independent and self-governing. Yet, by a different title each serves the personal and social vocation of the same human beings" (art. 76). Hence the need for "wholesome mutual cooperation." Even though it is quite distinct from the political community, the Church can be of great advantage to it: "By preaching the truth of the gospel and shedding light on all areas of human activity through her teaching and the example of the faithful, she shows respect for the political freedom and responsibility of citizens and fosters these values" (art. 76). As to its means of action, the Church utilizes "the means and helps proper to the gospel. In many respects these differ from the supports of the earthly city" (art. 76). She will even "renounce the exercise of certain legitimately acquired rights if it becomes clear that their use raises doubts about the sincerity of her witness or that new conditions demand some other arrangement" (art. 76). In any case, she can never fail to preach the faith and to teach her social doctrine, to pass moral judgments even on matters touching the political order when this is required by the fundamental rights of human persons and by the salvation of the souls, even though she can use only those means that conform to the gospel.

This has been an extremely rapid synthesis of the content of chapter 4, part II, of the *Constitution on the Church in the Modern World*, which treats of the "life of the political community." As we have said in our talk on culture, this chapter on the life of the political community leaves many problems unsolved. I would like to consider one point that seems to be of special actuality and importance: the task of the Christian in political life.

Christians cannot afford to be disinterested in political life. "Let Christians appreciate their special and personal vocation in the political community. This vocation requires that they give conspicuous example of devotion to the sense of duty and of service to the advancement of the common good" (art. 75). The Constitution recommends also that "those who are suited for it or can become so, prepare themselves for the difficult but most honorable art of politics. Let them work to exercise this art without thought of personal convenience and without benefit of bribery" (art. 75). These words of the Constitution echo what Pope Pius XI had to say December 18, 1927, when he addressed the Federation of Catholic Universities (F.U.C.I.): "They [the young people] often ask themselves if, being Catholics, they should not be doing something in politics. . . . [But] the greater and more important the field, the greater and heavier is the work itself. The political arena is such that it concerns the interests of the whole of society. In this respect it is also the field of the greatest charity, political charity, to which nothing else, except religion, is superior. It is under this aspect that Catholics should be engaged in politics."[1]

The Christian is therefore called to assume political responsibility according to his capabilities and availability. It is a duty which, if he is in any way capable, he must not shirk. It is clear that in such political activity he must not be guided by personal ambition, the pursuit of success at all costs, or the thirst for power and gain, since for the Christian politics is a service and, as Pope Pius XI said, "the field of the greatest charity, political charity." He will, of course, bring to the field of politics passion and enthusiasm, cultural and professional preparation and moral dedication without denying his own aspirations (a good dose of ambition is necessary and without a desire for success one cannot engage in politics), but elevating and purifying them in the fire of charity.

But once the Christian has pledged himself to political life, what sort of

---

[1] *Discorsi di Pio XI*, ed. by D. Bertetto (Turin: S.E.I., 1960) 1: 744–745.

politics is he to engage in? Christian politics? Evidently a "Christian" cannot engage in politics except in accord with his own Christian commitment. But what does this commitment mean in terms of political activity and in what sense can we still speak of "Christian" or "evangelical" politics?

Let us, first of all, clarify one idea: a Christian who engages in politics does not act as a fiduciary of the Church as a religious society, nor is he her deputy; he is not sent by the Church to protect her interests, neither material ones nor—I point this out especially—spiritual ones. He has not received any mandate whatsoever from the Church, since she is not in a position to give a political "mandate." He, therefore, acts in his own name alone and in his political action involves only himself and must follow his own conscience. It is true that the Church plays a great and decisive role in the formation of his conscience through her social teachings and the moral judgments she passes on things that pertain to the political order. Thus, in his political actions the Christian can never ignore these teachings and/or prescind from her moral judgments. Nevertheless, the social doctrine of the Church and the moral judgments she makes even regarding the political order do not refer to the technical aspects of political, social or economic problems, since the Church has no competence in political technique and concrete decisions. In such cases the Christian is independent of the Church and must follow solely his own conscience. It is evident that he must keep the social teachings of the Church and her moral judgments in mind while acting in the political sphere, but the application of these teachings and moral judgments to concrete cases is up to him and he must follow the dictates of his own conscience, on the one hand, and the dictates of his own professional competence, on the other. Thus, even while being autonomous in his political decisions, the Christian must obtain inspiration for his political actions from the social doctrine and moral judgments of the Church, and attempt to make them effective and bring political life into conformity with them.

But to what extent, and with what methods and means?

First of all, with regard to the just *autonomy of terrestrial realities* having their own laws and ends that must be respected, politics is a terrestrial reality with laws, means and methods of its own which the Christian is bound to respect, as expressed in the *Constitution on the Church in the Modern World* (art. 36): "By the very circumstance of their having been created, all things are endowed with their own stability, truth, goodness, proper laws, and order. Man must respect these." Therefore, also the Christian who engages in politics must "be a politician." This does not mean, however, that the "reason of State" or *Realpolitik* must take the upper hand in political decision-making; since politics is also subject to the moral law, there are values that cannot be sacrificed even for the collective interest of a nation or a state, such as the dignity of the person, religious liberty of individuals or religious communities, and the common good of all mankind.

Secondly, we must shun all *integralism*. The aim of Christian politics can no longer be the establishment of a *civitas christiana* or a *civitas Dei*, that is, the construction of a "Christian" order, imposed somehow from above, in which everything in the laws and institutions as well as in practical life would conform to the dictates of Christian faith and morals. The act of faith is in fact free, and Christian morals make demands that are not accepted by the non-Christian. It is impossible to impose a social and political order in harmony with Christian faith and morals upon a world that does not accept Christian faith and morals. On the other hand, both the state and politics are profane, terrestrial and lay realities that have as an end the temporal common good, not the attainment of man's supernatural end; they must not be opposed to the reaching of this goal, should even to some extent favor it, but they do not have as their own direct goal the propagation of faith and the promotion of Christian morals. What then is the aim of Christian politics? It is the creation of a human social and political order that is able to safeguard the dignity of the person and at the same time advance his development, open at the same time to the supernatural. In order to explain the meaning of this "openness to the supernatural," we may recall what was said in *Pacem in Terris* where Christians are urged to "endeavor, in the light of faith and with the strength of love, to ensure that the various institutions— whether economic, social, cultural or political in purpose—should be such as not to create obstacles, but rather to facilitate or render less arduous man's perfecting of himself both in the natural order as well as in the supernatural" (par. 146). Further on, the same encyclical notes that "in traditionally Christian nations, secular institutions, although demonstrating a high degree of scientific and technical perfection and efficiency in achieving their respective ends, not infrequently are but slightly affected by Christian motivation or inspiration" (par. 151). Therefore it will be the task of the Christian politician to make an effort to inject into political life and political achievements this "Christian motivation or inspiration."

Thirdly, we have the phenomenon of *positive acceptance of political and social pluralism* in modern society. It is not just a case of the Christian adapting himself to a *de facto* situation, such as the pluralism of modern society, but of seeing in it a value insofar as, because of it, society is enriched with the help of diverse ideological and practical contributions. Therefore, the Christian politician will be disposed to collaborate with others, forcing himself to make his own Christian contribution to the world of politics but also seeking to reconcile it with the contributions of others, without trying to make his own Christian viewpoint prevail through cunning, force or violence. Above all, he will respect the political and religious freedom of others.

Finally, in accepting the *rules* and *method* of democracy, even when it puts his cause at a disadvantage, it will be his duty to fight with all his forces, with the means a democratic system offers, to make the cause which he holds to be the true one triumph, but always aiming at the good of the whole community, with all the different currents of opinion existing in it.

In conclusion, it seems to me that we might also talk about a Christian politics in the sense of politics inspired by faith and the principles of the Church's social doctrine, one that tries to pervade social and political structures with "Christian motivation or inspiration," so that political and social life be, not an obstacle, but rather a means toward the perfection of the human person, not only on the natural but also on the supernatural plane. However, it is necessary that this spring from the Christian life and practice of the Christian politician and be a vital witness to the gospel lived in political life.

Rev. Roberto Tucci, S.J.

CULTURE

THE PASTORAL *Constitution on the Church in the Modern World* has confronted the problem of culture and has placed it among the more important problems of modern times. In this study we intend to offer some reflections on this problem and thus make our contribution to the debate that ought to accompany the study of the Conciliar documents. We shall center our considerations on three points: 1) the meaning of culture; 2) the answer Vatican Council II gave to the problems that culture raises for modern man; 3) the problems that still remain open.

I. The Meaning of Culture

Anyone who wants to discuss culture faces immediately the difficulty of clearly defining culture. Is culture synonymous with civilization? What is the relationship between culture and technology, culture and religion, culture and humanism?

What then is culture? In its etymological meaning, culture (from *colere*: to cultivate fields and, by extension, man's spirit and spiritual faculties) indicates the activity by which man, acting upon the surrounding world and transforming it, develops and transforms himself. Man is a being with certain physiological, affective and spiritual needs that must be satisfied. He needs to nourish, clothe, shelter and reproduce himself; he needs to establish affective relationships with his fellow men. He also has need of a spiritual order, namely, a thirst for knowledge, beauty, power. In order to satisfy these needs, unlike an animal, man must transform the world that surrounds him. An animal, in fact, finds what he needs already "prepared"; it need only search for it, collect it, and whenever necessary preserve it. Man instead must "prepare" what he needs by means of that specifically human activity called labor. Nature is the matter or object of man's labor; he applies his mind and hand to nature; he adapts it, transforms it according to his needs and makes it produce what he desires.

Man's hand, however, is incapable, by itself, of transforming nature, since its strength is too modest and limited and very restricted in its potentialities. To the aid of the hand, then, comes the mind; by it man creates the "tools" that multiply and prolong the hand's action. In this way he can confront nature. Nature, however, does not lend itself to easy domination; it throws up difficulties and obstacles to man's action and instruments. These obstacles can be either superable or insuperable. Superable are those obstacles that can be overcome by ordinary efforts, though hard and enduring, by facing them either directly or indirectly. The insuperable obstacles are those that no force or human ability can overcome as well as those that demand efforts so strenuous and enduring that no ordinary man can sustain.

Man, therefore, confronts nature with his instruments; if he finds no difficulty or insuperable obstacle, he makes progress in his conquest and adaptation of nature. In fact, inasmuch as he is endowed with intellect and will (two powers oriented toward the totality of being and directed toward knowing and willing "everything"), it is proper to man never to stop, never to limit himself to what has already been achieved or conquered. Rather, he always moves forward toward new goals and conquests. If he encounters insuperable obstacles, however, he stops and all progress is halted; man begins to center his attention on himself, to mark time in an immovable present that knows neither past nor future. But by overcoming one by one the obstacles presented by nature, man creates instruments ever more complex and perfect, and at the same time progress acts upon man as a source of energy and strength in such way that he becomes capable of overcoming ever greater obstacles until he surmounts even those difficulties that at one time seemed insuperable.

Nevertheless, in this effort of overcoming nature and subjecting it to his needs, man realizes that he cannot succeed alone, that he needs others, because only through united effort and the exchange of various instruments of labor can he overcome those obstacles of ever increasing complexity that nature places before him. Only in this way can progress be secured.

However, what urges man toward others is not simply material needs but also affective ones. Man is social by nature; he is meant to live with others, relating to others, not only on the level of interest, but also on that of solidarity and affection. In this way language is born as an instrument of communication of one's thoughts and sentiments. As this language assumes diversified forms and uses various symbols, various forms of society arise, from the basic (family, clan, tribe) to the more complex. And life together is made possible and human by means of law that sets up norms and regulations for civilized living.

In addition to physiological and affective needs, man has also spiritual needs. These come to light and are expressed all the more forcefully in proportion as man has satisfied his essential needs for food, clothing, shelter, security for present and future, and the more extensive his relations are. These spiritual needs are the measure of man's value and the sign of his elevation above the purely physical, physiological and social order that he shares with animals. These needs concern man's desire for learning, aesthetics and religion. The need for learning urges man to investigate the world that surrounds him in order to discover its structure and laws, to explore man's interior as well as his relations with others, to inquire into the history of the world and man, to attempt to establish the supreme principles that govern the universe and the profound meaning of man and history. In this manner the natural and human sciences, history and philosophy are born. The aesthetical need urges man to give expression to his inner life by means of artistic creations. Thus the arts are born, which vary according to their means of expression (poetry, music, painting, sculpture, drama, dance, and so forth). Finally, his religious need urges man to adopt formulas and symbolic rites in order to enter into relation with God, to express the need for the divine and for the infinite found in man. In this way are born ritual forms and expressions, which may be very simple but at the same time structurally complex.

In his effort to dominate nature and adapt it to his needs, in his effort to establish a community life, and finally in his effort to satisfy his need for learning, art and religion, man establishes, laboriously and at the cost of much endeavor, more or less successful, a vast complex of technology, instruments, customs, laws, juridical institutions, philosophical and scientific principles, artistic productions and religious expressions. This vast and manifold complex, endowed with a unity and structure of its own, forms the civilization of a people or of a social group.

The civilization of a social group is never the same as that of another social group. In fact, even though man is basically identical in his nature to all other men, he is nevertheless conditioned in his activity by a variety of external factors (climate, fertility and richness of the soil, nourishment, and the like) which profoundly affect his emotional and intellectual life. Man is, above all, conditioned by history and geography. It is not without significance for an individual or a social group to live in this or that moment in history, to live in this or that place on the globe. This means that time and space mark the rhythm of human civilizations and give them different expressions and forms. Hence the diversity and multiplicity of human civilizations.

With these premises in mind, let us now consider the meaning of culture.

Some believe that the terms "civilization" and "culture" are synonymous and therefore interchangeable. This is true particularly for German-speaking peoples, for whom *kultur* means "culture" and "civilization." Nonetheless, other languages also use the term "culture" where we would expect to find "civilization," due perhaps to the influence of German scholars. In general, this happens only when the terms are used in their etymological sense, as, for example, in the famous book *Primitive Cultures* (1872) by E. B. Tylor, and also in Italy when one speaks of "Algonquian culture" or "Bantu culture." Undoubtedly, between culture and civilization there are very close bonds and numerous points of contact. Culture seems to signify something more than civilization. In order to understand the meaning of this "something more," it is necessary to introduce the concept of "value." We must then affirm that culture comprehends and expresses the values of a civilization. Thus not the whole of civilization is included, nor all its manifestations, but only those manifestations that possess value of some kind, whether philosophical, artistic, religious, moral, scientific or technical. Culture not only expresses the values of a civilization; it also organizes and unifies them. Indeed, the concept of unity, together with that of value, is essential to the concept of culture. Culture is, therefore, the unity of the values of a civilization; it is an organic unity, and thus a living one.

This is the concept of culture understood in its objective sense. Its subjective aspect, the cultivated man, the man of culture, means the man who, by means of the study of a civilization and of its manifestations, has succeeded in assimilating the values of that civilization in an organic and unified way. But civilizations are different and manifold; consequently, also different and manifold are the values they express. Hence, a man will be the more cultured and his culture will be the more vast and profound, the more able he is to assimilate, in an organic synthesis, the values of different civilizations.

In order for one to speak of culture, and not simply of erudition, it is necessary that the elements and values of a civilization be vitally assimilated, namely, that they form one entity with his personality; in fact, they must become a principle and source of thought and action for the man who possesses them. This means that culture has an essentially formative and educative function, and that the cultured man is the "formed" man, the "educated" man. Precisely in this consists the human value of culture: it forms and develops the human person. Indeed, we must add that culture is necessary to the formation and development of the human person. Unlike

456

animals, man is born ignorant and destitute; if he had to learn, discover and verify everything by himself, he would remain on a crude and primitive human level. Instead, through culture man profits from the great, noble, beautiful or useful achievements of mankind of previous centuries, so that he can start not from zero but from a very high level and thus attempt new conquests. Culture is therefore the motivating principle of human progress.

II. The Council and Culture

In the Church's profound examination of her mission in the world conducted at Vatican Council II, she also took up the problem of culture. While one should remember the words of Pius XI to Bishop P. D. Roland Gosselin of Versailles—"Il ne faut jamais perdre de vue que l'objectif de l'Église est d'évangéliser et no de civiliser. Se elle civilise, c'est par l'évangélisation"[1] —although, in other words, her mission is not directly cultural, nevertheless the Church cannot be disinterested in culture. The reason is clear: culture is intimately connected with the dignity and formation of the human person, since only through culture is it possible for the human person to develop according to God's design for man and history. The Church has fully realized that it is part of her mission to promote the development of the human person as well as to defend his dignity. For this reason, whenever the opportunity presented itself the Church in Council has intervened in favor of culture. Indeed, it would be erroneous to believe that the Church has dealt with this problem only in the pastoral *Constitution on the Church in the Modern World*. While here culture is treated *ex professo* and in ample measure, other Conciliar documents also speak of it.

Thus in the Constitution *Lumen gentium*, one reads that the Church "takes nothing away from the temporal welfare of any people. . . . Rather does she foster and take to herself, insofar as they are good, the ability, resources, and customs of each people. Taking them to herself she purifies, strengthens, and ennobles them" (art. 13). Or again, "through her work whatever good is in the minds and hearts of men, whatever good lies latent in the religious practices and cultures of diverse peoples, is not only saved from destruction but is also healed, ennobled, and perfected unto the glory of God, the confusion of the devil, and the happiness of man" (art. 17).

In the *Constitution on the Sacred Liturgy* it is said that "anything in their way of life that is not indissolubly bound up with superstition and error she studies with sympathy and, if possible, preserves intact. Sometimes in fact she admits such things into the liturgy itself, as long as they harmonize with its true and authentic spirit" (art. 37). It further states that:

> Very rightly the fine arts are considered to rank among the noblest expressions of human genius. This judgment applies especially to religious art and to its

highest achievement, which is sacred art. By their very nature both of the latter are related to God's boundless beauty, for this is the reality which these human efforts are trying to express in some way. To the extent that these works aim exclusively at turning men's thoughts to God persuasively and devoutly, they are dedicated to God and to the cause of His greater honor and glory.

Holy Mother Church has therefore always been the friend of the fine arts and has continuously sought their noble ministry, with the special aim that all things set apart for use in divine worship should be truly worthy, becoming, and beautiful, signs and symbols of heavenly realities. For this purpose, too, she has trained artists. . . .

The Church has not adopted any particular style of art as her very own; she has admitted fashions from every period according to the natural talents and circumstances of peoples, and the needs of the various rites . . . the art of our own days, coming from every race and region, shall also be given free scope in the Church (art. 122, 123).

In the *Decree on the Church's Missionary Activity*, especially where the problems of missionary adaptation are examined, references to the respect due the cultural treasures of the various non-Christian peoples are very frequent. For example, the document strongly recommends that Christians, in order to give witness effectively to Christ, enter into relationships of esteem and love with non-Christians and

acknowledge themselves to be members of the group of men among whom they live. Let them share in cultural and social life by the various exchanges and enterprises of human living. Let them be familiar with their national and religious traditions, gladly and reverently laying bare the seeds of the Word which lie hidden in them. . . .

Christ Himself searched the hearts of men, and led them to divine light through truly human conversation. So also His disciples, profoundly penetrated by the Spirit of Christ, should know the people among whom they live, and should establish contact with them. Thus they themselves can learn by sincere and patient dialogue what treasures a bountiful God has distributed among the nations of the earth. But at the same time, let them try to illumine these treasures with the light of the gospel, to set them free, and to bring them under the dominion of God their Savior (art. 11).

Elsewhere the same Decree invites Catholics to cooperate fraternally with other Christians in order to achieve "a common profession of faith in God and in Jesus Christ. They can collaborate in social and in technical projects as well as in cultural and religious ones" (art. 15).

Finally, in the *Declaration on Christian Education*, the Church recognizes the inalienable right of every man "to an education corresponding to his proper destiny and suited to his native talents, his sex, his cultural background, and his ancestral heritage" (art. 1). She urges all Christians "to devote themselves generously to the whole enterprise of education, with the special aim of helping to bring more speedily to all men everywhere the worthy benefits of education and training" (art. 1). Furthermore, the Church recommends that Catholic schools strive "to relate all human culture eventually to the news of salvation, so that the light of faith will illumine the knowledge which students gradually gain of the world, of life, and of mankind" (art. 8). Finally she directs Catholic universities "to have individual branches of knowledge studied according to their own proper principles and methods, and with due freedom of scientific investigation. She intends thereby to promote an ever deeper understanding of these fields" so that "the students of these institutions may become men truly outstanding in learning" (art. 10).

As is evident, even in these documents, though in passing, the Church manifests her appreciation for culture in general as well as for particular cultures, which the Church wants to respect, preserve and even accept in her liturgy. She affirms the right of all to culture; she insists on the need for Catholics to be open to cultural dialogue and to work with competent effort for the promotion of culture, in a spirit of freedom proper to cultural research.

However, it is in the pastoral *Constitution on the Church in the Modern World* that the problem of culture is treated in all its amplitude. This is done in chapter 2 of part II, entitled "The Proper Development of Culture." Thus one who wants to know the thinking of the Church in this regard has to study this document. It is indeed significant that the problem of culture is placed among "particularly urgent needs characterizing the present age, needs which go to the roots of the human race . . . arousing universal concern" (art. 46). This indicates that, in the Church's mind, the problem of culture cannot be overlooked without serious consequences.

The chapter of the Constitution dedicated to culture opens with an important assertion: "It is a fact bearing on the very person of man that he can come to an authentic and full humanity only through culture" (art. 53). Thereby is shown the essential and intimate relation that exists between culture and the perfecting of the human person. But what really is culture? More than a definition, the Council gives a description of it first under the anthropological aspect and then under the sociological and ethnological aspect:

> The word "culture" in its general sense indicates all those factors by which man refines and unfolds his manifold spiritual and bodily qualities. It means his effort to bring the world itself under his control by his knowledge and his labor. It includes the fact that by improving customs and institutions he renders social life more human both within the family and in the civic community. Finally, it is a feature of culture that throughout the course of time man expresses, communicates, and conserves in his works great spiritual experiences and desires, so

that these may be of advantage to the progress of many, even of the whole human family (art. 53).

This is the *anthropological* aspect of culture. The fact is that man transcends the animal level and perfects his human qualities. By his intellect and work he achieves control over the land; in his family and social life he humanizes customs and institutions; in works of art he expresses his sentiments and spiritual experiences and transmits them to forthcoming ages, thus enriching the whole human race.

There is also the *sociological* and *ethnological* aspect of culture that allows us to speak of a "plurality of cultures." "Various conditions of community living, as well as various patterns for organizing the goods of life, arise from diverse ways of using things, of laboring, of expressing oneself, of practicing religion, of forming customs, of establishing laws and juridical institutions, of advancing the arts and sciences, and of promoting beauty. Thus the customs handed down to it form for each human community its proper patrimony" (art. 53). Culture, however, has also a *historical* character, since, as the Council affirms, each culture constitutes a "historical environment which enfolds the men of every nation and age and from which they draw the values which permit them to promote human and civic culture" (art. 53).

Following this consideration of culture in general, the Council turns to consider the place of culture in the modern world. It observes that such a culture is characterized, first of all, by a *critical* sense, which is notably refined by the development of the so-called exact sciences as well as by studies of psychology, which have contributed to a more profound understanding of human activity. It is further characterized by a *historical* sense arising from the development of historical sciences, which have been instrumental in bringing men to see reality under the aspect of its mutability and evolution. It is subsequently characterized by a certain *uniformity* of ideas, customs and tastes, which leads to *mass culture* by virtue of urbanization and industrialization. And finally, it is characterized by a certain cultural *universalism* due to the "growth of communication between the various nations and social groups [which] opens more widely to all the treasures of different cultures" (art. 54). The Council further observes that, more than in the past, man of today is conscious of being a craftsman of culture. Hence the sense of responsibility, which is so strong in him and which imprints a special character on modern culture, since it gives birth to "a new humanism, one in which man is defined first of all by his responsibility toward his brothers and toward history" (art. 55).

What then is the Church's judgment on modern culture thus characterized? The Church does not pronounce directly on the validity of modern culture but, after considering its contradictions, describes what culture ought to be and do: "In the thick of these tensions, human culture must evolve today in such a way that it can develop the whole human person harmoniously and at the same time assist men in those duties which all men . . . are called to fulfill" (art. 56).

"In the thick of these tensions . . . ," what are the difficulties and contradictions that culture faces today? The first contradiction comes from the actual intensification of cultural relations. While it may lead "to a real and fruitful dialogue between different classes and different nations," it may also cause a community to forget and overlook its sound tradition, and may endanger the character proper to each people by creating the mass-man lacking any originality and tradition, the anonymous man, the "assembly line" man. The danger that fidelity to the patrimony of tradition be lost in modern culture is aggravated by the difficulty of harmonizing "technical" culture and "classical" culture.

The second contradiction is to be found in the difficulty of harmonizing two requirements of modern culture: on the one hand, the necessity of specialization due to the vastness of the field of science, and on the other, the necessity of synthesis. Culture in fact, is essentially the unity and synthesis of a large and complex mass of data and knowledge, coming from various branches of learning as well as from diverse and meaningful human experiences. To culture belong also "those faculties of contemplation and wonder which lead to wisdom," and it is indeed difficult to maintain and develop in man such faculties in today's "technological" culture, one essentially directed to what is useful. Hence the importance of solving the problem of harmonizing "technological" culture and "classical" culture, namely, that culture which, being adapted to various traditions (the Greco-Latin culture, therefore, is not the only one referred to) is nourished by classical studies (cf. art. 56).

A third contradiction is found in the fact that while, on the one side, the urgency is felt of making all men participate in the riches of culture, leading necessarily to a simplification of culture (to so-called mass culture), on the other side, the culture of the more sophisticated grows evermore refined and complex, and therefore less and less accessible to the average man. Thus, the gap is increasingly widened between "mass culture," which tends to become more and more superficial and unvarying, and the culture of the more sophisticated, which tends to become evermore esoteric and clannish.

Finally, a fourth contradiction is brought about by the difficulty of reconciling the independence of culture with its necessary openness to truth and supernatural values; independence of culture, in fact, tends to restrict it to "a humanism which is merely earthbound and even contrary to religion itself" (art. 56).

Even though these difficulties and contradictions make the Church's judgment on culture more refined and complex (culture in fact, like all other human and worldly values, contains a dispensable ambiguity and thus cannot be accepted unconditionally), nevertheless the Church looks upon culture with interest. This is done, not for the sake of opportunism, but in virtue of the Christian faith, which recognizes and asserts the value of culture in the obligation of the Christian to work with all men in constructing a more human world. "In fact," says the Constitution, "the mystery of the Christian faith furnishes them [Christians] with excellent incentives and helps toward discharging this duty more energetically and especially toward uncovering the full meaning of this activity, a meaning which gives human culture its eminent place in the integral vocation of man" (art. 57).

What then is man's integral vocation? Faith, and faith alone, tells us that man is destined eternally to contemplate God and enjoy his happiness by entering into a relationship of sonship with God and by participating in his divine life. Man fulfills this destiny in his present life by subjugating the earth and perfecting creation, as well as by placing himself at the service of his brethren. At the same time, man prepares himself to receive God's wisdom and Christ's grace by means of contemplation, prayer and worship. In this task man is validly assisted by culture:

> For when, by the work of his hands or with the aid of technology, man develops the earth so that it can bear fruit and become a dwelling worthy of the whole human family, and when he consciously takes part in the life of social groups, he carries out the design of God. Manifested at the beginning of time, the divine plan is that man should subdue the earth, bring creation to perfection. . . . When a man so acts he simultaneously obeys the great Christian commandment that he place himself at the service of his brother men (art. 57).

Therefore, even in its lower forms culture helps man to follow his total vocation. Nevertheless, it is in its higher manifestations that culture prepares man to receive God's light:

> When a man applies himself to the various disciplines of philosophy, of history, and of mathematical and natural science, and when he cultivates the arts, he can do very much to elevate the human family to a more sublime understanding of truth, goodness, and beauty, and to the formation of judgments which embody universal values. Thus mankind can be more clearly enlightened by that marvelous Wisdom which was with God from all eternity (art. 57).

Indeed, culture is a force that liberates man from bondage to creatures. In virtue of this liberating ability, the cultured man "can be more easily drawn to the worship and contemplation of the Creator. Moreover, under the impulse of grace, man is disposed to acknowledge the Word of God. Before He became flesh . . . 'He was in the world' already as 'the true light that enlightens every man'" (art. 57). It would have been difficult perhaps to say more in order to show the esteem the Church has for culture. In any form of culture, but particularly in modern culture with its distinguishing positive values, the Church sees a *preparatio evangelica*: "All of these values," says the Constitution, after enumerating the positive values of modern culture, "can provide some preparation for the acceptance of the message of the gospel—a preparation which can be animated with divine love by Him who came to save the world" (art. 57). Between culture and grace there is, therefore, a reciprocal relationship: culture appeals to grace because only in grace can it find its fulfillment; grace looks to culture because the latter constitutes the ordinary way in which grace affects human life. This is why evangelization requires a minimum of life and cultural development, and why evangelization always brings with it a development of culture.

While exalting the positive values of modern culture, however, the Church is conscious of two grave dangers to which modern culture is exposed and which sometimes people justify very weakly: the danger of phenomenalism and agnosticism, and that of self-sufficiency. The Council says:

> Today's progress in science and technology can foster a certain exclusive emphasis on observable data, and an agnosticism about everything else. For the methods of investigation which these sciences use can be wrongly considered as the supreme rule for discovering the whole truth. By virtue of their methods, however, these sciences cannot penetrate to the intimate meaning of things. Yet the danger exists that man, confiding too much in modern discoveries, may even think that he is sufficient unto himself and no longer seek any higher realities (art. 57).

This kind of culture, therefore, is closed in upon itself, does not feel the need of higher enlightenment, and is not open to grace. At the same time, it is a culture incapable of grasping the inner meaning of man; it is agnostic in regard to everything that transcends mere phenomena, and thus the better part of man, namely, what is most noble, profound and authentic in man.

Does today's culture necessarily give rise to phenomenalism, agnosticism and skepticism, on the one side, and self-sufficiency, rejection of the divine, on the other? The Council firmly denies it: "These unfortunate results do not necessarily follow from the culture of today, nor should they lead us into the temptation of not acknowledging its positive values" (art. 57). Frankly, many Christians have fallen into this temptation, thus lumping together in a condemnation both the negative aspects and positive values of modern culture.

The esteem that the Church has for culture is motivated also by the fact that "there are many links between the message of salvation and human culture" (art. 58). On the one hand, revelation has taken the form expressive of the culture proper to different ages: thus, God spoke to the ancient Jews in the form proper to Semitic culture, Christ according to the cultural forms of late Judaism, and the apostles against the background of Hellenic culture. On the other hand, "living in various circumstances during the course of time, the Church, too, has used in her preaching the discoveries of different cultures to spread and explain the message of Christ to all nations, to probe it and more deeply understand it, and to give it better expression in liturgical celebrations and in the life of the diversified community of the faithful" (art. 58). In order to prove how true this is, let it suffice to point to the intimate relationship between the abstract formulation of the more important Christian dogmas—the dogma on the Trinity and the dogma of the hypostatic union—and Greek culture, as well as between the liturgy and medieval culture.

Even though the Church may be identified with different cultures, it nevertheless transcends them all: the Church may accept them and make them her own, after purifying them of those non-Christian elements that cannot be assimilated, but she "is not bound exclusively and indissolubly to any race or nation, nor to any particular way of life or any customary pattern of living, ancient or recent" (art. 58). This is so, not because the Church does not esteem cultural values, but because her mission is universal, having been "sent to all peoples of every time and place." Precisely because she is called to make all the cultural values of human history her own, the Church cannot bind herself definitively to any one of them. She operates like the human eye, which, simply because it is destined to see everything, cannot tie itself exclusively to any form and color; otherwise it would see either nothing or everything in one form and color, and therefore in a deformed way.

Though not bound to any culture, the message of the gospel, nevertheless, does not cease to exercise a highly cultural function:

> The good news of Christ constantly renews the life and culture of fallen man. It combats and removes the errors and evils resulting from sinful allurements which are a perpetual threat. It never ceases to purify and elevate the morality of peoples. By riches coming from above, it makes fruitful, as it were from within, the spiritual qualities and gifts of every people and of every age. It strengthens, perfects, and restores them in Christ. Thus by the very fulfillment of her own mission the Church stimulates and advances human and civic culture. By her action, even in its liturgical form, she leads men toward interior liberty (art. 58).

After having expressed the Church's profound esteem for culture and having recalled her relationship with it—a relationship that makes of Christianity and the Church authentic and beneficial forces of culture, though transcending the different cultures—the Constitution recalls a few principles that must preside over the development of an authentic culture. It mentions first of all its end: "Culture must be made to bear on the integral perfection of the human person, and on the good of the community and the whole of society" (art. 59). These words deserve a careful consideration. Culture cannot be limited to developing this or that faculty in man, but must tend toward a harmonious development of all the faculties of man, physical, affective and spiritual. In particular it must tend toward developing man as an intelligent and free being. In other words, culture must, above all, develop man's intellect and freedom, must help man to think, reason and judge, to form his personal opinions, to develop his sense of morality, to free himself from all prejudice and passions, and to develop his religious and social sense. In fact, the human person cannot be considered only in relationship to self and the world, but also in relationship to others and God; such a consideration is indeed essential to the human person. Culture, therefore, cannot disregard the social and religious dimensions of the human person.

If we now turn to modern culture, can we say that it is aimed "at the integral perfection of the human person"? The answer cannot be completely affirmative. Modern culture is, on the one hand, too dominated by technology and, on the other hand, too excessive a mass culture to give due consideration to "pure" intellectual values; it is too utilitarian and mechanized to leave room for the "useless" powers of contemplation and speculation; it is too commercialized and dependent on those who pay for it to preserve the freedom necessary for an autonomous development of thought.

Culture does indeed need freedom. This is a point raised by the Council with great emphasis:

> Because it flows immediately from man's spiritual and social nature, culture has constant need of a just freedom if it is to develop. It also needs the legitimate possibility of exercising its independence according to its own principles. Rightly, therefore, it demands respect and enjoys a certain inviolability, at least as long as the rights of the individual and of the community, whether particular or universal, are preserved within the context of the common good (art. 59).

Culture can vindicate freedom even with regard to faith. Accordingly the Council, recalling the teaching of Vatican Council I, declares that there are two orders of knowledge that are distinct, namely, faith and reason, and that "the Church does not forbid that 'when the human arts and sciences are practiced, they use their own principles and their proper method, each in its own domain.' Hence, 'acknowledging this just liberty,' this sacred Synod affirms the legitimate autonomy of human culture and especially of the sciences" (art. 59). This assertion is of great importance. First of all, it ought to dispel the conviction of many non-Catholics and non-Christians that faith deprives Catholics of the necessary cultural and scientific freedom, and that a scientist cannot accept faith without renouncing his free scientific research. According to them, faith would condition the scientist both in his process of research as well as in his conclusions, since he is required to conform the latter to the data of faith. These convictions have been greatly reinforced by some deplorable facts of the past, like the Galileo case. However, we must assert with emphasis that the Catholic enjoys the same freedom of research and investigation that his non-Catholic colleagues enjoy.

Obviously, like any other form of freedom, the freedom of research also has its limits. These, however, are moral limits, neither religious nor specifically Catholic. They are limits placed on any scientist who wants to preserve his human dignity and desires science to be a benefit to man rather than a source of destruction and ruin.

The Council's assertion of the freedom of culture and scientific research must be brought to bear even within the Church, where some want to put a muzzle on culture and scientific investigation for fear that certain limits, established more or less arbitrarily, might be transgressed or that faith itself might be put in danger. In this respect, it is proper to observe that one must not confuse the truths of faith, absolutely certain in virtue of the authority of God who revealed them and the confirmation of the Church which defined them, with the presentation that has been made of those truths during the course of centuries. Nor should they be confused with what has been more or less legitimately added to them, to the point of giving the impression either that the additions form a singular body with those truths or that *aut simul stabunt aut simul cadent*. Actually, we ought to point out that, in the area of faith, there are relatively few doctrines that are absolutely certain, while many points—even those believed to be definitely established—are open to investigation. The clearest proof of this is the fact that the Council reopened questions that seemed forever closed.

For the rest, faith is constantly in search of understanding (*fides quaerens intellectum*), and it cannot be said that investigations of past centuries have exhausted the task of illuminating faith and that, consequently, no new insight is to be expected from modern research. Therefore the dialogue between faith and culture, between faith and scientific research, is as open today as it was yesterday. It is by no means an easy dialogue, just as it was not easy in the past. The Council recognizes this when it asserts that "although the Church has contributed much to the development of culture, experience shows that, because of circumstances, it is sometimes difficult to harmonize culture with Christian teaching" (art. 62). The Council, however, remarks that these difficulties are stimulating: "these difficulties do not necessarily harm the life of faith. Indeed they can stimulate the mind to a more accurate and penetrating grasp of the faith. For recent studies and findings of science, history, and philosophy raise new questions . . . and demand new theological investigations" (art. 62).

This is why the Church looks with benevolence upon the vast work of scientific research that is accomplished outside as well as within her bosom. Not only does she not fear or suspect these endeavors, but she truly encourages them, since the Church knows that scientific progress, when authentic, leads to a more profound understanding of faith. Because man has been created in God's image, and the world is a reflection of his omnipotence and wisdom, a more profound knowledge of the mystery of man and of the enigma of the universe cannot but lead to a deeper understanding of the mystery of God, present with his creating Word in man and in the universe.

Science, however, is not alone in delving into the mystery of man; other branches of learning, especially literature and the arts, perform the same function. Accordingly, the Council affirms that "literature and the arts are also, in their own way, of great importance to the life of the Church. For they strive to probe the unique nature of man, his problems, and his experiences" (art. 62), in brief, his mystery. Consequently, "efforts must be made so that those who practice these arts can feel that the Church gives recognition to them in their activities, and so that, enjoying an orderly freedom, they can establish smoother relations with the Christian community" (art. 62). Indeed, the Church must receive "new forms of art" even into her places of worship (art. 62).

On their part, theologians must collaborate "through a sharing of resources and points of view . . . with men well versed in the other sciences" (art. 62). But, the Council concludes, "in order that such persons may fulfill their proper function, let it be recognized that all the faithful, clerical and lay, possess a lawful freedom of inquiry and of thought, and the freedom to express their minds humbly and courageously about those matters in which they enjoy competence" (art. 62).[2]

Having asserted the autonomy of culture from faith, the Council proceeds to affirm such an autonomy also from political and economic forces. It realizes, in fact, that these forces attempt to put culture at their service either by compulsion or bribery. In rejecting the claim proper to all the totalitarian states to create their own particular culture or to dictate norms and laws for culture, the Council affirms that "it is not the function of public authority to determine what the proper nature of forms of a human culture should be. It should rather foster the conditions and the means which are capable of promoting cultural life among all citizens and even within the minorities of a nation" (art. 59). Well aware of how economic forces strongly influence cultural life by demanding submission and services in exchange for the economic assistance that they, almost exclusively, can provide, the Council insists it is essential that culture be not diverted from its own purpose (to promote the total well-being of the human person, and not the interests of political and economic groups) "to serve political or economic interests" (art. 59).

The Council does not limit itself to enunciating the principles that should guide cultural life. Addressing itself to all Christians, it also specifies what must be done in order that culture progress. There are three most urgent tasks that the Council assigns to Christians in the cultural field.

The first is to work strenuously in order that "universal recognition and implementation . . . be given to the right of all men to a human and civic culture favorable to personal dignity" (art. 60). Every man has a right to culture, just as he has a right to nourishment. Ignorance is a form of spiritual misery that diminishes man's personal dignity. "Therefore," the Council continues, "it is necessary to provide every man with a sufficient abundance of cultural benefits, especially those which constitute so-called basic culture. Otherwise, because of illiteracy and a lack of responsible activity, very many will be prevented from collaborating in a truly human manner for the sake of the common good" (art. 60). Whoever considers how widespread the plague of illiteracy is in the modern world, will realize how great the responsibility of Christians is for what has been called the "waste of intelligence." However, seen under a less economic and utilitarian but more profoundly human aspect, illiteracy is first of all a permanent offense to the dignity of man, insofar as he is a human person before being a producer of goods and services. Under the religious and Christian aspect, illiteracy is an obstacle to the acceptance of faith and religious values, insofar as it is associated, both as cause and effect, with a materialism that ignores any spiritual exigency. Consequently, the struggle against illiteracy is, for the Christian, a struggle for man and for spiritual and religious values.

Man, however, has a right not only to basic culture, but also to whatever is necessary for the development of his person. Thus, men capable of higher studies must be given the opportunity to pursue them. To be sure, this possibility should not be given in view of services that one can render to society or with an implicit clause that the state will later have the right to assign a specific task, as is the case for example in the Soviet Union. This would amount to making the human person a servant of the state, to using the person as a means to an end. The human person, however, can never be used as a means.

However, culture is a duty before being a right. Indeed it is a right precisely because it is a duty. It is because man has a right to develop himself culturally and to improve himself according to all his potentialities and powers, that he has the right to employ whatever is necessary for him to accomplish such a duty. It is therefore extremely important that everyone be made "conscious of his right to culture and of the duty he has to develop himself culturally" (art. 60). The Council justly remarks that "existing conditions of life and of work sometimes thwart the cultural strivings of men and destroy in them the desire for self-improvement. This is especially true of country people and laborers" (art. 60). They need, therefore, to be provided with working conditions that will not hinder their cultural life but rather favor it. Similar preoccupation the Council shows for women: "Everyone should acknowledge and favor the proper and necessary participation of women in cultural life" (art. 60). There is a vast field for the cultural initiative of Christians wherein they can work in close cooperation with non-Christian or nonreligious cultural enterprises such as those promoted by UNESCO.

The second duty of Christians is to work toward the formation of man's whole culture, i.e., a culture that tends to develop the whole of man according to the scale of values proper to him. Man is a substantial and indissoluble unity of body and spirit; in him are found physical and spiritual faculties. A culture is integral when it leads to a harmonious development of man's physical and spiritual faculties. But there is also in man a scale of values. Spiritual values tower over material ones and must therefore obtain pre-eminence also in the cultural development of man. In other words, the development of intellectual and moral values ought to have priority over the development of physical values, otherwise proper and harmonious development will be damaged or impeded. Accordingly, the Council asserts that "it remains each man's duty to preserve a view of the whole human person, a view in which the values of intellect, will, conscience, and fraternity are pre-eminent. These values are all rooted in God the Creator and have been wonderfully restored and elevated in Christ" (art. 61).

Now, what is the present condition of culture? In general, culture appears as divided and dividing, lacking as it does a synthetic principle of unity. There are many specialists but "universal men" are becoming more and more rare, men who alone are capable of gathering under one principle the large mass of data and knowledge that mankind today possesses. Where there is no unity there is no culture, understood in its highest meaning. As the Council observes:

> Today it is more difficult than ever for a synthesis to be formed of the various branches of knowledge and the arts. For while the mass and the diversity of cultural factors are increasing, there is a decline in the individual man's ability to grasp and unify these elements. Thus the ideal of the "universal man" is disappearing more and more (art. 61).

Obviously, it is not a question of condemning specialization and specialists, but of integrating specialization into a wider, indeed global vision of reality, open to the great problems of human existence, as well as into a global vision of the world and of history. It is not a question of rejecting technical formation and technology, but of integrating them into the so-called classical or humanistic culture, so as to develop all human faculties: the physical, the intellectual and the emotional.[3] In other words, our task is to give modern culture, which, under the influence of a technological materialism, tends to become spiritually atrophied, a motivating spiritual principle. Consequently, the Council recommends that all Christians collaborate with others so as to "animate the cultural expressions and group activities characteristic of our times with a human and a Christian spirit" (art. 61).

The third duty of Christians in the cultural field is the establishment of a Christian culture. But what is a Christian culture? It is the result of the encounter of human culture with Christianity, the fruit of the permeation of a cultural world by the Christian faith, so that new cultural forms are created. Christopher Dawson writes:

> Christian culture is the embodiment of Christianity in social institutions and patterns of life and behavior. It is the nature of Christianity to act as leaven in the world and to transform human nature by a new principle of divine life.[4]

Actually, in order to understand what Christian culture is, one must look into history. History reveals that from the encounter of the Greco-Roman culture with Christianity there arose the first form of Christian culture. Its major exponents were the Fathers of the Church (Ambrose, Augustine, Gregory, Basil, Gregory of Nyssa, Gregory Nazianzen, John Chrysostom), Christian poets and philosophers like Prudentius and Boethius, jurists like Justinian. Marks of this first Christian culture are found in the major Roman basilicas, in St. Sophia in Constantinople and in St. Apollinaris in Classe. When this culture came into contact with the knowledge brought by the "barbarians" who had invaded and conquered the Roman empire, a new Christian culture was born, the result of a very laborious process: the medieval culture, whose highest expressions were Scholasticism, the *Summa Theologica* of St. Thomas, the *Divine Comedy* of Dante, the Crusades, St. Bernard and Gothic cathedrals, St. Francis and St. Dominic, the universities of Paris and Bologna, the *Decretum Gratiani*, and above all, the idea of a *Christianitas* that made of the whole Christian Western world one sole "People of God," i.e., a religious and political community governed by pope and emperor.

Creation of a medieval Christian culture was certainly Christianity's greatest cultural success. But with the end of the Middle Ages it lost its power to create a Christian culture. Thus, for example, coming into contact with highly developed pagan cultures, like the Indian, Chinese, Japanese and Arabian, it was unable to permeate them and to give rise to a Christian culture in those countries. It was successful only in its contacts with primitive cultures like those existing in America and Africa; but even here rather than create autochthonous Christian cultures, it transplanted the Christian culture of Western Europe. The cause of this failure is to be found in the fact that, in previous centuries, it was the conviction that the only form of Christian civilization, and therefore the only form of Christian culture, was that of the Western Christian world. Consequently, this civilization was considered as the one to impose on the whole world. In this regard, one should remember the both tragic and comical story of the Malabar and Chinese rites.

From the eighteenth century to present times, Christianity, though remaining a live theological and spiritual tradition, has gradually lost cultural weight and power. Consequently, modern culture has arisen and developed apart from Christian influence. It is certainly true that, indirectly and through many secondary and at times secret channels, the Christian cultural influence has made itself felt also on modern culture. Nevertheless such influence has not succeeded in giving it a Christian character. And yet only Christianity can give modern culture what it desperately needs, namely, a coordinating and unifying spiritual principle.

On this Dawson writes:

> Modern civilization in spite of its immense technical achievement is morally weak and spiritually divided. Science and technology in themselves are morally neutral and do not provide any guiding spiritual principle. They are liable to be used by any *de facto* power which happens to control society, for its own ends. And thus we see at the present time how the resources of science have been used by the totalitarian state as instruments of power, and how the technological order has been applied in the Western democratic world in the service of wealth and the satisfaction of material needs, even though these needs are artificially stimulated by the same economic powers which find their profit in their satisfaction.[5]

It is necessary, therefore, that modern culture and Christianity encounter each other and establish a mutually profitable dialogue. But who has the responsibility of realizing this meeting and this conversation? The Council states:

> While adhering to the methods and requirements proper to theology, theologians are invited to seek continually for more suitable ways of communicating doctrine to the men of their times. For the deposit of faith or revealed truths are one thing; the manner in which they are formulated without violence to their meaning and significance is another (art. 62).

And the Council goes on to say:

> Theological inquiry should seek a profound understanding of revealed truth without neglecting close contact with its own times. As a result, it will be able to help those men skilled in various fields of knowledge to gain a better understanding of the faith. This common effort will very greatly aid in the formation of priests. It will enable them to present to our contemporaries the doctrine of the Church concerning God, man, and the world in a manner better suited to them, with the result that they will receive it more willingly. Furthermore, it is to be

hoped that many laymen will receive an appropriate formation in the sacred sciences, and that some will develop and deepen these studies by their own labors (art. 62).

Therefore, theologians, priests with pastoral care, and theologically prepared laymen must put forth great effort to announce the gospel to the man of modern culture, to make it comprehensible and acceptable. Only by doing so will Christianity become a cultural leavening that can give rise to a new Christian culture truly expressive of our time.

III. OPEN PROBLEMS IN THE CULTURAL FIELD

In dealing with culture, the Council did not attempt to examine, and much less solve, all the problems that directly or indirectly concern culture. The Council set out, first of all, to show its regard for the values of culture and how important in its eyes culture is for the development of the human person. Furthermore, it has given some directives and suggestions that culture might truly be a factor of human development. Consequently, many problems concerning culture remain wide open and Christians will be called upon to solve them in collaboration with other men. In this regard the Council states:

> May the faithful . . . live in very close union with the men of their time. Let them strive to understand perfectly their way of thinking and feeling, as expressed in their culture. Let them blend modern science and its theories and the understanding of the most recent discoveries with Christian morality and doctrine. Thus their religious practice and morality can keep pace with their scientific knowledge and with an ever-advancing technology. Thus, too, they will be able to test and interpret all things in a truly Christian spirit (art. 62).

The first problem concerns the content that culture ought to have and the values it should promote in our technological age. In other words, it is a question of what type of man we should now create, so that today's man may live as man in a world increasingly dominated by technology. The really crucial problem in today's world is that of preserving man's characteristics of *homo sapiens*, of *human personality*, in a world that tends to make of him only a *homo faber*, a robot, a machine—yes, a link in a gigantic assembly line. How is man to survive as a person in a world that judges man, not according to what he is, but according to what he can produce, according to his output; in a world that tends to prevent him from thinking since one or a few do it for all; in a world that tends to deprive man of his freedom of judgment and choice by means of an intense propaganda hammering away in every field, from the political to the economic and commercial?

Since it is the task of culture to promote and develop the human person, what content is necessary and on what values must culture place greater stress in order to give rise to a humanism of the technological age? Obviously, no short answer can be given to this extremely complex problem. Let it suffice to state that, in our opinion, a culture that wants to serve toward the promotion of the human person in the technological age must emphasize above all "pure" intellectual values; it must develop man's ability to think both in abstract and in general terms; it must lead man to think "universally"; it must liberate man from the commonplace, from slogans, and teach him to think personally. This cannot be achieved, however, except through constant contact with the classics, not only the Greek and Latin classics, but also the classics of every age and people, ancient and modern, Western and Eastern—not only from the field of literature and art, but from every field: philosophical, political, scientific, juridical and religious. This means that even in our technological age classical culture, broadly understood, must be given pre-eminence (but we do not mean that it should be the only one) over technological and scientific culture; this latter cannot and must not be lacking, but should certainly not occupy the whole intellectual effort of man.

Contemporary man faces another grave risk, i.e., that of limiting himself solely to scientific research and to the study of objective facts without asking himself about the meaning and destiny of man and the world, and the ultimate purpose of life. Above all, there is a grave risk of seeing in man nothing but a natural being equal in everything to other living beings. In fact, today's scientific and technological man, especially if he is engaged in pure research, runs the risk of being engulfed in an agnostic positivism and in a narrower materialism. In order to avert this danger, culture, especially in our technological age, must bring to the fore the great problems concerning the meaning and destiny of man, the world and history.

At this point arises a second problem. Modern culture seems incapable of saving man of the technological age from positivism and materialism, since culture itself lacks spiritual vigor and moral force. In fact, it is to a great extent without spritual content; it is agnostic and skeptical with regard to moral and spiritual values, and sometimes it is even the prey of a radical pessimism concerning man and his destiny. Hence, there is an urgent need to reinvigorate culture spiritually in order for it to become a source of authentic development for men. How can this be achieved? It seems that such a goal cannot really be accomplished unless modern culture returns to its religious matrix, i.e., Christianity, for the spiritual and moral aridity of modern culture is due precisely to its withdrawal from this matrix.

Whence the problem of the encounter and dialogue between Christianity and modern culture, one of the most important and difficult problems of our times. Is such an encounter and dialogue possible today? Does Christianity today have the power and ability to inject new spiritual life into modern culture? Or can the gap between Christianity and modern culture ever be filled? These are some of the questions that we would like to raise without pretending to answer them exhaustively. We shall call attention only to the fact that today it is especially on the cultural level that Christianity and atheism confront each other in a decisive manner. For Christianity to lose the battle of culture means to lose in great part the battle for the construction of a more human and Christian world; it means to fade away as a force creative of a more noble humanism, Christian humanism, and to be confined to exclusively spiritual activity; it means, finally, to be excluded from the forces that move history. One of the more serious dramas of our time is that while, on the one hand, modern culture needs Christianity in order to draw the spiritual strength it lacks, and Christianity needs to insert itself into modern culture in order to reach man more profoundly and radically, on the other hand, modern culture nurtures diffidence—if not contempt—for Christianity, which in turn experiences an inferiority complex regarding culture that prevents a frank and serene dialogue.

In reality, a dialogue between Christianity and modern culture is more difficult than it might seem, even if the history of Western culture alone is taken into account. Undoubtedly, the origins of that culture are Christian, and Christian in most of its content, but beginning with the end of the Middle Ages, Christianity and culture began to separate and walk different paths, following an erratic course. Consequently, today they find themselves in clear opposition on many points, and spiritually very remote from each other.

As a proof of this assertion, we have only to analyze some fundamental characteristics of modern culture readily to see how opposed they are to Christianity. Modern culture is relativist and conditioned by history; it recognizes no absolute truths or laws applicable in every age, but submits everything to the flow of history and thus holds everything as changeable and relative to conditions of time and place. Christianity instead admits absolute truths and laws that are always valid, and even though it lives in history, it sees itself as transcending history, i.e., not subject to it, because of some of its essential aspects. Modern culture is immanentistic and anthropocentric, that is, it rejects transcendence and places man at the center of the universe, making him the measure of all things as well as the supreme norm of all values. Christianity, on the contrary, is essentially held to transcendence and places God at the core of everything as supreme norm of all values. Modern culture is fundamentally rationalistic, that is, it holds human reason as the supreme norm of truth. For Christianity, however, beyond reason there is faith that reaches where reason does not and sees where reason encounters only darkness. Modern culture distrusts anything that cannot be measured or tested, anything that cannot be scientifically analyzed and controlled; consequently it distrusts "mystery."

Finally, modern culture fluctuates between optimism and pessimism, between self-sufficiency and despair. On the one hand, it has total confidence in man and his ability and holds him capable of daring anything and over-coming all obstacles that stand between him and his complete conquest of nature, without having to have recourse to anyone in order to achieve a complete humanism. On the other hand, modern culture is radically pessimistic with regard to man and the world, judging man a "useless passion" (Sartre) and his human condition as "absurd" (Camus). In neither case does man need God: he either saves himself or is in such a situation that no one can save him. For Christianity, however, man is a sinner unable to save himself, but is saved by God through Christ. Christianity is thus essentially a message of salvation, an *evangelium salutis*.

To be sure, between modern culture and Christianity there are not only points of opposition and disagreements, but also many points of contact. Therefore, a dialogue between Christianity and modern culture is indeed possible today. However, one should not overlook the difficulties nor expect that such an encounter can take place soon or without great effort.

The technological age creates for today's man a third problem in the cultural field, namely, the problem of a truly universal or world-wide culture. In the past, when communication and cultural exchange among people was limited, the cultural world was divided into many particular cultures, each developing itself more or less independently from the other. Of course, even in the past there were universal cultures: the Hellenic, the Roman, and in the Middle Ages the Christian, which was divided into two sub-cultures: the Romano-Germanic in the West and the Byzantine in the East. But the universality of those cultures was limited to the then known world and actually did not even extend to all of that. Thus, in the Middle Ages, in the margin of the Christian culture there flourished an Arab culture. Only today, when contacts between people are so close that the world tends toward unification, in spite of obstacles that political and economical interests raise, is a relatively universal culture, or if you will a *superculture*, being born.

What are its characteristics? Certainly those of Western civilization and culture. Unfortunately, however, the emerging superculture of our technological age does not reveal all the characteristics of Western culture; in fact, it manifests the least significant and original ones. The scientific technological character is predominant, and this gives the emerging superculture a utilitarian and materialistic aspect. Furthermore, this superculture tends to suppress particular cultures, especially those which, because of their rich spiritual patrimony, attend less to material values and are, therefore, ill protected against the invading forces of a materialistic superculture which is so proud of its success.

An authentic superculture of the technological age should, instead, be born out of the encounter and dialogue between all the cultures of the world, each contributing its own value. In other words, it should be an *integrated* culture, rich with all the cultural values capable of being universalized and placed at the service of all mankind. Only in this way can a truly *universal* and planetary culture be achieved—universal not in the sense that it is the culture of all men, but rather universally formulated, i.e., representing a synthesis of the highest cultural values of all particular cultures.

Is such a superculture truly possible? And if so, where can we find the central nucleus around which the values of particular cultures could be rallied in a living synthesis? An answer to these questions is not easy. For our part, we think that such a nucleus could be represented by the principle, generally admitted today, of the sovereign dignity of the human person, as *imago Dei.* This could be the starting point for the creation of a new humanism, the humanism of the technological age.

Here, then, are some of the problems in the area of culture that the Council has left open. They constitute an invitation to Christians to reflect and to search for a solution in conformity with the new spirit the Council has promoted in the Church and with the directives it has given for the renewal of culture. In the area of culture too the principle applies that the Council marks not an end but a beginning, the opening of new paths that Christians must now courageously walk.

NOTES

1. In *Semaines sociales de France* (Versailles, 1936) 461–462.

2. With regard to the freedom of culture, noteworthy was the intervention at the Council of Archbishop Pellegrino, of Turin (Oct. 1, 1965). Having defended freedom of scientific inquiry not only for laymen, but for clerics as well, the Archbishop recalled how a few years earlier he had met a priest "who lived in involuntary exile simply because he had expressed certain views which we now find with satisfaction in papal and Conciliar documents." He added: "It is hardly necessary to remind you that, even in the theological sciences, it is discovered that many things, though unquestionably accepted for a long time, with the progress of inquiry appear to be in need of a revision. Indeed the range of possible or probable opinions is perhaps much more ample than those may think who are not expert in this difficult and often delicate type of inquiry. Only under this condition, namely, that all Catholics be given freedom in their search for truth, will it be possible to have within the Church that dialogue which Pope Paul VI, in *Ecclesiam suam,* recommended be 'frequent and familiar . . . ready to listen to the various voices of the men of our times, effective in making good, prudent, just, and strong Catholics.' I would like to add that if everyone understood that it is licit to express one's own opinion in a spirit of true and responsible freedom, it would be done with the truthfulness and sincerity that should always shine forth in the Church. Otherwise the grave evil of falsehood and hypocrisy will hardly be avoided. For these reasons, I propose that the following four simple words be inserted in the text of the schema: 'Christian freedom of inquiry should be recognized for all the faithful, *sive clericis sive laicis,* in order that they may fulfill their proper function'" (*La Civiltà Cattolica* [1966] 172).

3. In *The Crisis of Western Education* (New York: Sheed and Ward, 1961) 132, Christopher

Dawson writes: "The old domination of classical humanism has passed away, and nothing has taken its place except the scientific specialisms which do not provide a complete intellectual education, and rather tend to disintegrate into technologies. Every educator recognizes that this is unsatisfactory. A scientific specialist or a technologist is not an educated person. He tends to become merely an instrument of the industrialist or the bureaucrat, a worker ant in an insect society, and the same is true of the literary specialist, though his social function is less obvious."

4. *Ibid.*, 150.
5. *Ibid.*, 159.

Question: *Since mutual love belongs thus intrinsically to the nature of marriage, does this nullify marriages which are entered upon with no will to mutual love?*

Häring: Mutual love expresses itself in the indissoluble bond and structure of unity. Hence it belongs to the objective order, to the fundamental qualities of this covenant between one man and one woman. If the two should enter into marriage with the understanding that they will not love each other, they would deny the essence of marriage, and nothing could then be sanctified in their life. One example will show how essential is the will to express mutual love in conjugal intercourse. In a recent book I read. the author tells how he made an experiment new in human history. He decided to procreate a child with a Bohemian without any feeling, any affection, any expression of love. He found that it could be done. But here we are faced with the greatest bestiality. This shows how wrong it was not to make very clear to Christian couples that it is essential in conjugal intercourse to express love, authentic love.

Question: *From your talk, Father Häring, I conclude that no matter how high conjugal love is elevated in value, in com-*

478

parison with the transmission of life it is still Christian teaching that there is a moral bond between these goods. Perhaps the Church ought not to make judgments about specific methods of birth regulation. But must not the Church state very clearly that, while the communicative and procreative ends or goods belong together in the order or estate of marriage, these may nevertheless be separated "artificially" in single acts or a series of single acts of conjugal intercourse? How else can the Church break with the single act analysis of the past?

HÄRING: I think the single act analysis is done for because of our modern biological intelligence. In an earlier interpretation, even among medical authorities, it was thought that every act by its very nature is procreative; they knew of only the existence of the sperm. But today, we know that in the very intention of God the Creator, as manifested in biological function, there are only a few acts in which the procreative good is biologically intended. And the intention of man cannot go further. In the eighteenth century it was already evident that the procreative good need not be desired in every act of intercourse. St. Alphonsus of Ligouri taught explicitly that poor people are fully in accord with God's will if in the conjugal intercourse they deeply desire and pray that a new pregnancy will not occur.

Question: As soon as you assert the judgment of the couples, who are taught by their virtue and by their experience, is important, how can we expect that a categorical answer as to means will possibly cover all cases and be loyal to the criteria which you set forth in your talk?

HÄRING: I tried to keep the answer within general principles. But I failed to say that there is never a perfect solution that guarantees all values. The solution must be one that here and now, in this personal and cultural context, protects the higher values in the best possible way. For instance, indissolubility, unity and fidelity protect the harmony that is necessary for education. The proper solution must also appreciate the urgency of values. Another aspect I did not develop that is absolutely fundamental for Christian morality is the law of growth. If our pastoral directives do not allow people to take the first step toward growth, toward order, they never will take the other steps. If we demand of them a solution that respects only one value but neglects many others (even though they could put it into practice with the greatest heroism here and now) shows we would be wrong. Once more St. Alphonsus shows understanding in this respect. If there is no possibility of convincing people that they have to act on a certain principle, the confessor must weigh the matter carefully lest he only push them to rebellion or occasion a formal sin. He even goes further than I would dare when he declares that there are secondary principles of natural law that are very imperfectly worded, and that if the application of such a natural law would do great harm in view of other principles (cause evident evil or extraordinary distress), then epikeia can be used. I don't think that we can cover all possible cases with one principle.

CALLAHAN: Generally as a married lay person I liked your talk very much. Only one thing bothered me: you mentioned the necessity of purifying conjugal love. I am curious as to whether you believe conjugal love requires some special purification, or whether it is not the case that all love requires purification and hence also conjugal love. I ask this because I think many married people feel that they somehow exist in the constant occasion of sin, as that is the way the traditional doctrine has come across. We feel under terrible pressure to justify somehow our use of the sexual act and constantly show that it is all right for us to be married.

HÄRING: The answer is evident: purification is needed in the whole human life. Whatever a man does—even his intellectual efforts—needs further purification and deepening. There is no exception. There is, of course, a spiritualist trend in Christian thinking stemming from Manichaeism. I received just this week a series of letters from pious persons who explained to me that the first sin of Adam was a sexual sin. The Fathers of the early Church, great Christian thinkers and biblical scholars reject such an explanation. Manichaeism is responsible for this. Conjugal love, as a matter of fact, is meant by the creator to help people overcome egotism. Only because of man's general condition of sinfulness does it need purification, as does every kind of love.

LADY JACKSON: What I would like to ask Father Häring concerns another matter in this spectrum of natural values or values of the natural order. Is not one of the problems that we confront here the fact that the Church does not have a very clear picture of what it means by woman as a person. In other words, we hear much about the dignity of persons, but there are certain conditions I think involved in the whole problem of birth control, of sexual relations, of marriage, for which perhaps a better picture of woman would itself be a clarification or a help.

I would like to give two examples. One is in this urgency in the developing world. How very little we hear about the appalling life of women who have babies every year, pregnancies practically continuously, who then perhaps have to bring up five or six children under conditions of poverty and whom they can barely feed. This I think quite destroys their dignity as persons in a way that is existential, factual and has to be considered. I see a great deal more being said about the pressure of population rather than about the present destruction of persons. And this is a point to make.

HÄRING: Your concern that we must first appreciate the person is very drastically expressed in the Council Constitution. When it speaks of harmonizing conjugal love with the responsible transmission of life, it says that the question "must be determined by objective standards," and that these are "based on the nature of the human person and his acts" (art. 51). The accent is strongly placed on the person throughout. It is evident that in the past it was not always fully appreciated that the person of woman is worth as much as the person of man. The Constitution speaks of the acts of a person only after the nature of the person. Hence the physical expression is not without value, but it has to be integrated; it has to be seen as an expression of the personal action, love.

LADY JACKSON: My second point is that being a person means having a full function not just a biological one. My point here is that I think the teaching Church doesn't do very much to help women in this wider concept of the development of all their gifts. In other words, they may get very strictly caught into one side of their contribution in their function as mothers and wives but not as a full human person.

HÄRING: In the same article of the Constitution that lays such stress on the importance of the mother in the family, especially if there are little children to be educated, we are told that "the legitimate social progress of women should not be understood on that account" (art. 52). A one-sided insistence on the role of the mother would be wrong, if we neglect her personality and function to society.

HYSLOP: Father, you quote article 51 which states that a true contradiction cannot exist between the divine laws pertaining to the transmission of life and those pertaining to authentic conjugal love. Your comment is that the Council does not assert that the Church knows fully divine laws, but rather makes all possible effort to know them better. I appreciate the depth of that effort. Let me now refer you to article 48 of the Constitution in which it is stated that the institution of matrimony itself and conjugal love are ordained for the procreation and education of children, and find in them their ultimate crown. I am asking whether this does not seem to indicate to the reader that here is a definite declaration of the divine law and a choice which emphasizes the transmission of life rather than the expression of conjugal love.

HARING: By speaking in such a fundamental way about conjugal love, the Council has done the greatest service to the procreative good and put it on the right level. Here important progress has been made in comparison with older moralists. They taught that the institution of marriage is ordained to procreation, while married love is only a subjective end.

481

Question: Father Tucci, your paper and the Constitution seem to reflect the problems of government as whole and of administration of laws in particular. They don't distinguish these sufficiently from politics. Law is not politics. Politics has to do with the conflict of interest in the making of law and policy. The Constitution and the paper need to examine the generic dilemmas of politics in the sense of participating in party politics, looking toward the making and remaking of law. Please comment.

TUCCI: Well, I agree, fundamentally, with this observation. In the document there are some indications of those major preoccupations which the politician has to keep in mind when making and remaking laws. But it is true that in the text, as it is, the main preoccupation is to identify politics with law.

Question: In a pluralistic society like the United States is it permissible for a Christian Catholic politician to endorse a public policy and legislation in support of birth control? Is it permissible for him to oppose it on grounds of Catholic morality today? May official agencies of the Church oppose such a public policy in today's ecumenical and aggiornamento context?

TUCCI: Well, I think that really when the Catholic politician in general has to judge about making or remaking laws, he must not only consider what is the authentic and clear doctrine of the Church (I presume there is a clear doctrine of the Church on the subject, for you seem to suppose that), but he has to consider the common good of this historical, factual community in which he lives. He has to consider, according to his own competence and with great freedom, what is the best legislation that will really correspond to the needs of the whole community, with all the trends of different opinions represented in it. Hence, I don't think that you can say it is permissible for him to oppose it on the grounds of Catholic morality only. As for the question of an official agency of the Church, I would say that they have to be even more prudent than single politicians because they are more directly connected with the Church.

Question: If the priest and religious remains a Christian, must he not remain free and responsible to his own conscience and his own professional competence in speaking and acting in the social political sphere?

TUCCI: In a negative way, I would say he cannot be obliged to act against his conscience, or to defend in the social or political sphere, a position that is, from the point of view of the authentic doctrine of the Church, still open.

Positively, he might be asked not to express his opinion publicly if there is a danger to the discipline he has freely accepted, provided it is not on a matter of vital importance to which the Church as a whole is requested by God, through the signs of the times, to bear witness, e.g., in defense of human rights. It applies certainly to the state of oppression of religious liberty in the countries under communist rule. Why should this not be the case for the promotion of civil rights in a democratic country.

> *Question: To what extent do you think the process of secular-*
> *ization is in the line of the economy of salvation or the will of*
> *God as expressed in revelation?*

TUCCI: I would stress the transcendence and the uniqueness of revelation and the economy of salvation.

> *Question: Does the word "Church" mean hierarchy once*
> *more in your paper? Can the Christian not have a mandate of*
> *his own as a layman who is a citizen? Does not every Christian,*
> *therefore, represent the Church and does not the Church in*
> *this person engage very fallibly in politics?*

TUCCI: Well it may be that I sometimes used the word "Church" in the old, bad sense of identifying Church only with the hierarchy. If so, I apologize. But most of the time I was considering the whole community of faith, which is interpreted by hierarchy. I don't think there is opposition between the two points here.

As to the second question, I think the Christian can have a mandate of his own as a layman who is a citizen. And I think also we have to consider the prophetic mission of single Christians and groups. On religious grounds they may have a prophetic mission in the political sphere. They represent the Church in some way, certainly, because in the Church they receive their main mission, general or specific. But I would say that in matters not yet clear in the consciousness of the whole Church, they cannot represent, not yet represent, the faith or position of the whole community.

> *Question: My question has to do with the position that Père*
> *Daniélou reaffirmed in an editorial in the* Journal of Ecu-
> menical Studies, *in which he argued that the Church cannot*
> *really be secure or do its salvific work in a secular environ-*
> *ment (and here we touch the vexed word secular), but that*
> *the environment must be penetrated, through the Church's*
> *agency, with a generalized Christian and moral quality. Now I*
> *felt that the effort made in your paper struck substantially free*

of this. And the Constitution itself does not seem to me to support his position. But I would like you to comment on whether the decree sets aside, supports or rejects Père Daniélou's statement.

Tucci: Very frankly, I don't accept the view of Father Daniélou. He speaks mainly in terms of structures and institutions or closed, social Catholic communities. I would say that the state or juridical institutions of a civil community, or nation, have to allow the greatest possible freedom so that religion may develop itself in the best way—not favoring, in the sense of sponsoring, the viewpoint of the Catholic group or the Protestant group, again in the sense of an established Church. On the other hand, however, even if there isn't a law against religion, behind some secular views there is an opposition to religion, a certain prejudice against it. This is not the function of the state.

> Question: The concept of secularity as distinguished from the threat of secularism is functioning in some discussion in the United States. And a theology of the secular is on the tongues of many people. If the word secularity be understood to describe what you simply called the "profane, terrestrial and lay realities which have as an end the temporal common good," would you feel it just to say that the Church does its entire duty in relation to politics when it urges the Christian in politics to do his entire duty, by saying to him that the justice that exists in the secular state is the justice that is the proper end of the state, in the divine economy, and when the Christian seeks to realize that justice he aids the Holy Spirit, he does his full Christian duty in that sphere?

Tucci: I agree. This is the old distinction between laicism and laicity in my own language.

Stransky: I found something of this problem in your statement on culture where you seem to be stressing the point that the coordinating and unifying spiritual principles of the modern world can be achieved only by giving birth to a new Christian culture. The alternatives that you list in your paper are based on the either/or of Christianity and atheism. This sounds very fine if this is the only option, that is, if the Christianity as we have known it up to now doesn't continue a kind of corpus Christianum, we are going to have atheism. This brings up the problem of the secularization process that is going on in the world today. When you talk about modern culture having developed apart from Christian influence, I wonder. I think it is a deep theological question of the dialectic that, in fact, did take place within the *corpus Christianum* to produce a secular culture. In other words, the *corpus Christianum* that the Church built up collapsed from within under the impact of forces which the Church herself had stirred into active life. Hence, it seems to me that there was something within Christianity, not excluding the demonic, that has produced secularization in the good sense of the word. It is in fact this secularization that is becoming a world-wide force: global unification through global secularization. I don't think we should simplify the question by thinking that somehow the secularization process came about despite Christianity or in opposition to Christianity. Therefore, since this is here we had better face up to it. There is something very Christian in the secularization process that we are facing today. And when we ask what are we going to do about it, I don't think it's a question of Christianity as you are describing it here, but of a new form of the *Christian people.*

The point I want to bring out is that I think your excellent paper on politics still doesn't solve the problem that you bring up in the general area of the Christian Church in relation to the secular world in all its aspects. What is this new Christianity as the unifying principle of culture that you are proposing in your paper?

TUCCI: I think you are right in stressing that some elements that were part of Christianity in the past operated the transition to secularization. But I would say that was done not despite Christian principles, but certainly despite Christian institutions. It was providential, because I am convinced that every new situation of humanity, every new richness of history, must come in contact with Christian principles and create new forms of Christian culture. So it was good that some forms decayed. And the reason why they really were decaying was the fact that they were not able to understand the principles of secularization in the good sense; they were not able to break those crystallized institutions in order to make a new vital synthesis of Christian principles in this new situation.

HESCHEL: The sharp distinction between secular and sacred is not, I believe, quite valid according to the Bible. To me the most secular piece of literature ever written is the first chapter of Genesis. It doesn't say a word about worship, synagogues or sanctuaries. It is all about prosaic, secular things that God has created. Maybe God himself is a secular being. But I think this can be overstressed. It is certainly not biblical. And of course all of creation is just the direction toward the seventh day, toward the Sabbath. The ideal is to sanctify the secular. In other words, there is no absolute contradiction. It is a matter of degree. There is a separation but not a contradiction.

Now I am fully aware of the dreadful thing we face when secularization becomes defiance of the holy, when religion is under judgment. It pays the penalty for having been so isolated, for having isolated the holy instead of trying to sanctify the secular everywhere.

The answer to this, of course, if I may in all humility suggest one, is that, while the sacramental and priestly is vital, the prophetic is equally vital; the office of prophet is indispensable. In a sense the prophets of Israel were the most superfluous people that ever lived. The Law was known; the will of God was proclaimed. What did you need the other prophets for? Moses was there. Apparently there is no institution in the world that is not in need of repair from time to time. Apparently even the word of God can become stale. You need the outburst of prophetic protest and reminders. With all our dedication and loyalty to the permanence of sacraments in the Church and the permanence of the mitra in Judaism, we must be a prophetic outburst. Perhaps the secularization of the world is the greatest challenge we face now, and we have to try to learn that this secularization is our great opportunity for renewal in full prophetic exultation. Unless we learn how to celebrate within the secular we will forget how to worship within the sanctuary.

ERRATA

Session XII, Page 487:

Photograph over caption "NOR-RIS" is incorrect.

Correct picture of NORRIS appears above.

NORRIS

SESSION XII

Rt. Rev. George G. Higgins
Economic and Social Life

Mr. James J. Norris
International Order

Rt. Rev. George G. Higgins

ECONOMIC AND SOCIAL LIFE

Bishop Mark McGrath, the Chairman of our Conference, served in the Council as the *relator* on the *Introductio Expositiva* to the *Constitution on the Church in the Modern World*. In this capacity he was called upon to explain to the Conciliar Fathers the methodology that had been employed in the drafting of the Constitution. Because of the very nature of the document, he pointed out, it was necessary that the real condition of today's world be described, at least in a general way, before any judgments were made about it. This inductive or descriptive methodology, he indicated, was set forth in the *Introductio Expositiva* and was followed throughout the entire schema. "Finally," he noted in concluding his *Relatio*, "the very newness of many of the questions proposed and their diversity . . . impose limits on our document. General principles, either doctrinal or moral, are proposed, which principles frequently do not touch upon completely concrete solutions either because the problems involved require more mature examination, or because they must be considered by the faithful in a particular way in each region, under the guidance of their pastors."

The same point is made as follows in the text of the Constitution itself:

Undeniably this Conciliar program is but a general one in several of its parts— and deliberately so, given the immense variety of situations and forms of human culture in the world. Indeed while it presents teaching already accepted in the Church, the program will have to be further pursued and amplified, since it often deals with matters in a constant state of development. Still, we have relied on the word of God and the spirit of the gospel. Hence we entertain the hope that many of our proposals will be able to bring substantial benefit to everyone, especially after they have been adapted to individual nations and mentalities by the faithful, under the guidance of their pastors (art. 91).

This preliminary word of caution with regard to the inherent limitations of the Constitution is applicable to each of its several chapters, but to none so much as the particular chapter we are to discuss this afternoon—chapter 3 of part II, which deals with economic and social life. In the very nature of things, this chapter deals with highly contingent matters that are in "a constant state of development" and consequently do not lend themselves readily to a univocal application of general principles, either doctrinal or moral. This will explain why the Council decided—wisely, in my opinion—to confine itself to the restatement of certain general principles and proposals which, hopefully, to repeat the words of the Constitution, "will be able to bring substantial benefit to everyone . . . after they have been adapted to individual nations and mentalities by the faithful, under the guidance of their pastors" (art. 91).

The word "restatement" of principles is used here advisedly to suggest at the outset that this particular chapter of the Constitution does not pretend to break any new ground in the field of Catholic social teaching. For better or for worse, it is simply a brief restatement—or, if you will, a bringing up to date—of some, but by no means all of the key principles and ideals outlined in papal social pronouncements of the past seventy-five years and, more specifically, in the two major encyclicals of Pope John XXIII, *Mater et Magistra* and *Pacem in Terris*. It is the Council's hope that Christians may be led by these ideals "and all mankind enlightened, as they search for answers to questions of such complexity" (art. 46).

The Constitution's explicit reference to the fact that mankind must search for answers to the complex questions of the modern world and that the Church wishes only to be of service to mankind in carrying out this search was echoed in Bishop McGrath's *Relatio* on the methodology of the document. "Thus," he stated, "the *Introductio Expositiva* ought to serve the purpose of our schema, namely, to speak to the entire world, with a serious study of the problems which now concern its peoples, so that we may enter into a sincere dialogue with them, bringing forth the light of Christ for the solace, strength, peace, and more abundant life of all men in God."

The tone of the entire Constitution, then, derives from this purpose, namely, to enter into a dialogue with the modern world. In this respect, the document is closely modeled after the example set by John XXIII in his major encyclicals.

Mr. E. E. Y. Hales makes much of this point in his recent book entitled

Pope John and His Revolution. "John," he writes in this perceptive study, "was as anxious as any previous pope to reaffirm some continuity in papal teaching; but in fact, in his brief reign, he changed both its spirit and its content. Still more surprising, he introduced a quite new note of hesitancy. He even hinted that he could be wrong, that he was only expressing his own view . . . [yet] doubt where doubt is due, as it is in all questions of politics and economics, is both intellectually proper and persuasively effective, and part of the charm of Pope John was his refusal to pontificate on public affairs; one feels that he is only giving advice; with Leo XIII and with Pius XI one is not allowed to forget that they are laying down the law."[1]

To round out these introductory remarks about the methodology and the tone of the Constitution, I would call attention to still another similarity between the Constitution and John's encyclicals, namely, its spirit of Christian optimism. Again, what Mr. Hales says in this regard about John's pronouncements on contemporary social, economic and political developments can also be said, *mutatis mutandis,* about the Constitution: "The note of alarm is scarcely audible."[2]

Ernesto Balducci elaborates upon this point in his recent biographical study entitled *John—The Transitional Pope.* "Pope John's image of the Catholic of today," Balducci remarks, "is very different from that which was, for example, widely dominant in the era of his childhood, when the Catholic seemed to be more or less aware of being besieged within a 'Christian world,' which was to be opposed and defended against a 'modern world.'" As regards the modern world, Balducci continues,

> Pope John's Catholic does not feel himself alien to it; all that is good in it is his toc. He desires and does what he can to promote the rights of the working classes; not only towards better social conditions but also towards full and direct political responsibility; he opposes clericalism in all its forms, including those in which capitalism seeks to perpetuate it, in disguise; he prefers the democratic system to any other political system, and this not simply as a make-shift . . . but because it best corresponds to the dignity of the human person; . . . he does not condemn the process of socialization brought about by improved techniques, but sees also its positive contributions, once it has been adequately incorporated and directed towards forms beneficial to the community as a whole; he does not reject the collaboration of other men who do not share his ideas, but seeks to work with them, within the limits permitted by real and proven good will. In short, Pope John's Catholic is perfectly at home in the modern world, and if he opposes it, he does so, not because he is a Catholic, but because the modern world is in many of its aspects inhuman, smitten asunder by the onslaught of evil; he opposes it because he is a man like his fellows, a man among men."[3]

[1] (London: Eyre and Spottiswoóde, 1965) 28.
[2] *Ibid.,* 37.
[3] (New York: McGraw-Hill, 1965) 216–217.

Balducci's portrait of Pope John's modern Catholic—a portrait which, you will note, touches upon certain matters that lie outside the formal scope of our discussion this morning—can also serve as a portrait of the Council's modern Catholic: one who is at home in the modern world and seeks only to serve it and, more specifically, to collaborate with other men of good will in hastening the process of the unification of mankind, which, as Balducci points out, "has shown an almost miraculous progress in recent years."

These things having been said about the methodology, the tone and the self-imposed limitations of the Constitution's chapter on economic and social life, we can proceed, not indeed to summarize the chapter in detail—for this would serve no useful purpose at the present time—but rather to single out a few points that seem to be of particular importance or seem to require clarification or further development.

First of all, the chapter on economic and social life, following the Constitution's controlling methodology of starting inductively from the so-called *signa temporum*, takes note at the very outset of what has come to be called "the revolution of rising expectations"—a phenomenon of which one of our distinguished Conference participants, Barbara Ward, has written about so extensively and to such good effect in recent years. In summary, the chapter points out that, while the economy of today is "an apt instrument for meeting the intensified needs of the human family" . . . and while "the development of economic life could diminish social inequalities, if that development were guided and coordinated in a reasonable and human way . . . all too often it serves only to intensify the inequalities. In some places, it even results in a decline of the social status of the weak and in contempt for the poor" (art. 63). The lack of balance between social classes, between various sectors of economic life, between particular regions of individual countries and between rich and poor nations—these and other inequalities seriously jeopardize the peace of the world. "Our contemporaries," the document points out, "are coming to feel these inequalities with an ever sharper awareness. For they are thoroughly convinced that the wider technical and economic potential which the modern world enjoys can and should correct this unhappy state of affairs" (*ibid.*). According to the document, the basic cause of this unhappy state of affairs is the fact that "many people, especially in economically advanced areas, seem to be hypnotized, as it were, by economics, so that almost their entire personal and social life is permeated with a certain economic outlook. These people can be found both in nations which favor a collective economy as well as in others" (*ibid.*).

The legislative history of the Constitution makes it clear that this phrase "as well as in others" was meant to cover some of the leading capitalist nations of the world, including the United States presumably. This double-barrelled criticism of communist and capitalist nations will probably be resented by some Americans if the reaction to Père Lebret's recent book, *The Last Revolution*, is truly indicative of American sensitivity to such criticism. Père Lebret, of course, is much more explicit and much more pointed than the Constitution in his criticism of the western powers. "There are many reasons," he writes, "for the reluctance of the more advanced and consequently richer peoples to take an objective view of the world situation. The main reason is a certain kind of greed, that is, an immoderate love of possessions. The former Colonial powers were often steeped in this vice, and never succeeded in freeing themselves from it. But the new major powers are possessed by the same vice in an even more virulent form."[4]

Père Lebret's specific references to the United States, which are almost brutally frank, have rubbed a number of Americans the wrong way. I happen to think that Lebret is too critical of the United States or, in any event, is much too doctrinaire in his critique of American capitalism. Be that as it may, Americans, in my judgment, would be well advised to read his book with an open mind and, by the same token, would also be well advised to ponder the significance of the fact that a Conciliar Commission made up of some sixty bishops representing every part of the world felt it necessary to say in the *Constitution on the Church in the Modern World* that "theories which obstruct the necessary reforms [in economic life] in the name of a false liberty" are no less erroneous than "those theories which subordinate the basic rights of individual persons and groups to the collective organization of production" (art. 65).

The reforms advocated by the Constitution, under the heading of Economic Development, are aimed at "progress in the production of agricultural and industrial goods and in the rendering of services, . . . rightly aimed at making provision for the growth of a people and at meeting the rising expectations of the human race" (art. 64). "Economic development," the document insists, "must be kept under the control of mankind. It must not be left to the sole judgment of a few men or groups possessing excessive economic power, or of the political community alone, or of certain especially powerful nations. It is proper, on the contrary, that at every level the largest possible number of people have an active share in directing that development. When it is a question of international developments, all nations should so participate" (art. 65).

In this connection, a special word of warning is addressed to those people in the economically underdeveloped areas of the world who hold back their unproductive resources or who deprive the community of the material or spiritual aid that it needs. They are told very pointedly that "they gravely endanger the common good" (*ibid.*). While they are never identified, I think it would be fair to say that perhaps a disproportionate percentage of them

[4] (New York: Sheed and Ward, 1965) 135.

are to be found in certain traditionally Catholic countries, notably Latin America.

The section of the Constitution dealing with economic development is rounded off with a brief reference to the special problems of those workers who migrate from one country or district and contribute to the economic advancement of another nation or region. It would be safe to assume, I think, that this matter was included in the document at the request of bishops from the Mediterranean area who are understandably concerned about the plight of their own fellow citizens, who, in recent years, have migrated in such great numbers to Germany, Switzerland, England and even to Ireland.

Finally, under the heading of Economic Development, we find a fleeting, two-sentence reference to automation. This once-over-lightly treatment of automation will come as a disappointment to those who expected the Council to "solve" the major problems confronting the modern world. Their feeling of disappointment is understandable, but they need to be reminded that it was not the purpose of the Council to "solve" specific problems but merely, as previously indicated, to enter into a sincere dialogue with mankind about some of these problems from the point of view of Christian principles and ideals.

The second section of the chapter on economic and social life deals with certain principles concerning (1) the rights and duties of labor and (2) the subject of private property. It says nothing substantially new or original about either of these matters, but in general, simply paraphrases the teaching of the social encyclicals, notably *Mater et Magistra*. The right of labor to organize and, under certain circumstances, to strike is restated as follows:

> Among the basic rights of the human person must be counted the right of freely founding labor unions. These unions should be truly able to represent the workers and to contribute to the proper arrangement of economic life. Another such right is that of taking part freely in the activity of these unions without risk of reprisal. Through this sort of orderly participation, joined with an ongoing formation in economic and social matters, all will grow day by day in the awareness of their own function and responsibility. Thus they will be brought to feel that according to their own proper capacities and aptitudes they are associates in the whole task of economic development and in the attainment of the universal common good. When, however, socio-economic disputes arise, efforts must be made to come to a peaceful settlement. Recourse must always be had above all to sincere discussion between the parties. Even in present-day circumstances, however, the strike can still be a necessary, though ultimate, means for the defense of the workers' own rights and the fulfillment of their just demands. As soon as possible, however, ways should be sought to resume negotiations and the discussion of reconciliation (art. 68).

The chapter on economic and social life also favors the active sharing of all in the administration and profits of individual business enterprises, but it does not attempt to settle the old argument as to whether or not this is a requirement in strict justice. Significantly, however, it does make a further application, within the economic order, of the basic principle of participation in government by all members of a community or group. It says that since "decisions concerning economic and social conditions, on which the future of the workers and their children depends, are rather often made not within the enterprise itself but by institutions on a higher level . . . the workers themselves should have a share also in controlling these institutions, either in person or through freely elected delegates" (art. 68). This reference to workers being represented by "freely elected delegates" has meaning not only for workers where there are no workers' organizations, but also for countries that have them but, like Spain, do not yet allow for a genuinely free election by the workers of their own representatives.

Private property is upheld in the document as "an extension of human freedom" and "a kind of prerequisite for civil liberties" (art. 71), but the social nature of property and the common destination of earthly goods are stressed antecedently. As Donald Campion, S.J., points out in his commentary on the Constitution, "the immediately relevant significance of this deliberate choice to reaffirm the earliest Christian tradition concerning property appears from a Patristic citation made at this very point in the Constitution: 'Feed the man dying of hunger, because if you have not fed him, you have killed him' "[5]

Finally, the document, in three short sentences, also takes note of the fact that the forms of property ownership are varied today and are becoming increasingly diversified. These sentences were added to the final draft of the Constitution to meet the objections of those African and Asian bishops who had complained, with good reason, that earlier drafts were too Western or too European in tone and outlook and did not give due recognition to the various community patterns of ownership that are found in their particular countries. Similarly the document's concluding reference to the urgent need for land reform was inserted to take account of the situation in some of the economically underdeveloped areas of the world.

On balance, I think it must be said that the Constitution's treatment of the problem of private ownership barely scratches the surface of an enormously complicated problem. The basic principles outlined in the document with regard to private ownership are valid as far as they go, but if they are to be of "substantial benefit to everyone," as the Council hopes they will be, they will have to be adapted "to individual nations and mentalities by the faithful, under the guidance of their pastors." Under the guidance of their

[5] In W. M. Abbott, *The Documents of Vatican II* (New York: America Press, 1966) 192.

pastors, yes—but, no less important, with the technical assistance of highly trained experts who, if I am not mistaken, are in short supply at this moment within the Catholic community, at least in the United States.

The chapter on economic and social life closes with an appeal to Christians to play an active role in the field of social and economic reform. "Christians who take an active part in modern socio-economic development and defend justice and charity," the document reads,

> should be convinced that they can make a great contribution to the prosperity of mankind and the peace of the world. Whether they do so as individuals or in association, let their example be a shining one. After acquiring whatever skills and experience are absolutely necessary, they should in faithfulness to Christ and His gospel observe the right order of values in their earthly activities. Thus their whole lives, both individual and social, will be permeated with the spirit of the beatitudes, notably with a spirit of poverty.
>
> Whoever in obedience to Christ seeks first the kingdom of God, will as a consequence receive a stronger and purer love for helping all his brothers and for perfecting the work of justice under the inspiration of charity (art. 72).

These concluding paragraphs of the chapter recall an earlier reference to the same subject in the fourth chapter of the first section of the Constitution —a reference which reads in part as follows: "The Christian who neglects his temporal duties neglects his duties toward his neighbor and even God, and jeopardizes his eternal salvation. Christians should rather rejoice that they can follow the example of Christ, who worked as an artisan. In the exercise of all their earthly activities, they can thereby gather their humane, domestic, professional, social, and technical enterprises into one vital synthesis with religious values, under whose supreme direction all things are harmonized unto God's glory" (art. 43).

Whenever I read this section of the *Constitution on the Church in the Modern World*, I cannot help but recall the great Teilhard de Chardin's plaintive lament in his book, *The Divine Milieu*, about the tragic harm that has been done to so many good Christians by a truncated spirituality based on a false dichotomy between the spiritual and the temporal. "I do not think I am exaggerating," Chardin wrote almost a generation ago,

> when I say that nine out of ten practicing Christians feel that man's work is always at the level of a "spiritual encumbrance." In spite of the practice of right intentions, and the day offered every morning to God, the general run of the faithful dimly feel that time spent at the office or the studio, in the fields or in the factory, is time diverted from prayer and adoration. It is impossible not to work—that is taken for granted. But it is impossible, too, to aim at the deep religious life reserved for those who have the leisure to pray or preach all day long. A few moments of the day can be salvaged for God, yes, but the best hours are absorbed, or at any rate cheapened, by material cares. Under the sway of this

feeling, large numbers of Catholics lead a double or crippled life in practice: they have to step out of their human dress so as to have faith in themselves as Christians—and inferior Christians at that.[6]

In the spirit of the Council, then, we who are interested in Christian social action can make our own the advice that Chardin addressed to an earlier generation of committed Christians:

> Try, with God's help, to perceive the connection—even physical and natural—which binds your labour with the building of the Kingdom of Heaven; try to realise that heaven itself smiles upon you and through your works, draws you to itself; then, as you leave church for the noisy streets, you will remain with only one feeling, that of continuing to immerse yourself in God. If your work is dull or exhausting, take refuge in the inexhaustible and becalming interest of progressing in the divine life. If your work enthrals you, then allow the spiritual impulse which matter communicates to you to enter into your taste for God whom you know better and desire more under the veil of His works. Never, at any time, "whether eating or drinking," consent to do anything without first of all realising its significance and constructive value *in Christo Jesu*, and pursuing it with all your might. This is not simply a commonplace precept for salvation: it is the very path to sanctity for each man according to his state and calling. . . . Right from the hands that knead the dough, to those that consecrate it, the great and universal Host should be prepared and handled in a spirit of adoration.[7]

[6] *The Divine Milieu* (New York: Harper and Row, 1960) 34.
[7] *Ibid.*, 35–36.

Mr. James J. Norris

INTERNATIONAL ORDER

IT IS SAFE TO SAY THAT NO SECTION of the pastoral *Constitution on the Church in the Modern World* was awaited with more interest than chapter 5 on the fostering of peace and the promotion of a community of nations. Attention from the start was primarily focused on the chapter dealing with marriage and the family, but as the Council progressed, more and more attention was directed to the questions of war and peace.

This was due not only to the wide diversity of opinions expressed by the bishops on the floor of the Council and in their written interventions, but also to the opinions of men and women around the world. Governmental leaders especially were following with great interest the debate and the progress of the text.

The remarkable thing about the final text is that it faced up squarely to the problems of nuclear warfare, disarmament, nonviolent action and conscientious objection, and yet the Council was able to produce a document representing the consensus of 2,000 bishops. In spite of the strong, negative attitudes expressed during the debates and the preliminary voting, only 75 negative votes were cast in the final vote, whereas two days earlier there were 483 *nonplacets*. And it is certain that some of these 75 negative votes were against the text as a whole or chapters other than the fifth.

During the course of the debates and the working sessions of the mixed commission that edited this document, the bishops had in mind the fact that the encyclical *Pacem in Terris* had been a long step forward in the teaching of the Church on the subject of war and peace. The Council felt that in a solemn proclamation it could not say less than Pope John had done in his encyclical, but this was more easily said than done, in view of the strong currents of opinion that ran through the Council.

Of those who spoke their observations the majority wanted a strong statement against modern war, particularly nuclear war. Others hoped that the Council would solemnly condemn all war, and outlaw not only the use but also the possession of nuclear weapons. On the opposite side a few felt that the text went too far in appearing to condemn the powers that held atomic weapons, even if they were not looking for war, but had been forced to build up their atomic arsenal in order to act as a deterrent.

In producing the text, the Council Fathers endeavored to bring together in one document pronouncements on war and peace, scattered among papal statements of the last thirty or forty years. A large number of bishops felt that the idea of a "just war" no longer made sense in a modern context, and they strongly urged a "prophetic" type of text that would condemn violence and emphasize the importance of the Christian witness of peacemaking. The bishops concurred with the thinking of Pope Paul as expressed in his speech to the United Nations in recognizing that so long as man is weak and sinful, so long as he shows himself changeable and even at times wicked, defensive arms will always unfortunately be necessary. They preferred a text that would be pastoral and would not condemn any nation or person. They felt the Church could not repudiate the rights of those who defend their home-lands, because such a condemnation would make existing society impossible. (Incidentally, some of those who wanted specific condemnation were being inconsistent, as in other matters [e.g., communism] they had resisted the idea of condemnation by the Council.) In stressing the pastoral rather than the prophetic accent, the Council Fathers gave less attention to principles than to actions, for their immediate objective was to accomplish the task at hand, namely, to limit war and to build peace. While predominately pastoral, the text on war and peace is replete with formulations that raise fundamental questions which must be a challenge to theologians concerned with updating the theology of war and peace. Being on this platform only in the role of a substitute for a theologian, I leave these matters to the theologians for further elucidation.

While the text does not use the term international morality, does it not still provide all of the elements for a new Christian probing into the basis of international life and a study of a new theology in relation to the basic issues discussed in the text?

One of the key phrases of the document is found in article 80 which reads, "All these considerations compel us to undertake an evaluation of war with an entirely new attitude. The men of our time must realize that they will have to give a somber reckoning of their deeds of war. For the course of the future will depend largely on the decisions they make today." What are "all these considerations?" They are the various characteristics of modern warfare described throughout this entire section of the document: the precariousness of the balance of terror; the constant danger that every war, even if begun as a small one, will end in world-wide conflict; the terrible cruelty of scientific arms in the twentieth century; the possibility of massive and indiscriminate destruction going far beyond the bounds of legitimate defense; the constant threat of "an almost total and altogether reciprocal slaughter of each side by the other"; and the widespread devastation that threatens the world and the deadly aftereffects.

The Council does not deny the right of self-defense. On the contrary, in spite of its strong words, self-defense is considered both a right and a duty. The duty to military service for the security and freedom of one's country is recognized as is the right of individuals to refuse to bear arms for reasons of conscience; finally nonviolent action is recognized as a legitimate right. Keeping in mind these rights and duties, the Council formulated principles concerning modern warfare stating clearly that it is one thing to have arms for the proper defense of one's country, but it is altogether another thing to use those arms to subjugate other countries. The Council urged adherence to natural rights and rules of humanity when wars are conducted, insisting on respect for international conventions guaranteeing those rights. It likewise says that blind obedience in executing commands against these human rights cannot be excused, and gives high praise to those who resist such commands.

The Council supported the rights of those who for *reasons of conscience* refuse to bear arms, provided that they serve humanity in some other way. Originally the text on conscientious objection had the phrase "frequently for religious reasons," but this was suppressed in the final version since it was felt that the highest motivation for sincere objection to the bearing of arms is the appeal to conscience.

In its discussion of total war, the Council, having in mind the nature of modern war which kills far more innocent victims than military participants, joined with the last three popes in condemning total war, by declaring it a crime against God and man himself to engage in any act of war aimed indiscriminately at the destruction of entire cities or extensive areas along with their population. Will these words provide a dilemma of conscience for Catholic citizens of those nations owning weapons of such magnitude that their use perforce results in indiscriminate destruction of whole cities or regions? May Catholics now participate in a war that results in indiscriminate wiping out of whole cities or regions? With this in mind, undoubtedly, the bishops of the whole world begged all men, especially government officials and military leaders, to give "unremitting thought to the awesome responsibility which is theirs before God and the entire human race" (art. 80). An American commentator has said that in this condemnation of total indiscriminate war, the Council has protected the inerodible diamond of innocent life.

The Council warned all that "the arms race is an utterly treacherous trap for humanity" (art. 81), and the only way to avoid the trap is to have governments bring into being some universal public authority, acknowledged by all and endowed with power to safeguard the security of all. Until the time that such universal public authority can be created, all existing international agencies are urged to devote themselves vigorously to the pursuit of a better means to obtain common security. The ideal approach to peace advocated by the Council would be a common policy of progressive bilateral disarmament built on mutual trust between nations and not imposed on them through fear of weapons or by an equilibrium of terror (art. 82).

The Council places responsibility in the lap of every single individual in the world, because their leaders cannot work for peace so long as among men feelings of hostility, distrust, racial hatred and "unbending ideologies continue to divide men and place them in opposing camps" (art. 82). For this reason there is a great need for a renewed education of attitude and new inspiration in public opinion. The Council tells us that we all need a change of heart, if we are to meet the challenges that are presented to us to work together for the betterment of the entire human family.

Taking up the theme of the human family, the document moves into the second section of chapter 5, on the construction of an international community.

This section on the construction of an international community is intimately linked to the first section on war. There is first of all a brief review of the basic and deep causes of present-day instability, the primary cause being excessive economic inequalities and the constant putting off of adequate steps to remedy them. When Pope Paul returned to Rome from his United Nations visit, he struck the same note in speaking to the bishops gathered in St. Peter's when he asked, "Is not perhaps this awareness of the imbalance between classes, between nations, the gravest threat against peace?" On the previous day he told the United Nations that the only way peace can be built is by combating world hunger and meeting world needs. In spite of the fact that the world in our own day has shrunk to the point where we can go from Washington to Bombay faster than our ancestors of the last century could go from Washington to New York; in spite of the fact that we live in a world community and are so interdependent, there still exist envy, distrust and injustices crying to heaven. The Council, therefore, urged the community of nations to organize in such way that it can face up to its present responsibilities, especially toward the many parts of the world that are suffering hunger and are living in utter misery.

The note of great concern for the poor and the responsibility of the rich nations toward the poor nations appears as a constantly recurring theme in every chapter of the document, and it was stressed over and over in the bishops' speeches throughout the four sessions of the Council.

In a loving human family does one brother take what he needs and give only what is left over to his other brother? In our world human family, if a brother in India is starving, should not I too have an emptiness in me? Is it possible to bring home these simple notions of a human family whose binding force among all members is love? May I ask our theologians: Has our theology developed sufficiently the basic concept of the gospel as applied to justice and charity within a single human family? Can the human race, inspired by the Church, move to this realization or is it an idle dream in the light of man's unredeemed tendency to selfishness? The message of *Gaudium et Spes* is that it is possible and realizable but only by enduring, properly motivated efforts that stem from our commitment to Christ.

The Council in our document recognizes the international and regional agencies that are trying to lay the foundations for a community of men to work toward a solution of today's serious problems. But the Council urges still greater efforts in international cooperation so that the needs of the poor around the world will be met.

The Pope's visit to the United Nations supported the efforts of that agency, which, in spite of its ineffectiveness at times, is still today's best hope for promoting understanding among nations. The presence of Holy See observers at the United Nations offices in New York, Geneva, Paris and Rome indicates the importance attached by the Holy Father to the works of the U.N. One might fairly ask: If there were not a United Nations, would not the world situation demand the immediate formation of one? The activities carried on by the agencies of the U.N.—the International Labor Organization, the World Health Organization, the U.N. Childrens' Fund, the Food and Agricultural Organizations, UNESCO and the Special Fund—are all carrying out the works of understanding and peace.

Charity alone is not called for, but justice based on love must be accorded to the poor members of the human family by the rich members of that family. How different the pronouncement of Vatican Council II, about the great works of mercy being performed by individual governments and by the United Nations, from the frequent vocal criticisms, for the most part based on ignorance or sensational news stories, of the work of American development programs and the United Nations' agencies dedicated to stamping out illiteracy, hunger, poverty, economic underdevelopment and agricultural stagnation. The bishops in Council recognized the great good being done by all of these works of charity, mercy and justice, and urged that they be greatly increased in order to close the ever widening gap between the rich and the poor. The Council emphasizes the fact that the greater part of the wealth of the world is in the hands of so-called Christian nations, and the possession of this great wealth carries with it tremendous responsibility. At this point it would be fair to ask why it is that Catholics who should have a universal outlook seem frequently to be the greatest critics of international activities, foreign aid and the United Nations. Is there a "gap" in the education of our Catholic people?

Why is it that our document stresses so frequently the problem of poverty and misery in the world? Why is it that the Council has chosen to dedicate a third of the chapter on war and peace to the subject of aid to the developing countries? I should like to suggest at least an answer to this latter question. Firstly, the great gap between the rich and the poor nations is undoubtedly one of the most menacing causes of war. It could wind up in a class war on the international level, which in an atomic age would be disastrous for humanity. Just as within nations we have succeeded to a certain extent in reducing the gap between the rich and the poor, so today on the international scale peace will ultimately depend on closing the gap between the rich nations and the poor nations. Secondly, help for the underdeveloped countries is a type of action for peace that is immediately at hand for every citizen, whether he devotes himself through personal service or whether he supports organizations or governments involved in international aid activities. Lastly, I think that the great emphasis on the gap between rich and poor nations occurs in the Council document so frequently because of the large number of bishops from the underdeveloped areas of the world. They are like a "Lazarus Church" begging crumbs from the table of "Dives Church." This is the unreported story of Vatican Council II.

We read recently that the living expenses of more than half the bishops at the Council were paid by the Holy See, which had asked the bishops of the rich countries for such help. This is an indication of the economic condition of the Church and the countries from which the majority of the bishops at the Council came. These bishops are deeply conscious of the feeling of their political leaders that they are at the mercy of the rich nations in their efforts to develop, promote trade or bring about agricultural or economic development. These bishops understand well that the development of their countries depends upon human development, and that all progress in their country depends ultimately upon the work of their own people. They know that their own resources must be put to full use, but at the same time they need help from the well-to-do and wealthy lands.

In discussing the problem of development, the Council briefly touched on the subject of the rapid increase in population, which is considered by many to be the greatest obstacle to development. Originally the document had a much longer treatment of the population question, but it became quite apparent that when the texts were being reduced at the request of the Coordinating Commission, it would be impossible to give a thorough and adequate treatment to the population question. The Council then settled on a single paragraph stressing the gravity of the problem, the need for Catholic universities to be involved in scientific study and research at high level in trying to find a solution, at the same time confirming the right of parents to make the ultimate decision concerning the number of children they will have, and denying the right of any public authority to interfere with the parents' rights. Responsible parenthood is, of course, stressed, but it is also recognized that there cannot be responsible parenthood in many areas of the world until there is an improvement in educational and social conditions, and above all formation in religious and moral training in trying to find solutions.

Toward the end of the document, stress is laid on the responsibility of nations everywhere to alleviate as far as they are able the sufferings of our day. In doing so, they are encouraged to look back to the ancient Church in which it was the custom to give not only what is superfluous but of one's substance.

Catholic organizations working on the international level received encouragement from the Council. They were urged to work with all others in building up a peaceful community of nations. Especially urged was cooperation with our separated brothers in carrying out the social mission of the gospel. And as a final word, the document called for the creation of an organism of the Universal Church which would have the role of educating the Catholic community about the problems of the poor nations of the world, stimulate development in poor countries and promote social justice among nations. Why had so many bishops spoken on the subject of poverty and misery in the world in a forum like the Council, if they did not want some such action at the highest level of the Church? If the Secretariat had not been called for, the hundreds of statements on the subject would have had little meaning and would have been without response on the part of the Council.

The chapter ends here abruptly with a call for action. It has told all the People of God to reach out to the brother in need, to teach, to work and finally to found an organization that will bring justice to bear among men, which will ultimately accomplish the mission of the Church in the world. The chapter is both pastoral and practical. The constantly recurring theme is love of the poor. An international community must be present in order to serve the poor. All the works of peace are summed up in the word "service."

Pacem in Terris brought a new unity and hope to men of all faiths and of no faith. *Gaudium et Spes* in its unequivocal protection and support of the neediest and weakest of the human family, and in its clear teaching that we must protect innocent civilians threatened by the mercilessness of total war, built on the sense of unity and hope in Pope John's letter to humanity. Having probed the signs of the times, *Gaudium et Spes* brings "to the whole of humanity" a practical message of hope and renewal from men of every race and nation who are marked by the Holy Spirit to lead the People of God through their short terrestrial pilgrimage to a permanent peace that surpasses all understanding.

Question: The Constitution acknowledges but does not sufficiently wrestle with the world revolutionary situation. It deals
with developing nations and duties to help them, but it does
not adequately analyze the revolutionary character of the international order. Is not the international system in a revolutionary state? Is it not radically heterogeneous with respect to
the power of competing states, the economic policy of the various regions, the levels of development, and the ideological conflicts? In the face of these, and other factors, does not the
Constitution present an essentially Western and bland argument, insufficiently aware of the non-Western realities? What
does this mean for methodology in future ecumenical work?
Part of the above problematic may be put this way: Do not
Western world economic and cultural leaders assume that the
non-Western World will have primarily to adapt to what our
scientific, technological and economic powers are? Is there
even a faint recognition of the fact that in the long run the
Western political economic order is on trial with respect to
adapting to that other world?

HIGGINS: A very good question. I would, by way of preface before going into a specific answer, go back to the point I tried to make briefly in the paper, a point which has been made in another context by another speaker on this particular Constitution. The Constitution was never intended to be much more—at least in these sections we are talking about—much more than a preliminary essay opening up a dialogue that will have to go on indefinitely. I indicated in my paper that I thought the methodology that was supposed to control the entire document was inadequately reflected in this particular chapter. Therefore, by way of specific reply, I would say that it was definitely inadequate in its treatment of the point raised by Professor Muelder. There is no question about the fact that, in spite of what Jim Norris says, there was a large influence, in some ways, of the non-Western bishops. Nevertheless, the framework of thinking at the Conciliar level was, I think, inevitably Western, in spite of the best efforts of the Commission to overcome it. Now the paradox of the situation is that many Americans, with certain technical competence in sociology, economics and political science, regard the document as completely inadequate from the Western point of view. They regard it as being naive; in some respects perhaps it is, because it never intended or pretended to be anything like a complete reading of the signs of the times. But that doesn't discourage me too much, if we move on from there, using the same methodology in our work as Catholics and in the ecumenical area. Therefore, at the ecumenical level I think it would be most helpful if joint work could be done by the World Council of Churches and some appropriate international Catholic body addressing themselves specifically to the question of the West's inadequate understanding that we live in a revolutionary world and that we may have to adapt radically to the East.

> Question: Does the Constitution take sufficient account of the prepolitical requirements of world order for peace based on law? Does it take sufficient account of the political processes that precede true international law and organs of enforcement? Is it not really a hortatory appeal at points where analysis and guidelines are needed? This is a problem in methodology.

HIGGINS: To save time, I would give substantially the same answer. This was by design a pastoral chapter. The point is made quite explicitly in the notes that it was not the intention of the document to write a handbook of casuistry, and I think we can say then, by extension, that it was not its intention to write anything or even to pretend to write anything like an adequate political science background for this. However, I would agree quite substantially with the import of the question. Again, its reading of the prerequisites of the signs of the times and of the structural and political processes which are needed to get from exhortation to implementation leaves much to be desired. But I have a strong feeling myself—I know it is not shared by some who were at the Council—that it would have been a mistake for the Council to get too involved in this kind of secular (I use secular in the very best sense of the word) analysis, lest it leave the impression that the Council was trying to do something which, I personally think, a council has no business doing.

MUELDER: I appreciated very much those remarks. It seems to me that if the Council had had more time it could, on the prepolitical issue I raised, have related this to that very interesting chapter on culture, which in one sense is prepolitical in an area in which the Church has an enormous contribution to make in cooperation with all other agencies affecting the ethos in culture and the like.

Now what I missed, and what perhaps we all need to work on together, was seeing the nature of social systems, their structure, what kinds of things have to be done in relationship to other elements in a structure, in order that one doesn't simply have a very rich agenda of problems, but has some profile of those problems and the order in which they can be dealt strictly with.

HIGGINS: I would agree with you, Dr. Muelder, but I think it was the intention of the Council—and if not, it should have been, in my judgment—that this is the kind of work we have to do jointly, ecumenically and separately when necessary. And the scientists and sociologists and social scientists not attached to religion have to help us and we have to help them. It is this kind of continuing dialogue outside the framework of a Council that is so needed.

DR. BROWN: I'd like to make a brief comment and then ask one question of Msgr. Higgins. The comment would simply be to reinforce and underline his point of the importance of including in the document reiteration of such principles as the right to strike. Both Msgr. Quinn, who is in the audience, and I were at Delano within a week after the ending of the Council to be able to speak to the striking workers—almost all Mexican, American, Filipino, Roman Catholics—rallying, to be sure, under the banner of Our Lady of Guadalupe, to be able to say to them, with the ink barely dry on the mimeographed sheets, that within the week their bishops had affirmed the rightness of what they were now engaged in. This was very helpful to be able to do. I think it is very significant that on this kind of point the Council is still speaking to immediate issues that confront us.

Now the brief question I would like to ask is in terms of something out of Msgr. Higgins' speech, his quoting Mr. E. E. Y. Hales about the nature of Pope John's encyclicals: "Part of the charm of Pope John was his refusal to pontificate on public affairs. One feels that he is only giving advice. With Leo XIII and Pius XI one is not allowed to forget that they are laying down the law." I am made a little uneasy by this. I am quite pleased that this kind of principle should be applied to such things as *veterum sapientia*, for example. But I would be made unhappy if the impression got around, in either the Catholic world or the non-Catholic world, that because this is true one doesn't need to take *Pacem in terris* and *Mater et magistra* with the seriousness that one takes other papal encyclicals. I wonder if there is a psychological problem here, and that it will mean Pope John's teachings will in a sense be downgraded for this reason, and the very important social advances that his encyclicals register be lost.

HIGGINS: My initial comment will be facetious, and I know you will take it in the sense in which it is meant. I am a little intrigued that we have now come almost full circle, and most of the conversation in this meeting on the binding force of documents has come from the Protestants. My serious remark is that your comment would be a necessary balance to what Hales said. However, I think Hales protects himself, to some extent, by his own phrasing. He says: "It is both intellectually proper and persuasively effective to use the tone that John used." Now he is not suggesting for a moment that Pope John meant to be just giving advice in such a casual way that, as far as he was concerned, people could take or leave it. He was rather speaking of a tone and style which he feels is more appropriate to our day, and *de facto*, if I am any judge of reaction to encyclicals, the one encyclical of all modern encylicals that people have taken seriously is *Pacem in terris*. People do take his teaching authority seriously, because he tries to do what he exhorted the bishops to do in his opening address to the Council, that is, to speak in a style and a language and in a context which would have some meaning for the modern mind.

> Question: I do not address this question to Roman Catholics alone, but to all organized Christian churches. Could not the world also say to the Church, in many places and under many circumstances, what of authoritarianism in the Church's life, and secondly what of your responsible use of the Church's wealth and the scandal of economic waste caused by competition of churches, all too often competing for allegiances of the same group of people?

HIGGINS: I would answer the question, in the first instance, very briefly by saying that the world not only could but has said this. It has said it in various ways and in various places, and with varied tact. However, this raises a larger question of whether or not the Council should have gone in for breastbeating on this particular point. There were bishops who wanted, in many parts of many chapters to have more breastbeating than there is. It is an arguable point. I think on the whole the Council followed the wiser policy in not going in for too much public breastbeating and too much public confession of the Church's sins. There is some of it. To the substance of your questions, I think the answer is yes. The world could and has at times criticized certain authoritarian overtones and practices in the Church's life and certainly the irresponsible use of Church funds in the competition between Churches. However, if we were going to go into a serious discussion of the irresponsible use of Church funds, we would have to do a large amount of demythologizing of many of the liberal images of the Church's wealth in various parts of the world. Tourists see the large churches in some countries, and they conclude out of hand that the Church there is wealthy. It could be one of the poorer in the world. There is, I think, a certain exaggeration at times of the wealth of the Church in various parts of the world. On the other hand, where there are abuses in the use of Church funds, and particularly in the competition that you are talking about, certainly it should be examined and examined ecumenically.

SHEPHERD: Thank you very much. I wasn't thinking of poor countries; I was thinking particularly of our own. It seems to me that it is now a matter of scandal for the Christian conscience that in certain areas, where I live in California for example, there are only about 20 or 25 per cent of the people who have any Christian allegiance of any kind, and yet the churches continue to build on opposite corners tremendous buildings and educational plants that are not really necessary. In many areas in this country and other affluent countries, it seems to me, a great deal could be done by sharing common facilities, and this could start right now. I think the same thing is true in the field of theological education; there are entirely too many seminaries. I don't know the situation well enough to say much about it, but I have been told that in Italy there are entirely too many dioceses which are supported by the government in part. It seems to me if we would enter into dialogue with the world on political and economic matters, it is essential for the Church to acknowledge that she also must speak to herself of these things.

HIGGINS: With regard to Italy there are many people here who could speak quite definitively. Just as an outsider I get the impression that Pope Paul is trying to reverse this tendency of multiplying the number of dioceses. I agree with you quite specifically on the question of theological studies, and I assume that if anybody wants to talk with Dr. Shepherd afterwards, he will hear some very encouraging news about the possible developments in Berkeley in this regard.

McGRATH: The question about the third world not being adequately represented in the schema touches on the subcommittee, on which I worked, which was charged with reviewing the Constitution from that point of view.

I think it is very interesting that it be brought out in this particular chapter. There was a very serious problem which I mentioned in the *relatio* at the Council, that we didn't have theologians and experts from these areas of the world. We had just a handful compared to the hundreds from Europe, and they were for the most part, bishops presenting their problems, but without proper articulation. European experts had to try to understand and appraise these problems. We had the assistance of some persons like Father Lebret, Father Houtart and other Europeans who had traveled and worked a great deal in Africa, Latin America, and this was indispensable. But it is, nevertheless, a problem of articulation that is reflected in the document. Sometimes the European theologians tried to write texts referring to the poverty in the world, and African, Asian and Latin American bishops would read them and say: "These people have never seen poverty; they don't know what it is."

There was also a constant tendency, which our commission had to try hard to undo, to place the descriptions of one or other of these problems in Western, European or European and North American contexts. This was particularly true in this economic and social chapter, in which the whole labor situation was cast, by some of the European authors, under the aspect of very powerful labor unions. Hence, the question of the strike was treated in a series of admonitions to the effect that strikes can be engaged in when this, that and the other condition obtains. In other areas of the world the situation of unions is entirely different. When people from different areas get together for a common discussion, it is extremely difficult, for their mentalities are entirely different.

This points out the necessity of making an appropriate application of these documents for particular areas. For instance, there is the statement of the Cardinal Secretary of State sent to Cardinal Silva of Santiago, Chile, for a recent congress, which is far, far stronger in criticizing capitalism than anything that could be put in a universal document, precisely because it is criticizing capitalism as it exists in many of our Latin American nations.

One final point I would like to make concerns the authority of these documents. I think there are two points that are novel here and should be appreciated. First of all, there is an awareness that the moral authority of the Church at this time is of great importance for development. And there is a desire that this not be confused with the Church's getting into technical areas, making decisions that are not proper to any Church authority. I think that is one of the big points that is made in this document. Secondly, there is a new kind of awareness that, given the multiplicity and variety of problems, it is not up to the Church or any churchman to be making moral decisions that are proper to the individuals who are in these problems—

whether they are family problems, political problems, union problems, whatever they may be. The Church must pronounce on principles, yes; on the individual moral problems, no.

COLOMBO: I wonder whether, as Christians, we have sufficiently pondered on the need of Christ, not only as a Lord, but as a Savior of all the problems of humanity. No doubt, the text of the Constitution's second part devotes much space to Christ as Lord, and therefore you find applications of evangelical law, of charity especially, and it is in that light that we have been discussing our problem. But Christ is needed by humanity not only as Lord and Master of human wisdom, but also as the one who must give the strength so that mankind can solve these problems. He is Savior, not only for internal life, but he is also Savior in terms of the solution of problems in the light of the needs of God and men. I wonder whether we emphasize sufficiently the need and the necessity of this presence of Christ as Savior. The Christian solution to all these problems of mankind is perhaps not only a technical, sociological one. Otherwise we seem to be tending toward a somewhat Marxist solution in terms of ethics. I think that the Christian position requires that we emphasize the necessity of the moral effort, the presence of the necessary virtues, for the solution of these problems. These are Christian virtues, which man by himself cannot attain; nor can the human communities help purely by human effort. Christ's presence is required. No matter how good our human solutions are, we cannot afford to lose sight of the real historical perspective: original sin will never be eliminated from mankind. These problems will require of Christians a continuous moral effort and a wisdom and strength that come only from Christ. This is the problem I face, and I would like to have someone try to answer it.

HIGGINS: If I may comment, I would say that I agree again with the substance of what the Bishop is saying, but I myself am afraid that we may fall into the opposite mistake. In fact, we have. It is surely a necessity for a Christian to relate Christ to whatever he does. But my own experience would suggest to me that we have not been short on moral exhortation or an emphasis on the moral principles needed to bring about a Christian solution to problems. I think we have been rather short on the kind of dialogue that is needed to relate those principles to the facts (number one), to the techniques (number two), and to the whole evolving situation in which we find ourselves. And this is precisely why churchmen are often not taken very seriously, even when they speak of Christ and speak in the highest of moral terms. Both are necessary. I more or less took it for granted in my own presentation, as I think to some extent the document does, that we were agreed on the point that Bishop Colombo is making. Maybe it could be emphasized more, but I think it is not so much a question of emphasis, as it is a question of trying to relate the two. This is, I think, a continuing problem. For example, I have a very uneasy feeling myself that the appeals to morality, indeed to pure biblical categories, in the subject of war and peace, are frequently being used as a substitute for a serious, rational argument about the facts, about the situation, and about the application of these categories to the problems we face. The sheer, crude, almost fundamentalist appeal to biblical categories and to pure moral principles coupled with an easy transition to conclusions about extremely involved human problems strikes me as having very real dangers. On the other hand, I think that the point the Bishop makes is a very valid one, if it is kept in this kind of context.

> Question: What has been done to establish the organism of
> the universal Church you spoke of? What do you foresee to
> be the lines of its development?

NORRIS: The call for this organism goes back to the 1964 session of the Council, the third session. At the time a day was devoted to the subject of poverty and misery in the world. There were about six talks on that particular day. And after all of these interventions, the question was asked: What does the Church do now? The proposal was made that we have some kind of secretariat which would promote social justice in the world. Then during the last session of the Council this idea was supported by many bishops. As a result, the commission working on the document put this paragraph in. The thought behind it was that there should be a small, but very effective, organ that would, first of all, be educational and, secondly, would stimulate and inspire people to assist in this grave problem. The material that would go out from this agency would reach all levels of the Church; it would go down through Bishops' conferences to the parishes. It would influence the teaching in the seminaries. As it now stands, a working group is to meet during the second week of May to discuss the type of structure needed and make a proposal to the Holy See.

SMITH: I have a question relating to conscientious objection, and I will be glad to hear from anyone who will answer it. I quite understand all that Father Higgins has said about what was possible and wasn't possible in composing the document. My question really has to do with developing it. The statement is very sparse: "It seems right that laws make humane provisions for the case of those who for reasons of conscience refuse to bear arms, provided, however, that they accept some other form of service to the human community" (art. 79). A quite limited statement, although obviously sound in intention.

A much more pregnant passage is contained in the *Declaration on Religious Freedom*, which, though directed toward religious freedom, stands as a statement about the character of conscience. "Man perceives and acknowledges the imperatives of the divine law through the mediation of conscience. In all his activity a man is bound to follow his conscience faithfully, in order that he may come to God, for whom he was created. It follows that he is not to be forced to act in a manner contrary to his conscience. Nor, on the other hand, is he to be restrained from acting in accordance with his conscience, especially in matters religious" (art. 3).

This last phrase seems to indicate in the authors a consciousness that this was a statement that reaches much farther than the issues of religious freedom. Now may it be hoped, and indeed assumed, that there will soon be a much more extended development of Catholic thinking and perhaps statements, in the form of encyclicals and other comparably authoritative documents that will spell out a much more extended and significant support? I am a nonpacifist, and I am at the same time profoundly concerned that this tremendous power that is flowing from conscientious objection through channels of nonviolent protest in this messy problem of international relations should be preserved and safeguarded and thus protected just exactly as religious freedom itself is protected by this very significant statement. What prospect is there, in your judgment, of the development of this powerful position in that direction?

HIGGINS: Well, I would say first, and this time not so facetiously, that I think it would be a mistake to think in the first instance of an official statement. The problem we are faced with here is, I think, that there is nothing like an adequate, theoretical basis for the discussion among our own theologians. Insofar as I have any right to have an opinion on it, because I haven't studied the problem, I would be inclined to think that the whole theory, the whole *Declaration on Religious Freedom*, needs careful study in the light of the problem that you are raising. But that study has not been made yet. And while I would hope that it would be done very soon, I would at the same time hope it would be done first by the scholars. It would be unfortunate to come right out with some kind of official statement merely to solve the *ad hoc* problem of conscientious objection, in the present context of the Viet Nam war, or some other immediate or forthcoming crisis.

SMITH: May I propose that when this study group is formally set up, it be ecumenized. There is very much common ground here which could very well figure in discussions of that kind. I would hope it would not be pursued independently, but ecumenically.

HIGGINS: Well, I thought that now everything but meat on Friday was done ecumenically. I think we can assume that more and more things will be done ecumenically.

STRANSKY: I would just like to raise a question here. I've been noticing in international meetings—especially where Africans and South Americans are involved—that they feel we are always thinking about the whole problem of international peace, but are not facing up to even a casuistry of national revolution, which does not involve just the tranquility of order. I am thinking of a meeting we had last February in which some Christian leaders were wondering how to answer, for example, the questions of Christians on guerilla warfare in Mozambique. We are getting statements from the churches, from the World Council of Churches, on international peace and international politics, and yet when we talk to the people from Africa and South America they say, well, what about a theology of revolution. I'm just raising this as a question. I don't know what the answer is.

HOUTART: I am sorry to disagree with my friend George Higgins here. Since we are not living in a laboratory but in a concrete world, we cannot speak and think just as we have. We cannot wait until all those problems are solved in the laboratories of our universities and faculties of theology. We are living in a world where the concrete problems of underdevelopment and war really exist. And there Church and Christians must play a very concrete, prophetic role, even if we do not perhaps have as yet all the theories necessary to make a completely clear judgment, or to have a very clear-cut type of action. I am thinking now of this prophetic role of recalling certain fundamental values. A case like Camillo Torres in Columbia has some kind of prophetic value, even if we don't agree with all that he has said or done. I think the same thing is valuable for the peace movement, for the pacifist movement, and even for the participation of priests and religious in various kinds of manifestation. Because thereby we are really helping the Church to get involved in the problem of the concrete world.

TUCCI: I agree with Father Houtart that we do not have the time to build a definitive doctrine but have to face the problems immediately. Perhaps we cannot demand that the magisterium always have this prophetic mission. We have to trust individuals much more, bishops, individual priests, individual religious, and especially laymen; we have to allow them to be free now to play their prophetic role, even at the risk of making some mistakes.

GREMILLION: l want to have a word on the secretariat-organism that Mr. Norris spoke of. I want to emphasize the ecumenical dimension of this. There is envisioned a secretariat which is of the Catholic Church and which is official, but by all means we are hoping and anticipating and are discussing with leaders of World Council of Churches and National Council of Churches some sort of parallel development among them that could become a conjoint effort. Exactly one year ago this week Father Stransky and the Unity Secretariat asked a group of us to go to Geneva to meet with the World Council of Churches on a consulation regarding the Church in society. Some twenty of us were there together working on these issues, and we very specifically dealt with these questions of world poverty, justice, development and unity as areas of ecumenical collaboration. And this has continued.

I want to return to the revolutionary world; that is the first question that Dr. Muelder raised here. Obviously this isn't covered. We have to think then about Islam, Buddhism and Hinduism, all of which are undergoing enlightenment, their "French" revolution, their industrial revolution, their social revolution. We are a very small enclave of the human race that is represented in this cockpit here. Very small. We are all Westerners, for instance. In a few more years there will be four billions of non-Christians as compared to ourselves. As soon as we start speaking ecumenically, we Christians tend to think just of ourselves, and it is particularly in this social issue that we have to relate, I would suggest, to Islam and the others. Let us look toward the future, the thrust forward.

HIGGINS: My heart sank when François [Houtart] said he disagreed with me, because that would make me very unhappy; it would spoil my week. But I don't think we are so far apart, François. What I meant to say is that I am trying to safeguard prophetic witness. The question that was raised was raised about official statements. And official statements are very nice short cuts, and everybody likes them on specific points in which they are interested. Father Cronin and I are in the business, at times, of trying to get the bishops to take short cuts and help us do our job by making something official that isn't really official. Every liberal group in the United States which is opposed to the Church getting involved in the temporal order has at least a half dozen issues on which it wants the bishops to make official statements. But what I am suggesting is: by all means let us have free prophetic witness, let us have the people who feel strongly and can argue their point out on conscientious objection, say it with all freedom and with all respect from the Christian community. But let us likewise not pretend that that prophetic witness necessarily closes out the problem. I am reminded in this context that the chapter in Corinthians on charity is in the context of a discussion of the gifts of prophecy. And it was with the precise purpose of asking that charity override and overrule this use of prophecy. There has to be charity from both ends: charity of the Christian community, the Christian hierarchy and the authorities in the Church, and even justice in allowing people the maximum amount of freedom to exercise their prophetic witness; charity also on the part of the individual prophet who will not want his opinion to be made prematurely the official opinion. That's the only point I was trying to make. I know something about this question of getting official statements. This is the oldest game in the world, and I might say that it has nothing to do with Roman Catholicism as such; this is the most ecumenical vice of all our ecumenical vices.

DR. BROWN: I simply want to make a comment in response to Msgr. Gremillion and in courtesy also to Mr. Norris in terms of the proposals that are contained in article 90 of the Constitution about this Catholic agency for purposes of social involvement, and so forth. I think some of the defense that seemed to be needed for this has been in part from a criticism that I raised in my analysis of the document printed in the Abbot edition. I want to go on record as saying that my criticism was based on what I now clearly see as a misunderstanding of the intention. I promise that in subsequent editions of this work this paragraph of mine will be either revised or excised.

HYSLOP: I just wanted to add a word to the emphasis already put by Msgr. Gremillion on the ecumenical aspects of this agency of the universal Church and just comment that certainly the hour is now. It seems to me that God is working to bring us to the point of action together, despite the fact that we do not have the visible unity with which we theologians are so greatly concerned. I just wanted to point out that the document itself speaks of this agency of the universal Church as being set up for the world-wide promotion of justice for the poor, and of Christ's kind of love for them. And it seems to me that here we have the clue, because there is a universal Church in existence that is not identified with the Roman Catholic Church or with the ecclesial communities that are not in communion with Rome. This is the Church invisible, and it needs so badly to be made visible in simply and profoundly manifesting Christ's kind of love. I simply ask that we have the daring now to make visible our unity in this following of Christ in the expression of his kind of love in the world. And I am convinced, as a theologian, that then we will be able to answer your question: Has theology developed sufficiently the basic concept of the gospel as applied to justice and charity within a single human family? The answer to that now is no, because although the human family is there and Christ is there, we are not there. I think this is the way in which we must go in order to discover the unity which then will be made visible in the forms of the Church.

SISTER LUKE: I just want to add a note here from the Sisters' viewpoint. In regard to the value of the prophetic role, I think that Selma has been a proof that unless these things happen first the official opinion can't be easily formed. Unless there is the witness, unless there is the courage to move into an area where this kind of conviction can be shown, then we are delayed all the more at arriving at any sort of official statement. It seems to me that every episode in this direction moves the matter forward. And I don't think there are any superiors today who would hesitate to allow sisters to take part in demonstrations, and so forth, simply because we have had the example of successful demonstrations that took place before. We must not be so timid about truly evangelical witness; now that witness follows from points in the documents. We have official statements.

GREMILLION

HOUTART

SESSION XIII

VERY REV. JOSEPH GREMILLION
The Church in the World Today—Challenge to Theology

ABBÉ FRANÇOIS HOUTART
Suggestions for Doctrinal Development

Very Rev. Joseph Gremillion

THE CHURCH IN THE WORLD TODAY—
CHALLENGE TO THEOLOGY

I AM NOT HERE AS A THEOLOGIAN. Rather, the *social* sciences are my field of study and work; more specifically I am a social actionist, concerned with development programs in the seventy-five poorer nations of the world, an administrator, a bureaucrat, an "organization man" of the Church—concerned with the broad problems of world poverty, world justice and development.

I. THE PROBLEM OF WORLD POVERTY, JUSTICE AND DEVELOPMENT

THEOLOGY AND SOCIAL SCIENCE, ANOTHER NEW DIALOGUE

A most noteworthy breakthrough of schema 13[1] is the deepened interchange it has occasioned, and continues here, between theology and the social sciences, between the "down here" of concrete societal realities and strivings, daily experienced by flesh and blood men and social groupings, and the "up there" of theological reasoning and conceptualization, illuminated by "the light from above" of revelation.

During the Council, theology and the social sciences began—seriously, systematically, respectfully—to nourish each other at the very heart of the Church Universal, affecting the whole People of God, in the very mainstream of Christian life.

SOCIAL SCIENCES APPLY THE TRANSFORMING POWER OF THIS WORLD

By the social sciences I here mean principally economics, politics and sociology. Let us leave aside for the moment the intertwining kindred disciplines of history, anthropology, social psychology, and the like, all of which certainly throw much light on the human predicament. In this brief outline I will focus on economics, politics and sociology, because these are "the big three" through which, by and large, the far-reaching discoveries of the exact sciences, mathematics, physics, chemistry, biology, astronomy, and others, are *applied* today to all the human family, on massive scale, at very rapid pace, and for the first time in history.

Economics, politics and sociology deal with those societal motives and forces, structures and bodies that pull together coherent groupings of skilled men, physical resources and executive direction appropriate for forging the myriad findings of the exact sciences into manageable problem-solving units in order to beget and to implement the technology and society-wide planning, the *applied power*,[2] that now transforms the world, physically and culturally, through governmental bureaus, business enterprise, worker, farmer and professional associations, communications, social institutes, and the rest.[3] The social sciences, then, treat par excellence of the things of this world, and especially of the tranforming power in *this world of today*, upon which the Church has begun to reflect theologically in schema 13.

My thesis tonight is that in the post-Conciliar years theology and social science must learn to nourish each other in evermore meaningful manner and degree. My proposition here is to introduce some of the needs, some of the yearnings which I as a social actionist for world justice and development experience, and which I hope you theologians can help to satisfy in the years to come.

In the *Constitution on the Church in the Modern World* you have made a great start. But you have still much to do, far to go, if our concern as Christians and as humans for "the hopes, the griefs and the anxieties" of the poor half of the human family is to become anything but beautiful, plaintive groanings in the opening sentence of another Church document. The Church cannot become relevant to this world unless theology becomes relevant. And in this changing world relevancy is never fully attained, never accomplished once and for all. It is "a becoming," a continuing, never-ending, process, and today rapidly changing.[4]

That is why I applaud the serious dialogue which has but now begun in schema 13 among theologians and social scientists. I plead above all for its continuation and even for its institutionalization at all levels in the Church. Canon Houtart will address himself to this latter point: the institutionalization of change.[5]

RICH NATIONS AND POOR NATIONS

Most of the areas of interest of the Constitution have already been ably analyzed during this week. Without underplaying any of these, I will now concentrate on one major focus of the Constitution: the rich nations and the poor nations (in a phrase made household by a book of Lady Jackson, bearing this title).[6]

I need not detail here the stark realities of today's divided world, split into the affluent North and *les misérables* of the South: the economic aristocrats eating Marie Antoinette cake, Caucasian for the most part, in the heartland of Christianity; the poor with their crumbs, getting poorer by comparison, Dives and Lazarus on global scale, "a great gulf fixed between," in the thousands of millions (Lk 16:26).

To move the rich to concern for the poor nations, the Constitution calls upon the universal common good and the solidarity of all the human family, the justice and love of Christ for the poor. In detail remarkable for a Conciliar document, the remedies for world poverty and injustice—technical assistance, grants and loans by the industrialized nations, the restructuring of world trade, finance and investment systems—are all urged by the Council Fathers. The Constitution even calls for the establishment of an "agency of the universal Church . . . to stimulate the Catholic community to faster progress in needy regions, and social justice among nations on the international scene" (art. 90).

FROM COUNCIL DECREE TO HUMAN WILL AND SOCIETAL COMMITMENT

These offer excellent take-off platforms for our strivings as Christians, together with all men of good will, during the coming decades and generations which world development will require. These lay down the bases for forging the new international and the supranational structures that must undergird world justice and peace, for building up the juridic framework to realize the universal common good.

Let us suppose that man does possess the techniques for feeding and teaching, providing jobs and "the fullness of a more excellent life" to all the human family. Man and institutions *of his creation* must still shape this technology into problem-solving units; "organization man" must apply this transforming power of technology. Let us suppose that man does possess not only the techniques but also the political experience and ingenuity, the criteria for planning and decision-making, the organizational skill and managerial know-how needed to apply the technology. The big question remains: Do we humans have the required vision and the will to do it?

I fear that as of now, and of ourselves, we do not. It is all very well, and most commendable, to set forth the remedies of world poverty and misery, as does the *Constitution on the Church in the Modern World* (art. 83–90). But applying these creative remedies calls for Herculean strivings and sacrifices, and a new level of accord among nations and peoples. This demands a great new vision of God and man, of life and work, of society and world.

Let us recall how long it took the Western Church, and Christians as a whole, to accept the moral principles underlying *national* social justice, and how much longer to apply these teachings within each nation, among our own brother Christians and fellow citizens. The Socialists and Marxists grasped the reality and showed the will to act decades and generations before "the children of light."[7] How much more difficult to move now from justice *within* the nation to social justice *among* the nations, among the differing blocs and religio-cultural systems of the whole world.

A HUMAN ELAN CALLS FOR GOD

The human *élan* now called for—the fresh awareness and openness, love and determination required—is so great and all-embracing, of such dimension, that in view of the sad historic probabilities of human behavior, it seems well beyond reasonable human expectation. I believe God himself must needs enlighten and move man to generate this fresh human *élan* for bringing about the required commitment toward human unity and continuing creativity for justice and peace.

I believe that God might be presently giving the first glimmers of his light in that direction through men like Mahatma Gandhi, Pope John and Martin Luther King. I believe that God may be imparting his first gentle impulse to the pilgrim People of God and the whole human caravan in the this-world-of-the-here-and-now through the *aggiornamento*, Orthodox-Protestant-Catholic, and through the "openness" movements, both ecumenical among Christians and interreligious among all the religio-culture systems, and through today's world-wide yearning and striving for peace, based on justice and human betterment.

THEOLOGICAL QUESTIONS

I beg you theologians to answer me frankly. Am I merely "seeing things" which I wish to see in today's events? Can God act in such a manner in this world today? Does he do so? Is he likely to? Or do you really know? Are you already beginning to answer affirmatively in schema 13 and in comparable studies on the Church and society of the World Council of Churches?

From a theological point of view, can I, might I, validly hope for that new surge of vision and will, justice and accord—that fresh human *élan*—needed to deal with the misery and strife which are my daily preoccupations? Can I with integrity encourage *les misérables* of the world to ask with confidence for their daily bread, for justice and peace, for that "fullness of a more excellent life" promised by Pope John in the opening sentence of *Mater et Magistra?* My problem is, you understand, that I do not believe these can be attained without the intervening presence and action of God in our human here-and-now of this world. Is this what you are also saying in schema 13, and in the "new theology" of the *aggiornamento?* Is this what I hear in *The Secular City* of Harvey Cox and Van Leeuwen's *Christianity in World History?* And what then of secularity?[8]

I can imagine some of you thinking within yourselves: What a mixed-up mishmash in that man's head! How can we theologians, with our precise categories and structured patterns of thought-development, talk with these actionists, with this *pot-pourri* of yearnings, strivings and pragmatic goals? Worse yet, you must realize that I and many of my social-problem colleagues cannot approach you with a truly open mind, *tubula rasa.* Your *aggiornamento* theology, still very young, unripe and underdeveloped, does not yet reach and move Christians as a whole in their daily lives. Rather, most of us, clergy and laity, are still moved, or better yet, still rendered immobile, by the theology of my seminary days, the Prümmer, Noldin, Van Noort, Hervé, Tanquérey and Garrigou-Lagrange of twenty-five years ago.

TASK FORCE OF THEOLOGIANS

Now, to become effective in this world today you must, I submit, become more problem-oriented and consciously fashion a theology aimed at the several basic problems of today. And looming large, maybe largest, among these issues is that of world poverty, justice, development and peace—to say nothing of population.[9]

I submit, further, that, in the terminology of economics, politics and applied sociology, you should form appropriate task forces, or working parties, of theologians. These would, on behalf of the *conspiratio* (in Courtney Murray's sense) begotten here this week, address themselves variously to the large problem areas of this world, and particularly, of course, to "my" problem of justice and development.

A MORAL EQUIVALENT OF WAR

Your theological ancestors devoted a lot of time and space to that relation among religions and cultures, among nations and peoples that is called war. Perhaps you could redeem them, and theology's reputation, by giving more proximate attention to justice among nations, to cultural openness and exchange, to world unity and peace.

For many centuries theologians and churchmen have joined politicians and nationalist crusaders in proclaiming "God wills it!" Perhaps you could now help provide, in the phrase of William James, "a moral equivalent of war," a cause which could move man to that Herculean striving and sacrifice, that conjoint exertion and endurance that war can beget, and which the world-wide war on poverty must beget, if peace—and man—is to survive.

WHERE AND WHEN DOES MAN MEET GOD?

This issue, as do indeed all this-world issues, centers around the question: Where and when does man encounter God? Where and when does man *meet* God, learn of him, feel his creative strength and urgings, experience his unifying love and forgiveness? For these are so needed, I repeat, for man "to do the job" of world justice and development and peace.

Yes, I know that we meet God in and through and with Christ in his Church—in his word, in his unifying grace (sacraments and sacrifices), in his assembled people. But surely we can also meet God meaningfully out there in the world, particularly when we move toward the unity he desires for all and the creative power he shares with us, made to his image and likeness.

Does God perhaps in a special manner today *choose* to meet us down here in this world, where and when men meet men toward unity and continuing creation, to fulfill and to become more truly his image?

> God wills to meet man where and when men meet men toward unity and continuing creation.[10]

Will theologians allow this proposition,[11] and help give it flesh and blood, front and center in the Church in the arena of this world? Is there, in short, an "operative relation" between continuing creation in this world and continuing the incarnation?

II. CREATION AND INCARNATION AS CONTINUING IN THIS WORLD

WHY AND HOW DOES A SOCIAL ACTIONIST REFLECT THEOLOGICALLY?

Why and how does this social actionist reflect theologically, if, I should add, my reflections might be accorded such distinction at all? I am trying to convey the way I see things in this world, to explain how I see God in relation to the things of this world, to understand the steps I have gone through in reaching (or falling into) my present view of this world and Christ, to find out whether the theology of schema 13, coinciding so closely as it does with what I want, really says what I think it says, or whether I am reading my own mirror-image yearning and meaning into the root concepts of the *Constitution on the Church in the Modern World.*

Further, and there is the focus of this entire paper, I am trying to clarify and deepen my hazy and shallow grasp, and to find out whether the main theological currents of Vatican II (and of certain Protestant thinkers) *can be applied* to the problem for which I have daily responsibility—the issue of world poverty, justice, development, unity and peace. Then, if this theological light and motive power can be applied, I want to know how this theology can be strengthened and nourished, to grow and articulate itself into the respective elements required to respond to the respective needs of my problem.

This is what I mean by a problem-solving approach in theology. And by no means do I think that this is the only or principal approach. I know full well that just as applied research grows from pure research, and applied science (technology) derives from pure science, so does applied theology come forth from pure theology, that is, pure theology *plus* adequate grasp of reality from this world focused on an appropriate problem.

Until very recent years, I believe that theology has remained too often overly pure, i.e., lacking this adequate grasp of reality, overly isolated from the problems and yearnings and initiatives of man in this world, even snubbing them with disdainful hauteur. The sciences, especially the social sciences, responded on the whole with equal largesse.

THE THEOLOGY OF THIS WORLD COMPARED WITH NATURAL LAW

I will call the new currents I discern in schema 13 "the theology of this world." Its main elements, as I see them, will be commented upon a bit later. Just now I want to survey these very quickly as compared with "the theology of natural law," which I learned in the seminary.[12]

Now please understand that I am following a subjective approach with the *advertenda* "which I discern" and "which I learned." Also, I will use lay as distinct from theological terminology, nonprofessional as distinct from professional phraseology. And please be warned again, I am always picking and choosing in terms of my problem of world poverty, justice and development.

Natural Law Theology	*This-World Theology*
1. Creation is already finished: God has already fully expressed his will in creatures once and for all; his eternal mind and will found in creation is always the same.	Creation has not reached its terminus: God expresses himself in new ways in his unfinished creation; creation continues in this world.

527

Natural Law Theology	This-World Theology
2. Natural law uncovers to man in finished creation the "road signs" for conforming to God's will, but provides no "motor power" moving man to act creatively.	God shares his power over creation with man, made to his image, and thus co-creator with God; together they continue creation.
3. A whole view of life tends to see the world as static, unchanging, affecting all cultural expression.	A whole view of life tends to see the world as dynamic, more rapidly changing today than ever, affecting all cultural expression.
4. Such change as does occur tends to be repetitive, cyclical, seasonal, really "not going anywhere"; nature really does not change; old relations remain.	Change is developmental, step by step, moving in a general direction, growing, "going somewhere," evolutionary; nature itself changes; new relations are created.
5. Problems of man and society are basically the same, constantly repeated in history; responses, remedies are traditional, handed down generation after generation.	New issues, new questions, new challenges and opportunities arise, with roots in the past, but with shoots toward the future; pat answers from the past are inadequate; new responses are required.
6. Man's freedom to choose is badly restricted because of obvious and proven directives already inherited from past.	Man's freedom to choose is much expanded, ever changing and opening because of *continuing creation*; indeed since man *must* make new decisions based on new reality, new relations, he must be free.
7. God's mind is well expressed in finished creation, so nature is God's domain and sacral; man is almost a trespasser or squatter allowed by divine sufferance; he should not meddle too much in nature, including its social expressions.	Man receives dominion over nature from God; man has at least co-managerial responsibility; he can and must experiment, renew, create, reform nature, especially its social expressions.
8. Intellectual curiosity, spirit of investigation and research, joy of discovery are all suspect, contrary to psychology of passive acceptance of past solutions.	Curiosity, research, grasping reality anew are obligations; wonder and joy of discovery are highly valued human experiences and can be tied in with discovery of God. (Cardinal Montini on sharing God's vision of innards of matter and energy.)

528

Natural Law Theology	*This-World Theology*
9. Closed, withdrawn, defensive cultural, social and political atmosphere is apparent.	Openness, dialogue, seeking true and good wheresoever can be found is the mentality here.
10. There is a conservative, *status quo* attitude concerning societal structures; man must conform to society.	We find a progressive, experimental attitude concerning societal reform; society is to be formed and shaped by man "for the fullness of a more excellent life."

Perhaps these opposites are overdrawn. They are at least illustrative of the mental images or feelings I get while my mind ranges over the natural law approach of seminary days as compared with my intellectual picture-and-frame today. If these are merely caricatures, then I confess them nonetheless. It is well for theologians to know what misapprehensions Catholic social actionists are capable of today.

The sharp differences outlined here spring out of the sharp difference in the relationship between God and creation. For that reason they all have theological roots and content. And skipping over several possible approaches for discussing the subject, let us go directly to what I regard as the root concept and key emphasis of the new theology of this world in the Constitution —a concept that spans the whole of Scripture, beginning with Genesis through the gospels and the Apocalypse: man as the image of God, Christ as the perfect image of God.

Both of these are very biblical, with complementary stress in Old and New Testaments respectively. They are perhaps the most significant and pregnant truths of revelation in that they can impart so much meaning to Christian life on a continuing basis and in an ever deepening, broadening, more fruitful sense. They are replete with what we need and want to see and know, love and act for. (Please recall again that my theological lenses are adjusted to the optics needed for my problem.)

THE IMAGE OF GOD

The *Constitution on the Church in the Modern World* is anthropocentric; it centers around man, not around the abstract man of matter and form, but around his interests and experiences: "The joys and the hopes, the griefs and anxieties of the men of this age. . . . Indeed, nothing genuinely human fails to raise an echo in their hearts" of the followers of Christ, the Church (art. 1).

How astonishing and delightful to think that such human expressions and everyday feelings now enter that revered sanctuary of my seminary days, Denzinger's *Enchiridion Symbolorum*. Just imagine! Man's tears and laughter, frustrations and exaltations—the very stuff of life—side by side with Nicaea, Trent and Vatican I.

Still this is theology, not mere humanism. Perhaps we are beginning to see that all *theology*, rather paradoxically, must also be *anthropology*, because revelation is not God speaking to himself about himself, but God speaking to man, about both of themselves together, God and man. More significant still, *the* revelation of God to man is the God-Man, *Theos* and *Anthropos*. So to be more fully and truly Christian, our theology must be man-centered. And indeed, the purpose of it all is to move toward the One Center who is All-in-All, the Omega—and still man.[13]

Theology is not man talking to God. Rather, theology is man talking to man (including the God-Man) about the God who talks to man. Now I beg to have more of this "talking" focus expressly on certain particular human problems—which are also problems of the God-Man, because he is also human. "According to the almost unanimous opinion of believers and unbelievers alike, all things on earth should be related to man as their center and crown" (art. 12). In addition to confirming our present thesis, this passage of the Constitution illustrates well its constant awareness of and feeling for this world's opinion.

What the world thinks, its interests, concerns, problems, responses can no longer be ignored. The Church must be *au courant*, in communication with this world. And today this world centers around man. Let us face it, theology now becomes more anthropocentric because the world has become so, in a process stretching back over a couple of centuries, even dating back to the Renaissance. But theology and the Church are only now awakening to this as offering theological opportunities, and not just difficulties to be swept away by *auctores approbatae* as *opiniones falsae*.

"But what is man?" the Constitution continues. "About himself he has expressed, and continues to express, many divergent and even contradictory opinions. In these he often exalts himself as the absolute measure of all things or debases himself to the point of despair. The result is doubt and anxiety. The Church understands these problems" (art. 12). Well, it's about time. "The Church" here is a pretty broad statement. The Holy Spirit, yes. But only certain theologians and writers, a few pastors and spiritual directors. And the unconditioned indicative "understands" is much too strong. "Seeks now to begin to understand" would be closer to reality.

In any case, "What is man?" becomes in truth *the* one big question. And here the Church does have the one big answer: "Sacred Scripture teaches that man was created 'to the image of God,' is capable of knowing and loving his Creator, and was appointed by Him as master of all earthly creatures that he might subdue them and use them to God's glory" (art. 12). The consequences of "the image of God" are wonderfully rich and fulfilling. The Constitution begins to explore these magnanimously. They give hopeful, satisfying leads toward dealing with, or at least speaking intelligently about, many human problems, and particularly with my problems of world poverty, justice and development, unity and peace.

To summarize my interpretation of the Constitution, man as the image of God:

1) possesses, in God's name, dominion over the universe;
2) by means of work continues creation by transforming and perfecting reality;
3) constructs and enhances, cultivates and adorns the human community;
4) exercises his powers freely, capable of error and sin, among dramatic "ups and downs" of stupidity and genius, catastrophe and hope;
5) seeks solidarity with all the human family, in justice and love;
6) brings about socialization, the growing mutual interdependence of human groupings;
7) fills the dominant creative role in history;
8) is affected but not determined by the rest of creation;
9) "puts on Christ" during the development process in time;
10) aims at becoming, with, in and through Christ, who is the one full and perfect "Image of the invisible God" (Col 1:15), Alpha and Omega, partaker in the future restoration (recapitualtio) of all things,
11) in the eternal kingdom of God, already present in some way and degree in time and history,
12) here and now in the this-world of man, striving toward unity and continuing creation.

We can readily see what a contribution such a view of man and of life can make toward the problem of world justice and development. The human élan (and commitment) necessary may be generated from such vision and motivation. Toward that end, the theology of this world itself requires development and articulation. It must be applied to specific programs of aid, trade, finance and societal reform.

This theology and its application must enter the mainstream of the Church—divinity schools, seminaries, houses of study, retreat centers and lay spirituality, pulpits and liturgy, religious education, school curricula, universities, communications media, art and other cultural expression, leader-formation and professional associations, business, labor and governmental circles, opinion-forming and pressure groups.[14] How this could affect the Church as an institution, which not only reacts and adapts to change, but which embraces and promotes positive change, falls more directly within the companion paper of Canon Houtart.

CREATION AND INCARNATION: GOD AS CREATOR AND REDEEMER

My problem of world justice, unity and development revolves around whether or not man will have the vision and will to continue creation in the scale and scope necessary to make possible "the fullness of a more excellent life" for all the human family.

The root truth of the image of God, developed in terms of this-world theology, leads fittingly to a discussion of creation and incarnation as continuing today in this world. Because, from the viewpoint of man the most significant thing about creation is that he is made in the image of God; the most significant thing about the incarnation is that this Man Christ is *the* "Image of the invisible God."[15] Both are of and from God the Creator: man, his imperfect likeness; and *the* Man, his perfect image and Word.

Now today the same men of this world who continue creation by work and thought, by love and striving toward unity, are also the very same men who continue the incarnation, who continue to make Christ present here in this world, as the People of God. They strive toward the love and unity of all men, and toward the greater, ultimate unity of all men and all things with the All from whom we come, the creator and father of all. Because we come from the creator through his perfect image who is now man, creation and incarnation are very closely at one with each other.

St. John tells us that through Christ is made all that is made: the whole of creation, all electrons and atoms, viruses and cells, proteins and protozoa, plants, doves and dinosaurs, horses and humans. In the great arch of time's forward thrust, continuing today, all come forth from the mind of God the Father, from his own perfect image and idea, the Word and Logos, his Son who is Christ the Son of Man. And from the will of the Father and Son, from their love personified, who is the Holy Spirit.

God, and particularly the God-Man, knows and loves every bit of stuff that we call being. He conceives it, wills that it continue to exist, sees that it is good. And loving man, his image, his crowning creation of all the earth, God gives this creation to man, shares with man dominion over every other creature. (Quite a move toward decentralization of authority.)

God wills that man know and love all being, as he knows and loves all that is. God bids man to name the rest of creation, to call all by meaningful signs, to become aware of the nature and traits of each atom and cell, galaxy and social grouping. So God wants man to be curious, to investigate and research, to grasp the interrelations of creatures with each other and with man himself. Thus perceiving their being and relations, man learns the better who he is, and who God is.

God directs man to dress and cultivate creation, to bring raw matter and energy into new relationships, toward fuller perfection and order unto higher states of existence and unity—and, in the process, to dress and cultivate man, to free him from determinations that are merely creaturely, to bring him toward unity and fuller perfection, unto higher states of existence, even unto becoming perfect as the Father is perfect, through the restoring and renewing of creation, which the incarnation brings about and which the People of God continue today.

The incarnation is a sort of second love affair between God and creation, following a stormy courtship that lasted since the breakup of the first love affair in Eden.[16] The Old Testament recounts the repeated quarrels and temporary reconciliations of this long courtship held together by a betrothal that Israel repeatedly breaks, then renews. The Old Testament foreshadows the permanent reconciliation which the Redeemer signs and seals and empowers in the New Testament. But the ultimate consummation of union between God and creature will come about only at the end of time. True, it has already begun with the coming of Christ, his death and resurrection, but his incarnation, his reconciling union with man, must continue taking place, taking hold of and embracing creation in time and space, until the renewal and unity of all creation is fully complete. Then occurs the greater birth by which all creation becomes the complete Christ, the Omega.

"The whole universe is a womb, and history records the billion yeared period of gestation, until we who are Christ are born into eternity. The Last Day is the Day of Christ's Nativity."[17] During this "period of gestation" within the womb of the universe and history creation continues. As the good diffusive of himself, God constantly shares, expresses and exteriorizes his being and his goodness through his idea, the Logos, who by the incarnation becomes Christ. "All things were made through him, and without him was made nothing that has been made" (Jn 1:3). Hence, continuing creation and continuing incarnation deeply affect each other. In a sense they are inseparable, and even cause each other to continue—in Christ.

I believe that this incarnational view of continuing creation offers the source of vision and motive needed to beget that exceptional human *élan* which my problem of world justice, development and unity requires today and for the next century. I believe that the consequences of this incarnational view find wide and deep resonance among a broad spectrum of human thought today. Note that I do not say that this incarnational view *in itself*, in its doctrinal roots and premises of faith, receives sympathetic attention among others who have world views quite contrary to our Christian view of life. It is the *consequences* worked out and articulated from this incarnational view of continuing creation that others look upon with increasing attention and favor. At least they begin to see the bases of intelligent conversation about some of these consequences, such as outlined above under this-world theology and man as the image of God.

We must make a quick review of these basic world views, particularly since followers of two of these, the rational-technological and the technocratic, have on the whole shown deeper awareness of my problem of world misery, justice and development, and have done more toward its solution than Christians have.

EVIL, SIN, THE CROSS

Before pursuing this line of thought, we must very deliberately consider the fact and experience of evil and sin in the world, the truth in faith of Christ's saving action in the paschal mystery of his suffering and cross, death and resurrection.

Certainly this paper tends to be too optimistic and this-world centered. I admit that it is unbalanced in this respect. For brevity's sake, I will not try to amend this grievous fault, but only confess it. I have not given much thought as yet to the influence of sin on "my" problem, to the relation of moral evil to global injustice or hemispheric apathy or world social chaos. I do believe that Christ is *the* one who has conquered these sins, and has brought into the world the "wherewithal" for justice and concern and order —even love—among all men. And that the continuing incarnation gives these actuality today and tomorrow. That's the heart of the incarnational view which I profess.

But it is not all over and done with. The struggle to overcome sin persists to the end of time. Both within each person, and in society, the Christ-Good struggles with "the mystery of iniquity." To this great drama many leaders and thinkers of this world are blind. And a paper like this one, written of and in and for the faith, must witness to this reality of sin and evil, and of the saving Christ who comes particularly to redeem and to reorder creation from this sad condition.

I have not, I repeat, given much thought to these pervading and interlocking truths of history and of faith. I cannot of a sudden formulate something worthwhile saying. But the following quote from the Constitution is eminently appropriate and illuminating.

> For a monumental struggle against the powers of darkness pervades the whole history of man. The battle was joined from the very origins of the world and will continue until the last day, as the Lord has attested. Caught in this conflict, man is obliged to wrestle constantly if he is to cling to what is good. Nor can he achieve his own integrity without valiant efforts and the help of God's grace.
>
> That is why Christ's Church, trusting in the design of the Creator, acknowledges that human progress can serve man's true happiness. Yet she cannot help echoing the Apostle's warning: "Be not conformed to this world" (Rom 12:2). By the world is here meant that spirit of vanity and malice which transforms

into an instrument of sin those human energies intended for the service of God and man.

Hence if anyone wants to know how this unhappy situation can be overcome, Christians will tell him that all human activity, constantly imperiled by man's pride and deranged self-love, must be purified and perfected by the power of Christ's cross and resurrection. For, redeemed by Christ and made a new creature in the Holy Spirit, man is able to love the things themselves created by God, and ought to do so. He can receive them from God, and respect and reverence them as flowing constantly from the hand of God.

Grateful to his Benefactor for these creatures, using and enjoying them in detachment and liberty of spirit, man is led forward into a true possession of the world, as having nothing, yet possessing all things. "All are yours, and you are Christ's, and Christ is God's" (1 Cor 3:22–23).

For God's Word, through whom all things were made, was Himself made flesh and dwelt on the earth of men. Thus He entered the world's history as a perfect man, taking that history up into Himself and summarizing it. He Himself revealed to us that "God is love" (1 Jn 4:8). At the same time He taught us that the new command of love was the basic law of human perfection and hence of the world's transformation.

To those, therefore, who believe in divine love, He gives assurance that the way of love lies open to all men and that the effort to establish a universal brotherhood is not a hopeless one. He cautions them at the same time that this love is not something to be reserved for important matters, but must be pursued chiefly in the ordinary circumstances of life.

Undergoing death itself for all of us sinners, He taught us by example that we too must shoulder that cross which the world and the flesh inflict upon those who search after peace and justice. Appointed Lord by His resurrection and given plenary power in heaven and on earth, Christ is now at work in the hearts of men through the energy of His Spirit. He arouses not only a desire for the age to come, but, by that very fact, He animates, purifies, and strengthens those noble longings too by which the human family strives to make its life more human and to render the whole earth submissive to this goal (art. 37, 38).

FIVE PRIMORDIAL WORLD VIEWS

In severely truncated manner I will now introduce five basic world views, each of which deeply affects the culture and society of their respective peoples, and which may indeed be the prime genitors of their respective cultures and societies.

These five are the 1) ontocratic, 2) theocratic, 3) rational-technological, 4) technocratic, and 5) incarnational. There may well be others, or other ways of classifying, or denominating them. Again, allow me merely to begin an introduction of these ideas, which are far from being worked out in my own mind. And even such inadequate ideas as I do now have cannot be put forth in this short space.

Hardly anywhere today are any of these world views to be found in a pure state. Intercommunication among peoples, among cultural and societal ensembles causes increasing cross-fertilization, brings about many combination and hybrid views, conflicting currents and tensions.

Nor are they all the same "age." The ontocratic, for instance, goes back much farther than the others, to the beginnings of history and human civilization, and even back to the primitive cultures of prehistoric man. The technocratic view, on the other hand, is a comparative youngster, having become possible only with the industrial revolution, and having attained serious know-how and power only in our generation. The theocratic is situated between these two, having begun, of course, when Abraham heard God calling him to depart from Ur of the Chaldees and its ontocratic culture, which was already then some two thousand years old, dating back to the temple-city-states of Sumer. The rational-technological was introduced to man by the Greeks.

The incarnational view became possible with Christ's coming and has experienced an amazing succession of "ups and downs," cross-fertilizations with the other views, deformations and reformations, declines and renewals during its nineteen hundred years. Another renewal, nourished in part from the rational-technological view, and even by the technocratic, appears now to be beginning. But the incarnational view, tied in as explained above with continuing creation, will not reach full fruition until the end of this world as we now know it.

1. The *ontocratic* world view is monist: nature, man, gods are all one cosmic totality, forming one continuum. The Hindu religion, culture and society present a good example of the ontocratic view worked out and actualized by man through several millennia and still observable today. Discussing the subject in this same context, Van Leeuwen says:

> The classical Indian way of thinking . . . starts from the basic apprehension of the undivided Oneness of all that exists. That fundamental trend could be called *horror individuationis*, an urge to shy away from individualized existence and to seek to be absorbed in that sub-individual and super-individual Oneness in which all individual features are annihilated. . . . This ontocratic view is expressed clearly in the doctrine of Karma. All that exists has emanated from the primeval matter and, in the end, will be absorbed into it again . . . for every individual form is a transient manifestation of the undifferentiated primordial matter which alone is real and true, transcendent and eternal.[18]

A comparable ontocratic view was shared by primitive societies such as the Canaanite and Hittite and in certain measure by the animists of Africa and totemists of America. It also played a major role in shaping the great Babylonian, Egyptian and Chinese—Buddhist, Taoist, Confucian—civilizations. And it certainly seriously affected the theocratic view of Judaism and its spiritual and cultural offspring, Christianity.

2. The theocratic world view places stress on God as the absolute other in relation to creation. God exercises full physical dominance over nature, determining nature's operations in minutest detail and with ever vigilant constancy.

So awesome and ineffable that even his name should not be spoken, God wields full moral dominance over man. Man does remain free to rebel, however, to his eventual and eternal damnation, i.e., his complete separation from God, complete alienation between creature and creator. Still the absolute other, who determines all, enters into agreement with man by covenant or alliance, somewhat comparable to a truce between a king and rebellious subjects. As part of the alliance, man appeases the wrath of the almighty king with a courtly ritual of worship and sacrifice, performed publicly on behalf of the whole people and privately by each family and individual. Depending upon faithful completion of the alliance's prescriptions, the king sends good or evil, fruit or famine, victory or defeat, war or peace, health or plague upon his subjects. Through the covenant's ritual, then, man exercises some "influence" with the creator and through him over nature.

But man is not disposed toward "taking hold" of nature directly, to manipulate and mold and refashion it to his own this-world purposes. This seems due to the view that nature is sacral; it is both God's plaything and his workshop. Man is a sort of cowed child who has constantly been told by a domineering father, "Don't you dare touch my tools, or my golf clubs!" So the abject son does not fool around with the energies and forces of nature. He feels little scientific curiosity, no desire to experiment, no technical creativity and little social imagination.

Seldom, if ever, has this theocratic world view really taken complete hold of a people to the degree implied here. These are rather its currents, stresses and tendencies. They are found in the Old Testament, of course, in Islam, in much of Byzantine and Medieval Christianity, in early Calvinism, in the Iberian church as transplanted to Latin America, in the Jansenism of Europe and as transmuted into the popular piety of many Catholic ghetto parishes of the United States.

I wonder if the popularity of Mary the Mother and her intercession was not due largely to the need of humanizing the awesome King-Father of theocracy. And to what extent does this current in Catholicism account for our long suspicion of the natural sciences, our lack of curiosity and the spirit of research.

Perhaps, too, the work ethic of Calvinism, so lacking in the joyous sense of self-fulfillment, is more of an ascetic offering to the fearsome God, who rewards this righteousness by the fruitfulness of harvest and profit. At least this *furor laboris* resulted in new creation, in development and social experiment.

3. In the *rational-technological* world view, man takes hold of and determines nature directly, without God or indifferent to him. Power over nature is acquired through careful observation and controlled experiment, by reasoning out tentative hypotheses, which after repeated trial and error become general laws that predict the behavior of energy and matter. Known and predictable, these forces lose their mystery, their sacral aura. They can be controlled, manipulated, directed to man's use, through technology.

The Greeks, of course, are the primogenitors of this world view, which required a major break with the ontocratic milieu surrounding them. For Protagoras, "man is the measure of all things," especially the reason of man.

The mathematics of the Pythagoreans, Socrates' curiosity about societal structures, Aristotle's recorded observations and musings on natural phenomena, the experiments of Archimedes—all flow toward the renewed scientific curiosty of Renaissance man, of Francis Bacon and Da Vinci, to Galileo and Keppler, down the mainstream of the Enlightenment, and to the rational-technological world view of our modern age, of Dewey and Poincaré, Bertrand Russell, Julian Huxley and Sidney Hook.

Bergson gives this view intellectual formulation as a continuing *élan vital*, a continuing evolution that is self-generating and self-determining, that lacks both outer control and inner freedom. It just goes on and on and cannot do anything about it. Nor is there Anyone "out there" or "down here" who knows or cares or can do anything. God as creator and sustainer of all is extraneous to all serious thought and concern. Belief in him is tolerated since it makes some people sleep better. Or the whole question of God and the ultimate "whys" of life are put aside on the shelf, swept under the rug. It is the "how" of things that count.

The only measure is man—his needs, his awareness, his dignity, his freedom. These provide criteria for values and decisions. But they are short-term. In the long run the whole business has no ultimate meaning. We and the rest of creation are not going anywhere or becoming anything really new, truly significant or absolutely precious. Another two or three billion years and it will be all over for the human race. Another two or three decades and it will be all over for you and me.

4. In the *technocratic* world view technology and its power replace man as the measure and value, to assume dominance over man himself, society and nature. Technical power and process become so elevated that technology takes on the determining role, in the hands, of course, of an elite group of power-manipulators. These know also how to manipulate public opinion.

By a strange *tour de force*, technology, the creature of man's reason, seizes power from its human creator. The totalitarian state, and especially Nazism and Stalinism, are the most thorough-going examples of this view so far. But this technocratic spirit infiltrates so-called democratic societies as well, insofar as their mass culture and proliferating structures tend to reduce human dignity, freedom and creativity, without giving sufficient compensatory human dignity, freedom and creativity as promised. It accompanies that depersonalization and bureaucratization which can result from today's big business and big labor, big government and big research, mass communication and mass advertisement, big city and big church. This danger to the human person is innate to socialization, the multiplying of human interdependence. But it is not inevitable, especially if fully recognized.

The totalitarian expressions of technocracy are violently hostile to God and strive to expunge even the vestiges of religion. Hostility to its expressions in mass democracy is more subtle and rational. Its ideology is secularism, which feels at home too in the rational-technological world view. Secularism makes this world an absolute, leaving no intellectual room whatsoever for God and religion.

It is basic then to the secularist view that God and creation have no relationship at all, for the simple reason that God just simply is not. The very idea that God is, and especially the idea that he has any meaningful relation to man and society and this world, must be gotten rid of. This world (saeculum) is everything.

Secularization, as now occurring almost everywhere under the impact of technology and other influences, must, however, be sharply distinguished from secularism. The current process of secularization, insofar as it erodes the outer expressions and inner "imperialism" of an older, erroneous ontocratic and/or theocratic view of society (and a sacralist view of nature), could well be a purification of the visible Church and institutional religion, in full accord with the incarnational view, and consequently a positive gain. Secularism, on the other hand, is a basic ideology that cuts off all relation between creator and creature.

5. I have already introduced the incarnational world view of continuing creation above. I believe the incarnational view provides just those elements of vision and motive which my problem of world misery, justice and development requires. In the incarnational view God and nature (including man) are definitely distinct, radically other. In this respect it differs completely from the monism of the ontocratic view and accords fully with the theocratic view.

However, God and nature can and do communicate in a manner and degree much more profound than the theocratic view would allow. God and man (and nature) have been, in fact, and are now becoming totally reconciled and at one in and through the incarnation of Christ, true God becoming true man. In Christ, God, while remaining radically other, becomes "humanized," sharing the human life of his creature. While remaining radically creature and dependent on God, man becomes divinized, partaking in the divine life of God. This "humanization-divinization" process began with the incarnation of Christ, by his coming into the world, but by no means did it cease upon his physical departure. In the descent of his Spirit of love the "humanization-divinization" process really began on a grand scale and continues today through his Church to reach out toward all mankind. By sharing human life and making men partakers of divine life, Christ introduces to mankind new creative powers, tending especially toward a new relationship of love. This unites Christ-in-me with Christ-in-you to form one body in Christ. It renders the unity of all the human family more precious, more possible, more imperative.

God retains basic and residual responsibility over nature, but he freely shares his authority with man. Man becomes God's partner, with proximate managerial authority over creation. Made to the image of the creator, man has the duty to create, to exercise power over nature, and to seek greater creative power for continuing creation. This he does through thought and work, art and technology, justice and love, which move toward the unity of all men among each other, and as a whole toward God.

This movement toward unity, this convergence of all men and all creation toward the All, is *the* essential element and aim of continuing creation-and-incarnation. They are hyphenated, pulled together as one, because the creating God and the redeeming God-Man are one and the same God, the creatures he works with are the same, and basically the work itself is the same—the continuing incarnation redeems, renews, re-creates, continues all creation, elevating it to a new level of communication and participation with God.

CONTINUING CREATION AND MY PROBLEM

The problem of world misery, justice and development, unity and peace requires a massive new surge of vision and will, of imagination and work, of perseverance and sacrifice, of justice and accord. To beget the new juridic structures, to finance the cost, to create the new technology, to change old patterns of thought and duty, of treaty and trade, a fresh human élan must invigorate all the family of man. This élan must also enable all peoples to move toward consensus and unity, while retaining freedom, identity, diversity.

The incarnational view of continuing creation offers many of the key elements required to beget and to motivate this new surge of conjoined creative endeavor. This, I trust, begins to become sufficiently clear; a more detailed statement is not possible here.

But two major questions remain. Will the imperative of continuing creation, which is at the heart of our incarnational view, really be embraced by Christians, singly and as the People of God? Granting that non-Christians cannot accept our premises, rooted as these are in the Christian faith, are they able to form with us a working consensus embracing the consequences of our incarnational view? If both questions receive affirmative answers, then we have hope of moving together toward that unity and continuing creation which my problem requires.

In this paper I cannot explore these questions in detail. By way of conclusion I will give only some indications of possible responses and horizons for exploration. The Constitution states in the opening sentence of chapter 1: "According to the almost unanimous opinion of believers and unbelievers alike, all things on earth should be related to man as their center and crown" (art. 12).

Man is certainly accorded an increasingly central place in the ancient ontocratic cultures of Hinduism and Buddhism and among the primitive cultures of Africa. The same holds true in theocratic societies, like those of Islam, and in cultures that are rich amalgams of several world views, like those of certain Latin countries with their strong theocratic and/or ontocratic currents. The harsher technocratic aspects of Stalinist Russia are now transmuted so that Soviet society shows increasing concern for human dignity and need, at home and abroad. Step by step man becomes more the measure of things in Eastern Europe. Somehow all the seventeen nations of the United Nations were able to agree on a Declaration of Human Rights.

And at last, when Pope John clearly gave to the world some of the human consequences of the incarnational view, he was admired, acclaimed, even loved. When Pope Paul and the Council Fathers address themselves to man's needs and offer the Church to the service of the world, their efforts are followed avidly by world opinion. They receive constant criticism, comment and counsel. Similar this-world concerns by the World Council of Churches and other religious bodies receive comparable attention.

The centrality of man has always been the central thesis of the rational-technological view. Its progressive modern expressions through democracy, scientific advance, industrialization, social justice, human dignity and responsible participation, in concert with the Christian message, have played the main roles in begetting this new global awareness of the centrality of man. Some of the more notable thinkers of this view, like Julian Huxley, now wonder aloud whether they might join hands with fresh propounders of the incarnational view, like Teilhard de Chardin.[19]

There grows an atmosphere of openness among the respective views, an openness centered around man's needs and potential, which might be expressed in this way: Let us meet when and where men meet, let us meet in order that men may meet toward unity and continuing creation.

The distinctiveness of the incarnational view lies, as we have seen, in the meeting of God and man whereby they both continue creation and draw toward the ultimate union of all in the new creation, the new All, the Omega. Unbelievers, like Huxley, are not interested in these next-world aspects of the incarnational view.[20] But is it not possible that we encounter God whenever we move toward the unity he desires for all, wherever we humanly use the creative power he shares with us, made to his image and likeness? Whether or not Mr. Huxley or U Thant, Mr. Spaak or Mr. Kosygin want to meet God, whether or not they recognize his presence—there he is. Because God wills to meet man where and when men meet men toward unity and continuing creation.

Adherents of the Christian faith must guard against a concept of divine presence that is only in and of this world, only horizontal, in a man-meet-man encounter that is only human. Certainly man alone cannot make God present. But let us suppose that this meeting of men is in the context of seeking fulfillment of the man Christ, subject to and calling upon his power and grace, his light and strength. Then Christ ensures his presence, his light, his Spirit of Love. God is there.

God is sovereignly free. He can meet man anywhere, under any circumstances, privately or publicly, singly or in massed mobs. He has met man at work in the desert, at prayer in church, traveling on horseback. But perhaps today God in a special manner *chooses*, freely wills, to meet us down there amidst the problems of this world, where and when men meet men toward unity and continuing creation, to fulfill and to become together more truly his image.

If he does, then we who would follow and live by his perfect image have a great role to fill in the Herculean problem of world misery, justice and development, unity and peace. And I certainly hope that theologians and the Church as an institution will spend on this aspect of the God-man encounter more time and talent.

NOTES

1. In this paper the *Constitution on the Church in the Modern World* is sometimes referred to as schema 13.

2. Some of the theological and practical implications of the *applied power* now exercised by man are broached by Romano Guardini, especially in *Power and Responsibility* (Chicago: Regnery, 1961).

3. *Economics*, by Paul A. Samuelson (New York: McGraw-Hill, 1964), is the type of college-level primer which the theologians, as well as pastors and churchmen in general, should study to get some basic understanding of how economic forces and bodies actually apply today's science and technology to transform the world. For more detailed and explicit treatment of international de-

velopment, see Gunnar Myrdal's books, e.g., *An International Economy* (London: Routledge and Kegan Paul, 1956), *Economic Theory and Under-Developed Regions* (London: Duckworth, 1957). For an integrated view of some political and sociological aspects of applying technology through economics see John Kenneth Galbraith's *American Capitalism, The Concept of Countervailing Power* (Boston: Houghton Mifflin, 1957) and *The Affluent Society* (Boston: Houghton Mifflin, 1958). Peter Drucker's, *The New Society* (New York: Harper, 1949) gives more sociological emphasis in the economics-political context.

4. Josef Fuchs, S.J., discusses some aspects of this question in *Natural Law: A Theological Investigation* (New York: Sheed and Ward, 1965) 181–193. Cf. Karl Rahner, S.J., "Christianity and Ideology," *Concilium* 6 (Glen Rock, N. J.: Paulist Press, 1965) 41–59; see also Heinz Robert Schlette, "The Problem of Ideology and Christian Belief," *ibid.*, 107–129.

5. Canon Houtart has introduced some of these subjects in his book *The Challenge to Change* (New York: Sheed and Ward, 1964), and in "Le Schema 13 sera-t-il plus qu'un texte?" *Nouvelle Revue Théologique* 87 (1965) 849–856. The organs he refers to are at the international level, and especially in relation to the Vatican Curia.

6. Barbara Ward, *The Rich Nations and the Poor Nations* (New York: Norton, 1962). Besides numerous articles on this theme in periodicals such as *The Economist* and *New York Times Magazine*, Lady Jackson has four other books that are all most pertinent to this paper: *Faith and Freedom* (New York: Norton, 1954), *The Interplay of East and West* (New York: Norton, 1961), *Five Ideas That Change the World*, (Norton, 1959), and *India and the West* (Norton, 1959).

7. I introduce some of these issues in *The Other Dialogue* (Garden City, N. Y.: Doubleday, 1965) especially 135–164, 221–262.

8. Some of the major aspects of this paper are treated with admirable insight by Arend Van Leeuwen, *Christianity in World History: The Meeting of the Faiths of East and West* (London: Edinburgh House, 1964) and Harvey Cox, *The Secular City* (New York: Macmillan, 1965).

9. Cf. R. M. Fagley, *The Population Explosion and Christian Responsibility* (New York: Oxford University, 1960). Dr. Fagley is executive secretary of the Commission of the Churches on International Affairs, an associate body of the World Council of Churches, and he often represents the WCC at international discussions of the population question. See also Arthur McCormack, ed. *Christian Responsibility and World Poverty* (Westminster, Md.: Newman, 1963) for the view of some Catholics on these issues. Cf. also *World Council of Churches, Report of the General Secretary to the Central Committee* (Egunu, Nigeria, January, 1965) 161–170. This report states: "There have always been social problems, but in our time the basic problem of overcoming hunger or poverty and of social justice has become the issue which dominates all other issues and on the solution of which the future of mankind depends. . . . So the question is firstly a spiritual question. . . . The secret of solidarity is the secret of men living together as fellow-creatures and brothers for all of whom Christ died" (p. 166).

10. This is the way I sum up the position presented by Cox in *The Secular City*, as I read it in the context of *Gaudium et Spes*, and undoubtedly my own feeling of what my problem and the world, as I know it, need. Cf. also Hans Urs Von Balthasar, "Meeting God in Today's World," *Concilium* 6, 23–29. "In this continual confrontation, a confrontation to which the principal Christian commandment compels the believer, the believer must search for and find God in the neighbor and in this way recall and reveal God to him. All dogmatic propositions are implicit in this experience. Encounter, in the simple carrying out of Christian responsibility, is the 'sacrament' in which God wills 'to be among us' in an almost-experiential way. This encounter is also the center from which the cosmos, with all its miracles, laws and terrors, becomes theophanous" (38–39).

11. By no means is this a rhetorical question. I do not know whether my theology is doctrinally sound, because I do not know that much about theology today. I am, of course, especially concerned as to what Catholic theologians might say, but am also deeply interested in the judgment of Protestant, Orthodox and Jewish thinkers. I hope it is clear that I do not wish to identify the concept of the advance of the kingdom of God with evolution, or with merely human betterment. Cf. Gerard Philips, "The Church in the Modern World," *Concilium* 6, 14–15, on finding God "on the horizontal dimension . . . and yet God is not enclosed in creation."

12. I have since become acquainted with a more existential concept of natural law, for example, from J. Messner's *Social Ethics: Natural Law in the Modern World* (St. Louis: Herder, 1949). But despite some improvement, the static, guideline approach comes through heavily, rather than the surge of a creative *élan*, which we need so badly, besides being closer to the truth. Furthermore, fifteen years after ordination I had the blessing of a year's lectures on natural law by Father Gundlach, in person, in Latin! Jacques Maritain offered the principal light, especially *True Humanism*

543

(New York: Scribners, 1938); it too is quite static compared to the *Constitution on the Church in the Modern World.*

13. This thinking is very evident in Cardinal Suhard's two pastorals, "Growth or Decline?" and "Priests Among Men," *The Church Today* (Notre Dame, Ind.: Fides, 1953). And such thinking is clearly the leit-motif of Teilhard de Chardin's *The Phenomenon of Man* (New York: Harper, 1959) and *The Divine Milieu* (New York: Harper, 1960).

14. This should perhaps be a principal role of the "agency of the universal Church," called for by the Constitution in article 90, namely, to stimulate the Catholic community to foster progress in needy regions, and social justice on the international scene."

15. Col 1: 15. Knox translates this passage: "In the Son of God, in his blood, we find the redemption that sets us free from our sins. He is the true likeness of the God we cannot see; his is that first birth which precedes every act of creation. Yes, in him all created things took their being, heavenly and earthly, visible and invisible; what are thrones and dominions, what are princedoms and powers? They were all created through him and in him; he takes precedence of all, and in him all subsist. He too is that head whose body is the Church; it begins with him, since his was the first birth out of death; thus in every way the primacy was to become his. It was God's pleasure to let all completeness dwell in him, and through him to win back all things, whether on earth or in heaven, into union with himself, making peace with them through his blood, shed on the cross" (Col 1: 14–20).

Cf. Edward Schillebeeckx, O.P., "The Tridentine Decree on Justification: A New View," *Concilium* 5, 176–179, where he explains that "grace as an 'incarnation,' an historical reality," is essential to Christianity. "And so grace itself becomes a visible, tangible, *historical* reality *in* man's freedom. . . . That is why merit and grace are never opposed to each other: within the *telos* or end, given us as a pledge or *arrha* by the indwelling Spirit, we are borne toward the future *in* our historical existence." See also his "The Church and Mankind," *Concilium* 1: "Unequivocally, God loves man; and the being called man is not some abstract 'human nature' but a flesh-and-blood being who, together with his fellowmen, takes the fate of the world and of mankind into his own hands; he is a being who, by humanizing the world humanizes himself" (p. 86). "Creation in view of Christ, which includes the gift of grace, means that since creation all mankind carries within itself and anonymously this ecclesial orientation as a grace that is accepted or rejected. . . . Therefore, in the concrete, every free human act is one that works toward salvation or perdition" (p. 93).

16. A. Hulsbosch, O.S.A., in *God and Creation and Evolution* (New York: Sheed and Ward, 1965), seems to say that there was no historical Eden, and consequently no "first love affair." His treatment of creation and incarnation as continuing in time until the final fulfillment in Christ seems to accord wonderfully with the needs of my problem. About his views on original sin I cannot judge.

17. *The Journal of a Southern Pastor* (Notre Dame, Ind.: Fides, 1957) 202. Cf. Henri de Lubac, S.J., *La Pensée réligeuse du Père Teilhard de Chardin* (Paris: Aubier, 1962) especially chapter 18, "Création, Cosmogénèse, Christogénèse," 281–296.

18. Op. cit., (note 8) 179–183.

19. In his introduction to Teilhard's *The Phenomenon of Man*, Julian Huxley writes: "What is more, he [Teilhard] has helped to define the conditions of advance, the conditions which will permit an increase of fulfillment and prevent an increase of frustration. The conditions of advance are these: global unity of mankind's noetic organization or system of awareness, but a high degree of variety within that unity; love with goodwill and full cooperation; personal integration and internal harmony; and increasing knowledge" (p. 27).

20. "Though many scientists may, as I [Huxley] do, find it impossible to follow him [Teilhard] all the way in his gallant attempt to reconcile the supernatural elements in Christianity with the facts and implications of evolution, this in no way detracts from positive value of his naturalistic general approach" (*ibid.,* 19).

Abbé François Houtart

SUGGESTIONS FOR DOCTRINAL DEVELOPMENT

THE PASTORAL *Constitution on the Church in the Modern World* is of fundamental importance as a Conciliar document, because it gives the orientation to the forms of the Church's presence in the world and indicates the relations between the Church and creation. Several other documents of the Council have some important references to this matter, but this constitution offers a synthesis. Without schema 13, the Council would have been only half a Council.

This is not a matter of tactics. It would have been a scandal if the Church had organized such a meeting as a Council out of concern only for her own institution. It would have been an infidelity to the *raison d'être* of the Church, to her own mission.

Reflection on this problem was a necessity for the Church. The history of the last centuries shows how a real divorce has progressively come about between the Church and the world. The dynamism of humanity in the fields of science, politics, economy and social organization was not recognized by the Church and frequently was even opposed. Christians, often with reason, were not considered among the people "taking the world seriously," because this "world" was not integrated into their vision of faith.

At the same time a too exclusive attention has been given to the institutions of the Church herself, attributing an intrinsic value to many of them, overshadowing the fact they were purely instrumental for the salvation of

545

the world. The overemphasis put on certain roles (the clerical ones), the monopolization of too many functions by the clergy—all this is closely related to a distorted view of the relations between the Church and the world. Pietism and all the movements of withdrawal from the world as well as secularism are the fruit of it.

The main value of the *Constitution on the Church in the Modern World* is precisely that it offers a new approach and has laid the foundations not only for a renewed theological perspective, but also for a rejuvenated Christian attitude. And this was a doctrinal task. The task was not, however, easy. Many times during the preparatory period a dualism between the natural and supernatural orders, between body and soul, between matter and spirit, between Church and world, between redemption and creation kept reappearing, sometimes almost spontaneously. Hence, the theology elaborated especially in the first part of *Spes et Gaudium* is only a starting point.

I. READING THE SIGNS OF THE TIMES

Even if the introduction of the Constitution is short (6.2 per cent of the whole), its importance is great, for reasons of methodology as well as of the type of vision developed.

The introductory exposition is entitled "The Situation of Man in the Modern World." It is a description of the world and the evolution of mankind at the present stage of its history. Many have reacted against the idea of putting a descriptive part in a Conciliar document. They argued that this was not appropriate in a theological document; the Church has to provide doctrine, not to give a description. Others thought that it was useless, because the description would not be valid after a few years, or because in such a short text it could be only superficial. But the Council finally approved this introduction.

As a matter of fact the importance of the introduction lies first in the *method of thinking* it reveals, not only in the first part of the Constitution, but also in the introduction of the different chapters of the second part (marriage and family, culture, social and economic order, international community). In a certain sense, it is similar to the well-known "observe, judge and act" method developed by a specialized branch of Catholic Action.

John XXIII used the expression "reading the signs of the time" when alluding to the task of the Council. This means that the basic attitude must be one of facing reality, of looking at the facts before making a judgment. So often we have made our judgments before even knowing the facts, and this has led us to unrealistic attitudes and sometimes to the elaboration of slogans instead of doctrine. Then, too, this knowledge of the facts corresponds to a vision of faith: God is acting in the world, and for Christians the study of reality is a "reading of the signs of the time."

Knowledge of man's situation today is impossible without relevant means of information. In a complex society and in a changing civilization, systematic knowledge is a must, as much for thought as for action. Theological thinking has now developed with the help of the "human sciences," like demography, psychology, sociology and economics. Would it be conceivable today to make statements about family and marriage without demographic, sociological and psychological knowledge? Could we say anything worthwhile about war without a vivid knowledge of the conditions of modern warfare? All this has of course no influence on fundamental values but will influence their application and aid us in discovering some of their less known aspects.

This method of thinking, perhaps new for some theologians, should be more greatly developed in other theological fields, too, for example, ecclesiology; the study of the different institutions in the Church (the parish, religious congregations, the Roman Curia, the lay apostolate); the system of communication or of information in the Church; the roles in the Church (bishop, priest, laypeople), and others. The following branches of theology could also be cited: the need theology of the sacraments has of knowing the actual motivations of the recipient; how important it is for the theology of preaching to know the characteristics of the audience, the conditions of transmission of the message, the role of mass media.

There is a need for the Church to institutionalize research concerning relations between theology and the human sciences. Universities have a vital role to play in *basic research*. Without their help any progress in thought will be accidental and episodic. I consider it to be one of the most important tasks of Catholic universities today to establish permanent centers, with an interfaculty character, for interdisciplinary research.

Among the sciences of man I would rate psychology and sociology as most basic for reasons I would like to explain briefly. We must center our preoccupations in this area around the concrete conditions of the spread of the Christian message. This does not mean reducing theology to this field, nor does it mean reducing human reality to psychological and social facts. But this is the object of our concrete preoccupation. *Psychology*, because the human person is at the center of the mystery of creation and salvation (Part I, ch. 1), as both subject and actor: God has given his Church to men. Psychology, however, cannot work except in cooperation with biology and with reference to philosophy. *Sociology*, because man is living in community (Part I, ch. 2): the reception of Christ's message, the religious behavior of man and ecclesiastical institutions are all conditioned by the social character of the human being. Again sociology has to appeal to cultural anthropology, history, demography, economics, politics, social psychology and philosophy in order to elaborate adequate tools of research and its theories. The sources of information are very broad both for psychology and sociology, ranging from direct empirical research to the invaluable contribution of modern literature.

If we are looking for a specific task of Catholic universities today, or of theological faculties in the great secular universities, I do not hesitate to say that this is probably the most important. It lies completely in the line of the Constitution *Spes et Gaudium*, because it is at the focal point of the relations between the Church and the world. The universities would be the laboratories for the "servant Church's" service to the world and for the world's service to the Church.

Such a task should be undertaken on an ecumenical basis. Common work along this line would also help us to discover better the "nontheological" elements of our divisions, to relativize the expression of some of our theological positions, often influenced by the historical and cultural milieu of their elaboration, to work together to help man in the modern world in his search for orientation.

According to their geographical or cultural locations, universities would specialize in certain fields and eventually create some research centers out of their cultural areas.

The two other levels of contact between human sciences and the Church are more directly connected with action. The first is the organization of statistics on religious phenomena, and the second is applied socio-religious research.

But the introduction of the Constitution is not only a matter of methodology. The description is centered around the fact of change. We are living in a changing world. Some Council Fathers found this difficult to accept; some of them refused to recognize the fact of change. But they were a small minority. Others did not see why this had any importance for the Church. Is it not up to the Church to teach doctrine and thus indicate precisely what is not changing?

Change is too important a fact for the technical civilization in which we live to be ignored. It is so central that modern philosophy, social and political ideologies, the concept of history and the hopes of mankind are influenced by it. Today institutions that are not able to change are marginal and without meaning in the modern world. If the Church is not able to *institutionalize the change*, she will not be able to accomplish her mission, because instead of being a witness to the transcendent, and meaningful for all times and cultures, she will only be a witness to a particular time or culture.

Three remarks should be made at this point. First of all, this is a question of value, not of interest—in the sense of Sister Marie Augusta Neal's excellent book, *Values and Interests in Social Change*.[1] The motivation behind the Church's adaptation must be profoundly rooted in the salvation of mankind and not in a simple adaptation of an institutional system. It means a complete *remise en question* of the Church's whole life—going as far as a revision of the theological concept of mission; of the pattern of authority in the Church; of the relationship between hierarchy and laity, between bishops and priests; and of the contacts with other Christians, with other religions and with atheists, and among them with Marxists.

Merely to use modern tools to better ensure the Church's power over society, or to manipulate mass media in order to create an artificial image of a dynamic Church, to put a computer at the service of an autocratic and conservative chancery office, would only make things worse.

Secondly, this will allow the Church to play her prophetic role in society. The Church has been so identified with the "establishment" or with so-called western civilization, because of attachment to order and stability and because of the revolutionary flavor of change. The only way of judging the world from God's point of view is to be constantly aware of a changing reality where injustice, egotism and exploitation are always taking on new forms.

Thirdly, institutionalization of change means concrete measures. One of them on the level of the Universal Church should be the institutionalization of councils—let us say every ten years. This would help us avoid a new form of triumphalism, Vatican II triumphalism, which would serve as a tranquilizer for the Christian conscience.

Because of this rapid social change it is good that the introduction of the Constitution *Spes et Gaudium* will be out of date very soon. This will help to make people conscious of the need to be constantly at work and, for us, of being preoccupied not so much with applying the results of the Council as of continuing its work. We must not *follow* the Council; we must thrust forward from it.

II. A Theology of Creation and of the New Creation

If we ask what is the central theological point of the Constitution, the answer may be: a theology of creation, of the role of Christ in creation and the new creation. We must confess however that, like a small precious stone, this doctrine is well hidden in the present document; the Constitution gives only the embryo of such a doctrine. But there is here a tremendous power that post-Conciliar theology must develop.

In the new dimensions of man's history today, we are discovering some aspects of revelation. Indeed the central place of Christ in the world, through his action in history, is the fundamental fact we have to study in all its consequences. It will furnish the basis for a new Christian approach toward the world.

This new approach will require the development of three central theological themes: creation,[2] the role of Christ in the world,[3] and the new creation.[4]

Each of these themes is present in the text of the Constitution but all are far from being fully developed. Here we will address ourselves to each of them briefly.

1. CREATION

A dynamic concept of creation is provided by modern thinking on evolution now viewed as much better adapted to the reality of God's action. Creation is a vital action of a living God. It is alive with the development of what has been created, brought about under the impulse and with the cooperation of man. Only at the time of its consummation will it be possible to think of creation as perfected.

Historically our theological thought patterns were too committed to a frame of reference having a static vision of the world based on the Greek concept of *phusis*. This view, as H. Berkhof indicates in an outstanding contribution to this problem, failed to include a historical perspective.[5] As he writes, "It [the concept of creation] is the beginning of a chain in which nature, history and consummation are inseparable links."[6] And in this chain man has an active role. He is not only a subject, but also an actor. There is more to the picture than man playing in a garden, put at his disposal by God once and for all. God is calling man to associate himself with this creative work. Each new generation makes a contribution. Today's "mutation of mankind" is a living step of creation itself. Here is the basis of a profoundly religious meaning of the world's development and the realization of man's temporal task. This is why man is created in the image of God, of an active God, of a God-creator.

The whole question of secularization is also bound up with such a vision. It is what the Council called "the autonomy of the temporal realities." This involves recognition of the fact that "planet earth is the material given to man with which to fashion a human world" and that "the Bible refers to that divine act [creation] . . . as unmystifying the world handing it over to itself, into the hands of man for God's glory."[7] It helps man to cease identifying nature with the divine and to perceive his active role.[8]

2. THE ROLE OF CHRIST IN CREATION

From the very beginning the Word is associated with creation. He can be described as "the mediator of creation."[9] In him everything has been created (Col 1:16); through him everything has been created (Heb 1:2); without him nothing has been made (Jn 1:3). He was not only there at the beginning, but he ensures the continuity and full development of creation (Heb 1:3). The building up of all temporal reality comes through Christ. We cannot give the impression that by entering the world for his redemptive mission he came in as from the outside, as a foreigner, for an accidental mission.

This lordship of Christ over the world is a mystery transcending all historical expressions of mankind, and no identification between the kingdom and any concrete situation may be made.

The incarnation has, of course, more than an individual meaning. The whole of humanity in its relation to the whole of creation is ensured in the incarnation, and this relation is well expressed in the Constitution.[10] The sin of man affected the whole world, because of "the unity of man and nature and of soul and body, and the decisive role which man plays in the process of nature."[11] This central and dramatic event of human history is dominated by the "prince of this world" (Jn 2:31). The redemption wrought by Christ, as the true "covenant-partner,"[12] already announced in the promise made to Abraham, put a definitive, even if inchoative, end to the reign of sin. It is through his resurrection that he realized it. "The Resurrection means the full actualization of the Mystery of Christ: the total and glorious Incarnation of the Son of God, becoming even in his human character The New Adam, The Spirit source of life, The Saviour of mankind, The lord of history. It is the eschatological event par excellence: the coming of the Kingdom of God in and through Christ, who, through his Resurrection-Parousia, rules and achieves the entire human and cosmic future."[13]

3. THE NEW CREATION

In *Spes et Gaudium* there is an important section on the "new earth and new heavens."[14] This calls to mind the fact that for too long we have lived in a climate of pessimism, not only because of the reality of sin, but also because of a false vision of the value of "this world," of creation and of its destiny.

Modern theology has rediscovered the "project" of God. It has done this with the help of contemporary philosophical, scientific and humanistic knowledge of the dynamism of reality, of the notion of history, of possibility, of progress, of evolution, and so forth. The whole of creation will be renewed and recapitulated in Christ. There exists a certain, however mysterious, link between present creation and the new era. H. Berkhof does not hesitate to speak about a continuity. "The new world will be this earth renewed."[15] There is a distinction, of course, says the Constitution, between earthly progress and the growth of the kingdom of Christ, but this progress has a meaning in reference to the kingdom. "Within that God-centered life, albeit anonymous, the construction of the world and the promotion of peoples, those two great hopes of mankind on earth, become an activity which is not only intentionally but intrinsically relevant to the kingdom of God."[16]

CONCLUSIONS

A serious reading of the signs of the times and the development of these three theological themes will provide the basis for Christians' participation in the history of creation and in the work of Christ in the world. For today's Christian the world becomes an integral part of his vision of faith.

NOTES

1. Englewood Cliffs, N. J.: Prentice-Hall, 1965.
2. Art. 12, 34, 36.
3. Art. 57, 22, 38, 39, 45.
4. Art. 38, 45.
5. Dr. H. Berkhof, "God in Nature and History," *Study Encounter* 1, no. 3, p. 8.
6. *Ibid.,* 5.
7. E. Schillebeeckx, "The Church and Mankind," *Concilium* 1, no. 1 (January, 1965) 39.
8. Important literature exists on this matter, for example, Arend Th. Van Leeuwen, *Christianity in World History,* (Edinburgh: House Press, 1965) 66; Harvey Cox, *The Secular City,* (New York: Macmillan, 1965); Pastoral *Constitution on the Church in the Modern World,* art. 36.
9. H. Berkhof, *op. cit.,* 6.
10. Art. 38.
11. H. Berkhof, *op. cit.,* 7.
12. H. Berkhof, *op. cit.,* 5.
13. P. Hitz, "Jesus Risen, Mankind and the Church," *Lumen Vitae* 20 (September, 1965) 412.
14. Art. 39.
15. H. Berkhof, *op. cit.,* 19.
16. E. Schillebeeckx, *op. cit.*

Dr. Brown: Father Houtart, in your early pages you make a splendid plea for reading the signs of the times, studying demography, sociology, and so forth, insisting that we cannot properly make theological utterances apart from a willingness to listen to what other disciplines tell us. Then you go on to say all this has, of course, no influence on the fundamental principles, by which I presume you mean the fundamental theological principles. This strikes me perhaps as being too timid. Perhaps this is taking back what you have already offered, to be assuring the Christian that nothing he hears through the signs of the times need really shake him to the roots. The Christian always has four aces. Must we not risk more than this, I would ask, in our encounter with the world today? Is there not a real sense in which we really lay our faith on the line in this encounter with the world, with the genuine possibility that it may be shattered in a very deep and fundamental way, that we may even have more in our day to receive from the world than to give?

Houtart: Well, I must say I was almost expecting that question, because when I wrote this passage I felt the question. I think it is a matter of knowing what fundamental principle means. Here I do not mean to say that what we in the Church have called fundamental principle will not be affected by the fundamental change in the world, but rather the fundamental reality of God and God's action in revelation. Even what we have called *dogmas*, principles, expressions of fundamental principles of Christianity—these are also to a certain extent affected by social change and the development of mankind, in the sense that we understand them better and are expressing them in completely new ways. In this sense, of course, what we have called fundamental principles may also change.

SISTER LUKE: Would you then agree that there is great continuity throughout the doctrinal changes brought about by succeeding councils?

HOUTART: Well, I am not a theologian, so I would like to have a theologian answer that.

HÄRING: Of course, Karl Rahner would be the one to answer this question. For my part, I think some people have an impression of continuity in the Church that is too optimistic. There is a fundamental continuity guaranteed by God, but to some extent there is also discontinuity occasioned by the condition of the human instrument, for instance, because of the lack of fidelity to God's grace. The Church owes it to the absolutely unmerited grace of God that God protects her in the fundamental things. But there would be greater continuity in the Church, if all were more open to the Holy Spirit. For instance, there is discontinuity between the epoch of Constantine and the insistence on the two swords of the Church by Boniface VIII, on the one hand, and the final declaration on religious liberty, on the other. There is certainly a difference between the emphasis in earlier centuries that no one outside the Church could be saved, and the later qualification that only those remaining outside the Church in bad faith could not be saved. Of course, there is a continuity in this case because the fundamental truth remains that God has chosen the Church as the instrument of salvation, and all salvation is linked to it. But there is, nevertheless, great variety. I think we should be honest and recognize there is a very deep problem of discontinuity, not so much that it can disturb our faith, but that it can shake us and make us more cautious and more prayerful and more obedient to the working of the Holy Spirit.

HOUTART: I think this is true and we have to recognize that there is a whole method of writing in the Church that always appeals to preceding popes and councils in order to show the continuity. But in fact almost the contrary is true. *Mater et Magistra* is a good example. Pope John takes all that was said by previous popes on social affairs to show that there is a continuity. Here is a kind of method at work that is quite disagreeable for modern minds.

DR. BROWN: I realize we must not prolong this too much longer. But I think we have located here a very fundamental point of difference in theological methodology and approach that might be fruitful for further discussion sometime. I can only speak for myself, of course, but I think that as a Protestant one accepts a greater kind of risk in this adventure of encountering the world and what it says to us than I think is possible even with the much more resonant remarks that Father Häring made about this problem. I think we have here a fundamental difference in this problem of the degree of continuity.

MINEAR: I should like to illustrate that risk. As was pointed out, in the methodology of every modern historical science the dissolution of the Christian faith is almost inevitable risk. Now for many of us, modern psychology and sociology depend upon a methodology that threatens the very basis of the Christian view of man. How can we even use sociology and psychology to apply our faith when they are rooted in a methodology that challenges the faith?

CONGAR: Two brief questions, Father Houtart. Toward the end of your paper, I do not really see the connection between the quotation from the *Constitution on the Church in the Modern World* and the quotation from Father Schillebeeckx; it seems to me they are saying something a little different. It seems to me that Father Schillebeeckx sees complete continuity between human doings on the natural level and the progress of the kingdom of God.

HOUTART: I do think that Father Schillebeeckx is going a little further than the text of the Constitution.

CONGAR: My second point is that you said yourself that the concept of mission needs to be reconsidered. Could you explain? How?

HOUTART: Well, I was alluding to a very particular concept of mission that I would call quantitative concept, developed especially during the last century: the statistical approach, how many people were baptized, and so forth. With the revolution of the whole third world, with our present awareness of the Asian and African cultures, we see much better now that missions must mean something more than just quantity.

CONGAR: That is very important because now the concept of mission is changing; now it is more and more a question of the presence of Christians as signs of the redemptive act and presence of God. I think it goes in the direction Msgr. Gremillion mentioned. In that direction, however, also lies the danger that missionaries will consider their mere presence as sufficient, somewhat in the sense of Père de Foucauld who simply lived among Moslems as a pure sign of the charity of Christ. There is a danger of that sort of thing. Not that there isn't some truth here. Upon hearing Msgr. Gremillion, I remembered a small book written by one of my Dominican brethren living among the Moslems who probably never made any conversions. He conceived of his presence among the Moslems as a sign of Christ as he shared bread and hospitality with them. But the point is he was a sign of Christ because he explained to them the significance of this presence whenever he could. I think it is in that direction that missions should now be developed.

MOELLER: I want to say a few words about this question of continuity and discontinuity. The theological teaching of the *Constitution on the Church in the Modern World* is quite traditional. It is a good example of our problem, however, for it seems to me that the principle of solution to the problem was always the same. In each authentic renewal of the Church, of the Christian witness in the world, we must feel at one and the same time a sense of continuity in the most profound truths of revelation (e.g., man is created to the image of God) and a sense of rediscovery (e.g., Christian anthropology). It is because we are asking new questions of the Church, and it is because we are listening to the new questions that we are rediscovering in the most profound depths of Christian tradition such themes as the image of God, the word of God, and so forth. And so it seems to me that the principle of solution for this problem is that while we experience discontinuity, prophetic discontinuity, or renewal, if you will, at the same time we discover that this renewal is only the rediscovery of what Christ was telling us in the beginning.

COOKE: I would like to speak on that same point. I think the problem as raised by Dr. Brown is a little more acute. For many people in the contemporary situation, it is not just a question of seeing more explicitly things that perhaps hadn't been discovered that clearly before; it is a very radical situation we are facing. We are under the impact of things happening in our world. There is really the threat of having radically to rethink many of the positions that seemed very firm and secure. I wonder if part of the problem has not been that we thought of the process of continuity much too simply, as something rather unilinear going from less clear to more clear as light was given out by certain human disciplines along the way. I think that part of what is indicated by some non-Catholic thought is that it may be much more of a dialectical process, in which things come out and then, as it were, recede into the background, then come out again only out of the impact of certain needs that arise in a different age. Oftentimes the influences that contribute to the understanding of things may, for the moment at least, even appear to be anti-Christian, but may have in themselves the germs of very profound Christian understanding. I would like to hear your reaction to that.

HOUTART: Well, I would agree fundamentally with what you said. I should perhaps have said more about this dialectical process between reality and theological thinking. In order to make this dialectical process possible, we must be aware of it and have always our instruments of knowledge ready.

One of the things which is most impressive in past history, even in the present history, is the interval between the reality of the world and the moment we take cognizance of it. Tools of modern science will help greatly to reduce the span of this interval and make the dialectical process possible.

BURGHARDT: I have the same problem without that Dr. Brown had. I really think it's highly important that what Father Houtart said should be expunged, at least as it stands, namely, that demographic, psychological and sociological knowledge has no influence upon fundamental principles. [Since the discussion Houtart has changed the term "principles" in his text to "values."] It is at least conceivable, in fact I think more than that, that in many instances the knowledge we derive from empirical research reveals that what we thought were fundamental principles are not really such, or at least have to be redefined and modified. In the area of human love and procreation, for instance, is it not quite likely that we have misconceived some fundamental principles, for example, the so-called artificial interference with natural processes. As Msgr. Gremillion says so well in his paper, we have discovered newly what nature is and in fact that nature itself changes. If this is true, I think then that we have to say that empirical discoveries have a profound influence on fundamental principles, unless we limit or restrict fundamental principles to certain very basic things, such as the basic Christian facts and such things as good is to be done and evil is to be avoided.

LADY JACKSON: I notice that the question raised by Dr. Minear, whether new discoveries and new methods and methodology in general of such sciences as psychology do not in fact undermine Christianity, has not been taken up by our panel, and I'm sure it is not because they can't.

HOUTART: First, I must say I am very happy to hear theologians say what they said about fundamental principles, because I like to agree with that. But we are really here in a very difficult situation in which we lack understanding about words and about epistemology. Secondly, regarding Dr. Minear's question I would like to say that there is a danger, of course, that sociology and psychology, like history, may render a disservice not only to religious values but also to society. That is true, but it is not necessarily true, because like every human reality these tools of the mind are ambivalent and may be used in either way.

SITTLER: As I reflect on the course of this argument, it seems to me that at long last, after several days, we have—really without perhaps meaning to—uncovered what in a famous moment in the World Council development was called "our deepest difference." That moment arrived when we became aware of falling right into the abyss of disclosure, when I gulped, as Robert Brown did, at the sentence about principles remaining unchanged by all exposure to fact. It seemed to argue against the main point of the paper. It seems to me that we have only to ask how does a principle get to be a principle—even in Roman Catholic thought—to see that that statement must be expunged.

Very briefly it seems to me that, if we have summarized in the last fifteen minutes our deepest difference, it ought certainly to be the subject for the next time we get together. And it can be stated in several ways. What has been exposed here in the last fifteen minutes is really what a non-Catholic theologian means by the *theologia crucis*, which means a pointing not only to the episode of the cross, but to the sign of the cross that remains over the life of the mind. That means exactly that the life of the mind must lead the believer to the very edge of falling into unbelief in order that his belief may be dialectically matured precisely in that risk of faith. And if we talk about participation in sociology, political science, economics, if we simply want to learn these disciplines in order to use them, in order to certify an uncriticized principle, this is neither honest nor good. And there, it seems to me, that Protestant Christians must say: at this point we must really intersect and get some real good thinking done.

STRANSKY: I would like to bring up a point, which I think is related, namely, concentration on theology for the sake of preaching the gospel. I think that Vatican Council II skirted the very major crisis that is going on in terms of the relationship between service of the Church and its mission of preaching the gospel. One of the very underlying reasons, if we are honest with ourselves, why we may be stressing so much service to the world is that we are becoming much more confident of our techniques than we are of our faith. The scandal of the gospel is the scandal of the gospel and not the scandal of Christians stumbling over the gospel within the churches. We have enough of a real problem if we face up to the command of preaching the gospel. Serving mankind, building up the human family, and all of what Msgr. Gremillion said, I would wholeheartedly go along with. But we still are facing the question: What is the gospel that we are to preach and what is the gospel as a stumbling block? The World Council of Churches solved this by having two separate departments, and we had two separate schemata. But I think we have to face up to the relation in the Church between a Church that serves in building up the human family and also serves to build up the kingdom of God with the preaching of the word. Despite all our pretenses about a theology for the sake of the modern man, we must remember that it is a theology which is also evangelistic. And so I repeat that I think we may be getting a little less confident of our faith and are therefore stressing so much the competence of Western techniques.

STANLEY: Coming after Dr. Sittler this will be in the nature of a public confession. But I have been concerned for some time about the same type of thing that he mentioned. To relate it to Canon Houtart's paper, I would like to point out that, rather than the new Adam, Christ in St. Paul is called the *eschatos Adam*—quite a different concept from what at least we often made of the *new Adam*. Christ is the last; he is the incarnation of judgment. And it is as this that he is present in history, as the *eschatos Adam*. Therefore, he is the embodiment, as I understand it, of this continuity in history. Hence, he is a *scandalum* in this sense that he is the contradiction or the discontinuity of history, and, as such, is the Lord of history. Now this seems to me to be an element that is lacking in incarnational theologies as I read them often, or as I hear them expressed by the two papers that we have just heard. I think that this perhaps is an element that we, as Catholics, should be more aware of than we actually are if we are going to be faithful to the New Testament data.

I could say the same thing about the word *kainos* in the New Testament, which says *new* in the sense of discontinuity. That is why it is different from *neos*, it seems to me. We come to the same conclusion: the new creation is a contradiction, the new creation is a discontinuity. And that perhaps, if I am saying somewhat the same as Dr. Brown earlier, it is precisely this that makes our faith necessary, that makes our faith operative in this world. And I was rather interested that Canon Houtart spoke of the resurrection. He almost doesn't speak of the cross; he does in a sense speak of the redemption performed by Christ as true covenant partner. But it seems to me that this is the element that is precisely needed in this development, if I may be so brash as to say so. It is what Christ did in dying; by this act of obedience he said yes to the Father, and thereby said no to everything that went before. Therefore, precisely by the fact of dying and of rising he constitutes the question of the Jesus of history and the Christ of faith.

McGRATH: This is strictly a historical note. What Father Stanley has said reflects quite similarly some of the things stated on the Council floor in the last discussion, particularly by several German bishops. There was a serious attempt to augment some of these points of view in the final rendition of the schema. And really I think both speakers tonight professedly are giving their interpretation and going a bit beyond in a certain direction. I think much of what you have said is found in the Constitution.

MUELDER: I want to get back to the issue that really started the discussion on continuity or discontinuity, as it related to Msgr. Houtart's paper, that is, the relationship of the social sciences to theology. I am amazed at what some of the Protestant theologians have said here, because it is characteristic of Protestant theologians, in dealing with this question, to say that theology operates at one level and the sciences at another. And they do not really bring them into relationship with each other. because they keep theology safely in its sphere and the social sciences safely in their sphere, they want a pure methodology for each, and they really don't run very many risks.

If they run out of first principles, they pull back into faith, so that really they haven't come to terms with this problem to put first principles fully under the cross. Really they are not risking it, because faith comes in at the last to save the whole show. I am really wondering whether we have therefore come to terms with the issue on this whole matter of continuity and discontinuity. Actually, I think the social sciences are in a dialogue with theology, and it is this dialogical character that has to be preserved.

MURRAY

SESSION XIV

REV. JOHN COURTNEY MURRAY, S.J.
The Declaration on Religious Freedom
with an Introduction by
DR. ROBERT MCAFEE BROWN

Dr. Robert McAfee Brown

INTRODUCTION

I NOW ENTER INTO unbroken apostolic succession with her excellency Sister
Mary Luke, who now becomes my favorite Catholic bishop. And the fact
that she has made her way now into the inner circle assures me that her
orders are indeed indelible. If this choice of a Presbyterian parson to replace
a Catholic bishop as one of the chairmen at an ecumenical gathering is a
symbol of the religious indifferentism the opponents of the *Declaration on
Religious Freedom* were worried about, I think we must certainly make the
most of it. I shall now exercise my conciliarly validated freedom by including
one item into the agenda which is not scheduled.

There is no indication that there will be another Protestant chairman in
subsequent sessions. Therefore, I want to seize this opportunity to speak on
behalf of my fellow Protestant, Orthodox, Anglican and Jewish friends on
the panel. I have not, as a bishop should, consulted the faithful on this
matter of doctrine, but I assume, as a bishop should not, their wholehearted
concurrence in what they have yet to hear me say. This is simply to express
on their behalf and mine our heartfelt thanks to all responsible for this
Conference, in particular to Father Hesburgh, Father Schlitzer and Bishop
McGrath, for all the time, effort and patience, let alone money that they
have invested in this week. To some present this experience has been a
brand new experience. To others it has been a remarkable kind of old home
week, at which experiences spread over four years in Rome have quite magi-

cally been rekindled and discussions held there have been deepened and continued. We are pleased to discover that there is indeed development in the Roman Catholic Church, and that simultaneous translation can indeed be instituted under Roman Catholic auspices. We are filled with amazement that we who sat silent in the observer's tribune at St. Peter's while bishops talked should here have the privilege of the floor in the presence of bishops who sit silent in the observer's tribune in this aula. But most of all we appreciate the openness that this week has represented and which it is representing more and more with each succeeding round of debate, and the openness that is manifested by your invitation to us and the recognition thereby that Vatican II is not an exclusively Roman Catholic affair, but an affair for all Christians and Jews, and indeed all men of goodwill. To whatever degree we must still walk separate paths, we discover in an experience like this, as both Father Cooke and Dr. Sittler pointed out, that there are increasing areas in which we walk together, and in which we not only want one another's company but desperately need one another's company. So to Father Hesburgh, Father Schlitzer, Bishop McGrath and all those responsible for this week, I offer *in nomine fratrum seiunctorum* our heartfelt thanks.

Now after that long but very sincere parenthesis, to the matter at hand. We have not taken time at these meetings to give lengthy introductions to our speakers, and I need inform no one in this audience of the credentials of Father John Courtney Murray to speak to us about the *Declaration on Religious Freedom*. I will only say that to the non-Roman Catholic world watching the Council from near and from afar with certain breathlessness, no more important *immediate* test of ecumenical sincerity was debated at the Council than this Declaration, and I think it is eminently fair to say that no single person in the Council, therefore, held the ecumenical balance more in the palm of his hand at Vatican II than tonight's speaker. After Bishop De Smet's *relatio* at the second session got the religious freedom Declaration on to the floor of the Council, a limerick went around as follows: "A Bishop named Emil De Smet put the Curia crowd in a sweat, by appealing to those who in conscience oppose being forced to be Catholics just yet." Now, that this whole matter was so creatively resolved by the Council is, I would want to assert, a triumph of the Holy Spirit over what at times seemed insurmountable odds. And I hope that neither the Holy Spirit nor Father Murray will be offended, if I introduce Father Murray as the one from whom the Holy Spirit received his greatest help in overcoming an area of concern that for centuries has been divisive but now becomes one which we can creatively explore together, Father John Courtney Murray.

564

Rev. John Courtney Murray, S.J.

THE DECLARATION ON RELIGIOUS FREEDOM

O N DECEMBER 7, 1965, in the section of his discourse directed to the
statesmen of the world, Pope Paul VI spoke of the *Declaration on Religious
Freedom* as "one of the major texts" of the Council. The characterization is
correct, for a variety of reasons. It must be said, however, that the Declaration
was, in the first instance, an exercise in *aggiornamento* in the strict sense. Its
achievement was simply to bring the Church abreast of the developments
that have occurred in the secular world.

The fact is that the right of man to religious freedom has already been
accepted and affirmed by the common consciousness of mankind. Before the
year 1947 it had been guaranteed in the constitutions of more than fifty
nations. Since that time some fifty more nations—notably those which have
recently emerged into statehood—have made constitutional acknowledgment
of it. Moreover, the right was affirmed in the Universal Declaration of Human
Rights adopted by the General Assembly of the United Nations in 1948. The
Declaration was not at the time a legally binding international instrument.
However, as Egon Schwelb has pointed out,[1] the "recommendations" of the
Declaration have gradually been acquiring the force of law—a sort of customary law—by reason of their general acceptance in civilized political
communities throughout the world. The Declaration has inspired some
twenty-three other instruments of world-wide or regional significance; in par-

[1] *Human Rights and the International Community* (Chicago: Quadrangle, 1964).

ticular, the Convention of the Council of Europe, adopted in Rome in 1950, and the Charter of the Organization of African Unity, adopted in Addis Ababa in 1963. Pope John XXIII was entirely right when he spoke of the Declaration as "an act of the highest importance," which "represents an important step toward the juridical-political organization of the world community. For in it, in most solemn form, the dignity of the person is acknowledged to all human beings" (*Pacem in terris*, 143–144). Finally, the World Council of Churches has long set the weight of its authority behind the affirmation of religious freedom as a human right, notably in the Amsterdam Declaration of 1948 and in the New Delhi Statement of 1961.

Securus iudicat orbis terrarum. One must surely agree with the conclusion reached by Msgr. Pietro Pavan, after a review of the constitutional evidence, in his book, *Libertà religiosa et pubblici poteri*: "One must regard it as legitimate to conclude that religious freedom, understood and exercised as a right, answers to a universal conviction. And one must consider it to be a universal persuasion that the emergence of this right in the human consciousness marks a step forward in civilization." By the *Declaration on Religious Freedom* the Church assembled in Council also took a step forward, matching the step already taken by the civilized world.

Hence the Declaration was a major text of the Council for the initial reason that it was a major act of humility on the part of the teaching Church—an act of the humility that is always inherent in a willingness to learn. The Declaration was, in fact, the most striking proof offered by the Council of the disposition of the Church, noted in the *Constitution on the Church in the Modern World*, to recognize "how richly she has profited by the history and development of humanity. Thanks to the experience of past ages, the progress of the sciences, and the treasures hidden in the various forms of human culture, the nature of man himself is more clearly revealed and new roads to truth are opened. These benefits profit the Church too" (art. 44). So Vatican Council II profited by the secular experience of religious freedom, whereby the exigencies of human dignity have been more fully disclosed.

It was high time, of course, for the Church to take the step forward. The need for it could be amply demonstrated from the first and longer draft-text of chapter 9 of the first schema on the Church, composed by the Theological Commission during the preparatory phase of the Council. The chapter was entitled "On the Relations between Church and State and on Religious Tolerance." (A shorter text appeared later, entitled simply "On the Relations between Church and State.") The first text proposed, in somewhat mild form, the opinion that had come to be accepted in the canonistic school. It was based on a doctrinal distinction between "thesis" and "hypothesis," which was itself based on the historical distinction between the "Catholic state" and the "non-Catholic state." In the Catholic state the right to religious freedom in public life is neither acknowledged nor granted to those who do not belong to the one "religion of the state." Their lot is simply tolerance, or intolerance, in greater or lesser measure. In the non-Catholic state, on the other hand, the legal institution of religious freedom is defended as a lesser evil, to be accepted on grounds of necessity and expediency, in the interests of the Church, and for the sake of the public peace, which would be seriously disturbed by application of the thesis of legal intolerance.

The archaism of this opinion and its remoteness from the political-social realities of the present moment are entirely evident. It exhibits the thought of the Church as imprisoned in a particular segment of history and in a limited geographical area—in the nineteenth-century conflict with continental European laicism, which had become a corrosive force in the Catholic nations, so called. On the basis of this received opinion there could be no dialogue between the Church and the peoples of the contemporary world, in whose personal and political consciousness the principle of religious freedom has taken firm root. If this opinion were to be accepted as the permanent doctrine of the Church, Catholic thought would suffer its worst fate—that of being irrelevant to the world, and to that perennial problem of the world, which is the problem of the freedom of the human person.

Fortunately, in the early summer of 1963 the competence to draft a schema on religious freedom was finally accorded by Pope John XXIII to the Secretariat for the Promotion of Christian Unity. The move was made against strong opposition, at the courageous instance of Cardinal Augustin Bea, strongly seconded by the able secretary of the Secretariat, Msgr. Jan Willebrands.

The first two schemata prepared by the Secretariat were strongly influenced by the fact that they were conceived within the context of ecumenism. The first schema appeared as chapter 5 of the schema of ecumenism; the second, as a declaration appended to the schema. The result was a certain confusion between two distinct problems: the moral-ecumenical problem of relationships between Catholics and non-Catholics, and the juridical-political problem of religious freedom in its contemporary technical sense. Both schemata were, in effect, a declaration of the rights of conscience. They ventured into a treacherous problematic by asserting that the right to religious freedom is based on the dictates of conscience, and that its content is both positive and negative—action according to conscience and also immunity from coercion in such action. This doctrinal line was severely criticized by the Conciliar Fathers in the full discussion held September 23–25, 1964. In consequence, the third schema installed a new doctrinal line, which remained substantially unaltered through the three successive revisions of the schema.

The final Declaration has two essential doctrinal components, juridical and political. The juridical affirmation is that every man has a right to religious freedom—a right that is based on the dignity of the human person, and is therefore to be formally recognized as a civil right and protected by an armature of constitutional law. The political affirmation is that the powers of government are to be employed in the safeguard of this right and are not to be used to limit its free exercise, except in cases of proved necessity.

Affirmation, however, is one thing. The conception embodied in an affirmation is a matter for distinct consideration. In the first place, the Declaration presents the content or object of the right to religious freedom as simply negative, namely, immunity from coercion in religious matters. Thus the Declaration moves onto the solid ground of the constitutional tradition of the West, whose development, in what concerns religious freedom, was first effected by the Constitution of the United States in 1789 and by the First Amendment in 1791. The fundamental freedoms of the First Amendment, including the "free exercise of religion," were conceived to be not claims upon government or society, but assurances against government and society. They were, what the Fourteenth Amendment would later call them, certain specified "immunities of the citizens of the United States."

This is good juridical philosophy. It is proper to a juridical formula—such as the constitutional formulas of freedom of speech, press, religion, assembly and civic protest—that it should define the outside limits of a sphere of human activity and guarantee the integrity of this sphere against coercive intrusion from without, but that it should not enter, as it were, into the sphere itself, there to pass moral or theological judgments on the beliefs expressed, or on the actions performed, within the sphere. Such judgments are "unconstitutional," beyond the competence of purely juridical authority. In our case the juridical formula, "the free exercise of religion," contains no positive evaluation of the religious phenomenon in any of its manifestations. It simply defines the immunity of these manifestations from interference, as long as they remain within the outside limits of lawful freedom. Therefore the only matters of juridical relevance are, first, the definition of the limits beyond which the exercise of freedom is socially unacceptable and unlawful and, second, the duty of others, including government, to respect the integrity of action that goes on within these limits.

Here, of course, it is possible to see the vast difference between religious freedom in its contemporary juridical meaning and "freedom of conscience" and "freedom of cult" in the sense of nineteenth-century continental laicism. These latter formulas were not simply juridical; they were ideological. Inherent in them was the moral judgment that the individual conscience is absolutely autonomous, and the further theological-social judgment that religion is a purely private affair, irrelevant to any of the public concerns of the political community. In the laicist view, freedom of conscience and freedom of cult were instrumental concepts—but concepts instrumental to an ideological negation of the public status and of the social function of religion. On the contrary, in the contemporary constitutional conception religious freedom is still an instrumental concept, but instrumental simply to the freedom of religion as a public phenomenon, whose manifestations are of a transcendent order, and consequently of such high personal and public interest that no repressive coercion may be brought to bear upon them, unless there be some transgression of penal statutes which are necessary for the protection of fundamental social values against abuses of freedom.

In the second place, the Declaration conceives religious freedom to be a twofold immunity. First, no man is to be coercively constrained into belief or action contrary to his own convictions; second, no man is to be coercively restrained from action—that is, from public witness, worship, observance and practice—according to his own convictions. In distinguishing this twofold immunity, the Declaration indicates the structure of the problem, both historical and also theoretical.

Historically, the right of man not to be compelled to believe or to act in a manner contrary to his own convictions came to be acknowledged in the post-Reformation era as the iniquity of the territorial principle—that the religion of the prince is to be a religion of his people—came to be commonly recognized. Historically, however, the right of man not to be forcibly restrained from acting in a manner conformable to his own convictions, in public as well as in private, has not been so readily recognized. Among the Conciliar Fathers at Vatican II there were those who were still unwilling to recognize this right. They wished to defend the historic religious prerogative of the Catholic state—its right to repress public manifestations of non-Catholic belief and worship in the name of the common good, of which the religious unity of the people is an integral element, to be protected by the coercive force of law and government.

At that, the theoretical aspect of the problem is the more important. If an authority exists that is empowered to restrain men from public action in accordance with their religious beliefs, this authority can reside only in government, which presides over the juridical and social order. Therefore, in order to prove the validity of the moral claim of the human person to immunity from such restraint, it is necessary to show that no valid counterclaim can be entered by government. Here the political issue in the question of religious freedom appears. It is the crucial issue. It concerns functions and the limits of government in the order of religion. It may perhaps be doubted whether the Declaration manifests sufficient awareness that this political issue is the crucial issue. Fortunately, however, it states the two principles which avail for the solution of the issue. This will appear.

As the foundation of the right of man to the twofold immunity just described the Declaration proposes the dignity of the human person, as known by human reason and as more fully illuminated by the light of the Christian revelation. By this doctrine the Declaration makes contact with Catholic tradition. It also makes contact with the contemporary fact noted in the Introduction—that rising consciousness of human dignity which is prominent among the signs of the times. This new personal consciousness has shown itself particularly in the demand "that constitutional limits should be set to the powers of government, in order that there may be no encroachment on the rightful freedom of the person and of associations" (art. 1). Through the satisfaction of this political demand, religious freedom, as an idea and as an institution, became a reality in the modern world. Hence the dignity of the person is the primary locus of argument for the right of man to religious freedom. This brings us to the argument proposed in the Declaration. And two remarks are in order.

In the first place, it was altogether necessary that the Declaration should make an argument. Some of the Conciliar Fathers were unwilling that it should do so, chiefly on the ground that it is the function of a Council simply to affirm, not to argue. In this case, however, a simple affirmation of the right to religious freedom would not do. It was necessary to make clear that the affirmation was being made in principle, as a matter of truth, not as a concession, motivated by expediency, to historical circumstances. Furthermore, it was necessary to indicate that an argument for religious freedom can be made in terms of rational and Christian principle. Other men, in other times, and even today, have made the argument otherwise—in terms of skepticism with regard to religious truth, or of moral relativism, or of religious indifferentism, or of laicist or secularist conceptions of the functions of government. The Christian cannot acquiesce in these arguments; he must have his own argument, if his affirmation of religious freedom is to be authentically his own. Hence the Council made an argument. The first part of it was directed to the intelligent world at large, whether religious or nonreligious. The other part was directed to those who believe in God.

In the second place, however, it is not necessary to believe that the Conciliar argument is the best one that can be made. It did not pretend, in fact, to be apodictic. The Conciliar intention was simply to indicate certain lines that an argument might validly follow. Moreover, the doctrinal authority of the Declaration falls upon its affirmation of the human right to religious freedom, not on the arguments advanced in support of this affirmation. This has been traditional conciliar custom.

Hence it is legitimate to raise questions about the Conciliar argument. One might question, for instance, the prominence given to man's moral obligation to search for the truth, as somehow the ultimate foundation of the right to religious freedom. The notion occurs four times in the text. But behind this insistence on it, one may suspect, there lay a preoccupation that was rather more pastoral than theoretical. The concern was lest a divorce seem to be instituted between the juridical order of man's relationship to other men and to political authority and the moral order of man's relationship to the transcendent order of truth and to the authority of God. More briefly, the concern was lest religious freedom be misunderstood to mean a freedom from the claims of truth—in particular, as these claims are declared by the Church. This pastoral concern may well have been legitimate. But it seems to reveal that some of the Conciliar Fathers were still living in the long shadow of the nineteenth century. The fact is that this misunderstanding of religious freedom is impossible for anyone who grasps the twentieth-century state of the question.

The real difficulty, however, is that the argument from man's duty to search for the turth, whatever its value, does not deserve the fundamental place in the structure of a demonstration of the right to religious freedom. The reason is that it fails to yield the necessary and crucial political conclusion, namely, that government is not empowered, save in the exceptional case, to hinder men or religious communities from public witness, worship, practice, and observance in accordance with their own convictions. The classical Catholic government, for instance, or the contemporary communist government, for another instance, does not greatly bother about man's duty to search for the truth. They simply maintain that they already have the truth; that they represent the truth, which is also the good of the people; that consequently they are empowered to repress public manifestations of error. Against this conception of government as the representative of the truth, the argument from man's duty to search for the truth can make little headway.

A more cogent argument for the right to religious freedom can be constructed from the principles of the Declaration itself, assembled into an organic structure. The argument begins from the dignity of man as a moral subject. Man is intelligent. Therefore he is capable of, and called to, an understanding of the sense of his own existence—its meaning and purpose, as these are accessible to reason in the total reality of human existence itself, and as they are more luminously declared in divine revelation. Man is free. Therefore he is called personally to realize, in love and through a lifelong process of choice, the sense of his own existence. Hence the mark of man as a person is his personal autonomy. Inseparable, however, from personal autonomy is personal responsibility. This is twofold. First, man is responsible for the conformity between the inner imperatives of his conscience and the transcendent order of truth. Second, man is responsible for the conformity between his external actions and the inner imperatives of conscience. These responsibilities are moral and altogether stringent. Man bears them as a moral subject, as he confronts, so to speak, his vertical relationship to the transcendent order of truth. However, on the horizontal plane of intersubjective relationships, and within the social order, which is the order within which human rights are predicated, man's fulfillment of his personal moral responsibilities is juridically irrelevant. The major reason is that no authority exists within the juridical order that is capable or empowered to judge in this regard. This is a matter of traditional jurisprudence. (It is recognized in the Declaration, where it is said that the right to religious freedom does not have its foundation "in the subjective disposition of the person"; subjective dispositions are juridically irrelevant.)

What is juridically relevant, however, and relevant in the most fundamental sense, is the personal autonomy which is constituent of man's dignity. More exactly, resident in man's dignity is the exigence to act on his own initiative and on his own responsibility. This exigence is of the objective order; it is simply the demand that man should act according to his nature. And this exigence is the basic ontological foundation, not only of the right to religious freedom, but of all man's fundamental rights—in what concerns the search for truth, the communication of opinions, the cultivation of the arts and sciences, the formation and expression of political views, association with other men for common purposes, and, with privileged particularity, the free exercise of religion.

All these rights are immunities from coercion. Given the exigence of the person to act on his own initiative and responsibility, coercion appears as a thing of no value to the person. No man can be endowed with moral worth from the outside, as it were, and under compulsion. What is more important, man's fundamental exigence to act according to his nature makes coercion an injury, an attempted intrusion into the sanctuary of personality, a violation of the inviolability that attaches to the moral subject. Hence the basic exigence of the person is for immunity from coercion, chiefly, as the Declaration says, in what regards the quest for the values proper to the human spirit, and more particularly, in what regards the free exercise of religion in society. Religion has to do with man's relation to God. And this relation is personal. That is to say, it is immediate, directly between the finite moral subject and the infinite moral Subject; consequently, it is to be freely entered upon by both parties—by man in free response to the free and imperative initiative of God. Therefore, man himself must bear the responsibility for the acceptance or rejection of the divine demand of love, knowing that the penalty for rejection is the eternal loss of his own identity.

The argument so far is only preliminary and partial. It does not yet avail to constitute the right to religious freedom or to any other fundamental human right. It merely lays the foundation for a moral claim on others, that they should abstain from coercive action with regard to the human subject and respect his inner exigence to act on his own initiative and responsibility. To speak of a right, however, is to imply a juridical relationship, within which to the right of one there corresponds a duty on the part of others with regard to whatever the object of the right is—in our case, immunity from coercive action. A right, as a moral claim on others, is not fully constituted, until it is established that no one else may validly enter a counterclaim—in our case, legitimately to invade an asserted immunity.

This further step in the argument is easily taken with regard to the first immunity claimed by the human person in religious matters, that is, immunity from compulsion to believe against one's will or to act in a manner contrary to one's religious beliefs. Obviously, no human power can rightfully compel such action. The assertion of an empowerment to do so would instantly be rejected by the common consciousness of mankind. The first immunity is absolutely inviolable, and to the moral claim to it there corresponds a universal duty on the part of others, including government, to respect the claim.

A difficulty, however, arises with regard to the second immunity: not to be forcibly restrained from acting in accordance with one's religious beliefs. The fact is that in so acting a man may, in all good faith, be doing what is wrong —spreading religious errors or performing religious actions that are not consistent with the divine law. Here the political dimension of religious freedom comes to view. The question is, whether some special characteristic or attribute attaches to government that empowers it to repress erroneous religious opinions or practices from public life. And if not, on what principle is this power denied to government?

The Declaration supplies two principles. Both of them are rooted in the dignity of the person, and each of them is intimately related to the other. The first is the political principle of the free society: "Let there be as much freedom as possible, and only as much restraint as necessary." Or as the text puts it, "The usages of society are to be the usages of freedom in their full range. These require that the freedom of man be respected as far as possible, and curtailed only when and insofar as necessary" (art. 7). This principle follows directly from the conception of the human person as a moral subject, who can achieve his perfection only by love of the truth and by free obedience to its demands, not by coercive constraints or restraints. By incorporating this principle the Declaration importantly fulfills its promise to advance still further the development of the Church's socio-political doctrine that has been going on under recent popes.

It has always been traditional doctrine that human society is to be based on truth, directed toward justice, and animated by love. Pius XII brought the tradition to a new perfection of understanding and statement by his teaching that the truth upon which human society is to be based is the truth about the human person; that justice to the human person is the goal of society; that love is the basic principle of social unity, since it is the proper bond among persons, which alone can lift their living together above the level of sheer coexistence. Then to the traditional trinity of social values John XXIII added the fourth—freedom. The truth about the human person is that his fundamental exigence is to act on his own initiative and responsibility. The truth therefore requires that in society there should be as much freedom as possible. Moreover, that which is primarily due in justice to the human person is his freedom—as much freedom as possible. Finally, love of the human person and love among human persons require that the freedom of each and of all should be respected as far as possible, and not curtailed except when and insofar as necessary.

Freedom, therefore, is the political method par excellence. Only by the usages of freedom in their full range can society, like the human person, make progress toward the equal justice that is its goal, toward that "more human equality (of rights)" of which *Pacem in terris* speaks. Furthermore, freedom is not only the primary method of politics; it is also the highest political goal. So it was once most truly written: "We, the People . . . , in order to . . . secure the blessings of liberty to ourselves and our posterity, do ordain and establish this Constitution. . . ."

Cognate with the political principle of the free society, and inseparable from it, is the juridical principle of equality before the law. As the Declaration puts it, speaking of the duties of government: "Finally, government is to see to it that the equality of citizens before the law, which is itself an element of the common welfare, is never violated for religious reasons, whether openly or covertly" (art. 6). The principle of equality before the law has its foundation in the metaphysical and theological truth stated in *Pacem in terris*, that "all men are equal by reason of their natural dignity" (articles 44, 48, 89, 132). This truth, the Pope notes, has come to pervade, and to be firmly established in the consciousness of men today. Its juridical consequence— what the Fourteenth Amendment calls the "equal protection of the laws"— has always been capital in the constitutional tradition of the West, as the complement of the principle of the free society. There is no freedom in society unless there is equal freedom for all, recognized as equally due in justice to all, and equally protected by law.

These two principles, political and juridical, furnish the solution to the political issue raised by the question of religious freedom as the immunity of the person from coercive restraint of action in accordance with his own beliefs. Together they require that government should be "constitutional." In the case, this means four essential things.

First, the powers of government are limited by a higher order of truth and justice—the truth about the human person, the justice due to the human person and the respect or love also due to the human person—which requires reverence for the basic exigence of human dignity, which is to act on one's own initiative and responsibility. This exigence, therefore, brings into being a juridical relationship. The immunity of the person from coercive restraint emerges as the object of a strict right, to which there corresponds on the part of government a strict duty to recognize the right and to respect its free exercise. Second, not only are the powers of government limited by the higher order of the rights of the person; they are also to be primarily employed "to secure these rights" (in the phrase of the Declaration of Independence) against invasion by others. Third, the protection and vindication of these rights are to be carried out by government in accord with the principle of equality before the law. This principle forbids classification of citizens according to their religious beliefs or lack thereof. Hence government may not recognize the right of some citizens to immunity from coercive restraint of action in accordance with their religious beliefs, and deny this right to other citizens. Fourth, the equal freedom of the people in the exercise of their rights in religious matters is to be respected as far as possible, and is not to be restricted except when and insofar as necessary. In principle, the freedom of the citizen is in possession. It is not to be restricted except in cases of proved necessity. And the onus rests on government to prove the necessity in the particular case. This requires a legal showing that there is question in the case of a violation of public order, a civil offense which the force of law must necessarily prohibit or punish.

In its quest for a juridical criterion narrow enough to warrant limitations of the free exercise of religion the Declaration finally adopted, after some hesitation and in spite of some opposition, the concept of public order. The concept of the common good, and—what is much the same—the concept of the purpose of society, had been advanced in the first two Conciliar schemata. Neither of them was acceptable, given the notion of society and government adopted in the Declaration from the doctrine of Pius XII. In this doctrine the common good itself and the purpose of society require the fullest possible free exercise of all human and civil rights, and government has the primary duty, not of limiting, but rather of promoting the freedom of the human person as far as possible.

In principle, the criterion for the restriction of freedom must be the necessity of such restriction. And the concept of public order meets this test of principle. The formula itself has broad constitutional status, even though it seems to lack full constitutional definition, commonly agreed on. The Declaration, therefore, gives it as clear and precise a definition as may be possible. Public order is the fundamental component of the common good. The common good is the broader concept that embraces the totality of those conditions of social life and the entire complex of those realized social values whereby men, as human persons, may achieve their proper perfection with all possible fullness and ease. Public order, in contrast, embraces only those fundamental social values that are necessary for the sheer coexistence of the citizenry—values without which society would cease to be an order and verge toward conditions of chaos. Three such socially necessary values are commonly distinguished in the constitutional tradition: the value of justice, which consists in the effective safeguard of the equal rights of all citizens; the value of public peace, which is the work of justice, achieved when means are available for the pacific settlement of conflicts among the citizenry; and the value of public morality, in the measure in which morality can be realized by the coercive discipline of law. In three cases, therefore, the exercise of the right of religious freedom may be legitimately restrained by coercive measures, mainly, when there is a violation of the rights of others, or a serious disturbance of the public peace, or a grave offense against public morality. In these three cases the exercise of freedom becomes in fact an abuse of freedom, and restraint becomes a matter of public necessity. The concept of public order, thus defined, satisfies the demands of moral, political and juridical principle.

The conclusion is that the doctrine of the Declaration forms an organic whole. All of it hangs suspended from the supreme principle of the dignity of the human person. Inherent in this dignity is the exigence that a man should act on his own initiative and responsibility, not under coercion, but from inward motivation, by his sense of duty toward the transcendent order of truth and morality. This exigence in turn founds the political principle that the freedom of the person is to be respected as far as possible and restricted only in cases of necessity. The equality of this exigence in all men, who are equal in their dignity as human persons, founds the further juridical principle of the equality of all citizens before the law. And from these two principles in conjunction two sets of conclusions follow with equal immediacy. The first juridical conclusion is that the full immunity of the human person from coercion in religious matters is the object of a genuine human right. The corresponding first political conclusion is the duty of government itself to respect this right and to ensure respect for it in society. The second juridical conclusion is that the exercise of the right to religious freedom is to be as free as possible. And the second political conclusion is that governmental or legal limitation of the exercise of the right is warranted only by the criterion of necessity.

Much further comment would need to be made on the Declaration. It raises a number of serious issues. And it is fraught with theological significance in ways that go far beyond the narrow context of the single problem with which it deals. This essay, however, was concerned simply with showing the organic wholeness of its central doctrinal content.

WOLF: I would just like to raise the question of the right of disbelief, which I believe the document never quite admits. And I wonder whether in the fullness of a statement on the right to religious freedom there ought to be included—not only because of expediency, say, for dialogue with secular man, but simply because it is part of the dignity of the human person— an affirmation of the right of disbelief, not only because it is a fundamental right, but because, from the point of view of revelation, the fullness of the free act of faith may require the possibility of disbelief.

MURRAY: This question was argued at considerable length in the Secretariat. Some of you at least know there were petitions made by many bishops, notably among the French hierarchy, that explicit mention should be made of the atheists. It was very carefully considered. There were many reasons for it, but the reasons against it seemed to be decisive. I don't know that I can remember all that they were; I wouldn't want to put words in the mouths of anybody else. One reason, of course, was the change of state of the question between the eighteenth century and now. In the happy days—if they were happy—of the Enlightenment, freedom of religion was proclaimed in the name of freedom of unbelief. It was considered today that things have come round: freedom of religion now has come in favor of those who wish to believe. The other people on the whole, by and large, are doing fairly well, I would think at the moment. The other question was whether or not it would be appropriate in a conciliar statement of an ecumenical council thus to single out the atheists. And the third reason is that the atheists are properly provided for in the principles of the Declaration itself, because the phrase that is used in the definition of religious freedom is used with great breadth. Indeed, in the Latin text of article 2 the word *conscientia* is used, not in a technical sense of the moral faculty of judgment, but rather in its broad sense, namely, a man's whole inner world, the inner forum as such, the fullness of a man's own beliefs, desires, hopes, wishes, and so on. That is why it was translated in English "in accordance with his own beliefs," not "conscience," because that would be misleading.

SMITH: Father Murray, you state that the protection and vindication of the rights named in the Declaration of Independence is to be carried out by government in accord with the principle of equality before the law, and this principle forbids classification of citizens according to their religious beliefs or the lack thereof. I recall two cases before the Supreme Court: the Everson and Sherbert cases. The New Jersey law in the Everson case, the bus transportation law, was written to benefit the children in Catholic parochial schools. If you recall Justice Jackson was opposed to the law on that ground. That was a case of classification according to religion in vindication of free exercise and the protection of children on the streets.

The Sherbert case, more recently, is completely distinct. It was directed that the South Carolina Social Security Commission should pay social security benefits to Mrs. Sherbert, who is a Seventh-Day Adventist and had refused work on her Sabbath, Saturday. She was singled out for this benefit, because her reasons for refusing to work on that day were religious, and it was expressly stated that if her reasons had had to do with family care that the case would not have gone favorably to her. The second and more telling instance of classification according to religion in vindication of free exercise.

Now my question is: Does your principle stand when it applies to the vindication of free exercise, so that it favors religion, and not stand when the case is opposite?

MURRAY: First of all, my recollections of the Everson case are vague. It was in 1947 that it was decided. I seem to recall that one of the lawyers was trying to make the point that the law should be struck down, precisely because it was an unreasonable classification according to religious beliefs. The court decided to play it the other way: that not to admit Catholic children to enjoy these benefits, transportation by buses, would have been to classify them out on grounds of religion. I would want my principle to hold in full universality.

578

SMITH: Professor Kurland has argued this same point: classification according to religion should never be done, and that would have meant that Mrs. Sherbert would have been out of work and out of social security because her religious principles forbade her to work on her Sabbath day. So the Court went against that general counsel contained in this principle in order to vindicate her freedom of exercise against the indirect pressure of denial of unemployment compensation.

MURRAY: The problem of classification is a delicate and needed one, in its thrust, in its direction, and then of course in verifying the famous adjective that goes with it, "reasonable" classification. You are saying then that if this principle were to be held with full universality, then the Court was wrong in the second case that you are mentioning. Is this right?

SMITH: I think that is the impression I would draw. I myself think that maybe we ought to go this far: the universality of this rule can be broken when a free exercise matter is in question. But that also is a delicate matter.

MURRAY: Yes, very delicate at the moment in American courts, because it is not entirely clear whether or not the presumption today does stand for free exercise, or for no aid to religion.

CROSSEN: I would like to ask two brief questions. The first is whether you think that the substance of the argument you have presented here could be translated adequately into the language of "what is right" as distinguished from what is "rights"—for example, to speak of the "rightness" of following one's own conscience, and consequently the obligation of others to acknowledge one's response to "rightness."

And the second question concerns what seemed to me possible limitations on the sense of freedom in your remarks and perhaps in the document. You speak of the obligation of government to safeguard the freedom of the religious conscience. Is "safeguard" here taken as a minimal term, or as a term that would exclude a positive action on the part of government to promote the free exercise? What I am concerned with here is the negative cast of the conception of freedom in your relating it to the obligations of the state. I think you probably know what I'm driving at here.

MURRAY: Yes, I was afraid somebody might head toward difficult and somewhat troubled waters, that the Declaration itself tried to skate around. It wanted to insist, in the first instance, that the content or object of the right was an immunity. On the other hand, one of the great preoccupations of the Council as well as the Secretariat was that this Declaration might be construed as somehow, rather belatedly, canonizing what is usually known as laicism, or what—I don't like to use the term because it is so ambiguous— some call an exaggerated conception of the separation of Church and state. In order to avoid this possible misinterpretation of the Declaration, that rather general and somewhat enigmatic phrase was put in at the end of article 3. It says: "Government, therefore, ought indeed to take account of the religious life of the people and show it favor, since the function of government is to make provision for the common welfare. However, it would clearly transgress the limits set to its power were it to presume to direct or inhibit acts that are religious."

You see, here is the difficulty, at least my difficulty. I don't see how you can promote an immunity—making somebody more and more immune. This just doesn't make any sense to me; it never has. Therefore, as I understand the doctrine of the Declaration, it is this: the right to religious freedom, its content, is simply an immunity. However, government has not done its full duty to society when it has guaranteed this immunity and protected it with the legal armature of law. There is the further fact of religion in society, and this fact, as a sheer religio-social fact, claims the attention of government; it is not to be denied, certainly, is not even to be disregarded, but is to be taken account of and indeed shown favor on grounds that are mentioned later on, namely, that society itself may benefit in terms of justice and order, and so on. Therefore, the duty of government to favor religion in society does not derive from the rights to religious freedom, but from another root. So at least I understand the matter. But, you see, one of the difficulties with the whole declaration is that it did not want to get into the broader problem of Church and state; it simply wanted to prevent such a Declaration from appearing to favor an older laicist or secularist conception of the problem of Church and state. That is why this little sentence was put in.

CROSSON: Let me just add one remark to that. I wonder if some of this problem is not smuggled into your remark about freedom being the highest political goal, and you quote the preamble to the Constitution of the United States, though of course dropping out the other political goals which the Constitution enumerates. I wonder if the ambiguity here isn't hidden in whether we take freedom in the sense of immunity or in the sense of freedom for certain goals, and understand government to be concerned, not with coercion, but with the making accessible to its people the means for the exercise of the guaranteed immunities.

MURRAY: I am not at all sure that that second interpretation was in the minds of our founding fathers. When they wanted to insure the blessings of equal liberty to ourselves and our posterity, they were thinking in terms of immunity; they had not yet got on to the days of the Great Society in which we live; wherein the criterion of governmental action seems to be providing the possibility. I am perfectly willing to admit that this is progress; I am not, therefore, sneering at the Great Society by any means. You may have noticed as I was talking I left out highest political goal, because I am not at all sure freedom is the highest political goal. I would fully accept your interpretation of that freedom as a goal in society *as inclined*, the duty on the part of government being to supply the fullest possible measure of what Mortimer Adler, for instance, would call the freedom of self-realization, by providing a multitude of opportunities in terms of which people could pursue, through their own choice, their own higher perfection.

COTTRELL: Father Murray, one afternoon at the American Bishops' press panel in Rome last fall, I believe you made the suggestion that the *Declaration on Religious Freedom* might be considered a first step in the direction of religious freedom, implying that other steps might be taken. I wonder if you could suggest what further steps in this direction might well be taken.

MURRAY: Well, there was one suggested by Dr. Wolf here in a paper that he gave me and as a matter of fact was suggested in what, I take it, was the official report on Vatican Council II made by the World Council of Churches. In the section on religious freedom they mentioned this possibility: namely, that now that this Declaration is out, would it not be possible to have a joint declaration made by the World Council of Churches, through some appropriate organ, and the Catholic Church, again through some appropriate organ, in order that they might be a common Christian witness in the world today, a world in which religious freedom is still so largely flouted. This was actively discussed in Rome, as a matter of fact. This would be one further step. There is the possible second further step, namely, ecumenical dialogue with regard to the bases of religious freedom. This was discussed, you remember, at a meeting of the observers when we were all in Rome in those good old nostalgic days. What are we all going to do next fall, by the way? I would consider a joint declaration almost a certainty. I don't know just when it would happen. We are all sort of catching our breath at the moment.

COTTRELL: I believe that afternoon at the Bishops' press panel the suggestion had been made that there might be further steps in the direction of internal religious freedom within the Church. Would you care to comment further on that as an outgrowth of the present Declaration?

MURRAY: This is most important. I certainly believe that the problem of freedom within the Church is one of the theological implications of the *Declaration on Religious Freedom*, one of the four that I mentioned. The second is the secularity of the secular. The third is the development of this particular doctrine. And the fourth is the transition from classicism to historical consciousness which is the broadest problem of all. Having declared religious freedom in the civil and social order, we've got simply to face up to the problem of freedom within the Church. I see no reason why, *mutatis mutandis*, the principles of the Declaration itself—notably the dignity of

581

man and that there be as much freedom as possible and only as much restriction as necessary—should not also be valid within the Church as well as within civil and social society.

COOKE: I simply wanted to raise that same question about the application of these principles to the situation within the Church and to ask more specifically if that implication arose at the Council in the discussion of this matter?

MURRAY: Very much so; so much so that it was the express wish of Pope Paul himself, that the Declaration should make a clear distinction between two distinct problems: the problem of religious freedom in the technical sense, and the problem of freedom within the Church. And that is why certain changes were made within the text—notably the omission of a proemium on freedom in the history of salvation, which at one time occupied a place within the text. They very seriously considered this matter and the decision was that the Declaration would confine itself to the narrower issues and clear up, first of all, this dreadful ambiguity in Catholic doctrine, before we get on to the other shopping.

LITTELL: When the discussion starts with the political issue on the matter of separation of Church and state, it inevitably ends in the ditch. Either we argue that separation is impossible because some kind of ideological Christianity is necessary to shore up a society, or we argue that separation is essential because we want that kind of a state. In the last years we certainly learned that you can have separation without having religious liberty; that is the lesson from the Third Reich, and the lesson now from communist areas. The great strength of this Declaration is that it puts the whole claim on higher ground, but it puts it on the ground chiefly of the dignity of the human person, of natural law, rights, dignities and immunities of the person. I would like to know what your conviction is as to the dignities and immunities and rights of groups, if you will? The General Board of the National Council of Churches discussed this matter recently. In Protestant thinking, too, there is a great deal more certainty about the integrity of the individual conscience than there is about the autonomy or integrity of groups of dissenters. How would you feel on that point?

MURRAY: Well, it seems to me that the Declaration is extremely explicit and also extremely detailed with regard to the religious rights of religious groups, churches, or whatever they choose to call themselves. That section was composed with considerable care in order that it might be the charter of the freedoms that the Catholic Church considers herself entitled to, and also that it might cover the substantially identical social freedoms, collective corporate freedoms, which the great statements of the World Council of Churches speak of. And it has been acknowledged that, by and large, give or take a freedom or two, the two things do pretty much cover the same list.

LITTELL: But then may I press the real point? Doesn't this have very clear ecclesiological implications? Isn't a certain doctrine of the Church, or a set of doctrines, implied, that emphasizes voluntaristic membership (not voluntarism) rather than the traditions of establishment? At the time of the founding fathers there was the natural law tradition which comes through very clearly, it seems to me, in terms of the integrity of the human person. There was also very strong free Church that argued on entirely different grounds than the state Church and the establishment, argued that the true Church is, by its very nature, a voluntary association, one separate from Church support or control of any kind. Now in this Declaration the one tradition comes through loud and clear and is elaborated in terms of wisdom accumulated subsequently. But when we speak of the immunities, rights and dignities of groups of religious conscience and concern and discipline, isn't there a very clear implication as to the doctrine on the Church?

MURRAY: If you get into the problem of separation of Church and state, obviously ecclesiological presumptions become vastly important. However, if you stay simply arguing the question of the free exercise of religion, I am not so sure that ecclesiology gets into it all that much. You can afford to leave it aside. When you talk about separation of Church and state it matters terribly what you mean by the Church. But it doesn't matter so terribly much what you mean by the Church when you are talking about religious freedom— not in the first instance; in the farthest instance, of course, it matters like mad, like anything in the world.

LITTELL: I don't talk about separation of Church and state, because it seems to me when you start with a political issue you inevitably end up with the wrong solution of one kind or another. But if you start with the question of the nature of religion, and the integrity and dignity of group conscience and witness, as well as the rights of the person, then you are going to end up with a certain kind of a church as over against other kinds of churches, aren't you?

MURRAY: I suppose so. It all depends, however, on how you read, not any political tradition, but the word of God. Doesn't it?

GREMILLION: What are the implications of the Declaration for the whole system of concordats and diplomatic relations and ambassadorial apparatus in the Catholic Church?

MURRAY: That calls for prognosis. I don't know. I haven't really thought about it too profoundly, but my guess is that concordats don't have much of a future.

HÄRING: The question was proposed: if the state must promote religious liberty, why then not the Church? In your short answer I saw some difficulty, Father Murray. One of the reasons in the Council was that the state has no competence whatsoever in declaring what is truth. The Church does have.

Can there therefore be a comparison of religious freedom in the state with that within the Church? Therefore, must there not be a very profound distinction between the kind of freedom there is within the Church and within the state?

Murray: Of course. We are not confronted here with univocity, but only with analogy. The Church is a society only in a sense analogous to the way in which civil society is a society. So too the Church is an order of law; the Church has authority. So your beginning of discussion of the problem of freedom in the Church must lay down these theological premises for the institution. In other words, we are here confronted with a situation which is somewhat the same and yet completely different from that which obtains in civil society.

Häring: I think just the opposite: because the Church has competence in truth, she must give the greatest freedom where she cannot definitely propose the truth. Since the fundamental obligation of the Church is to seek truth, when she cannot speak the truth infallibly, she must promote the greatest liberty for the search for truth. Would you agree with this?

Murray: I would surely agree with that. It is not only the *in dubiis libertas* of St. Augustine that you are asserting, but something more. I would include this under the principle I mentioned before, namely, as much freedom as possible should obtain within the Church, under the guidance, obviously, of prudence. I think that one of the great effects of the Council has been precisely that there was no great preoccupation with the authority of the documents, nor with the degree of certainty that attaches to them. We've been plagued for years in the schools with deciding is this *certa et Catholica*, is it *certa communis*, is it *proxima heresi*. What matters is that the thing is true. A lot of this goes back to the Cartesian era, to the pursuit of the clear and distinct idea, and to the quest of certainty; this was *the* human quest, more inspired by rationalism than by Catholicism. Now, however, we are in the era of understanding; these affirmations are made and the affirmations are true. It is not a question of how certain they are; what is true is true, and why don't we leave it at that at the moment and get on to something more important, which is to understand what has been said.

Sister Jacqueline: If Catholic children are baptized in infancy and educated both in formal schooling and in their family situation with the conviction that they *have* the faith, and are in danger of losing the faith and have a responsibility for keeping the faith, do they possess the psychic freedom to place a free act of disbelief?

Murray: The answer is yes. I don't see how one's psychological freedom is in any sense diminished by the fact that one has been baptized in infancy and brought up a Catholic.

Hyslop: In the last paragraph of article 4, it is stated: "It comes within

the meaning of religious freedom that religious bodies should not be pro-
hibited from freely undertaking to show the special value of their doctrine
in what concerns the organization of society and the inspiration of the whole
human activity." I read it to be a magnificent charter for Christian social
action, and I am going to quote it in our next issue of *Social Action*, in
answer to all of our critics who are many, I assure you. But I now wonder
if it could not be stated in support of the continuing freedom of the exponents of the very doctrine you have exposed and discredited to continue to
advocate that doctrine, and freely to do so in the future, both Catholics and
Protestants. Would this not be a necessary part of the freedom which is
assured to religious bodies, that they continue to advocate a doctrine which
you feel is opposed to proper understanding of religious freedom?

MURRAY: That would seem to me a highly arbitrary interpretation of this
particular statement of the Declaration. The intention of this statement was
to make sure that it was well understood that while the message of the
Church is religious, indeed theological, a message of faith, the Church has,
nonetheless, a word to say on all social issues in which a religious issue arises.
Now it seems to me that would take a good bit of straining to use this principle as the premise to get some action to restore the old thesis.

HYSLOP: No, I certainly don't want to see it restored, but I think it
should continue to be discussed. That might be an option that your Declaration would make possible. Is that not the fact?

MURRAY: Oh, the discussion would certainly go on, lively, blissfully!

RAHNER

SESSION XV

Rev. Karl Rahner, s.j.
The Task of Theology after the Council

Rev. Karl Rahner, S.J.

THE TASK OF THEOLOGY AFTER THE COUNCIL

VATICAN COUNCIL II IS, without doubt, a challenge for Catholic theology, since it sets up new tasks, provides it with a stronger dynamic and affords more for freedom of movement. The Council is, first of all, of the greatest importance for Catholic theology, because the positive teachings of its decrees are theologically very significant. What some Roman theologians expected and others feared before the Council never came to pass, namely, that the Council would merely repeat what for a century had already been the established and explicitly professed doctrine of official papal teachings and traditional theology of Neo-Scholastic origin. And thus theology, after politely alluding to the Conciliar text in new editions of Denzinger, would merely have to hand on what it has always taught. True, the Council was very cautious and careful in all its doctrinal statements and even avoided giving new definitions; but it still said many things that before had not been a part of the obvious repertoire of the theology of the schools. What is crucial in this situation is not that many hitherto disputed questions were taken up and, to a certain extent, decided, thus obliging theology to think through and justify the decision and further clarify what remained unclear. Much more important is the fact that many topics appear, in the Council's teachings that, while not having been actually controversial in traditional theology, nevertheless did not exist as clear issues in it and thus had not at all, or only marginally, been brought to the attention of the faithful in catechisms influenced by it

589

and in average every-day faith consciousness. From this point of view, the Council sets up important themes and tasks for theology and obliges it to broaden and considerably restructure its over-all subject matter in many aspects. Moreover, the Council is of great importance to theology in two more ways: the Council deliberately left open and even opened up many questions, or clearly acknowledged that they require further theological consideration. And by this we mean not only questions that are without actual meaning for the church's concrete life or man's Christian existence, those theological subtleties meant only for the theological specialist and his introvert kind of work.

Secondly, the Council in its whole mentality displays a spirit of freedom, a desire first to study and only then to decide (as Paul VI urged), an awareness of problems, and a respect for specialists (without cowardly letting their "professional" one-sidedness have the last word). Thus the theological routine, which was widespread in the Church during the last century and believed that everything important in theology had already been solved, is now old-fashioned theology, so long as theology now takes advantage of the opportunity provided by the spirit of the Council. The Council has certainly furnished theology with a sharpened awareness of the problems and more room for free theological activity.

Moreover, in addition to this formal general theological viewpoint, theology has received further benefit from the Council. The Council has opened up a dialogue with the world. It actually did not and, of course, could not itself carry out this dialogue. But during its sessions the Council clearly began to see the world of the modern mind, that is, the world of a pluralistic, scientific, technically oriented society of vast scope and multiplicity of insights and tendencies, a world of a contrasted and divided Christianity, one of world religions, a world with an immense future waiting to be planned. The Council did not view this world as one within which one simply lives—joyfully or fearfully—in order to dedicate oneself, while living in it, to traditional activities and goals. Rather it saw it as a world with which one must enter into an open dialogue whose result is not fixed beforehand, as a world that the Church has to help shape and that will also help brand the Church of tomorrow in a way the Church wants and not merely endures. This situation, recognized and accepted by the Church, means not only a new, but partial, task for an area of theology—in other words, doing the task only insofar as it is explicitly called for and thematically defined by the *Constitution on the Church in the Modern World*. The dialogue with the world that the Church is expressly setting up is rather a task for theology in all of its branches and themes, even in those that seem the most esoteric. The whole of theology must become conscious of this situation. What this means more exactly will be taken up later.

With these presuppositions as a basis, let us say a few things about the tasks of post-Conciliar theology. In doing so, we are aware of the fragmentary and subjective character of our explanations and realize that it is embarrassing to make demands, that it is easier to give advice than to follow it, and that only they give true recipes who actually apply them in practice.

First, as to historical theology in general, its continuation and further development should be urgently and seriously emphasized. If Catholic theology—and we prescind here from the biblical sciences; they will be treated later—has made any progress in the last century, this progress was achieved above all, if not almost exclusively, in the area of historical theology, the history of dogma and theology, the history of patristic literature, the editing of texts, the history of law, and so on. Doubtlessly, much more remains to be done. Today especially, no science can dispense with its own history, and theology owes it to its own sublime dignity to continue such efforts. Wherever there are talents for these tasks (and there are talents that are more or less oriented only in this direction), they should be furthered. And it would not hurt for Church authorities to be more broadminded in regard to financial support (for the edition of texts, the publishing of special historical investigations, and the like) than has been customary.

However, one must not think it an affront to historical theology's dignity and to the objective search for truth if future historical theology becomes more conscious of its function and responsibility in regard to "systematic" theology (including "practical"), the true nature of which is to serve the living proclamation of the gospel and the Christian existence of today urged on by awareness of the problems of practical pastoral care. When we think of the leaders of historical theology in the last century, of Ehrle, Denifle, Bardenhewer, Grabmann, Pelster, Landgraf, and others, we must realistically state, if we are honest, that their great and scholarly work is today of almost no use for the proclamation of Christ's salvific message, even if we take into account some very anonymous and indirect results. This kind of historical theology was theology in retrospect. That does not have to be so, as modern examples show. Think only of Congar, Chenu, de Lubac, to mention only a few.

Historical theology (as a whole) must no longer be so antiquarian and retrospective. It must become much more prospective; it must look backward in order to go forward to a new future of theology and proclamation. Historical theology should not merely ask what has been, but it must investigate the past in order to find the answer to the question: What ought to be, what should be proclaimed tomorrow? Historical theology, too, must have its theologians who feel, bear and suffer the anxiety, burden and risk of today's theology for tomorrow's proclamation. In the work of tomorrow, determined by the Council and by our day, historical theology must of course question with complete objectivity what has been, but it can no longer afford the art-for-art's-sake attitude of unlimited historical curiosity for everything. Its questioning of the past must be related to the life-and-death questions with which the future confronts theology, even though many *quaestiones quodlibetales* of second- and third-rate medieval theologians remain unedited and undiscussed. A theologian of our day, even in the field of history, should not have to prove his scientific acumen by writing books—that no one except his closest professional colleague or disciple will read—about questions that interest nobody but the author himself.

Historical theology can contribute much at least to loosening up and expanding current theology's awareness of problems for tomorrow, even though the past can hardly yield ready-made answers for the questions of our day. This holds true today especially for the history of moral theology and Church law. As contemporary examples show, here is an area where historical theology can do a lot of very useful work by renewing systematic theology's all too simple and settled theses with good historical awareness and subjecting them once again to debate and thus preparing answers that are better, more expert and more nuanced. This is perhaps true also of Church history, although its application may be difficult. During the Council one sometimes got the impression that quite a few of the leading Church men had heard little about or learned little from the history of the Church, her institutions and customs, as well as many of her doctrines.

The biblical sciences face great new problems after the Council. Not that these problems did not exist before, but the climate has become more favorable to their solution—above all, safer. The *Constitution on Divine Revelation* was certainly very cautious and conservative in its exposition of doctrine. This is certainly of great positive significance, since in the area of biblical science too the newest is not necessarily the truest and most lasting. In the next decades we will also need courage to maintain intact the faith of Christianity, which will always be a scandal and under attack. Courage is necessary, not in order to defend positions that are merely traditional, but to withstand the method of solution and historical scepticism (methodically—almost unavoidably—inherent in every modern historical science) that lack a true religious experience and believe that they can properly derive the living whole of the reality of faith from its parts and historical conditions.

Nevertheless, the *Constitution on Divine Revelation* has sanctioned the development in this discipline already begun under Pius XII (*Divino afflante Spiritu* and several statements of the Bible Commission). In exegesis and in the biblical theology of the Old and the New Testaments, one can use the methods first developed in Protestant biblical science, especially that of *Formgeschichte*, since they are not by their nature connected with unacceptable implications. Even if one adheres to the "historicity" of the four gospels, this somewhat global judgment must be nuanced, a fact that the Constitution clearly sees when it acknowledges a "vario modo historicum" (art. 12) and points out that post-resurrection theology influenced the apostles' report concerning the earlier life of Jesus (art. 19). The pressing task of a proper investigation is to show that there is a profound difference and yet true relationship, satisfying the demands of Catholic dogma, between the Jesus of history and the Christ of faith according to John and Paul; that, in other words, modern man, in spite of his historical realism and his eye for differences and development, with the eyes of faith can recognize in the history of Jesus more than merely the tragic facet of a religious enthusiast.

Of course, this requires a closer cooperation between exegesis and dogma than has been customary in the last decades. The dogmatic theologian must not expect conclusions from the exegete that the latter, if he is historically honest, cannot draw, and he must show, more than he has done in the past, that, in a right understanding of Christological dogma (without mythological overtones), the authentic findings of the exegete are a completely satisfactory point of departure and foundation for dogma. The decree concerning the training of future priests has ascribed to biblical science a greater and more original task in Catholic theology than merely to provide the *dicta probantia* for the theses (and their selection and system) that are already drawn up prior to exegetical work. It is now up to biblical science to do justice to this official mandate.

Something more must be said about "systematic" theology, above all, about dogmatic and moral theology.

It is clear that the Council hands to the theologian many tasks already through its express teachings. The Council's ecclesiology will, above all, be a concern of theology. Naturally, the Council formulated its teaching according to tradition, but this does not mean that it did not move many ecclesiological themes into the foreground of theological awareness, themes that deserve and need further reflection and that have very practical consequences. The precise relationship of the primary to the entire episcopate, the nature of the ordinary magisterium, the relationship between Scripture and tradition, the pneumatic-sacramental basis of law in the Church, the role of charisms within the Church, the theology of the diaconate, the Church's eschatological character, the possibility of salvation for the non-Christian, the ecclesiological aspect of penance (and of the sacraments in general), the nature of revelation and salvation history, the synodal principle of the constitution of the Church in general, the ecclesiological place of the evangelical counsels and religious communities in the Church, the meaning and significance of speaking about the hierarchy of truths of revelation, the theology of the missions, the possibility of a "communicatio in sacris" among separated Christians, the function of non-Christian religions in the collective and individual history of salvation, the obligation of the pope (even if jurid-ically it cannot be determined any further) to make use of collegial organs within the Church, the theology of the local community and altar com-munity as Church, the possibility of a historical development of the *jus divinum* in apostolic times, the theology of the word and theological herme-neutics—these and many other ecclesiological (in the broadest sense) themes newly confront theology because of the Council!

Aside from direct commentary on the theological texts of the Council, these ideas will occupy systematic theology doubtlessly to a considerable degree. To fulfill this task, theology must certainly do and say more than the maxims that had been explicit and traditional in theology before the Council. Considering only this explicit Conciliar thematic one really can no longer maintain that systematic theology today (besides dogmatic-historical retro-spection) has no new lands to conquer except in border areas or in special questions as, for instance, in Mariology, since everything else has already been clarified and cannot be said any better.

Perhaps I am wrong, but I feel that the description of the moral theology of the future in the *Decree on Priestly Formation* is a severe but just criticism of the moral theology taught in many seminaries. The Decree understands the task and method of moral theology differently from what has hitherto been actually practiced.

It would, however, be an easy and tempting—but for the future, fatal—error to think that the paramount task of systematic theology of the next decades would be to comment on the Conciliar texts, to justify historically and systematically to deepen the themes explicitly treated by the Council. Such a development of theology in the near future would completely con-tradict the spirit and intention of the Council. The Council did not invite theology to become the means and mode of an introversion of the Church to herself. The Council wanted an inexorable and at the same time coura-geous confrontation of the Church with our time. This was the actual intention of the Council. Out of the Church's desire to meet the men of our day and not to remain a historical relic of the sociological past arise questions that are completely different and much more radical than those of a more subtle ecclesiology.

The newest questions are the oldest and are radically fundamental for Christianity. First there is the question of God, whose answer implies a theology of atheism and general unbelief; in the unity of a transcendent (yet bringing into focus man's true and entire nature) formulation of the question the theologian must inquire after both God and the possibility of and "training" in a true experience of God for modern man, for whom God does not "appear" in the world. Then comes the question of Christ seen within an evolutionary *Weltanschauung* on the horizon of a salvation history that embraces all mankind; with conceptions that avoid anything that might have mythological overtones for the ears of modern man; and with a method that goes the way of the earliest Christology (before Paul and John): from the historical Jesus to the Christ of faith. Theology is also in search of an anthropology that interprets modern man as he actually experiences himself with an existence that comprises more than the "animal rationale" of an abstract metaphysics; a Christian anthropology that understands the original union of nature and grace and does not remove what we call grace in a Christian sense from the realm of concrete existence; an anthropology that does not leave intercommunication, love and the experience of the absurd and of death up to moral theology or to pious literature. Finally, we must take a hard look at all that goes under the title of dogmatic eschatology, and here we even lack a true hermaneutics of eschatological statements. More intensive reflection on the relationship between individual and collective eschatology is needed, if the proclamation of the "last things" is to be truly believable. The basic atmosphere of modern man's existence is such that it does not eliminate the danger of his falling back into the attitude of Old Testament man towards "the other world"; the hope and postulate of eternal individual life are not self-evident points of departures, as in the time of rationalistic enlightenment, but are attitudes to which man of today and tomorrow must again be carefully introduced. Christian eschatology is far from adequately confronting the eschatology of a future worldly Utopia of the dawning era of united humanity, an eschatology of the humanization of environment and of man's planned self-manipulation. A theology of hope is still waiting to be developed out of the arid beginnings of scholastic theologians concerning the theological virtue of hope. The dialogue desired by the decree of Vatican Council II between the hope of the world and the hope of Christianity must still be realized.

In short, the thematic set by the Council for tomorrow's theology is not the thematic with which the Council itself explicitly deals (if we prescind from the allusions of the *Constitution on the Church in the Modern World*), but is the thematic of the ultimate foundations of the Christian message on which the entire hierarchically structured edifice of Catholic dogma rests— the very last, which is at once the ultimate need and the most sublime vocation of man. This is what tomorrow's theology must consider if it wants to be a theology worthy of the Council; it must consider it with a faith ready to be attacked, a faith that always breaks up the clear definition of formulas into the incomprehensibility of God, and thus, while forced into this incomprehensibility, becomes simple and uncomplicated.

I mean that from such a starting point we could gain a truly correct understanding of "ecumenical theology" that is ready for the demands of the future. Naturally, there must be direct ecumenical theology, a dialogical controversial theology that deals with the differences in doctrine among Christian denominations, that eliminates misunderstandings and gradually learns to mutually translate the different languages of these separated theologies—a controversial theology that aims at a union of the churches, and not at an ever more subtle justification of their separation. Certainly in this respect much successful work has been done within the last decades, more than earlier. And still more can and must be done. But if it is true that ecumenism as such holds out a real hope for the union of Christianity only through a movement toward a Church of the future (which a Catholic can also admit, if he believes in the enduring obligation of the defined dogma of his Church and is convinced that the true Church of Christ "subsists" in the Roman Catholic Church), this holds true all the more of ecumenical theology. All churches and Christian communities will find the same language and a common confession only if they do not in the first place converse about present doctrinal differences that stem from the past, but strive to learn to speak the new language of the future in which the gospel of Christ (without any cheap subtractions à la Robinson) has to be proclaimed to the man of tomorrow so that he can understand it aright. The Christian theology for today's "pagan" is also the best ecumenical theology.

We still have to speak about another branch of theology and its future tasks, namely, practical theology, usually called "pastoral theology." After a Council desiring to be a pastoral one that explicitly considered the Church of the future, one that spoke about the collegiality of bishops, the office of bishop, episcopal conferences, the responsibility of the entire Church for the missions, the responsibility of each part of the Church for the whole Church —after all that pastoral theology can no longer be a collection of pious counsels for the simple clergy regarding the holy and effective performance of their duties. Practical theology must consider today the entire life and action of the Church with the help of theological reflection on the Church's present situation. Church law alone cannot do this—not only because, as we know, it is more inclined toward the history and interpretation of existing law than to the question *de lege condenda*, but above all, because the entire life of the Church is not identical with the observance of explicitly established juridical norms, either existing or to come. Questions as to how the Church as a whole is to live and act, how the central Roman offices are to be organized, how mission strategy (not just tactics) are to be dealt with, how a diocese is to be structured, how a large-scaled "politics" of mind and culture is to be influenced—such matters, in the cybernetic era of a society of large organizations and their reflex controls, can no longer be entrusted in a paternalistic way to the wisdom, prudence and experience of the leading Churchmen. True enough, the decision is theirs, but the thinking and study that precede a decision necessarily requires today a scientific method and a systematic execution. A practical theology is needed, and a theology within the thematic we are talking about does not yet exist. The pastoral Council calls for a new pastoral theology with a considerably broader objective and a more profound method, which, within the unchanging maxims of an ecclesiology of essence, attempts, with a theologically enlightened view of the present situation, to reach, at least approximately, the imperatives that must determine the concrete actions of the Church as a whole. Almost everything is still to be done in the area of such scientific practical theology with its own formal object and its own method.

The challenge theology has been given by the Council is great, even greater than the Council Fathers explicitly realized. This renewal of theology, its *aggiornamento*, should (by way of conclusion) be officially furthered by the Church. This means not only that regional episcopal conferences should soon, and thoroughly, carry out the task given them by the Council and formulate and initiate a new *ratio studiorum* for the training of priests; it means not only that bishops, home once again in their dioceses, should, according to circumstances, maintain the contact with the theologians that they, to their mutual pleasant surprise, had established in Rome, to their own benefit and to the benefit of theology itself; it means not only that the papal secretariats of ecumenism, of non-Christian religions and of modern unbelief can fulfil their task only through a renewed theology and thus should further it. It means that in a world, which has become a world of science, eggheads and experts, the Church should be officially concerned about theology and further its progress, over and beyond what has been said, in many more ways and institutions. There could still be considerable progress in the internationalization of Catholic theology. Would it not be possible to have, on the basis of international agreement and organization, specialized centers of theology (no individual can do everything) for the benefit of Catholic theology and with the participation of all Catholic theologians? Could there not be (although to a smaller extent) a collection for Catholic theology throughout the Church like that for Catholic missions? Could not the contact between Church administration and ecclesiastical sciences be closer and institutionally fixed? Could not the Congregation for the Doctrine of Faith, which originated in the Holy Office, also positively further theology by "commissioning research" regarding important questions (and ones of interest to the Congregation), and, more precisely, give these commissions to theologians outside Rome, who eventually could work in teams?[1] In short, one could and should ask whether the Church's theologians could and should not, with less constraint and to a greater extent than has been customary,

---

[1] When one studies the *Constitution on the Liturgy*, for example, one begins to doubt whether the Holy Office's 1957 decision on concelebration would have been the same if the question had been studied beforehand by an international commission of expert theologians and liturgists.

take over her organizational offices and institutions that are conditioned by sociological and practical factors, just as it has become customary because necessary in other areas of modern scholarship.

Programs and institutions cannot replace creative men. This applies above all to theology. Thus theology will, also in the future, be the Spirit's gift to the Church. But it is out of the longing and needs of the times that he will call to her and give her strength. Theology must exist so that "the word of the Lord may run and be glorified" (2 Thes 3:1). When theology trusts in God's grace and is truly permeated by its mission to the world of tomorrow, it will become good theology and will fulfill what it has been authorized for by this Council.

RAHNER: One question concerns the relationship between theology and sociology. I cannot, of course, answer this question very well, because it is beyond my competence, but I would have to define first what sociology is, and then ask what the role of sociology in theology is. Undoubtedly, there is an application of sociology in ecclesiology, and there is very great application of a sound and deep sociology in practical theology, and perhaps sociology has a critical role to play in regard to an understanding of Church dogma that is sociologically conditioned and not identified with dogma. Many teachings of the Church can be justified in a manner conditioned by time but perhaps erroneously understood, and, in view of the possibility of such misunderstanding of Church dogmas, sociology can play a very important role under certain circumstances.

MINEAR: What I am asking for is a suggestion in the area of method. The Council had to use lay experts in the social sciences in order to do some of its theological work on documents such as the *Constitution on the Church in the Modern World*. One gets the impression from the Constitution that a method has not yet been worked out to relate what has been called theology to the disciplines that have to be used by these lay experts. The question

599

is whether there are suggestions as to how the bridge between theology and these sciences used by the lay experts can be made?

RAHNER: Well, frankly speaking, I can't make any specific suggestions, but I can merely point out that sociologists should indeed be listened to in all questions dealt with by the Church and that have to be solved within the Church, whether by theologians or Church authorities. But I also believe that such a critical and concrete function of sociology has broader implications than appear at first glance. There is a sociology of knowledge and similar things, and such a science must have a place in theology. But how to organize it in practice I do not really know; sociologists should make recommendations to us.

There are many questions here that pertain in one way or another to the relationship of philosophy and theology in theology. Now it is a very vast and broad area, and one in which I am very much interested. But I need at least an hour to say something intelligent about it. The difficulty lies in the need to distinguish between the basic relationship, between theology and philosophy as sciences, or between philosophy and faith, and the other matter of the relationship of philosophy to theology as a training period in theology.

With regard to this second question I would like to say briefly that I do not believe the relationship between philosophy and theology in the training of theologians will remain what it has been so far, at least not for long. I am fully aware of the great significance of philosophy, even for theology, and I would consider it a serious danger—and here may I ask the indulgence of my Evangelical brethren—if Catholic theology were to fall back into a pure biblicism. This danger is undoubtedly already at hand in our Catholic theology, and I feel that we must be aware of this danger and overcome it. I am for a thinking theology, a theology in dialogue with the nonbeliever, and one that gives him an opportunity to raise questions in theology from his point of view. Therefore, I do not want to see theology based on biblical sciences alone.

On the other hand, however, I do not believe that in the future we will simply study three years philosophy first, as though we were not Christians, as though the real, basic problems of our existence could be solved philosophically, and then afterwards squeeze within this set and fixed framework some secondary issues of theology. Without denying the distinction between philosophy and theology, without abandoning a well-understood rational philosophy, we must determine the relationship between philosophy and theology (I am speaking not only theoretically but also about the practical training of our theologians) differently than was done in the Neo-Scholastic tradition, which is not very old at that. One cannot—at least in Germany—begin by studying pure philosophy for two or three years. First of all, most of the young theologians are intellectually fully incapable of it, if one does it honestly and reasonably. Secondly, it does not meet the concrete existential questions of the faith of these young people, or their over-all resolve of entering upon a priestly life. I know that even in Germany I am attacked regarding my skepticism of pure philosophy, but I believe that my views are correct. I believe that after a relatively short introduction of a more philosophical kind which is not yet reflective philosophy but an *introduction* to the concrete Christian and human situation of modern man, the young students can study theology right away, and some philosophy within theology. And then later those who are really capable can study a truly reflective philosophy that considers the formal structures of what we as Christians experience. But we should not put at the beginning a philosophy that is neutral in its *Weltanschauung*.

HAY: Is not the major stumbling block or difficulty for modern man Christianity's basis in historical revelation? How is the breakthrough to be made?

RAHNER: Your question is undoubtedly one of the essential and basic ones. It is the old question that was raised for the first time during the Enlightenment: How can a history of revelation tied to a certain time and place be necessary and meaningful as the basis for the life and salvation of a human being?

To my way of thinking, to answer such a question, one must first make inquiry into the nature of man as a real and necessarily historical being in his personal existence. Secondly, adhering to the official explicit revelation history of the Old and New Testaments, it should be demonstrated that this history is imbedded in a salvation and revelation history that exists in humanity as a whole and is thus co-existent with the spiritual and cultural history of mankind. It is at least a Catholic view that has very clearly emerged during Vatican Council II, namely, that God's grace solicits, enlightens, supernaturally raises everyone who comes into this world, and presents him with salvation in Christ for his acceptance. This implies a supernatural history of salvation that co-exists with spiritual history, both individual and collective, of mankind. And then if I presuppose theologically along with St. Thomas and Thomists, contrary to the usual Jesuit conception, that the supernatural elevation of man's being because of God's universal salvific will also brings with it a new formal object for the whole of spiritual existence (or put in modern terms, a peculiar and nonreflective horizon for man's entire spiritual existence), I have thereby already said history of revelation in a certain sense. Hence, this would already justify, I think this statement: there is, even if nonreflective and not yet historically objectified, a history of revelation and salvation that co-exists with the history of mankind. With all this as a basis, we should be able to make it more comprehensible for modern man that,

601

because of this universal history of revelation and salvation, there is also an official, reflective and explicit history of revelation bound by time and space, and that it reaches its climax in Jesus Christ.

Hay: Thank you sir, very much. I might understand then that perhaps our best procedure is to latch onto the growing consciousness, even in what you have called the pagan mind, that man is a historical phenomenon. Is this the point of contact, so to speak, by which the Christian theologian will try to initiate the dialogue with the man of tomorrow?

Rahner: I believe that the starting point is what St. Paul indicated. As a Christian I do not preach what has been until now absolutely beyond the horizon of man's existence. Rather I proclaim what basically man already knows, experiences and is in the depth of his consciousness touched by grace. I proclaim that God who already lies in the depths of man's existence as the God of absolute reality and as the God of grace because of his universal salvific will. When I evangelize as a Christian, I make a man reflectively, explicitly and in social, objectified, historical dimensions what by the grace of God he already is or can become.

Meyendorff: I would like to ask Father Rahner for a brief comment along the same line about the possible relationship that exists between philosphy and the dogma. Some earlier dogmatic statements have been made in philosophical terms. I am speaking of both some of the ancient councils as well as the Council of Trent. What happens? Is it possible to disengage absolute revelation in these cases from philosophy, and in what sense?

Rahner: Well, you see, first of all, I would say that there is no clear-cut border or limit between the normal human and philosophical conceptions. There is a certain difference, of course, but the difference is only of degree and fluent interchange. Consequently, I do not believe—and I think it Utopian to assume—that sometime in the future the Church's dogmas can be proclaimed without using philosophical concepts. Such concepts will never be those that are absolute in a clear and fixed function of dependence on a very specific philosophical system. But in theology we cannot avoid speaking of formal, material, cause, sign, act and substance. These are concepts that cannot be avoided in everyday language; in fact, the more humanity moves forward the less these concepts can be avoided. Thus, for instance, a person who only three weeks ago climbed about trees like an ape can perhaps live without these philosophical concepts, but our specific cultural situation necessarily calls for philosophical concepts in everyday life. And such concepts are to be found in the New Testament: *logos, alētheia, charis, esoanthropos*—thousands of such things have had a long history that is basically philosophical. A theology that is not implicitly philosophy, even if perhaps to a different degree, is not theology! Of course, theology has the function of critically examining the philosophical concepts it uses, and perhaps it has not always adequately coped with that task. However, I deem it impossible to practice a theology that tries to avoid being philosophical. The ultimate conviction that God's truth as God's can be expressed in human terms and the possibility of God's coming to man essentially imply the possibility of using philosophical concepts in theology, because philosophical and other human concepts are only different degrees of reflection, not basically different modes of human thought and speech.

Question: Would you please give us your opinion regarding Teilhard de Chardin.

RAHNER: I hesitate to do so for two reasons: I understand nothing of Teilhard's, and there is such an eminent interpreter of Teilhard de Chardin among us, Father de Lubac. Let me merely point out that there is no doubt that in a Christian's or theologian's work we can distinguish two questions: Is he, on the one hand, providing a great, basic vision that is meaningful and significant for the Church, theology and the Christian life? On the other hand, is a theologian or philosopher in every single one of his positions and formulations offering a refined and exact statement that does adequate justice to Catholic dogma? I am of the opinion that if someone is making mere statements that are certainly orthodox and must not and cannot arouse the slightest contradiction on the part of the magisterium, then such a person must ask himself whether he is not merely a sterile repeater of statements which, while they may be correct, he himself has not properly understood and cannot express in a way so as to be comprehended by modern man. To be orthodox in such a scholastic way is no work of art, is it? Let us agree that even if Teilhard de Chardin has not in every respect succeeded in doing justice to dogma, then I would say *in magnis voluisse sat est.* That it isn't as bad as when we teachers of theology give forth with a very orthodox but sterile theology that is of interest to no one.

Lastly, I believe that the Church should rejoice that a person like Teilhard de Chardin has reached the ear of so many people. He has certainly not set these people against Christianity, against the Church, but has interested them in Christianity and the Church. But withal, I have said really nothing about Teilhard de Chardin but made only a general comment on the subject. Let me repeat that I am not an expert on Teilhard and can, therefore, not go into detail.

Question: What do you mean by specialized centers of theology?

RAHNER: Nowadays, a normal theological faculty department can no longer provide that sort of theology in which all areas and disciplines can really be carried forth with genuinely scholarly investigation. We can, of course, have school theology—in the positive sense of the word—with which future priests are given an idea of what is going on in the individual disciplines of theology. However, genuinely scientific investigation and research in all disciplines cannot be carried out within the framework of one center of theological study. Consequently, would it not be useful to consider the possibility of setting up in a meaningful way such centers of gravity without coercive measures? Let us give some examples: one department of theology could emphasize patristic studies, another center moral theology, and still another medieval theology, and a fourth one perhaps practical theology in the more narrow sense. Then libraries that do not have unlimited means at their disposal could be developed accordingly. Then we should provide a reasonable opportunity for those who are interested in any given area to study at the corresponding faculty. I cannot see any harm—I say this with tongue in cheek—in a Jesuit's studying pastoral or moral theology under Father Häring at the Alphonsiana. I do not know whether this has happened yet. What? [Father Häring: "The Jesuits are doing that."] Well, then you are better than I thought. But that is what I meant when I referred to centers of gravity. Our difficulty in Germany lies in the fact that, though a need for such meaningful centers of gravity has been theoretically recognized, practically it has not been implemented, whether because of local patriotism or self-will, or the individuality of professors. Such local patriotism should really be overcome. Of course this involves many complex problems. In Germany, for instance, to mention an analogous problem, the Catholic theological faculties of universities, because of the present shortage of priests and the cost of study, would like religious to study in these faculties as much as possible; on the other hand, these same universities are not very willing to let religious teach in their faculties. These are some of the contradictions that naturally create difficulty in any attempt to organize well the theological enterprise.

OUTLER: This paper is a very rich and instructive charter for theological work, both for Roman Catholics and for non-Roman Catholics. Hence, I would not wish to appear as though I were complaining, if I mention two omissions that seem to appear in it. And I mention them only because of their relevance to the ecumenical dialogue. I put them in the form of two separate questions.

Is it true that Roman Catholic theologians have so little to learn from non-Roman Catholic theology, Protestant, Anglican and Orthodox, as would seem to be implied by the paper and presentation? One listens to understand what is the future task of Roman Catholic theology with respect to the very large body of theologizing in historical, biblical, systematic, dogmatic, practical spheres that has been going on, that is going on and will continue to go on. From the paper, with one or two rather casual exceptions, one wonders if this theology exists, or if it exists if it is of any real interest and instructive value to Roman Catholic theologians. I would have thought that one of the great consequences of Vatican II is that the ecumenical dialogue now has become a two-way street. We non-Roman Catholics have got to read the Roman Catholic theology. It is high time and a very good thing. But are Roman Catholics going to read Protestant, Anglican and Orthodox theology? And if they are not why are they not, and on what grounds will it be decided that this isn't worth doing? That is my first question.

RAHNER: May I answer this first question right away. It is quite possible that my paper has given that impression, but may I solemnly and explicitly declare that it is not my viewpoint. Of course, we Catholic theologians must and can learn not only from the biblical theology of non-Catholics, without which we cannot practically and concretely live, but also from the systematic theology of Protestant, Anglican and Orthodox Churches. There is no doubt about it. I believe that to a substantial degree it is being already done, certainly not enough. I believe that there are relatively many Catholic theologians who read Karl Barth and Ebeling, for instance. If I am properly informed, Rudolf Bultmann has explicitly acknowledged that he is studied and understood by Catholic theologians. I do not want to praise Catholic theology, for it has not earned that much praise. But I believe that if we are to dialogue not only with each other but with the modern, so-called pagan world, we must study theology together, learn from each other, read each other, talk to each other, and that we could find and say many really theological things in common. It goes without saying that Catholic theology is to a certain extent—and please understand me properly, for I say this as a Catholic without being ashamed—more tied down; it has a binding magisterium alongside and behind it, and to that degree Catholic theology is, in a certain sense, more clearly set apart from Protestant theology. But I believe that it is to a much lesser extent than it is generally assumed. Let me give you an example: I believe that there is a relationship between word and sacrament that could be developed in Catholic theology, one that would seem Protestant to a Protestant theologian without being unorthodox in the Catholic Church. And if we do something like that, we will, of course, have also learned something from Protestant theology. And so it simply isn't true that all theological problems have either a Catholic or a Protestant solution. Today there are countless problems in theology for which even within different confessions themselves different solutions are found, so that under certain circumstances the Catholic solution A agrees better with the Protestant solution B than the Catholic solution A does with the Catholic solution B. There are many instances of that. Let me merely emphasize once more that I would regret it very much indeed if my paper gave the impression that systematic Catho-

lic theology cannot or must not learn anything from Protestant theology. It
can and should.

Outler: First, let me say how much I welcome this statement, because
to me it does seem to belong to the very genius of what now lies before us
all in the post-Conciliar period. The second question has to do with my
impression that one of the great unfinished tasks of Vatican Council II is
what to do about the fact that the Council has, in some of its documents,
created some very drastic changes in the line and continuity of conventional
Catholic teaching on a fair number of important points. One need not elaborate them or argue how much change or how much development there is
involved. But it seems to some of us that the present question is to deal in
a proper theological way with the fact that Catholic teaching on at least four
or five crucial questions now represents a kind of breach with its own immediate past, if not long past, and that this requires a theory of discontinuity
as well as continuity in the magisterium. Since this is a tortured problem
for non-Roman Catholics and is a central problem for the ecumenical dialogue and possible convergence of the divided parts of Christendom, it seems
that this is one of the crucial, urgent, constant tasks of the post-Vatican
period in theology and theological method.

Rahner: I must say that, generally speaking, the Catholic theologian
does not get that impression, but rather—and I am convinced he is right—
the impression of a very intensive continuity. Speaking personally, if I may, I
have never found my opinions to be in any special discontinuity with school
theology, and I really cannot say that I have the impression—and I didn't
have even during the Council—that a particular discontinuity is present.
Certain problems, of course, were recognized, that perhaps the Church's
teaching authority had not recognized before; aspects were developed which
have never been handled with such clarity and explicitness. But I do not
believe that we can speak of a genuine discontinuity. The Catholic theologian can admit, in individual cases, that the official Church had defended a
certain doctrine which it later abandoned, and there, of course, we have a
certain discontinuity. If for thirty years I as a Catholic teacher of Scripture
have not been allowed to teach that there is a Deutero-Isaiah, and now I
am allowed to do so, that shows clearly that the old position has been abandoned and that a new position has been accepted. In such a case we cannot
simply speak of continuity, but here in a certain question—not in a dogmatic one, however—a change has taken place. Take, for instance, what the
Constitution on the Church says about the collegiality of bishops and their
relationship to the pope; it is precisely what was already said at Vatican
Council I by the official spokesmen for the pope, Gasser, Cinelli, Kleutgen,
etc. If, when Vatican Council II teaches something like this explicitly, the
world gets the impression that a tremendous revolution has taken place, the

Catholic theologian says to himself: thank God, the Church has stated officially what was earlier basically accepted as evident. Hence, I cannot really share the impression of such a radical discontinuity.

DUNNE: The question I wanted to ask was about the plurality of theologies, how one might evaluate the fact that there are many theologies. I wonder what Father Rahner's position would be on this. I wonder if it would be possible to give an almost completely affirmative evaluation of this, for instance, to say that, just as in the New Testament, in addition to kerygma and didache, there are the theologies of St. Paul and St. John, because of the different theological languages and conceptual systems. On that type or model, plurality of theologies is a good thing, a necessary thing, something we can say yes to in some fundamental way.

RAHNER: May I say briefly that, first of all, the *Decree on Eastern Catholic Churches* has explicitly acknowledged such a plurality of theologies. Secondly, the theology of this plurality of theologies has not actually been worked out. Theologians have hardly given thought to it. Although the Church, by means of her approbation of Bonaventure on the one hand, and St. Thomas Aquinas on the other, and similar things, has tolerated, in fact expressly recognized a plurality of schools in theology, a theology of theologies does not exist, unfortunately. This is undoubtedly a very important matter.

Thirdly, one must say that the plurality of schools in a Catholic understanding of faith and theology cannot be considered in such a manner that the theologies absolutely contradict each other in a tangible, clear way on the conceptual level, and that the unity of theologies lies, as it were, in some absolutely intangible meaning. On the other hand, I do not believe that the different schools can be so positively synthesized with each other and can be integrated into a higher system, that the plurality of schools would essentially be abolished. But in Catholic theology there is no reflective theology, whether in regard to biblical theology, or in regard to other theologies in the Church. The problem of many theologies in the New Testament is still, unfortunately, one that has been given very little thought by Catholics. Protestant theologians have done much more work on that, perhaps often with an extremism that, in my opinion, is false. There is not only an external canon with absolutely heterogeneous theologies in the New Testament, but a real unity among them, without their being synthesized into a common, positive system—and in New Testament times they were considered heresies.

CONGAR: My question really refers to a point already passed in the discussion. It seems to me that Father Rahner identifies the extension of the history of salvation with that of the history of revelation. It is quite clear that the history of salvation began with the first man. But as for the history of revelation, the question is whether Father Rahner thinks of revelation as beginning with Abraham or with a primitive revelation. Which one?

RAHNER: Well, naturally, it is a complex problem. If there is a universal history of salvation that coexists with the history of mankind, then it must, first of all, be a history of faith, and a history of faith is, in the last analysis, unthinkable apart from a history of revelation. Vatican Council II says in its *Decree on the Church's Missionary Activity* that we may assume that God, in ways known to him, can lead to a saving faith even those people who are not reached by the explicit preaching of the gospel. Now in terms of the whole tradition of theology, I can see that faith only is an answer to a genuine revelation of God. And this faith cannot be replaced by a *bona voluntas*. Therefore, for my humble logic tells me that if there is a universal history of salvation that exists with the history of man, there must be a history of revelation that also coexists with the history of man. The question then arises for the theologian, how can I bring this universal history of salvation or history of revelation into an orthodox relationship with that history of revelation that reaches from Moses to Jesus Christ, and is, therefore, tied to time and space, is regional and particular. This requires more thought; for my part I have tried to give my views here and there on this complex and dark problem, but I cannot do it here, because it would tax your patience too much.

MEYENDORFF

BURGHARDT

OUTLER

SESSION XVI

VERY REV. JOHN MEYENDORFF
Vatican II and Orthodox Theology in America

DR. ALBERT OUTLER
Vatican II and Protestant Theology in America

REV. WALTER J. BURGHARDT, S.J.
Vatican II and Catholic Theology in America

Very Rev. John Meyendorff

VATICAN II AND ORTHODOX THEOLOGY IN AMERICA

C HRISTIAN EAST AND CHRISTIAN WEST have had an entire millennium of common history. And it would be utterly wrong to believe that all of a sudden history ceased to be common when the schism took place. Actually, as modern historians have shown, the date itself of the schism cannot be established: for quite a number of centuries, nobody was sure whether there had been a real schism, or a simple jurisdictional squabble between patriarchs. And of course, in theology, in traditions of worship and piety, in all the essential elements of Christian life, the common past remained alive in East and West. Despite the Crusades and the hatreds they created, despite all the cultural estrangement that had already taken place, no one doubted, as late as the middle of the fifteenth century in East or West, that union between the two churches could be restored easily, if only a common council could meet and re-establish the kind of relationship that existed before the schism.

And it seems to me extremely important to realize that even after the total interruption of official communication between the churches, which occurred in the fifteenth century and lasted until our day, *theology* remained fundamentally ecumenical, in its very nature, even when it was polemical or apologetic.

When I mention this ecumenical *nature* of theology, I mean simply that both Eastern and Western theologians have used the same Scriptures, the same Fathers, the same tradition, and, more recently, the same tools of historical research. If you consult any Orthodox theological textbook or monograph, Greek, Russian, Romanian, or other, you will discover there a profuse Western bibliography. What is true today in biblical scholarship, to be defined as either "Catholic" or "Protestant," is even more true for the entire area of tradition that remains between Orthodox and Catholics, an essentially ecumenical area of research and thought. And even if a sense of self-sufficiency, often created by linguistic barriers, limits mutual knowledge between contemporary Orthodox and Catholic theologians, the ecumenical nature of theology is maintained by the common reference to the past.

It is also important to realize that this ecumenical fact, on the level of theological research, was a reality even before Vatican II. The real tragedy between us Orthodox and you Roman Catholics is that from this tremendous treasure of scriptural, traditional, sacramental realities, which we have in common, we draw conclusions that still clearly separate us. The irritation we occasionally feel toward each other arises precisely when we suddenly discover that our brother, who knows what I know, who feels so much the same way, rejects what appears to us as the obvious and only possible conclusion from the premises we have in common.

Now there is no doubt that Vatican II has begun a new era—an era in which the Roman Catholic Church is, in many ways, beginning to see in our common past the same realities as we do. I am sure, however, that many of you have been disappointed by the lack of response in so many Orthodox circles; many of you were irritated by what appeared as stubbornness among precisely those Orthodox from whom you expected a more positive response to some of the Vatican's ecumenical approaches. May I express in all frankness my belief that this Orthodox cautiousness sometimes comes, not from negativism or fear, but from the simple conviction that the premises of our common past, which Vatican II has done so much to recover, have not yet been exploited to their fullest; that many statements have been made on the basis of the obvious common tradition of the ancient Church, without reaching all the possible implications for the present. The affirmation of Christ's full presence in the sacramental community of the local Church, the affirmation of the collective and collegiate infallibility of the episcopate, the participation of the entire body of the People of God in the preservation of the faith—all these statements of the Constitution on the Church, which are the very foundation of Orthodox ecclesiology, are not yet totally integrated into a coherent whole. They will, however, lead to more progress in mutual understanding, provided no misleading short cuts are taken. It is therefore out of an optimistic respect for the growing and evolving theological aggiornamento of the Roman Church, still in its beginning stage, that those Orthodox who —as one of my Catholic friends said recently—"should know better" are still waiting for the decisive steps that will make our total unity a reality.

All this, of course, has a tremendous importance for us in America. I have just spoken of the ecumenical nature of theological science, which has and still succeeds—on the scholarly academic level—to transcend cultural barriers. These barriers, however, were still very strong as late as the beginning of this century. But now in America, the results of Vatican II reach us in a situation which is totally new, sociologically and culturally: an Orthodox Church, quite sizable in numbers, is taking shape in a Western country. Even if today it is still largely dependent upon conditions of recent immigration, it will certainly be totally "American" in twenty years. But even today, the traditional categories of "East" and "West" have very little meaning for American-born generations. They speak and think exactly as other Americans, and understandably refuse to determine their Orthodoxy solely on the basis of their grandparents' having been Greek or Russian. The Orthodox Church in this country cannot and will not identify itself as an "Eastern" Church, any more than a Protestant will allow his convictions to be explained exclusively by the social conditions of sixteenth-century Europe, or a Catholic see his allegiance to the pope presented only as a vestige of ancient Roman religion that considered the emperor as *Pontifex Maximus*. An American, living in a pluralistic and essentially free society, will himself personally determine his religious allegiance on the basis of what he considers to be the truth.

This new American situation creates totally new conditions of ecumenical witness and action, especially for the Orthodox who are newcomers on the scene. The former dialogue between East and West was constantly obstructed by cultural misunderstandings, by linguistic barriers, by human "traditions": History itself is now contributing to the disappearance of all this, and we are confronted *in common* with the real, basic issues of Christian witness in the world today.

May I therefore suggest three areas in which, it seems to me, the decisions of Vatican II compel us urgently to cooperate.

1. DEVELOPMENT OF A COMMON ECUMENICAL METHODOLOGY

I have alluded to ecumenical *short cuts* that may be a harmful result of our era of youthful and inexperienced ecumenical enthusiasm. True ecumenism is dialogue, which implies that each party take the other seriously, respect the sincerity of his convictions and try to understand them in depth without necessarily agreeing with them. In order to realize the conditions of such true ecumenism, both Orthodox and Roman Catholics must modify some of their traditional attitudes toward each other.

The Orthodox, for example, must abandon their deep-seated conviction that Roman ecclesiology can be reduced to a search for power on behalf of the popes, a sort of imperialism. Even if the medieval papacy did act in a way that lends some credibility to this view, in its essence and in the belief of millions of the faithful, it is nothing of the sort, but rather an article of faith, a gift of God, which Roman Catholics want out of love to share with us Orthodox. The Orthodox, therefore, must take their Roman Catholic brethren seriously on this point and stop dreaming up Utopian and naive schemes, according to which the Roman Church would cease to encourage Catholicism of Eastern rite and restrict its jurisdiction to Latin Christians. To dictate such conditions to Rome amounts to requiring of it an immediate conversion to Orthodoxy, which is obviously premature and would exclude ecumenical dialogue *today*.

The Roman Catholics, on the other hand, must also avoid pseudo-ecumenical attitudes, which usually amount to an exaltation of the "venerable Eastern rites," to their delatinization and to the conviction that the only true reason for Orthodox refusal to accept Roman primacy is their fear of losing their Eastern traditions. Even if "Latinization" of the Uniate Churches was an issue in the past and still is an issue today, no responsible Orthodox believes, or has ever believed, that the issue between Orthodoxy and Rome concerns only liturgical rites or traditional customs. And American Orthodox will believe it even less. The existence of churches of Eastern rite in the Roman Church symbolizes the *tension* between Orthodoxy and Rome, a tension which the Orthodox must learn to cope with. But this is not in itself the starting point of dialogue, but rather its ready-made solution as presented to the Orthodox by Rome; for *doctrinal* reasons, for reasons that arise from the understanding of the Christian gospel itself, it remains unacceptable and even irritating in its naiveté.

If the message of Vatican II is truly that of dialogue, one should not delay in setting up *ecumenical methodology* that excludes these slippery side issues.

2. THEOLOGICAL COOPERATION IN CONFRONTING THE MODERN WORLD

The modern ecumenical movement started among missionaries who recognized the scandal of division among Christians competing for the souls of non-Christians. And the *aggiornamento* of John XXIII starts with the vision of a modern world that ignores God.

It is widely assumed that the Christian East has a tradition of passivity toward the world. And the present critical condition of the Orthodox world, when compared with the dynamism of the Catholic *aggiornamento*, seems to raise doubts about interest in searching together with Orthodoxy for any fruitful cooperation in the crucial issue of dealing with the world. It is said that the Eastern Church was passive before the state, passive in its desperate fight for survival in the Moslem Middle East, and passive again today in communist countries where it cannot publish, cannot teach and, therefore, is radically restricted even in the possibility of thinking.

However, the extraordinary fact of the persistence of religion in Russia, after half a century of violent anti-religious "re-education" of two successive generations, and the no less extraordinary fact that leading Russian intellectuals, both old and young—like Boris Pasternak, Anna Akhmatova, Sozhelnitzyn, or Senyavsky-Tertz—could profess their Christian convictions and find in the Christian faith the apex of their literary inspiration, seem to show that the Orthodox Church's attitude toward the world has not been a total failure. And the Russian experience is certainly of relevance to America, since we all know that these two great countries and civilizations tend more and more to face the same human problem, that of a technologically affluent society dehumanizing man.

Now, in schema 13 the Council meets directly the essential inspiration of the Greek patristic tradition when it refuses to recognize the profanity of the world, when it affirms between creation and redemption a unity that, in the light of Christology, can be called *hypostatic*, for the Logos, "through whom all things were made," and the Redeemer Christ are *one* hypostatically and personally. It follows from this that salvation is nothing but a re-establishment of the original relationship between the Prototype, the Plan, and creation itself in the very person of the Logos, and that in this unity lies the beginning of the road that leads to the transfigured cosmos of the *eschaton*. Agreement of Christians today—Catholic, Protestant and Orthodox—on these essential lines of thought would perhaps be the most solid foundation for our common action in the world.

Another area in which dialogue is badly needed is the idea of knowledge of God, essential for the encounter with atheism. The Orthodox Church committed itself in the late Middle Ages to affirming that God is absolutely and totally unknown in his essence, that no human faculty, not even the "beatific vision," is able to grasp the essence of God. Knowledge of God is possible only inasmuch as the living God manifests himself in the free acts of this love toward man. Between the honest agnostic and the Christian there is therefore this capital point of agreement: God is unknown to the human mind. And their dialogue consists in the responsibility of the Christian not to prove, but to *show* what divine life is, what divine love is, and where and how man encounters them.

So, if we Orthodox join our Catholic brethren in confronting modern agnostic man, we are immediately led into the discussion between the Palamite and the Thomist on the issue of our knowledge of God, on the making of the "spiritual senses," which are, according to the Fathers, our means of contact with the Living God; and whose existence we cannot *prove* to the atheist, or even to ourselves, but whose reality we experience, both intellectually and otherwise, in the Church of God as those things that, Paul said, "are prepared by God for those who love him."

And if the knowledge of God is ultimately the very content of Christian faith, and if this knowledge can be shown and accepted only *in the total freedom* of the human person responding with love to God's love, is the Roman Church always correct in its traditional preoccupation—certainly not totally absent in Vatican II's decisions—of *administering* to human society, of finding solutions for all human problems, of guiding, of feeding, of· advising, of ruling and of directing instead of *showing?* In any case, here we are, the passive East and the activistic West standing together, side by side, confronting a mounting secularism. In America perhaps, where there is neither East nor West, we will be able to learn better from each other.

3. THEOLOGICAL COOPERATION IN UNDERSTANDING MAN

The problem of the knowledge of God is essentially connected with anthropology. To speak of "spiritual senses," able to encounter God's acts and life, implies not only a theology but also a dimension in man himself, which a secularized anthropologist would normally ignore. The argumentation of the schema 13, based, as Canon Moehler has so brilliantly shown, upon the notion of the image of God in man, implies therefore a specific Christian anthropology as a starting point of what man is in general, and what modern man is in particular.

In the tradition of the Greek Fathers since Irenaeus the notion of the divine image implies that man is *by nature* a participant in God's life. It is through this participation that he is immortal and free, and it is by rejecting this participation that death "entered into the world" (Rom 5:12). It is only in this participation that man is truly man. There is no such thing, therefore, as "pure nature," which is the object of God's wrath and punishment, the recipient of justification, and the beneficiary of grace. There is only man in various states of being, determined by his attitude and relation to God. And man without God is not only nature without grace; he is a dehumanized man, enslaved to powers that have usurped God's lordship over creation. Nature and grace are not opposed to each other, but complementary in defining what man truly is.

It seems to me it is over against this theology of man that the whole problem dividing us so bitterly—that of Church *authority*, of "continuity" and "discontinuity"—is to be treated.

In falling away from participation in God, man did not lose freedom, but his freedom became a fallen one: that of *choosing* between good and evil, that of hesitating between right and wrong. This fallen freedom needs guidance, requires obedience and, as Dostoyevsky has shown, finds great satisfaction and relief in renouncing itself, thus escaping the suffering of doubt by submitting to external power. But this is not the original and true human freedom: one that participates in God's truth, sees God, one that was given back to man in Christ. Here man is "taught by God," participates in the life of the Spirit of Truth, and the ultimate point of his being as a Christian, the knowledge of God, does not depend upon obedience to any external criterion. It is on the level of this knowledge of God that the Church's *continuity* lies.

Now what happens in the Church while it is still *in via?* Is it still based on authority and obedience? Or is the Spirit, and therefore *true freedom*, already present in the entire body, whose members are somehow joined together and coordinated through the various ministries of the Spirit? What are these ministries? Are they simply the necessary elements of a "fallen" order of things where there is still no freedom and where obedience is the rule? Or do they express and realize an order of the Spirit, the new life that has already become a historic reality? And if the latter is true, can these ministries—episcopate, Roman primacy—limit in any sense redeemed human freedom and responsibility? Can they add anything to it? In other words, does law still have a place in the redeemed community of the Church, and if so, is this place an absolute, or only a relative one?

Here are some of the issues that start with a pleasant ride of Orthodox and Catholic together on the train of scriptural and patristic tradition but end in a bifurcation that catches the Orthodox (or the Catholic) by surprise. On the basis of Vatican II we can and indeed must go on several of these rides together and try to avoid bifurcation as long as we can. With our common return to the sources, our common concern for unity in truth, the ride will become longer and longer, and then *perhaps*, without our expecting it, on a day and at an hour we *cannot* know the Lord will catch us himself on the same train and end the journey in his heavenly kingdom.

I have discussed in this paper the relevance of Council decisions directly for Orthodox theology. However, the Orthodox-Catholic dialogue, in order to reach its total ecumenical dimension, must also include Protestants. Not that methodologically it is not possible to dialogue bilaterally—we have spent long years alone with Protestants in the ecumenical movement, and on many issues it is wise, even at this time, to prefer bilateral talks—but ultimately we Orthodox must realize the magnitude of our failure in the sixteenth century to participate in and to contribute a solution to the drama of the Reformation.

If, as Father Stransky said, Vatican II represents a way back from the Counter-Reformation toward a more integrated conception of Christian tradition than negativistic fear of Protestantism, then the reintegration must be a true one and must transcend the categories of the Council of Trent. The affirmation of this principle is indeed one of the most magnificent achievements of the Council, not only as an overture to Protestantism, but because a return to Pre-Tridentine Catholicism inevitably encounters Orthodoxy. Unfortunately, the very deep crisis in which the Orthodox Church finds itself in its traditional geographical territories of Eastern Europe may again prevent it from taking an active role in the exciting processes occurring in Western Christianity. And here again we discover the particular responsibility of the encounter which will, can, and must take place here in America, beyond all traditional walls and misunderstandings.

Dr. Albert Outler

VATICAN II AND PROTESTANT THEOLOGY IN AMERICA

Tʜɪs ᴡᴇᴇᴋ ɪɴ ᴄᴏɴꜰᴇʀᴇɴᴄᴇ ʜᴀꜱ ᴘʀᴏᴠᴇᴅ—as if further proof were needed—that Vatican II was itself the effect of a pre-Conciliar theological revival in the Roman Catholic Church that came to providential focus in the Council, and also the cause of a yet more widely expanding revival in theology that is spreading throughout the Roman Catholic Church and far beyond, now in the post-Conciliar epoch. Whatever else it was, Vatican II was a *theological* event of major magnitude, and in our papers and discussions here we have had a rich sampling of its first fruits.

The genius of Vatican II may be indicated (with suitable vagueness) by the catchword *aggiornamento*. The *theological* gist of this slogan, I take it, is the deliberate decision to expose the Roman Catholic mind to the spectrum of challenge and danger in *today's* world—and to do this with confidence that Christian truth is still mighty and will prevail even in *this* world. This means, among other things, the exposure of a conventionally immobilist manner of theologizing to the assumptions of modern *historical criticism* (which is to say, relativism and change), to modern *inconoclasm* (which is to say, radical skepticism and antitraditionalism), to modern *secularism* (which is to say, contemporary man's narcissist claim to autonomy and self-sufficiency—a secularism that is very much more than a reaction against otherworldliness but humanist to the bone). That those exposures will leave traditional Catholic thought-forms intact is not even mildly probable. How far they will lead to what sort of developments is not yet clear.

This much, however, *is* certain. This post-Conciliar phase of Roman Catholic theology is newly and vitally connected with contemporary Protestant theology as has not been the case since the rude polemics of the seventeenth century. It is an interaction that has little by way of common history in our recent past (and this is its deficit on both sides!), but it has already begun to take up the burden of a common fate. Its forms and prospects are unpredictable, but we have seen their beginnings—in this conference and elsewhere—and the omens are honestly hopeful.

As we all know, however, this is not an especially glorious moment in the history of Protestant theology for this convergence to take place. At a time when the Roman Catholics are excitedly riding the crest of a theological boom (not to say inflation) the Protestants are milling about in a corresponding slump (not to say depression). We stand, as you must know, in the aftermath of a generation of titans with no comparable successors left or emerging. We stand in the midst of a noisy outburst of theological panic and arson that obscures the broader and more solid enterprises that are still actually going forward at a more modest level in the Protestant communions. We stand before an ecumenical future of interaction with the Roman Catholics and Orthodox, with whom we are scarcely acquainted—and we are not yet prepared to pull our full weight in the ecumenical projects that are proliferating all over.

Historical perspective is a very present help in time of theological confusion. It is, therefore, useful to recall that our equivalent of *aggiornamento* began a long time ago with F. D. E. Schleiermacher's *Lectures on Religion to Its Sophisticated Despisers*—an essay on the Church in the *modern* world of 1799. This involvement of Protestant theology with the Enlightenment mentality has had a strange history, in its divagations and developments, and we cannot even summarize it here. But it should be remembered that it was a history quite apart from the parallel development—or lack of development—in Roman Catholic teaching in the same period.

For in decisive contrast to the liberalizing tendencies of nineteenth-century Protestantism, the Roman Catholic Church reacted defensively toward the Enlightenment and all its works. The century between De Maistre and Garrigou-Lagrange was an era of siege-mentality in the Roman Catholic Church, of the stifling of "modernist" tendencies whenever they challenged the immobilist monopoly. This was the century of *Mirari Vos*, the *Syllabus Errorum*, the *Pascendi Dominici Gregis*, the *Antistitum* and the *Mortalium Animos*—each in turn a conscious rejection of "the *modern* world."

The catastrophe of World War I seems to have generated a strange reversal of roles in the Protestant and Catholic camps, still estranged, as they were, by an armed truce. The shattering of the optimisms of liberal Protestantism made way for a generation of titans and epigones who, although all sons of the Enlightenment, now began to turn against it in a variety of reactive patterns, each with its peculiar syndrome of Enlightenment, Reformation and biblical motifs. This, I suggest, is the best formula for understanding— and differentiating—the dominant theologies in Protestantism since Barth's *Römerbrief* (1919): Barth and Brunner, Kierkegaard *redivivus*, the brothers Niebuhr, Tillich (especially in his American phase) and even Bultmann, when he finally got to us and became indigenized. Between them, these neo-orthodox theologians managed to discredit the older liberalism and to revive an older strain of theological *fideism* that snatches faith from the very jaws of doubt, a dangerous game that helped open the way to the skeptical reaction we are now wallowing in.

While Protestant liberalism was in eclipse, Roman Catholic liberalism was assuming a new lease on life after its debacle in the days of St. Pius X. It was, however, a chastened liberalism and kept half-hidden from the generality of Catholics, and Protestants as well. If you take the names and books reviewed in Elmer O'Brien's bibliographical symposium, *Theology in Transition*,[1] and trace their backgrounds over the past generation, you begin to see a pattern: a "new" theology as fully open to the modern mind as an immobilist Church would allow, a theology aimed at tomorrow but not certain as to when, or even if, tomorrow would ever come. It was this *preparatio theologica* that set the stage for Vatican II. It was Vatican II that gave this "new" theology its first main chance to register on the Church as a whole. Thus, the theology of Vatican II and the new theological perspectives of the post-Conciliar epoch are the improbable outcome of three decades of prior development, now almost suddenly dominant. One has only to review the roster, and careers, of the Vatican *periti* here at this conference (and add a score of other pioneers: Weigel, Guardini, Chenu, Lonergan *et al.*), in order to real-ize how much was made possible by how few in what unlikely circumstances. It is, of course, an illusion to suppose that what has happened thus far is more than a new frontier opened; the territory is far from being settled or developed.

Meanwhile, in Protestantism (with the passing of our titans) we have witnessed a rejuvenescence of the humanist motifs of nineteenth-century Enlightenment liberalism. This helps partially to explain the current *brou-haha* over "the death of God" and "the secular city"; it helps to explain the crisis of morale among Protestant churchmen in reaction to our unmet demands for our equivalents of *aggiornamento*. Each of these current clamors ("death of God," "secular city," "the new morality") represents a caricature of elements in the classical Protestant syndrome that are authentic only when

---

[1] New York: Herder and Herder, 1965.

they hang together in the whole syndrome: a triumphant skepticism that is
the corruption of a long-standing motif of radical fideism (Altizer), a house-
wrecking anti-institutionalism that is the distortion of a valid Protestant
emphasis upon "prophecy" and the freedom of the Holy Spirit in the Church
and the world (Cox), a new "essence of Christianity" (Hamilton) that has
now been whittled down to the bleeding stub of what once was a vital core—
a reckless *reductio* of the Protestant emphasis on the distinction between
fundamenta and *adiaphora*.

For better or for worse, however, this is the time when Catholicism and
Protestantism have been thrown together in the convergence I mentioned
earlier. I take it as the consequence of Vatican II that we are now involved
in a mutually interdependent dialogue and in various tasks of common labor,
with more hope than certainty that our work together will bear fruit to the
glory of God and the recovery of Christian community. No one can predict
the changes that are in store for us on either side. Even so, the very effort
to understand our prospects is bound to sharpen our theological perceptions.
I mention five items out of a possible dozen.

In the first place, I think it likely that Protestant theology will be recalled
to new essays in fundamental Christian doctrine by the joint challenges of
Vatican II on the one hand, and the "death of God" hullabaloo on the other.
Christology and anthropology have been our staples for a century, as our heritage of classical theism was being slowly eroded away. Now, the *reality* of
God becomes the central issue once more, and new patterns of inquiry in
religious epistemology, religious metaphysics, ontology, and theology proper
are the obvious tasks of the new generation that aims to convince men of the
reality of God (of his presence and grace) in a world come of age and gone
to pot. It is no accident that there is a crop of able younger men engaged in
one or another aspect of this effort to shape up a *neoclassical theism* (Ogden,
Cobb, Lindbeck, Harvey, Gilkey *et al.*), and their efforts will be worth a
careful watch.

In the second place, because of the joint pressures from our own "secular-
city" prophets and the new frontiersmen of the social gospel in Roman Catholicism—the men who take *Gaudium et Spes* as their chief charter—there
is a growing awareness amongst Protestant theologians that the time is ripe
for a major mutation in the Protestant tradition of *sola gratia* in the direction
of a radically reformulated doctrine of creation and grace. One could still
maintain that the Protestant suspicions of the medieval versions of the *gratia-
non-tollit-naturam* maxim were justified and then agree that the cluster of
anomalies in the currently fashionable concepts of "God in history" are more
likely to confirm than to convert modern secular skepticism. Every really
fruitful notion of the creator in his creation, the premise of the social *gospel*,
must have its matrix in the *via negativa* and every valid doctrine of God's

redemption of man-in-society must be rooted in a vivid awareness of *history* as the theater of providence. To explore these complexities is a task that can best be done by Catholics and Protestants together—in the post-Vatican atmosphere and outlook.

In the third place, as never before and in ways still unfamiliar to most of us, Protestant theology is being reoriented (by Vatican II and other ecumenical stimuli) toward *ecclesiology*. The twin problem of ecclesiology looks, on the one hand, toward a koinonia of *redemption* and, on the other, to a koinonia of *authority*. Protestantism, since the stabilization of the fragmentation of Western Christianity in the seventeenth century, has been loathe to join these two communities, preferring to locate *authority* in Scripture alone and then to relate *redemption* to the Church conceived chiefly in metahistorical terms (*ecclesia invisibilis*). But where *is* the authority of Scripture, and how is it to be determined? What are we to make of radical disagreements in the interpretation of Scripture on matters fundamental? This, it seems to me, is the real basis of the new urgency we can notice in the questions of hermeneutics—essentially, the effort to identify, locate and make available the true and valid authority of God's word in and for man's religious reflections, wherever that word may be sought and heard. But this marks the end of Protestant biblicism.

For hermeneutics has long since passed from its locus in Scripture alone and has become ecclesiological in the strict sense. Where is there, if there is, an authoritative community that allows (or provides) for the reliable interpretation of Scripture—for the adjudication of contrary traditions of *sola Scriptura*? Or, to put the same question another way, is there a court of appeal for the hermeneuts—an obstreperous crew!—other than the ecclesial community? Subjective certainty is not a viable norm, nor are theological fads and fashions any more decisive. Thus, the question of "the infallibility of the Church" has taken on new poignancy as a problem for Protestant theology and, curiously enough, this coincides with a new nervousness about this same problem as it is being reviewed by Roman Catholics.

It was the *Decree on Ecumenism* and the *Declaration on Religious Freedom* that defined the rules for this continuing dialogue between Catholics and Protestants, but the substantive issues in that dialogue were established by the *Constitutions on the Church, on Divine Revelation, on the Sacred Liturgy,* and on *The Church in the Modern World,* as well as the *Decree on the Church's Missionary Activity,* which we have neglected this week. If we are to conceive of even the initial terms of the eventual unity of Christians, we Protestants must match the essays of *Lumen Gentium* with something like our own equivalents. In no other way can we really get beyond the present impasse, in which we are able to criticize the evident ambiguities of, say, *Lumen Gentium,* but not to promise much by way of a comparable mutation on our part, in our own sadly deficient ecclesiological traditions. Thus, for hermeneutics to serve the ecumenical cause means that, especially in Protestant circles, it must transcend its conventional perimeters of biblical theology and get past its present triflings with canons within the classical canon and of its advertisements of "solutions" that dispel the confusions of biblical doctrine without avowed ecclesiological presuppositions, and so forth and so on. Only so can we develop a truly biblical hermeneutics that includes the reality of the Church as the matrix of *truth* as well as *salvation*.

Fourthly, Vatican II has jolted the Protestant theological enterprise in the area of worship and liturgy—and not just in relation to our old stereotypes about ritual and true piety. Indeed, it may be the Romans will help us get over our recent muddlings in the "enrichment" of our rites and ceremonies and aid in the recovery of the biblical and patristic sense of liturgy as the creation, re-creation and sustenance of *the sacramental community*, not by the magical effects of ritual but by the miraculous action of God's grace in Christ in the community of faith and grace. This would bring with it a revival and re-presentation of many ancient notions—native, though, to classical Protestantism—notions about the People of God, the household of faith, the laity as the general priesthood who are the Church *in the world*, the Church in history and of history in the Church, eschatology as the *present* action of divine providence, the continuity and identity of the Christian message through the vicissitudes of the Church's historical experience.

Finally, this theological collaboration between Catholics and Protestants might just possibly give an impetus to the development of new patterns in the study and writing of Church history that would produce what I have elsewhere called "an ecumenical historiography," the history of the Christian *community*. History, so conceived, would not gloss over the ghastly truth about our estrangements, but it would not be as much concerned to justify them or to defend their consequences as to help us reconstruct them with a view to our being liberated from their entailments of prejudice. Thus, we might open up a new future in which we could transcend the past through the discovery of our common history as Christians. How else can we ever hope to find our way toward unity?

It would be worth another conference to extend and develop these tendencies and directions in Protestant theology today and tomorrow in the light of Vatican II and in the new theological atmosphere that is beginning to change our accustomed theological weather system. In these comments I have sketched them in barest outline, partly because of the pressures of time in an overloaded program, partly because I do not suppose that my half-formed notions here are magisterial, partly because the preconditions for a genuine theological consensus in the post-Conciliar age are still unclear and uncertain.

It is, however, clear enough that Roman Catholic and Protestant theology have now been brought into a new, dynamic interdependency; that the future of Roman Catholic and Protestant theologizing will parallel each other in the tasks and risks of communicating the gospel to the modern mind; that Protestant theology will be greatly strengthened and enriched in the dialogue; that the way back to the *status quo erat ante concilium* has been blocked, for you and for us too. For this new future and its prospects, we can thank Vatican II and its *partial* victory for what is now no longer "the new theology." But if we are to make much of this future—its call to renewal and the reintegration of the Christian community—we shall have to move forward together, in the love that casts out the fear of honest disagreement, in a sustained and mutual endeavor of study and dialogue, of Christian witness and service that may prepare us, or those who follow after, for God's gift of unity when it comes. This is, as far as I can see, our only hope; since Vatican II it has become a good hope that can uphold us in our labors and prayers. In the interim and on the way, we shall have to learn, better than we have known, how to speak and listen to each other so that we are able to share our mutual love as well as our respective notions. This, as I finally came to understand, was what Vatican II was trying to teach us all—and why it stands as *exemplum* for what may come hereafter.

Rev. Walter J. Burghardt, S.J.

VATICAN II AND CATHOLIC THEOLOGY IN AMERICA

I SUGGEST THAT, FOR A ROMAN CATHOLIC, the stuff of tomorrow's theology is compounded of three factors. There is, first, the primordial fact, the Christ-event, the blinding epiphany of God-in-flesh, witnessed by human eyes, heard by human ears, touched by human hands, preached by human lips, recorded in human letters on imperishable parchment. There is, second, the ceaseless effort of nineteen centuries, over an ever-expanding earth, to grasp this event and express it, to experience this person and respond to him, to explore that once-written word and lay open its wisdom, to deepen and broaden man's understanding of the once-for-all-given. There is, third, the immediate problem that confronts us in the present, that grows out of our situation: What meaning has the Christ-event for us? What relation has the revelation for the sixties, Christian theology for a post-Christian world, the re-presentation of a risen God for a world convinced that God is dead?

I am persuaded, therefore, that a realistic discussion of tomorrow's theology must grapple with these three facets of Christian experience. In consequence, my paper will deal successively with three points: the original revelation, the developing tradition, and the contemporary challenge. I shall spend relatively little time on the first two areas—not because they are relatively insignificant, but because a body of theologians such as sits in loving judgment before me may be presumed familiar with the significance of Scripture and tradition.

626

Rev. Walter J. Burghardt, s.j.

Vatican II and Catholic Theology in America

1. The Original Revelation

In theology man speaks about God. But before man could speak about God, God had to speak to man. The root of all theologizing is revelation, God's epiphany, his self-manifestation to men. Theology stems from a centuries-long wedding of words and deeds whereby an invisible, inaccessible God revealed and realized his plan to redeem man's intelligence and his freedom, to show himself to the creatures of his shaping and to draw them into fellowship with the Father through the Son in the Spirit.

This epiphany, this self-disclosure of God, goes back to the first dialogue of God with men: to the first love, the first sin, the first death. It goes back to Abraham ("I will make of you a great nation"), to God's choice of Israel to play a decisive role in the history of salvation, to Abraham's response in faith as he leaves his country and his kindred and his father's house. It goes back to Moses and the prophets, as God teaches his people through exile and exodus, through tears and laughter, through life and death, to confess the one living Lord and wait with hushed expectancy for the savior he has promised. It goes back to the midpoint of history, when God speaks to man not through angels or prophets but through his Son, when the spoken word is the eternal Word, God meeting man in the womb of a virgin. It goes back to a feeding trough in Bethlehem and an empty tomb outside Jerusalem.

It is this revelation, this self-disclosure of God, that lies at the root of theology. The work of theology does not begin in abstraction; the theologian does not operate with both feet firmly planted in mid-air. Theology begins with, has its roots in, fact—fact that is at once history and mystery: something was done, something was said, someone appeared. That is why one of the critical questions in contemporary theology is, what precisely is revelation? And that is why one of the crucial documents for tomorrow's theology is the *Constitution on Divine Revelation*.[1]

What, in the view of Vatican II, is revelation? It is the invisible, hidden God emerging from the mystery that is God, breaking his eternal silence to enter into dialogue with men, inviting man to share in the intimate life of Father, Son, and Holy Spirit. To define revelation, the Council retains an age-old analogy, familiar to Old Testament and New: revelation is word. God has spoken to man; it is by his word that God breaks the infinite barrier that separates him from all that is not God. Revelation as word, however, should not be narrowly conceived. In point of fact, as the Council makes clear, revelation is an intimate wedding of words and works: "This plan of revelation is realized by deeds and words having an inner unity: the deeds wrought by God in the history of salvation manifest and confirm the teaching and realities signified by the words, while the words proclaim the deeds and clarify the mystery contained in them" (art. 2).

627

The Council's *Constitution on Divine Revelation* stresses several insights that are basic for Catholic theology. In the first place, the high point of revelation, its apex, its fullness, its consummation, is Christ. Why? Because Christ is *the* Word of God who as man speaks to men the words of God. Crucial here is the realism and the uniqueness of the incarnation. The new revelation is indeed continuous with the old, but it surpasses the old beyond human telling, for God in person is the revelation. "He who sees me sees my Father."

Second, the way in which the Word of God disclosed the mystery of God is consonant with God's self-disclosure through all the Old Testament: it was a remarkable junction of words and works:

> Jesus perfected revelation by fulfilling it through His whole work of making Himself present and manifesting Himself: through His words and deeds, His signs and wonders, but especially through His death and glorious resurrection from the dead and final sending of the Spirit of truth. Moreover, He confirmed with divine testimony what revelation proclaimed, that God is with us to free us from the darkness of sin and death, and to raise us up to life eternal (art. 4).

Third, this revelation that was God-in-flesh is not a passing phase, a transitory stage, in God's self-disclosure; it will not be supplanted by another disclosure that is more perfect. In Christ God has spoken his unique Word, his perfect Word, his total Word. "The Christian dispensation, therefore, as the new and definitive covenant, will never pass away, and we now await no further new public revelation before the glorious manifestation of our Lord Jesus Christ" (art. 4).

This is revelation, the original revelation, at its sketchiest, in skeleton form.[2] I mention it even so sketchily because apart from the original revelation of God in Christ *Christian* theology is impossible. I may indeed be talking about God, but I am not talking about God as he has manifested his mystery to me in history, as he has shown his face to me in the person of his Son. The theological enterprise, therefore, demands of me a ceaseless effort to understand what revelation really is, to grasp what it means to say that Jesus Christ is the fullness of God's revelation, the complete and perfect expression of God's communication with man. It demands that I immerse myself more and more deeply in one book, because in that one book the original revelation is recorded—recorded by men, of course, but under the inspiration of the Holy Spirit. An imperative demand, for, as St. Jerome remarked bluntly fifteen centuries ago, "Ignorance of Scripture is ignorance of Christ." For the sake of tomorrow's theology, I dare not proclaim proudly that I have searched *The Secular City* if I have not plumbed the sacred page, that Harvey Cox has spoken to me but Jesus Christ has not.

2. THE DEVELOPING TRADITION

A second facet of Christian theology is the developing tradition. I mean the anguished effort of the centuries to apprehend the epiphany of God and express it, to experience the person of Christ and respond to him, to explore that once-written word and relate it to the changing problems of the ages.

As I see it, a present peril to theology is a narrowness that is not uncommon. All too many Christians today—committed Christians too—are persuaded that nothing of substance has happened between the original revelation and their own experience, nothing of consequence has taken place between God's blinding disclosure of himself and their own vision of what is real and relevant.

In this connection an editorial that appeared in *Life* Magazine some years back is splendidly suggestive.[3] The editorial was entitled "Welcome, Son, Who Are You?" The subtitle ran: "Self-knowledge is helped by the study of history, starting with one's own." Pointing to the fact that the American college undergraduate was about to come home for the Easter vacation, the writer observed that at the moment "the young sobersides" were above all concerned with knowing themselves; their first question as students was "Who am I?" The editorial went on to say:

> Lest this useful search [for identity] be suspended for the holidays, we suggest a suitable ice-breaking topic for tongue-tied parents. It is the role of history, not only in the college curriculum but in the outlook for Western man today. Anyone who wants to know who he is should start by finding out where he came from and where he's been. The quest will also tell him something about the present world and his relation to it. For an individual or a nation, there lies the utility of historical knowledge.

"Anyone who wants to know who he is should start by finding out where he came from and where he's been." This is true of every man, of every Christian; it is strikingly true of the college or university man, the college or university Christian. If the student of theology, the educated Christian, is to answer the question "Who are you?" he must be prepared to answer the question "Where do you come from?" The point is: as believing Christian on the one hand, as questing Christian on the other, I come in large measure from the past, from tradition—tradition understood as the movement of Christian thought and life down the ages.[4]

Here two aspects of the past are of supreme significance for the future. The first is dogma. Take, as one example from among many, the First Council of Nicaea in 325. Here is where dogma is first proclaimed: "One Lord Jesus Christ . . . out of the substance of the Father . . . begotten, not made . . . consubstantial with the Father. . . ." Now it is not my contention that a dogma is the last word on some facet of God's revelation; it is often enough only a springboard for theology, for the unending effort to understand. This much, however, must be said: within Catholic theology, there is no going back on a dogma, no retreating from Nicaea. Nicaea may not be unchangeable, but it is irreversible. Very bluntly: having come this far, we cannot refuse to come this far.[5] And so it is with all dogma: with the Council of Ephesus and the dogma of one person in Christ, with the Council of Florence and the dogma of the procession of the Spirit from the Father and the Son, with Vatican I and the dogma of papal infallibility, with Pius XII and the dogma of the assumption. Dogma, in the Catholic sense, stems from a progressively deeper understanding by the Church of the revelation once and for all given in Christ, an understanding open to change but not to contradiction. Unless Catholic theology takes seriously the dogmas of the past, the theology is not quite Catholic.

A second crucial issue that involves historical understanding, an issue intimately linked with the problem of dogma, is the issue of doctrinal development. To be concrete, take the question of Mary. After the concept of the Church, the single theological issue that most effectively strangles the ecumenical dialogue is the Catholic vision of our Lady. For Mary is "the wall"—if only because she is, for many a Protestant, the visible symbol of Catholic idolatry: the Roman abandonment of Scripture, of history, of Christ.[6]

Here the Catholic theologian is confronted with a serious problem. How do I justify on theological lines, on the level of faith in quest of understanding, the transition from the biblical mode of conception and expression to the conciliar, the pontifical, the dogmatic? The humble maid of Nazareth, bringing forth in a stable, deeply perplexed at one moment and highly confident at another, silent beneath a cross and articulate in common prayer, seeking her Son in sorrow as boy and as man—how do I explain the transition from this descriptive mode of expression to the articulated, technical, definitional propositions which make of Mary the mother not merely of a finite man but of a timeless God, virgin not only before Gabriel but days without end, sinless not simply from the age of reason but from the very womb of Anne, glorious before the face of God not simply in soul but in body incorruptible?

It is not the function of this paper to answer these questions. The point I am making, by select examples, is that the Catholic theology of tomorrow dare not leap lyrically from the first century to the twentieth, from the original revelation to the latest experience, from the pulsing page of Scripture to the living heart of contemporary man. Catholic theology is inescapably involved in tradition, in the Church's ceaseless effort over the centuries to plumb the meaning of God's self-disclosure to men. Original revelation and developing tradition—these lead naturally to my third and perhaps most significant point: today's theological crisis.

3. Today's Theological Crisis

For me as a theologian, one of the most frightening and at the same time most stimulating articles I have ever read appeared in *New Blackfriars* this past September. The author is a perceptive Dominican, Fergus Kerr. The title of his article is "Theology in a Godforsaken Epoch."[7] Kerr begins with a presupposition:

> all Catholic theology occurs in the first place within the context of some Church-mediated experience of God. This does not mean reducing theology to spirituality or to the conceptual elaboration of personal piety. It is simply saying that theology requires a starting-point, a source of intelligibility, which is encounter with God himself: for without some prior relationship to its "object" theology can never be anything more fundamental than the philological investigation of more or less ancient documents. . . . Doing theology at all depends on hearing the word of God: God must be allowed to speak to us before we can begin to speak about him.[8]

Given this presupposition, Kerr's root affirmation is that today the experience of God, our encounter with God, the way God speaks to us, is radically different from yesterday. We live in a different epoch.

> An epoch occurs when the role of some of our most basic activities is transformed, when the very sense of some of our keywords changes. It is no use having an abstract conception of human nature which is supposed to define what is essential about man in any epoch. . . . If we were to speak of man in terms of "rational animal" we should have to allow for the enormous differences between what we mean by reason now and what *ratio* meant for the medievals; while *logos* meant something related, yet something very different again, for the Greeks, and none of these notions had any meaning for Jeremiah and Amos.[9]

A new epoch, however, is not arbitrary—just as, Kerr points out, painting is not arbitrary:

> We don't simply *choose* to paint in some particular style . . . : of course we could paint like the ancient Egyptians if we wanted to, but this would only be imitation and reproduction, it would not be "our" sort of painting because we simply don't "see" the world any longer in the way they apparently did—we don't see it any better or any worse, only very differently. . . . An epoch is a whole generation rising to the occasion and showing the requisite energy in responding to what has befallen it.[10]

An epoch, Kerr observes, has "its genius, its particular creative and inventive capacities, its prevalent feeling, taste, ideology, its character and spirit—

its vocation even."[11] What is this genius of an epoch, this something unique, something original, something unrepeatable?

It is . . . the consensus about ideals and standards in human experience which is registered and communicated in the anonymity of the common language of a generation. It is a consensus about what is meaningful at all, about what counts as sense in the first place. . . . It is a consensus about what is . . . obvious and simply beyond argument; it is a consensus manifested in one's sense of priorities, in one's sense of what counts as relevant, worthwhile and significant, or pointless and ridiculous. It is one's perception in community of the totality of meaning which constitutes the context in which words like "real," "true," "beautiful," "Nature," "history," "love," "God," etc., can have any sense [i.e., direction] in the first place.[12]

It is this sense of what is meaningful "which generates an epoch—and it is this which changes. It is only in this total context that we can have any experience at all, that we can talk and think and make love and make bombs and do theology. It is this instinct for what matters, this preliminary sense of direction, which changes from one epoch to another."[13]

In this new epoch, how does one, how can one, experience God? He "seems to have withdrawn, to have ceased to make himself accessible in many of the ways that have hitherto been viable. The way of life as a whole is not affording the experience of God it would seem to be the structure for."[14] The traditional treatises in theology not only fail to make God more intelligible, more "visible," more available; they sometimes make it more difficult to discover him. The institutions we take for granted, the institutions in which we exist, seem to be Godforsaken. What does this mean?

A Godforsaken form of life is a form of life from which God has withdrawn, in which God gives himself now only in ways which either run counter to the traditions and customs of the particular form of life in question or anyway in ways which are more or less unrelated to them.[15]

It is in this experience that theology must renew itself—that is, in the experience of the present Godforsakenness of the milieu itself. The point is, "for believers at large, and particularly for religious, *encounter with God seems to occur now primarily in experiencing his absence*."[16] In other words, "it is the fate of our epoch that the encounter we have with God, the encounter which must precede and sustain all theological exploration and understanding, takes the form mostly of failing to find him in the system of institutions and structures which constitutes our tradition."[17]

With reference primarily to the vocation to religious life—but implicitly too for the life of the whole Church—Kerr concludes on a note that is paradoxically depressing and promising:

We have just to be patient, to wait, to practise a very provisional sort of theology (pro-visional = forward-looking, not "progressive" but eschatological), to create meanwhile whatever real personal relations, whatever fraternity in depth, it may be given to us to experience. St. Augustine once said that *veritas est in caritate*: perhaps one might translate that as meaning that the truth which is theology will occur only in the context of personal relationships, only in and from the community experience which Christian love is surely still capable of originating and sustaining even in a milieu which seems formally "Godforsaken."[18]

In line with this insight into a new era, the historian Thomas Berry has focused on three characteristics of the contemporary world that differentiate it radically from the old. First, its universalism. There simply are no isolated islands—whether nations or cultures or continents. "The thoughts and problems of one man are now the thoughts and problems of the entire world. The creative work of one part of the world is shared almost instantly by the entire world." Second, this new world is not fixed, not static; it is developmental, dynamic. The reality of structures is change. And so we speak "not of cosmos but of cosmogenesis, not of fixed species but of biogenesis, not of mankind as a determined reality but of anthropogenesis, for man is making himself at the same time as he is in a manner making the world." Third, humanism. Contemporary man centers not on some cosmic order, not on the divine, not on God, but on man.[19]

Given this root newness in contemporary man and his world, tomorrow's theology dare not simply mouth yesterday's. Vatican II has suggested broad lines of direction which a theology in tune with the times must take. Such a theology will be at once more authentically *biblical and historical*; for it will wrestle with the once-for-all-given (not as isolated proof-texts, but as the biblical "event" in its original contexts) and the progressive (and retrogressive) efforts of the Christian ages to grasp it and express it and live it and touch it to new generations—the problem of history-and-theology of which Joseph Sittler has spoken so eloquently. Tomorrow's theology will be more *anthropological*, in that it will search out man as he is, with flesh and bones, inwardly divided because at once sin-full and still God's image, alternating between hope and despair, love and hate, life and death. It will be more *pastoral*, not in the sense of "instant application," fast-working bromides for confessor and counselor, rather in that its burning questions will rise in significant measure from the anguish of contemporary man, and will never lose from sight the People of God in whose service theology operates—yes, even the vast and growing majority of men who know not Christ and care not. It will be more *ecumenical*, in that "Protestants and Others Disunited" will not be primarily adversaries but co-operators in a common concern, the effort of faith not simply to understand but to unite in love. It will be more *eschatological*, not in a lyric leap to a more abiding abode, but in its awareness of a pilgrim people in movement now and tomorrow and every day, through the demonic and the salvific, to the consummation of their corporate oneness in Christ.

Tomorrow's theology will be different from yesterday's. Paradoxically, it is already different. If any single expression can focus the difference, I suggest it is the *person;* more accurately, *person within community.* I mean person as set over against thing; truth as it touches me in contrast to truth in itself; reality in its relation to living persons rather than reality somewhere "out there"; interpersonal encounter in place of isolated independence.

Let me concretize what may have sounded dreadfully abstract. In dealing with *revelation,* it is no longer legitimate for the theologian to put the major stress on God's formal utterance, be it the commandments from Sinai or the Sermon on the Mount. The words are important, of course—as are the events of salvation history; but the words, like the events, are only the vehicle of revelation, not the revelation itself. Revelation is God's self-disclosure, whereby a divine person communicates himself, a community of divine persons communicate themselves, to a human person, to a community of persons, and the human person and human community react with a personal response that is intelligent love.[20]

In *Trinitarian* theology, the primary emphasis will no longer fall on what is called the "ontological" Trinity—the inner relations between the three persons, origin, procession, consubstantiality. It will fall rather on the "functional" Trinity—the mission of the Spirit from the Father through the Son into the heart of the believer. Correspondingly, the treatment of *grace* will give less place to created grace as an accident, a quality, a habit modifying the substance of the soul. The stress will be (where indeed the more perceptive theologian has put it in the past) on Trinitarian presence, on uncreated grace, on the promise of Christ: "If any man love me, my Father will love him, and we will come to him and make our home with him." Grace will be seen more and more as, on God's side, God offering himself to man, communicating his life to man, demanding from man love and fidelity; on man's side, man offering himself to God, man transformed, shaped to Christ. A profoundly personal encounter, therefore: not simply or primarily a Scholastic category, but living persons intimately linked in loving union.[21]

In *sacramental* theology, the accent can no longer fall on the number seven, on the external rite or ceremony, on validity, on efficacity *ex opere operato,* important as these issues are. What will be stressed is that in these symbolic acts, more than anywhere else, the Church encounters the individual, and in this encounter with the Church the individual encounters Christ. Not simply in some idea of him, some image or picture of him; not only the ontological oneness that is so crucial; but even an intuition of him (dark, yes, but thrillingly true) that comes from loving surrender to him—

an interaction of knowledge and love.[22] Just as Christ is the sacrament of God's love, so all the sacraments which Christ has designed within his Church are the presence of the same Christ in the remarkable richness of his love for the human persons purchased with his blood.

Faith itself will be seen not primarily as an intellectual assent to propositions (integral as such assent is to faith), but as total response to divine initiative, commitment of the whole person to Christ.

In the area of *ecclesiology* too, the direction will be different. This fresh development was heralded in the early days of Vatican II, when Emile De Smedt, Bishop of Bruges, took serious issue with the original schema on the Church. After taxing the draft with triumphalism and clericalism, he leveled against it the charge of legalism. What we need to recapture from the primitive Church, he said, is the concept of the Church as mother:

> All the baptized are children of the Church. By valid baptism all Christians are born of Mother Church. However they live, in whatever Christian community, they are by right children of the Church. Her children they remain always; Christian blood they have always in their veins. In point of fact, they are all brothers and sisters, and they remain brothers and sisters even when they are separated from the rest of the brethren. The bond of birth is never lost; they never lose the love of Mother Church for her children, be they close by or far off.

In the light of all this, the Bishop continued, read the draft and you will see how far wrong you can go if you look at the Church in a sheerly juridical—better, an aprioristic—fashion. Take the matter of membership in the Church. The schema begins by establishing, a priori, what is demanded if the notion of member is to be applied to any individual. He alone is a member of the Church who . . . *Atqui* . . . *Ergo*. The rest are not members in the proper sense.

> This way of speaking [the Bishop lashed out] is not good theology, nor is it worthy of the Church if she is genuinely a mother. What mother has ever asserted about the son to whom she gave birth, whom she cherishes with her love —if for some sorrow-laden reason he no longer lives in his father's house and with his brothers and sisters—what true mother has ever asserted: he is no longer a member of my family? Blood speaks with a different voice. It is not proper for Mother Church to speak like this. Unworthy of Mother Church is such apriorism, such an exercise in minor logic.

In line with Vatican II's *Constitution on the Church*, tomorrow's ecclesiology will lay less stress on the juridical elements in the Church, more on the transcendent, the Church as mystery, because filled with the presence of God; less emphasis on the vertical, the hierarchical, the Church as pyramid from pope to people, more emphasis on the horizontal, on the community of all the baptized, on the common priesthood of the faithful

635

as prior in God's design to the structure that divides—emphasis, therefore, on the whole People of God as one community of service, of worship, of love. Emphasis, consequently, on what unites the churches, the sects, the denominations, the Christian communities; separated brethren seen more as brethren than as separated.

The theology of redemption, *soteriology*, will pay less heed to retributive justice, will stress as the goal of Christ's redeeming activity the new covenant between God and man—a covenant that puts in clear relief the loving initiative of the Father, revealed and made present in the Son enfleshed, and the need of the human community and the individual person to add their love-laden yes to Christ's filial response to the Father.

The "last things," *eschatology*, will take on new personal dimensions. Death for a Christian has never been a biological fact that calls for a "stiff upper lip." But over and above that, death must be seen not primarily as a punishment for sin to be accepted with Christian resignation, but rather as something *I do*: it is my final option, my definitive decision, to share in the redemptive death of Christ or to abide inescapably in sin. Even hell will appear in a more personalist perspective: utter frustration of the whole person, endless alienation from Life, endless absence of Love—such total aloneness that even creation is hostile, even flesh and blood will not comfort. And heaven? The emphasis will hardly be on the vision of God "face to face," mind in immediate contact with the living God, significant as this is. The accent will fall on perfect fulfillment in loving union: *I, this selfsame person*, ceaselessly and ecstatically one with Father, Son, and Holy Spirit, one with the community of love—never a cold thing, abstract, depersonalized, always a warm relationship that touches the core of each person, human and divine.

Tomorrow's *moral* theology will be more obviously based on the gospel. It will find its center in New Testament love: Christian morality is a loving response to the love of God revealed in Christ, a response tested and proved indeed in day-to-day fidelity to the law of Christ, but still and always a response of love.

This is not to say that love can ever be all-sufficient, that traditional concepts like right and justice are outmoded. Wilfrid Cross put it pungently when he wrote:

> Bishop Robinson seems in *Honest to God* to think that we can dispense with all this paraphernalia of right and justice because love has an inbuilt compass that "homes" it on to the gist of the issue. Canon Rhymes endorses the compass theory of love with enthusiasm. Canon Demant in answer to the compass theory refers to a loving elephant who seeing an ostrich leave her nest to get a drink of water went and sat on her eggs to keep them warm. Love can be a fuddy-duddy elephantine thing.[23]

In the new morality love will surely be primary, because love alone can ensure a person-to-person relationship with Christ; but even in the new morality love will need direction: from justice, from law, from conscience, from the accumulated experience of men, from the Church.[24]

Such, on very broad lines, promises to be tomorrow's theology; such is already in some measure today's theology. The original revelation, of course, remains in all its pristine power; the developing tradition too, with its doctrinal formulations and its ceaseless effort to understand—but all this in a fresh context, where the moving forces, the thrilling ideas, are person and community, commitment and action, responsibility and response, encounter and experience, liberty and love, and so on and so forth.

A theology thus orientated, so structured, calls for a manner of philosophizing adequate to its specialized demands. It means, in the first place, that every theologian in yesterday's tradition (and I say frankly "include me in") must face up to (not admit uncritically, but face up to) a serious charge: traditional Scholasticism, because it conceives too narrowly the experiential foundation of philosophy, cannot sustain tomorrow's theology. The Jesuit philosopher Robert Johann, first-rate metaphysician and no iconoclast, has seen the problem clearly and expressed it incisively.[25]

First, traditional Thomism is built solely on cognitive experience; man is essentially a knower. But "an age like our own, increasingly concerned with man's temporal destiny and inclined to view theory only as a function in the process of man's temporal development, will find this identification of human perfection with abstract knowledge quite unacceptable."[26]

Second, the experience that founds traditional Scholastic philosophy is limited to the experience of making judgments, and so the philosophy that results is a philosophy of natures. "To an age, however, that has newly discovered the person and is passionately concerned with the emphatically personal realms of responsibility, identity, liberty and love, such a limitation will appear intolerable."[27]

Third, traditional Scholastic philosophy seems "unable in principle to fulfil the traditional aspiration of philosophy, namely, to grasp the whole of the real and the real as a whole." For it comes to grips "only with the objective face of the real. Being as subject [eludes] its grasp."[28] "Is it then surprising that contemporary man, so desperately in search of wholeness, is not attracted to a philosophy which cannot in principle provide what he looks for?"[29]

This is not a call to abandon Scholastic philosophy. It does demand, however, that the Scholastic philosopher and the Scholastic theologian face honestly a question crucial to their very existence: Can Scholasticism so broaden its base of experience as to incorporate the experience that is so meaningful to modern man? I mean the experience which Johann defines as "the dynamic interrelation of the self and the world, grasped, not objectively, but from within, insofar as the self, as self, is present to both itself and the world as co-constituents of an open yet all-inclusive whole."[30] I mean the experience in which the world "is not merely the world of things" but "also, and more importantly, the world of persons, of other selves."[31] I mean that experience which is "never a closed circle" but "always open to further development."[32] I mean not simply the experience that is "expressed and formulated in judgments" but the experience that is "knowledge in action, in terms of which the world is present, not as expressly known, but as lived in."[33] I mean the experience that permits philosophy to achieve its "aspiration to grasp the whole of the real and the real as a whole."[34]

It is the contention of respected philosophers and respectable theologians that a philosophy responsive to these demands must shun two extremes: at one pole, simple relegating Scholasticism without further ado to the slag pile of the past; at the other pole, simply attaching contemporary insights like some tail to Scholasticism's posterior. It is their contention that philosophy must be radically restructured, that without such root renewal theologians will go on talking to themselves and not to the world they breathe, and theology itself will fail to fulfil its exciting function: to be, oh not the queen of the sciences, but their servant.

It is the function of theology to be a servant. In our time this demands service on three levels: the City of God, the City of Man, and what I can only call the No-City.[35] Theology must serve, as she has always served, the man committed above all to God; theology must serve, as she has rarely served, the man committed only to man; and theology must serve, as she has never served, the man committed to Nothing (Nothing with a capital N).

This man committed to Nothing is a frightening phenomenon of our time. It is an attitude toward reality that stems from at least four sources: (1) a creeping collectivism, where "the people" suppresses the individual; (2) a growing dehumanization, symbolized by Dachau, the mushroom cloud, and the shelter doorway; (3) an increasing automation, represented by the IBM card; (4) the apparent failure of organized religion to redeem the world. In this attitude, man's dignity and his hope lie in his ability to confront, with courage and indeed with joy, a life and a reality that is senseless, useless, absurd. Man is alone, isolated, a stranger to himself, to the world, to God. The hell of Jean Paul Sartre—hell is other people—has given place to the hell of Ingmar Bergman—hell is being alone.

This affirmation of Nothing leaps out at you from the creative arts: from the painting of a Pollock, through the music of a Cage, to the poetry of a Kazantzakis. It is splendidly epitomized by Samuel Beckett: two times anything equals zero.

This affirmation of Nothing does not necessarily lead to despair. Quite the contrary, if we can believe, as I think we must, the self-disclosure of Kazantzakis in a letter written some years ago:

> In man's world, the success or defeat of the spirit depends on man himself, and the upward path is one of unceasing, ruthless, and bloody strife. To a man who erects his home on the Abyss, this challenge does not lead to despair or suicide but to acceptance of necessity in joy, to laughter on the highest peaks of existence, and finally to a creative "play" with tragic elements in an ecstasy of joy.[36]

The challenge to tomorrow's theology of service is provocative, intoxicating, somewhat frightening. Let me close with a moving paragraph in which Avery Dulles has recently voiced his concern over an ecumenism in danger of overemphasizing the past, an ecumenism of interest to only an elite because it does not take its stand in the midst of living men:

> From many quarters . . . one hears the call for a new ecumenism—one less committed to historical theological controversies and more in touch with contemporary secular man; one less turned in upon itself, more open to the world and its concerns. The great decisions affecting man's future are being made in the sphere of the secular; and Christianity does not seem to be there. A cry to all the churches rises up from the heart of modern man: "Come to us where we are. Help us to make the passage into the coming technocratic age without falling into the despair and brutality of a new paganism. Teach us sincere respect and affection for our fellow men. If the charity of the Good Samaritan burns in your hearts, show that you share our desires and aspirations. In our struggle to build the city of man, we need the support which your faith and hope alone can give. If you remain comfortably in your churches and cloisters, we are much afraid that God will become a stranger to modern life. Christianity, secluded in a world of its own, will turn into a mere relic to be cherished by a few pious souls."[37]

NOTES

1. See the helpful commentary by René Latourelle, S.J., "La révélation et sa transmission selon la constitution 'Dei verbum,'" *Gregorianum* 47 (1966) 5–40.

2. For a more adequate treatment of revelation and the problems it raises, cf. Gabriel Moran, F.S.C., "What Is Revelation?" *Theological Studies* 25 (1964) 217–31. The standard Catholic monograph on the subject is Latourelle's *Théologie de la révélation* (Bruges: Desclée de Brouwer, 1963); see the careful summary and critique by Avery Dulles, S.J., "The Theology of Revelation," *Theological Studies* 25 (1964) 43–58.

3. *Life* (March 16, 1959) 32.

4. Cf. Walter J. Burghardt, S.J., "The Fathers of the Church: Obsolete or Relevant?" *Proceedings of the Society of Catholic College Teachers of Sacred Doctrine, Tenth Annual Convention, 1964* (Weston, Mass.: Regis College, 1964) 17–35, esp. 30 ff.

5. Cf. John Courtney Murray, S.J., *The Problem of God Yesterday and Today* (New Haven: Yale University Press, 1964) 33–60.

6. Cf. Walter J. Burghardt, S.J., "Mary and Reunion," *Catholic Mind* 60 (1962) 13–18.

7. Fergus Kerr, O.P., "Theology in a Godforsaken Epoch," *New Blackfriars* 46 (1965) 665–72.

8. *Ibid.*, 665.

9. *Ibid.*, 667.

10. *Ibid.*, 668.

11. *Ibid.*

12. *Ibid.*

13. *Ibid.*

14. *Ibid.*, 670.

15. *Ibid.*

16. *Ibid.*, 671; italics mine.

17. *Ibid.*

18. *Ibid.*, 672.

19. Cf. Thomas Berry, C.P., "The Threshold of the Modern World," *Proceedings of the Teilhard Conference 1964* (New York: Fordham University, n.d.) 57–69, esp. 57–59. From our "radically new ways of seeing the world" and from his conviction that our "new knowledge is not derived from the old but emerges from immediate experience of reality such as man has apparently never known before," Berry draws a provocative conclusion: "This time no simple adjustment can be made between the old and the new. Certainly the new cannot be considered as merely an addendum to the old" (57).

20. Cf. Moran, *art. cit.*, 225: "Both Catholic and Protestant writers today insist that revelation does not consist in doctrines or in statements but in the historical saving actions of God. Although this is a step forward in the understanding of divine revelation, this still leaves room for misunderstanding. Revelation does not consist in doctrines, revelation does not consist in statements; but neither does revelation consist in historical events. The *magnalia Dei* is, of course, a richer expression and a wider category than doctrinal statement; but whatever happens in history or whatever is in a book can only be a symbol mediating revelation. Our irrespressible tendency to objectify makes us think and speak of God 'up there,' man 'down here,' and revelation 'out there.' But there is no revelation 'out there'; there is God revealing, man believing, and there is no revelation unless it is received. When the word 'revelation' is used as a noun in the objective sense and when one asks where this exists, the only answer would seem to be: in the consciousness of man. Man does not believe in statements or truths, nor does he believe in events; he believes in God revealed in human experience and consciousness." See also the intriguing thesis of Karl Rahner that the history of revelation is not just a series of discrete, arbitrary interventions from on high, but, from the human side, may be viewed as the self-transcending action by which man, under the leading of God's salvific providence, progressively interprets to himself his own inner ordination to the divine (cf. Karl Rahner and Joseph Ratzinger, *Offenbarung und Überlieferung* [Freiburg: Herder, 1965] 11–24).

21. Cf. Pierre Fransen, "Towards a Psychology of Divine Grace," *Cross Currents* 8 (1958) 211–32.

22. Cf. Walter J. Burghardt, S.J., "Christian Encounter," *Catholic Mind* 63 (1965) 15–22.

23. Wilfrid O. Cross, "The No-New Morality," *American Church Quarterly* 5 (1965) 223.

24. I have been speaking, obviously, in terms of traditional theological "tracts," and it may well be that the "Christian in action," from Appalachia to Africa, will shake his head sadly at such monstrous irrelevance. This is indeed theology, for it is talking about God and about the image of God; but is it saying anything *to man*? To this question I would at present address two remarks, while recognizing that the hard-core issues implied in the objection merit serious discussion. First, the "tract" examples I have selected are simply that—examples, and nothing more: examples of the fresh personal dimension that is enriching theology and cannot but have a strong impact in recasting whole areas of theology that concern, e.g., the social worker and the sociologist. Second, in the post-Conciliar age there must be intimate interaction between theology and the sciences; they must, in Msgr. Joseph Gremillion's burning yearning, "learn to nourish each other in ever more meaningful manner and degree"; there must be "task forces, working parties, of theologians who address themselves variously to the large problem areas of this-world."

25. See Johann's article "Experience and Philosophy," in *Experience, Existence, and the Good: Essays in Honor of Paul Weiss*, ed. Irwin C. Lieb (Carbondale: Southern Illinois University Press, 1961) 25–38.

26. *Ibid.*, 26.

27. *Ibid.*

28. *Ibid.*

29. *Ibid.*, 27.

30. *Ibid.*

31. *Ibid.*

32. *Ibid.*, 28.

33. *Ibid.*, 29.

34. *Ibid.*, 37.

35. The remarks that follow on modern man committed to Nothing owe much to an insightful article by Karl Welton Kleinz, S.J., soon to appear in the journal *Renascence*.

36. See the Introduction to Nikos Kazantzakis, *The Odyssey: A Modern Sequel*, tr. Kimon Friar (New York: Simon and Schuster, 1958) xxi.

37. From a sermon at the National Shrine of the Immaculate Conception, Washington, D.C., Jan. 22, 1966; quoted in *Catholic Mind* 64, no. 1203 (May, 1966) 31–32.

CONFERENCE PRINCIPALS

Rev. Barnabas Ahern is a member of the Passionist Fathers, ordained 1941. He studied Scripture at the Ecole Biblique, Jerusalem, and in Rome, where he received his doctorate in 1958. His writings include: *New Horizons, Commentary on Romans and Galatians;* he is co-editor of the *Bible Today.* He is past president of the American Catholic Biblical Association. He was "peritus" to the Council; consultor to the Secretariat for Christian Unity and to the mixed commission for the drafting of the Conciliar document *On Revelation;* and "peritus" to the commission on the Church in the modern world. He is a permanent consultor to the pontifical Biblical Commission.

Rev. Walter J. Burghardt, a Jesuit priest, studied theology at the Catholic University of America, where he received his S.T.D. He has been teaching patristic theology at Woodstock College since 1946. He is managing editor of *Theological Studies,* and co-editor of the series *Ancient Christian Writers.* He is author of several books and of many articles in theological journals. He is a member of the Baltimore Archdiocesan Commission on Christian Unity; of the Catholic Commission on Intellectual and Cultural Affairs; of the Ecumenical Institute for Advanced Theological Studies in Jerusalem.

Abbot Christopher Butler, a member of the English Benedictines, studied at Oxford University 1920-1925. Received in the Catholic Church 1928. Ordained priest 1933. He served as Head Master of Downside School 1940-1946. He was

643

elected Abbot of Downside Abbey in 1946. He has been president of the English Benedictine Congregation since 1961. He was a member of the Doctrinal Commission of the Vatican Council. For years Abbot Butler has been a leading churchman in England.

MOST REV. CARLO COLOMBO was ordained priest of the archdiocese of Milan, Italy, in 1931. He was consecrated bishop of the titular diocese of Vittoriana in 1964. He was president of the Istituto "Giuseppe Toniolo," in Milan. He is now president of the faculty of theology of the archdiocese of Milan. He edited and wrote articles for the two-volume work, *Problemi e Orientamenti di Teologia Dommatica*.

REV. YVES M. J. CONGAR is a member of the Order of Preachers in France. An internationally known theologian, he is the author of such outstanding books as *Lay People in the Church; The Mystery of the Church; Christ, Our Lady and the Church*, and has contributed many articles to scholarly theological journals. He is also editor of the *Unam Sanctam* series, of which some forty volumes have appeared to date. He was active as a "peritus" in the Council. His book, *Chrétiens Déunis*, written decades ago, pioneered in ecumenism among Catholics.

REV. HENRI DE LUBAC, a Jesuit priest, is honorary professor of the Faculté de Théologie Catholique, Lyons, France, and member of the Institut de France (Académie des sciences morales). He was consultor to the theological commission for the preparation of the Council, and served actively as "peritus" to the Council's sessions. Among his many writings are *The Splendour of the Church* and *The Drama of Atheistic Humanism*.

REV. GODFREY L. DIEKMANN, a member of the Order of Benedictines, received his S.T.D. from the College of Sant' Anselmo, Rome, and pursued further graduate studies in liturgy at the Abbey of Maria Laach in Germany. He was associated with Father Virgil Michel in editing *Orate Fratres*, and has been editor-in-chief of *Worship* since 1938. He is professor of patrology in the Benedictine Major Seminary at Collegeville, and of theology at St. John's University. He served as consultor to the preparatory commission on the liturgy and as a "peritus" to the Council itself. He is a member of the Post-Conciliar Commission for the Implementation of the *Constitution on the Sacred Liturgy*.

VERY REV. JOSEPH GREMILLION was born in Moreauville, Louisiana, and ordained to the priesthood in 1943. He did graduate studies at the Catholic University of America, and the Gregorian University, Rome, where he received his doctorate. He wrote: *The Catholic Movement of Employers and Managers, The Journal of a Southern Pastor*, and *The Other Dialogue*. He served as pastor 1949-1958. For years he was associated with the Catholic Rural Life Conference. Since 1960 he has served on the Catholic Relief Services of the NCWC and directs its program for socio-economic development. In 1964 he was appointed observer to the U.S. Conference for the World Council of Churches. He is secretary to the post-

Conciliar group which is to promote development of the poor regions and social justice among nations.

REV. BERNARD HÄRING, a Redemptorist priest, was born in Böttingen, Germany. He studied theology at the University of Tübingen, and was closely associated with Prof. Romano Guardini. For a time he taught canon law and moral theology at the Redemptorist theologate in Germany. He had much to do with the founding of the Alphonsian Institute of graduate studies in moral theology. He is well known for his initiative and work toward the renewal of moral theology. Among his numerous writings is the three-volume *The Law of Christ*. He served as "peritus" to the Council. At present he is visiting professor of theology at Brown University.

RIGHT REV. GEORGE G. HIGGINS, ordained priest for the archdiocese of Chicago in 1940. Pursued graduate studies in economics and political science at the Catholic University of America, where he received his Ph.D. in 1944, and where he also taught for some years. He has been associated with the staff of the Social Action Department of the National Catholic Welfare Council since 1944, and was appointed director in 1954. He was a member of the preparatory commission on the lay apostolate for the Council, and served as "peritus" to the Council. He is the author of the weekly syndicated column, "The Yardstick."

ABBE FRANÇOIS HOUTART was born in Brussels, and ordained priest at Malines in 1949. He did graduate studies in social and political sciences at Louvain, and in America at the Universities of Indiana and Chicago. He has been director of the *Centre de Recherches Socio-Religieuses* since 1956. He is secretary-general of the *International Federation of Institutes of Social and Socio-Religious Research* (FERES). Since 1953 he has been in close contact with Latin American affairs.

DR. GEORGE A. LINDBECK was born in Loyang, China. He received his B.A. from Gustavus Adolphus College, his B.D. from Yale in 1946 and his Ph.D. in 1955. He has taught at Augustana and Upsala College. He has been teaching at Yale since 1949, where he is at present associate professor of historical theology. His major interest is in the history of medieval thought and contemporary Roman Catholicism. He is co-author of *The Papal Council and the Gospel*, and *Dialogue On The Way*.

MOST REV. MARK G. McGRATH, a member of the Congregation of Holy Cross, was born in Panama. He was ordained to the priesthood in 1949. He pursued graduate studies in theology at Paris, and the Angelicum, Rome, where he received his S.T.D. in 1953. He was dean of the faculty of theology at the Catholic University of Chile 1959-1961. He was appointed auxiliary bishop of Panama in 1961. In 1964 he was transferred to the Diocese of Santiago di Veraguas in the Republic of Panama. He served actively on the Council's Doctrinal Commission. He is member of the Post-Conciliar Commission for Nonbelievers and president of the Episcopal Commission of the Latin American Bishops for University Pastoral Action.

645

Right Rev. Jorge Medina Estevez was born in Santiago, Chile, and ordained to the priesthood in 1954. He studied theology at the Catholic University of Chile, where he received his doctorate in 1955. He has been professor of theology at the same university since 1956, and at present is dean of the faculty of theology. He has written articles for the journal, *Teologia y Vida*, on the diaconate and on the history of the Constitution "Lumen Gentium." He served as "peritus" to the Council, and is consultor to the Pontifical Commission for the Revision of Canon Law.

Very Rev. John Meyendorff was born in Paris, France, was educated at the Orthodox Theological Institute of Paris, and pursued graduate studies at the Sorbonne, where he received his doctorate. He came to the United States in 1959. He is professor of patristics and church history at St. Vladimir's Orthodox Theological Seminary. He is also lecturer in Byzantine theology at the Harvard Center for Byzantine Studies, and lecturer on Eastern Orthodox theology at Union Theological Seminary in New York. He is the author of *A Study of Gregory Palamas; The Orthodox Church, Its Role in the World Today; Orthodoxy and Catholicity*. He is a member of the Faith and Order Commission of the World Council of Churches.

Dr. Paul S. Minear was born in Mount Pleasant, Iowa. He studied at Wesleyan University, Garrett Biblical Institute, Northwestern University, and Yale where he received his Ph.D. in 1932. He was ordained to the ministry in the Methodist Church in 1938. He has taught at Garrett and Andover Newton Theological School. He has been professor of New Testament at the Yale Divinity School since 1956. Among his many writings are: *An Introduction to Paul, Eyes of Faith; The Kingdom and the Power; Christian Hope and the Second Coming; Images of the Church in the New Testament*. He was director of the Faith and Order Commission, World Council of Churches, in 1961, and chairman in 1963.

Canon Charles Moeller was born in Brussels. He received his doctorate in theology at Louvain in 1941, and has been professor of theology there since 1956. He served as "peritus" to the Council and collaborated in the formulation of the *Dogmatic Constitution On the Church, On Revelation, On Ecumenism, On Non-Christian Religions*. He is consultor to the Secretariat for Nonbelievers. He was recently appointed undersecretary of the Congregation for the Doctrine of the Faith (the reorganization of the former "Supreme Sacred Congregation of the Holy Office").

Rev. John Courtney Murray, a Jesuit priest, was born in New York City. He received his doctorate in theology at the Gregorian University in Rome in 1937, and since then has been professor of theology at Woodstock College, Maryland. Among his many writings are: *St. Augustine: Admonition and Grace; We Hold These Truths; The Problem of God; The Problem of Religious Freedom*. He is editor of *Theological Studies*. He served as "peritus" to the Council, where his work for the *Declaration on Religious Freedom* is well known. He is consultant to the Secretariat for the Promotion of Christian Unity and to the Secretariat for Nonbelievers.

JAMES J. NORRIS attended high school in Elizabeth, N. J., and received his A.B. degree at the Catholic University of America. He studied at the Fordham University School of Social Service 1938-1941. During World War II he was Commander, U. S. Naval Armed Guard, and saw service in European, Atlantic, and Pacific theaters of war. He is assistant to the Executive Director of Catholic Relief Services of NCWC (the Catholic Bishops' Overseas Relief Agency); president of The International Catholic Migration Commission; member of the Board of Directors of the American Council of Voluntary Agencies for Foreign Service, Inc. He was among the twenty laymen invited to participate in discussion on the first draft of the *Pastoral Constitution on the Church in the Modern World*. In 1963 he was named Catholic lay auditor to the Council. He took an active part in the subcommissions of the Council. He is consultant to the Post-Conciliar Lay Commission.

DR. ALBERT OUTLER was born in Thomasville, Georgia. He studied at Wofford College, Emory University, and Yale, where he received his Ph.D. in 1938. He taught theology at Duke and at Yale. He has been professor of theology at Southern Methodist since 1951. He was delegate of the Methodist Church to the Third World Council on Faith and Order, Lund, Sweden in 1952. He was also delegate at New Delhi in 1962. He was vice-chairman of the Fourth World Council on Faith and Order, Montreal in 1963. He was official observer at the Vatican Council. He is the author of *College Faculties and Religion; Psychotherapy and the Christian Message; The Christian Tradition and the Unity We Seek*.

RIGHT REV. GERARD PHILIPS, a native of Truiden, Belgium, received his S.T.D. from the Gregorian University. He has been professor of dogmatic theology at Louvain since 1943, and is a member of the Belgian Senate. He also served as chaplain to the National Catholic Action Association, and as "peritus" to the Council. He is the author of numerous writings, predominantly on the Church, grace, and Catholic Action.

REV. KARL RAHNER, a Jesuit priest, was born in Freiburg, Germany. He studied philosophy and theology in Munich, Freiburg, Innsbruck, and Valkenburg. After his ordination in 1932 he spent two years studying under the well-known existentialist Martin Heidegger. His first published work was *Geist in Welt*. This has been followed by a constant stream of books and articles in learned journals. He is editor of the monumental *Lexikon für Theologie und Kirche*. He served throughout the Council as a "peritus." He has taught theology at Innsbruck, and at present is professor of theology at Munich.

DR. JOSEPH SITTLER, born in Upper Sandusky, Ohio, studied at Wittenberg College, Hamma Divinity School, Wagner College, and Alfred University. He pursued graduate studies at Oberlin, University of Chicago, Western Reserve, and University of Heidelberg. He was ordained minister of the United Lutheran Church in 1930. He taught systematic theology at Chicago Lutheran Theological Seminary in 1943-1957, and at the Divinity School, The University of Chicago, 1957-. He was a delegate to the Ecumenical Conference on Faith and Order at Lund, Montreal, and New Delhi. He is author of *The Doctrine of the Word*; *Structure of Christian Ethics*; *The Ecology of Faith*; *The Care of the Earth*.

Rev. Thomas F. Stransky was born in Milwaukee. He is a member of the Congregation of St. Paul, ordained in 1956. He did graduate studies at the Catholic University of America, University of Münster, and the Gregorian University. In 1960 Pope John appointed him one of the original staff members of the Secretariat for Promoting Christian Unity where he helped in the drafting of the Council documents *On Ecumenism*; *On Non-Christian Religions*; and *On Religious Liberty*. He also worked very closely with Orthodox, Anglican and Protestant observers at the Council. He is a permanent member of the staff of the Secretariat for the Promotion of Christian Unity.

Rabbi Marc H. Tanenbaum was born in Baltimore, Md. He received his B.A. at Yeshiva University in 1945; M.A. at the Jewish Theological Seminary in New York. He undertook graduate studies at Johns Hopkins and at the New School for Social Research, 1953. He has been a free-lance writer since 1952; public relations counsel, Eternal Light radio program, 1951. He was literary editor and public relations director of Henry Schuman, Inc., publishers, and of Farrar, Straus, and Young, publishers. He is director of the Interreligious Affairs Department, The American Jewish Committee. He was executive director of the Synagogue Council of America. He is a member of the Rabbinical Assembly of America, and on the board of directors of Religion in American Life.

Rev. Roberto Tucci, a Jesuit priest, was born in Naples, Italy. He studied at Naples, Milan, Louvain, and Rome. He has a doctorate of philosophy from the State University of Naples, and a doctorate of theology from the Gregorian University. Since 1959 he has been editor of the fortnightly periodical *La Civiltà Cattolica*. He was a member of the preparatory commission on the apostolate of the laity, and served as "peritus" to the Council. He was also consultor to the Pontifical Commission for Social Communications. He is a member of the Post-Conciliar Commission for the Apostolate of the Laity.

CONFERENCE PARTICIPANTS

Rev. Louis Bouyer, *University of Paris*

Rev. Raymond Brown, s.s., *St. Mary's Seminary*

Dr. Robert McAfee Brown, *Stanford University*

Rev. Eugene Burke, c.s.p., *Catholic University of America*

Mr. Daniel Callahan, *The Commonweal*

Rev. Bernard Cooke, s.j., *Marquette University*

Mr. Raymond F. Cottrell, *The Review and Herald*

Dr. Frederick J. Crosson, *University of Notre Dame*

Most Rev. John F. Dearden, *Archbishop of Detroit*

Rev. John Dunne, c.s.c., *University of Notre Dame*

Mr. Edwin Espy, *National Council of Churches*

Rev. Dr. Eugene Fairweather, *Trinity College*

Rev. Dr. Georges Florovsky, *Princeton University*

Rev. Piet Fransen, s.j., *University of Louvain*

Dr. Reginald Fuller, *Seabury-Western Theological Seminary*

Sister Mary Ann Ida Gannon, b.v.m., *Mundelein College*

Sister Jacqueline Grennon, s.l., *Webster College*

Most Rev. Paul J. Hallinan, *Archbishop of Atlanta*

Dr. David H. Hay, *Knox College*

Rabbi Abraham J. Heschel, *Jewish Theological Seminary*

Dr. Ralph D. Hyslop, *Union Theological Seminary*

Lady Jackson, *Cambridge, Massachusetts*

Dr. James Kritzeck, *University of Notre Dame*

Very Rev. Germain M. Lalande, c.s.c., *Superior General*

Right Rev. Luigi Ligutti, *National Catholic Rural Life Conference*

Dr. Franklin Littell, *Chicago Theological Seminary*

Dr. Frederick McManus, *Catholic University of America*

Dr. Martin Marty, *University of Chicago*

Dr. Paul Minus, *Methodist Theological Seminary*

Dr. Walter G. Muelder, *Boston University*

Dr. John T. Noonan, Jr., *University of Notre Dame*

649

DR. JOHN VON ROHR, *Pacific School of Religion*

REV. DR. JOHN ROMANIDES, *Brookline, Massachusetts*

REV. ALEXANDER SCHMEMANN, *St. Vladimir's Orthodox Theological Seminary*

REV. DR. MASSEY SHEPHERD, *Church Divinity School of the Pacific*

DR. GEORGE N. SHUSTER, *University of Notre Dame*

DR. ELWYN SMITH, *Pittsburgh Theological Seminary*

REV. DAVID STANLEY, S.J., *Regis College*

SISTER MARY LUKE TOBIN, S.L., *Webster College*

DR. WILLIAM WOLF, *Episcopal Theological School*

INDICES

COMPREHENSIVE INDEX

651

DISCUSSION INDEX